D1058734

FINITE MATHEMATICS

With Business Applications

FINITE MATHEMATICS

With Business Applications

SECOND EDITION

John G. Kemeny

President
Dartmouth College

Arthur Schleifer, Jr.

Professor of Business Administration
Director of the Division of Computer Services
Graduate School of Business Administration
Harvard University

J. Laurie Snell

Chairman
Department of Mathematics
Dartmouth College

Gerald L. Thompson

Professor of Applied Mathematics
and Industrial Administration
Carnegie-Mellon University

Prentice-Hall, Inc. *Englewood Cliffs, New Jersey*

HF
5695
K4
1972

© 1972, 1962 by PRENTICE-HALL, INC., Englewood Cliffs, New Jersey

All rights reserved. No part of this book may be reproduced
in any form without permission in writing
from the publisher.

Printed in the United States of America

ISBN   0-13-317321-6

Library of Congress Catalog Number: 75-171841

10 9 8 7 6 5 4 3 2

PRENTICE-HALL INTERNATIONAL, INC., *London*
PRENTICE-HALL OF AUSTRALIA, PTY., LTD., *Sydney*
PRENTICE-HALL OF CANADA, LTD., *Toronto*
PRENTICE-HALL OF INDIA PRIVATE LIMITED, *New Delhi*
PRENTICE-HALL OF JAPAN, INC., *Tokyo*

CONTENTS

194419

v

CHAPTER 4
VECTORS AND MATRICES

CHAPTER 5
LINEAR PROGRAMMING

CHAPTER 6
DECISION THEORY AND ANALYSIS

CHAPTER 7
MATHEMATICS OF FINANCE

PREFACE
to the Second Edition

The first edition of this book was published in 1962. At that time it was widely felt that business school students should be exposed to topics in finite mathematics in the course of their undergraduate training, and it was that need which motivated us to write the first edition.

In the subsequent decade we have seen many schools adopting formal requirements in this subject area, and many new applications of mathematics to the business curriculum and to business practice. Perhaps the most significant change has been the computer revolution, and especially the development of time-shared computers, which has made it possible for students as well as practitioners to apply the results of mathematical analysis to practical problems. Because digital computers are machines which are capable of performing only finite mathematics calculations, the relevance of this subject has greatly increased. All of these developments have contributed to making a new edition of the work desirable.

Unfortunately one of the original authors (JGK) was unable to participate in writing the revision, but his beneficial influence on the first edition of the work shows clearly throughout the second edition.

Two entirely new chapters were written for the second edition, one on decision theory and another on Markov decision processes. In addition, the chapters on linear programming and the theory of games have been entirely rewritten in order to emphasize a new approach (due to A. W. Tucker) to the simplex method, and to add the transportation model. In the remaining chapters some material that we have come to regard as having marginal interest has been dropped, and new material added. Also we have included new exercise material at the ends of most sections.

To be more specific we list the chapter by chapter changes from the first to the second edition. Parts of Chapters 1 and 2 of the first edition have been deleted and the remainder combined into Chapter 1 of the second edition. We felt that this change would emphasize the relationships between logic and set theory and permit fast coverage of the two topics. Chapter 2 of the new edition approaches counting problems by means of labeling techniques (instead of partitions as in Chapter 3 of the first edition), and other simplifying changes have been made in this chapter, again to make it easier to cover. Chapter 3 of the new edition covers probability theory in much the same way as in the previous edition but with some rearrangement of topics and the exchange of the gambler's ruin problem for reliability theory. Chapter 4 covers vectors and matrices much as before, and a new section containing two examples from finance and economics has been added. Chapter 5 is a complete revision of the linear programming chapter of the first edition, and includes an approach to the simplex method recently developed by Professor A. W. Tucker of Princeton University. We would like to thank him for permission to use this approach, and are also grateful for his other suggestions and criticisms for this chapter. Also in Chapter 5 are two new sections on the transportation method and its applications. Chapter 6 is the newly written chapter on decision theory and analysis. This is an important new area in the application of probability theory which reflects the emphases and results developed by members of the managerial economics area at Harvard Business School. The subjects covered here include utility theory, risk analysis, and portfolio selection. In Chapter 7 we have retained the first half on the mathematics of finance from Chapter 7 of the first edition. Another new area of application of mathematics is the Markov decision processes exposited in Chapter 8. Readers may be especially interested in the stock market example covered there. Finally in Chapter 9 the theory of games is covered, first by a geometric method for small games, and then using the simplex method of Chapter 5. The section on nonzero sum games is retained from the first edition.

The authors thank Professor Robert A. Mills and Dr. Perri Stinson who acted as reviewers of the first edition. The authors would also like to thank other readers of the first edition who have sent us suggestions, many of which have been incorporated into the second edition. We would like to encourage users of the second edition to respond likewise. In particular we would be interested in opinions concerning the changes we have made in going from the first to the second edition. Finally, the authors would like to thank Mr. David Griffeath for his aid in the preparation of Chapter 8.

ARTHUR SCHLEIFER, JR.

J. LAURIE SNELL

GERALD L. THOMPSON

PREFACE
to the First Edition

Mathematics has, in recent years, been widely applied to the fields of business and industrial administration. The growth and development of such mathematically oriented subjects as operations research, statistical decision theory, management science, and mathematical programming, and the application of these subjects to business problems, make it desirable that students of business and industrial administration take courses in applied mathematics in their undergraduate training. The Gordon and Howell[1] and Pierson[2] reports, and a number of articles and symposia[3] have reviewed the current state of mathematics training for business students and have suggested the directions in which such training might proceed in the future. While most agree that students of business should be exposed to some traditional mathematics, such as is given in precalculus and calculus courses, they all have called for a course which would provide a sophisticated introduction for the non-mathematician to topics in modern mathematical analysis—what has come to be known as finite mathematics.

The book, *Introduction to Finite Mathematics*, written by three of us, was conceived as an answer to a similar gap in the mathematical training of behavioral and social scientists. Another version of that book, *Finite Mathematical Structures*, written by three of us together with H. Mirkil, was directed to the mathematical training of students in the physical

[1] R. A. Gordon and J. E. Howell, *Higher Education for Business*, New York: Columbia University Press, 1959, pp. 159–163.
[2] F. C. Pierson *et al.*, *The Education of American Businessmen*, New York: McGraw-Hill Book Co., Inc., 1959, pp. 186–190.
[3] See, for example, S. Goldberg, "Mathematics for Business Students" in *Views on Business Education*, School of Business Administration, Chapel Hill, University of North Carolina, 1960; R. K. Gaumnitz and O. H. Brownlee, "Mathematics for Decision Makers," *Harvard Business Review*, **34**, 3 (May–June 1956), p. 48; G. A. W. Boehm, "Mathematics II: The New Uses of the Abstract," *Fortune*, **LVIII**, 1 (July 1958), p. 124.

sciences. These two books, together with the present one, have used the same central theme: to develop material from the *finite* point of view, that is, without resorting to infinite sets, limiting processes, continuity, etc. We have found that the basic ideas of finite mathematics are easier to state and theorems about them considerably easier to prove than is the case with their infinite counterparts. And we believe that, for the class of problems with which we are here concerned, the task of abstracting from the real world to a mathematical model is much easier with finite mathematics.

In the present book we have treated topics in finite mathematics in the context of business and industrial administration. The basic mathematics core of the book remains as in the previous books, but most of the applied exercises and examples have been set in the context of business. In addition, more than one-third of the book is completely new. The new material consists partly of new mathematical ideas, but it also treats a large number of applications of mathematics to business and administration problems. Among the applications discussed are computer circuits, critical path analysis, flow diagrams for computing and accounting procedures, Monte Carlo simulation of decision processes, reliability, decision theory, waiting line theory, a simple approach to mathematics of finance, and the simplex method for solving linear programming problems and matrix games.

Besides "tree diagrams," a pedagogical device found to be of great usefulness in *Introduction to Finite Mathematics*, we have utilized other diagrammatic devices. For instance, the graph of the jobs in a project is used in the critical path analysis of Chapter II. And in Chapter III there is a discussion of flow diagrams, which permit the easy description of complicated computational processes, such as the Monte Carlo simulation calculations of Chapter IV, the accounting procedures of Chapter VI, and the simplex calculations of Chapter VII. In addition, the ability to construct a good flow diagram is perhaps seventy per cent of the work of writing a computer program in one of the algebraic languages commonly used to program modern computers.

The basic core of the book consists of the unasterisked sections of the first five chapters. This material should be covered in every introductory course and constitutes a basic mathematics course. The optional (asterisked) sections of these chapters, together with Chapters VI, VII, and VIII, can be used to enrich the basic course in various directions, depending upon the interests of the instructor and class. These additional sections can also be used for supplementary material in the functional business courses, for seminar study, and for self-study on the part of a student. The entire book can be used for a year's course in mathematics and its applications to business and administration problems. Furthermore, the optional material contains many of the topics which are taught under such titles as Operations Research, Quantitative Methods, etc.

In organizing the book, we have included major applications within each chapter. We hope that the ordering of material in this book will motivate the student by demonstrating immediately the relevance of the mathematical theory contained herein to applied problems.

Recognizing the possibility that some instructors may want to skip some sections of the book and take up topics in an order different from that in which the book was laid out, however, we have included in the Contents the prerequisites for each section. Generally, we have listed only immediate prerequisites. We have, however, permitted for emphasis a certain amount of redundancy in our listing. It is hoped that this listing of prerequisites will also help the student who has difficulty with a particular section to trace back to the source of his difficulty.

It occasionally happens that a detail which is not crucial to the assimilation of the principal subject matter of a section depends on some previous section. For example, in Section 4 of Chapter VI, we discuss how to interpolate in Table III by using approximate formulae developed from the binomial theorem (Section 8 of Chapter III). This discussion is not, however, crucial for an understanding of the main theme of the section, although it permits wider application of the theory. Dependencies of this sort are shown by putting in parentheses the number of the prerequisite section.

The only prerequisite for this book itself is the mathematical maturity obtained from two and a half or more years of high school mathematics. It can, therefore, be used at any stage in the curriculum from the beginning of the freshman year on. Most of the material in the book has been tested in some version at Dartmouth College, Carnegie Institute of Technology, and a number of other institutions.

We would like to thank H. Mirkil who kindly permitted us to utilize parts of the book three of us wrote with him. The Dartmouth Computation Center provided help in preparing the Appendix Tables and in obtaining solutions for some of the examples in the text. Also, the following people have been kind enough to read and criticize parts of the manuscript or have suggested problem material to us: N. Churchill, G. Cooke, R. M. Cyert, H. J. Davidson, D. Dearborn, M. W. Herriott, R. H. Klein, M. Miller, L. E. Morrissey, Jr., R. Schlaifer, R. Trueblood, and P. R. Winters. We are grateful to them for their suggestions. We would also like to thank the production staff of Prentice-Hall for their usual careful attention to editing and printing.

J. G. K.
A. S., Jr.
J. L. S.
G. L. T.

1

STATEMENTS
AND SETS

1. PURPOSE OF THE THEORY

A *statement* is a verbal or written assertion. In the English language such statements are made by means of declarative sentences—for instance, "Business is good," and "Stock prices are high."

The two statements just quoted are *simple statements*. A combination of two or more simple statements is a *compound statement*—for instance, "Business is good, and stock prices are high."

It might seem natural to study simple statements before studying compound ones. However, because of the tremendous variety of simple statements, the theory of such statements is very complex. We can use here an approach that has been found fruitful in mathematics: to assume for the moment that a difficult problem has been solved and then to go on to the next problem. Therefore we shall proceed as if we knew all about simple statements and study only the way they are compounded. The latter is a relatively easy problem.

While the first systematic treatment of such problems is found in the writings of Aristotle, mathematical methods were first employed by George Boole only about a century ago. The more polished techniques now available are the product of twentieth-century mathematical logicians.

The fundamental property of any statement is that it is either true or false (and it cannot be both). Naturally, we are interested in finding out which is the case. For a compound statement it is sufficient to know which of its components are true, since the truth values (that is, the truth or falsity) of the components determine, in a way to be described later, the truth value of the compound.

Our problem then is twofold: (1) In how many different ways can statements be compounded? (2) How do we determine the truth value of a compound statement given the truth values of its components?

Let us consider ordinary mathematical statements. In any mathematical formula we find three kinds of symbols: *constants, variables,* and *auxiliary symbols.* For example, in the formula $(x + y)^2$ the plus sign and the exponent are constants, the letters x and y are variables, and the parentheses are auxiliary symbols. Constants are symbols whose meanings in a given context are fixed. Thus in the formula $(x + y)^2$, the plus sign indicates that we are to form the sum of the two numbers x and y, while the exponent 2 indicates that we are to multiply $(x + y)$ by itself. Variables always stand for entities of a given kind, but they allow us to leave open just which particular entity we have in mind. In $(x + y)^2$ the letters x and y stand for unspecified numbers. Auxiliary symbols function somewhat like punctuation marks. Thus if we omit the parentheses we obtain the formula $x + y^2$, which has quite a different meaning than the formula $(x + y)^2$.

In this chapter we shall use variables of only one kind. We indicate these variables by the letters $p, q, r,$ and so on, which stand for unspecified statements. These statements frequently will be simple statements but may also be compound. In any case we know that, since each variable stands for a statement, it has an (unknown) truth value.

The constants that we shall employ will stand for certain connectives used in the compounding of statements. We will have one symbol for forming the negation of a statement and several symbols for combining two statements. It will not be necessary to introduce symbols for the compounding of three or more statements, since we can show that the same combination can also be formed by compounding them two at a time. In practice only a small number of basic constants are used and the others are defined in terms of these. It is even possible to use only a single connective!

The auxiliary symbols that we shall use are, for the most part, the same ones used in elementary algebra. Any different usage will be explained when it first occurs.

Examples. As examples of simple statements let us take "Business is good" and "Stock prices are high." We will let p stand for the former and q for the latter.

Suppose we wish to make the compound statement that both are true: "Business is good *and* stock prices are high." We shall symbolize this statement by $p \wedge q$. The symbol $\wedge$, which can be read "and," is our first connective.

In place of the strong assertion above we might want to make the weak (cautious) assertion that one or the other of the statements is true: "Business is good *or* stock prices are high." We symbolize this assertion by $p \vee q$. The symbol $\vee$, which can be read "or," is the second connective that we shall use.

Suppose we believed that one of the statements above was false—for example, "Stock prices are *not* high." Symbolically we would write $\sim q$. Our third connective is then $\sim$, which can be read "not."

More complex compound statements can now be made. For example, $p \wedge \sim q$ stands for "Business is good *and* stock prices are *not* high."

EXERCISES

1. The following are compound statements or may be so interpreted. Find their simple components.
   a. Business is bad and stock prices are high.
   b. Business is good but stock prices are not high.
   c. Business will improve or stock prices will decline.
   d. Stock prices and bond prices are high.
   e. We should sell common or preferred stock.
   f. We should sell neither common nor preferred stock.
   g. Either business is going to improve or we should liquidate our inventories now.

2. In Exercise 1 assign letters to the various components, and write the statements in symbolic form. [*Ans. b. $p \wedge \sim q$.*]

3. Write the following statements in symbolic form, letting p be "Jones' productivity is higher than Smith's" and q be "Jones earns more money than Smith."
   a. Jones' productivity is higher than Smith's but Jones earns no more money than Smith.
   b. Jones' productivity is no higher than Smith's, but he earns more money than Smith.
   c. Jones' wages and productivity are both lower than Smith's.
   d. Either Jones produces more than Smith or Smith earns more money than Jones.
   e. Jones neither produces more nor earns more money than Smith.
   f. Jones does not produce more than Smith but he earns less money.
   g. It is not true that Jones both produces less and earns less money than Smith.

4. Assume that Jones' productivity is higher than Smith's and that he earns more money. Which of the seven compound statements in Exercise 3 are true? [*Ans. d., g.*]

5. Write the following in symbolic form.
   a. The Acme Company sells to Brown and Company (statement p).
   b. Brown and Company sells to the Acme Company (statement q).
   c. Acme and Brown sell to each other.
   d. Acme and Brown do not sell to each other.
   e. Brown buys from Acme but Acme does not reciprocate.
   f. Brown buys from Acme but Acme does not buy from Brown.
   g. Neither Acme nor Brown fails to sell to the other.
   h. It is not true that Acme and Brown fail to sell to one another.

6. Suppose Acme sells to Brown but Brown does not sell to Acme. Which of the eight statements in Exercise 5 are true?

7. For each statement in Exercise 5 give a condition under which it is false. [*Ans. c. Acme does not sell to Brown.*]

8. Let p be "Stock prices are high," and q be "Stocks are rising." Give a verbal translation for each of the following.

a. $p \land q$.
b. $p \land \sim q$.
c. $\sim p \land \sim q$.
d. $p \lor \sim q$.
e. $\sim(p \land q)$.
f. $\sim(p \lor q)$.
g. $\sim(\sim p \lor \sim q)$.

9. Using your answers to Exercise 8, parts *e.*, *f.*, *g.*, find simpler symbolic statements expressing the same idea.

10. Let p be "Jones is Treasurer" and q be "Smith is Controller." Translate into English and simplify:

$$\sim[\sim p \lor \sim\sim q] \land \sim\sim p.$$

2. THE MOST COMMON CONNECTIVES

The truth value of a compound statement is determined by the truth values of its components. When discussing a connective we will want to know just how the truth of a compound statement made with this connective depends upon the truth of its components. A very convenient way of tabulating this dependency is by means of a *truth table*.

Let us consider the compound $p \land q$. Statement p could be either true or false and so could statement q. Thus there are four possible pairs of truth values for these statements, and we want to know in each case whether or not the statement $p \land q$ is true. The answer is straightforward: if p and q are both true, then $p \land q$ is true, and otherwise $p \land q$ is false. This seems reasonable, since the assertion $p \land q$ says no more and no less than that p and q are both true.

Figure 1 gives the truth table for $p \land q$, the *conjunction* of p and q. The truth table contains all the information that we need to know about the connective $\land$—namely, it tells us the truth value of the conjunction of two statements given the truth values of each of the statements.

p	q	$p \land q$
T	T	T
T	F	F
F	T	F
F	F	F

Figure 1

p	q	$p \lor q$
T	T	?
T	F	T
F	T	T
F	F	F

Figure 2

We next look at the compound statement $p \lor q$, the *disjunction* of p and q. Here the assertion is that one or the other of these statements is true. Clearly, if one statement is true and the other false, then the disjunction is true, while if both statements are false, then the disjunction is certainly false. Thus we can fill in the last three rows of the truth table for disjunction (see Figure 2).

Observe that one possibility is left unsettled: what happens if both components are true? Here we observe that the everyday usage of "or" is ambiguous. Does "or" mean "one or the other or both" or does it mean "one or the other but not both"?

Let us seek the answer in examples. The sentence "Brown or Smith is a foreman" allows for the possibility that both men may be foremen. However, the sentence "I will go to Dartmouth or to Princeton" indicates that only one of these schools will be chosen. "I will buy a TV set or a phonograph next year" could be used in either sense; the speaker may mean that he is trying to make up his mind which one of the two to buy, but he could also mean that he will buy *at least one* of these—possibly both. We see that sometimes the context makes the meaning clear but not always.

A mathematician would never waste his time disputing which usage "should" be called the disjunction of two statements. Rather he recognizes two perfectly good usages, calling one the *inclusive disjunction* (p or q or both) and the other the *exclusive disjunction* (p or q but not both). The symbol $\vee$ will be used for inclusive disjunction, and the symbol $\underline{\vee}$ will be used for exclusive disjunction. The truth tables for these are found in Figures 3 and 4. Unless we state otherwise, our disjunctions will be inclusive disjunctions.

p	q	$p \vee q$
T	T	T
T	F	T
F	T	T
F	F	F

Figure 3

p	q	$p \underline{\vee} q$
T	T	F
T	F	T
F	T	T
F	F	F

Figure 4

The last connective we shall discuss in this section is *negation*. If p is a statement, the symbol $\sim p$, called the negation of p, asserts that p is false. Hence $\sim p$ is true when p is false, and false when p is true. The truth table for negation is shown in Figure 5.

Besides using these basic connectives singly to form compound statements, we can use several to form a more complicated compound statement, in much the same way that we form complicated algebraic expressions by using the basic arithmetic operations. For example, $\sim(p \wedge q)$, $p \wedge \sim p$, and $(p \vee q) \vee \sim p$ are all compound statements. They are to be read "from the inside out" in the same way that algebraic expressions are: quantities inside the innermost parentheses are first grouped together, then these parentheses are grouped together, and so on. Each compound statement has a truth table, which can be constructed in a routine way. The examples that follow show how to construct truth tables.

p	$\sim p$
T	F
F	T

Figure 5

Example 1. Consider the compound statement $p \lor \sim q$. We begin the construction of its truth table by writing in the first two columns the four possible pairs of truth values for the statements p and q. Then we write the proposition in question, leaving plenty of space between symbols so that we can fill in columns below. Next we copy the truth values of p and q in the columns below their occurrences in the proposition. This completes step 1 of the construction (see Figure 6).

p	q	$p \lor \sim q$	
T	T	T	T
T	F	T	F
F	T	F	T
F	F	F	F
Step No.		1	1

Figure 6

Next we treat the innermost compound, the negation of the variable q, completing step 2 (see Figure 7).

p	q	p	$\lor$	$\sim$	q
T	T	T		F	T
T	F	T		T	F
F	T	F		F	T
F	F	F		T	F
Step No.		1		2	1

Figure 7

Finally we fill in the column under the disjunction symbol, which gives us the truth value of the compound statement for various truth values of its variables. To indicate this we place two parallel lines on each side of the final column, completing step 3 (Figure 8).

p	q	p	$\lor$	$\sim$	q
T	T	T	T	F	T
T	F	T	T	T	F
F	T	F	F	F	T
F	F	F	T	T	F
Step No.		1	3	2	1

Figure 8

The next two examples show truth tables for more complicated compounds worked out in the same manner. There are only two basic rules that the student must remember when working these: first, work from the "inside out"; and second, find the truth values of the compound statement in the last column filled in during this procedure.

Example 2. The truth table for the statement $(p \lor \sim q) \land \sim p$ together with the numbers indicating the order in which the columns are filled in appears in Figure 9.

p	q	$(p$	$\lor$	$\sim$	$q)$	$\land$	$\sim$	p
T	T	T	T	F	T	F	F	T
T	F	T	T	T	F	F	F	T
F	T	F	F	F	T	F	T	F
F	F	F	T	T	F	T	T	F
Step No.		1	3	2	1	4	2	1

Figure 9

Two compound statements having the same variables are said to be *equivalent* if and only if they have exactly the same truth table. It is always permissible, and sometimes desirable, to replace a given statement by an equivalent one.

Example 3. The first of DeMorgan's laws asserts that the statements $\sim(p \land q)$ and $\sim p \lor \sim q$ are equivalent. The truth tables in Figure 10 show

p	q	$\sim$	$(p \land q)$	$\sim p$	$\lor$	$\sim q$
T	T	F	T	F	F	F
T	F	T	F	F	T	T
F	T	T	F	T	T	F
F	F	T	F	T	T	T
Step No.		2	1	1	2	1

Figure 10

that this is indeed true. The reader will notice that we wrote the truth tables for $p \land q$, $\sim p$, and $\sim q$ directly on the first step to shorten the work. Notice that the two columns marked on step 2 are identical, so that $\sim(p \land q)$ and $\sim p \lor \sim q$ are equivalent statements.

Let us give an interpretation of the equivalence just mentioned. Consider, "It is false that business is good and stocks are high." The equivalent statement derived from DeMorgan's law is: "Either business is bad or stocks are low." Intuitively the equivalence of these two compound statements is clear.

The other of DeMorgan's laws is that the statements $\sim(p \lor q)$ and $\sim p \land \sim q$ are equivalent. This law is discussed in Exercises 6 and 7.

Example 4. It is also possible to form compound statements from three or more simple statements. The next example is a compound formed from three simple statements p, q, and r. Notice that there will be a total of eight possible triples of truth values for these three statements, so that the truth table for our compound will have eight rows as shown in Figure 11.

p	q	r	[p	$\wedge$	(q	$\vee$	r)]	$\wedge$	$\sim$	[p	$\vee$	$\sim$	r]
T	T	T	T	T	T	T	T	F	F	T	T	F	T
T	T	F	T	T	T	T	F	F	F	T	T	T	F
T	F	T	T	T	F	T	T	F	F	T	T	F	T
T	F	F	T	F	F	F	F	F	F	T	T	T	F
F	T	T	F	F	T	T	T	F	T	F	F	F	T
F	T	F	F	F	T	T	F	F	F	F	T	T	F
F	F	T	F	F	F	T	T	F	T	F	F	F	T
F	F	F	F	F	F	F	F	F	F	F	T	T	F
Step No.			1	3	1	2	1	5	4	1	3	2	1

Figure 11

EXERCISES

1. Give a compound statement that symbolically states "p or q but not both," using only $\sim$, $\vee$, and $\wedge$.

2. Construct the truth table for your answer to Exercise 1, and compare this with Figure 4.

3. Construct the truth table for the symbolic form of each statement in Exercise 3 of Section 1. How does Exercise 4 of Section 1 relate to these truth tables?

4. Construct a truth table for each of the following:
   a. $\sim(p \wedge q)$.   [*Ans.* FTTT.]
   b. $p \wedge \sim p$.   [*Ans.* FF.]
   c. $(p \vee q) \vee \sim p$.   [*Ans.* TTTT.]
   d. $\sim[(p \vee q) \wedge (\sim p \vee \sim q)]$.   [*Ans.* TFFT.]

5. Let p stand for "Jones passed the course" and q for "Smith passed the course" and translate into symbolic form the statement: "It is not the case that Jones and Smith both passed the course." Use DeMorgan's law to derive an equivalent compound statement, and translate the latter back into words.

6. DeMorgan's second law is that $\sim(p \vee q)$ and $\sim p \wedge \sim q$ are equivalent. Use truth tables to prove that this is true.

7. Let p and q be the statements given in Exercise 5. Translate into symbolic form the statement, "It is not the case that Jones and Smith both failed the course." Use DeMorgan's second law to derive an equivalent symbolic statement and translate back into words.

8. Let p be the statement: "Acme bid low," and q the statement: "Acme got the contract." Translate the following statements into symbolic form, find equivalent statements, and translate back into word form.

     a. Acme bid high and got the contract.
     b. Acme bid low but did not get the contract.
     c. Either Acme bid high or Acme got the contract.
     d. Acme did not bid high and did not get the contract.
     e. Acme did not bid high or did not get the contract.

9. Construct truth tables for:
     a. $\sim p \lor (q \lor r)$.   [*Ans.* TTTFTTTT.]
     b. $(p \lor r) \land (\sim p \lor q)$.   [*Ans.* TTFFTFTF.]
     c. $(p \lor q) \lor (\sim p \land \sim q)$.   [*Ans.* TTTT.]
     d. $p \land \sim p$.   [*Ans.* FF.]
     e. $\sim(p \land \sim p)$.   [*Ans.* TT.]
     f. $(p \lor \sim q) \land r$.   [*Ans.* TFTFFFTF.]
     g. $\sim(\sim p \lor \sim q \lor r) \lor [\sim(\sim p \lor q) \lor (\sim p \lor r)]$.
                                          [*Ans.* TTTTTTTT.]

10. The truth table for a statement compounded from two simple statements has four rows, and the truth table for a statement compounded from three simple statements has eight rows. How many rows would the truth table for a statement compounded from four simple statements have? How many for five? For n? Devise a systematic way of writing down these latter truth tables.

11. A statement is logically true if its truth table consists of all T's, and it is logically false if its truth table consists of all F's. Prove that each of the following statements is either logically true or logically false.
     a. $(p \land q) \lor (\sim p \lor \sim q)$.   *b.* $\sim(p \land q) \lor p$.
     c. $p \land \sim p$.   *d.* $\sim(p \land (\sim p \lor q) \lor q$.

12. Construct a truth table for $\sim[(\sim p \land \sim q) \land (p \lor r)]$.
                                      [*Ans.* TTTTTTFT.]

13. Find a simpler statement having the same truth table as the one constructed in Exercise 12.

14. Show that the statements $p \land (q \lor r)$ and $(p \land q) \lor (p \land r)$ are equivalent—that is, have the same truth table.

15. Show that the statements $p \lor (q \land r)$ and $(p \lor q) \land (p \lor r)$ are equivalent.

3. LOGICAL POSSIBILITIES, SETS, AND SUBSETS

A well-defined collection of objects is known as a *set*. This concept, in its complete generality, is of great importance in mathematics, since all of mathematics can be developed by starting with it.

    The various pieces of furniture in a room form a set. So do the books in a given library, the students in a classroom, the integers between 1 and 1,000,000, the members of the board of directors of a company, or the products that a company sells. These are all examples of *finite* sets—sets having a finite number of elements. All the sets discussed in this book will be finite sets.

    There are two essentially different ways of specifying a set. One can give a rule for determining whether or not a given object is a member of the set, or one can give a complete list of the elements in the set. We shall say that the former is a *description* of the set and the latter is a *listing* of the set. For instance, we can define a set of four people as either (a) the members of the executive committee of the XYZ Corporation, or (b) the people whose names are Jones, Smith, Brown, and Green. It is customary to use braces to surround the listing of a set; thus the set above should be listed {Jones, Smith, Brown, Green}. The order in which the members are listed is not important; thus {Brown, Green, Jones, Smith} is the same set.

One of the most important occurrences of sets is in the analysis of the logical possibilities for a scientific problem. By the *set of logical possibilities* we shall mean a listing or description of all the possibilities (or outcomes) for a problem (or experiment). Mathematics can provide such a set of logical possibilities, and it is the role of science to discover facts that will eliminate all but one possibility. Or, if this cannot be achieved, at least science tries to estimate the probabilities of occurrence of the various outcomes.

An example we have already seen is the set of logical possibilities for the truth or falsity of compound statements involving three variables, say p, q, and r. Here the set of logical possibilities is just the eight truth-table cases. And if we had four statements, p, q, r, and s, there would be 16 truth-table cases—that is, the set of logical possibilities has 16 elements.

As another more applied example, if we want to talk about the various bridge hands, then the set of logical possibilities consists of all 13-card hands that can be dealt from a bridge deck. Or if we wish to discuss chess moves, we must consider the set of all possible legal positions of the chess pieces on the board.

Suppose that we have determined the set of logical possibilities for a given problem. That is, we have a list of outcomes such that one and only one of them can possibly be true. We know this partly from the framework in which the problem is considered and partly as a matter of pure logic. We then consider *statements relative to this set of possibilities*. These are statements whose truth or falsity can be determined for each logical possibility.

For example, if we consider the eight truth-table cases for variables p, q, and r, then statements relative to these possibilities are the various compound statements that can be formed from them. Or, for the 13-card bridge hands, statements such as "The hand contains at least one ace" or "The hand has all black cards" and so on are relative to this set. Finally, relative to the set of all legal chess positions, we can consider statements such as "Black Knight can take White Queen" or "White has lost more pieces than Black" and so on.

Example 1. The following problem is of a type often studied in probability theory. "There are two urns; the first contains two black balls and one white ball, while the second contains one black ball and two white balls. Select an urn at random and draw two balls in succession from it. What is the probability that . . . ?" Without raising questions of probability, let us ask

Case	Urn	First Ball	Second Ball
1	1	black	black
2	1	black	white
3	1	white	black
4	2	black	white
5	2	white	black
6	2	white	white

Figure 12

what the possibilities are. Figures 12 and 13 give us two ways of analyzing the logical possibilities.

Case	Urn	First Ball	Second Ball
1	1	black no. 1	black no. 2
2	1	black no. 2	black no. 1
3	1	black no. 1	white
4	1	black no. 2	white
5	1	white	black no. 1
6	1	white	black no. 2
7	2	black	white no. 1
8	2	black	white no. 2
9	2	white no. 1	black
10	2	white no. 2	black
11	2	white no. 1	white no. 2
12	2	white no. 2	white no. 1

Figure 13

In Figure 12 we have analyzed the possibilities in terms of colors of balls drawn. Such an analysis may be sufficient for many purposes. In Figure 13 we have carried out a finer analysis, distinguishing between balls of the same color in an urn. For some purposes the finer analysis may be necessary.

It is important to realize that the possibilities in a given problem may be analyzed in many different ways, from a very rough grouping to a highly refined one. The only requirements on an analysis of logical possibilities are:

1. that under any conceivable circumstances one and only one of these possibilities must be the case, and
2. that the analysis is fine enough so that the truth value of each statement under consideration in the problem is determined in each case.

It is easy to verify that both analyses (Figures 12 and 13) satisfy the first condition. Whether the rougher analysis will satisfy the second condition depends on the nature of the problem. If we can limit ourselves to statements such as "Two black balls are drawn from the first urn," then it suffices. But if we wish to consider "The first black ball is drawn after the second black ball from the first urn," then the finer analysis is needed.

A set that consists of some members of another set is called a *subset* of that set. A subset is determined by either its description or its listing. For instance, let p be the statement "The first ball drawn was black" relative to the set of possibilities in Figure 12. We see that the statement "p is true" is true in the first, second, and fourth cases. Hence "p is true" is a description of the subset of the set in Figure 12 whose listing is {case 1, case 2, case 4}.

In order to discuss all the subsets of a given set, let us introduce the following terminology. Call the original set the *universal set*, $\mathcal{U}$, call one-element subsets *unit sets*, and call the set that contains no members of $\mathcal{U}$ the *empty set*, $\mathcal{E}$. If p is any statement relative to $\mathcal{U}$, then the *truth set* of p consists of all elements of $\mathcal{U}$ for which p is true. For instance, if p is logically true, then the truth set of p is $\mathcal{U}$ itself. And if p is logically false, the truth set of p is the empty set $\mathcal{E}$. If p is neither logically true nor logically false, then its truth set will contain some but not all elements of $\mathcal{U}$ and will be called a *proper subset* of $\mathcal{U}$. Of course, we can also define proper subsets by listing their members.

As an example, let the universal set $\mathcal{U}$ consist of the three elements $\{a, b, c\}$. The proper subsets of $\mathcal{U}$ consist of three two-element sets, namely, $\{a, b\}$, $\{a, c\}$, and $\{b, c\}$ and three unit sets, namely, $\{a\}$, $\{b\}$, and $\{c\}$. To complete the picture we also consider the universal set a subset (but not a proper subset) of itself, and we also consider the empty set $\mathcal{E}$, that contains no elements of $\mathcal{U}$, as a subset of $\mathcal{U}$. One reason for including $\mathcal{U}$ and $\mathcal{E}$ as subsets of $\mathcal{U}$ is to have the truth sets of logically true and logically false statements well defined (as $\mathcal{U}$ and $\mathcal{E}$, respectively).

In order to see another reason let us return to the set $\{a, b, c\}$. We saw that this three-element set has $8 = 2^3$ subsets. In general, a set with n elements has 2^n subsets, as can be seen in the following manner. We form subsets P of $\mathfrak{U}$ by considering each of the elements of $\mathfrak{U}$ in turn and deciding whether or not to include it in the subset P. If we decide to put every element of $\mathfrak{U}$ into P we get the universal set, and if we decide to put no element of $\mathfrak{U}$ into P we get the empty set. In most cases we will put some but not all the elements into P and thus obtain a proper subset of $\mathfrak{U}$. We have to make n decisions, one for each element of the set, and for each decision we have to choose between two alternatives. We can make these decisions in $2 \cdot 2 \cdot \ldots \cdot 2 = 2^n$ ways, and hence this is the number of different subsets of $\mathfrak{U}$ that can be formed. Observe that our formula would not have been so simple if we had not included the universal set and the empty set as subsets of $\mathfrak{U}$.

Two sets are said to be *equal* if and only if they have exactly the same members. For instance, if $P = \{a, b\}$ in the example above, and $Q = \{b, a\}$, then $P = Q$.

A set Q is contained in a set P if every element of Q is also a member of P; we symbolize this by $Q \subseteq P$ or, equally well, $P \supseteq Q$. Thus in the three-element example above if $P = \{a, b\}$ and $Q = \{b\}$, then $P \supseteq Q$. Note also that $P \supseteq \mathcal{E}$ for every set P, and $\mathfrak{U} \supseteq P$ for every set P.

Example 2. The Miracle Filter Company conducts an annual survey of the smoking habits of adult Americans. The results of the survey are organized into 25 files, corresponding to the 25 cases in Figure 14. First, figures are kept separately for men and women. Second, the educational level is noted according to the following code:

> 0   did not finish high school
> 1   finished high school, no college
> 2   some college, but no degree
> 3   college graduate, but no graduate work
> 4   did some graduate work

Finally, there is a rough occupational classification: housewife, salaried professional, or salaried nonprofessional.

The Miracle executives have found this classification—that is, this set of logical possibilities—adequate for their purposes. For instance, to get figures on all adults in their survey who did not go beyond high school, they pull out the files numbered 1, 2, 3, 4, 11, 12, 13, 14, 15, and 16. Or they can locate data on male professional workers by looking at files 1, 3, 5, 7, and 9.

According to their analysis, the statement "The person is a housewife, professional, or nonprofessional" is logically true, while the statement "The person has educational level greater than 3, is neither professional nor nonprofessional, but not a female with graduate education" is a self-contradiction. The former statement is true about all 25 files, the latter about none.

Of course, the company may at some time be forced to consider a finer analysis of logical possibilities. For instance, "The person is a male with annual income over $10,000" is *not* a statement relative to the given possibilities. We could choose a case—say case 6—in which the given statement may be either true or false. Thus the analysis is not fine enough.

Of all the logical possibilities, one and only one represents the facts as they are. That is, for a given person, one and only one of the 25 cases is a correct description. To know which one, we need factual information. When we say that a certain statement is "true," without qualifying it, we mean that it is true in this one case. But, as we have said before, what the case actually is lies outside the domain of logic. Logic can tell us only what the circumstances (logical possibilities) are under which a statement is true.

Case	Sex	Educational Level	Occupation
1	male	0	prof.
2	male	0	non-prof.
3	male	1	prof.
4	male	1	non-prof.
5	male	2	prof.
6	male	2	non-prof.
7	male	3	prof.
8	male	3.	non-prof.
9	male	4	prof.
10	male	4	non-prof.
11	female	0	housewife
12	female	0	prof.
13	female	0	non-prof.
14	female	1	housewife
15	female	1	prof.
16	female	1	non-prof.
17	female	2	housewife
18	female	2	prof.
19	female	2	non-prof.
20	female	3	housewife
21	female	3	prof.
22	female	3	non-prof.
23	female	4	housewife
24	female	4	prof.
25	female	4	non-prof.

Figure 14

We conclude by illustrating various statements and their corresponding truth sets. The truth set of "The person is a nonprofessional male with a college degree" is {8, 10}. The truth set of "The person is a housewife who has completed high school" is {14, 17, 20, 23}.

We can also turn the problem around by first specifying a subset and then trying to find a statement that describes it. For instance, to describe the subset {5, 18} we note that it consists of nondegree professionals with some college. And to describe the set {2, 4, 6, 8, 10} we observe that it consists of male nonprofessionals. However, it is difficult to furnish a statement that describes the subset {1, 4, 8, 13, 20}, since this subset does not have a "natural" interpretation within the context of the problem. To specify such subsets we may have to be content with the listing method.

EXERCISES

1. Figure 14 gives the possible classifications of one person in the survey. How many cases do we get if we classify two people jointly? [*Ans.* 625.]

2. For each of the 25 cases in Figure 14 state whether the following statement is true: "The person has had some college education, and if the person is female then she is a housewife."

3. In Example 1, with the logical possibilities given by Figure 12, state the cases in which the following statements are true.
   a. Urn one is selected.
   b. At least one white ball is drawn.
   c. At most one white ball is drawn.
   d. Either the first ball drawn is not white, or the second is black.
   e. Two balls of different color are drawn, or urn one is selected.

4. In Example 1 give two logically true and two logically false statements (other than those in the text).

5. In a college using grades A, B, C, D, and F, how many logically possible report cards are there for a student taking four courses?   [*Ans.* 625.]

6. Two dice are rolled. Which of the following analyses satisfy the first condition for logical possibilities? What is wrong with the others?
      The sum of the numbers shown is:
   a. (1) 6, (2) not 6.
   b. (1) an even number, (2) less than 6, (3) greater than 6.
   c. (1) 2, (2) 3, (3) 4, (4) more than 4.
   d. (1) 7 or 11, (2) 2, 3, or 12, (3) 4, 5, 6, 8, 9, or 10.
   e. (1) 2, 4, or 6, (2) an odd number, (3) 10 or 12.
   f. (1) less than 5 or more than 8, (2) 5 or 6, (3) 7, (4) 8.
   g. (1) more than 5 and less than 10, (2) at most 4, (3) 7, (4) 11 or 12.
      [*Ans. a., c., d., f.* satisfy the condition.]

7. A company wishes to run three different advertisements of product A, which we shall designate A1, A2, and A3, and two different advertisements, B1 and B2, of product B, in successive issues of a weekly magazine. If it is decided to alternate advertisements of product A and product B, list the set of all possibilities.

8. In Exercise 7, list the following subsets. Let the words "is next to" mean either "immediately precedes" or "immediately follows."
   a. The set in which A1 is next to B2.
   b. The set in which B2 is next to A2 and A3.
   c. The set in which A2 is the third advertisement.
   d. The set in which B1 is the third advertisement.
   e. The set in which an advertisement of product A starts and ends the series.

9. Pick out all pairs in Exercise 8 in which one set is a subset of the other.

10. A TV producer is planning a half-hour show. He wants to have a combination of comedy, music, and commercials. If each is allotted a multiple of five minutes, construct the set of possible distributions of time. (Consider only the total time allotted to each.)

11. In Exercise 10, list the following subsets.
   a. The set in which more time is devoted to comedy than to music.

b. The set in which no more time is devoted to commercials than to either music or comedy.

c. The set in which exactly five minutes is devoted to music.

d. The set in which all three of the above conditions are satisfied.

12. In Exercise 10, find two sets, each of which is a proper subset of the set in 11*a.* and also of the set in 11*c.*

13. A man has nine coins totaling 78 cents. What are the logical possibilities for the distribution of the coins? [*Hint:* There are three possibilities.]

14. In Exercise 13, which of the following statements are logically true and which are logically false?

a. He has at least one penny. [*Ans.* Logically true.]

b. He has at least one nickel. [*Ans.* Neither.]

c. He has exactly two nickels. [*Ans.* Logically false.]

d. He has exactly three nickels if and only if he has exactly one dime. [*Ans.* Logically true.]

15. In Exercise 13 we are told that the man has no nickel in his possession. What can we infer from this?

Exercises 16 through 20 refer to the following example: There are three urns. The first contains two black balls, the second contains one black and two white balls, and the third contains two black and two white balls We select an urn and draw two balls.

16. Construct a table of the logical possibilities, similar to Figure 12.
[*Partial Ans.* There are eight cases.]

17. In which cases is the statement "One black and one white ball is drawn" true?

18. What is the status of the statement: "Urn one is selected, and two different color balls are drawn"? [*Ans.* Logically false.]

19. Find the cases in which the statement "Urn one is selected if and only if two black balls are drawn" is true.

20. How does the list of possibilities change if we don't care about the order in which the balls are drawn?

4. TREE DIAGRAMS

A very useful tool for determining the set of logical possibilities is the drawing of a "tree." This device will be illustrated by several examples.

Example 1. Consider again the survey of the Miracle Filter Company. They keep two large filing cabinets, one for men and one for women. Each cabinet has five drawers, corresponding to the five educational levels. Each drawer is subdivided according to occupations; drawers in the filing cabinet for men have two large folders, while in the other cabinet each drawer has three folders.

When a clerk files a new piece of information, he first has to find the right cabinet, then the correct drawer, and then the appropriate folder. This three-step process of filing is shown in Figure 15. For obvious reasons we shall call a figure like this, which starts at a point and branches out, a *tree.*

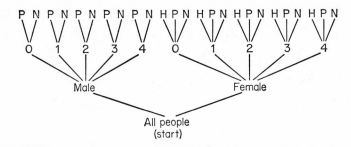

Figure 15

Observe that the tree contains all the information relevant to classifying a person interviewed. Each *path* in the tree from the start to the end (bottom to top) represents a logical possibility. There are 25 ways of starting at the bottom and following a path to the top. The 25 paths represent the 25 cases in Figure 14. The order in which we performed the classification is arbitrary. We might as well have classified first according to educational level, then according to occupation, and then according to sex. We would still obtain a tree representing the 25 logical possibilities, but the tree would look quite different. (See Exercise 1.)

Example 2. Next let us consider the example of Figure 12. This is a three-stage process; first we select an urn, then draw a ball, and then draw a second ball. The tree of logical possibilities is shown in Figure 16. We note that six

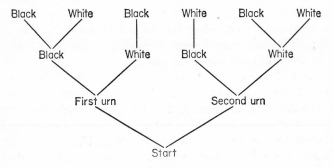

Figure 16

is the correct number of logical possibilities. The reason for this is: if we choose the first urn (which contains two black balls and one white ball) and draw from it a black ball, then the second draw may be of either color; however, if we draw a white ball first, then the second ball drawn is necessarily black. Similar remarks apply if the second urn is chosen.

Example 3. As a final example, let us construct the tree of logical possibilities for the outcomes of a World Series played between the Dodgers and the Yankees. Figure 17 shows half of the tree, corresponding to the case when the Dodgers win the first game (the dotted line at the bottom leads to the other half of the tree). A "D" stands for a Dodger win and "Y" for a Yankee win. There are 35 possible outcomes (corresponding to the circled letters) in the half-tree shown, so that the World Series can end in 70 ways.

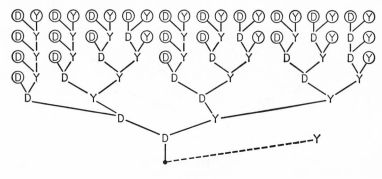

This example is different from the previous two in that the paths of the tree end at different levels, corresponding to the fact that the World Series ends whenever one of the teams has won four games.

Not always do we wish as detailed an analysis as that provided in the examples above. If, in Example 2, we wanted to know only the color and order in which the balls were drawn and not which urn they came from, then there would be only four logical possibilities instead of six. Then in Figure 16 the second and fourth paths (counting from the left) would represent the same outcome, namely, a black ball followed by a white ball. Similarly, the third and fifth paths would represent the same outcome. Finally, if we cared only about the color of the balls drawn, not the order, then there would be only three logical possibilities: two black balls, two white balls, or one black and one white ball.

A less detailed analysis of the possibilities for the World Series is also possible—for example: Dodgers in four, five, six, or seven games, and Yankees in four, five, six, or seven games. The new classification reduces the number of possibilities from 70 to eight. The other possibilities have not been eliminated but merely grouped together. Thus the statement "Dodgers in four games" can happen in only one way, while "Dodgers in seven games" can happen in 20 ways (see Figure 17). A still less detailed analysis would be a classification according to the number of games in the series. Here there are only four logical possibilities.

The student will find that it often requires several trials to reveal the "best" way of listing logical possibilities for a given problem.

EXERCISES

1. Construct a tree for Example 1, if people are first classified according to educational level, then according to profession, and finally according to sex. Is the shape of the tree the same as in Figure 15? Does it represent the same possibilities?

2. In 1965 the Dodgers lost the first two games of the World Series, but won the series in the end. In how many ways can the series go so that the losing team wins the first two games?   [*Ans.* 10.]

3. In how many ways can the World Series be played (see Figure 17) if the Dodgers win the first game and
   a. No team wins two games in a row.   [*Ans.* 1.]
   b. The Dodgers win at least the odd-numbered games.   [*Ans.* 5.]
   c. The winning team wins four games in a row.   [*Ans.* 4.]
   d. The losing team wins four games.   [*Ans.* 0.]

4. A man is considering the purchase of one of three types of stocks. Each stock may go up, go down, or stay the same after his purchase. Draw the tree of logical possibilities.

5. For the tree constructed in Exercise 4 give a statement that:
   a. Is true in two-thirds of the cases.
   b. Is false in all but one case.
   c. Is true in all but one case.
   d. Is logically true.
   e. Is logically false.

6. We set up an experiment similar to that of Figure 16, but urn one has two black balls and two white balls, while urn two has one white ball and four black balls. We select an urn and draw three balls from it. Construct the tree of logical possibilities. How many cases are there?   [*Ans.* 10.]

7. From the tree constructed in Exercise 6 answer the following questions.
   a. In how many cases do we draw three black balls?
   b. In how many cases do we draw two black balls and one white ball?
   c. In how many cases do we draw three white balls?
   d. How many cases does this leave?   [*Ans.* 3.]

8. In Exercise 6 we wish to make a rougher classification of logical possibilities. What branches (in the tree there constructed) are identified if:
   a. We do not care about the order in which the balls are drawn.
   b. We care neither about the order of balls, nor about the number of the urn selected.
   c. We care only about what urn is selected, and whether the balls drawn are all the same color.

9. Work Exercise 7 of the last section by sketching a tree diagram.

10. Let us define three arithmetical operations. The operation A adds 2 to a given number, the operation R raises the number to the second power, and D divides the number by 2. Draw a tree showing the possible orders in which the operations can be applied (using each operation once). How many orders are there?   [*Ans.* 6.]

11. Use the tree constructed in Exercise 10 to show the result of applying all three operations to the number 0, in various orders.

12. Use the tree of Exercise 10 to show what happens if the tree operations are applied to a number x, in various orders. For each of the six cases decide whether there is an x that is left unchanged after the three operations.

13. Demand for an item on a particular day can vary between 0 and 3 units. Draw a tree diagram to show the possible demands on each of two successive days.

14. An item can be *sold* if it is *demanded* and if there is sufficient stock to *supply* the demand. For the tree constructed in Exercise 13, what are

the possible sales in each of the two days if the initial stock is: (a) 4 units? (b) 6 units?

15. Suppose the initial inventory of the item of Exercise 13 is 2 units, but that after the first day an additional 2 units arrive from the factory. Now what are the possible sales at the end of two days?

16. The inventory at the end of a period is the inventory at the beginning of the period diminished by the sales during the period and augmented by new stock that arrives prior to the end of the period. In Exercise 15 list the inventory at the end of the first day and at the end of the second day for each of the possible combinations of two days' demand.

17. Sampling to determine which of two courses of action to take is often performed according to a "decision rule." In acceptance sampling to determine whether a lot purchased from a vendor is acceptable, for example, a decision rule may be of the form: "Take a sample of size n from the lot and determine how many pieces in the sample are defective and how many are good. If the number of defectives is less than or equal to some number c, accept the lot; otherwise reject the lot." Such a decision rule can be characterized simply by the sample size n and the "acceptance number" c; it is called an (n, c) decision rule.

Draw a tree diagram for the decision rule $(7, 3)$, given that the first item in the sample is good, and that each item can be classified as either "good" or "defective." Indicate the outcomes that lead to acceptance of the lot and those that lead to rejection.

18. In the decision tree of Exercise 17, it is often possible to apply the decision rule and conclude what to do with the lot before all seven items have been sampled. If, for example, the first four items are classified as defective, the lot will be rejected according to the decision rule, and hence the sampling operation may as well be curtailed at this earlier stage.

Redraw the tree diagram of Exercise 17, curtailing the sampling operation as soon as a decision about the lot can be reached. Compare this diagram with Figure 17.

19. An electric utility bills its residential customers bimonthly. Reminders or warnings are issued on overdue accounts on the basis of the amount of the uncollected balance, number of days overdue, the customer's credit rating, and whether or not the customer has a deposit. Classify these variables as follows:

$$\text{Uncollected balance} \begin{cases} \text{under \$25} \\ \text{\$25 or over} \end{cases}$$

$$\text{Days overdue} \begin{cases} \text{30 to 60} \\ \text{over 60} \end{cases}$$

$$\text{Credit rating} \begin{cases} \text{good} \\ \text{fair} \\ \text{poor} \end{cases}$$

$$\text{Deposit} \begin{cases} \text{yes} \\ \text{no} \end{cases}$$

Construct the tree of logical possibilities.

20. In Exercise 19 it is desired to send a reminder to all overdue accounts whose uncollected balance is less than \$25 except for (a) poor credit risks with no deposit and (b) fair credit risks with no deposit whose accounts are overdue more than 60 days; the latter two exceptions will receive strong warnings. For overdue accounts whose uncollected balance is \$25

or more, warnings are to be sent to all except (a) the good credit risks and (b) accounts that are overdue 60 days or less and that are covered by deposits; these exceptions will receive reminders.

Are these criteria logically consistent? If so, indicate which of the logical possibilities receive warnings and which receive reminders.

5. OPERATIONS ON SUBSETS

In Sections 1 and 2 we considered the ways in which one could form new statements from given statements. Now we shall consider an analogous procedure: the formation of new sets from given sets. We shall assume that each of the sets we use is a subset of some universal set, and we shall also want the newly formed set to be a subset of the same universal set. As usual, we can specify the newly formed set either by a description (that is, as a truth set of a compound statement) or by a listing of its members.

As a fairly complicated example we shall consider the leadership possibilities of three companies, A, B, and C, competing with each other in four territories, North, South, East, and West. We want to determine the possibilities for market leadership in each territory, where a company is the market leader if its share of the market is larger than that of any competitor. Assume that Company A markets in all territories, Company B does not market in the East, and Company C does not market in the North. Figure 18 lists the set of logical possibilities. Since there are only two possible market leaders in the East and North, while there are three possibilities in the South and three in the West, there are in all $2 \cdot 2 \cdot 3 \cdot 3 = 36$ different logical possibilities, as listed in Figure 18. We shall use this example to illustrate the operations on subsets that we shall define next.

If P and Q are two sets, we shall define a new set $P \cap Q$, called the *intersection* of P and Q, as follows: $P \cap Q$ is the set containing those and only those elements that belong to both P and Q. As an example, consider the logical possibilities listed in Figure 18. Let P be the subset in which Company A is the market leader in at least three territories—that is, the set

$$\{P1, P2, P3, P4, P7, P13, P19\}.$$

Let Q be the subset in which A is the leader in the East and the South— that is, the set

$$\{P1, P2, P3, P4, P5, P6\}.$$

Then the intersection $P \cap Q$ is the set in which both events take place— where A is the leader in the East and the South *and* is the leader in at least three territories. Thus $P \cap Q$ is the set

$$\{P1, P2, P3, P4\}.$$

Possibility Number	Winner in New Hampshire	Winner in Minnesota	Winner in Wisconsin	Winner in California
P1	A	A	A	A
P2	A	A	A	B
P3	A	A	A	C
P4	A	A	B	A
P5	A	A	B	B
P6	A	A	B	C
P7	A	B	A	A
P8	A	B	A	B
P9	A	B	A	C
P10	A	B	B	A
P11	A	B	B	B
P12	A	B	B	C
P13	A	C	A	A
P14	A	C	A	B
P15	A	C	A	C
P16	A	C	B	A
P17	A	C	B	B
P18	A	C	B	C
P19	C	A	A	A
P20	C	A	A	B
P21	C	A	A	C
P22	C	A	B	A
P23	C	A	B	B
P24	C	A	B	C
P25	C	B	A	A
P26	C	B	A	B
P27	C	B	A	C
P28	C	B	B	A
P29	C	B	B	B
P30	C	B	B	C
P31	C	C	A	A
P32	C	C	A	B
P33	C	C	A	C
P34	C	C	B	A
P35	C	C	B	B
P36	C	C	B	C

Figure 18

If P and Q are two sets, we shall define a new set $P \cup Q$, called the *union* of P and Q, as follows: $P \cup Q$ is the set that contains those and only those elements that belong either to P or to Q (or to both). In the example in the paragraph above, the union $P \cup Q$ is the set of possibilities for which either A is the leader in the East and the South *or* is the leader in at least three territories—that is, the set

$$\{P1, P2, P3, P4, P5, P6, P7, P13, P19\}.$$

To help in visualizing these operations we shall draw illustrative diagrams, called Venn diagrams. We let the universal set be a rectangle and let subsets be circles drawn inside the rectangle. In Figure 19 we show two

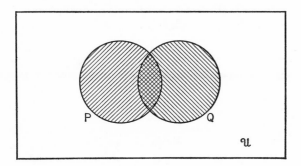

Figure 19

sets P and Q as shaded circles. Then the doubly crosshatched area is the intersection $P \cap Q$, and the total shaded area is the union $P \cup Q$.

If P is a given subset of the universal set $\mathcal{U}$, we can define a new set $\tilde{P}$, called the *complement* of P, as follows: $\tilde{P}$ is the set of all elements of $\mathcal{U}$ that are *not* contained in P. For example, if, as above, Q is the set in which Company A is the market leader in the East and the South, then $\tilde{Q}$ is the set {P7, P8, ... , P36}. The shaded area in Figure 20 is the complement of the set P. Observe that the complement of the empty set $\mathcal{E}$ is the universal set $\mathcal{U}$, and also that the complement of the universal set is the empty set.

Sometimes we shall be interested in only part of the complement of a set. For example, we might wish to consider the part of the complement of the set Q that is contained in P—that is, the set $P \cap \tilde{Q}$. The shaded area in Figure 21 is $P \cap \tilde{Q}$.

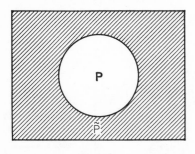

Figure 20

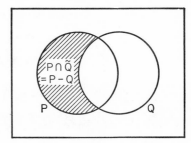

Figure 21

A somewhat more suggestive definition of this set can be given as follows: let $P - Q$ be the *difference* of P and Q—that is, the set that contains those elements of P that do not belong to Q. Figure 21 shows that $P \cap \tilde{Q}$ and $P - Q$ are the same set. In the market-leadership example above the set $P - Q$ can be listed as $\{P7, P13, P19\}$.

The complement of a set is a special case of a difference set, since we can write $\tilde{Q} = \mathfrak{u} - Q$. If P and Q are nonempty sets whose intersection is the empty set ($P \cap Q = \mathcal{E}$), then we say that they are *disjoint* sets.

Example 1. In the market-leadership example, consider the four territories in the order East, South, North, West, and let R be the set in which A is the leader in the first three territories—that is, the set $\{P1, P2, P3\}$; let S be the set in which A is the leader in the last two territories—that is, the set

$$\{P1, P7, P13, P19, P25, P31\}.$$

Then $R \cap S = \{P1\}$ is the set in which A is the leader in the first three territories and also the last two; that is, he is the leader in all the territories. We also have

$$R \cup S = \{P1, P2, P3, P7, P13, P19, P25, P31\},$$

which can be described as the set in which A is the leader in the first three territories or the last two. The set in which A is not the leader in the first three territories is

$$\tilde{R} = \{P4, P5, \ldots, P36\}.$$

Finally, we see that the difference set $R - S$ is the set in which A is the market leader in the first three territories but not both of the last two. This set can be found by taking from R the element $\{P1\}$ that it has in common with S, so that

$$R - S = \{P2, P3\}.$$

Example 2. Sometimes shading of subsets of a Venn diagram becomes complicated. Instead of shading them, we can number them. Figure 22 shows

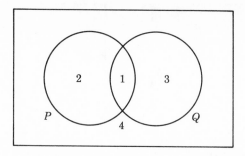

Figure 22

the Venn diagram of Figure 19 but with the parts numbered. It is easy to see that the areas included in each of the sets listed below are as indicated.

Set	Numbered areas included in the set
P	1, 2
Q	1, 3
$P \cap Q$	1
$P \cup Q$	1, 2, 3
$\tilde{P}$	3, 4
$\overbrace{(P \cup Q)}$	4

Example 3. Venn diagrams are also useful for three subsets. Such a diagram with numbered areas is shown in Figure 23. Again we can identify the num-

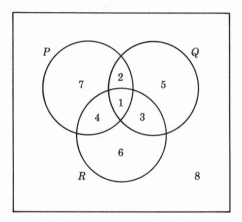

Figure 23

bered areas included in each of the sets below.

Set	Numbered areas included in the set
P	1, 2, 4, 7
$P \cup Q \cup R$	1, 2, 3, 4, 5, 6, 7
$P - Q$	4, 7
$R \cup \tilde{Q}$	1, 3, 4, 6, 7, 8
$P \cap Q \cap \tilde{R}$	2

EXERCISES

1. Draw Venn diagrams for $P \cap Q$, $P \cap \tilde{Q}$, $\tilde{P} \cap Q$, and $\tilde{P} \cap \tilde{Q}$, shading in each of these areas. Also identify each area in terms of the numbers of Figure 22.

2. Give a step-by-step construction of the diagram for the set $(P - Q) \cup (P \cap \tilde{Q})$. Identify this set in terms of the numbers of Figure 22.

3. Identify each of the following sets by using the numbers of Figure 23.
   a. $R - (P \cap Q)$.   b. $R \cup (P \cap Q)$.
   c. $(P \cup Q \cup R) - (P \cap Q \cap R)$.   d. $(R \cap \tilde{Q}) \cup (P \cap \tilde{Q})$.
   e. $(P \cup \tilde{Q}) \cap R$.

4. In testing blood, three types of antigens are looked for: A, B, and Rh. Every person is classified doubly. He is Rh positive if he has the Rh antigen, and Rh negative otherwise. He is type AB, A, or B depending on which of the other antigens he has, with type O having neither A nor B. Draw a Venn diagram, and identify each of the eight areas.

5. Considering only two subsets, the set X of people having antigen A, and the set Y of people having antigen B, define (symbolically) the types AB, A, B, and O.

6. A person can receive blood from another person if he has all the antigens of the donor. Describe in terms of X and Y the sets of people who can give to each of the four types. Identify these sets in terms of blood types.

7. The accompanying tabulation records the reaction of a number of spectators to a television show. All the categories can be defined in terms of the following four: M (male), G (grown-up), L (liked), Vm (very much). How many people fall into each of the categories (a) through (j)?

	Liked Very Much	Liked Slightly	Disliked Slightly	Disliked Very Much
Men	1	3	5	10
Women	6	8	3	1
Boys	5	5	3	2
Girls	8	5	1	1

    a. M.   [*Ans.* 34.]
    b. $\tilde{L}$.
    c. Vm.
    d. $M \cap \tilde{G} \cap \tilde{L} \cap Vm$.   [*Ans.* 2.]
    e. $\tilde{M} \cap G \cap L$.
    f. $(M \cap G) \cup (L \cap Vm)$.
    g. $\widetilde{(M \cap G)}$.   [*Ans.* 48.]
    h. $(M \cup \tilde{G})$.
    i. $(M - G)$.
    j. $[\tilde{M} - (G \cap L \cap \tilde{Vm})]$.

8. In a survey of 100 families, the numbers that read the most recent issues of various magazines were found to be: *Look*, 28; *Time*, 30; *Life*, 42; *Look* and *Time*, 8; *Look* and *Life*, 10; *Time* and *Life*, 5; all three magazines, 3.
    a. How many read none of the three magazines?   [*Ans.* 20.]
    b. How many read *Life* as their only magazine?   [*Ans.* 30.]
    c. How many read both *Time* and *Life* or neither *Time* nor *Life*?
                                                [*Ans.* 38.]

9. In another survey of 100 families, the numbers that had read recent issues of a certain monthly magazine were found to be: September only, 18; September but not August, 23; September and July, 8; September, 26; July, 48; July and August, 8; none of the three months, 24.
    a. How many read the August issue?   [*Ans.* 18.]

    b. How many read two consecutive issues?   [*Ans.* 8.]

    c. How many read both the July and August issues or neither the July nor the August issues?   [*Ans.* 50.]

    d. How many read the September and August issues but not the July issue?   [*Ans.* None.]

10. The report of an inspector who inspected a lot of 100 pieces and reported the number of hardness, finish, and dimensional defects of pieces in the last lot was as follows: all three defects, 5; hardness and finish, 10; dimensional and finish, 8; dimensional and hardness, 20; finish, 30; hardness, 23; dimensional, 50. The inspector was fired. Why?

11. The workers in a factory were classified according to skill, number of years in the employ of the factory, and whether they performed direct or indirect labor. If they had worked less than three years in the factory, they were categorized as short-term workers; if they had worked ten years or more, they were considered long-term, and all others were medium-term employees. The data are summarized in the following table:

	Skilled and Direct	Unskilled and Direct	Skilled and Indirect	Unskilled and Indirect
Short	6	9	10	20
Medium	7	11	15	9
Long	2	3	8	0

Let SH = short, M = medium, L = long, SK = skilled, I = indirect. Determine the number of workers in the following classes.

    a. $SH \cap SK \cap I$.   [*Ans.* 10.]

    b. M.

    c. $L \cap I$.

    d. $(M \cup L) \cap (SK \cup I)$.   [*Ans.* 41.]

    e. $\widetilde{SH} \cup (\widetilde{SK \cap I})$.

12. In Exercise 11, which set of each of the following pairs has more workers as members?

    a. $(\widetilde{SH \cup M})$ or L.

    b. $I \cap \widetilde{SK}$ or $SH - (I \cap \widetilde{SK})$.

    c. $\mathcal{E}$ or $L \cap \widetilde{SK} \cap I$.

6. THE RELATIONSHIP BETWEEN SETS AND COMPOUND STATEMENTS

In Section 3 we defined the truth set of the statement p to be the subset P of the set of all logical possibilities for which p was true. Now we want to consider the truth sets of compound statements.

    If p and q are statements, then $p \lor q$ and $p \land q$ are also statements and hence must have truth sets. To find the truth set of $p \lor q$ we observe that it is true whenever p is true or q is true (or both). Therefore we must assign to $p \lor q$ the logical possibilities that are in P or in Q (or both); that is, we must assign to $p \lor q$ the set $P \cup Q$. On the other hand, the statement $p \wedge q$ is true only when both p and q are true, so that we must assign to $p \wedge q$ the set $P \cap Q$.

Thus we see that there is a close connection between the logical operation of disjunction and the set operation of union, and also between conjunction and intersection. A careful examination of the definitions of union and intersection shows that the word "or" occurs in the definition of union and the word "and" occurs in the definition of intersection. Thus the connection between the two theories is not surprising.

Since the connective "not" occurs in the definition of the complement of a set, it is not surprising that the truth set of $\sim p$ is $\tilde{P}$. This follows since $\sim p$ is true when p is false, so that the truth set of $\sim p$ contains all logical possibilities for which p is false, that is, the truth set of $\sim p$ is $\tilde{P}$.

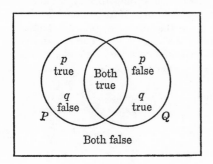

The truth sets of two statements p and q are shown in Figure 24. Also marked on the diagram are the various logical possibilities for these two statements. The reader should pick out in this diagram the truth sets of

Figure 24

the statements $p \vee q$, $p \wedge q$, $\sim p$, and $\sim q$.

The connection between a statement and its truth set makes it possible to "translate" a problem about compound statements into a problem about sets. It is also possible to go in the reverse direction. Given a problem about sets, think of the universal set as being a set of logical possibilities and think of a subset as being the truth set of a statement. Hence we can "translate" a problem about sets into a problem about compound statements.

In order to make the translation from statement language to set language carry out the following replacements:

Replace statements $p, q, r, \ldots$ by their truth sets $P, Q, R, \ldots$.
Replace the and symbol $\wedge$ by the intersection symbol $\cap$.
Replace the or symbol $\vee$ by the union symbol $\cup$.
Replace the negation symbol $\sim$ in front of a statement by the complement symbol over the corresponding sets.

Figure 25 gives several examples of this replacement.

The translation from set language to compound-statement language is just as easy, since we need only write the set in terms of $\cup$, $\cap$, and complements and then go back to statement language by making the reverse replacements indicated above.

The closeness of these two languages suggests that it might be possible to prove two statements are equivalent (have the same truth table) by means of Venn diagrams—or, equally well, to prove the equality of sets

Statement	Truth set
p	P
$\sim p$	$\widetilde{P}$
$p \wedge q$	$P \cap Q$
$p \vee q$	$P \cup Q$
$\sim p \vee q$	$\widetilde{P} \cup Q$
$\sim(p \wedge \sim q)$	$\widetilde{(P \cap \widetilde{Q})}$
$(p \wedge q) \vee (\sim p \wedge \sim q)$	$(P \cap Q) \cup (\widetilde{P} \cap \widetilde{Q})$

Figure 25

by using truth-table analysis. Indeed, the following examples show that both these procedures are possible.

Example 1. Prove by means of a Venn diagram that the statement $[p \vee (\sim p \vee q)]$ is logically true. The assigned set of this statement is $[P \cup (\widetilde{P} \cup Q)]$, and its Venn diagram is shown in Figure 26. The set P is

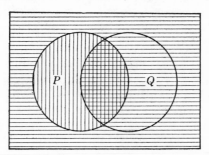

Figure 26

shaded vertically, and the set $\widetilde{P} \cup Q$ is shaded horizontally. Their union is the entire shaded area, which is $\mathfrak{U}$, so that the compound statement is logically true.

Example 2. Prove by means of Venn diagrams that $p \vee (q \wedge r)$ is equivalent to $(p \vee q) \wedge (p \vee r)$. The truth set of $p \vee (q \wedge r)$ is the entire shaded area of Figure 27, and the truth set of $(p \vee q) \wedge (p \vee r)$ is the doubly shaded area in Figure 28. Since these two sets are equal, we see that the two statements are equivalent.

Example 3. Prove that $P \cap (Q \cup R) = (P \cap Q) \cup (P \cap R)$ by truth-table analysis. In Exercise 14 of Section 2 the reader was asked to show that the statements $p \wedge (q \vee r)$ and $(p \wedge q) \vee (p \wedge r)$ have the same truth table. Hence these statements are both true for a given logical possibility or both false, and therefore their truth sets are equal. The set equality above merely states the latter.

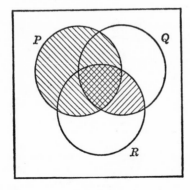

Figure 27

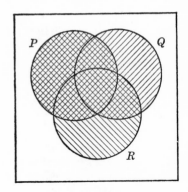

Figure 28

EXERCISES

In Exercises 1 and 2 find first the truth set of each statement.

1. Use Venn diagrams to test which of the following statements are logically true or logically false.

a. $p \vee \sim p$.

b. $p \wedge \sim p$.

c. $p \vee (\sim p \wedge q)$.

d. $\sim p \vee \sim (q \wedge \sim p)$.

e. $p \wedge \sim (\sim q \vee p)$.

[*Ans. a., d.* logically true; *b., e.* logically false.]

2. Use Venn diagrams to test the following statements for equivalences.

a. $p \vee \sim q$.

b. $\sim (p \wedge q)$.

c. $\sim (q \wedge \sim p)$.

d. $\sim (\sim (\sim p \vee \sim q))$.

e. $\sim p \vee \sim q$.

[*Ans. a.* and *c.* equivalent; *b.* and *d.* and *e.* equivalent.]

In Exercises 3–5 assign to each set a statement having it as a truth set.

3. Use truth tables to find which of the following sets are empty.

a. $(P \cup Q) \cap (\tilde{P} \cup \tilde{Q})$.

b. $(P \cap Q) \cap (\tilde{Q} \cap R)$.

c. $(P \cap Q) - P$.

d. $(P \cup R) \cap (\tilde{P} \cup \tilde{Q})$.

[*Ans. b.* and *c.*]

4. Use truth tables to find out whether the following sets are all different.

a. $P \cap (Q \cup R)$.

b. $(R - Q) \cup (Q - R)$.

c. $(R \cup Q) \cap (\widetilde{R \cap Q})$.

d. $(P \cap Q) \cup (P \cap R)$.

e. $(P \cap Q \cap \tilde{R}) \cup (P \cap \tilde{Q} \cap R) \cup (\tilde{P} \cap Q \cap \tilde{R}) \cup (\tilde{P} \cap \tilde{Q} \cap R)$.

5. Use truth tables for the following pairs of sets to test whether one is a subset of the other.

a. $P; P \cap Q$.

b. $P \cap \tilde{Q}; Q \cap \tilde{P}$.

c. $P - Q; Q - P$.

d. $\tilde{P} \cap \tilde{Q}; P \cup Q$.

6. Show, both by the use of truth tables and by the use of Venn diagrams, that $\sim p \wedge (q \vee \sim r)$ is equivalent to $(\sim p \wedge q) \vee (\sim p \wedge \sim r)$.

7. A pair of statements p and q are said to be *inconsistent* if they cannot both be true. Devise a test for inconsistency.

[*Ans.* $p \wedge q$ is logically false and $P \cap Q = \mathcal{E}$.]

8. Three or more statements are said to be inconsistent if they cannot all be true. What does this say about their truth sets?

9. In the following three compound statements (*a*) assign variables to the components, (*b*) bring the statements into symbolic form, (*c*) find the truth sets, and (*d*) test for consistency.

Either this is not a good product, or I will work hard selling it.
Either this is a good product, or I will not sell a lot of it.
I will not work hard, but I will sell a lot of it.

[*Ans.* Inconsistent.]

10. Suppose you had a set of ten inconsistent statements. How would you go about selecting a subset that could be believed?

*7. CRITICAL PATH ANALYSIS

Whenever tasks are performed by many different people, or groups of people, perhaps with the aid of machines, their activities must be planned and coordinated. Some pairs of tasks can be carried on simultaneously (in parallel), others must be done in a certain order (in series). Commonly, the planning is left to some person who is director of the project and who keeps track of the progress of the job.

If all goes well with the project, this method of coordination is satisfactory. But if the project is falling behind schedule, or if for some reason it must be speeded up, a better approach is desirable. The basic tool for such an approach is a project graph, which we will describe below. The entire approach is known as *critical path analysis*.

We first need to introduce a number of technical terms.

DEFINITION. A *project* is a nonempty set of jobs $\{a, b, c, \ldots\}$, for each of which a *time* is assigned and a relationship of being a *predecessor* of other jobs is determined.

For example, the jobs may be all the individual tasks that have to be completed in building a house or constructing an airplane. The time of a job is the number of time units (in some conveniently chosen units) required to finish the job, and a is a predecessor of b (or b is a *successor* of a) if a must be completed before b can be started. For instance, in constructing a house, pouring the foundation is a predecessor of putting up the roof.

To specify the predecessors of a given job, it suffices to specify the *immediate predecessors*, which is the smallest set of jobs such that once they are completed the given job may be started. The predecessors of a job are its immediate predecessors, the immediate predecessors of these, and so on.

DEFINITION. A *project graph* is a set of boxes in the plane with arrows connecting some of the boxes. There is one box for each job, and if a is an immediate predecessor of b, then there is an arrow from a to b. Predecessors appear at a lower level than their successors.

It is also helpful to introduce the following convention: We add to the list of jobs the pseudo-jobs "start" and "finish." Each requires 0 time to carry out, and "start" is a predecessor of all other jobs, while "finish" is a successor of all other jobs. These will be very convenient for bookkeeping purposes.

Example 1. Our project is the manufacture of a machine component that consists of two parts, P and Q. Each part must be turned on a lathe and Q must also be polished. Two types of raw materials, A and B, are needed. The project is specified by Figure 29. Its project graph is shown in Figure 30.

Job	Description	Immediate Predecessors	Time
a	Start	none	0
b	Order A	$\{a\}$	2
c	Order B	$\{a\}$	1
d	Turn P	$\{b, c\}$	2
e	Turn Q	$\{b, c\}$	1
f	Polish Q	$\{e\}$	2
g	Assemble component	$\{d, f\}$	1
h	Finish	$\{g\}$	0

Figure 29

As may be seen in Figure 30, the project graph is a convenient and concise way of tabulating all the relevant information. In fact, such a graph represents a common language that can be understood not only by foremen, superintendents, and project directors, but also by workmen and even by someone not involved in the project. We shall now show that a great deal more may be learned from a project graph.

As a first task we shall try to find the earliest possible completion date for our project. To do this, we carry out the following simple computations, beginning at "start," and working our way up one level at a time. (1) Write 0 to the right of "start." (2) Take a new job, and write to the *left* of it the largest number written to the right of any immediate predecessor. (3) Add to this number the time of the project, and record this to the *right* of the job. (4) Stop when "finish" is reached.

The interpretation of this simple routine is as follows: the number to the left of a job is the earliest that it can be started, and the number to the right of it is the earliest that it can be completed. We begin by saying that "start" comes at time 0, and then we compute the other figures using the fact that a project can start as soon as its immediate predecessors have been completed. We call the times computed the *early start time* (e.s.t.)

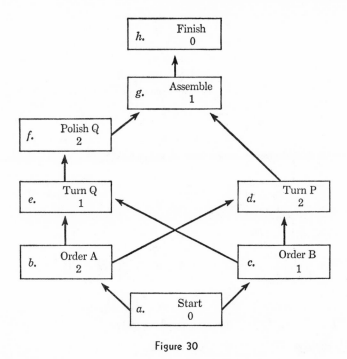

Figure 30

and *early finish time* (e.f.t.) for the various jobs. The e.s.t. for "finish" (or e.f.t., which is the same) is the answer to our problem, namely the earliest time at which the project can be completed. We refer to this as the *target time.*

> **Example 1 (continued).** Figure 31 shows the e.s.t. and e.f.t. of all the jobs. These may be computed by the four-step method described above. The target time turns out to be 6.

We would next like to know how much freedom we have in scheduling various tasks. For this we want the latest times at which a project can be started or finished without delaying the target time. These will be the *late start times* (l.s.t.) and *late finish times* (l.f.t.) of various jobs. We again put the starting times to the left and the finish times to the right of jobs, separating e.s.t. from l.s.t. and e.f.t. from l.f.t. by a hyphen. Our computation is very similar to the other four-step method, but this time we start with "finish" and work down one level at a time. (1) The l.s.t. of "finish" is the target time. (2) Take a new job, and assign to it as l.f.t. the smallest of the l.s.t.'s of its immediate successors. (3) Obtain the l.s.t. by subtracting the time of the project. (4) Stop when "start" is reached. Note that all that we have really used is the fact that a job must be finished before any of its successors are started.

> **Example 1 (continued).** Figure 32 shows the results of the new four-step computation. We note that we ended up with 0 as the late starting time for

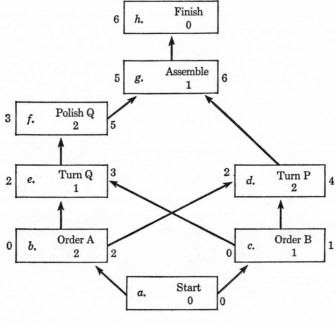

Figure 31

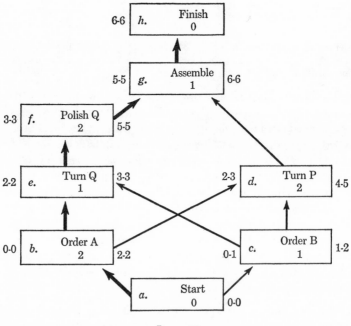

Figure 32

"start." This must always be the case, since the target time is the earliest possible target assuming that we start at 0. If a later starting time were possible for the project, then we should have been able to find an earlier target time.

DEFINITION. The *slack time* of a job is the difference between its l.s.t. and its e.s.t. A job with 0 slack time is a *critical job.*

The slack time may be thought of as the amount of freedom we have in scheduling that particular job, if all other jobs are scheduled suitably. Of course this could also be computed by taking the difference between l.f.t. and e.f.t. A critical job is a bottleneck in the project. The target date can be decreased only by decreasing the time required for one or more critical jobs (see Exercise 1).

DEFINITION. A *critical path* is a path (following the arrows) from "start" to "finish" that consists entirely of critical jobs.

THEOREM. Every critical job (not counting "start" and "finish") has at least one critical immediate predecessor and at least one critical immediate successor. Every project has at least one critical path, and every critical job lies on one or more critical paths.

Proof. Let us first show that "finish" has at least one critical immediate predecessor. If it did not, then each of its immediate predecessors would have an e.f.t. less than the l.f.t. Hence each of these could be finished at least one unit before its l.f.t. But the l.f.t. of an immediate predecessor of "finish" is the target time, hence the target time could be reduced, which is impossible.

In exactly the same way we show that we get a contradiction by assuming that all immediate predecessors of any critical job have slacks. Thus we conclude that a critical job must have at least one critical immediate predecessor.

We can also show in much the same way that "start" and all critical jobs have critical immediate successors. This completes the first part of the theorem. It also shows that there are critical jobs other than "start" or "finish." Take any such job a, and pick an immediate predecessor of a and an immediate successor of a that are critical. Continue this process in both directions till "start" and "finish" are reached, yielding a critical path that contains a. This completes the proof.

Example 1 (continued). The darkened path in Figure 32 shows the one critical path of our example. All critical jobs lie on this path. Thus, reducing job d to one time unit will not speed the project, since this job had a slack of 1, anyway. Job g would still have to wait for the completion of the critical predecessors b, e, and f, which are not helped by a change in d.

Example 2. In Figure 33 we redraw the figure of Example 1, but with a changed job time for d. Here the critical jobs are b, d, and g, and the critical path is shown darkened. The noncritical jobs, which are c, e, and f, each have total slack equal to 1. Note that we cannot use up the slack in jobs e and f both, without delaying the finish time of the project. For if e is delayed by one unit, then the early start time for f becomes 4 and hence f becomes a critical job.

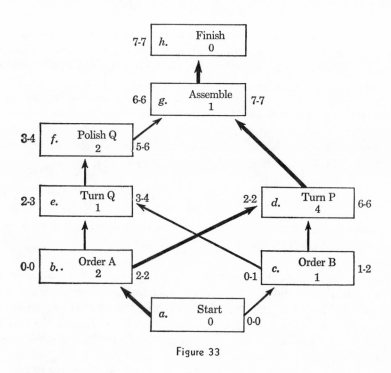

Figure 33

Other kinds of slack that can be defined for jobs are discussed in the exercises (see Exercises 9–11).

Example 3. A student wishes to major in mathematics and minor in physics. He must take seven mathematics courses, two statistics courses, and two physics courses, plus a mathematical physics course. These are all one-term courses. What is the minimum number of terms it will take for him to finish his requirements, ignoring all other course requirements and constraints? The twelve courses are listed with their immediate predecessors (usually called prerequisites) in Figure 34. Except for "start" and "finish," which take no time, each course takes one unit of time (a term). The project graph is shown in Figure 35. In the figure the early and late start and completion for each job, as well as the slack ($s = \ldots$) are marked. The minimum time to complete the project is six terms. The critical path, which in this case is unique, is shown as a darkened line. The critical courses (jobs) are seen to be M101, M102, M104, M108, M110, and M111. Delaying the taking of any critical course will delay the completion of the major. On the other hand, some courses have quite a bit of slack. Statistics 1 and 2 have three units of slack each. M103 has one term slack, but if it is delayed for that term, then both statistics

No.	*Courses*	*Immediate Predecessors* *(Prerequisites)*
	Start	None
M101	Calculus I	Start
M102	Calculus II	M101
M103	Finite Mathematics	Start
M104	Calculus III	M102, M103
S1	Elementary Statistics	M103
S2	Advanced Statistics	S1, M102
P1	Elementary Physics	M101
P2	Advanced Physics	P1, M102
M108	Advanced Calculus	M104
M109	Mathematical Physics	M108, P2
M110	Complex Variable	M108
M111	Real Variable	M110
	Finish	M109, M111, S2

Figure 34

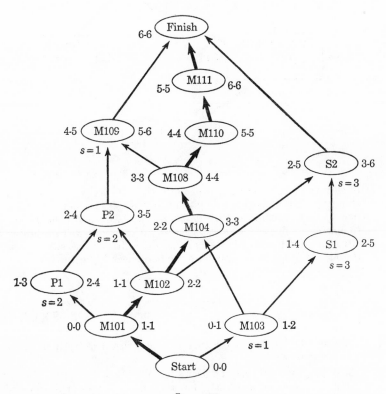

Figure 35

courses have one less unit of slack. Many other observations can be made from the figure.

Example 4. One of the important uses for critical path analysis is in the planning and monitoring of the development of new kinds of equipment. Figure 36 shows an example of such a plan for the development of a new piece

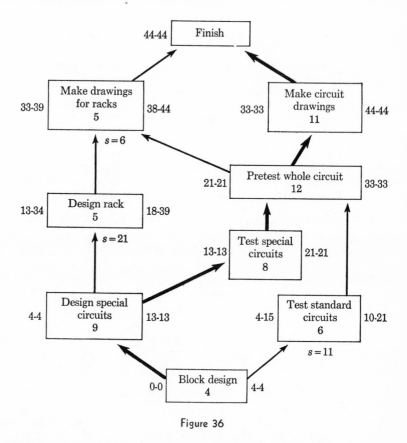

Figure 36

of electronics equipment. It is assumed that the design involves some quite standard kinds of circuits that take little time, plus the development of some new kinds of circuits, and the design of the chassis and panel racks for the completed product. The times in weeks are given, as well as the early and late times, and the slack times for noncritical jobs. We see that the design and testing of the special circuits form the bottleneck in the project.

EXERCISES

1. Prove that reducing the time of a noncritical job does not reduce the target time.

2. A project graph may be drawn as an "arrow diagram," in which jobs are represented as arrows. Job x is an immediate predecessor of job y if the tip of the arrow representing job x touches the end of the arrow for job y. For instance, consider the project arrow diagram in Figure 37. Here job a is a predecessor of jobs c and d, job c is a predecessor of job e, and job b is a predecessor of job f. Adding the dummy jobs of Start and Finish, draw the project graph for the project whose arrow diagram is given in Figure 37.

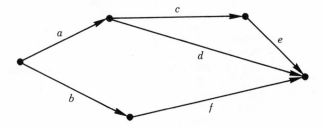

Figure 37

3. Try to draw the arrow diagram for the project graph shown in Figure 38. Show that it is impossible to complete it without adding one "dummy job" to avoid unintended precedence relations among jobs. Show also that the arrow diagrams for Figures 35 and 36 require dummy jobs. The main advantage of the project graph as defined here is that there is no need for adding this kind of dummy job to prevent the occurrence of unintended precedence relations.

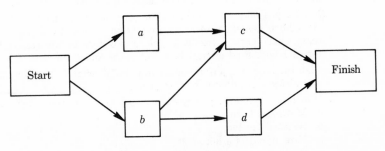

Figure 38

4. Winters, a house contractor, has listed the jobs needed to build a house. They are shown below together with their predecessors and their times. Draw the project graph. Compute the e.s.t., e.f.t., l.f.t., and e.f.t. for each job. Mark critical paths and show slacks.

Job	Description	Predecessors	Time (Days)
a	Start	None	0
b	Lay foundation	{a}	6
c	Wooden frame including rough roof	{b}	4
d	Brickwork	{b}	4
e	Basement drains and plumbing	{b}	1
f	Pour basement floor	{e}	2
g	Rough plumbing	{c, f}	3
h	Rough wiring	{c, f}	2
i	Heating and ventilating	{c, f}	4
j	Plaster board and plaster (drying)	{i, h, g}	10
k	Install finish flooring	{j}	3
l	Install kitchen fixtures	{j}	2
m	Install finish plumbing	{j}	2
n	Finish carpentry	{j}	3
o	Roofing and flashing	{d, c, f}	2

Job	Description	Predecessors	Time (Days)
p	Gutters and downspouts	$\{o\}$	1
q	Storm drains for rain water	$\{p\}$	1
r	Sand and varnish flooring	$\{k, l, m, n\}$	2
s	Paint	$\{r\}$	3
t	Finish electrical work	$\{s\}$	2
u	Finish grading	$\{q\}$	2
v	Walks and landscaping	$\{u\}$	5
w	Finish	$\{v, t\}$	0

5. In Example 3 assume that the student delays the following courses by the amounts indicated, but elects all other courses as early as possible. By how much is the final completion time of his major delayed?
   a. M103 one term.
   b. M103 one term and S1 four terms.
   c. M101 two terms and M108 one term.
   d. P2 two terms and M109 one term.   [*Ans. a.* 0; *b.* 2; *c.* 3; *d.* 1.]

6. Draw a project graph for the task of cooking a meal in a kitchen with two stove burners and one oven, assuming that the menu will consist of: soup, roast, baked potato, vegetables, pie, and coffee. Assume reasonable times for each job. Find critical jobs and paths and total slack for each job.

7. Plan the following job: repair an automobile engine, installing new rings and pistons, grinding valves, replacing spark plugs, etc.

8. Which of the following projects are suitable for critical path analysis?
   a. Mowing a lawn.
   b. Writing a letter.
   c. Moving out of a house.
   d. Repairing a watch.
   e. Servicing an airplane.
   f. Building a bridge.
   g. Getting dressed in the morning.

9. The *free slack* of a job is defined to be the smallest of the early start times of the successors of *a* minus the early finish time of *a*. For instance, in Figure 33 job *e* has 0 free slack while job *f* has 1 free slack. Free slack measures the amount a job can be displaced assuming all other jobs are started as early as possible.
   a. Find the free slacks of noncritical jobs in Figure 35.
   b. Find the free slacks of the noncritical jobs in Figure 36.
   [*Partial Ans.* In Figure 35, M109 has free slack of 1, and S2 has free slack of 3.]

10. The *independent slack* of a job *a* is defined to be the minimum of the early start times of successors of *a* minus the maximum of the late finish times of predecessors of *a* minus the time for *a*, *providing* this quantity is nonnegative; otherwise the independent slack of *a* is defined to be zero. Independent slack measures the amount a job can be displaced regardless of all other jobs, providing only that the other jobs remain within their early and late times.
   a. In Figure 32 show that job *d* has independent slack 1.
   b. Find the independent slacks for noncritical jobs in Figure 35.
   c. Find the independent slacks of noncritical jobs in Figure 36.

11. Devise a project having at least one job that has different slack, free slack, and independent slacks.

12. A group of authors laid out the following plans for writing a book jointly. The project is still not completed. Why?

Job	Description	Immediate Predecessors	Time (Weeks)
a	Start	none	0
b	Write Chapter 1	{a}	2
c	Write Chapter 2	{a}	1
d	Write Chapter 3	{b, c}	4
e	Write Chapter 4	{c}	2
f	Draw diagrams	{d, e, h}	1
g	Compile index	{f}	2
h	Write preface	{d, e, i}	1
i	Compile bibliography	{g}	2
j	Finish	{h, i}	0

SUGGESTED READING

Tarski, A., *Introduction to Logic*, Oxford, New York, 2nd rev. ed., 1946, Chapters I, II.

Church, A., *Introduction to Mathematical Logic*, Volume I, Princeton University Press, 1956.

Suppes, P., *Introduction to Mathematical Logic*, Van Nostrand, Princeton, 1957.

Johnstone, H. W., Jr., *Elementary Deductive Logic*, Crowell, New York, 1954, Parts 1, 2, and 3.

Breuer, Joseph, *Introduction to the Theory of Sets*, Prentice Hall, Englewood Cliffs, N. J., 1958.

Fraenkel, A. A., *Abstract Set Theory*, North-Holland Publishing Co., Amsterdam, 1953.

Levy, F. K., G. L. Thompson, and J. D. Wiest, "The ABC's of the Critical-Path Method," *Harvard Business Review*, 41 (1963), pp. 98–108.

2

COUNTING
PROBLEMS

1. PERMUTATIONS

The first step in the analysis of a scientific problem is the determination of the set of logical possibilities. Next it is often necessary to determine how many different possible outcomes there are. We will find this particularly important in probability theory. Hence it is desirable to develop general techniques for solving counting problems. In this section and the next we shall discuss the two most important cases in which it is possible to achieve formulas that solve the problem. When a formula cannot be derived, one must resort to certain other general counting techniques, tricks, or, in the last resort, complete enumeration of the possibilities.

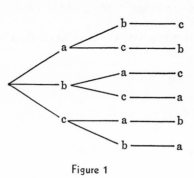

Figure 1

As a first problem let us consider the number of ways in which a group of n different objects can be arranged. A *listing* of n different objects *in a certain order* is called a *permutation* of the n objects. We consider first the case of three objects, a, b, and c. We can exhibit all possible permutations of these three objects as paths of a tree, as shown in Figure 1. Each path exhibits a possible permutation, and there are six such paths. We could also list these permutations as follows:

abc,   bca,
acb,   cab,
bac,   cba.

If we were to construct a similar tree for n objects, we would find that the number of paths could be found by multiplying together the numbers n, $n-1$, $n-2$, continuing down to the number 1. The number obtained in this way occurs so often that we give it a symbol, namely $n!$, which is read "n factorial." Thus, for example, $3! = 3 \cdot 2 \cdot 1 = 6$, $4! = 4 \cdot 3 \cdot 2 \cdot 1 = 24$, and so on. For reasons that will be clear later, we define $0! = 1$. Thus we can say *there are $n!$ different permutations of n distinct objects.*

Example 1. Seven different machining operations are to be performed on a part, but they may be performed in any sequence. We may then consider $7! = 5040$ different orders in which the operations may be performed.

Example 2. Ten workers are to be assigned to 10 different jobs. In how many ways can the assignments be made? The first worker may be assigned in 10 possible ways, the second in any of the 9 remaining ways, the third in 8, and so forth: there are $10! = 3,628,800$ possible ways of assigning the workers to the jobs.

Example 3. A company has n directors. In how many ways can they be seated around a circular table at a board meeting, if two arrangements are considered different only if at least one person has a different person sitting on his right in the two arrangements? To solve the problem, consider one director in a fixed position. There are $(n-1)!$ ways in which the other people may be seated. We have now counted all the arrangements we wish to consider different. Thus there are also $(n-1)!$ possible seating arrangements.

For many counting problems it is not possible to give a simple formula for the number of possible cases. In many of these the only way to find the number of cases is to draw a tree and count them (see Exercise 4). In some problems, the following general principle is useful.

A GENERAL PRINCIPLE. *If one thing can be done in exactly r different ways, for each of these a second thing can be done in exactly s different ways, for each of the first two, a third can be done in exactly t ways, and so on, then the sequence of things can be done in $r \cdot s \cdot t \ldots$ ways.*

The validity of this general principle can be established by thinking of a tree representing all the ways in which the sequence of things can be done. There would be r branches from the starting position. From the ends of each of these r branches there would be s new branches, and from each of these t new branches, and so on. The number of paths through the tree would be given by the product $r \cdot s \cdot t \ldots$

Example 4. The number of permutations of n distinct objects is a special case of this principle. If we were to list all the possible permutations, there would be n possibilities for the first, for each of these $n-1$ for the second, etc., until we came to the last object, and for which there is only one possibility. Thus there are $n(n-1) \ldots 1 = n!$ possibilities in all.

Example 5. An automobile manufacturer produces four different models; models A and B can come in any of four body styles—sedan, hardtop,

convertible, and station wagon—while models C and D come only as sedans
or hardtops. Each car can come in one of nine colors. Thus models A and B
each have $4 \cdot 9 = 36$ distinguishable types, while C and D have $2 \cdot 9 = 18$
types, so that in all

$$2 \cdot 36 + 2 \cdot 18 = 108$$

different car types are produced by the manufacturer.

Example 6. Suppose there are n applicants for a certain job. Three interviewers are asked independently to rank the applicants according to their
suitability. It is decided that an applicant will be hired if he is ranked first
by at least two of the three interviewers. What fraction of the possible
reports would lead to the acceptance of some candidate? We shall solve this
problem by finding the fraction of the reports that do not lead to an acceptance and subtract this answer from 1. Frequently an indirect attack of this
kind is easier than the direct approach. The total number of reports possible
is $(n!)^3$, since each interviewer can rank the men in $n!$ different ways. If a
particular report does not lead to the acceptance of a candidate, it must
be true that each interviewer has put a different man in first place. By our
general principle, this can be done in $n(n - 1)(n - 2)$ different ways. For
each possible first choice, there are $[(n - 1)!]^3$ ways in which the remaining
men can be ranked by the interviewers. Thus the number of reports that
do not lead to acceptance is

$$n(n - 1)(n - 2)[(n - 1)!]^3.$$

Dividing this number by $(n!)^3$, we obtain

$$\frac{(n - 1)(n - 2)}{n^2}$$

as the fraction of reports that fail to accept a candidate. The fraction that
leads to acceptance is found by subtracting this fraction from 1, which gives

$$\frac{3n - 2}{n^2}.$$

For the case of three applicants, we see that $\frac{7}{9}$ of the possibilities lead to acceptance. Here the procedure might be criticized on the grounds that even if
the interviewers are completely ineffective and are essentially guessing, there
is a good chance that a candidate will be accepted on the basis of the reports.
For n equal to ten, the fraction of acceptances is only .28, so that it is possible
to attach more significance to the interviewers' ratings, if they reach a
decision.

EXERCISES

1. A salesman is going to call on five customers. In how many different
   sequences can he do this if he
   a. calls on all five in one day?
   b. calls on three one day and two the next?   [*Ans.* 120; 120.]

2. A machine shop has two milling machines, four lathes, seven drill presses, and three grinders. In how many ways can a part be routed that must first be ground, then milled, then turned on a lathe, and then drilled? In how many ways can it be routed if these four operations can be performed in any order?

3. Show the possible arrangements of machines A, B, C, and D in a circle. How many are there?

4. How many possible ways are there of seating six people, A, B, C, D, E, and F, at a circular table if
    a. A must always have B on his right?   [*Ans.* 24.]
    b. A must always have either B or C on his right?   [*Ans.* 48.]
    c. A must always have either B or C on his right, and B either C or D?
                                                                    [*Ans.* 18.]

5. In seating n people around a circular table, suppose we distinguish between two arrangements only if at least one person has at least one different person sitting next to him in the two arrangements. That is, we do not regard two arrangements as different simply because the righthand and lefthand neighbors of a person have interchanged places. Now how many distinguishable arrangements are there?

6. In how many ways can six people be assigned to offices if
    a. there are six offices, and one person is assigned to each office?
    b. there are three offices, and two people are assigned to each?
    c. there are four offices, two accommodating two people and two one person each?

7. A company has six officers and six directors; two of the directors are officers. List the possible memberships of a committee of four men who are either officers or directors in terms of the number of members who are (a) just officers, (b) just directors, and (c) both officers and directors.

8. In Exercise 7, how many ways are there of obtaining a committee of four consisting of
    a. two who are just officers, one who is just a director, and one who is an officer and a director?   [*Ans.* 48.]
    b. two who are just officers and two who are officers and directors?
                                                                    [*Ans.* 6.]
    c. two who are just officers and two who are just directors?   [*Ans.* 36.]

9. In Exercise 7, suppose a committee of four is to consist of at least two officers and at least two directors, where a man who is both an officer and a director satisfies both quotas. In how many ways can such a committee be formed?

10. Modify Example 6 so that, to be accepted, an applicant must be first in two of the interviewers' ratings and must be either first or second in the third interviewer's rating. What fraction of the possible reports lead to acceptance in the case of three applicants? In the case of n?
                                                                    [*Ans.* $\frac{4}{9}$; $4/n^2$.]

11. Find the number of arrangements of the five symbols that can be distinguished. (The same letters with different subscripts indicate distinguishable objects.)
    a. A_1, A_2, B_1, B_2, B_3.   [*Ans.* 120.]
    b. A, A, B_1, B_2, B_3.   [*Ans.* 60.]
    c. A, A, B, B, B.   [*Ans.* 10.]

12. Show that the number of distinguishable arrangements possible for n objects, n_1 of type 1, n_2 of type 2, and so on for r different types is

$$\frac{n!}{n_1!n_2! \cdots n_r!}.$$

13. *a.* How many four-digit numbers can be formed from the digits 1, 2, 3, 4, using each digit only once?

   b. How many of these numbers are less than 3000?   [*Ans.* 12.]

14. How many license plates can be made if they are to contain five symbols, the first two being letters and the last three integers?

15. How many signals can a ship show if it has seven flags and a signal consists of five flags hoisted vertically on a rope?   [*Ans.* 2520.]

16. We must arrange three green, two red, and four blue books on a single shelf.

   a. In how many ways can this be done if there are no restrictions?

   b. In how many ways if books of the same color must be grouped together?

   c. In how many ways if, in addition to the restriction in (*b*), the red books must be to the left of the blue books?

   d. In how many ways if, in addition to the restrictions in (*b*) and (*c*), the red and blue books must not be next to each other?   [*Ans.* 288.]

17. A young lady has three shades of nail polish with which to paint her fingernails. In how many ways can she do this (each nail being one solid color) if there are no more than two different shades on each hand?

[*Ans.* 8649.]

2. LABELING PROBLEMS

The second general type of counting problem that we want to consider may be described as follows. We have n objects and we wish to label each of these objects with one of r different types of labels. To be more specific, we wish to determine the total number of ways that we can label the n objects with r labels if n_1 of the objects are to be given the first type of label, n_2 the second type, and so on, where $n_1, n_2, \ldots, n_r$ are given nonnegative integers such that $n_1 + n_2 + \cdots + n_r = n$.

As an example assume that we have eight customers, A, B, C, D, E, F, G, and H, and we wish to assign to each of them one of three salesmen, Brown, Jones, or Smith. And we want to make this assignment so that Brown is assigned to three customers, Jones to three, and Smith to two. Notice that we can interpret the problem as that of assigning a label— Brown, Jones, or Smith—to each of the eight customers. In how many ways can this assignment be made?

One way to assign the customers is to list them in some arbitrary order (that is, select a permutation of them) and then assign Brown to the first three, Jones to the next three, and Smith to the last two. There are 8!

permutations or listings of the customers, but not all of these lead to different assignments. For instance, consider the following assignment

$$| \text{ BCA } | \text{ DFE } | \text{ HG } |.$$

Here, Brown is assigned to B, C, and A, Jones to D, F, and E, and Smith to H and G. Notice that another permutation such as

$$| \text{ ABC } | \text{ DEF } | \text{ GH } |$$

gives the same customer assignments, since it differs only in the sequences for particular salesmen. There are $3! \cdot 3! \cdot 2!$ such listings, since we can arrange the three customers of Brown in $3!$ different ways, and for each of these, the customers of Jones in $3!$ different ways, and for each of these, the customers of Smith in $2!$ different ways. Since there are $3! \cdot 3! \cdot 2!$ different listings that lead to the same assignments and $8!$ listings in all, there are $8!/(3! \cdot 3! \cdot 2!)$ different assignments of customers to salesmen.

The same argument could be carried out for r salesmen and n customers with n_1 assigned to the first salesman, n_2 to the second, and so on. In fact there is really nothing special about the argument for this example, so we have the following basic result. Let $n_1, n_2, \ldots, n_r$ be nonnegative integers with $n_1 + n_2 + \cdots + n_r = n$. Then:

The number of ways that n objects can be labeled with r different types of labels, n_1 with the first type, n_2 with the second, and so on, is

$$\frac{n!}{n_1! n_2! \cdots n_r!}.$$

We shall denote this number by the symbol

$$\binom{n}{n_1, n_2, \ldots, n_r}.$$

The special case when $r = 2$, meaning that there are just two types of labels, is particularly important. The problem is often stated in the following way. We are given a set of n elements; in how many ways can we choose a subset with r elements? If we interpret the problem to mean labeling each element as either "in the set" or "not in the set," we see that it is just a labeling problem whose answer is

$$\binom{n}{r, \, n - r} = \frac{n!}{r!(n - r)!};$$

and hence this is also the number of subsets with r elements. The notation $\binom{n}{r, \, n - r}$ is commonly shortened to $\binom{n}{r}$. These numbers are known as *binomial coefficients*.

Notice that every time we choose a subset of r elements to put in our subset we are also choosing a subset of $n - r$ elements to leave out. In this way we see that

$$\binom{n}{r} = \binom{n}{r,\, n-r} = \binom{n}{n-r}.$$

Example 1. A company buys a certain electronic component from three vendors. In how many ways can it place six orders, two with vendor A, three with vendor B, and one with vendor C? This is just the problem of labeling each of the six orders with one of three labels, A, B, or C. There are

$$\binom{6}{2,\,3,\,1} = \frac{6!}{2!3!1!} = 60$$

ways of carrying out the labeling.

Example 2. On August 20, 1970, 1551 different stock issues were traded on the New York Stock Exchange. Of these, 701 advanced, 530 declined, and 320 closed unchanged from the previous day. In how many ways could this have happened? We must label each stock as "advanced," "declined," or "unchanged." There are

$$\frac{1551!}{701!530!320!}$$

different ways in which this particular result could occur. This number is approximately equal to $1.1 \cdot 10^{705}$.

Example 3. This example will be important in probability theory, which we take up in the next chapter. If a coin is tossed six times, there are 2^6 possibilities for the outcome of the six throws, since each throw can result in either a head or a tail. How many of these possibilities result in four heads and two tails? We can interpret each assignment of outcomes to be a labeling of each integer from 1 to 6 with either H or T, corresponding to whether heads or tails came up on that toss. Since we required that four be labeled H and two T, the answer is $\binom{6}{4} = 15$. For n throws of a coin, a similar analysis shows that there are $\binom{n}{r}$ different sequences of H's and T's of length n that have exactly r heads and $n - r$ tails.

EXERCISES

1. Compute the following numbers.

a. $\binom{7}{5}$. [*Ans.* 21.]

b. $\binom{3}{2}$.

c. $\binom{7}{2}$.

d. $\binom{250}{249}$. [*Ans.* 250.]

e. $\binom{5}{0}$.

f. $\binom{5}{1, 2, 2}$.

g. $\binom{4}{2, 0, 2}$.   [*Ans.* 6.]

h. $\binom{2}{1, 1, 1}$.

2. Give an interpretation for $\binom{n}{0}$ and also for $\binom{n}{n}$. Can you now give a reason for making $0! = 1$?

3. How many ways can nine accounts be assigned to three different salesmen so that each one gets three accounts? How many ways if the same salesman cannot be assigned to one particular pair of accounts.
[*Ans.* 1680·1260.]

4. A group of seven workers is to be assigned to seven of ten available jobs. If we are only interested in which jobs are assigned, and not the specific worker-job assignments and if all of the workers are assigned jobs, in how many ways can the jobs be assigned to the workers? How many possibilities are there for the unassigned jobs, if three of the jobs are sure to be assigned?

5. Customers of the ABC Company may have their orders delivered from one of three field warehouses. If fifteen customers place orders,
   a. how many possibilities are there for assigning the warehouses from which the orders are delivered?   [*Ans.* 3^{15}.]
   b. how many of these possibilities would result in the assignment of the same number of orders from each warehouse?   [*Ans.* 756,756.]

6. A brewing company contracts with a television station to show three spot commercials a week for 35 weeks. The commercials consist of a series of cartoons. It is decided that in no two weeks will exactly the same three cartoons be shown. What is the minimum number of cartoons that will accomplish this? What is the minimum number if it is determined never to show the same commercial twice?

7. In how many ways can a machine produce ten pieces, half of which are good and half defective? In how many ways if no two consecutive pieces are both good or both defective?

8. From a lot containing six pieces, three good and three defective, a sample of three pieces is drawn. If we distinguish each piece, find the number of possible samples that can be formed:
   a. with no restrictions.   [*Ans.* 20.]
   b. with three good pieces and no defectives.   [*Ans.* 1.]
   c. with two good pieces and one defective.   [*Ans.* 9.]
   d. with one good piece and two defectives.   [*Ans.* 9.]
   e. with no good pieces and three defectives.   [*Ans.* 1.]
   What is the relation between your answer in part (*a*) and the answers to the remaining four parts?

9. Exercise 8 suggests that the following should be true:

$$\binom{2n}{n} = \binom{n}{0}\binom{n}{n} + \binom{n}{1}\binom{n}{n-1} + \binom{n}{2}\binom{n}{n-2} + \cdots + \binom{n}{n}\binom{n}{0}$$

$$= \binom{n}{0}^2 + \binom{n}{1}^2 + \cdots + \binom{n}{n}^2.$$

Show that it is true.

10. Show that

$$\binom{a}{b} = \frac{a \cdot (a-1) \cdot (a-2) \cdot \ldots \cdot (a-b+2) \cdot (a-b+1)}{b \cdot (b-1) \cdot (b-2) \cdot \ldots \cdot 2 \cdot 1},$$

where there are exactly b terms in both the numerator and the denominator.

11. Consider a town in which there are three plumbers, A, B, and C. On a certain day six residents of the town telephone for a plumber. If each resident selects a plumber from the telephone directory, in how many ways can it happen that

 a. three residents call A, two residents call B, and one resident calls C? [*Ans.* 60.]

 b. the distribution of calls to the plumbers is three, two, and one? [*Ans.* 360.]

12. Two committees (a labor relations committee and a quality control committee) are to be selected from a board of nine men. The only rules are (1) the two committees must have no members in common, and (2) each committee must have at least four men. In how many ways can the two committees be appointed?

13. A group of ten people is to be divided into three committees of three, three, and six members, respectively. The chairman of the group is to serve on all three committees and is the only member of the group who serves on more than one committee. In how many ways can the committee assignments be made? [*Ans.* 756.]

14. In a class of 20 students, grades of A, B, C, D, and F are to be assigned. Omit arithmetic details in answering the following.

 a. In how many ways can this be done if there are no restrictions? [*Ans.* 5^{20}.]

 b. In how many ways can this be done if the grades are assigned as follows: 2 A's, 3 B's, 10 C's, 3 D's, and 2 F's?

 c. In how many ways can this be done if the following rules are to be satisfied: exactly 10 C's; the same number of A's as F's; the same number of B's as D's; always more B's than A's?

$$\left[Ans. \ \binom{20}{5, \, 10, \, 5} + \binom{20}{1, \, 4, \, 10, \, 4, \, 1} + \binom{20}{2, \, 3, \, 10, \, 3, \, 2}. \right]$$

15. Establish the identity

$$\binom{n}{r}\binom{r}{k} = \binom{n}{k}\binom{n-k}{r-k}$$

for $n \geq r \geq k$ in two ways, as follows:

 a. Replace each expression by a ratio of factorials and show that the two sides are equal.

 b. Consider the following problem: From a set of n people a committee of r is to be chosen, and from these r people a steering subcommittee of k people is to be selected. Show that the two sides of the identity give two different ways of counting the possibilities for this problem.

3. SOME PROPERTIES OF BINOMIAL COEFFICIENTS

The binomial coefficients $\binom{n}{j}$ introduced in Section 2 will play an important role in our future work. We give here some of the more important properties of these numbers.

A convenient way to obtain these numbers is given by the famous Pascal triangle, shown in Figure 2. To obtain the triangle we first write

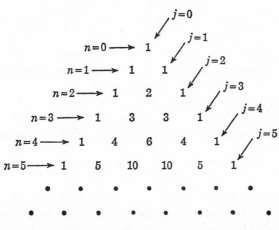

Figure 2

the 1's down the sides. Any of the other numbers in the triangle has the property that it is the sum of the two adjacent numbers in the row just above. Thus the next row in the triangle is 1, 6, 15, 20, 15, 6, 1. To find the binomial coefficient $\binom{n}{j}$ we look in the row corresponding to the number n and see where the diagonal line corresponding to the value of j intersects this row. For example, $\binom{4}{2} = 6$ is in the row marked $n = 4$ and on the diagonal marked $j = 2$.

The property of the binomial coefficients upon which the triangle is based is

$$\binom{n+1}{j} = \binom{n}{j-1} + \binom{n}{j}.$$

This fact can be verified directly (see Exercise 6), but the following argument is interesting in itself. The number $\binom{n+1}{j}$ is the number of subsets with j elements that can be formed from a set of $n + 1$ elements. Select one of the $n + 1$ elements, x. Of the $\binom{n+1}{j}$ subsets some contain x, and some do not. The latter are subsets of j elements formed from n objects, and hence there are $\binom{n}{j}$ such subsets. The former are constructed by adding x to a subset of $j - 1$ elements formed from n elements, and hence there are $\binom{n}{j-1}$ of them. Thus

$$\binom{n+1}{j} = \binom{n}{j-1} + \binom{n}{j}.$$

If we look again at the Pascal triangle, we observe that the numbers in a given row increase for a while, and then decrease. In fact, they increase to a unique maximum when n is even or to two equal maxima when n is odd.

An important application of binomial coefficients is in the expansion of products of the form $(x + y)^3$, $(a - 2b)^{10}$, and so on. We shall derive a general formula for these by making use of the binomial coefficients.

Consider first the special case $(x + y)^3$. We write this as

$$(x + y)^3 = (x + y)(x + y)(x + y).$$

To perform the multiplication, we choose either an x or y from each of the three factors and multiply our choices together; we do this for all possible choices and add the results. To state this as a labeling problem, note that we want to label each of the three factors with the two labels x and y. In how many ways can we do this using two x labels and one y? The preceding section gives the answer $\binom{3}{2} = 3$. Hence the coefficient of x^2y in the expansion of the binomial is 3. More generally, the coefficient of the term of the form x^jy^{3-j} will be $\binom{3}{j}$ for $j = 0, 1, 2, 3$. Thus we can write the desired expansion as

$$(x + y)^3 = \binom{3}{3} x^3 + \binom{3}{2} x^2y + \binom{3}{1} xy^2 + \binom{3}{0} y^3$$
$$= x^3 + 3x^2y + 3xy^2 + y^3.$$

Binomial Theorem. The expansion of $(x + y)^n$ is given by

$$(x + y)^n = x^n + \binom{n}{n-1} x^{n-1}y + \binom{n}{n-2} x^{n-2}y^2$$
$$+ \cdots + \binom{n}{1} xy^{n-1} + y^n.$$

Example 1. Let us find the expansion for $(a - 2b)^3$. To fit this into the binomial theorem, we think of x as being a and y as being $-2b$. Then we have

$$(a - 2b)^3 = a^3 + 3a^2(-2b) + 3a(-2b)^2 + (-2b)^3$$
$$= a^3 - 6a^2b + 12ab^2 - 8b^3.$$

EXERCISES

1. Extend the Pascal triangle to $n = 16$. Save the result for later use.
2. Prove that

$$\binom{n}{0} + \binom{n}{1} + \binom{n}{2} + \cdots + \binom{n}{n} = 2^n,$$

using the fact that a set with n elements has 2^n subsets.

3. For a set of ten elements prove that there are more subsets with five elements than there are subsets with any other fixed number of elements.

4. Using the fact that

$$\binom{n}{j+1} = \frac{n-j}{j+1} \cdot \binom{n}{j},$$

compute $\binom{30}{s}$ for $s = 1, 2, 3, 4$ from the fact that $\binom{30}{0} = 1$.

[*Ans.* 30; 435; 4060; 27,405.]

5. There are $\binom{52}{13}$ different possible bridge hands. Assume that a list is made showing all these hands, and that in this list the first card in every hand is crossed out. This leaves us with a list of twelve-card hands. Prove that at least two hands in the latter list contain exactly the same cards.

6. Prove that

$$\binom{n+1}{j} = \binom{n}{j-1} + \binom{n}{j},$$

using only the fact that

$$\binom{n}{j} = \frac{n!}{j!(n-j)!}.$$

7. Expand by the binomial theorem
   a. $(x + y)^4$.
   b. $(1 + x)^5$.
   c. $(x - y)^3$.
   d. $(2x + a)^4$.
   e. $(2x - 3y)^3$.
   f. $(100 - 1)^5$.

8. Using the binomial theorem, prove that

   a. $\binom{n}{0} + \binom{n}{1} + \binom{n}{2} + \cdots + \binom{n}{n} = 2^n.$

   b. $\binom{n}{0} - \binom{n}{1} + \binom{n}{2} - \binom{n}{3} + \cdots \pm \binom{n}{n} = 0$ for $n > 0$.

*4. FLOW DIAGRAMS

A flow diagram is a graphical device for showing the logical structure of a computation. A good flow diagram enables anyone familiar with arithmetical operations to carry out a computation, without the necessity of understanding the problem that gives rise to it. Thus, for example, it is easy to convert a flow diagram into a detailed set of instructions for a computing machine.

Flow diagrams have many advantages. Although a set of instructions (program) for one computer would be meaningless to a different kind of machine, the same flow diagram may be used to prepare a program for a variety of machines. It also enables a nonexpert to use computers, since he may hand his flow diagram to a professional programmer. This division of labor, having the customer write a flow diagram and having an expert change this to a program, is followed by many businesses.

But flow diagrams are extremely useful even in the absence of computing machines. They are an ideal way of clarifying a systematic or computational procedure.

A flow diagram consists of four types of components. The basic component is a *box*, which contains an arithmetical order. For example, the box

$$\boxed{x+2 \ \longrightarrow \ y}$$

instructs one to take x (some given or previously computed quantity), to add 2 to it, and assign this value to y. The quantity y may be one of the desired answers, or a quantity to be used in a later step in the computation. In general a box orders us to carry out arithmetical operations on known quantities, and to assign the answer to some variable. Note that a statement such as $x + 2 \rightarrow y$ is an *imperative* sentence, since it commands the carrying out of an instruction. This should be contrasted with a statement such as $x + 2 = y$, which is a *declarative* sentence indicating that a certain relation holds. These two statements are entirely different and should not be confused.

The next component in a flow diagram is the *circle*, which contains a question to be answered. These questions normally ask whether two known quantities are equal, or whether a certain inequality holds between them. For example, the circle

asks whether the number y is now bigger than 5. The outcome of a circle is a "yes" or "no," and we use circles to create a fork in the flow diagram.

That is, we may have one set of instructions if the answer is "yes," and a different set for a "no" answer.

We are now almost ready to write a simple flow diagram, but we must make provisions for starting and stopping. For this we use *terminals*, which are indicated by dashed boxes. Thus

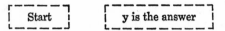

are typical terminals. The logical flow in the diagram will be indicated by arrows, which must start with a terminal and end in a terminal on each branch of the diagram.

Example 1. Suppose that we wish to compute $\sqrt{|a-2|}$, for some given number a. We wish to write a flow diagram that will work for any value of a. Such a diagram is shown in Figure 3. In this problem a is given, and we have

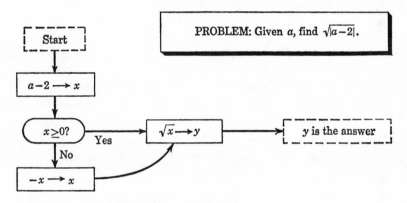

Figure 3

chosen y to represent the answer; that is, $y = \sqrt{|a-2|}$. We have introduced x for convenience, as a name for a partial answer. The flow diagram may be replaced by the following verbal instructions: "Subtract 2 from a. If the result is nonnegative, then take its square root, and this will be the answer. But if the result is negative, first replace the answer by minus the answer, and then take its square root." Even in so simple a problem the advantages of the flow diagram are clear.

This example illustrates a major need for flow diagrams. The formula $\sqrt{|a-2|}$ is static. It does not carry with it instructions on how the formula should be evaluated. This becomes more obvious in a more complex formula; a high school student may be baffled as to "where to start" in a formula such as

$$\frac{\sqrt{-(a+3b)(5-7)}}{((a-2b)^2+3)^3}.$$

But the flow diagram is dynamic; it gives step-by-step procedural directions.

Although a flow diagram of this sort may at first appear rather unfamiliar, one of the most useful ways to gain an understanding of a particular diagram is to replace the symbols with numbers and actually carry out the instructions in the diagram. By choosing numbers that will cause each possible path to be followed, we can informally check the adequacy of a flow diagram. Thus, we can try $a = 100$. The flow diagram says set $100 - 2 = 98$ equal to x. It then asks is $x = 98 \geq 0$? The answer is "yes." Therefore set $\sqrt{x} = \sqrt{98}$ equal to y. Then $y = \sqrt{98}$ is the answer. Try the same step-by-step analysis with $a = \frac{1}{2}$; with $a = -17.43$.

The great advantage of a computing machine is its tremendous speed in repetitive processes—that is, in carrying out essentially the same instructions a large number of times. Such repetitive patterns, or "loops," are diagrammed by means of the *diamond*, the fourth type of component. For example, the diamond

instructs us to let $i = 1$, and carry out the instructions below till these bring us back to the diamond. Then let $i = 2$, and carry out the same instructions. We keep repeating this procedure until we have carried the instructions out for $i = 100$, then we go on to the instructions to the right of the diamond. The letter i in the diamond is known as an *index*.

Example 2. Let us illustrate this in terms of finding the sum of 100 given numbers. The flow diagram is shown in Figure 4. We start with 0, and keep

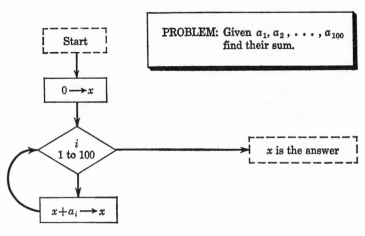

Figure 4

adding the 100 numbers one at a time (since adding a single number to a given number is one of the basic operations of any computer), till we have added all 100. Then we have the desired sum.

It is instructive to follow Figure 4 step by step. First we set $x = 0$. This step is called "initializing." Then we enter the diamond, and choose $i = 1$. Hence in the box below the diamond we compute $0 + a_1 = a_1$, and assign this to x. Then we return to the diamond, and let $i = 2$. This time in the box below we compute $a_1 + a_2$, and assign this to x. The next time we let $i = 3$, and compute $(a_1 + a_2) + a_3$, and so on. Clearly, after looping 100 times, x will have assigned to it the sum of all the numbers.

Example 3. A similar but slightly more complicated diagram is shown in Figure 5. The computation shown will play a key role in Chapter 4. The figure

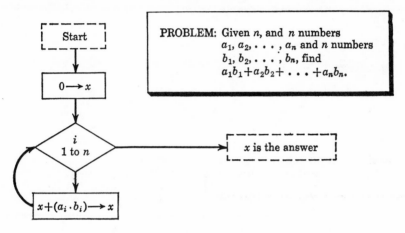

Figure 5

shows an interesting variation in the use of the diamond. We do not have to specify in the diagram how many times the computation should loop; we simply state that i goes from 1 to n, where n will be one of the numbers supplied to us. This gives us much greater flexibility. Not only may we vary the values of the a's and b's, but we may also vary their number, and still the same flow diagram will apply.

Example 4. Figure 6 illustrates a very important procedure, in which no arithmetical operation needs to be carried out. Given the n numbers a_1, a_2, ..., a_n we are interested in finding the largest number. Of course there may be repetitions in the sequence, but there is always a unique largest one—which may occur more than once. Thus, for example, the *maximum* (or *max*) of the sequence 1, 5, 11, 8, 11, 9, 0, 10, 5, 4, 5 is 11. Similarly, the *minimum* (or *min*) is 0. Figure 6 gives directions for finding the max of n given numbers. The basic idea is very simple: Start with the first number and look at the remaining numbers one at a time. For each, check whether it is larger than the largest previous number, till you have checked all n. In the flow diagram x stands for the largest number found up to that step in the computation, so that at the end x is equal to the max.

Example 5. The full power of flow diagramming can best be seen in a problem that requires a loop within a loop. Let us consider the problem of taking n given numbers a_1, a_2, ..., a_n and arranging them in decreasing order—that is, so that in the new order $a_1 \geq a_2$, $a_2 \geq a_3$, etc. Figure 7 describes one such method. We go through our list of numbers, and compare each number with

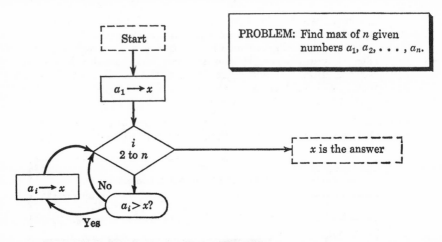

Figure 6

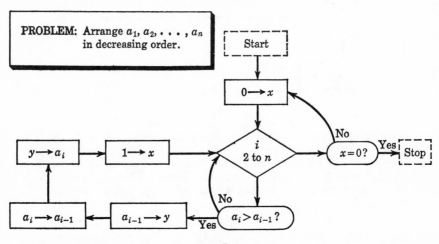

Figure 7

the preceding one. If it is greater than the preceding one, we interchange them. Since we must go through the entire list, this is one loop, and it is accomplished by the diamond in Figure 7. At the end of the loop we have a "better" order, but we are probably not done. We must now go through the same loop again, getting a further improvement, and repeat the loop till we find that no change is necessary. This repetition of loops cannot be achieved by a diamond, since we do not know how many times we have to go through the list. Instead, we keep track of whether any change occurred during the loop, and keep on until we get through the list for the first time without a change. This "keeping track" is accomplished by a *signal*, which in Figure 7 is the variable x. Variable x is set equal to 0 at the beginning of each loop, but is changed to 1 if the order of two of the numbers in the list is changed.

EXERCISES

1. Write a flow diagram to compute $(2a + 5)^2$ for an arbitrary a.
2. In Figure 3, for what values of a will we get a "no" in the circle?
3. Write a flow diagram to find the geometric mean of five numbers—that is, $\sqrt[5]{a_1a_2a_3a_4a_5}$.
4. In Figure 5, let $n = 3$, and $a_1 = 1$, $a_2 = 0$, $a_3 = -1$, $b_1 = 2$, $b_2 = 5$, $b_3 = 2$. Follow the flow diagram step by step to find the answer. Check your answer.
5. Write a flow diagram to find the min of n numbers.
6. Write a flow diagram to find the arithmetic mean (or average) of n numbers—that is, $(a_1 + a_2 + \cdots + a_n)/n$.
7. Write a flow diagram for arranging 100 given numbers in increasing order.
8. Write a flow diagram for taking n given numbers in increasing order, and removing duplications. The answer should be a number m, giving how many different numbers there were, and an increasing sequence a_1, a_2, $\ldots$, a_m.
9. Use the results of Exercises 7 and 8 to write a flow diagram for removing duplicates from 100 given numbers.
10. Why is the variable y introduced in Figure 7? Why not interchange a_{i-1} and a_i by the two boxes given below?

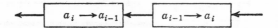

11. Show that a diamond can always be replaced by a combination of boxes and a circle.

*5. FLOW DIAGRAMS FOR COUNTING PROBLEMS

The purpose of this section is to give further examples of flow diagrams, applying this technique to the types of computational problems treated earlier in the chapter.

Example 1. The computation of $n!$ is ideally suited for flow diagramming. It requires just a simple loop, as shown in Figure 8.

Let us raise the question of what happens in Figure 8 if we ask for $0!$. Inside the diamond we then ask for i to go from 1 to 0. For this one needs a convention, and the standard convention is that if we ask i to go from a up to b, but $a > b$, then the loop is simply omitted. Thus our program will yield $0! = 1$. If we let $n = 1$, then the diamond instructs us to go from 1 to 1, hence we loop just once, with $i = 1$. Thus $1! = 1 \cdot 1 = 1$.

Example 2. A more interesting problem is the computation of the binomial coefficients $\binom{n}{j}$. We shall use the method of the Pascal triangle, computing

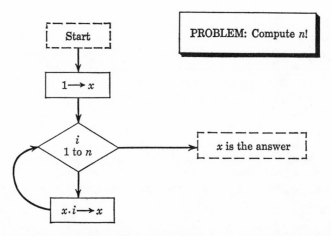

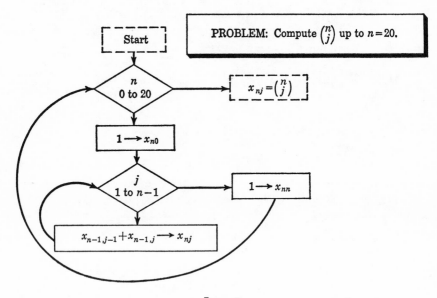

Figure 8

one row of the triangle at a time. This is shown in Figure 9. In this example we again make use of the convention that when $1 > n - 1$, the second diamond's loop is omitted. (See Exercise 3.)

Figure 9

Let us next consider three types of averages. Given a sequence of numbers $a_1, a_2, \ldots, a_n$, by their "average" we usually mean the *arithmetic mean*, which is $(a_1 + a_2 + \cdots + a_n)/n$. But many other types of averages are in common use. For example, the *median* is the "middle number" if we arrange our numbers in decreasing order. If there are an odd number of numbers, then this is precisely defined, but with an even number of a's, there are two candidates for the median. Thus, more precisely, we arrange our numbers in decreasing order and then one of three things can happen: (1) There are an odd number of a's, in which case the median is the middle one. (2) There are an even number and the two middle numbers are the same; then this number is the median. (3) The two middle numbers are different; then both are called medians. Often, in this case, one defines the set of medians to be the interval having the two middle numbers as end points.

Another commonly used "average" is the mode. This is defined as the commonest number in the sequence—that is, the number occurring the largest number of times in the sequence. In case of a tie we may have several modes.

Before diagramming the computation of the three types of averages, let us introduce an important shortcut in flow diagrams. It often occurs that a previously diagrammed computation occurs as part of a larger computation. Instead of duplicating the previous diagram, we simply insert an instruction to carry out that computation at the specified place in the new diagram. (On a computing machine this usually requires only a single instruction.) We then refer to the small computation as a *subroutine* of the larger one. In the diagram we indicate this by inserting a box or circle containing a verbal instruction to use a previously defined routine.

Example 3. To diagram the arithmetic mean we need only compute the sum and divide by n. Suppose that we want the arithmetic mean of the given numbers $a_1, a_2, \ldots, a_{100}$. We can easily accomplish this by using Figure 4 of the last section as a subroutine. The diagram is shown in Figure 10.

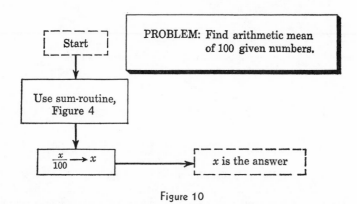

Figure 10

Example 4. To find the median of n numbers we will have to test whether the positive integer n is even or odd. Some computers have automatic tests for this. But just in case this is not available, we will write a subroutine for

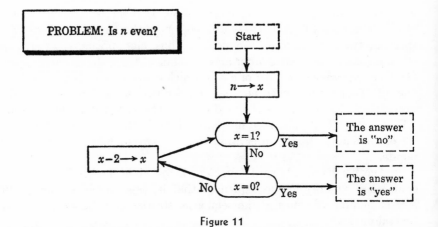

Figure 11

testing evenness. This is shown in Figure 11. Here the output is "yes" or "no," and the subroutine is used as a circle in Figure 12.

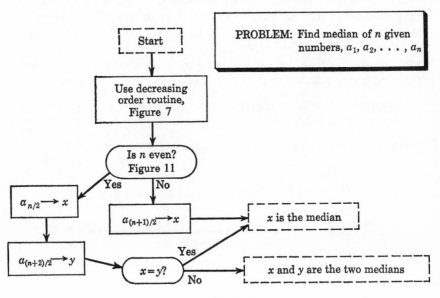

Figure 12

Example 5. To find a routine for determining modes, we will first write a very useful subroutine that counts the frequency (number of occurrences) of all numbers in a sequence. This is shown in Figure 13. The basic idea of the routine is the following: We first write $a_1, a_2, \ldots, a_n$, the given numbers, in decreasing order. Then we run through this list (using index i), noting whether we have hit a new number. Since the numbers have been ordered, a number different from the previous one is new. If we find a new number, we assign this to a new variable y_j (where j indexes the *different* numbers) and set up a counter z_j. But if the number is not new, then we increase z_j by 1. This explains the fork in Figure 13. The three instructions preceding the loop simply get us started; that is, these are initializing instructions.

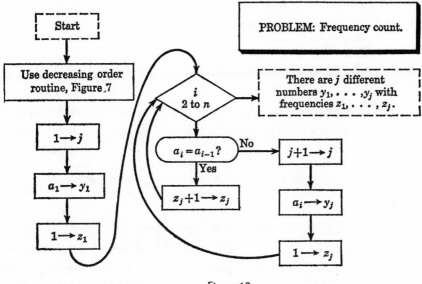

Figure 13

Given the frequency count routine, it is easy to find the modes. We need only pick out the number or numbers having the largest frequency. The flow diagram is drawn in Figure 14.

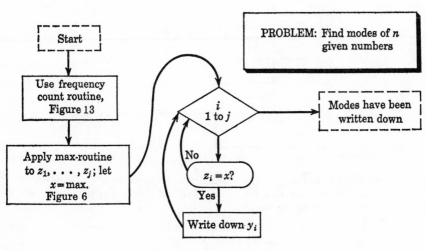

Figure 14

EXERCISES

1. Write a flow diagram for the computation of 2^n. Does it give the correct answer for $n = 0$ and $n = 1$?

2. Suppose that a machine can do only sums and not products. Write a flow diagram for computing na, where n is an integer and a any number. Does it give the correct answer for $n = 0$ and $n = 1$?

3. Check Figure 11 for the cases of $n = 0$ and $n = 1$, by following the diagram step by step.

4. Write a flow diagram for computing $\binom{n}{j}$ using the factorial routine as a subroutine.

5. Find the arithmetic mean, the medians, and the modes of each of the following sequences. Use the flow diagrams in Figures 10–13.
   a. 1, 2, 2, 2, 3, 3, 8.   b. 1, 1, 1, 2, 2, 3, 3, 3.
   c. 1, 2, 2, 2, 3.   d. 1, 2, 3, 4, 5, 6.
   e. 2, 5, 0, 9, 2, 1.

6. Write a flow diagram to test whether n is divisible by 3.

7. Write a flow diagram to test whether a given integer n is a perfect square.

8. Write a routine which for given positive number a will find the greatest integer whose cube is less than a. What does your routine do if $a < 1$?

9. Given the n numbers $a_1, a_2, \ldots, a_n$, what does the following routine do?

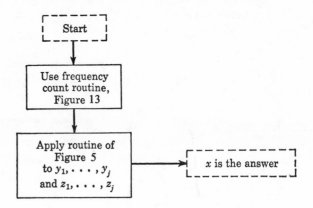

10. Write a flow diagram for testing whether among n given numbers there are at least two that are equal. Make the diagram as simple as possible, without using subroutines.

11. Let x be any positive number and carry out each of the following programs. In each case determine y.

[*Ans.* $y = 13$.]

(a)

(b)

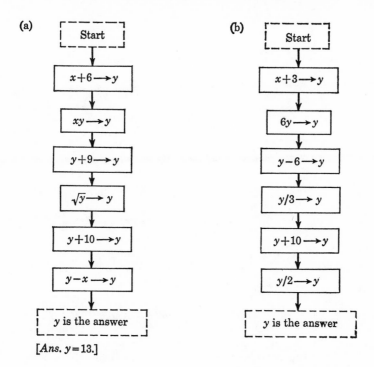

[*Ans. y*=13.]

12. Let a, b, c, and x be given numbers. Carry out the following program and identify the result.

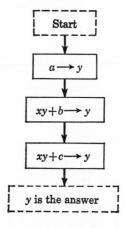

13. Let x and y be given numbers and carry out the following program. Note that the program terminates by indicating either a yes or a no answer. What is the significance of each answer?

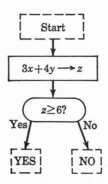

SUGGESTED READING

Whitworth, W. A., *Choice and Chance, with 1000 Exercises*, Stechert, New York, 1934.

Goldberg, S., *Probability, An Introduction*, Prentice-Hall, Englewood Cliffs, N. J., 1960.

Parzen, E., *Modern Probability Theory and Its Applications*, Wiley, New York, 1960.

Kemeny, J. G., J. L. Snell, and G. L. Thompson, *Introduction to Finite Mathematics*, 2nd Edition, Prentice-Hall, Englewood Cliffs, 1966.

3

PROBABILITY
THEORY

1. INTRODUCTION

We often hear statements of the following kind: "The missile is likely to fire successfully," "We have a fair chance of making the sale," "There is an even chance that a coin will come up heads." In each case our statement refers to a situation in which we are not certain of the outcome, but we express some degree of confidence that our prediction will be verified. The theory of probability provides a mathematical framework for such assertions.

Consider an experiment whose outcome is not known. Suppose that someone makes an assertion p about the outcome of the experiment, and we want to assign a probability to p. When statement p is considered in isolation, we usually find no natural assignment of probabilities. Rather, we look for a method of assigning probabilities to all conceivable statements concerning the outcome of the experiment. At first this might seem to be a hopeless task, since there is no end to the statements we can make about the experiment. However, we are aided by a basic principle:

FUNDAMENTAL ASSUMPTION. Any two equivalent statements will be assigned the same probability.

As long as there are a finite number of logical possibilities, there are only a finite number of truth sets, and hence the process of assigning probabilities is a finite one. We proceed in three steps: (1) we first determine $\mathfrak{U}$, the possibility set, that is, the set of all logical possibilities, (2) to each subset X of $\mathfrak{U}$ we assign a number called the measure $\mathbf{m}(X)$, (3) to each statement p we assign $\mathbf{m}(P)$, the measure of its truth set, as a probability. The probability of statement p is denoted by $\mathbf{Pr}[p]$.

The first step, that of determining the set of logical possibilities, is one that we considered in the previous chapters. It is important to recall that there is no unique method for analyzing logical possibilities. In a given problem we may arrive at a very fine or a very rough analysis of possibilities, causing $\mathfrak{U}$ to have many or few elements.

Having chosen $\mathfrak{U}$, we next assign a number to each subset X of $\mathfrak{U}$, which will in turn be taken to be the probability of any statement having truth set X. We do this in the following way.

Assignment of a Measure

Assign a positive number (weight) to each element of $\mathfrak{U}$, so that the sum of the weights assigned is 1. Then the measure of a set is the sum of the weights of its elements. The measure of the set $\mathcal{E}$ is 0.

In applications of probability to business problems, the assignment of measures and the analysis of the logical possibilities may sometimes depend upon masses of data that are best obtained, analyzed, and interpreted by a professional statistician; at other times the task depends more on qualitative knowledge and judgment of facts with which the businessman himself is most familiar, so that he is the person best qualified to assign measures and analyze the logical possibilities. Very often a combination of objective fact and subjective judgment makes it important for the statistician and the businessman to work together on this job.

Once the weights are assigned, to find the probability of a particular statement we must find its truth set and find the sum of the weights assigned to elements of the truth set. This problem, which might seem easy, can often involve considerable mathematical difficulty. The development of techniques to solve this kind of problem is the main task of probability theory.

Example 1. An ordinary die is thrown. What is the probability that the number that turns up is less than 4? Here the possibility set is $\mathfrak{U} = \{1, 2, 3, 4, 5, 6\}$. The symmetry of the die suggests that each face should have the same probability of turning up. To make this so we assign weight $\frac{1}{6}$ to each of the outcomes. The truth set of the statement, "The number that turns up is less than 4," is $\{1, 2, 3\}$. Hence the probability of this statement is $\frac{3}{6} = \frac{1}{2}$, the sum of the weights of the elements in its truth set.

Example 2. Three computer manufacturers, A, B, and C, are trying to contract for the installation of a computer system with the X Company. The sales manager of A feels that his company has the same chance of winning the contract as B, but that A (and hence also B) is twice as likely to win it as C is. What is the probability that A or C wins the contract? We take as $\mathfrak{U}$ the set $\{A, B, C\}$. If we were to assign weight a to the outcome C, then we would assign weight $2a$ to each of the outcomes A and B. Since the sum of the weights must be 1, we have $2a + 2a + a = 1$, or $a = \frac{1}{5}$. Hence we assign weights $\frac{2}{5}, \frac{2}{5}, \frac{1}{5}$ to the outcomes A, B, and C, respectively. The truth set of the statement "Company A or Company C wins the contract" is $\{A, C\}$. The sum of the weights of the elements of this set is $\frac{2}{5} + \frac{1}{5} = \frac{3}{5}$. Hence the probability that A or C wins the contract is $\frac{3}{5}$.

EXERCISES

1. Assume that there are n possibilities for the outcome of a given experiment. How should the weights be assigned if it is desired that all outcomes be assigned the same weight?

2. Let $\mathfrak{U} = \{a, b, c\}$. Assign weights to the three elements so that no two have the same weight, and find the measures of the eight subsets of $\mathfrak{U}$.

3. In an election Jones has probability $\frac{1}{2}$ of winning, Smith has probability $\frac{1}{3}$, and Black has probability $\frac{1}{6}$.
   a. Construct $\mathfrak{U}$.
   b. Assign weights.
   c. Find the measures of the eight subsets.
   d. Give a pair of nonequivalent predictions that have the same probability.

4. Give the possibility set $\mathfrak{U}$, for each of the following experiments.
   a. An election between candidates A and B is to take place.
   b. A number between 1 and 5 is chosen at random.
   c. A two-headed coin is thrown.
   d. A student is asked for the day of the year on which his birthday falls.
   e. A sample of five pieces is taken from a lot of 1000 and inspected to see how many defectives there are.
   f. An item is offered for sale on a day when there are four units in inventory.

5. For which of the cases in Exercise 4 might it be appropriate to assign the same weight to each outcome?

6. Job applicants are given an aptitude test to determine their qualifications for performing a certain skilled task. For an applicant selected at random the following probabilities have been assigned to the results of taking the test and of actual job performance: The probability that the applicant would perform unsatisfactorily both on the test and on the job is $\frac{1}{2}$. The probability that his performance would be satisfactory either on the test or on the job (but not both) is $\frac{1}{3}$.
   a. What is the probability that the applicant would perform satisfactorily both on the test and on the job?
   b. From the information given, is it possible to find the probability that the applicant would perform satisfactorily on the job?   [*Ans.* No.]

7. A die is loaded in such a way that the probability of each face is proportional to the number of dots on that face. (For instance, a 6 is three times as probable as a 2.) What is the probability of getting an even number in one throw?   [*Ans.* $\frac{4}{7}$.]

8. If a coin is thrown three times, list the eight possibilities for the outcomes of the three successive throws. A typical outcome can be written (HTH). Determine a probability measure by assigning an equal weight to each outcome. Find the probabilities of the following statements:
   r. The number of heads that occur is greater than the number of tails.
   [*Ans.* $\frac{1}{2}$.]
   s. Exactly two heads occur.   [*Ans.* $\frac{3}{8}$.]
   t. The same side turns up on every throw.   [*Ans.* $\frac{1}{4}$.]

9. For the statements given in Exercise 8, which of the following equalities are true?

  a. $\mathbf{Pr}[r \vee s]$ $= \mathbf{Pr}[r] + \mathbf{Pr}[s]$.
  b. $\mathbf{Pr}[s \vee t]$ $= \mathbf{Pr}[s] + \mathbf{Pr}[t]$.
  c. $\mathbf{Pr}[r \vee \sim r] = \mathbf{Pr}[r] + \mathbf{Pr}[\sim r]$.
  d. $\mathbf{Pr}[r \vee t]$ $= \mathbf{Pr}[r] + \mathbf{Pr}[t]$.

10. Which of the following pairs of statements (see Exercise 8) are inconsistent? (Recall that two statements are inconsistent if their truth sets have no element in common.)
  a. $r, s.$ *b.* $s, t.$
  c. $r, \sim r.$ *d.* $r, t.$ [*Ans.* *b.* and *c.*]

11. State a theorem suggested by Exercises 9 and 10.

12. An experiment has three possible outcomes, a, b, and c. Let p be the statement "the outcome is a or b," and q be the statement "the outcome is b or c." Assume that weights have been assigned to the three outcomes so that $\mathbf{Pr}[p] = \frac{2}{3}$ and $\mathbf{Pr}[q] = \frac{5}{6}$. Find the weights. [*Ans.* $\frac{1}{6}, \frac{1}{2}, \frac{1}{3}$.]

13. Repeat Exercise 12 if $\mathbf{Pr}[p] = \frac{1}{2}$ and $\mathbf{Pr}[q] = \frac{3}{8}$.

14. The weather man on the morning weather report states that there is a 10 percent chance for rain today. What do you think he means by this:
  a. if you see no clouds in the sky.
  b. if you see that it is raining when he makes the prediction.

2. PROPERTIES OF A PROBABILITY MEASURE

Before studying special probability measures, we shall consider some general properties of such measures that are useful in computations and in the general understanding of probability theory.

Three basic properties of a probability measure are:

A. $\mathbf{m}(X) = 0$ if and only if $X = \mathcal{E}$.
B. $0 \leq \mathbf{m}(X) \leq 1$ for any set X.
C. For two sets X and Y,

$$\mathbf{m}(X \cup Y) = \mathbf{m}(X) + \mathbf{m}(Y)$$

if and only if X and Y are disjoint—that is, have no elements in common.

The proofs of properties A. and B. are left as an exercise (Exercise 16). We shall prove C.

We observe first that $\mathbf{m}(X) + \mathbf{m}(Y)$ is the sum of the weights of the elements of X added to the sum of the weights of Y. If X and Y are disjoint, then the weight of every element of $X \cup Y$ is added once and only once; hence $\mathbf{m}(X) + \mathbf{m}(Y) = \mathbf{m}(X \cup Y)$.

Assume now that X and Y are not disjoint. Here the weight of every element contained in both X and Y—that is, in $X \cap Y$—is added twice in the sum $\mathbf{m}(X) + \mathbf{m}(Y)$. Thus this sum is greater than $\mathbf{m}(X \cup Y)$ by an amount $\mathbf{m}(X \cap Y)$. By A. and B., if $X \cap Y$ is not the empty set, then $\mathbf{m}(X \cap Y) > 0$. Hence in this case we have $\mathbf{m}(X) + \mathbf{m}(Y) > \mathbf{m}(X \cup Y)$. Thus if X and Y are not disjoint, the equality in C. does not hold. Our proof shows that in general we have

C'. For any two sets X and Y,

$$m(X \cup Y) = m(X) + m(Y) - m(X \cap Y).$$

Since the probabilities for statements are obtained directly from the probability measure $m(X)$, any property of $m(X)$ can be translated into a property about the probability of statements. For example, the above properties become, when expressed in terms of statements:

a. $Pr[p] = 0$ if and only if p is logically false.
b. $0 \le Pr[p] \le 1$ for any statement p.
c. The equality

$$Pr[p \vee q] = Pr[p] + Pr[q]$$

holds if and only if p and q are inconsistent.
c'. For any two statements p and q,

$$Pr[p \vee q] = Pr[p] + Pr[q] - Pr[p \wedge q].$$

Another property of a probability measure that is often useful in computation is

D. $m(\tilde{X}) = 1 - m(X)$,

or, in the language of statements,

d. $Pr[\sim p] = 1 - Pr[p]$.

The proofs of D. and d. are left as an exercise (Exercise 17).

It is important to observe that our probability measure assigns probability 0 only to statements that are logically false—that is, that are false for every logical possibility. Hence, a prediction that such a statement will be true is certain to be wrong. Similarly a statement is assigned probability 1 only if it is true in every case—that is, logically true. Thus the prediction that a statement of this type will be true is certain to be correct. (While these properties of a probability measure seem quite natural, it is necessary, when dealing with infinite possibility sets, to weaken them slightly. We consider in this book only the finite possibility sets.)

We shall now discuss the interpretation of probabilities that are not 0 or 1. We shall give only some commonly held intuitive ideas. These ideas can be made mathematically more precise; we offer them here only as a guide to intuitive thinking.

Suppose that, relative to a given experiment, a statement has been assigned probability p. From this it is often inferred that if a sequence of such experiments is performed under identical conditions, the fraction of experiments that yield outcomes making the statement true would be approximately p. The mathematical version of this is the "law of large numbers" of probability theory (which will be treated in Section 10). In cases where there is no natural way to assign a probability measure, the probability of a statement is estimated experimentally. A sequence of experiments is performed, and the fraction of the experiments that make the statement true is taken as the approximate probability for the statement.

A second and related interpretation of probabilities is concerned with betting. Suppose that a certain statement has been assigned probability p. We wish to offer a bet that the statement will in fact turn out to be true. We agree to give r dollars if the statement does not turn out to be true, provided that we receive s dollars if it does turn out to be true. What should r and s be to make the bet fair? If it were true that in a large number of such bets we would win s a fraction p of the time and lose r a fraction $1 - p$ of the time, then our average winning per bet would be $sp - r(1 - p)$. To make the bet fair we should make this average winning 0. This will be the case if $sp = r(1 - p)$ or if $r/s = p/(1 - p)$. Notice that this determines only the ratio of r and s. Such a ratio, written $r:s$, is said to give *odds* in favor of the statement.

DEFINITION. The *odds* in favor of an outcome are $r:s$ (r to s), if the probability of the outcome is p, and $r/s = p/(1 - p)$. Any two numbers having the required ratio may be used in place of r and s. Thus 6:4 odds are the same as 3:2 odds.

Example. Assume that a probability of $\frac{3}{4}$ has been assigned to a certain horse's winning a race. Then the odds for a fair bet would be $\frac{3}{4}:\frac{1}{4}$. These odds could be equally well written as 3:1, 6:2 or 12:4, and so on. A fair bet would be to agree to pay $3 if the horse loses and receive $1 if the horse wins. Another fair bet would be to pay $6 if the horse loses and win $2 if the horse wins.

EXERCISES

1. Let p and q be statements such that $\mathbf{Pr}[p \wedge q] = \frac{1}{4}$, $\mathbf{Pr}[\sim p] = \frac{1}{3}$, and $\mathbf{Pr}[q] = \frac{1}{2}$. What is $\mathbf{Pr}[p \vee q]$? [*Ans.* $\frac{11}{12}$.]

2. Using the result of Exercise 1, find $\mathbf{Pr}[\sim p \wedge \sim q]$.

3. Let p and q be statements such that $\mathbf{Pr}[p] = \frac{1}{2}$ and $\mathbf{Pr}[q] = \frac{2}{3}$. Are p and q consistent? [*Ans.* Yes.]

4. Show that, if $\mathbf{Pr}[p] + \mathbf{Pr}[q] > 1$, then p and q are consistent.

5. The Acme Company has submitted bids on two projects. The Controller assigns a probability of .4 to being awarded the first project, a probability of .6 to obtaining at least one, and a probability of .1 to obtaining both. What is the probability that the company will be awarded the second project?

6. An automobile dealer believes that within the next week he will sell at least four cars with probability .9, but less than seven cars with probability .6. What is the probability that he will sell four, five, or six? [*Ans.* .5.]

7. What odds should a person give on a bet that a six will turn up when a die is thrown?

8. Referring to Example 2 of Section 1, what odds should the sales manager of Company A be willing to give for a bet that either A or B will win the contract?

9. Prove that if the odds relative to a given statement are $r:s$, then the probability that the statement will be true is $r/(r + s)$.

10. Using the result of Exercise 9 and the definition of "odds," show that if the odds are $r:s$ that a statement is true, then the odds are $s:r$ that it is false.

11. A man is willing to give 5:4 odds that the Dodgers will win the World Series. What must the probability of a Dodger victory be for this to be a fair bet?   [$Ans.$ $\frac{5}{9}$.]

12. It has been found through long experience that 85 percent of the pieces a certain machine produces are good. What odds should be given that the next piece produced will be good?

13. A man offers 1:3 odds that A will occur, 1:2 odds that B will occur. He knows that A and B cannot both occur. What odds should he give that A or B will occur?   [$Ans.$ 7:5.]

14. A man offers 3:1 odds that A will occur, 2:1 odds that B will occur. He knows that A and B cannot both occur. What odds should he give that A or B will occur?

15. Show from the definition of a probability measure that $\mathbf{m}(X) = 1$ if and only if $X = \mathfrak{U}$.

16. Show from the definition of a probability measure that properties A., B. of the text are true.

17. Prove property D. of the text. Why does property D. follow from this property?

18. Prove that if R, S, and T are three sets that have no element in common,

$$\mathbf{m}(R \cup S \cup T) = \mathbf{m}(R) + \mathbf{m}(S) + \mathbf{m}(T).$$

19. If X and Y are two sets such that X is a subset of Y, prove that $\mathbf{m}(X) \leq \mathbf{m}(Y)$.

20. Suppose you know that when statement p is true, statement q is necessarily true. What can you say about the relation of $\mathbf{Pr}[p]$ to $\mathbf{Pr}[q]$?

21. Suppose that you are given n statements and each has been assigned a probability equal to r. Prove that the probability of the disjunction of these statements is less than or equal to nr.

22. The following is an alternative proof of property C'. of the text. Give a reason for each step.
    a. $X \cup Y = (X \cap \tilde{Y}) \cup (X \cap Y) \cup (\tilde{X} \cap Y)$.
    b. $\mathbf{m}(X \cup Y) = \mathbf{m}(X \cap \tilde{Y}) + \mathbf{m}(X \cap Y) + \mathbf{m}(\tilde{X} \cap Y)$.
    c. $\mathbf{m}(X \cup Y) = \mathbf{m}(X) + \mathbf{m}(Y) - \mathbf{m}(X \cap Y)$.

23. If X, Y, and Z are any three sets, prove that, for any probability measure

$$\mathbf{m}(X \cup Y \cup Z) = \mathbf{m}(X) + \mathbf{m}(Y) + \mathbf{m}(Z) - \mathbf{m}(X \cap Y)$$
$$- \mathbf{m}(Y \cap Z) - \mathbf{m}(X \cap Z) + \mathbf{m}(X \cap Y \cap Z).$$

24. Translate the result of Exercise 23 into a result concerning three statements p, q, and r.
25. Prove that for any two statements p and q,
    a. $\mathbf{Pr}[p \wedge q] = \mathbf{Pr}[q \wedge p]$.
    b. $\mathbf{Pr}[p \wedge q] + \mathbf{Pr}[p \wedge \sim q] = \mathbf{Pr}[p]$.
    c. $\mathbf{Pr}[p \wedge q] + \mathbf{Pr}[\sim p \wedge q] = \mathbf{Pr}[q]$.

3. THE EQUIPROBABLE MEASURE

We have already seen several examples where it was natural to assign the same weight to all possibilities in determining the appropriate probability measure. The probability measure determined in this manner is called the *equiprobable measure*. The measure of sets in the case of the equiprobable measure has a very simple form. In fact, if $\mathfrak{U}$ has n elements and if the equiprobable measure has been assigned, then for any set X, $\mathbf{m}(X)$ is r/n, where r is the number of elements in the set X. This is true since the weight of each element in X is $1/n$; hence the sum of the weights of elements of X is r/n.

The particularly simple form of the equiprobable measure makes it easy to work with. In view of this it is important to observe that a particular choice for the set of possibilities in a given situation may lead to the equiprobable measure, while some other choice will not. For example, consider the case of two throws of an ordinary coin. Suppose that we are interested in statements about the number of heads that occur. If we take for the possibility set the set $\mathfrak{U} = \{HH, HT, TH, TT\}$, then it is reasonable to assign the same weight to each outcome, and we are led to the equiprobable measure. If, on the other hand, we were to take as possible outcomes the set $\mathfrak{U} = \{no\ H, one\ H, two\ H\}$, it would not be natural to assign the same weight to each outcome, since one head can occur in two different ways, while each of the other possibilities can occur in only one way.

The phrase "at random" is often associated with the equiprobable measure. Strictly speaking, one out of a set of possibilities is chosen "at random" provided *any* probability measure whatsoever has been assigned to the set of possibilities. When there is no further qualification, however, a choice "at random" from a set of possibilities usually means that the set has assigned to it the equiprobable measure. Thus, if we say, for example, that a number has been chosen "at random" from the set of integers from 1 through 100, we imply that the equiprobable measure has been assigned to the set, i.e., that the probability of choosing any particular number—say 29—is .01.

Example 1. Suppose that we throw two ordinary dice. Each die can turn up a number from 1 to 6; hence there are $6 \cdot 6$ possibilities. We assign weight $\frac{1}{36}$ to each possibility. A prediction that is true in j cases will then have probability $j/36$. For example, "The sum of the dice is 5," will be true if we get $1 + 4$, $2 + 3, 3 + 2$, or $4 + 1$. Hence the probability that the sum of the dice is 5 is

$\frac{4}{36} = \frac{1}{9}$. The sum can be 12 in only one way, 6 + 6. Hence the probability that the sum is 12 is $\frac{1}{36}$.

Example 2. A lot contains 80 good pieces and 20 defectives. A sample of two is drawn at random from the lot. What is the probability that both pieces are defective? There are 100 possibilities for the first piece, and for each of these there are 99 possibilities for the second. Hence there are $100 \cdot 99$ possibilities for the result of two draws. We assign the equiprobable measure. The statement "both pieces are defective" is true in $20 \cdot 19$ of the $100 \cdot 99$ possibilities. Hence the probability of the statement is $20 \cdot 19/100 \cdot 99$ or .0384.

Example 3. Assume that, on the basis of a predictive index applied to salesmen A, B, and C when applying for a job, it is predicted that after one year the sales of A will be the highest, C the second highest, and B the lowest of the three. Suppose, in fact, that these predictions turn out to be exactly correct. If the predictive index has no merit at all, and hence the predictions were made simply at random, what is the probability that such a prediction will be correct? There are 3! = 6 orders in which the men might finish. If the predictions were really made at random, then we would assign an equal weight to each of the six outcomes. In this case the probability that a particular prediction is true is $\frac{1}{6}$. Since this probability is reasonably large, we would hesitate to conclude that the predictive index is in fact useful, on the basis of this one experiment. Suppose, on the other hand, it predicted the order of six men correctly. Then a similar analysis would show that, by guessing, the probability is 1/6! = 1/720 that such a prediction would be correct. Hence, we might take this to be strong evidence that the index has some merit.

EXERCISES

1. A letter is chosen at random from the word "random." What is the probability that it is an n? That it is a vowel?   [*Ans.* $\frac{1}{6}$; $\frac{1}{3}$.]

2. An integer between 3 and 12 inclusive is chosen at random. What is the probability that it is an even number? That it is even and divisible by three?

3. A card is drawn at random from a pack of playing cards.
   a. What is the probability that it is either a heart or the king of clubs?   [*Ans.* $\frac{7}{26}$.]
   b. What is the probability that it is either the queen of hearts or an honor card (that is, ten, jack, queen, king, or ace)?   [*Ans.* $\frac{5}{13}$.]

4. A word is chosen at random from the set of words $\mathfrak{U}$ = {men, bird, ball, field, book}. Let p, q, and r be the statements:

   > p: The word has two vowels.
   > q: The first letter of the word is "b."
   > r: The word rhymes with "cook."

   Find the probability of the following statements:
   a. p.   *b. q.*
   c. r.   *d. $p \wedge q$.*
   e. $(p \vee q) \wedge \sim r$.

5. A single die is thrown. Find the probability that
   a. An odd number turns up.

b. The number that turns up is greater than two.

c. A seven turns up.

6. In the market-leadership example of Chapter 1, Section 5, assume that all 36 possibilities for leadership in the four territories are equally likely. Find the probability:

    a. That Company A is the leader in more territories than either of its rivals.   [*Ans.* $\frac{7}{18}$.]

    b. That the same company is the leader in all the territories.

                                                    [*Ans.* $\frac{1}{36}$.]

    c. That every territory has a different market leader.   [*Ans.* 0.]

7. A single die is thrown twice. What value for the sum of the two outcomes has the highest probability? What value or values of the sum have the lowest probability of occurring?

8. In December 1960 the E. I. duPont de Nemours Company had 210,840 common stockholders, and General Motors Corporation had 830,873 common stockholders. Assume that 50,000 investors held common stock in both companies. If a person is selected at random from the list of common stockholders of duPont, what is the probability that he is also a stockholder of General Motors? If a General Motors stockholder is selected at random, what is the probability that he is *not* a duPont stockholder?

9. A certain part can be defective because it has one or more out of three possible defects: insufficient tensile strength, a burr, or a diameter outside tolerance limits. In a lot of 1000 pieces it is known that

        120 have a tensile-strength defect.
         80 have a burr.
         60 have an unacceptable diameter.
         22 have tensile-strength and burr defects.
         16 have tensile-strength and diameter defects.
         20 have burr and diameter defects.
          8 have all three defects.

If a piece is drawn at random from the lot, what is the probability that the piece

    a. is not defective?   [*Ans.* .79.]

    b. has exactly two defects?   [*Ans.* .034.]

10. Parts A, B, C, D, E, and F are to be produced one after the other on a machine. If all permutations are equally likely, what is the probability that

    a. the permutation will be D, B, F, A, E, C?

    b. part A will directly precede part B?

    c. part D will directly either follow or be followed by part F?

11. In Exercise 10, answer questions (*a*), (*b*), and (*c*) if part A must be directly followed by either B or C and all permissible permutations are equally likely.

12. A lot contains 20 pieces, of which 14 are good and 6 are defective. If the equiprobable measure is assigned to all possible samples of given size, what is the probability of obtaining a sample of five with

    a. no defectives?   [*Ans.* .129.]

    b. one defective?

    c. two defectives?

    d. three defectives?   [*Ans.* .117.]

  e. four defectives?
  f. five defectives?
  g. three or more defectives?
  h. less than two defectives?
  i. between two and four (inclusive) defectives?
  j. less than six defectives?
  k. two good pieces?
  l. between one and three (inclusive) good pieces?   [*Ans.* .483.]

13. A room contains a group of n people who are wearing badges numbered from 1 to n. If two people are selected at random, what is the probability that the larger badge number is a 3? Answer this problem assuming that $n = 5, 4, 3, 2$.   [*Ans.* $\frac{1}{5}; \frac{1}{3}; \frac{2}{3}; 0.$]

14. In Exercise 13, suppose that we observe two men leaving the room and that the larger of their badge numbers is 3. What might we guess as to the number of people in the room?

15. Find the probability that a bridge hand will have suits of:

  a. 5, 4, 3, and 1 cards. $\left[Ans.\ \dfrac{4!\binom{13}{5}\binom{13}{4}\binom{13}{3}\binom{13}{1}}{\binom{52}{13}} \cong .129. \right]$

  b. 6, 4, 2, and 1 cards.   [*Ans.* .047.]
  c. 4, 4, 3, and 2 cards.   [*Ans.* .216.]
  d. 4, 3, 3, and 3 cards.   [*Ans.* .105.]

16. There are $\binom{52}{13} = 6.35 \times 10^{11}$ possible bridge hands. Find the probability that a bridge hand dealt at random will be all of one suit. Estimate *roughly* the number of bridge hands dealt in the entire country in a year. Is it likely that a hand of all one suit will occur sometime during the year in the United States?

17. Find the probability of obtaining each of the following poker hands (a poker hand is a set of five cards chosen at random from a deck of 52 cards):

  a. royal flush (ten, jack, queen, king, ace in a single suit).
     [*Ans.* $4/\binom{52}{5} = .0000015.$]
  b. straight flush (five in a sequence in a single suit, but not a royal flush).
     [*Ans.* $(40 - 4)/\binom{52}{5} = .000014.$]
  c. four of a kind (four cards of the same face value).
     [*Ans.* $624/\binom{52}{5} = .00024.$]
  d. full house (one pair and one triple of the same face value).
     [*Ans.* $3744/\binom{52}{5} = .0014.$]
  e. flush (five cards in a single suit but not a straight or royal flush).
     [*Ans.* $(5148 - 40)/\binom{52}{5} = .0020.$]
  f. straight (five cards in a row, not all of the same suit).
     [*Ans.* $(10{,}240 - 40)/\binom{52}{5} = .0039.$]
  g. straight or better.   [*Ans.* .0076.]

18. Find the probability of *not* having a pair in a hand of poker.

19. Find the probability of a "bust" hand in poker. [*Hint:* A hand is a "bust" if there is no pair, and it is neither a straight nor a flush.]
     [*Ans.* .5012.]

20. In poker, find the probability of having
  a. exactly one pair.   [*Ans.* .4226.]
  b. two pairs.   [*Ans.* .0475.]
  c. three of a kind.   [*Ans.* .0211.]

21. A certain French professor announces that he will select three out of

eight pages of text to put on an examination and that each student can choose one of these three pages to translate. What is the minimum number of pages that a student should prepare in order to be certain of being able to translate a page that he has studied?

Smith decides to study only four of the eight pages. What is the probability that one of these four pages will appear on the examination?

*4. TWO NONINTUITIVE EXAMPLES

Sometimes one finds a problem for which the answer, based on probability theory, is not at all in agreement with one's intuition. It is usually possible to arrange a few wagers that will bring one's intuition into line with the mathematical theory. A particularly good example of this is provided by the matching-birthdays problem.

Assume that we have a room with r people in it and we propose the bet that at least two people in the room have the same birthday (the same month and day of the year). We ask for the value of r that will make this a fair bet. Few people would be willing to bet even money on this wager unless there were at least 100 people in the room. Most people would suggest 150 as a reasonable number. However, we shall see that with 150 people the odds are approximately 4,500,000,000,000,000 to 1 in favor of two people's having the same birthday, and that one should be willing to bet even money with as few as 23 people in the room.

Let us first find the probability that in a room with r people, no two have the same birthday. There are 365 possibilities for each person's birthday (neglecting February 29). There are then 365^r possibilities for the birthdays of r people. We assume that all these possibilities are equally likely. To find the probability that no two have the same birthday we must find the number of possibilities for the birthdays that have *no* day represented twice. The first person can have any of 365 days for his birthday. For each of these, if the second person is to have a different birthday, there are only 364 possibilities for his birthday. For the third man, there are 363 possibilities if he is to have a different birthday than the first two, and so on. Thus the probability that no two people have the same birthday in a group of r people is

$$q_r = \frac{365 \cdot 364 \cdot \ldots \cdot (365 - r + 1)}{365^r}.$$

The probability that at least two people have the same birthday is then $p_r = 1 - q_r$. In Figure 1 the values of p_r and the odds for a fair bet, $p_r : (1 - p_r)$, are given for several values of r.

We consider now a second problem in which intuition does not lead to the correct answer. We have seen that there are $n!$ permutations of the numbers from 1 to n. Let us consider a rearrangement of these numbers

Number of People in the Room	Probability of at Least Two with Same Birthday	Approximate Odds for a Fair Bet
5	.027	
10	.117	
15	.253	
20	.411	70:100
21	.444	80:100
22	.476	91:100
23	.507	103:100
24	.538	117:100
25	.569	132:100
30	.706	242:100
40	.891	819:100
50	.970	33:1
60	.994	169:1
70		1,200:1
80		12,000:1
90		160,000:1
100		3,300,000:1
125		31,000,000,000:1
150		4,500,000,000,000,000:1

Figure 1

as the operation of placing each of the numbers in one of n boxes or *positions* (one number to a position). The positions are assumed to be numbered in serial order. We shall say that the ith number is unchanged by the permutation if, after the rearrangement, number i is still in the ith position. For example, if we consider the permutations of the numbers 1, 2, and 3, then the permutation 123 leaves *all* numbers fixed, the permutation 213 leaves *one* number fixed, and the permutations 312 and 231 leave *no* numbers fixed. It is obviously impossible, in this example, to leave exactly two numbers fixed. (Why?)

DEFINITION. A *complete permutation* is one that leaves no numbers fixed.

The problem that we now consider can be stated as follows. If a permutation of n numbers is chosen at random, what is the probability that the permutation chosen is a complete permutation? A more colorful but equivalent problem is the following. A hat-check girl has checked n hats, but they have become hopelessly scrambled. She hands back the hats at random. What is the probability that no man gets his own hat? For this problem some people's intuition would lead them to guess that for a large number of hats this probability should be small, while others guess that it should be large. Few people guess that the probability is neither large nor small and essentially independent of the number of hats involved.

To find the desired probability, we assume that all $n!$ permutations are equally likely, and hence we need only count the number of complete permutations there are for n elements. Let w_n be the number of such permutations. Then the desired probability is $p_n = w_n/n!$. If this procedure is carried out (see Exercise 14), the answer is found to be

$$p_n = \frac{1}{2!} - \frac{1}{3!} + \frac{1}{4!} - \cdots \pm \frac{1}{n!}$$

where the plus sign is chosen if n is even and the minus sign if n is odd. Figure 2 gives these numbers for the first few values of n.

Number of Hats	Probability p_n That No Man Gets His Hat
2	.500000
3	.333333
4	.375000
5	.366667
6	.368056
7	.367857
8	.367882

Figure 2

It can be shown that, as the number of hats increases, the probabilities approach a number $1/e = .367879\ldots$, where the number $e = 2.718281\ldots$. The number e plays an important role in many branches of mathematics.

EXERCISES

1. What odds should you be willing to give on a bet that at least two people in the United States Senate have the same birthday?
   [*Ans.* 3,300,000:1.]

2. What is the probability that in the House of Representatives at least two men have the same birthday?

3. What odds should you be willing to give on a bet that at least two of the Presidents of the United States have had the same birthday? Would you win the bet?
   [*Ans.* More than 3:1; Yes. Polk and Harding were born on Nov. 2.]

4. What odds should you be willing to give on the bet that at least two of the Presidents of the United States have died on the same day of the year? Would you win the bet?
   [*Ans.* More than 2.4:1; Yes. Jefferson, Adams, and Monroe all died on July 4.]

5. Statistical evidence indicates that not all dates are equally likely to produce birthdays; for example, there tend to be more births in the summer

than in the winter. Qualitatively, how does this affect the probabilities of Figure 1 (does it tend to increase them or decrease them)?

6. What is the qualitative effect on the probabilities of Figure 1 of including the possibility of a person's having a birthday on February 29?

7. By assigning the equiprobable measure to births in each of the twelve months of the year, derive a table like Figure 1 showing the probability that at least two out of a group of r randomly selected people have birthdays in the same month for $r = 1, 2, 3, 4, 5$. What side would you take of an even-money bet that there were at least two people in the room who had birthdays in the same month if there were five people in the room? If there were four? What is the qualitative effect on the probabilities that you derived of the fact that the months have different numbers of days?

8. Four men check their hats. Assuming that the hats are returned at random, what is the probability that exactly four men get their own hats? Calculate the answer for exactly 3, 2, 1, 0 men. [*Ans.* $\frac{1}{24}$; 0; $\frac{1}{4}$; $\frac{1}{3}$; $\frac{3}{8}$.]

9. A group of 50 men and their wives attend a dance. The partners for a dance are chosen by lot. What is the approximate probability that no man dances with his wife?

10. Show that the probability that, in a group of r people, *exactly* one pair has the same birthday is

$$t_r = \binom{r}{2} \frac{365 \cdot 364 \ldots (365 - r + 2)}{365^r}.$$

11. Show that $t_r = \binom{r}{2} \dfrac{q_r}{366 - r}$, where t_r is defined in Exercise 10, and q_r is the probability that no pair has the same birthday.

12. Using the result of Exercise 11 and the results given in Figure 1, find the probability of exactly one pair of people with the same birthday in a group of r people, for $r = 15, 20, 25, 30, 40$, and 50.
[*Ans.* .22; .32; .38; .38; .26; .12.]

13. What is the approximate probability that there has been exactly one pair of Presidents with the same birthday?

14. Let w_n be the number of complete permutations of n numbers.
  a. Show that

$$w_1 = 0, \qquad w_2 = 1, \ldots,$$
$$w_n = (n - 1)w_{n-1} + (n - 1)w_{n-2}, \qquad n = 2, 3, \ldots.$$

  [*Hint:* Any complete permutation of n numbers can be obtained from a complete permutation of $n - 1$ numbers or from a permutation of $n - 1$ numbers that leaves one number fixed. Describe how this can be done, and show that the two terms on the right side of the equation represent the number that can be obtained from each of these methods.]

  b. Let p_n be the probability that a permutation of n numbers chosen at random is a complete permutation. From part a. show that

$$p_1 = 0, \qquad p_2 = \tfrac{1}{2},$$
$$p_n = \frac{n - 1}{n} p_{n-1} + \frac{1}{n} p_{n-2} \qquad \text{for } n = 3, 4, \ldots.$$

c. Let $v_n = p_n - p_{n-1}$ for $n = 2, 3, 4, \ldots$. From part b., show that

$$n(p_n - p_{n-1}) = -(p_{n-1} - p_{n-2}), \qquad n = 3, \ldots,$$

and hence that

$$nv_n = -v_{n-1}, \qquad n = 3, \ldots.$$

d. Using the fact that $p_1 = 0$, and $p_2 = \frac{1}{2}$, find v_2. From the result of part c. find $v_3, v_4, \ldots, v_n$.

e. Using the result of part d., show that

$$p_n = \frac{1}{2!} - \frac{1}{3!} + \cdots \pm \frac{1}{n!}.$$

5. FINITE STOCHASTIC PROCESSES

We have seen that in the case of the equiprobable measure the assignment of a probability measure and the computation of probabilities required only counting problems. We are now going to consider a more general situation, which we will again specialize in later sections.

We deal with a sequence of experiments where the outcome on each particular experiment depends on some chance element. Any such sequence is called a *stochastic process*. (The Greek word "stochos" means "guess.") We shall assume a finite number of experiments and a finite number of possibilities for each experiment. We assume that, if all the outcomes of the experiments that precede a given experiment were known, then both the possibilities for this experiment and the probability that any particular possibility will occur would be known. We wish to make predictions about the process as a whole. For example, in the case of repeated throws of an ordinary coin we would assume that on any particular experiment we have two outcomes, and the probabilities for each of these outcomes is one-half regardless of any other outcomes. We might be interested, however, in the probabilities of statements of the form, "More than two-thirds of the throws result in heads," or "The number of heads and tails that occur is the same." These questions can be answered only when a probability measure has been assigned to the process as a whole. In this section we show how a probability measure can be assigned, using the given information. In the case of coin tossing, the probabilities (hence also the possibilities) on any given experiment do not depend upon the previous results. We will not make any such restriction here, since the assumption is not true in general.

We shall show how the probability measure is constructed for a particular example, and the procedure in the general case is similar.

We assume that we have a sequence of three experiments, the possibilities for which are indicated in Figure 3. The set of all possible outcomes that might occur on any of the experiments is represented by the set $\{a, b, c, d, e, f\}$. Note that if we know that outcome b occurred on the first experiment, then we know that the possibilities on experiment two are $\{a, e, d\}$. Similarly if we know that b occurred on the first experiment and a on the second, then the only possibilities for the third are $\{c, f\}$. We denote by p_a the probability that the first experiment results in outcome a, and by p_b the probability that outcome b occurs in the first experiment. We denote by $p_{b,d}$ the probability that outcome d occurs on the second experiment, which is the probability computed on the assumption that outcome

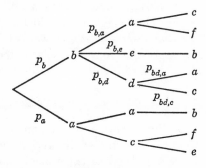

Figure 3

b occurred on the first experiment. Similarly for $p_{b,a}$, $p_{b,e}$, $p_{a,a}$, $p_{a,c}$. We denote by $p_{bd,c}$ the probability that outcome c occurs on the third experiment, the latter probability being computed on the assumption that outcome b occurred on the first experiment and d on the second. Similarly for $p_{ba,c}$, $p_{ba,f}$, and so on. We have assumed that these numbers are given, and the fact that they are probabilities assigned to possible outcomes would mean that they are positive and that

$$p_a + p_b = 1, \quad p_{b,a} + p_{b,e} + p_{b,d} = 1, \quad \text{and} \quad p_{bd,a} + p_{bd,c} = 1,$$

and so on. It is convenient to associate each probability with a branch of the tree. We have done this in Figure 3 for several branches. The sum of the numbers assigned to branches from a particular branch point is one; for example, $p_{b,a} + p_{b,e} + p_{b,d} = 1$.

A possibility for the sequence of three experiments is indicated by a path through the tree. We define now a probability measure on the set of all paths. We call this a *tree measure*. To the path corresponding to outcome b on the first experiment, d on the second, and c on the third, we assign the weight $p_b \cdot p_{b,d} \cdot p_{bd,c}$—that is, the *product* of the probabilities associated with each branch along the path being considered.

To justify this assignment mathematically we need only show that it leads to a probability measure on the set of paths. We shall do this, but we first indicate the following intuitive justification. Assume that we were to make a large number of repetitions of this sequence of three experiments. Then, from the frequency interpretation of probability, we could expect approximately p_b of the experiments to result in a b for the first outcome. Of these we could expect approximately $p_{b,d}$ to result in d for the second outcome. Thus we could expect approximately $p_b \cdot p_{b,d}$ to start with b, d. Finally, of these we would expect approximately $p_{bd,c}$ to have c for the third outcome. Hence we would expect approximately $p_b \cdot p_{b,d} \cdot p_{bd,c}$ of the experiments to follow the path.*b*, *d*, *c*. Thus if we wish to preserve our frequency interpretation we must make the assignment that we have chosen.

We now show that the weights are positive and the sum of the weights is one. The weights are product of positive numbers and hence positive. To see that their sum is one, we first find the sum of the weights of all paths corresponding to a particular outcome, say *b*, on the first experiment and a particular outcome, say *d*, on the second. We have

$$p_b \cdot p_{b,d} \cdot p_{bd,a} + p_b \cdot p_{b,d} \cdot p_{bd,c} = p_b \cdot p_{b,d}[p_{bd,a} + p_{bd,c}] = p_b \cdot p_{b,d}.$$

For any other first two outcomes we would obtain a similar result. For example, the sum of the weights assigned to paths corresponding to outcome *a* on the first experiment and *c* on the second is $p_a \cdot p_{a,c}$. Notice that when we have verified that we have a probability measure, this will be the probability that the first outcome results in *a* and the second experiment results in *c*.

Next we find the sum of the weights assigned to all the paths corresponding to the cases where the outcome of the first experiment is *b*. We find this by adding the sums corresponding to the different possibilities for the second experiment. But by our preceding calculation this is

$$p_b \cdot p_{b,a} + p_b \cdot p_{b,e} + p_b \cdot p_{b,d} = p_b[p_{b,a} + p_{b,e} + p_{b,d}] = p_b.$$

Similarly the sum of the weights assigned to paths corresponding to the outcome *a* on the first experiment is p_a. Thus the sum of all weights is $p_a + p_b = 1$. Therefore we do have a probability measure. Note that we have also shown that the probability that the outcome of the first experiment is *a* has been assigned probability p_a in agreement with our given probability.

Example 1. Suppose that we have two urns. Urn 1 contains two black balls and three white balls. Urn 2 contains two black balls and one white ball. An urn is chosen at random and a ball chosen from this urn at random. What is the probability that a white ball is chosen? A hasty answer might be $\frac{1}{2}$, since an equal number of black and white balls are involved and everything is done at random. However, it is hasty answers like this one (which is wrong) that show the need for a more careful analysis.

We are considering two experiments. The first consists in choosing the urn and the second in choosing the ball. There are two possibilities for the first experiment, and we assign $p_1 = p_2 = \frac{1}{2}$ for the probabilities of choosing the first and the second urn, respectively. We then assign $p_{1,w} = \frac{3}{5}$ for the probability that a white ball is chosen, under the assumption that urn 1 is chosen. Similarly we assign

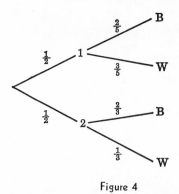

Figure 4

$p_{1,B} = \frac{2}{5}$, $p_{2,W} = \frac{1}{3}$, $p_{2,B} = \frac{2}{3}$. We indicate these probabilities on the possibility tree in Figure 4. The probability that a white ball is drawn is then found from the tree measure as the sum of the weights assigned to paths that lead to a choice of a white ball. This is $\frac{1}{2} \cdot \frac{3}{5} + \frac{1}{2} \cdot \frac{1}{3} = \frac{7}{15}$.

Example 2. We may treat the process of sampling two-valued items from a finite set as a stochastic process. Suppose, for example, we draw a sample of three pieces from a lot of ten containing two defectives. In Figure 5 each of the three possible draws is shown as an experiment. The first piece drawn can be either good or defective, so that there are initially two branches. Given that the first is good, the second can be either good or defective, so that there are again two branches. This is the case at each experiment, except that which follows the initial drawing of two defectives. Since there are only two defectives in the lot, there is only one possible outcome on the third experiment.

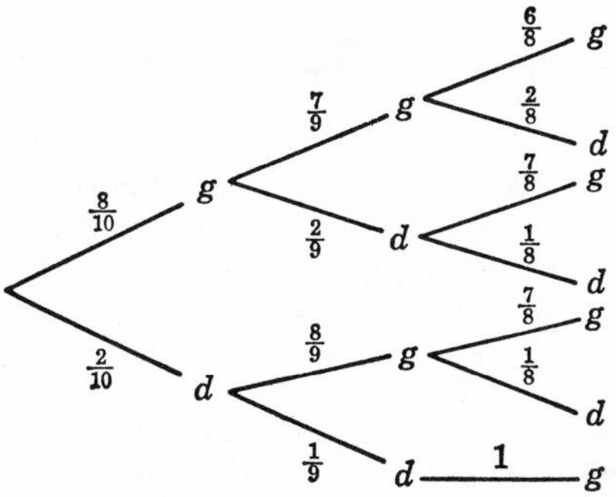

Figure 5

On the first experiment we assign $p_g = \frac{8}{10}$ and $p_d = \frac{2}{10}$, since eight out of the ten pieces are good and each piece has the same probability of being drawn. We then assign $p_{g,d} = \frac{2}{9}$ for the probability that the second piece chosen is defective, given that the first piece was good, since in the second experiment there are only nine pieces remaining of which, under these conditions, two are defective. Similarly we find the other probabilities on the tree.

The probability that the sample will consist of three good pieces is the probability that the first, second, and third pieces will all be good. This is simply the path weight of the uppermost path of the tree, or $\frac{8}{10} \cdot \frac{7}{9} \cdot \frac{6}{8} = \frac{7}{15}$.

To obtain the probability that the sample contains exactly one defective, we must obtain the sum of the path weights that result in two good pieces and one defective. There are three such paths—ggd, gdg, and dgg. The first has probability $\frac{8}{10} \cdot \frac{7}{9} \cdot \frac{2}{8} = \frac{7}{45}$, the second $\frac{8}{10} \cdot \frac{2}{9} \cdot \frac{7}{8} = \frac{7}{45}$, and the third $\frac{2}{10} \cdot \frac{8}{9} \cdot \frac{7}{8} = \frac{7}{45}$. (Why are the probabilities of the three paths the same?) Thus the probability of exactly one defective in the sample is $\frac{7}{45} + \frac{7}{45} + \frac{7}{45} = \frac{7}{15}$.

Example 3. A psychology student once studied the way mathematicians solve problems and contended that at times they try too hard to find symmetries in a problem. To illustrate this she asked a number of mathematicians to solve the following problem: Fifty balls (25 white and 25 black) are to be put in two urns, not necessarily the same number of balls in each. How should the balls be placed in the urns so as to maximize the chance of drawing a black ball, if an urn is chosen at random and a ball is drawn from it? A quite surprising number of mathematicians answered that you could not do any better than $\frac{1}{2}$, by the symmetry of the problem. But in fact one can do a good deal better.

To see this let us assume that we put one black ball in urn I and the rest of the balls in urn II. Then the appropriate tree diagram is shown in Figure 6. Let p be the statement, "A black ball is drawn." Then from Figure 6 we have

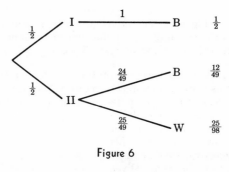

Figure 6

$$\mathbf{Pr}[p] = \tfrac{1}{2} + \tfrac{12}{49} = \tfrac{73}{98} = .745.$$

Shown this solution, many of the mathematicians then said, "But I assumed it was necessary to put the same number of balls in each urn," thus imposing symmetry into the problem even though it was carefully stated to be unnecessary.

That the solution above is the best one can do can be seen as follows. If each urn has the same number of black and white balls the answer is clearly $\tfrac{1}{2}$, and the solution above already does better than that. Thus we can assume that one of the urns has more black than white balls and the other has more white than black. We shall argue that the solution above (one black ball in urn I) does the best that can be done in either urn. For consider the urn (call it urn I) with more black than white. In the solution above we already have achieved probability 1 of getting a black ball when urn I is chosen; clearly we can do no better. Consider urn II, which has more white than black balls. Suppose it has j black balls; in order to maximize the probability of getting a black ball we should have only $j + 1$ white balls in the urn. Then the probability of picking a black ball if urn II is chosen is $j/(2j + 1)$. As j increases, this probability increases (see Exercise 8). Thus we should make j as large as possible, and we have already done this by choosing $j = 24$ in the solution above. Hence the scheme that puts one black ball in urn I and the rest in urn II does the best that can be done regardless of which urn is chosen.

EXERCISES

1. The fractions of Republicans, Democrats, and Independent voters in cities A and B are

    City A: .30 Republican, .40 Democratic, .30 Independent;
    City B: .40 Republican, .50 Democratic, .10 Independent.

    A city is chosen at random and two voters are chosen successively and at random from among its voters. Construct a tree measure and find the probability that two Democrats are chosen. Find the probability that the second voter chosen is an independent. [*Ans.* .205; .2.]

2. A coin is thrown. If a head turns up, a die is rolled; if a tail turns up, the coin is thrown again. Construct a tree measure to represent the two experiments and find the probability that the die is thrown and a six turns up.

3. A man wins a certain tournament if he can win two consecutive games out of three played alternately with two opponents A and B. A is a better player than B. The probability of winning a game when B is the opponent is $\frac{2}{3}$. The probability of winning a game when A is his opponent is only $\frac{1}{3}$. Construct a tree measure for the possibilities for three games, assuming that he plays alternately but plays A first. Do the same assuming that he plays B first. In each case find the probability that he will win two consecutive games. Is it better to play two games against the strong player or against the weaker player?

   [*Ans.* $\frac{10}{27}$; $\frac{8}{27}$; better to play strong player twice.]

4. Construct a tree measure to represent the possibilities for four throws of an ordinary coin. Assume that the probability of a head on any toss is $\frac{1}{2}$ regardless of any information about other throws.

5. A student claims to be able to distinguish beer from ale. He is given a series of three tests. In each test he is given two cans of beer and one of ale and asked to pick out the ale. If he gets two or more correct we will admit his claim. Draw a tree to represent the possibilities (either right or wrong) for his answers. Construct the tree measure that would correspond to guessing and find the probability that his claim will be established if he guesses on every trial.

6. A box contains three defective light bulbs and seven good ones. Construct a tree to show the possibilities if three consecutive bulbs are drawn at random from the box (they are not replaced after being drawn). Assign a tree measure and find the probability that at least one good bulb is drawn out. [*Ans.* $\frac{119}{120}$.]

7. In Example 3 if urn 1 contains j black balls and k white balls, find the probability of obtaining a black ball.

8. Show that if in the expression $j/(2j + 1)$ you replace j by $j + 1$, the ratio will increase—that is, that $j/(2j + 1) < (j + 1)/(2j + 3)$.

9. A chess player plays three successive games of chess. His psychological makeup is such that the probability of his winning a given game is $(\frac{1}{2})^{k+1}$, where k is the number of games he has won so far. (For instance, the probability of his winning the first game is $\frac{1}{2}$, the probability of his winning the second game *if he has already won the first game* is $\frac{1}{4}$, and so on.) What is the probability that he will win at least two of the three games?

10. Before a political convention, a political expert has assigned the following probabilities. The probability that the President will be willing to run again is $\frac{1}{2}$. If he is willing to run, he and his Vice-President are sure to be nominated and have probability $\frac{3}{5}$ of being elected again. If the President does not run, the present Vice-President has probability $\frac{1}{10}$ of being nominated, and any other presidential candidate has probability $\frac{1}{2}$ of being elected. What is the probability that the present Vice-President will be reelected? [*Ans.* $\frac{13}{40}$.]

11. Assume that in the World Series each team has probability one-half of winning each game, independently of the outcomes of any other game. Assign a tree measure. (See Chapter 1, Section 4, for the tree.) Find the probability that the series ends in 4, 5, 6, and 7 games, respectively.

12. Assume that in the World Series one team is stronger than the other and has probability .6 for winning each of the games. Assign a tree measure and find the following probabilities.

 a. The probability that the stronger team wins in 4, 5, 6, and 7 games, respectively.

 b. The probability that the weaker team wins in 4, 5, 6, and 7 games, respectively.

 c. The probability that the series ends in 4, 5, 6, and 7 games, respectively. [*Ans.* .16; .27; .30; .28.]

 d. The probability that the strong team wins the series. [*Ans.* .71.]

13. Redo Exercise 12 for the case of two poorly matched teams, where the better team has probability .9 of winning a game.

[*Ans.* c. .66; .26; .07; .01; d. .997.]

14. In the World Series from 1905 through 1970 (excluding series of more than seven games) there were 12 four-game, 16 five-game, 13 six-game, and 22 seven-game series. Which of the assumptions in Exercises 11–13 comes closest to predicting these results? Is it a good fit?

[*Ans.* .6; no.]

15. Consider the following assumption concerning World Series: 90 percent of the time the two teams are evenly matched, while 10 percent of the time they are poorly matched, with the better team having probability .9 of winning a game. Show that this assumption comes closer to predicting the actual outcomes than those considered in Exercise 13.

16. A and B play a series of games for which they are evenly matched. A player wins the series either by winning two games in a row or by winning a total of three games. Construct the tree and the tree measure.

 a. What is the probability that A wins the series?

 b. What is the probability that more than three games need to be played?

6. CONDITIONAL PROBABILITY AND BAYES' THEOREM

Suppose that we have a given $\mathfrak{U}$ and that measures have been assigned to all subsets of $\mathfrak{U}$. A statement p will have probability $\mathbf{Pr}[p] = \mathbf{m}(P)$. Suppose we now receive some additional information, say that the statement q is true. How does this additional information alter the probability of p?

The probability of p after the receipt of the information q is called its *conditional probability*, and it is denoted by $\mathbf{Pr}[p \mid q]$, which is read "the probability of p given q." In this section we will construct a method of finding this conditional probability in terms of the measure $\mathbf{m}$.

If we know that q is true, then the original possibility set $\mathfrak{U}$ has been reduced to Q and therefore we must define our measure on the subsets of Q instead of on the subsets of $\mathfrak{U}$. Of course, every nonempty subset X of Q is a subset of $\mathfrak{U}$, and hence we know $\mathbf{m}(X)$, its measure before q was discovered. Since q cuts down on the number of possibilities, its new measure $\mathbf{m}'(X)$ should be larger.

The basic idea on which the definition of $\mathbf{m}'$ is based is that, while we know that the possibility set has been reduced to Q, we have no new information about subsets of Q. If X and Y are subsets of Q, and

$\mathbf{m}(X) = 2 \cdot \mathbf{m}(Y)$, then we will want $\mathbf{m}'(X) = 2 \cdot \mathbf{m}'(Y)$. This will be the case if the measures of subsets of Q are simply increased by a proportionality factor $\mathbf{m}'(X) = k \cdot \mathbf{m}(X)$, and all that remains is to determine k. Since we know that $1 = \mathbf{m}'(Q) = k \cdot \mathbf{m}(Q)$, we see that $k = 1/\mathbf{m}(Q)$, and our new measure on subsets of $\mathcal{U}$ is determined by the formula

$$(1) \qquad \mathbf{m}'(X) = \frac{\mathbf{m}(X)}{\mathbf{m}(Q)}.$$

How does this affect the probability of p? First of all, the truth set of p has been reduced. Because all elements of $\tilde{Q}$ have been eliminated, the new truth set of p is $P \cap Q$, and therefore

$$(2) \qquad \mathbf{Pr}[p \mid q] = \mathbf{m}'(P \cap Q) = \frac{\mathbf{m}(P \cap Q)}{\mathbf{m}(Q)} = \frac{\mathbf{Pr}[p \wedge q]}{\mathbf{Pr}[q]}.$$

Note that if the original measure $\mathbf{m}$ is the equiprobable measure, then the new measure $\mathbf{m}'$ will also be the equiprobable measure on the set Q.

We must take care that the denominators in (1) and (2) be different from zero. Observe that $\mathbf{m}(Q)$ will be zero if Q is the empty set, which happens only if q is self-contradictory. This is also the only case in which $\mathbf{Pr}[q] = 0$, and hence we make the obvious assumption that our information q is not self-contradictory.

> **Example 1.** In Example 2 of Section 1, in which three computer manufacturers, A, B, and C, are trying to contract for the installation of a computer system with the X Company, the probability assigned to A, B, or C's winning the contract was $\frac{2}{5}$, $\frac{2}{5}$, and $\frac{1}{5}$, respectively. Suppose it is learned that B has decided not to compete on this contract. What are the chances of A and C now? Let q be the statement that B will not win—that is, that either A or C will win the contract. *Prior* to the receipt of the information that B has withdrawn from competition, $\mathbf{Pr}[q] = \frac{3}{5}$, while *subsequent* to receipt of this information, $\mathbf{Pr}[q] = 1$. Hence the other two probabilities are increased by a factor of $1/(\frac{3}{5}) = \frac{5}{3}$. Company A now has a $(\frac{2}{5})(\frac{5}{3}) = \frac{2}{3}$ chance of winning the contract, while C has a $(\frac{1}{5})(\frac{5}{3}) = \frac{1}{3}$ chance.

> **Example 2.** A family is chosen at random from the set of all families having exactly two children (not twins). What is the probability that the family has two boys, if it is known that there is a boy in the family? Without any information, we would assign the equiprobable measure on the set $\mathcal{U} = \{BB, BG, GB, GG\}$, where the first letter of the pair indicates the sex of the younger child and the second that of the older. The information that there is a boy causes $\mathcal{U}$ to change to $\{BB, BG, GB\}$, but the new measure is still the equiprobable measure. Thus the conditional probability that there are two boys given that there is a boy is $\frac{1}{3}$. If, on the other hand, we know that the first child is a boy, then the possibilities are reduced to $\{BB, BG\}$ and the conditional probability is $\frac{1}{2}$.

A particularly interesting case of conditional probability is that in which $\mathbf{Pr}[p \mid q] = \mathbf{Pr}[p]$. Here the new information q has no effect on the probability of p, and we then say that p is *independent* of q. If in (2) we replace $\mathbf{Pr}[p \mid q]$ by $\mathbf{Pr}[p]$, and cross-multiply, we get

$$(3) \qquad\qquad \mathbf{Pr}[p \wedge q] = \mathbf{Pr}[p] \cdot \mathbf{Pr}[q].$$

On the other hand, if we express the condition that q is independent of p, we arrive at the same result. Hence the two statements are independent of each other. We can therefore say that p and q are independent if and only if (3) holds.

> **Example 3.** Consider three throws of an ordinary coin, where we consider the eight possibilities to be equally likely. Let p be the statement, "A head turns up on the first throw," and q be the statement, "A tail turns up on the second throw." Then $\mathbf{Pr}[p] = \mathbf{Pr}[q] = \frac{1}{2}$ and $\mathbf{Pr}[p \wedge q] = \frac{1}{4}$ and therefore p and q are independent statements.
>
> While we have an intuitive notion of independence, it can happen that two statements, which may not seem to be independent, are in fact independent. For example, let r be the statement "The same side turns up all three times." Let s be the statement "At most one head occurs." Then r and s are independent statements (see Exercise 10).

An important use of conditional probabilities arises in the following manner. We wish to find the probability of a statement p. We observe that there is a complete set of alternatives $q_1, q_2, \ldots, q_n$ such that the probability $\mathbf{Pr}[q_i]$ as well as the conditional probabilities $\mathbf{Pr}[p \mid q_i]$ can be found for every i. Then in terms of these we can find $\mathbf{Pr}[p]$ by

$$(4) \quad \mathbf{Pr}[p] = \mathbf{Pr}[q_1]\mathbf{Pr}[p \mid q_1] + \mathbf{Pr}[q_2]\mathbf{Pr}[p \mid q_2] + \cdots + \mathbf{Pr}[q_n]\mathbf{Pr}[p \mid q_n].$$

The proof of this assertion is left as an exercise (see Exercise 12).

Conditional probabilities play an important role in many business problems; we may start with a probability assigned to a prediction p, and then revise our probability on the basis of added information q. It is customary to refer to the original probability $\mathbf{Pr}[p]$ as the *prior* probability, and the resulting conditional probability $\mathbf{Pr}[p \mid q]$ as the *posterior* probability.

For instance, in Example 1 the prior probability that Company A will win the contract was $\frac{2}{5}$, while the posterior probability is $\frac{2}{3}$.

This kind of problem occurs so often that it is convenient to have a formula for the computations involved. Our examples so far involve only two alternatives, but we shall consider the more general case of n alternatives. We assume that we have the following situation. A possibility space $\mathfrak{U}$ has been assigned with a probability measure. A complete set of alternatives, $p_1, p_2, \ldots, p_n$, has been singled out. Their probabilities are determined by the assigned measure. (A *complete set of alternatives* is a set of statements such that for any possible outcome one and only one of the statements is true.) We are now given that a statement q is true. We wish to compute the new probabilities for the alternatives relative to this information. That is, we wish the conditional probabilities $\mathbf{Pr}[p_j \mid q]$ for each p_j. We shall give two different methods for obtaining these probabilities.

The first is by a general formula. We illustrate this formula for the case of four alternatives: p_1, p_2, p_3, p_4. Consider $\mathbf{Pr}[p_2 \mid q]$. From the definition of conditional probability,

$$\mathbf{Pr}[p_2 \mid q] = \frac{\mathbf{Pr}[p_2 \wedge q]}{\mathbf{Pr}[q]}.$$

But since p_1, p_2, p_3, p_4 are a complete set of alternatives,

$$\mathbf{Pr}[q] = \mathbf{Pr}[p_1 \wedge q] + \mathbf{Pr}[p_2 \wedge q] + \mathbf{Pr}[p_3 \wedge q] + \mathbf{Pr}[p_4 \wedge q].$$

Thus

$$\mathbf{Pr}[p_2 \mid q] = \frac{\mathbf{Pr}[p_2 \wedge q]}{\mathbf{Pr}[p_1 \wedge q] + \mathbf{Pr}[p_2 \wedge q] + \mathbf{Pr}[p_3 \wedge q] + \mathbf{Pr}[p_4 \wedge q]}$$

$$= \frac{\mathbf{Pr}[p_2]\mathbf{Pr}[q \mid p_2]}{\mathbf{Pr}[p_1]\mathbf{Pr}[q \mid p_1] + \mathbf{Pr}[p_2]\mathbf{Pr}[q \mid p_2] + \mathbf{Pr}[p_3]\mathbf{Pr}[q \mid p_3] + \mathbf{Pr}[p_4]\mathbf{Pr}[q \mid p_4]}.$$

This result is sometimes known as "Bayes' theorem" after the Reverend Thomas Bayes, who first published it in 1763.

Example 4. Suppose a freshman must choose among mathematics, physics, chemistry, and botany as his science course. On the basis of the interest he expressed, his adviser assigns probabilities of .4, .3, .2, and .1 to his choosing each of the four courses, respectively. His adviser does not hear which course he actually chose, but at the end of the term the adviser hears that he received A in the course chosen. On the basis of the difficulties of these courses the adviser estimates the probability of the student's getting an A in mathematics to be .1, in physics .2, in chemistry .3, and in botany .9. How can the adviser revise his original estimates as to the probabilities of the student taking the various courses? Using Bayes' theorem, we get

$$\mathbf{Pr}[\text{He took math} \mid \text{He got an A}] = \frac{(.4)(.1)}{(.4)(.1) + (.3)(.2) + (.2)(.3) + (.1)(.9)}$$

$$= \frac{4}{25} = .16.$$

Similar computations assign probabilities of .24, .24, and .36 to the other three courses. Thus the new information, that he received an A, had little effect on the probability of his having taken physics or chemistry, but it has made it much less likely that he took mathematics, and much more likely that he took botany.

It is important to note that knowing the conditional probabilities of q relative to the alternatives is not enough. Unless we also know the probabilities of the alternatives at the start, we cannot apply Bayes' theorem. However, in some situations it is reasonable to assume that the alternatives are equally probable at the start. In this case the factors $\mathbf{Pr}[p_1], \ldots, \mathbf{Pr}[p_4]$ cancel from our basic formula, and we get the special form of the theorem:

If $\mathbf{Pr}[p_1] = \mathbf{Pr}[p_2] = \mathbf{Pr}[p_3] = \mathbf{Pr}[p_4]$, then

$$\mathbf{Pr}[p_2 \mid q] = \frac{\mathbf{Pr}[q \mid p_2]}{\mathbf{Pr}[q \mid p_1] + \mathbf{Pr}[q \mid p_2] + \mathbf{Pr}[q \mid p_3] + \mathbf{Pr}[q \mid p_4]}.$$

Example 5. In a sociological experiment the subjects are handed four sealed envelopes, each containing a problem. They are told to open one envelope and try to solve the problem in ten minutes. From past experience, the experimenter knows that the probability of their being able to solve the hardest problem is .1. With the other problems, they have probabilities of .3, .5, and .8. Assume the group succeeds within the allotted time. What is the probability that they selected the hardest problem? Since they have no way of knowing which problem is in which envelope, they choose at random, and we assign equal probabilities to the selection of the various problems. Hence the above simple formula applies. The probability of their having selected the hardest problem is

$$\frac{.1}{.1 + .3 + .5 + .8} = \frac{1}{17}.$$

The second method of computing Bayes' probabilities is to draw a tree, and then to redraw the tree in a different order. This is illustrated in the next example.

Example 6. A car manufacturer makes three types of cars: sedans, stationwagons, and convertibles. The same number of sedans and stationwagons are manufactured, but only half as many convertibles as sedans. It is found that 50 percent of the people who buy sedans buy a second car from the same manufacturer, while 75 percent of those who buy stationwagons and 25 percent of those who buy convertibles buy a second car from the manufacturer. What is the probability that a customer returning for a second car will already have a specified type of car?

We first construct a tree and tree measure for the type of the first car and for whether or not the customer returns for a second car (Figure 7).

We next construct the tree in reverse order, putting first whether the customer returns, and then the type of his old car. We have the same six branches as in Figure 7, only the order of description has been changed. Hence the path weights may be obtained from Figure 7. Furthermore, we know that the probability of the customer's returning is

$$\tfrac{4}{20} + \tfrac{6}{20} + \tfrac{1}{20} = \tfrac{11}{20};$$

hence we obtain the branch weights for the "first experiment" (Figure 8). We may now fill in the missing branch weights by simple division. For

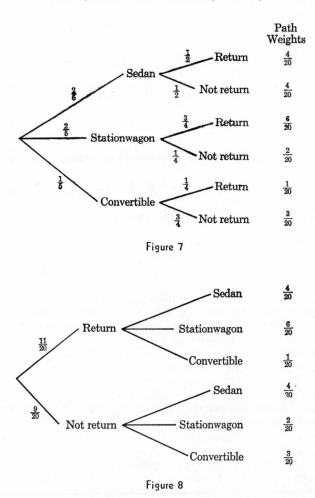

Figure 7

Figure 8

example, let x be the probability that the customer has a sedan, given that he returns. Then $\frac{11}{20}x = \frac{4}{20}$ on the first path in Figure 8. Hence

$$x = \frac{4}{20} \div \frac{11}{20} = \frac{4}{11}.$$

The completed tree is shown in Figure 9. From this we can find the posterior probabilities. For example, if the customer does not return, then the probabilities of his having the three types of cars have changed to $\frac{4}{9}$, $\frac{2}{9}$, and $\frac{3}{9}$, respectively.

It is important to realize in all of this use of Bayes' theory that we are simply computing ordinary conditional probability. Bayes' formula is mostly of historical interest. The method of reversing the order of the tree is a convenient computational method when we receive new information and want to compute the new conditional probabilities for all alternatives.

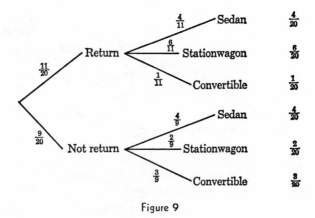

Figure 9

EXERCISES

1. Daily demand for a certain product can vary between one and thirteen units. If the equiprobable measure is assigned to all possible demands, what is the probability that on a particular day the demand was for exactly five units, given that on that day demand was between two and seven units inclusive?

2. There are seven potential bidders for a certain contract. It is believed that every bidder has about the same chance of winning. Just before the closing date, three of the potential bidders decide not to submit bids. How much does this increase the chance of one of the remaining four bidders to win the contract?

3. Let d_i be the statement, "The demand for product X today was for i units." Suppose $\mathbf{Pr}[d_0] = .1$, $\mathbf{Pr}[d_1] = .2$, $\mathbf{Pr}[d_2] = .4$, $\mathbf{Pr}[d_3] = .3$, and $\mathbf{Pr}[d_i] = 0$ for $i > 3$. Assume that demands on successive days are independent. What is the probability that total demand on two successive days will be for more than three units, given that:
   a. On one of the days demand was for one unit?   [*Ans.* $\frac{1}{3}$.]
   b. On the first day, demand was for one unit?   [*Ans.* .3.]

4. Referring to Section 3, Exercise 9, what is the probability that a given piece selected at random has a burr if:
   a. It has a tensile-strength defect?
   b. It has tensile-strength and diameter defects?   [*Ans.* $\frac{1}{2}$.]
   c. It has neither a tensile-strength nor a diameter defect?

5. In the market-leadership example of Chapter 1, Section 5, assuming that the equiprobable measure has been assigned, find the probability that A is the leader in at least two territories given that B discontinues marketing in the North.

6. If $\mathbf{Pr}[\sim p] = \frac{1}{4}$ and $\mathbf{Pr}[q \mid p] = \frac{1}{2}$, what is $\mathbf{Pr}[p \wedge q]$?   [*Ans.* $\frac{3}{8}$.]

7. The American Experience Table of Mortality shows that of 100,000 people alive at the age of ten, 57,917 will survive until their sixtieth year, and 56,371 will survive until their sixty-first year. What is the probability that a person selected at random at the age of sixty will die during the next year?

8. A researcher examines the output of an automatic machine by looking at the pieces produced in sequence and determining whether they are good or defective. He then partitions a sequence into *runs*, where a run is a sequence of pieces that ends whenever a defective occurs. For example, in the sequence *gggdgdggddggggd*, the runs are (*gggd*), (*gd*), (*ggd*), (*d*), (*ggggd*). He finally looks at the length of various runs and assigns probabilities to the future occurrences of runs of various lengths. In the example above, there are runs of length 4, 2, 3, 1, and 5. Let r_i be the statement, "The length of a run is i *or more*," $i = 1, 2, 3, \ldots$. After considerable research, the following probabilities are assigned to r_i:

i	$\mathbf{Pr}[r_i]$
1	1.00
2	.90
3	.81
4	.73
5	.66
6	.59

a. Let p_i be the statement, "The run is *precisely* of length i." Show that $\mathbf{Pr}[p_i] = \mathbf{Pr}[r_i] - \mathbf{Pr}[r_{i+1}]$. Calculate $\mathbf{Pr}[p_i]$ for $i = 1, 2, 3, 4, 5$.
b. Show that $\mathbf{Pr}[p_i \wedge r_i] = \mathbf{Pr}[p_i]$.
c. Calculate $\mathbf{Pr}[p_i \mid r_i]$ for $i = 1, 2, 3, 4, 5$. What can you say regarding independence or dependence about $\mathbf{Pr}[p_i \mid r_i]$?
[*Partial Ans.* All approximately .1.]

9. Let a deck of cards consist of the jacks and queens chosen from a bridge deck, and let two cards be drawn from the new deck. Find:
a. The probability that the cards are both jacks, given that one is a jack. [*Ans.* $\frac{3}{11} = .27$.]
b. The probability that the cards are both jacks, given that one is a red jack. [*Ans.* $\frac{5}{13} = .38$.]
c. The probability that the cards are both jacks, given that one is the jack of hearts. [*Ans.* $\frac{3}{7} = .43$.]

10. Prove that statements r and s in Example 3 are independent.

11. The following example shows that r may be independent of p and q without being independent of $p \wedge q$ and $p \vee q$. We throw a coin twice. Let p be "The first toss comes out heads," q be "The second toss comes out heads," and r be "The two tosses come out the same." Compute $\mathbf{Pr}[r]$, $\mathbf{Pr}[r \mid p]$, $\mathbf{Pr}[r \mid q]$, $\mathbf{Pr}[r \mid p \wedge q]$, $\mathbf{Pr}[r \mid p \vee q]$. [*Ans.* $\frac{1}{2}, \frac{1}{2}, \frac{1}{2}, 1, \frac{1}{3}$.]

12. Prove formula (4).

13. Urn A contains three white balls and seven black balls; urn B contains twelve white balls and eight black balls. One of the urns is chosen at random and a ball is drawn from it.
a. What is the probability that the ball is white *given* that it was drawn from urn A? *Given* that it was drawn from urn B?
b. What is the (unconditional) probability that the ball is white?
c. *Given* that the ball is white, what is the probability that it was drawn from urn A? [*Ans.* $\frac{1}{3}$.]

14. In Exercise 13, five balls are drawn from one of the urns chosen at random.

    a. What is the probability that two of the balls are white and three are black *given* that they were drawn from urn A? *Given* that they were drawn from urn B?

    b. What is the (unconditional) probability of obtaining two white and three black balls?

    c. Given that the sample of five consists of two white and three black balls, what is the probability that it was drawn from urn A?

                                             [*Ans.* .636.]

15. Three men, Smith, Jones, and Brown, are in jail; one is to be executed the next day and the others are to be freed. While they do not know who is the unlucky one, the guard does. Brown takes the guard to one side and says, "I know, of course, that either Smith or Jones will be freed tomorrow. Would you tell me the name of one of them who will go free? If by bad luck I am the one to be executed, just toss a coin to give me a name." The guard replies, "No, I don't think I should do that, since you now think you have probability $\frac{1}{3}$ of being executed. If I tell you the name of one who will be freed, there will only be two left, and your probability will change to $\frac{1}{2}$. Then you certainly won't sleep as well tonight!" Was the guard's reasoning correct?   [*Ans.* No.]

16. Three urns, A, B, and C, contain mixtures of white, red, and black balls in the following numbers:

Urn	White	Red	Black	Total
A	2	3	5	10
B	12	6	2	20
C	8	15	7	30

An urn is chosen by the following randomizing device: a six-faced die is thrown; urn A is chosen if the die comes up 1, urn B if it comes up 2 or 3, and urn C otherwise.

    a. Given that a single ball drawn from an urn selected in this manner is red, what is the probability that the urn is urn A? urn B? urn C?

                                              [*Ans.* $\frac{1}{8}$, $\frac{2}{8}$, $\frac{5}{8}$.]

    b. Given that three balls drawn in sequence from the urn are (in order) white, white, and black, what is the probability that the urn is urn A? urn B? urn C?

17. Urn A contains 2 white balls and one black ball; urn B contains 1001 white balls and 1000 black balls. One of the urns is selected at random. What is the probability that it was urn A if:

    a. One ball is drawn from the urn and it is white?   [*Ans.* $\frac{1334}{2335}$.]

    b. Two balls are drawn from the urn, the first of which is white and the second black?

    c. Two balls are drawn from the urn, both of which are white? What information does the second ball give about the contents of the urn if the first ball drawn was white?   [*Ans.* None.]

18. In Exercise 17, suppose the first ball drawn had been black. What is the probability that it was drawn from urn A? What is the probability for the sequences black-black and black-white? Does the second drawing give any information about the contents of the urn given that the first ball drawn was black?

19. A lot of ten pieces contains R defectives. A sample of five is drawn and two defectives are found. Suppose that the following prior probabilities are assigned to the number of defectives R in the lot: $\mathbf{Pr}[R = 3] = .2$; $\mathbf{Pr}[R = 5] = .8$. What are the posterior probabilities of the number of defectives in the lot given the sample result? What are the posterior probabilities of the number of defectives among the five pieces not sampled given the sample result?   [*Partial Ans.* $\mathbf{Pr}[R = 3] = \frac{21}{101}$.]

20. In a consumer panel in which records are kept of individuals' coffee purchases by brands, Consumer A purchases Brand X with probability .6 and other brands with probability .4, while Consumer B purchases X with probability .3 and other brands with probability .7. Assume that for both A and B each purchase is independent of all previous purchases.

    a. Construct a tree diagram for three consecutive purchases by A; for three consecutive purchases by B.

    b. Find the probability that A will buy Brand X exactly twice in three purchases; that B will buy X twice in three purchases.

    c. Given that either A or B was chosen at random and that in three consecutive purchases Brand X was bought exactly twice, find the posterior probability that the consumer chosen was A.

                                                 [*Ans.* .696.]

21. In Exercise 20, Consumer C has a pattern of purchasing coffee brands in which the probability of purchasing a particular brand depends on which brand was last purchased. If X was the last brand purchased, the probability of repurchasing X is .8 and the probability of purchasing some other brand is .2. If the last brand purchased was not X, the probability of buying X on the next purchase is .3, while the probability of buying some brand other than X is .7. Construct a tree diagram for the next three consecutive purchases of coffee and find the probability that Brand X is purchased exactly twice, given that Consumer C's last purchase was

    a. Brand X.

    b. not Brand X.

22. In Exercise 21, assume that a prior probability of .6 has been assigned to Consumer C's last purchase being Brand X, and that we then observe that of C's next three purchases, two were of Brand X. What is the posterior probability that the purchase preceding these last three was Brand X given that

    a. we do not know the order of the three purchases?

    b. the purchases were made in the order X, $\sim$X, X?   [*Ans.* .8.]

    c. the purchases were made in the order $\sim$X, X, X?

23. In blending whiskey, a panel of taste experts is often used to determine whether a given batch is distinguishable from previous batches. One well-known method of testing ability to distinguish is the "triad test," in which an expert is presented with two samples from the same batch and one from a different batch and asked to pick the odd sample. Suppose a given expert is given three such triad tests, and we are willing to concede that two batches are different if the expert picks the odd sample on at least two of the tests. Draw a tree to represent the possibilities (either right or wrong) for his answers. Construct the tree measure that will be applicable if the two batches are in fact indistinguishable and find the probability that two batches that are indistinguishable will be treated as if they were different.

24. Three economic theories are proposed at a given time, which appear to be equally likely on the basis of existing evidence. The state of the American economy is observed the following year, and it turns out that its actual development had probability .6 of happening according to the first theory; and probabilities .4 and .2 according to the others. How does this modify the probabilities of correctness of the three theories?

25. Let p_1, p_2, p_3, and p_4 be a set of equally likely alternatives. Let $\mathbf{Pr}[q \mid p_1] = a$, $\mathbf{Pr}[q \mid p_2] = b$, $\mathbf{Pr}[q \mid p_3] = c$, $\mathbf{Pr}[q \mid p_4] = d$. Show that if $a + b + c + d = 1$, then the revised probabilities of the alternatives relative to q are a, b, c, and d, respectively. Show also that $\mathbf{Pr}[p_i] = \mathbf{Pr}[q]$ for $i = 1, 2, 3, 4$.

26. In poker, Smith holds a very strong hand and bets a considerable amount. The probability that his opponent, Jones, has a better hand is .05. With a better hand Jones would raise the bet with probability .9, but with a poorer hand Jones would raise only with probability .2. Suppose that Jones raises, what is the new probability that he has a winning hand?   [*Ans.* $\frac{9}{47}$.]

27. One coin in a collection of 8 million coins has two heads. The rest are fair coins. A coin chosen at random from the collection is tossed ten times and comes up heads every time. What is the probability that it is the two-headed coin?

28. Referring to Exercise 27, assume that the coin is tossed n times and comes up heads every time. How large does n have to be to make the probability approximately $\frac{1}{2}$ that you have the two-headed coin?
                                                                      [*Ans.* 23.]

29. A man will accept job a with probability $\frac{1}{2}$, job b with probability $\frac{1}{3}$, and job c with probability $\frac{1}{6}$. In each case he must decide whether to rent or buy a house. The probabilities of his buying are $\frac{1}{3}$ if he takes job a, $\frac{2}{3}$ if he takes job b, and 1 if he takes job c. Given that he buys a house, what are the probabilities of his having taken each job?
                                                            [*Ans.* .3; .4; .3.]

30. Assume that chest X-rays for detecting tuberculosis have the following properties. For people having tuberculosis the test will detect the disease 90 out of every 100 times. For people not having the disease the test will in 1 out of every 100 cases diagnose the patient incorrectly as having the disease. Assume that the incidence of tuberculosis is 5 persons per 10,000. A person is selected at random, given the X-ray test, and the radiologist reports the presence of tuberculosis. What is the probability that the person in fact has the disease?

7. EXPECTED VALUE AND VARIANCE

In this section we shall discuss two important concepts associated with chance experiments where the outcomes are numbers. The first concept that we consider is that of expected value. Although it originated in the study of gambling games, it enters into almost any detailed probabilistic discussion.

DEFINITION. If in an experiment the possible outcomes are numbers, $a_1, a_2, \ldots, a_k$, occurring with probability $p_1, p_2, \ldots, p_k$, then the *expected value* is defined to be

$$E = a_1 p_1 + a_2 p_2 + \cdots + a_k p_k.$$

The term "expected value" is not to be interpreted as the value that will necessarily occur on a single experiment. For example, if a person bets $1 that a head will turn up when a coin is thrown, he may either win $1 or lose $1. His expected value is $(1)(\frac{1}{2}) + (-1)(\frac{1}{2}) = 0$, which is not one of the possible outcomes. The term, expected value, had its origin in the following consideration. If we repeat an experiment with expected value E a large number of times, and if we expect a_1 a fraction p_1 of the time, a_2 a fraction p_2 of the time, and so on, then the average that we expect per experiment is E. In particular, in a gambling game E is interpreted as the average winning expected in a large number of plays. Here the expected value is often taken as the value of the game to the player. If the game has a positive expected value, the game is said to be favorable; if the game has expected value zero, it is said to be fair; and if it has negative expected value, it is described as unfavorable. These terms are not to be taken too literally, since many people are quite happy to play games that, in terms of expected value, are unfavorable. For instance, the buying of life insurance may be considered an unfavorable game that most people choose to play.

Example 1. For the first example of the application of expected value we consider the game of roulette as played at Monte Carlo. There are several types of bets the gambler can make, and we consider two of these.

The wheel has the number 0 and the numbers from 1 to 36 marked on equally spaced slots. The wheel is spun and a ball comes to rest in one of these slots. If the player puts a stake, say of $1, on a given number, and the ball comes to rest in this slot, then he receives from the croupier 36 times his stake, or $36. The player wins $35 with probability $\frac{1}{37}$ and loses $1 with probability $\frac{36}{37}$. Hence his expected winnings are

$$35 \cdot \tfrac{1}{37} - 1 \cdot \tfrac{36}{37} = -\tfrac{1}{37} = -.027.$$

This can be interpreted to mean that in the long run he can expect to lose about 2.7 percent of his stakes.

A second way to play is the following. A player may bet on "red" or "black." The numbers from 1 to 36 are evenly divided between the two colors. If a player bets on "red," and a red number turns up, he receives twice his stake. If a black number turns up, he loses his stake. If 0 turns up, then the wheel is spun until it stops on a number different from 0. If this is black, the player loses; but if it is red, he receives only his original stake, not twice it. For this type of play, the gambler wins $1 with probability $\frac{18}{37}$, breaks even with probability $\frac{1}{2} \cdot \frac{1}{37} = \frac{1}{74}$, and loses $1 with probability $\frac{18}{37} + \frac{1}{2} \cdot \frac{1}{37} = \frac{37}{74}$. Hence his expected winning is

$$1 \cdot \tfrac{18}{37} + 0 \cdot \tfrac{1}{74} - 1 \cdot \tfrac{37}{74} = -.0135.$$

In this case the player can expect to lose about 1.35 percent of his stakes in the long run. Thus the expected loss in this case is only half as great as in the previous case.

Example 2. A player rolls a die and receives a number of dollars corresponding to the number of dots on the face that turns up. What should the player pay for playing, to make this a fair game? To answer this question, we note that the player wins 1, 2, 3, 4, 5 or 6 dollars, each with probability $\frac{1}{6}$. Hence, his expected winning is

$$1(\tfrac{1}{6}) + 2(\tfrac{1}{6}) + 3(\tfrac{1}{6}) + 4(\tfrac{1}{6}) + 5(\tfrac{1}{6}) + 6(\tfrac{1}{6}) = 3\tfrac{1}{2}.$$

Thus if he pays \$3.50, his expected winnings will be zero.

Example 3. In the game of craps a pair of dice is rolled by one of the players. If the sum of the spots shown is 7 or 11, he wins. If it is 2, 3, or 12, he loses. If it is another sum, he must continue rolling the dice until he either repeats the same sum or rolls a 7. In the former case he wins, in the latter he loses. Let us suppose that he wins or loses \$1. Then the two possible outcomes are $+1$ and -1. We will compute the expected value of the game. First we must find the probability that he will win.

We represent the possibilities by a two-stage tree shown in Figure 10.

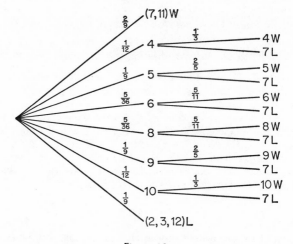

Figure 10

While it is theoretically possible for the game to go on indefinitely, we do not consider this possibility. This means that our analysis applies only to games that actually stop at some time.

The branch probabilities at the first stage are determined by thinking of the 36 possibilities for the throw of the two dice as being equally likely and taking in each case the fraction of the possibilities which correspond to the branch as the branch probability. The probabilities for the branches at the second level are obtained as follows. If, for example, the first outcome was a 4, then when the game ends, a 4 or 7 must have occurred. The possible outcomes for the dice were

$$\{(3, 1), (1, 3), (2, 2), (4, 3), (3, 4), (2, 5), (5, 2), (1, 6), (6, 1)\}.$$

Again we consider these possibilities to be equally likely and assign to the branch considered the fraction of the outcomes which correspond to this branch. Thus to the 4 branch we assign a probability $\frac{3}{9} = \frac{1}{3}$. The other branch probabilities are determined in a similar way. Having the tree measure assigned, to find the probability of a win we must simply add the weights of all paths leading to a win. If this is done, we obtain $\frac{244}{495}$. Thus the player's expected value is

$$1 \cdot \left(\frac{244}{495}\right) + (-1) \cdot \left(\frac{251}{495}\right) = -\frac{7}{495} = -.0141.$$

Hence he can expect to lose 1.41 percent of his stakes in the long run. It is interesting to note that this is just slightly less favorable than his losses in betting on "red" in roulette.

To see more clearly that the expected value of an experiment may not give a good prediction for the outcome of a single occurrence of the experiment, consider the following three experiments.

Experiment I:

$$\text{possible outcomes} \begin{cases} 1 & 2 & 3 & 4 & 5 \\ .1 & .2 & .4 & .2 & .1 \end{cases}$$
$$\text{probabilities}$$

Experiment II:

$$\text{possible outcomes} \begin{cases} 1 & 2 & 3 & 4 & 5 \\ .2 & .2 & .2 & .2 & .2 \end{cases}$$
$$\text{probabilities}$$

Experiment III:

$$\text{possible outcomes} \begin{cases} 1 & 2 & 3 & 4 & 5 \\ .3 & .15 & .1 & .15 & .3 \end{cases}$$
$$\text{probabilities}$$

The graphs of these probabilities are shown in Figure 11.

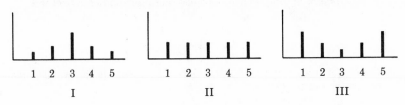

I   II   III

Figure 11

All three of these experiments have the same expected value, $E = 3$. However, as we go from experiment I to experiment III we see that we are less certain that on a single experiment we will get a 3 or a number near to 3 such as 2 or 4. For many purposes it is convenient to have a measure of the uncertainty that the outcome of an experiment will be near its expected value. There are several ways this could be given; the most commonly used measure is called the *variance* and defined as follows:

For an experiment with possible outcomes the numbers $a_1, a_2, \ldots, a_k$ occurring with probability $p_1, p_2, \ldots, p_k$ the *variance* is defined to be

$$V = (a_1 - E)^2 p_1 + (a_2 - E)^2 p_2 + \cdots + (a_k - E)^2 p_k.$$

Thus we measure the distance from the expected value by squaring the difference of the value from E and weight this with the probability that this difference will occur.

For experiment I:

$$V = (1 - 3)^2(.1) + (2 - 3)^2(.2) + (3 - 3)^2(.4)$$
$$+ (4 - 3)^2(.2) + (5 - 3)^2(.1)$$
$$= 1.2.$$

For experiment II:

$$V = (1 - 3)^2(.2) + (2 - 3)^2(.2) + (3 - 3)^2(.2)$$
$$+ (4 - 3)^2(.2) + (5 - 3)^2(.2)$$
$$= 2.0.$$

For experiment III:

$$V = (1 - 3)^2(.3) + (2 - 3)^2(.15) + (3 - 3)^2(.1)$$
$$+ (4 - 3)^2(.15) + (5 - 3)^2(.3)$$
$$= 2.7.$$

We note that the variances increase as we move to the experiments that are less likely to result in an outcome near the expected outcome— that is, as we move from experiment I to experiment III. In general, experiments that have high variances are those that are less likely to result in an outcome close to the expected value.

Example 1 (continued). In the roulette game of Example 1 under the first method of betting we had outcomes and probabilities given by

$$\text{outcomes} \quad \begin{Bmatrix} -1 & 35 \\ \frac{36}{37} & \frac{1}{37} \end{Bmatrix}$$
$$\text{probabilities}$$

The expected winning was $-.027$. Hence the variance for his winning under this method of play is

$$(-1 - (-.027))^2 \tfrac{36}{37} + (35 - (-.027))^2 \tfrac{1}{37} = 34.08.$$

Under the second method of play, red or black, the outcomes and probabilities were

$$\text{outcomes} \quad \begin{Bmatrix} -1 & 0 & 1 \\ \frac{37}{74} & \frac{1}{74} & \frac{18}{37} \end{Bmatrix}$$
$$\text{probabilities}$$

The expected winning was in this case $-.0135$. The variance is then

$$V = (-1 + .0135)^2 \tfrac{37}{74} + (0 + .0135)^2 \tfrac{1}{74} + (1 + .0135)^2 \tfrac{18}{37}$$
$$= .986$$

While the mean values for both games are nearly the same, there is a large difference in the variance. In the first case the player stands to win a lot more than his expected value, and this reflects itself in a larger variance.

Assume that we have an experiment with outcomes $a_1, a_2, \ldots, a_k$ occurring with probabilities $p_1, p_2, \ldots, p_k$. Let us multiply each of the outcomes by a constant c and find the effect of this on the mean and variance of the experiment. The new expected value E' is given by

$$\begin{aligned} E' &= ca_1p_1 + ca_2p_2 + \cdots + ca_kp_k \\ &= c(a_1p_1 + a_2p_2 + \cdots + a_kp_k) \\ &= cE. \end{aligned}$$

The new variance V' is given by

$$\begin{aligned} V' &= (ca_1 - cE)^2p_1 + (ca_2 - cE)^2p_2 + \cdots + (ca_k - cE)^2p_k \\ &= c^2[(a_1 - E)^2p_1 + (a_2 - E)^2p_2 + \cdots + (a_k - E)^2p_k] \\ &= c^2V. \end{aligned}$$

Thus we see that the effect of multiplying the outcomes by a constant c is to multiply the expected outcome by c and the variance by c^2.

A similar computation shows that if we add a constant c to each outcome, the new expected value is $E' = E + c$. However, the variance remains unchanged—which is quite reasonable, since all outcomes and the expected value are shifted by the same amount, so that the variation around the expected value remains unchanged.

Finally, suppose that we perform two experiments, each having numerical outcomes, and consider the new experiment obtained by simply adding the outcomes of these two experiments. Then it can be proved that the expected value of the sum experiment is simply the sum of the expected values of the individual experiments. However, it is not in general true that the variance of the sum experiment is the sum of the variances of the separate experiments. This will be the case only if the experiments are independent in the sense that the knowledge of the outcome of one experiment in no way affects the predictions about the outcome of the other. We shall not prove the latter properties, but rather illustrate them by examples.

Example 4. Assume that we toss a coin twice. On each experiment we have the following possibilities and probabilities for the number of heads that turn up:

$$\text{possibilities} \quad \begin{Bmatrix} 0 & 1 \\ \tfrac{1}{2} & \tfrac{1}{2} \end{Bmatrix}$$
$$\text{probabilities}$$

Thus if E_1 and V_1 are the mean and variance of the first toss, we have

$$E_1 = 0 \cdot (\tfrac{1}{2}) + 1 \cdot (\tfrac{1}{2}) = \tfrac{1}{2},$$

and

$$V_1 = (0 - \tfrac{1}{2})^2 \cdot \tfrac{1}{2} + (1 - \tfrac{1}{2})^2 \cdot (\tfrac{1}{2}) = \tfrac{1}{4}.$$

The second experiment will also have $E_2 = \frac{1}{2}$ and $V_2 = \frac{1}{4}$. The experiment obtained by adding the results has outcomes and probabilities given by

$$\begin{array}{l} \text{possibilities} \\ \text{probabilities} \end{array} \left\{ \begin{array}{ccc} 0 & 1 & 2 \\ \frac{1}{4} & \frac{1}{2} & \frac{1}{4} \end{array} \right\}$$

and hence the expected value E_3 and variance V_3 are

$$E_3 = 0 \cdot (\tfrac{1}{4}) + 1 \cdot (\tfrac{1}{2}) + 2 \cdot (\tfrac{1}{4}) = 1$$
$$= E_1 + E_2,$$

$$V_3 = (0 - 1)^2 \tfrac{1}{4} + (1 - 1)^2 \tfrac{1}{2} + (2 - 1)^2 \cdot \tfrac{1}{4} = \tfrac{1}{2}$$
$$= V_1 + V_2.$$

Thus in this case both the mean and variance are simply the sum of the results of the two individual experiments.

Example 5. Suppose now that we play the following two games. On the first game we win 1 dollar with probability $\frac{1}{2}$ and 0 with probability $\frac{1}{2}$. On the second game we are given 1 dollar if we lost on the first game and nothing if we won on the first game. Then the appropriate tree and tree measure for the two games are given in Figure 12.

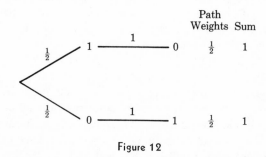

Figure 12

We notice that each game by itself has expected value $\frac{1}{2}$ and the game consisting of the sum of the two games has expected value 1, the sum of the two expected values. However, each individual game has variance $\frac{1}{4}$, while the sum has variance 0. Any experiment whose outcome is always the same will have variance 0 (see Exercise 15). Thus the variances do not add. However, the experiments are not independent; in fact in this case they are completely dependent.

Since the variance was defined in terms of the squares of the outcomes it is often more natural to deal with the square root of the variance, called the *standard deviation*: $D = \sqrt{V}$.

EXERCISES

1. Smith and Jones are matching coins. If the coins match, Smith gets \$1, and if they do not, Jones gets \$1.
    a. If the game consists of matching twice, what are the expected value and variance of the game for Smith?

    b. Suppose that if Smith wins the first round he quits, and if he loses the first he plays the second. Jones is not allowed to quit. What are the expected value and variance of the game for Smith?

2. A missile is fired successfully with probability p and fails with probability $q = 1 - p$. For one experiment find the expected number of successes, the variance, and the standard deviation.

$$[Ans. \; p, \; pq, \; \sqrt{pq}.]$$

3. For the situation in Exercise 2 find the expected value and the variance for n firings if the individual firings can be considered to be independent of one another.

4. In bets in which the probability of winning is .5, a popular betting "system" is to continue to bet each time one loses, doubling the stake at each stage, until a win occurs. Suppose the first bet is for \$1, and that the bettor's capital is \$3, so that if he loses twice in a row he must stop the procedure. What is the expected value of the game?   [*Ans.* 0.]

5. In Exercise 4, what is the expected value of the game if the bettor's capital is limited to (*a*) \$7? (*b*) \$15? (*c*) \$31? (*d*) Suppose a bettor has enough capital to play 20 times, doubling his stake each time. What is the expected value of the game? How much capital is required?

6. A man wishes to purchase a 5-cent newspaper. He has in his pocket one dime and five pennies. The newsman offers to let him have the paper in exchange for one coin drawn at random from the customer's pocket.
    a. Is this a fair proposition and, if not, to whom is it favorable?

$$[Ans. \; \text{Favorable to man.}]$$

    b. Answer the same questions as in (*a*) assuming that the newsman demands two coins drawn at random from the customer's pocket.

$$[Ans. \; \text{Fair proposition.}]$$

7. A bets 50 cents against B's x cents that, if two cards are dealt from a shuffled pack of ordinary playing cards, both cards will be of the same color. What value of x will make this bet fair?

8. Prove that if the expected value of a given experiment is E, and if a constant c is added to each of the outcomes, the expected value of the new experiment is $E + c$, and the variance is unchanged.

9. Suppose that we modify the game of craps as follows: on a 7 or 11 the player wins \$2, on a 2, 3, or 12 he loses \$3; otherwise the game is as usual. Find the expected value of the new game, and compare it with the old value.

10. Suppose that in roulette at Monte Carlo we place 50 cents on "red" and 50 cents on "black." What is the expected value of the game? Is this better or worse than placing \$1 on "red"?

11. Betting on "red" in roulette can be described roughly as follows. We win with probability .49, get our money back with probability .01, and lose with probability .50. Draw the tree for three plays of the game, and compute (to three decimals) the probability of each path. What is the probability that we are ahead at the end of three bets?   [*Ans.* .485.]

12. A man plays the following game: he draws a card from a bridge deck; if it is an ace he wins \$5; if it is a jack, a queen, or a king, he wins \$2; for any other card he loses \$1. What are his expected winnings and the variance per play?

13. An urn contains two black and three white balls. Balls are successively drawn from the urn without replacement until a black ball is obtained. Find the expected number of draws required.

14. Using the result of Exercises 12 and 13 of Section 5, find the expected number of games in the World Series (*a*) under the assumption that each team has probability $\frac{1}{2}$ of winning each game and (*b*) under the assumption that the stronger team has probability .6 of winning each game.

[*Ans.* 5.81; 5.75.]

15. Assume that an experiment has a constant outcome *c*. Show that the variance of the experiment is 0.

16. A royal family have children until they have a boy or until they have had three children. Find the expected number and variance for the number of girls for such a royal family. Do the same for the number of boys.

17. Show that the following alternative formula may be used for computing the variance for an experiment with numerical outcomes $a_1, a_2, \ldots, a_k$ with probabilities $p_1, p_2, \ldots, p_k$:

$$V = a_1^2 \cdot p_1 + a_2^2 \cdot p_2 + \cdots + a_k^2 \cdot p_k - E^2,$$

where E is the expected value of the experiment.

8. INDEPENDENT TRIALS

In Section 5 we developed a way to determine a probability measure for any sequence of chance experiments where there are only a finite number of possibilities for each experiment. While this provides the framework for the general study of stochastic processes, it is too general to be studied in complete detail. Therefore, in probability theory we look for simplifying assumptions that will make our probability measure easier to work with. It is desired also that these assumptions be such as to apply to a variety of experiments that would occur in practice.

In this book we shall limit ourselves to the study of two additional types of stochastic processes. The independent-trials process, the first one to be studied extensively in probability theory, will be considered in the present section. The Markov-chain process, which is finding increasing application, particularly in the behavioral sciences, will be considered in the next section.

A process of independent trials applies to the following situation. Assume that there is a sequence of chance experiments, each of which consists of a repetition of a single experiment, carried out in such a way that the results of any one experiment in no way affect the results in any other experiment. We label the possible outcome of a single experiment by $a_1, \ldots, a_r$. We assume that we are also given probabilities $p_1, \ldots, p_r$ for occurrence of each of these outcomes on any single experiment, the probabilities being independent of previous results. The tree representing the possibilities for the sequence of experiments will have the same outcomes from each branch point, and probability p_j will be assigned to any branch leading to outcome a_j. The tree measure determined in this way is the measure of an *independent-trials process*. We shall consider first the important case of two outcomes for each experiment.

In the case of two outcomes we arbitrarily label one outcome "success" and the other "failure." For example, in repeated throws of a coin we might call heads success, and tails failure. We assume there is given a probability p for success and a probability $q = 1 - p$ for failure. The tree measure for a sequence of three such experiments is shown in Figure 13. The weights

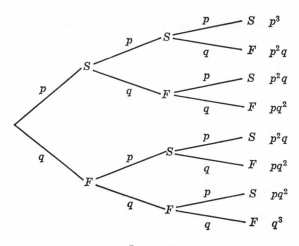

Figure 13

assigned to each path are indicated at the end of the path.

We now ask the following question. Given an independent-trials process with two outcomes, what is the probability of *exactly r successes* in n experiments? We denote this probability by $\mathbf{b}(r; n, p)$ to indicate that it depends upon r, n, and p.

Assume that we had a tree for this general situation, similar to the tree in Figure 13 for three experiments, with the branch points labeled S for success and F for failure. Then the truth set of the statement, "Exactly r successes occur," consists of all paths that go through r branch points labeled S and $n - r$ labeled F. To find the probability of this statement we must add the weights for all such paths. We are helped first by the fact that our tree measure assigns the same weight to any such path, namely $p^r q^{n-r}$. The reason is that every branch leading to an S is assigned probability p, and every branch leading to F is assigned probability q, and in the product there will be r p's and $n - r$ q's. To find the desired probability we need only find the number of paths in the truth set of the statement, "Exactly r successes occur." But this is just the number of ways that we can label the n outcomes with r S's and $n - r$ F's. We know that this is $\binom{n}{r}$. Thus we have proved:

In an independent-trials process with two outcomes the probability of exactly r successes in n experiments is given by

(1)
$$\mathbf{b}(r; n, p) = \binom{n}{r} p^r q^{n-r}.$$

A probability computed by the formula (1) is called a *binomial* probability. In Table I, p. 514, values of $\mathbf{b}(r; n, p)$ are given to three decimal places for $p = .01, .02, .05, .10, .15, .20, .25, .30, .40, .50$, for $n = 2, 3, 4, 5, 6, 7, 8, 9, 10, 12, 16, 20$, and for r between 0 and n inclusive, except where $\mathbf{b}(r; n, p) < .0005$.

Example 1. Consider n throws of an ordinary coin. We label heads "success" and tails "failure," and we assume that the probability is $\frac{1}{2}$ for heads on any one throw independently of the outcome of any other throw. Then the probability that exactly r heads will turn up is

$$\mathbf{b}(r; n, \tfrac{1}{2}) = \binom{n}{r}\left(\frac{1}{2}\right)^n.$$

For instance, in 100 throws the probability that exactly 50 heads will turn up is $\mathbf{b}(50; 100, \tfrac{1}{2}) = \binom{100}{50}(\tfrac{1}{2})^{100}$, or approximately .08. Thus we see that it is quite unlikely that exactly one-half of the tosses will result in heads. On the other hand, suppose that we ask for the probability that *nearly* one-half of the tosses will be heads. To be more precise, let us ask for the probability that the number of heads does not deviate by more than 10 from 50. To find this we must add $\mathbf{b}(r; 100, \tfrac{1}{2})$ for $r = 40, 41, \ldots, 60$, and we obtain a probability of approximately .96. Thus, while it is unlikely that exactly 50 heads will occur, it is very likely that the number of heads will not deviate from 50 by more than 10.

Example 2. An electronic component is mass-produced and then tested unit by unit on an automatic testing machine. According to the electrical characteristics of each component, the machine automatically classifies it as "good" or "defective." If the same unit is tested twice, the machine should, theoretically, classify it in the same way both times. We assume, however, that because of electrical or mechanical failure the machine has a certain probability q of misclassifying a part on any given trial. To improve the accuracy of our classification we may have the machine test the same unit not just once but r times, and finally classify a unit according to the classification that a majority of the tests give. To avoid ties we assume that r is odd. Let us see how this process decreases the probability of classification error.

Consider r experiments on each unit, where the jth experiment results in success if the jth test classifies the unit without error. The probability of success is then $p = 1 - q$. The majority decision will classify a unit correctly if we have more than $r/2$ successes. Suppose, for example, that we test each unit five times, and that the probability of misclassification on any single test is .1. Then the probability for success is .9, and the probability that the majority of the test results will correspond with the true state of the unit is

$$\mathbf{b}(3; 5, .9) + \mathbf{b}(4; 5, .9) + \mathbf{b}(5; 5, .9),$$

which is found to be approximately .991 [see Exercise 3(d)].

Thus the procedure above decreases the probability of misclassification from .1 in the case of one test to .009 in the case of five.

We have now found a formula for the probability of exactly j successes in n trials. It is natural to ask for the descriptive quantities, the mean and variance for the number of successes. For one trial the mean and variance are easily computed as follows:

$$\text{possibilities} \quad \begin{Bmatrix} 0 & 1 \\ q & p \end{Bmatrix}$$
$$\text{probabilities}$$

$$E = 0 \cdot q + 1 \cdot p = p,$$
$$V = (0 - p)^2 \cdot q + (1 - p)^2 \cdot p$$
$$= p^2 q + q^2 p = pq(p + q) = pq.$$

Since the expected value of the sum of n experiments is the sum of the expected value for each of the experiments, we find from this that the expected number of successes in n experiments is np. We know that the variances do not in general add unless the experiments are independent. We are in such a case. Thus the variance for the number of successes in n independent trials is npq and the standard deviation is $\sqrt{npq}$. It is interesting to consider also the mean and variance for the proportion of success. We obtain the proportion by multiplying the number of successes by $1/n$. Thus the expected value of the proportion of successes is $1/n \cdot (np) = p$. The variance is $(1/n)^2 (npq) = pq/n$. We notice that for large n the variance tends to 0. This means that for large n we can expect the fraction of successes to be very close to the expected value p. This is the first justification we have had for the frequency interpretation of probability. We shall see more justification for this interpretation in later sections.

> **Example 1 (continued).** In n throws of an ordinary coin the expected number of heads is $n/2$, the variance for the number of heads is $n/4$, and the standard deviation is $\sqrt{n}/2$. If we consider instead the fraction of the outcomes that are heads, then the expected value is $\frac{1}{2}$, the variance is $1/(4n)$, and the standard deviation is $1/(2\sqrt{n})$. Thus the variance of the *number* of heads increases with n while the variance of the *fraction* of heads tends to 0.

Consider next the case of independent trials with more than two outcomes. We assume that on each experiment the possible outcomes are $a_1, a_2, \ldots, a_k$, occurring with probabilities $p_1, p_2, \ldots, p_k$, respectively. We denote by

$$\mathbf{m}(r_1, r_2, \ldots, r_k; p_1, p_2, \ldots, p_k)$$

the probability that, in $n = r_1 + r_2 + \cdots + r_k$ such trials, there will be r_1 occurrences of a_1, r_2 of $a_2, \ldots$, and r_k of a_k. By exactly the same reasoning we used in the two-outcome case we are led to the following.

The probability for r_1 occurrences of a_1, r_2 occurrences of a_2, . . . , is given
by

$$\mathbf{m}(r_1, r_2, \ldots, r_k; p_1, p_2, \ldots, p_k) = \binom{n}{r_1, r_2, \ldots, r_k} p_1^{r_1} \cdot p_2^{r_2} \cdot \ldots \cdot p_k^{r_k}.$$

Example 3. A die is thrown 12 times. What is the probability that each number will come up twice? Here there are six outcomes, 1, 2, 3, 4, 5, 6, corresponding to the six sides of the die. We assign each outcome probability $\frac{1}{6}$. We are then asked for

$$\mathbf{m}(2, 2, 2, 2, 2, 2; \tfrac{1}{6}, \tfrac{1}{6}, \tfrac{1}{6}, \tfrac{1}{6}, \tfrac{1}{6}, \tfrac{1}{6}),$$

which is

$$\binom{12}{2, 2, 2, 2, 2, 2}(\tfrac{1}{6})^2(\tfrac{1}{6})^2(\tfrac{1}{6})^2(\tfrac{1}{6})^2(\tfrac{1}{6})^2(\tfrac{1}{6})^2 = .0034.$$

Example 4. Suppose that we have a repeated-trials process with four outcomes, a_1, a_2, a_3, a_4, occurring with probability p_1, p_2, p_3, p_4, respectively. It might be that we are interested only in the probability that r_1 occurrences of a_1 and r_2 occurrences of a_2 will take place with no specification about the number of each of the other possible outcomes. To answer this question we simply consider a new experiment where the outcomes are a_1, a_2, $\bar{a}_3$. Here $\bar{a}_3$ corresponds to an occurrence of either a_3 or a_4 in our original experiment. The corresponding probabilities would be p_1, p_2, and $\bar{p}_3$ with $\bar{p}_3 = p_3 + p_4$. Let $\bar{r}_3 = n - (r_1 + r_2)$. Then our question is answered by finding the probability in our new experiment for r_1 occurrences of a_1, r_2 of a_2, and $\bar{r}_3$ of $\bar{a}_3$, which is

$$\binom{n}{r_1, r_2, \bar{r}_3} p_1^{r_1} \cdot p_2^{r_2} \cdot p_3^{r_3}.$$

The same procedure can be carried out for experiments with any number of outcomes where we specify the number of occurrences of such particular outcomes. For example, if a die is thrown ten times, the probability that a one will occur exactly twice and a three exactly three times is given by

$$\binom{10}{2, 3, 5}(\tfrac{1}{6})^2(\tfrac{1}{6})^3(\tfrac{4}{6})^5 = .043.$$

EXERCISES

1. Verify by direct computation the entries in Table I (p. 514) for $\mathbf{b}(0; 2, .5)$, $\mathbf{b}(4; 6, .1)$, $\mathbf{b}(7; 8, .2)$, $\mathbf{b}(10; 10, .3)$.

2. Use Table I to compute the probability of
   a. Three or more successes when $n = 6$ and $p = .1$.
   b. Less than two successes when $n = 10$ and $p = .2$.
   c. Between three and five (inclusive) successes when $n = 10$ and $p = .3$.

3. Prove that $\mathbf{b}(r; n, p) = \mathbf{b}(n - r; n, 1 - p)$. Using this relationship and Table I, calculate the probability of

    a. Four successes when $n = 6$ and $p = .9$.
    b. More than eight successes when $n = 10$ and $p = .8$.
    c. Between six and eight (inclusive) successes when $n = 10$ and $p = .7$.
    d. More than two successes when $n = 5$ and $p = .9$.

In all the exercises that follow, use Table I wherever appropriate.

4. Compute for $n = 4$, $n = 8$, $n = 12$, and $n = 16$ the probability of obtaining exactly $\frac{1}{2}$ heads when an ordinary coin is thrown.
[*Ans.* .375; .273; .226; .196.]

5. Compute for $n = 4$, $n = 8$, $n = 12$, and $n = 16$ the probability that the fraction of heads deviates from $\frac{1}{2}$ by less than $\frac{1}{5}$.
[*Ans.* .375; .711; .854; .923.]

6. Assume that Peter and Paul match pennies four times. (In matching pennies, Peter wins a penny with probability $\frac{1}{2}$, and Paul wins a penny with probability $\frac{1}{2}$.) What is the probability that Peter wins more than Paul? Answer the same for five throws. For the case of 12,917 throws.
[*Ans.* $\frac{5}{16}$; $\frac{1}{2}$; $\frac{1}{2}$.]

7. If an ordinary die is thrown four times, what is the probability that exactly two 6's will occur?

8. In Example 2, if the probability for the machine's misclassifying a unit on a single trial is .2, how many times should a unit be tested on the machine to make the probability at least .90 that the answer obtained is correct?

9. A machine is set up to produce a lot of parts in sequence. Each piece has a certain fixed but unknown probability of being defective; this probability is independent of the quality of the preceding pieces produced. If the setup of the machine is bad, and therefore p is high, it is desired that the machine be set up again. If p is low, on the other hand, a small number of defectives in the lot can be tolerated better than the expense of setting up the machine again. To determine what to do, a sample of size n is taken from the process; if more than c defectives are found in the sample, the machine is set up again; otherwise, it is allowed to run as is. This is called an "(n, c) decision rule." For $p = 0$, .05, .1, .2, .3, .4, .5 find the probability of setting up the machine again using the following decision rules:

    a. $(10, 0)$ *b.* $(10, 1)$
    c. $(20, 0)$ *d.* $(20, 1)$
    e. $(20, 2)$.

10. The diameter of a particular piece may be within tolerance limits, or too large, or too small. If a machine produces pieces of which 10 percent have too large a diameter and 20 percent have too small a diameter, what is the probability that if three pieces are chosen at random, one will be too big, one too small, and one will be within tolerance limits?

11. In Exercise 10, suppose pieces whose diameters are within tolerance limits are classified as good, and all others as defective. What is the probability of obtaining one good piece and two defectives in a sample of three?

12. The most recent purchases of coffee by members of a consumer panel were distributed among brands as follows:

Brand	Percent
A	20
B	30
C	40
All other	10

What is the probability that in a random sample of five drawn (with replacement) from the panel, the most recent purchase of two of the members will have been Brand C, two Brand B, and one Brand A?

[*Ans.* .0864.]

13. In Exercise 12 what is the probability that in the sample of five, exactly two most recent purchases were Brand C and exactly one Brand A?

[*Ans.* .154.]

14. In Exercise 12 what is the probability that in the sample of five, more than one of the most recent purchases was some brand other than A, B, or C?   [*Ans.* .082.]

15. Assume that the following percentages apply to the daily coffee-drinking habits of the population of the United States:

25 percent do not drink coffee,
30 percent drink 1–3 cups per day,
30 percent drink 4–6 cups per day,
15 percent drink more than 6 cups per day.

What is the probability that in a random sample of four people in the United States, two will not be coffee drinkers, one will drink one to three cups per day, and one will drink more than six cups per day?

16. In a ten-question true-false exam, what is the probability of getting 70 percent or better by guessing?   [*Ans.* $\frac{11}{64}$.]

17. Assume that, every time a batter comes to bat, he has probability .3 for getting a hit. Assuming that his hits form an independent-trials process and that he comes to bat four times, what fraction of the games would he expect to get at least two hits? At least three hits? Four hits?

[*Ans.* .348; .084; .008.]

18. A coin is to be thrown eight times. What is the most probable number of heads that will occur? What is the number having the highest probability, given that the first four throws resulted in heads?

19. A small factory has ten workers. The workers eat their lunch at one of two diners, and they are just as likely to eat in one as in the other. If the proprietors want to be more than .95 sure of having enough seats, how many seats must each of the diners have?   [*Ans.* Eight seats.]

20. Suppose that five people are chosen at random and asked if they favor a certain proposal. If only 30 percent of the people favor the proposal, what is the probability that a majority of the five people chosen will favor the proposal?

21. In Example 2, if the probability of a machine's reversing its answer owing to a parts failure is .2, how many machines would have to be used to make the probability greater than .89 that the answer obtained would be the one that a machine with no failure would give?

[*Ans.* Three machines.]

22. It is estimated that a torpedo will hit a ship with probability $\frac{1}{3}$. How many torpedoes must be fired if it is desired that the probability for at least one hit should be greater than .9?

23. A student estimates that, if he takes four courses, he has probability .8 of passing each course. If he takes five courses, he has probability .7 of passing each course, and if he takes six courses, he has probability .5 for passing each course. His only goal is to pass at least four courses. How many courses should he take for the best chance of achieving his goal?

[*Ans.* 5.]

24. An urn contains five white balls, three black balls, and two red balls. What is the probability that a sample of five will consist of one black, one red, and three white balls if the sample is drawn (*a*) with replacement? (*b*) without replacement?

25. In an independent-trials process with three possible outcomes, a_1, a_2, and a_3, the following prior probabilities are assigned to p_1, p_2, p_3:

$$\mathbf{Pr}[(p_1 = .1) \wedge (p_2 = .2) \wedge (p_3 = .7)] = .6,$$
$$\mathbf{Pr}[(p_1 = .4) \wedge (p_2 = .2) \wedge (p_3 = .4)] = .4.$$

In $n = 6$ experiments, a_1 was observed $r_1 = 1$ time, a_2 was observed $r_2 = 4$ times, and a_3 was observed $r_3 = 1$ time.

a. What is the posterior probability

$$\mathbf{Pr}[(p_1 = .1) \wedge (p_2 = .2) \wedge (p_3 = .7) \mid (r_1 = 1) \wedge (r_2 = 4) \wedge (r_3 = 1)]?$$

[*Ans.* .396.]

b. What effect do the $r_2 = 4$ observations of a_2 have on the calculation of the posterior probability? Why?

c. Suppose the six observations were in the order a_1, a_2, a_3, a_2, a_2, a_2. How does this information affect the posterior probability?

26. In Exercise 25 suppose that a_1 was observed exactly $r_1 = 1$ time in $n = 6$ experiments, but that the values of r_2 and r_3 are not known. Now what is the posterior probability that

$$(p_1 = .1) \wedge (p_2 = .2) \wedge (p_3 = .7)?$$

In Exercise 25, what is the probability that in four trials we will observe $r_1 = 1$, $r_2 = 1$, $r_3 = 2$? [*Ans.* .132.]

27. In a certain board game players move around the board, and each turn consists of a player's rolling a pair of dice. If a player is on the square *Park Bench*, he must roll a seven or doubles before he is allowed to move out.

a. What is the probability that a player stuck on *Park Bench* will be allowed to move out on his next turn?

b. How many times must a player stuck on *Park Bench* roll before the chances of his getting out exceed $\frac{3}{4}$? [*Ans.* (*a*) $\frac{1}{3}$; (*b*) 4.]

28. Show that it is more probable to get at least one ace with four dice than at least one double ace in 24 throws of two dice.

9. MARKOV CHAINS

In this section we shall study a more general kind of process.

We assume that we have a sequence of experiments with the following properties. The outcome of each experiment is one of a finite number of possible outcomes a_1, a_2, ..., a_r. It is assumed that the probability of outcome a_j on any given experiment is not necessarily independent of the outcomes of previous experiments but depends at most upon the outcome of the immediately preceding experiment. We assume that there are given numbers p_{ij} that represent the probability of outcome a_j on any given experiment, given that outcome a_i occurred on the preceding experiment. The outcomes a_1, a_2, ..., a_r are called *states*, and the numbers p_{ij} are called *transition probabilities*. If we assume that the process begins in some particular state, then we have enough information to determine the tree measure for the process and can calculate probabilities of statements relating to the overall sequence of experiments. A process of the above kind is called a *Markov-chain process*.

The transition probabilities can be exhibited in two different ways. The first way is a square array. For a Markov chain with states a_1, a_2, and a_3, this array is written as

$$P = \begin{pmatrix} p_{11} & p_{12} & p_{13} \\ p_{21} & p_{22} & p_{23} \\ p_{31} & p_{32} & p_{33} \end{pmatrix}.$$

Such an array is a special case of a *matrix*. Matrices are of fundamental importance to the study of Markov chains as well as other branches of mathematics. They will be studied in detail in the next chapter.

A second way to show the transition probabilities is by a *transition diagram*. Such a diagram is illustrated for a special case in Figure 14. The

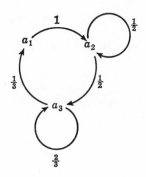

Figure 14

arrows from each state indicate the possible states to which a process can move from the given state.

The matrix of transition probabilities that corresponds to this diagram is

$$P = \begin{array}{c} \\ a_1 \\ a_2 \\ a_3 \end{array} \begin{array}{ccc} a_1 & a_2 & a_3 \\ \left(\begin{array}{ccc} 0 & 1 & 0 \\ 0 & \frac{1}{2} & \frac{1}{2} \\ \frac{1}{3} & 0 & \frac{2}{3} \end{array}\right). \end{array}$$

An entry of 0 indicates that the transition is impossible.

Notice that in the matrix P the sum of the elements of each row is 1. This must be true in any matrix of transition probabilities, since the elements of the ith row represent the probabilities for all possibilities when the process is in state a_i.

The kind of problem that most interests us in the study of Markov chains is the following. Suppose that the process starts in state i. What is the probability that after n steps it will be in state j? We denote this probability by $p_{ij}^{(n)}$. Notice that we do *not* mean by this the nth power of the number p_{ij}. We are actually interested in this probability for all possible starting positions i and all possible terminal positions j. We can represent these numbers conveniently again by a matrix. For example, for n steps in a three-state Markov chain we write these probabilities as the matrix

$$P^{(n)} = \begin{pmatrix} p_{11}^{(n)} & p_{12}^{(n)} & p_{13}^{(n)} \\ p_{21}^{(n)} & p_{22}^{(n)} & p_{23}^{(n)} \\ p_{31}^{(n)} & p_{32}^{(n)} & p_{33}^{(n)} \end{pmatrix}.$$

Example 1. Let us find for a Markov chain with transition probabilities indicated in Figure 14 the probability of being at the various possible states after three steps, assuming that the process starts at state a_1. We find these probabilities by constructing a tree and a tree measure as in Figure 15.

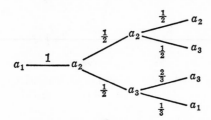

Figure 15

The probability $p_{13}^{(3)}$, for example, is the sum of the weights assigned by the tree measure to all paths through our tree that end at state a_3. That is,

$$1 \cdot \tfrac{1}{2} \cdot \tfrac{1}{2} + 1 \cdot \tfrac{1}{2} \cdot \tfrac{2}{3} = \tfrac{7}{12}.$$

Similarly

$$p_{12}^{(3)} = 1 \cdot \tfrac{1}{2} \cdot \tfrac{1}{2} = \tfrac{1}{4} \quad \text{and} \quad p_{11}^{(3)} = 1 \cdot \tfrac{1}{2} \cdot \tfrac{1}{3} = \tfrac{1}{6}.$$

By constructing a similar tree measure, assuming that we start at state a_2, we could find $p_{21}^{(3)}$, $p_{22}^{(3)}$, and $p_{23}^{(3)}$. The same is true for $p_{31}^{(3)}$, $p_{32}^{(3)}$, and $p_{33}^{(3)}$. If this is carried out (see Exercise 7) we can write the results in matrix form as follows:

$$P^{(3)} = \begin{matrix} & \begin{matrix} a_1 & a_2 & a_3 \end{matrix} \\ \begin{matrix} a_1 \\ a_2 \\ a_3 \end{matrix} & \begin{pmatrix} \frac{1}{6} & \frac{1}{4} & \frac{7}{12} \\ \frac{7}{36} & \frac{7}{24} & \frac{37}{72} \\ \frac{4}{27} & \frac{7}{18} & \frac{25}{54} \end{pmatrix} \end{matrix}.$$

Again the rows add up to 1, corresponding to the fact that if we start at a given state we must reach some state after three steps. Notice now that all the elements of this matrix are positive, showing that it is possible to reach any state from any state in three steps. In the next chapter we will develop a simple method of computing $P^{(n)}$.

Example 2. Suppose that we are interested in studying the process by which a given consumer purchases a certain product. We wish to make long-term predictions and so will not consider conditions peculiar to a particular purchase, such as an unusually intensive advertising campaign, or a special price reduction. We shall base our predictions only on past history of previous purchases, which would be available, for example, from consumer panels. We shall consider past purchases, and classify our data into purchases of Brand A (which we shall symbolize by A) and purchases of some other brand (which we shall symbolize by X). It is clear that a knowledge of past behavior would influence our predictions for the future. As a first approximation, we assume that the knowledge of the past beyond the last purchase would not cause us to change the probabilities for the outcomes on the next purchase. With this assumption we obtain a Markov chain with two states A and X and a matrix of transition probabilities

$$\begin{matrix} & \begin{matrix} A & \quad X \end{matrix} \\ \begin{matrix} A \\ X \end{matrix} & \begin{pmatrix} 1-a & a \\ b & 1-b \end{pmatrix} \end{matrix}.$$

The numbers a and b could be estimated from past results as follows. We could take for a the fraction of the purchases of A that were followed by X, and similarly for b.

We can obtain a better approximation by taking into account the previous two purchases. In this case our states are AA, AX, XA, and XX, indicating the outcome of two successive purchases. Being in state AA means that the last two purchases were of Brand A. Being in state XX means that the last two purchases were of brands different from A; it does not necessarily mean that the last two purchases were of the same brand. If we are now in state XX and the next purchase is of Brand A, we will be in state XA. If a series of purchases can be represented by $XXXAXAA$, then our process has moved from state XX to XX to XA to AX to XA, and finally to AA. Notice that the first letter of the state to which we move must agree with the second letter of the state from which we came, since these refer to the same purchase. Our matrix of transition probabilities will then have the form

$$
\begin{array}{cccc}
 & AA & XA & AX & XX \\
\begin{array}{c} AA \\ XA \\ AX \\ XX \end{array} &
\left(\begin{array}{cccc}
1-a & 0 & a & 0 \\
b & 0 & 1-b & 0 \\
0 & 1-c & 0 & c \\
0 & d & 0 & 1-d
\end{array}\right).
\end{array}
$$

Again the numbers a, b, c, and d would have to be estimated. The study of this example is continued in Chapter 4, Section 8.

Example 3. The following example of a Markov chain has been used in physics as a simple model for diffusion of gases.

We imagine n black balls and n white balls put into two urns so that there are n balls in each urn. A single experiment consists in choosing a ball from each urn at random and putting the ball obtained from the first urn into the second urn, and the ball obtained from the second urn into the first. We take as state the number of black balls in the first urn. If at any time we know this number, then we know the exact composition of each urn. That is, if there are j black balls in urn 1, there must be $n-j$ black balls in urn 2, $n-j$ white balls in urn 1, and j white balls in urn 2. If the process is in state j, then after the next exchange it will be in state $j-1$ if a black ball is chosen from urn 1 and a white ball from urn 2. It will be in state j if a ball of the same color is drawn from each urn. It will be in state $j+1$ if a white ball is drawn from urn 1 and a black ball from urn 2. The transition probabilities are then given by (see Exercise 14):

$$
p_{ij-1} = \left(\frac{j}{n}\right)^2, \qquad j > 0,
$$

$$
p_{ij} = \frac{2j(n-j)}{n^2},
$$

$$
p_{ij+1} = \left(\frac{n-j}{n}\right)^2, \qquad j < n,
$$

$$
p_{jk} = 0 \qquad\qquad \text{otherwise.}
$$

A physicist would be interested, for example, in predicting the composition of the urns after a certain number of exchanges have taken place. Certainly any predictions about the early stages of the process would depend upon the initial composition of the urns. For example, if we started with all black balls in urn 1, we would expect that for some time there would be more black balls in urn 1 than in urn 2. On the other hand, it might be expected that the effect of this initial distribution would wear off after a large number of exchanges. We shall see later, in Chapter 4, Section 8, that this is indeed the case.

EXERCISES

1. Draw a transition diagram for the Markov chain with transition probabilities given by the following matrices.

$$\begin{pmatrix} \frac{1}{2} & \frac{1}{2} & 0 \\ 0 & 1 & 0 \\ \frac{1}{2} & 0 & \frac{1}{2} \end{pmatrix}, \quad \begin{pmatrix} \frac{1}{3} & \frac{1}{3} & \frac{1}{3} \\ \frac{1}{3} & \frac{1}{3} & \frac{1}{3} \\ \frac{1}{3} & \frac{1}{3} & \frac{1}{3} \end{pmatrix},$$

$$\begin{pmatrix} 0 & 1 \\ 1 & 0 \end{pmatrix}, \quad \begin{pmatrix} 0 & 1 & 0 & 0 \\ 1 & 0 & 0 & 0 \\ 0 & 0 & \frac{1}{2} & \frac{1}{2} \\ 0 & 0 & \frac{1}{2} & \frac{1}{2} \end{pmatrix}.$$

2. Give the matrices of transition probabilities corresponding to the following transition diagrams.

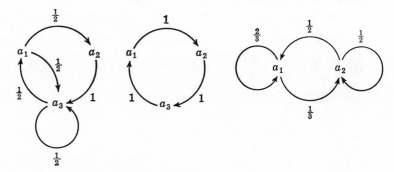

3. Find the matrix $P^{(2)}$ for the Markov chain determined by the matrix of transition probabilities

$$P = \begin{pmatrix} \frac{1}{2} & \frac{1}{2} \\ \frac{1}{3} & \frac{2}{3} \end{pmatrix}. \qquad \left[Ans. \ \begin{pmatrix} \frac{5}{12} & \frac{7}{12} \\ \frac{7}{18} & \frac{11}{18} \end{pmatrix}. \right]$$

4. What is the matrix of transition probabilities for the Markov chain in Example 3, for the case of two white balls and two black balls?

5. Find the matrices $P^{(2)}, P^{(3)}, P^{(4)}$ for the Markov chain determined by the transition probabilities

$$\begin{pmatrix} 1 & 0 \\ 0 & 1 \end{pmatrix}.$$

Find the same for the Markov chain determined by the matrix

$$\begin{pmatrix} 0 & 1 \\ 1 & 0 \end{pmatrix}.$$

6. Suppose that a Markov chain has two states, a_1 and a_2, and transition probabilities given by the matrix

$$\begin{pmatrix} \frac{1}{3} & \frac{2}{3} \\ \frac{1}{2} & \frac{1}{2} \end{pmatrix}.$$

By means of a separate chance device we choose a state in which to start the process. This device chooses a_1 with probability $\frac{1}{2}$ and a_2 with probability $\frac{1}{2}$. Find the probability that the process is in state a_1 after the first step. Answer the same question in the case that the device chooses a_1 with probability $\frac{1}{3}$ and a_2 with probability $\frac{2}{3}$.   [Ans. $\frac{5}{12}$; $\frac{4}{9}$.]

7. Referring to the Markov chain with transition probabilities indicated in Figure 14, construct the tree measures and determine the values of

$$p_{21}^{(3)}, p_{22}^{(3)}, p_{23}^{(3)} \quad \text{and} \quad p_{31}^{(3)}, p_{32}^{(3)}, p_{33}^{(3)}.$$

8. In Example 2, suppose we wanted to predict brand purchasing behavior by taking into account the last three purchases. Construct the matrix of transition probabilities. How many numbers would have to be estimated from the data? How many if we wanted to take into account the last four purchases? The last n purchases? What does this suggest about obtaining more and more complex "models" of purchasing behavior?   [Partial Ans. For n purchases, 2^n.]

9. Suppose that in Example 2 we wanted to predict the purchasing behavior of a consumer with respect to three named brands, A, B, and C, and "all other" brands, symbolized by X. If we assume a Markov-chain process and take into account only the last purchase, construct the matrix of transition probabilities. How many numbers must be estimated from the data? Construct the matrix of transition probabilities based on taking into account the last two purchases. How many numbers must be estimated from the data?

10. A certain calculating machine uses only the digits 0 and 1. It is supposed to transmit one of these digits through several stages. However, at every stage there is a probability p that the digit that enters this stage will be changed when it leaves. We form a Markov chain to represent the process of transmission by taking as states the digits 0 and 1. What is the matrix of transition probabilities?

11. For the Markov chain in Exercise 10, draw a tree and assign a tree measure, assuming that the process begins in state 0 and moves through three stages of transmission. What is the probability that the machine after three stages produces the digit 0—that is, the correct digit? What is the probability that the machine never changed the digit from 0?

12. Assume that a man's profession can be classified as professional, skilled laborer, or unskilled laborer. Assume that of the sons of professional men 80 percent are professional, 10 percent are skilled laborers, and 10 percent are unskilled laborers. In the case of sons of skilled laborers, 60 percent are skilled laborers, 20 percent are professional, and 20 percent are unskilled laborers. Finally, in the case of unskilled laborers, 50 percent of the sons are unskilled laborers, and 25 percent each are in the other two categories. Assume that every man has a son, and form a Markov chain by following a given family through several generations. Set up the matrix of transition probabilities. Find the probability that the grandson of an unskilled laborer is a professional man.   [Ans. .375.]

13. In Exercise 12 we assumed that every man has a son. Assume instead that the probability a man has a son is .8. Form a Markov chain with four states. The first three states are as in Exercise 12, and the fourth state is such that the process enters it if a man has no son, and that the state cannot be left. This state represents families whose male line has died out. Find the matrix of transition probabilities and find the probability that an unskilled laborer has a grandson who is a professional man.

[Ans. .24.]

14. Explain why the transition probabilities given in Example 3 are correct.

15. Five points are marked on a circle. A process moves clockwise from a given point to its neighbor with probability $\frac{2}{3}$, or counterclockwise to its neighbor with probability $\frac{1}{3}$.

 a. Considering the process to be a Markov-chain process, find the matrix of transition probabilities.

 b. Given that the process starts in a state 3, what is the probability that it returns to the same state in two steps?

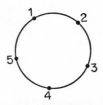

16. In northern New England, years for apples can be described as good, average, or poor. Suppose that following a good year the probabilities of good, average, or poor years are respectively .4, .4, and .2. Following a poor year the probabilities of good, average, or poor years are .2, .4, and .4, respectively. Following an average year the probabilities that the next year will be good or poor are each .2, and of an average year, .6.

 a. Set up the transition matrix of this Markov chain.

 b. 1971 was a good year. Compute the probabilities for 1972, 1973, and 1974.   [*Partial Ans. For* 1973: .28, .48, .24.]

17. In Exercise 16 suppose that there is probability $\frac{1}{4}$ for a good year, $\frac{1}{2}$ for an average year, and $\frac{1}{4}$ for a poor year. What are the probabilities for the following year?

18. A teacher in an oversized mathematics class finds, after grading all homework papers for the first two assignments, that it is necessary to reduce the amount of time spent in such grading. He therefore designs the following system: Papers will be marked satisfactory or unsatisfactory. All papers of students receiving a mark of unsatisfactory on any assignment will be read on each of the two succeeding days. Of the remaining papers, the teacher will read one-fifth, chosen at random. Assuming that each paper has a probability of one-fifth of being classified "unsatisfactory,"

 a. Set up a three-state Markov chain to describe the process.

 b. Suppose that a student has just handed in an unsatisfactory paper. What are the probabilities for the next two assignments?

19. In another model for diffusion, it is assumed that two urns together contain N balls numbered from 1 to N. Each second a number from 1 to N is chosen at random, and the ball with the corresponding number is moved to the other urn. Set up a Markov chain by taking as state the number of balls in urn 1. Find the transition matrix.

10. THE LAW OF LARGE NUMBERS

In this section we shall study some further properties of the independent trials process with two outcomes. In Section 8 we saw that the probability for x successes in n trials is given by

$$\mathbf{b}(x; n, p) = \binom{n}{x} p^x q^{n-x}.$$

In Figure 16 we show these probabilities graphically for $n = 8$ and $p = \frac{3}{4}$.

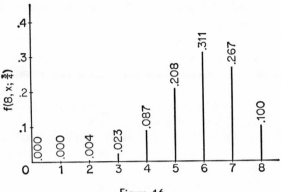

Figure 16

In Figure 17 we have done similarly for the case of $n = 7$ and $p = \frac{3}{4}$.

We see in the first case that the values increase up to a maximum value at $x = 6$ and then decrease. In the second case the values increase up to a maximum value at $x = 5$, have the same value for $x = 6$, and then decrease. These two cases are typical of what can happen in general.

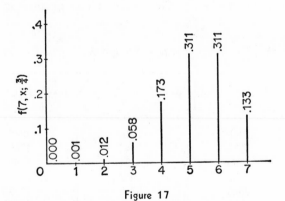

Figure 17

Consider the ratio of the probability of $x + 1$ successes in n trials to the probability of x successes in n trials, which is

$$\frac{\binom{n}{x+1} p^{x+1} q^{n-x-1}}{\binom{n}{x} p^x q^{n-x}} = \frac{n-x}{x+1} \cdot \frac{p}{q}.$$

This ratio will be greater than one as long as $(n - x)p > (x + 1)q$ or as long as $x < np - q$. If $np - q$ is not an integer, the values $\binom{n}{x} p^x q^{n-x}$

increase up to a maximum value, which occurs at the first integer greater than $np - q$, and then decrease. In case $np - q$ is an integer, the values $\binom{n}{x} p^x q^{n-x}$ increase up to $x = np - q$, are the same for $x = np - q$ and $x = np - q + 1$, and then decrease. We recall that np is the expected number of successes in n trials.

Thus we see that, in general, values near the expected value np will occur with the largest probability. It is not true that one particular value near np is highly likely to occur, but only that it is relatively more likely than a value further from np. For example, in 100 throws of a coin, $np = 100 \cdot \frac{1}{2} = 50$. The probability of exactly 50 heads is approximately .08. The probability of exactly 30 is approximately .00002.

More information is obtained by studying the probability of a given deviation of the proportion of successes x/n from the number p; that is, by studying for $\epsilon > 0$,

$$\mathbf{Pr}\left[\left|\frac{x}{n} - p\right| < \epsilon\right].$$

For any fixed n, p, and ϵ, the latter probability can be found by adding all the values of $\mathbf{b}(x; n, p)$ for values of x for which the inequality $p - \epsilon < x/n < p + \epsilon$ is true. In Figure 18 we have given these probabilities for the case $p = .3$ with various values for ϵ and n. In the first column we have the case $\epsilon = .1$. We observe that as n increases, the proba-

$$\mathbf{Pr}\left[\left|\frac{x}{n} - p\right| < \epsilon\right] \text{ for } p = .3 \text{ and } \epsilon = .1, .05, .01.$$

n	$\mathbf{Pr}\left[\left\|\frac{x}{n} - .3\right\| < .10\right]$	$\mathbf{Pr}\left[\left\|\frac{x}{n} - .3\right\| < .05\right]$	$\mathbf{Pr}\left[\left\|\frac{x}{n} - .3\right\| < .02\right]$
20	.5348	.1916	.1916
40	.7738	.3945	.1366
60	.8800	.5184	.3269
80	.9337	.6068	.2853
100	.9626	.6740	.2563
200	.9974	.8577	.4107
300	.9998	.9326	.5116
400	1.0000	.9668	.5868
500	1.0000	.9833	.6461
600	1.0000	.9915	.6944
700	1.0000	.9956	.7345
800	1.0000	.9977	.7683
900	1.0000	.9988	.7970
1000	1.0000	.9994	.8216

Figure 18

bility that the fraction of successes deviates from .3 by less than .1 tends to the value 1. In fact to four decimal places the answer is 1 after $n = 400$. In column two we have the same probabilities for the smaller value of $\epsilon = .05$. Again the probabilities are tending to 1 but not so fast. In the third column we have given these probabilities for the case $\epsilon = .02$. We see now that even after 1000 trials there is still a reasonable chance that the fraction x/n is not within .02 of the value of $p = .3$. It is natural to ask if we can expect these probabilities also to tend to 1 if we increase n sufficiently. The answer is yes, and this is assured by one of the fundamental theorems of probability called the *law of large numbers*. This theorem asserts that, for any $\epsilon > 0$,

$$\mathbf{Pr}\left[\left|\frac{x}{n} - p\right| < \epsilon\right]$$

tends to 1 as n increases indefinitely.

It is important to understand what this theorem says and what it does not say. Let us illustrate its meaning in the case of coin tossing.

We are going to toss a coin n times and we want the probability to be very high, say greater than .99, that the fraction of heads that turn up will be very close, say within .001 of the value .5. The law of large numbers assures us that we can have this if we simply choose n large enough. The theorem itself gives us no information about how large n must be. Let us, however, consider the above expression.

To say that of the total number of trials the fraction of successes is near p is the same as saying that the actual number of successes x does not deviate too much from the expected number np. To see the kind of deviations that might be expected we can study the value of $\mathbf{Pr}[|x - np| \geq d]$. Figure 19 tabulates these values for $p = .3$ and various values of n and d. Let us ask how large d must be before a deviation as large as d could be considered surprising. For example, let us see for each n the value of d that makes $\mathbf{Pr}[|x - np| \geq d]$ about .04. From the table, we see that d should be 7 for $n = 50$, 9 for $n = 80$, 10 for $n = 100$, etc. To see deviations that might be considered more typical we look for the values of d that make $\mathbf{Pr}[|x - np| \geq d]$ approximately $\frac{1}{3}$. Again from the table, we see that d should be 3 or 4 for $n = 50$, 4 or 5 for $n = 80$, 5 for $n = 100$, and so on. The answers to these two questions are given in the last two columns of the table. An examination of these numbers shows us that deviations that we would consider surprising are approximately $\sqrt{n}$, while those that are more typical are about one half as large or $\sqrt{n}/2$.

This suggests that $\sqrt{n}$, or a suitable multiple of it, might be taken as a unit of measurement for deviations. Of course, we would also have to study how $\mathbf{Pr}\left[\left|\frac{x}{n} - p\right| \geq d\right]$ depends on p. When this is done, one finds that $\sqrt{npq}$ is a natural unit—that is, the standard deviation for the number

$p = .3;$ $\Pr\left[|x - np| \geq d\right].$

d \ n	1	2	3	4	5	6	7	8	9	10	11	12	13	14	15	16	17	Pr near to .04	Pr near to $\frac{1}{3}$
50	.878	.644	.441	.280	.164	.088	.043	.020	.008									7	3-4
80	.903	.715	.542	.393	.272	.179	.112	.066	.037	.020	.010							9	4-5
100	.913	.744	.586	.445	.326	.230	.155	.101	.063	.037	.021	.012						10	5
120	.921	.765	.619	.486	.370	.273	.195	.135	.090	.058	.036	.022	.012					11	5-6
140	.927	.782	.645	.519	.407	.310	.230	.166	.116	.079	.052	.033	.021	.012				12	6
170	.933	.802	.676	.558	.451	.357	.276	.209	.154	.111	.078	.054	.036	.024	.015	.009		13	6
200	.939	.817	.700	.589	.488	.396	.316	.247	.189	.142	.105	.076	.053	.037	.025	.017	.011	14	7

Figure 19

of successes. A second fundamental theorem of probability, the central limit theorem (to be studied in the next section), implies that the following approximations hold for large n.

$$\mathbf{Pr}[|x - np| \geq \sqrt{npq}] \approx .3174,$$
$$\mathbf{Pr}[|x - np| \geq 2\sqrt{npq}] \approx .0455,$$
$$\mathbf{Pr}[|x - np| \geq 3\sqrt{npq}] \approx .0027.$$

That is, a deviation from the expected value of one standard deviation is rather typical, while a deviation of as much as two standard deviations is quite surprising and three very surprising. For values of p not too near 0 or 1, the value of $\sqrt{pq}$ is approximately $\frac{1}{2}$. Thus these approximations are consistent with the results we observed from our table.

For large n, $\mathbf{Pr}[x - np \geq k\sqrt{npq}]$ or $\mathbf{Pr}[x - np \leq -k\sqrt{npq}]$ can be shown to be approximately the same. Hence these probabilities can be estimated for $k = 1$, 2, and 3 by taking $\frac{1}{2}$ the values given above.

Example 1. In throwing an ordinary coin 10,000 times, the expected number of heads is 5000, and the standard deviation for the number of heads is $\sqrt{10,000(\frac{1}{2})(\frac{1}{2})} = 50$. Thus the probability that the number of heads deviates from 5000 by as much as one standard deviation, or 50, is approximately .317. The probability of a deviation of as much as two standard deviations, or 100, is approximately .046. The probability of a deviation of as much as three standard deviations, or 150, is approximately .003.

Example 2. Assume that in a certain large city 900 people are chosen at random and asked whether they watched a certain television program the previous night. Of the 900 asked, 150 say they saw the program and 750 say they did not. If, in fact, 10 percent of the people in the city saw the program, would it be unlikely that as many as 150 would say they had seen it in a sample of 900? We assume that the 900 people asked would form approximately an independent-trials process with probability .1 for a "yes" answer and .9 for a "no" answer. (The process is, strictly speaking, one of sampling *without* replacement, hence the trials are not actually independent. If the population of the city is large relative to the sample size of 900, however, the independent-trials process is a good approximation.) Then the standard deviation for the number of "yes" answers in 900 trials is

$$\sqrt{(900)(.1)(.9)} = 9.$$

It would therefore be very unlikely that we would obtain a deviation of more than 27 from the expected number of 90. The fact that in the sample the deviation from the expected number was 60, then, is evidence that the hypothesis that 10 percent of the people in the city saw the program is incorrect. The assumption that the true proportion is any value less than .1 would also lead to the fact that a number as large as 150 out of 900 saying they had seen the program is very unlikely. Thus we are led to suspect that the true proportion is greater than .1. On the other hand, if the number who reported seeing the program in the sample of 900 were 99, we would have only a deviation of one standard deviation, under the assumption that 10 percent of all the residents of the city saw the show. Since such a deviation is not unlikely, we could not rule out this possibility on the evidence of the sample.

Suppose we let p be the fraction of people in the city who did, in fact, see the program. If we started with prior probabilities that p had certain values, then we could use the sample evidence to compute posterior probabilities of those values of p. We could then make somewhat more precise statements about p than simply saying that a certain sample result does or does not rule out the possibility that $p = .1$.

Example 3. A certain Ivy League college would like to admit 800 students in its freshman class. Experience has shown that if it accepts 1250 students, it will have acceptances from approximately 800. If it accepts as many as 50 too many students, it will have to provide additional dormitory space. Let us find the probability that this will happen, assuming that the acceptances by the students can be considered to be an independent-trials process. We take as our estimate for the probability of an acceptance $p = \frac{800}{1250} = .64$. Then the expected number of acceptances is 800 and the standard deviation for the number of acceptances is $\sqrt{1250 \times .64 \times .36} \approx 17$. The probability that the number accepted is three standard deviations or 51 from the mean is approximately .0027. This probability takes into account a deviation above the mean or below the mean. Since in this case we are interested only in a deviation above the mean, the probability we desire is half of this or approximately .0013. Thus we see that under the assumptions we have made it is highly unlikely that the college will have to have new dormitory space.

We finish this discussion of the law of large numbers with some final remarks about the interpretation of this important theorem.

Of course no matter how large n is we cannot prevent a coin from coming up heads every time. If this were the case, we would observe a fraction of heads equal to 1. However, this is not inconsistent with the theorem, since the probability of its happening is $(\frac{1}{2})^n$, which tends to 0 as n increases. Thus a fraction of 1 is always possible, but becomes increasingly unlikely.

The law of large numbers is often misinterpreted in the following manner. Suppose that we plan to toss the coin 1000 times and after 500 tosses we have already obtained 400 heads. Then we must obtain less than one-half heads in the remaining 500 tosses to have the fraction come out near $\frac{1}{2}$. It is tempting to argue that the coin therefore owes us some tails and it is more likely that tails will occur in the last 500 tosses. Of course this is nonsense, since the coin has no memory. The point is that something very unlikely has already happened in the first 500 tosses. The final result can therefore also be expected to be a result not predicted before the tossing began.

We could also argue that perhaps the coin is a biased coin, but this would make us predict more heads than tails in the future. Thus the law of averages, or the law of large numbers, should not give you great comfort if you have had a series of very bad hands dealt you in your last 100 poker hands. If the dealing is fair, you have the same chance as ever of getting a good hand.

Early attempts to define the probability p that success occurs on a single experiment sounded like this. If the experiment is repeated indefinitely, the fraction of successes obtained will tend to a number p, and this number p is called the probability of success on a single experiment. While this fails to be satisfactory as a definition of probability, the law of large numbers captures the spirit of this frequency concept of probability.

EXERCISES

1. If an ordinary die is thrown 20 times, what is the expected number of times that a 6 will turn up? What is the standard deviation for the number of 6's that turn up? [*Ans.* $\frac{10}{3}$; $\frac{5}{3}$.]

2. Suppose that an ordinary die is thrown 450 times. What is the expected number of throws that result in either a 3 or a 4? What is the standard deviation for the number of such throws?

3. In 16 tosses of an ordinary coin, what is the expected number of heads that turn up? What is the standard deviation for the number of heads that occur? [*Ans.* 8; 2.]

4. In 16 tosses of a coin, find the exact probability that the number of heads that turn up differs from the expected number by (a) as much as one standard deviation, and (b) by more than one standard deviation. Do the same for the case of two standard deviations, and for the case of three standard deviations. Show that the approximations given for large n lie between the values obtained, but are not very accurate for so small an n. [*Ans.* .454; .210; .077; .021; .004; .001.]

5. Consider n independent trials with probability p for success. Let s and t be numbers such that $p < s < t$. What does the law of large numbers say about

$$\mathbf{Pr}\left[s < \frac{r}{n} < t\right]$$

as we increase n indefinitely? Answer the same question in the case that $s < p < t$.

6. It is known that 20 percent of purchases of frozen orange juice are of a certain brand. Following an intensive advertising campaign, a random sample of 900 purchases revealed 250 purchases of this brand of frozen orange juice. What can be said about the effectiveness of the advertising campaign?

7. In a large number of independent trials with probability p for success, what is the approximate probability that the number of successes will deviate from the expected number by more than one standard deviation but less than two standard deviations? [*Ans.* .272.]

8. A gasoline company has a large list of automobile owners to whom it intends to mail credit cards. It is undecided whether to offer as an incentive for supplying the necessary credit information (a) five free gallons of gasoline, or (b) a free car wash. In a sample mailing, half the addressees, selected at random, are offered the first premium, and half are offered the second. If it really makes no difference which incentive is offered, what is

the probability that in 10,000 returns, between 4850 and 5150 will consist of people who were offered five free gallons of gasoline?

9. Suppose that it is desired that in the situation of Example 2 the probability be approximately .95 that the fraction of people in a sample of size n who say they saw the program deviate by no more than .01 from the fraction p of city residents who saw the show, when $p = .20$. How large should n be?　　　　　　　　　　　　　[*Ans.* Approximately 6400.]

10. Two railroads are competing for the passenger traffic of 1000 passengers by operating similar trains at the same hour. If a given passenger is as likely to choose one train as the other, how many seats should the railroad provide if it wants to be sure that its seating capacity is sufficient in roughly 999 out of 1000 cases?　　　　　　　　　　　[*Ans.* 547.

11. Assume that 20 percent of the subscribers to a certain magazine can recall having seen a certain cigarette advertisement in that magazine. If 1600 of the subscribers are selected at random from the mailing list, what is the expected number who will recall having seen the advertisement? What is the standard deviation? What is the approximate probability that more than 352 of the 1600 chosen remember having seen the advertisement?　　　　　　　　　　　　　　　　　[*Ans.* 320; 16; .023.]

12. Suppose that in Exercise 11 the 1600 people are chosen at random from those subscribers to the magazine who smoke. Under the hypothesis that smoking has no effect on a person's recollection of the advertisement, what is the expected number in the 1600 who will recall having seen the advertisement? Suppose that more than 370 of the 1600 recall having seen the advertisement. What might be said concerning the hypothesis that smoking has no effect on a person's ability to remember having seen the advertisement?

13. In Example 2 we assumed in our calculations that, if the true proportion of people who saw the television program were p, then the 900 people chosen at random represented an independent-trials process with probability p for a "yes" answer, and $1 - p$ for a "no" answer. Give a method for choosing the 900 people that would make this a reasonable assumption. Criticize the following methods:
    a. Choose the first 900 people in the list of registered Republicans.
    b. Choose 900 names at random from the telephone book.
    c. Choose 900 houses at random and ask one person from each house, the houses being visited in the mid-morning.
    d. Choose 30 representative blocks in the city and choose 30 representative houses in each block.

14. For n throws of an ordinary coin, let t_n be such that

$$\mathbf{Pr}\left[-t_n < \frac{r}{n} - \tfrac{1}{2} < t_n\right] = .997,$$

where x is the number of heads that turn up. Find t_n for $n = 10^4$, $n = 10^6$, and $n = 10^{20}$.　　　　　　　[*Ans.* .015, .0015, .000,000,000,15.]

15. Assume that a calculating machine carries out a million operations to solve a certain problem. In each operation the machine gives the answer 10^{-5} too small, with probability $\tfrac{1}{2}$, and 10^{-5} too large, with probability $\tfrac{1}{2}$. Assume that the errors are independent of one another. What is a reasonable accuracy to attach to the answer? What if the machine carries out 10^{10} operations?　　　　　　　　　　　[*Ans.* ±.01; ±1.]

16. The Dartmouth Computer tossed a coin 1 million times. It obtained 499,588 heads. Is this number reasonable?

11. THE CENTRAL LIMIT THEOREM

We continue our discussion of the independent-trials process with two outcomes. As usual, let p be the probability of success on a trial, and $\mathbf{b}(x; n, p)$ be the probability of exactly x successes in n trials.

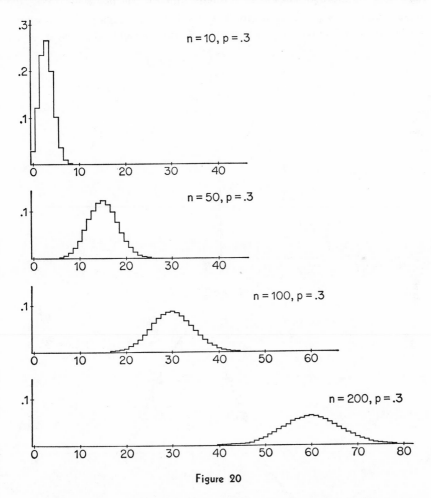

Figure 20

In Figure 20 we have plotted bar graphs that represent $\mathbf{b}(x; n, .3)$ for $n = 10$, 50, 100, and 200. We note first that the graphs are drifting off to the right. This is not surprising, since their peaks occur at np, which is steadily increasing. We also note that while the total area is always 1, this area becomes more and more spread out.

We want to redraw these graphs in a manner that prevents the drifting and the spreading out. First, we replace x by $x - np$, assuring that our peak always occurs at 0. Next we introduce a new unit for measuring the deviation, which depends on n, and which gives comparable scales. As we saw in Section 10, the standard deviation $\sqrt{npq}$ is such a unit.

We must still insure that probabilities are represented by areas in the graph. In Figure 20 this is achieved by having a unit base for each rectangle, and having the probability $b(x; n, p)$ as height. Since we are now representing a standard deviation as a single unit on the horizontal axis, we must take $b(x; n, p)\sqrt{npq}$ as the heights of our rectangles. The resulting curves for $n = 50$ and 200 are shown in Figures 21 and 22, respectively.

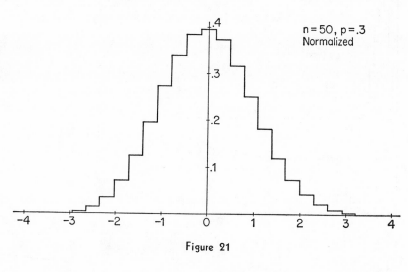

Figure 21

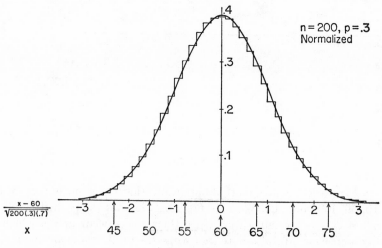

Figure 22

We note that the two figures look very much alike. We have also shown in Figure 22 that it can be approximated by a bell-shaped curve. This curve represents the function

$$\mathbf{f}(x) = \frac{1}{\sqrt{2\pi}} e^{-x^2/2},$$

and is known as the *normal curve*. It is a fundamental theorem of probability theory that as n increases, the appropriately rescaled bar graphs more and more closely approach the normal curve. The theorem is known as the *central limit theorem*, and we have illustrated it graphically.

More precisely, the theorem states that for any two numbers a and b, with $a < b$,

$$\mathbf{Pr}\left[a < \frac{x - np}{\sqrt{npq}} < b \right]$$

approaches the area under the normal curve between a and b, as n increases. This theorem is particularly interesting in that the normal curve is symmetric about 0, while $\mathbf{b}(x; n, p)$ is symmetric about the expected value np only for the case $p = \frac{1}{2}$. It should also be noted that we always arrive at the same normal curve, no matter what the value of p is.

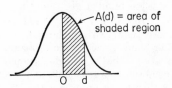

$A(d)$ = area of shaded region

d	$A(d)$	d	$A(d)$	d	$A(d)$	d	$A(d)$
.0	.000	1.1	.364	2.1	.482	3.1	.4990
.1	.040	1.2	.385	2.2	.486	3.2	.4993
.2	.079	1.3	.403	2.3	.489	3.3	.4995
.3	.118	1.4	.419	2.4	.492	3.4	.4997
.4	.155	1.5	.433	2.5	.494	3.5	.4998
.5	.191	1.6	.445	2.6	.495	3.6	.4998
.6	.226	1.7	.455	2.7	.497	3.7	.4999
.7	.258	1.8	.464	2.8	.497	3.8	.49993
.8	.288	1.9	.471	2.9	.498	3.9	.49995
.9	.316	2.0	.477	3.0	.4987	4.0	.49997
1.0	.341					5.0	.49999997

Figure 23

In Figure 23 we give a table for the area under the normal curve between 0 and d. Since the total area is 1, and since it is symmetric about the origin, we can compute arbitrary areas from this table. For example, suppose that we wish the area between -1 and $+2$. The area between 0 and 2 is given in the table as .477. The area between -1 and 0 is the same as between 0 and 1, and hence is given as .341. Thus the total area is .818. The area outside the interval $(-1, 2)$ is than $1 - .818 = .182$.

Example 1. Let us find the probability that x differs from the expected value np by as much as d standard deviations.

$$\mathbf{Pr}[|x - np| \geq d\sqrt{npq}] = \mathbf{Pr}\left[\left|\frac{x - np}{\sqrt{npq}}\right| \geq d\right],$$

and hence the approximate answer should be the area outside the interval $(-d, d)$ under the normal curve. For $d = 1, 2, 3$ we obtain

$$1 - (2 \times .341) = .318, \qquad 1 - (2 \times .477) = .046$$

and

$$1 - (2 \times .4987) = .0026,$$

respectively. These agree with the values given in Section 10, to within rounding errors. In fact, the central limit theorem is the basis of those estimates.

Example 2. In Section 10 we considered the example of throwing a coin 10,000 times. The expected number of heads that turn up is 5000, and the standard deviation is $\sqrt{10{,}000 \cdot \frac{1}{2} \cdot \frac{1}{2}} = 50$. We observed that the probability of a deviation of more than two standard deviations (or 100) was very unlikely. On the other hand, consider the probability of a deviation of less than .1 standard deviation—that is, of a deviation of less than five. The area from 0 to .1 under the normal curve is .040; hence the probability of a deviation from 5000 of less than five is approximately .08. Thus, while a deviation of more than 100 is very unlikely, it is also very unlikely that a deviation of less than five will occur.

Example 3. The normal approximation can be used to estimate the individual probabilities $\mathbf{b}(x; n, p)$ for large n. For example, let us estimate $\mathbf{b}(65; 200, .3)$. The graph of the probabilities $\mathbf{b}(x; 200, .3)$ was given in Figure 23 together with the normal approximation. The desired probability is the area of the bar corresponding to $x = 65$. An inspection of the graph suggests that we should take the area under the normal curve between 64.5 and 65.5 as an estimate for this probability. In normalized units this is the area between

$$\frac{4.5}{\sqrt{200(.3)(.7)}} \quad \text{and} \quad \frac{5.5}{\sqrt{200(.3)(.7)}},$$

or between .6944 and .8487. Our table is not fine enough to find this area, but from more complete tables, or by machine computation, this area may be found to be .046 to three decimal places. The exact value to three decimal places is .045. This procedure gives us a good estimate.

If we check all of the values of $\mathbf{b}(x; 200, .3)$, we find in each case that we would make an error of at most .001 by using the normal approximation. There is unfortunately no simple way to estimate the error caused by the use of the central limit theorem. The error will clearly depend upon how large n is, but it also depends upon how near p is to 0 or 1. The greatest accuracy occurs when p is near $\frac{1}{2}$.

Example 4. Suppose that a drug has been administered to a number of patients and found to be effective a fraction $\bar{p}$ of the time. Assuming an independent-trials process, it is natural to take $\bar{p}$ as an estimate for the unknown probability p for success on any one trial. It is useful to have a method of estimating the reliability of this estimate. One method is the following. Let x be the number of successes for the drug given to n patients. Then by the central limit theorem

$$\mathbf{Pr}\left[\left|\frac{x - np}{\sqrt{npq}}\right| \le 2\right] \approx .95.$$

This is the same as saying

$$\mathbf{Pr}\left[\left|\frac{x/n - p}{\sqrt{pq/n}}\right| \le 2\right] \approx .95.$$

Putting $\bar{p} = x/n$, we have

$$\mathbf{Pr}\left[|\bar{p} - p| \le 2\sqrt{\frac{pq}{n}}\right] \approx .95.$$

Using the fact that $pq \le \frac{1}{4}$ (see Exercise 12), we have

$$\mathbf{Pr}\left[|\bar{p} - p| \le \frac{1}{\sqrt{n}}\right] \ge .95.$$

This says that no matter what p is, with probability $\ge .95$, the true value will not deviate from the estimate $\bar{p}$ by more than $1/\sqrt{n}$. It is customary then to say that

$$\bar{p} - \frac{1}{\sqrt{n}} \le p \le \bar{p} + \frac{1}{\sqrt{n}}$$

with confidence .95. The interval $[\bar{p} - (1/\sqrt{n}), \bar{p} + (1/\sqrt{n})]$ is called a 95 percent *confidence interval*. Had we started with

$$\mathbf{Pr}\left[\left|\frac{x - np}{\sqrt{npq}}\right| \le 3\right] \approx .99,$$

we would have obtained the 99 percent confidence interval

$$\left[\bar{p} - \frac{3}{2\sqrt{n}}, \bar{p} + \frac{3}{2\sqrt{n}}\right].$$

For example, if in 400 trials the drug is found effective 124 times, or .31 of the times, the 95 percent confidence interval for p is

$$[.31 - \tfrac{1}{20}, .31 + \tfrac{1}{20}] \quad \text{or} \quad [.26, .36],$$

and the 99 percent confidence interval is

$$[.31 - \tfrac{3}{40}, .31 + \tfrac{3}{40}] \quad \text{or} \quad [.235, .385].$$

EXERCISES

1. Let x be the number of successes in n trials of an independent trials process with probability p for success. Let $x^* = (x - np)/\sqrt{npq}$. For large n estimate the following probabilities.
   a. $\Pr[x^* < -2.5]$.   [*Ans.* .006.]
   b. $\Pr[x^* < 2.5]$.
   c. $\Pr[x^* \geq -.5]$.
   d. $\Pr[-1.5 < x^* < 1]$.   [*Ans.* .774.]

2. A coin is biased in such a way that a head comes up with probability .8 on a single toss. Use the normal approximation to estimate the probability that in a million tosses there are more than 800,400 heads.

3. Plot a graph of the probabilities $b(x; 10, .5)$. Plot a graph also of the normalized probabilities as in Figures 21 and 22.

4. An ordinary coin is tossed one million times. Let x be the number of heads that turn up. Estimate the following probabilities.
   a. $\Pr[499,500 \leq x \leq 500,500]$.
   b. $\Pr[499,000 \leq x \leq 501,000]$.
   c. $\Pr[498,500 \leq x \leq 501,500]$.
               [*Ans.* .682; .954; .997 (approximate answers).]

5. Assume that a baseball player has probability .37 of getting a hit each time he comes to bat. Find the probability of getting an average of .388 or better if he comes to bat 300 times during the season.   [*Ans.* .242.]

6. A true-false examination has 48 questions. Assume that the probability that a given student knows the answer to any one question is $\tfrac{3}{4}$. A passing score is 30 or better. Estimate the probability that the student will fail the exam.

7. In Example 3 of Section 10, assume that the school decides to admit 1296 students. Estimate the probability that they will have to have additional dormitory space.   [*Ans.* Approximately .115.]

8. Peter and Paul each have 20 pennies. They agree to match pennies 400 times, keeping score but not paying until the 400 matches are over. What is the probability that one of the players will not be able to pay? Answer the same question for the case that Peter has 10 pennies and Paul has 30.

9. In tossing a coin 100 times, the probability of getting 50 heads is, to three decimal places, .080. Estimate this same probability using the central limit theorem.   [*Ans.* .080.]

10. A standard medicine has been found to be effective in 80 percent of the cases where it is used. A new medicine for the same purpose is found to be effective on 90 of the first 100 patients on whom the medicine is

used. Could this be taken as good evidence that the new medication is better than the old?

11. In the Weldon dice experiment, 12 dice were thrown 26,306 times and the appearance of a 5 or a 6 was considered to be a success. The mean number of successes observed was, to four decimal places, 4.0524. Is this result significantly different from the expected average number of 4? [*Ans.* Yes.]

12. Prove that $pq \leq \frac{1}{4}$. [*Hint:* Write $p = \frac{1}{2} + x$.]

13. Suppose that out of 1000 persons interviewed 650 said that they would vote for Mr. Big for mayor. Construct the 99 percent confidence interval for p, the proportion in the city that would vote for Mr. Big.

14. Opinion pollsters in election years usually poll about 3000 voters. Suppose that in an election year 51 percent favor candidate A and 49 percent favor candidate B. Construct 95 percent confidence limits for candidate A's fraction of votes. [*Ans.* .492, .528.]

15. In an experiment with independent trials we are going to estimate p by the fraction $\bar{p}$ of successes. We wish our estimate to be within .02 of the correct value with probability .95. Show that 2500 observations will always suffice. Show that if it is known that p is approximately .1, then 900 observations would be sufficient.

16. An experimenter has an independent trials process and he has a hypothesis that the true value of p is p_0. He decides to carry out a number of trials, and from the observed $\bar{p}$ calculate the 95 percent confidence interval for p. He will reject p_0 if it does not fall within these limits. What is the probability that he will reject p_0 when in fact it is correct? Should he accept p_0 if it does fall within the confidence interval?

17. A coin is tossed 100 times and turns up heads 61 times. Using the method of Exercise 16, test the hypothesis that the coin is a fair coin. [*Ans.* Reject.]

*12. GAMBLER'S RUIN

In this section we shall study a particular Markov chain, which is interesting in itself and has far-reaching applications. Its name, "gambler's ruin," derives from one of its many applications. In the text we shall describe the chain from the gambling point of view, but in the exercises we shall present several other applications.

Let us suppose that you are gambling against a professional gambler, or gambling house. You have selected a specific game to play, on which you have probability p of winning. The gambler has made sure that the game is favorable to him, so that $p < \frac{1}{2}$. However, in most situations p will be close to $\frac{1}{2}$. (The cases $p = \frac{1}{2}$ and $p > \frac{1}{2}$ are considered in the exercises.)

At the start of the game you have A dollars, and the gambler has B dollars. You bet \$1 on each game, and play until one of you is ruined. What is the probability that you will be ruined? Of course, the answer depends on the exact values of p, A, and B. We shall develop a formula for the ruin-probability in terms of these three given numbers.

First we will set the problem up as a Markov chain. Let $N = A + B$,

the total amount of money in the game. As states for the chain we choose
the numbers 0, 1, 2, . . . , N. At any one moment the position of the chain
is the amount of money *you* have. The initial position is shown in Figure 24.

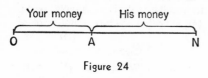

Figure 24

If you win a game, your money
increases by \$1, and the gambler's
fortune decreases by \$1. Thus the new
position is one state to the right of
the previous one. If you lose a game,
the chain moves one step to the left.
Thus at any step there is probability p of moving one step to the right, and
probability $q = 1 - p$ of one step to the left. Since the probabilities for the
next position are determined by the present position, it is a Markov chain.

If the chain reaches 0 or N, we stop. When 0 is reached, you are
ruined. When N is reached, you have all the money, and you have ruined
the gambler. We will be interested in the probability of *your* ruin—that is,
the probability of reaching 0.

Let us suppose that p and N are fixed. We actually want the probability of ruin when we start at A. However, it turns out to be easier to
solve a problem that appears much harder: find the ruin-probability for
every possible starting position. For this reason we introduce the notation
x_i, to stand for the probability of your ruin if you start in position i (that
is, if you have i dollars).

Let us first solve the problem for the case $N = 5$. We have the un-
knowns x_0, x_1, x_2, x_3, x_4, and x_5. Suppose that we start at position 2. The
chain moves to 3, with probability p, or to 1, with probability q. Thus

$$\mathbf{Pr}[\text{ruin} \mid \text{start at } 2] = \mathbf{Pr}[\text{ruin} \mid \text{start at } 3] \cdot p + \mathbf{Pr}[\text{ruin} \mid \text{start at } 1] \cdot q,$$

using the conditional probability formula, with a set of two alternatives.
But once it has reached state 3, a Markov chain behaves just as if it had
been started there. Thus

$$\mathbf{Pr}[\text{ruin} \mid \text{start at } 3] = x_3.$$

Similarly,

$$\mathbf{Pr}[\text{ruin} \mid \text{start at } 1] = x_1.$$

We obtain the key relation

$$x_2 = px_3 + qx_1.$$

We can modify this as follows:

$$(p + q)x_2 = px_3 + qx_1,$$
$$p(x_2 - x_3) = q(x_1 - x_2),$$
$$x_1 - x_2 = r(x_2 - x_3),$$

where $r = p/q$, and hence $r < 1$. When we write such an equation for each of the four "ordinary" positions, we obtain

(1)
$$x_0 - x_1 = r(x_1 - x_2),$$
$$x_1 - x_2 = r(x_2 - x_3),$$
$$x_2 - x_3 = r(x_3 - x_4),$$
$$x_3 - x_4 = r(x_4 - x_5).$$

We must still consider the two extreme positions. Suppose that the chain reaches 0. Then you are ruined, hence the probability of your ruin is 1. If the chain reaches $N = 5$, the gambler drops out of the game, and you can't be ruined. Thus

(2)
$$x_0 = 1, \qquad x_5 = 0.$$

If we substitute the value of x_5 in the last equation of (1), we have $x_3 - x_4 = rx_4$. This in turn may be substituted in the previous equation, and so on. We thus have the simpler equations

(3)
$$x_4 = 1 \cdot x_4,$$
$$x_3 - x_4 = rx_4,$$
$$x_2 - x_3 = r^2 x_4,$$
$$x_1 - x_2 = r^3 x_4,$$
$$x_0 - x_1 = r^4 x_4.$$

Let us add all the equations. We obtain

$$x_0 = (1 + r + r^2 + r^3 + r^4)x_4.$$

From (2) we have that $x_0 = 1$. We also use the simple identity

$$(1 - r)(1 + r + r^2 + r^3 + r^4) = 1 - r^5.$$

And then we solve for x_4:

$$x_4 = \frac{1 - r}{1 - r^5}.$$

If we add the first two equations in (3), we have that $x_3 = (1 + r)x_4$. Similarly, adding the first three equations, we solve for x_2, and adding the first four equations we obtain x_1. We now have our entire solution,

(4) $$x_1 = \frac{1 - r^4}{1 - r^5}, \quad x_2 = \frac{1 - r^3}{1 - r^5}, \quad x_3 = \frac{1 - r^2}{1 - r^5}, \quad x_4 = \frac{1 - r}{1 - r^5}.$$

The same method will work for any value of N. And it is easy to guess from (4) what the general solution looks like. If we want x_A, the answer is a fraction like those in (4). In the denominator the exponent of r is always N. In the numerator the exponent is $N - A$, or B. Thus the ruin-probability is

$$(5) \qquad\qquad x_A = \frac{1 - r^B}{1 - r^N}.$$

We recall that A is the amount of money you have, B is the gambler's stake, $N = A + B$, p is your probability of winning a game, and $r = p/(1 - p)$.

In Figure 25 we show some typical values of the ruin-probability. Some of these are quite startling. If the probability of p is as low as .45 (odds against you on each game 11:9) and the gambler has 20 dollars to put up, you are almost sure to be ruined. Even in a nearly fair game, say $p = .495$, with each of you having \$50 to start with, there is a .731 chance for your ruin.

It is worth examining the ruin-probability formula, (5), more closely. Since the denominator is always less than 1, your probability of ruin is at least $1 - r^B$. This estimate does not depend on how much money you have, only on p and B. Since r is less than 1, by making B large enough, we can make r^B practically 0, and hence make it almost certain that you will be ruined.

Suppose, for example, that a gambler wants to have probability .999 of ruining you. (You can hardly call him a gambler under those circumstances!) He must make sure that $r^B < .001$. For example, if $p = .495$, the gambler needs \$346 to have probability .999 of ruining you, even if you are a millionaire. If $p = .48$, he needs only \$87. And even for the almost fair game with $p = .499$, \$1727 will suffice.

There are two ways in which gamblers achieve this goal. Small gambling houses will fix the odds quite a bit in their favor, making r much less than 1. Then even a relatively small bank of B dollars suffices to assure them of winning. Larger houses, with B quite sizable, can afford to let you play nearly fair games.

EXERCISES

1. An urn has nine white balls and eleven black balls. A ball is drawn and replaced. If it is white, you win 5 cents, if black, you lose 5 cents. You have \$1 to gamble with, and your opponent has 50 cents. If you keep on playing till one of you loses all his money, what is the probability that you will lose your dollar?   [*Ans.* .868.]

2. Suppose you are shooting craps, and you always hold the dice. You have \$20, your opponent has \$10, and \$1 is bet on each game; estimate your probability of ruin.

3. Two government agencies, A and B, are competing for the same task. A has 50 positions and B has 20. Each year one position is taken away

Ruin-probabilities for $p = .45, .48, .49, .495$.

$p = .45$

A \ B	1	5	10	20	50
1	.550	.905	.973	.997	1
5	.260	.732	.910	.988	1
10	.204	.666	.881	.984	1
20	.185	.638	.868	.982	1
50	.182	.633	.866	.982	1

$p = .48$

A \ B	1	5	10	20	50
1	.520	.865	.941	.981	.999
5	.202	.599	.788	.923	.994
10	.131	.472	.690	.878	.990
20	.095	.381	.606	.832	.985
50	.078	.334	.555	.801	.982

$p = .49$

A \ B	1	5	10	20	50
1	.510	.850	.926	.969	.994
5	.184	.550	.731	.871	.972
10	.110	.402	.599	.788	.951
20	.069	.287	.472	.690	.921
50	.045	.204	.363	.586	.881

$p = .495$

A \ B	1	5	10	20	50
1	.505	.842	.918	.961	.989
5	.175	.525	.699	.838	.948
10	.100	.367	.550	.731	.905
20	.058	.242	.402	.599	.839
50	.031	.143	.259	.438	.731

Figure 25

from one of the agencies and given to the other. If 52 percent of the time the shift is from A to B, what do you predict for the future of the two agencies?

[*Ans.* One agency will be abolished. B survives with probability .8, A with probability .2.]

4. What is the approximate value of x_A if you are rich, and the gambler starts with $1?

5. Consider a simple model for evolution. On a small island there is room for 1000 members of a certain species. One year a favorable mutant appears. We assume that in each subsequent generation either the mutants take one place from the regular members of the species, with probability .6, or the reverse happens. Thus, for example, the mutation disappears in the very first generation with probability .4. What is the probability that the mutants eventually take over? [*Hint:* See Exercise 4.]   [*Ans.* $\frac{1}{3}$.]

6. Verify that the proof of the text is still correct when $p > \frac{1}{2}$. Interpret formula (5) for this case.

7. Show that if $p > \frac{1}{2}$, and both parties have a substantial amount of money, your probability of ruin is approximately $1/r^4$.

8. Modify the proof in the text to apply to the case $p = \frac{1}{2}$. What is the probability of your ruin?   [*Ans.* B/N.]

9. You are matching pennies. You have 25 pennies to start with, and your opponent has 35. What is the probability that you will win all his pennies?

10. Mr. Jones lives on a short street, about 100 steps long. At one end of the street is his home, at the other a lake, and in the middle a bar. One evening he leaves the bar in a state of intoxication and starts to walk at random. What is the probability that he will fall into the lake if

    a. he is just as likely to take a step to the right as to the left?
    [*Ans.* $\frac{1}{2}$.]

    b. he has probability .51 of taking a step towards his home?
    [*Ans.* .119.]

11. You are in the following hopeless situation: You are playing a game in which you have only $\frac{1}{3}$ chance of winning. You have $1, and your opponent has $7. What is the probability of your winning all his money if

    a. You bet $1 each time?   [*Ans.* $\frac{1}{255}$.]
    b. You bet all your money each time?   [*Ans.* $\frac{1}{27}$.]

12. Repeat Exercise 11 for the case of a fair game, where you have probability $\frac{1}{2}$ of winning.

13. Modify the proof in the text to compute y_i, the probability of reaching state $N = 5$.

14. Verify, in Exercise 13, that $x_i + y_i = 1$ for every state. Interpret.

Exercises 15–18 deal with the following ruin problem: A and B play a game in which A has probability $\frac{2}{3}$ of winning. They keep playing until either A has won six times or B has won three times.

15. Set up the process as a Markov chain whose states are (a, b), where a is the number of times A won, and b the number of B wins.

16. For each state compute the probability of A's winning from that position. [*Hint:* Work from higher a- and b-values to lower ones.]

17. What is the probability that A reaches his goal first?   [*Ans.* $\frac{1024}{2187}$.]

18. Suppose that payments are made as follows: If A wins six games, he receives $1; if B wins three games then A pays $1. What is the expected value of the payment, to the nearest penny?

*13. MONTE CARLO SIMULATION

So far we have studied only very simple stochastic processes—the independent-trials process with two outcomes and with more than two outcomes, and the Markov-chain process. There are other stochastic processes that are mathematically tractable, but we shall not study them here. Others are inherently so difficult that a purely mathematical treatment, no matter how advanced, is not practical. A method for analyzing stochastic processes of any degree of complication is the so-called *Monte Carlo simulation method.*

We have already seen that any stochastic process can be described by a tree diagram. The Monte Carlo method substitutes for a real-world stochastic process a simulated process with the same tree diagram. And in order to simulate the outcomes of real-world events that are probabilistic in nature, it uses random devices. In order to describe Monte Carlo simulations, we will commonly use flow diagrams.

The random devices used in the simulation may be mechanical devices such as a roulette wheel, a pair of dice, or a spinning pointer. For instance, since the roulette wheel has 37 equally spaced slots, we assume that the 37 possible outcomes are equally likely. Accordingly, the roulette wheel can be used as a randomizing device for any stochastic process for which the probability of each outcome of each experiment is an integral multiple of $\frac{1}{37}$.

> **Example 1.** Consider a machine that produces good pieces and defectives according to an independent-trials process with two outcomes. Let the probability that a defective is produced be $\frac{2}{37} = .054$. Then we may simulate the production process by spinning the roulette wheel and saying that a defective is produced if the numbers 0 or 1 turn up, but a good piece is produced if any other number turns up. We could then simulate the process of examining a sample of three pieces produced by the process of spinning the roulette wheel three times. And we could approximate the binomial probabilities $\mathbf{b}(r; 3, \frac{2}{37})$ by observing the relative frequency with $r = 0, 1, 2,$ and 3 "defectives" in a large series of such trials. The fraction of cases in which 1 defective is found in 10,000 such tries will differ from the expected number 10,000 $\mathbf{b}(1; 3, \frac{2}{37})$ in a way that is described in the law of large numbers.
>
> Observe that we could have used the outcomes 16 and 23, say, to represent the drawing of a defective, instead of the numbers 0 and 1. Such changes do not alter the basic probability process.

Reliance on mechanical random devices would be very slow and clumsy, especially if a large number of trials is to be made. For this reason, random-digit tables, such as Table II, p. 516, have been prepared, and by properly using them we can simulate any chance device. A random-digit table is, in principle, created by recording the results of an independent-trials process with ten outcomes—the digits $0, 1, \ldots, 9$. The probability assigned to each of the ten possible outcomes is $\frac{1}{10}$. Since the probability of each digit's occurring is $\frac{1}{10}$, the probability for a two-digit number is $\frac{1}{100}$, for a three-digit number $\frac{1}{1000}$, and so on.

Then to simulate an event whose occurrence has probability .173, all we do is to assign any 173 of the 1000 possible three-digit numbers as representing a success. For instance, we could say that the numbers 000 through 172 represent success. But we could equally well have chosen the sequence 827 through 999 to represent success. We then select from the random-number table a number and record the experiment as success or failure depending upon whether the chosen number corresponds with one of the numbers we have labeled success.

In using the table of random numbers it is important not to use the same part of the table over and over again, since this will lead to a repetition of the same series of experiments. Instead, start at some arbitrary place in the table and move up or down a column, or right or left across a row, or take every other number group, and so on. It is a good idea to use a different rule each time the table is used. However, it is necessary to pick the rule in advance and, once it is chosen, to stick to it.

Example 2. Let us simulate the brand-purchasing behavior of a consumer who buys three brands of coffee, A, B, and C, according to the Markov-chain process whose transition matrix P is given by

$$P = \begin{array}{c} \\ A \\ B \\ C \end{array} \begin{array}{ccc} A & B & C \\ \left(\begin{array}{ccc} .8 & .1 & .1 \\ .1 & .7 & .2 \\ .2 & .2 & .6 \end{array} \right). \end{array}$$

Assume that the last brand purchased was C. Then for the next purchase we assign the numbers 0 and 1 to choosing A, 2 and 3 to choosing B, and 4 through 9 to choosing C. In Figure 26 we show the calculations for 15 trials where we chose the random digits to be the first figure in each five-figure group starting in the first row and working from left to right. The first random number chosen was 6, so that according to our convention stated above we choose Brand C again. The next three numbers are 5, 8, and 4, so that we continue to choose Brand C. The fifth number is 2, so we shift to Brand B and look at the second row of P. Here we let 0 represent choosing A, the numbers 1 through 7 represent choosing B, and the numbers 8 and 9 represent choosing C. The next number 0 indicates that we choose Brand A, and so on. The reader should check the rest of the entries in Figure 26.

Example 3. In a factory, machinists have to obtain tools at a tool crib that is serviced by a clerk, and hence a queue tends to form. The clerk takes three minutes to service a machinist. We are interested in the problem of how many new machinists arrive during three minutes. We assume that only one can arrive in any one-minute interval; and if there are s machinists, the probability of a machinist's joining the queue during a given minute when it is of length q is given by

$$p \left(\frac{s - q}{s} \right),$$

Trial	Random Number	Brand Chosen
1	6	C
2	5	C
3	8	C
4	4	C
5	2	B
6	0	A
7	6	A
8	0	A
9	7	A
10	7	A
11	4	A
12	5	A
13	9	C
14	9	C
15	1	A

Figure 26

where p is a fixed number between 0 and 1. We get a new queue length of 0, 1, 2, or 3; the probability of getting each of these when $p = \frac{1}{2}$ and $s = 5$ is given in the table of Figure 27.

q	0	1	2	3
Probability	.125	.455	.360	.060

Figure 27

We now have the choice of simulating the formation of queues either by using the distribution of Figure 27 or by actually simulating the process of deciding when a machinist is to be added to the queue. Figure 28 shows a flow diagram for carrying out the latter simulation. This diagram will be used again as a subroutine in a simulation problem of the next section.

In Figure 28 we have set up a simulation for deciding whether a new person is to be added to the queue, given that there are q people already in the queue and s people in all who can be chosen in M minutes. The three initial pieces of data to be used are a_1, which is the value of p; a_2, which is s, the number of machinists; and a_3, which is the number of trials to be run. The reader should study the figure to see that it simulates the process above.

In Figure 29 we show 16 runs of the simulation diagrammed in Figure 28, for $p = \frac{1}{2}$, $s = 5$, $M = 3$. The random numbers were taken to be the first two digits of the third column in Table II. The observed frequencies for queues of length 0, 1, 2, and 3 were $\frac{3}{16} = .19$, $\frac{7}{16} = .44$, $\frac{6}{16} = .38$, and $\frac{0}{16} = 0$, respectively. These are in surprisingly good agreement with Figure 27—better than could normally be expected in so short a run. However, the law of large numbers guarantees with high probability excellent agreement in sufficiently long runs. But queues of length 3 should turn up only with probability .06; thus in 16 runs the expected number is only .96, or less than 1. Hence we would expect to have to run a much larger number of trials than 16 to obtain a reasonable estimate for this probability.

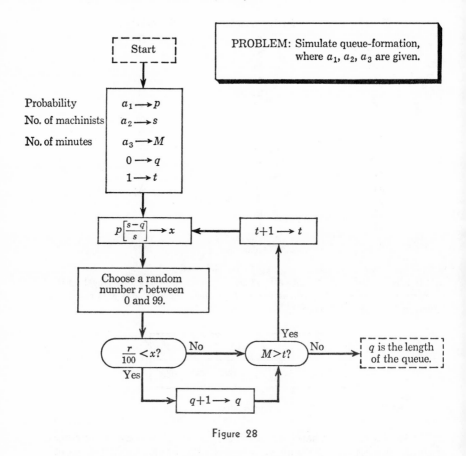

Figure 28

It should be reemphasized that simulation techniques are designed for much more complex problems than here illustrated. They are useful when explicit probabilistic calculations are too cumbersome to carry out. The examples above illustrate the use of simulation, but the examples are simple enough to have been treated by the methods discussed in earlier sections.

EXERCISES

1. Draw a tree diagram of the possibilities for the queueing situation of Example 3 when $p = \frac{1}{2}$, $s = 5$, and $M = 3$. Assign probabilities and show that the numbers in Figure 27 are correct.

2. Use the flow diagram of Figure 28 and the random-number table (Table II) to carry out 16 more simulations of the queueing situation of Example 3 when $p = \frac{1}{2}$, $s = 5$, and $M = 3$. Compute the observed frequencies of queue lengths and compare your numbers with those in Figure 27.

Trial	Random Number	x	q	Trial	Random Number	x	q
1	80	.50	0	1	58	.50	0
2	07	.50	1	2	14	.50	1
3	95	.40	1	3	11	.40	2
1	40	.50	1	1	05	.50	1
2	54	.40	1	2	91	.40	1
3	64	.40	1	3	67	.40	1
1	60	.50	0	1	64	.50	0
2	08	.50	1	2	56	.50	0
3	26	.40	2	3	86	.50	0
1	59	.50	0	1	61	.50	0
2	88	.50	0	2	13	.50	1
3	54	.50	0	3	30	.40	2
1	57	.50	0	1	08	.50	1
2	88	.50	0	2	78	.40	1
3	28	.50	1	3	42	.40	1
1	83	.50	0	1	09	.50	1
2	05	.50	1	2	00	.40	2
3	56	.40	1	3	47	.30	2
1	83	.50	0	1	70	.50	0
2	74	.50	0	2	48	.50	1
3	96	.50	0	3	06	.40	2
1	40	.50	1	1	57	.50	0
2	61	.40	1	2	89	.50	0
3	05	.40	2	3	12	.50	1

Figure 29

3. In Exercise 2, compute the relative frequencies of queue lengths observed in the simulations of all the students in the class and again compare with the table of Figure 27.

4. A machine produces good pieces and defectives according to an independent-trials process, where the probability of a defective is $p = .4$. Use the random-number table to simulate a sample of 20, and count the number of "defectives" in the simulated "sample." What is the binomial probability of obtaining this number of defectives? What is the probability that this number of defectives *or more* would be obtained?

5. A lot of 20 pieces contains six defectives. A sample of five is taken from the lot. Simulate the sampling operation and count the number of "defectives" in the sample. What is the hypergeometric probability of obtaining this number of defectives? What is the probability of obtaining this number of defectives *or less?*

6. A person buys Brand X of coffee according to a Markov-chain process, with the following matrix of transition probabilities:

$$
\begin{array}{cc}
 & \text{X} \quad \text{Not X} \\
\begin{array}{c} \text{X} \\ \text{Not X} \end{array} &
\left(\begin{array}{cc} .6 & .4 \\ .2 & .8 \end{array} \right)
\end{array}
$$

Simulate ten consecutive purchases given that (a) the last purchase was X; (b) the last purchase was not X; (c) the last purchase was X with probability $\frac{1}{3}$ and not X with probability $\frac{2}{3}$.

7. A model for the behavior of a stock traded on the New York Stock Exchange is that its price goes up, stays the same, or goes down from day to day according to a Markov-chain process, with the following matrix of transition probabilities:

$$
\begin{array}{cccc}
 & \text{Up} & \text{Unchanged} & \text{Down} \\
\begin{array}{c} \text{Up} \\ \text{Unchanged} \\ \text{Down} \end{array} &
\left(\begin{array}{ccc}
.7 & .2 & .1 \\
.3 & .4 & .3 \\
.1 & .3 & .6
\end{array} \right)
\end{array}
$$

Suppose, in addition, that *if* the price goes up or down, the *amount* by which it changes is given by the following probabilities:

Amount of Change	Probability
$\frac{1}{2}$	.30
1	.40
$1\frac{1}{2}$	.20
2	.05
$2\frac{1}{2}$	.05

Simulate the next 20 days' trading on the assumption that the stock closed yesterday unchanged at 100.

8. A common model for predicting a company's sales volume by periods is to assume that sales are affected by four factors: trend, cycle, seasonal, and random fluctuations. Suppose that the trend of sales is increasing by 2000 units per quarter, that the business cycle is expected to affect sales in the next twelve quarters according to Table 1 below, that the deviation

Table 1		Table 2		Table 3	
Qtr.	*Cyclical deviations*	*Qtr.*	*Seasonal deviations*	*Random fluctuations*	*Probability*
1	+ 3000	1	− 8000	−10,000	.02
2	+ 5000	2	− 2000	−8,000	.04
3	+ 6000	3	+ 1000	−6,000	.08
4	+ 7000	4	+ 9000	−4,000	.11
5	+ 7000			−2,000	.15
6	+ 6000			0	.20
7	+ 4000			+2,000	.15
8	+ 2000			+4,000	.11
9	− 1000			+6,000	.08
10	− 3000			+8,000	.04
11	− 4000			+10,000	.02
12	− 4000				

of sales from average in each of the four quarters is given by Table 2, and that the probabilities of various random fluctuations are given by Table 3. Simulate three years' sales by quarters if the next season's basic sales level, including trend, but excluding cyclical, seasonal, and random factors, is 150,000 units.

9. The X company supplies Companies A, B, C, and D with a certain part. A orders 3 units every 5 days; B orders every 3 days, but the size of its order varies according to Table 1 below. C orders 5 units whenever it orders, but the interval between successive orders varies according to Table 2. D orders varying amounts at varying intervals, the amount ordered being independent of the time interval since the last order; Tables 3 and 4 show D's variation in amount and interval between orders. Simulate 20 days' demand for the part.

Table 1		Table 2		Table 3		Table 4	
Size of B's order	*Prob- ability*	*Days btwn. C's orders*	*Prob- ability*	*Size of D's orders*	*Prob- ability*	*Days btwn. D's orders*	*Prob- ability*
3	.2	2	.4	2	.2	1	.1
5	.3	3	.3	4	.2	2	.2
7	.4	4	.2	6	.3	3	.3
10	.1	5	.1	8	.3	4	.4

10. Suppose consumers buy Brand X of coffee according to a Markov-chain process, with the matrix of transition probabilities given in Exercise 6. Assume that each consumer buys one pound a week, every week. At a certain time the X Company initiates a three-week advertising campaign. This may change a consumer's matrix of transition probabilities to

$$\begin{array}{c} \\ X \\ \text{Not X} \end{array} \begin{array}{cc} X & \text{Not X} \\ \begin{pmatrix} .7 & .3 \\ .4 & .6 \end{pmatrix} \end{array}$$

but it is not certain when the change will occur or whether it will take place at all. There is a .7 probability that the change will occur, but it may happen after the first, second, or third weeks of the campaign according to the following probabilities:

Number of Weeks After Start of Campaign	*Probability*
1	.2
2	.2
3	.3

Suppose each of five consumers last bought Brand X with probability $\frac{1}{3}$ and some brand other than X with probability $\frac{2}{3}$. Simulate ten weeks' purchases for the five consumers under the assumption that the advertising campaign begins after the third purchase.

11. Toss a coin 100 times, recording the results by writing 1 each time the coin comes up heads, and 0 each time it comes up tails. The resulting table may be considered a table of random bits (binary digits). Use this table to simulate
    a. A sample of five drawn from an independent-trials process where the probability of success is .5.
    b. A sample of ten drawn from an independent-trials process where the probability of success is .125.

12. In Exercise 11 arrange the bits in the table you have created into groups of four. Interpret each such group as a binary-coded decimal number. Where a particular group has no interpretation as a binary-coded decimal, disregard it. Show that the method produces random decimal digits. Can you think of a way of converting a table of random bits into a table of random decimal digits that makes more efficient use of the bits?

*14. MONTE CARLO ANALYSIS OF DECISION RULES

Although the Monte Carlo technique is useful as a method of simulating a stochastic process for purely descriptive purposes, it is most important for the analysis of decision rules applied to complex systems. In recent years there has been considerable development of advanced mathematical techniques to handle systems such as inventory control, waiting lines, and so forth; however, these techniques can usually be applied only when the system in question obeys certain carefully defined probabilistic laws. And when these laws do not apply to a given situation, the best method of analysis available is often the Monte Carlo method.

We shall illustrate the application of this technique to decision problems in inventory control and waiting lines. The reader will quickly observe that the number of trials that can be simulated by hand calculation seldom will be sufficient to permit any firm conclusions about the adequacy of a particular decision rule. However, the ability to perform these calculations very rapidly on computers makes the Monte Carlo method a practical way to analyze decision rules. Here we shall simply illustrate the method by means of hand calculations, but the flow diagrams we draw can easily be translated into computer programs. And those readers who have a computer available can try them out.

Example 1. *Waiting Line.* Machinists in a factory have to obtain new tools as a result of tool wear or because of setup requirements for new jobs. They obtain these tools at a tool crib, which is serviced by clerks. Suppose that it takes exactly two minutes for a clerk to service a single machinist's request. Then one clerk can handle up to 30 requests an hour, two clerks can handle up to 60 requests, and so on.

A clerk in the tool crib is paid $2 an hour. The cost of having a machinist wait in line while his machine is idle is assessed at $24 an hour. Figure 30 shows a flow chart for calculating the total cost of running a tool bin with r

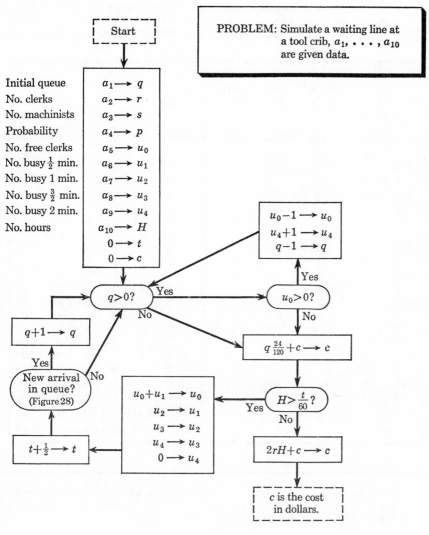

Initial queue	$a_1 \longrightarrow q$
No. clerks	$a_2 \longrightarrow r$
No. machinists	$a_3 \longrightarrow s$
Probability	$a_4 \longrightarrow p$
No. free clerks	$a_5 \longrightarrow u_0$
No. busy $\frac{1}{2}$ min.	$a_6 \longrightarrow u_1$
No. busy 1 min.	$a_7 \longrightarrow u_2$
No. busy $\frac{3}{2}$ min.	$a_8 \longrightarrow u_3$
No. busy 2 min.	$a_9 \longrightarrow u_4$
No. hours	$a_{10} \longrightarrow H$

Figure 30

clerks for H hours, in a shop having s machinists. A subroutine in this program is the flow diagram of Figure 28 for $M = 1$, in which the new arrival in the queue is simulated. It is assumed that time is measured in intervals of $\frac{1}{2}$ minute. The quantity u_0 counts the number of idle clerks, u_1 the number who will be busy for another $\frac{1}{2}$ minute servicing a particular machinist, u_2 the number who will be busy for 1 minute, u_3 the number who will be busy for $\frac{3}{2}$ minutes, and u_4 the number who will be busy for 2 minutes. The quantity q is the length of the queue at any time, p is the probability needed in the queue arrival subroutine, and t is the current time, measured in $\frac{1}{2}$-minute intervals. The reader should study the flow chart until he is convinced that it simulates the problem described in words above.

In Figures 31 and 32 a simulation is carried out for 10 minutes of the problem, assuming that there are 2 and 3 clerks, respectively. It is also assumed that there are 20 machinists. It is initially assumed that two people

Time	q^*	"Arrival" 001 to	Random No.	No. Arriving	q	u_0	u_1	u_2	u_3	u_4	c
0				0	0	0	0	1	1	0	
1/2	2	450	430	1	1	0	1	1	0	0	.20
1	3	425	776	0	0	0	1	0	0	1	.20
3/2	2	450	990	0	0	1	0	0	1	0	.20
2	1	475	186	1	0	0	0	1	0	1	.20
5/2	2	450	612	0	0	0	1	0	1	0	.20
3	2	450	297	1	0	0	0	1	0	1	.20
7/2	2	450	467	0	0	0	1	0	1	0	.20
4	2	450	806	0	0	1	0	1	0	0	.20
9/2	1	475	783	0	0	1	1	0	0	0	.20
5	1	475	273	1	0	1	0	0	0	1	.20
11/2	1	475	128	1	0	0	0	0	1	1	.20
6	2	450	155	1	1	0	0	1	1	0	.40
13/2	3	425	111	1	2	0	1	1	0	0	.80
7	4	400	823	0	1	0	1	0	0	1	1.00
15/2	3	425	392	1	1	0	0	0	1	1	1.20
8	3	425	056	1	2	0	0	1	1	0	1.60
17/2	4	400	275	1	3	0	1	1	0	0	2.20
9	5	375	602	0	2	0	1	0	0	1	2.60
19/2	4	400	540	0	1	0	0	0	1	1	2.80
10	3	425	772	0	1	0	0	1	1	0	3.00

Cost of 2 clerks for 10 min.   .67

Total cost for 10 min. $3.67

Figure 31

are being served. The entry q^* in the tables counts the total number of people who were being served or were waiting to be served in the previous period. The probability of a machinist's arriving is

$$\frac{1}{2}\left(\frac{20 - q^*}{20}\right).$$

The random numbers were chosen between 000 and 999 from Table II.

Note that the total cost with 2 clerks is $3.67 for 10 minutes, which would mean that the hourly cost would be $22.02. On the other hand, the total cost with 3 clerks is $1.40 for 10 minutes, which would mean that the hourly cost would be $8.40. Clearly, it pays to have 3 rather than 2 clerks. It might just barely pay to add a fourth clerk, since the cost for the clerks would be $8.00 per hour and it is unlikely that any machinist would ever have to wait with 4 clerks. However, the greatest possible savings are only $.40 per hour, so the decision as to whether or not to add the fourth clerk may depend upon other factors.

The results of one short simulation run are not, of course, sufficient to assure that the conclusions drawn will always hold. However, with a fast computer it is possible to make very long simulation runs, studying the

Time	q^*	"Arrival" 001 to	Random No.	No. Arriving	q	u_0	u_1	u_2	u_3	u_4	c
0				0	0	1	0	1	1	0	0
1/2	2	450	430	1	0	0	1	1	0	1	0
1	3	425	776	0	0	1	1	0	1	0	0
3/2	2	450	990	0	0	2	0	1	0	0	0
2	1	475	186	1	0	1	1	0	0	1	0
5/2	2	450	612	0	0	2	0	0	1	0	0
3	1	475	297	1	0	1	0	1	0	1	0
7/2	2	450	467	0	0	1	1	0	1	0	0
4	2	450	806	0	0	2	0	1	0	0	0
9/2	1	475	783	0	0	2	1	0	0	0	0
5	1	475	273	1	0	2	0	0	0	1	0
11/2	1	475	128	1	0	1	0	0	1	1	0
6	2	450	155	1	0	0	0	1	1	1	0
13/2	3	425	111	1	1	0	1	1	1	0	.20
7	4	400	823	0	0	0	1	1	0	1	.20
15/2	3	425	392	1	0	0	1	0	1	1	.20
8	3	425	056	1	0	0	0	1	1	1	.20
17/2	3	425	275	1	1	0	1	1	1	0	.40
9	3	425	602	0	0	0	1	1	0	1	.40
19/2	3	425	540	0	0	1	1	0	1	0	.40
10	2	450	772	0	0	2	0	1	0	0	.40

Cost of 3 clerks for 10 min.	1.00
Total cost for 10 min.	$1.40

Figure 32

effects of a particular situation over days or even months or years of operation. From such large-scale simulations, the law of large numbers assures us that reliable conclusions can be drawn. The main problem for such studies is to be certain that the simulation accurately describes the situation under study.

Example 2. *Inventory Control.* A distributor observes that the daily demand for an item varies probabilistically. At the beginning of any day an order can be placed for any number of units of the item at a total cost of $2, regardless of the number of units ordered. But if no order is placed, the $2 cost is not incurred. Units ordered are delivered and available for sale on the third day after the order is made. It costs the distributor $.20 per day for each item held in inventory. If demand exceeds inventory on a given day, the excess demand constitutes a negative inventory or a "back order." If the inventory becomes negative in this manner, there is a cost of $1 for each day per item. As soon as an order arrives, it is used first to reduce back orders. The remainder of an order, if any, is then used to fill current demand. Thus, when an order arrives, it is simply added to the (negative or positive) inventory.

The distributor observes that the probabilities of various sizes of demand are as shown in Figure 33. Given the table, it is easy, using the tech-

Random numbers	1–8	9–21	22–37	38–57	58–74	75–85	86–94	95–00
Demand	0	1	2	3	4	5	6	7
Probability	.08	.13	.16	.20	.17	.11	.09	.06

Figure 33

niques of the preceding section, to simulate the demand.

The flow diagram for the simulation of the situation above is shown in Figure 34. The names of the variables are given on the diagram. I_t is the inventory at time t. Time $t = 4$ is chosen as the starting time. The box labeled "Find demand d_t" is simulated, using the data in Figure 33. We assign to the event "demand is 0" the two-digit random numbers 01 through 08, to the

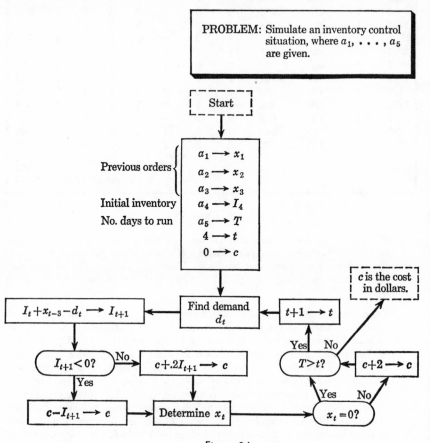

Figure 34

event "demand is 1" we assign the numbers 09 through 21, and so on, and finally we assign the numbers 95 through 00 to the event "demand is 7." These numbers are marked in Figure 33.

The box labeled "Determine x_t" may be simulated in several ways. One way is to permit a person to make this decision on the basis of the previous orders and the back orders. When we do this we have what is commonly known as a *business game*, since part of the simulation involves the decisions of a person. Such games have recently come into the fore as useful tools for teaching as well as for simulation and research; it is likely that they will be of increasing importance in the future. The example above is a business game involving only one person, but larger games involving several players have been devised.

The other way of simulating the box labeled "Determine x_t" is to replace it by a decision rule, which automatically determines x_t for each possible given set of values of the various variables. Examples of decision rules are the following:

1. Order 7 units every other day, starting today.
2. Order every fourth day so that the total number of units on order plus in inventory is equal to 16.
3. Order 5 units whenever previous orders plus present inventory falls below 10 units.
4. Order 10 units whenever previous orders plus present inventory falls below 15 units.

The first two of these rules are called "cyclical ordering" rules, since an order is always placed at a predetermined time. Rules 3 and 4 are called "trigger level" rules since no action is taken until the sum of previous orders plus present inventory falls below a preset trigger level. In rule 3 the trigger level is 10 while in rule 4 the trigger level is 15. In these rules the amount ordered— 5 or 10—is called the "reorder quantity."

We summarize the results of 20 days' simulation in Figure 35. This simulation was based on rule 3 to determine x_t. (See Exercises 8–10.) It was assumed that the initial inventory is 10 and that 5 units were ordered 3 days ago. For the determination of the demand d_t the last two digits of the numbers in column two of Table II were used.

Of course, a run of 20 days is too short to make an accurate estimate. A run of 500 days was carried out on a high-speed computer. This run indicates that there is a tendency for back orders to pile up. The results can be improved by increasing either the reorder quantity or the trigger level. Figure 36 shows the result of eight different runs of 500 days each, in which these two quantities were varied. We note, for example, that by increasing the reorder quantity to 11, we can cut the average daily cost from \$2.62 to \$1.93, which is a saving of more than 25 percent.

There is evidence in Figure 36 that even a run of 500 days is subject to considerable variance. For example, we would expect that back-order costs would decrease in the first six lines of the table. (Why?) Back-order costs were recomputed for trigger level 10 and reorder quantities 10, 11, 12 on a run of 12,000 days. The results were 152, 147, 127 per 500 days, as opposed to the figures 175, 99, 132 given in the table. On the other hand, the new estimates for the average daily costs differed from Figure 36 by less than 5¢ in each case. Hence the runs of 500 days may be useful for many purposes.

Day	Ran-dom No.	De-mand	I_t	x_{t-3}	x_{t-2}	x_{t-1}	I_{t+1}	x_t	c
1 ($t = 4$)	45	3	10	5	0	0	12	0	$ 2.40
2	32	2	12	0	0	0	10	0	4.40
3	07	0	10	0	0	0	10	0	6.40
4	52	3	10	0	0	0	7	5	9.80
5	59	4	7	0	0	5	3	5	12.40
6	33	2	3	0	5	5	1	0	12.60
7	23	2	1	5	5	0	4	5	15.40
8	92	6	4	5	0	5	3	5	18.00
9	70	4	3	0	5	5	−1	5	21.00
10	80	5	−1	5	5	5	−1	5	24.00
11	85	5	−1	5	5	5	−1	5	27.00
12	38	3	−1	5	5	5	1	0	27.20
13	63	4	1	5	5	0	2	5	29.60
14	59	4	2	5	0	5	3	5	32.20
15	06	0	3	0	5	5	3	0	32.80
16	29	2	3	5	5	0	6	0	34.00
17	07	0	6	5	0	0	11	0	36.20
18	01	0	11	0	0	0	11	0	38.40
19	62	4	11	0	0	0	7	5	41.80
20	80	5	7	0	0	5	2	5	44.20

Figure 35

Trigger Level	Reorder Quantity	Average Total Cost Per Day	Costs for 500 Days*			
			Total	Ordering	Back Orders	Inven-tory
10	5	$2.62	$1312	$656	$412	$244
10	8	2.11	1054	422	244	388
10	10	2.02	1011	330	175	506
10	11	1.93	965	284	99	582
10	12	2.00	998	272	132	594
10	14	2.11	1055	246	155	654
10	5	2.62	1312	656	412	244
12	5	2.38	1191	632	115	444
15	5	2.76	1381	646	26	709

* Totals to nearest dollar.

Figure 36

EXERCISES

1. In Example 1, suppose that at the time of the first arrival there are five machinists waiting, including those who are being serviced, and that

servicing has just begun on all who can be served. Recompute the waiting-line data.

2. In Example 1, suppose that the service time is not a constant two minutes, but can vary between one and four minutes with the following probabilities:

Service Time (Minutes)	Probability
1	.20
$1\frac{1}{2}$	.25
2	.25
$2\frac{1}{2}$	.15
3	.05
$3\frac{1}{2}$	.05
4	.05

Simulate the service time as well as the arrival time, and find the cost of using two or three clerks. What is the expected service time?

3. In Example 2, fill in the data in Figure 35 for the twenty-first day.
   [*Ans.* 42, 3, 2, 0, 5, 5, −1, 5, 47.20.]

4. In Example 2, modify the flow chart (Figure 34) to include decision rule 3.

5. In Example 2, suppose the lead time between the placement and delivery of an order can vary between two and four (inclusive) days, with probabilities as follows:

Lead Time (Days)	Probability
2	.3
3	.4
4	.3

Simulate the lead time and, using the data of Figure 35, find the cost of the third decision rule. What is the expected lead time?

6. In Example 2, suppose once again that the lead time is constant, but that demand that occurs during a stockout is not back-ordered but lost. Let the foregone profit on an item that is demanded but cannot be supplied be $3. In Figure 35 revise the costs of using the third decision rule.

7. Suppose that in Example 2 a unit demanded during a stockout is sometimes back-ordered, but sometimes the sale is lost. Let the probability of back-ordering decrease as the number of units back-ordered (and hence the expected delay in filling the order) increases. Discuss how you would modify the flow chart of Figure 34 and how you would modify the simulation procedure to take this into account, but do not perform any calculations.

8. In Example 2 simulate decision rule 1 for 20 days.

9. In Example 2 simulate decision rule 2 for 20 days.

10. In Example 2 simulate decision rule 4 for 20 days.

11. Play Example 2 as a business game making the decisions yourself for the amounts to reorder. Simulate your decision for 20 days and compare your results with each of the four decision rules. Did you do better?

12. Use the results of Exercises 8–11 to formulate a decision rule that is superior to rules 1 through 4. Make your rule as simple as possible.

13. In Example 2 compute the expected total demand in 20 days and compare this with the result obtained in Figure 35. By how many standard deviations did the obtained value differ from the expected value?
[*Ans.* 64.8; less than one standard deviation.]

SUGGESTED READING

Cramer, Harold, *The Elements of Probability Theory*, Wiley, New York, 1955, Part I.

Feller, W., *An Introduction to Probability Theory and Its Applications*, Wiley, New York, 1950.

Goldberg, S., *Probability: An Introduction*, Prentice-Hall, Inc., Englewood Cliffs, N. J., 1960.

Mosteller, F., *Fifty Challenging Problems in Probability with Solutions*, Addison-Wesley, Reading, Mass., 1965.

Parzen, E., *Modern Probability Theory and Its Applications*, Wiley, New York, 1960.

Blackwell, D., *Basic Statistics*, McGraw-Hill, New York, 1969.

4

VECTORS
AND MATRICES

1. COLUMN AND ROW VECTORS

A *column vector* is an ordered collection of numbers written in a column. Examples of such vectors are

$$\begin{pmatrix} 1 \\ -2 \end{pmatrix}, \quad \begin{pmatrix} .6 \\ .4 \end{pmatrix}, \quad \begin{pmatrix} 0 \\ 0 \\ 0 \end{pmatrix}, \quad \begin{pmatrix} 3 \\ -4 \\ 0 \end{pmatrix}, \quad \begin{pmatrix} 1 \\ -1 \\ 2 \\ 4 \end{pmatrix}.$$

The individual numbers in these vectors are called *components*, and the number of components a vector has is one of its distinguishing characteristics. Thus the first two vectors above have two components; the next two have three components; and the last has four components. When talking more generally about n-component column vectors we shall write

$$u = \begin{pmatrix} u_1 \\ u_2 \\ \cdot \\ \cdot \\ \cdot \\ u_n \end{pmatrix}.$$

Analogously, a *row vector* is an ordered collection of numbers written in a row. Examples of row vectors are

$$(1, 0), \quad (-2, 1), \quad (2, -3, 4, 0), \quad (-1, 2, -3, 4, -5).$$

Each number appearing in the vector is again called a *component* of the vector, and the number of components a row vector has is again one of its important characteristics. Thus, the first two examples are two-component, the third a four-component, and the fourth a five-component vector. The vector $v = (v_1, v_2, \ldots, v_n)$ is an n-component row vector.

Two row vectors, or two column vectors, are said to be *equal* if and only if corresponding components of the vector are equal. Thus for the vectors

$$u = (1, 2), \quad v = \begin{pmatrix} 1 \\ 2 \end{pmatrix}, \quad w = (1, 2), \quad x = (2, 1)$$

we see that $u = w$ but $u \neq v$, and $u \neq x$.

If u and v are three-component column vectors, we shall define their sum $u + v$ by componentwise addition as follows:

$$u + v = \begin{pmatrix} u_1 \\ u_2 \\ u_3 \end{pmatrix} + \begin{pmatrix} v_1 \\ v_2 \\ v_3 \end{pmatrix} = \begin{pmatrix} u_1 + v_1 \\ u_2 + v_2 \\ u_3 + v_3 \end{pmatrix}.$$

Similarly, if u and v are three-component row vectors, their sum is defined to be

$$\begin{aligned} u + v &= (u_1, u_2, u_3) + (v_1, v_2, v_3) \\ &= (u_1 + v_1, u_2 + v_2, u_3 + v_3). \end{aligned}$$

Note that the sum of two three-component vectors yields another three-component vector. For example,

$$\begin{pmatrix} 1 \\ -1 \\ 2 \end{pmatrix} + \begin{pmatrix} 2 \\ 3 \\ -1 \end{pmatrix} = \begin{pmatrix} 3 \\ 2 \\ 1 \end{pmatrix}$$

and

$$(4, -7, 12) + (3, 14, -14) = (7, 7, -2).$$

The sum of two n-component vectors (either row or column) is defined by componentwise addition in an analogous manner, and yields another n-component vector. Observe that we do not define the addition of vectors unless they are both row or both column vectors, having the same number of components.

Because the order in which two numbers are added does not affect the answer, it is also true that the order in which vectors are added does not matter; that is,

$$u + v = v + u,$$

where u and v are both row or both column vectors. This is the so-called *commutative law of addition*. A numerical example is

$$\begin{pmatrix} 1 \\ -1 \\ 2 \end{pmatrix} + \begin{pmatrix} 2 \\ 3 \\ -1 \end{pmatrix} = \begin{pmatrix} 3 \\ 2 \\ 1 \end{pmatrix} = \begin{pmatrix} 2 \\ 3 \\ -1 \end{pmatrix} + \begin{pmatrix} 1 \\ -1 \\ 2 \end{pmatrix}.$$

Once we have the definition of the addition of two vectors, we can easily see how to add three or more vectors by grouping them in pairs as in the addition of numbers. For example,

$$\begin{pmatrix} 1 \\ 0 \\ 0 \end{pmatrix} + \begin{pmatrix} 0 \\ 2 \\ 0 \end{pmatrix} + \begin{pmatrix} 0 \\ 0 \\ 3 \end{pmatrix} = \begin{pmatrix} 1 \\ 0 \\ 0 \end{pmatrix} + \begin{pmatrix} 0 \\ 2 \\ 3 \end{pmatrix} = \begin{pmatrix} 1 \\ 2 \\ 3 \end{pmatrix}$$

$$= \begin{pmatrix} 1 \\ 2 \\ 0 \end{pmatrix} + \begin{pmatrix} 0 \\ 0 \\ 3 \end{pmatrix} = \begin{pmatrix} 1 \\ 2 \\ 3 \end{pmatrix},$$

and

$$(1, 0, 0) + (0, 2, 0) + (0, 0, 3) = (1, 2, 0) + (0, 0, 3) = (1, 2, 3)$$
$$= (1, 0, 0) + (0, 2, 3) = (1, 2, 3).$$

In general, the sum of any number of vectors (row or column), each having the same number of components, is the vector whose first component is the sum of the first components of the vectors, whose second component is the sum of the second components, and so on.

The multiplication of a number a times a vector v is defined by componentwise multiplication of a times the components of v. For the three-component case we have

$$au = a \begin{pmatrix} u_1 \\ u_2 \\ u_3 \end{pmatrix} = \begin{pmatrix} au_1 \\ au_2 \\ au_3 \end{pmatrix}$$

for column vectors and

$$av = a(v_1, v_2, v_3) = (av_1, av_2, av_3)$$

for row vectors. If u is an n-component vector (row or column), then au is defined similarly by componentwise multiplication.

If u is any vector, we define its negative $-u$ to be the vector $-u = (-1)u$. Thus in the three-component case for row vectors we have

$$-u = (-1)(u_1, u_2, u_3) = (-u_1, -u_2, -u_3).$$

Once we have the negative of a vector it is easy to see how to subtract vectors: we simply add "algebraically." For the three-component column-vector case we have

$$u - v = \begin{pmatrix} u_1 \\ u_2 \\ u_3 \end{pmatrix} - \begin{pmatrix} v_1 \\ v_2 \\ v_3 \end{pmatrix} = \begin{pmatrix} u_1 - v_1 \\ u_2 - v_2 \\ u_3 - v_3 \end{pmatrix}.$$

Specific examples of subtraction of vectors occur in the exercises at the end of this section.

An important vector is the zero vector, all of whose components are zero. For example, three-component zero vectors are

$$0 = \begin{pmatrix} 0 \\ 0 \\ 0 \end{pmatrix} \quad \text{and} \quad 0 = (0, 0, 0).$$

When there is no danger of confusion we shall use the symbol 0, as above, to denote the zero (row or column) vector. The meaning will be clear from the context. The zero vector has the important property that, if u is any vector, then $u + 0 = u$. A proof for the three-component column-vector case is as follows:

$$u + 0 = \begin{pmatrix} u_1 \\ u_2 \\ u_3 \end{pmatrix} + \begin{pmatrix} 0 \\ 0 \\ 0 \end{pmatrix} = \begin{pmatrix} u_1 + 0 \\ u_2 + 0 \\ u_3 + 0 \end{pmatrix} = \begin{pmatrix} u_1 \\ u_2 \\ u_3 \end{pmatrix} = u.$$

One of the chief advantages of the vector notation is that we can denote a whole collection of numbers by a single letter such as u, v, . . . , and treat such a collection as if it were a single quantity. By using the vector notation we can state very complicated relationships in a simple manner. The student will see many examples of this in the remainder of the present chapter and the three succeeding chapters.

EXERCISES

1. Compute the quantities below for the vectors

$$u = \begin{pmatrix} 3 \\ 1 \\ 2 \end{pmatrix}, \quad v = \begin{pmatrix} -2 \\ 3 \\ 0 \end{pmatrix}, \quad w = \begin{pmatrix} -1 \\ -1 \\ 1 \end{pmatrix}.$$

a. $2u$. $\qquad\qquad\qquad\qquad\qquad\qquad\qquad$ $\left[Ans. \begin{pmatrix} 6 \\ 2 \\ 4 \end{pmatrix} . \right]$

b. $-v$.
c. $2u - v$.

d. $v + w$. $\qquad\qquad\qquad\qquad\qquad\qquad\qquad$ $\left[Ans. \begin{pmatrix} -3 \\ 2 \\ 1 \end{pmatrix} . \right]$

e. $u + v - w$.

f. $2u - 3v - w$.

g. $3u - v + 2w$.   [*Ans.* $\begin{pmatrix} 9 \\ -2 \\ 8 \end{pmatrix}$.]

2. Compute *a.* through *g.* of Exercise 1 if the vectors u, v, and w are

$$u = (7, 0, -3), \qquad v = (2, 1, -5), \qquad w = (1, -1, 0).$$

3. *a.* Show that the zero vector is not changed when multiplied by any number.
   b. If u is any vector, show that $0 + u = u$.

4. If u and v are two row or two column vectors having the same number of components, prove that $u + 0v = u$ and $0u + v = v$.

5. If $2u - v = 0$, what is the relationship between the components of u and those of v?   [*Ans.* $v_i = 2u_i$.]

6. Answer the question in Exercise 5 for the equation $-3u + 5v + u - 7v = 0$. Do the same for the equation $20v - 3u + 5v + 8u = 0$.

7. When possible compute the following sums; when not possible give reasons.

a. $\begin{pmatrix} -1 \\ 3 \end{pmatrix} + \begin{pmatrix} 6 \\ -2 \\ 5 \\ -4 \end{pmatrix} = ?$

b. $(2, -1, -1) + 0(4, 7, -2) = ?$

c. $(5, 6) + 7 - 21 + \begin{pmatrix} 0 \\ 1 \end{pmatrix} = ?$

d. $1\begin{pmatrix} 1 \\ 0 \\ 1 \end{pmatrix} + 2\begin{pmatrix} 1 \\ 1 \\ 0 \end{pmatrix} + 3\begin{pmatrix} 0 \\ 1 \\ 1 \end{pmatrix} = ?$

8. If $\begin{pmatrix} 1 \\ 1 \\ 2 \end{pmatrix} + \begin{pmatrix} u_1 \\ u_2 \\ u_3 \end{pmatrix} = \begin{pmatrix} 1 \\ -1 \\ 0 \end{pmatrix}$, find u_1, u_2, and u_3.   [*Ans.* $0; -2; -2$.]

9. If $2\begin{pmatrix} v_1 \\ v_2 \\ v_3 \end{pmatrix} = \begin{pmatrix} 0 \\ 1 \\ 3 \end{pmatrix}$, find the components of v.

10. If $\begin{pmatrix} 0 \\ 0 \\ 0 \end{pmatrix} + \begin{pmatrix} u_1 \\ u_2 \\ u_3 \end{pmatrix} = \begin{pmatrix} 0 \\ 0 \\ 0 \end{pmatrix}$, what can be said concerning the components u_1, u_2, u_3?

11. If $0 \cdot \begin{pmatrix} u_1 \\ u_2 \\ u_3 \end{pmatrix} = \begin{pmatrix} 0 \\ 0 \\ 0 \end{pmatrix}$, what can be said concerning the components u_1, u_2, u_3?

12. In a certain school students take four courses each semester. At the end of the semester the registrar records the grades of each student as a row vector. He then gives the student 4 points for each A, 3 points for each B, 2 points for each C, 1 point for each D, and 0 for each F. The sum of these numbers, divided by 4 is the student's grade point average.
    a. If a student has a 4.0 average, what are the logical possibilities for his grade vector?
    b. What are the possibilities if he has a 3.0 average?
    c. What are the possibilities if he has a 2.0 average?

13. Consider the vectors

$$x = \begin{pmatrix} x_1 \\ x_2 \end{pmatrix}, \qquad y = \begin{pmatrix} y_1 \\ y_2 \end{pmatrix}.$$

Show that the vector

$$\tfrac{1}{2}(x + y)$$

has components that are the *averages* of the components of x and y. Generalize this result to the case of n vectors.

14. a. Show that the vector equation

$$x \begin{pmatrix} 3 \\ -4 \end{pmatrix} + y \begin{pmatrix} -4 \\ 5 \end{pmatrix} = \begin{pmatrix} 2 \\ -3 \end{pmatrix}$$

represents two simultaneous linear equations for the two variables x and y.
    b. Solve these equations for x and y and substitute into the vector equation above to check your work.

15. Write the following simultaneous linear equations in vector form

$$ax + by = e$$
$$cx + dy = f.$$

[*Hint:* Follow the form given in Exercise 14.]

16. Suppose that we associate with each person a three-component row vector having the following entries: age, height, and weight. Would it make sense to add together the vectors associated with two different persons? Would it make sense to multiply one of these vectors by a constant?

17. Suppose that we associate with each person leaving a supermarket a row vector whose components give the quantities of each available item that he has purchased. Answer the same questions as those in Exercise 16.

18. Let us associate with each supermarket a column vector whose entries give the prices of each item in the store. Would it make sense to add together the vectors associated with two different supermarkets? Would it make sense to multiply one of these vectors by a constant? Discuss the differences in the situations given in Exercises 16, 17, and 18.

19. Let $x = \begin{pmatrix} x_1 \\ x_2 \end{pmatrix}$. Define $x \geq 0$ to be the conjunction of the statements $x_1 \geq 0$ *and* $x_2 \geq 0$. Define $x \leq 0$ analogously. Now prove that if $x \geq 0$, then $-x \leq 0$.

20. Using the definition in Exercise 19, define $x \geq y$ to mean $x - y \geq 0$, where x and y are vectors of the same shape. Consider the following four vectors:

$$x = \begin{pmatrix} -1 \\ 2 \\ 0 \end{pmatrix}, \qquad y = \begin{pmatrix} -4 \\ 0 \\ -1 \end{pmatrix}, \qquad u = \begin{pmatrix} 1 \\ 1 \\ 1 \end{pmatrix}, \qquad v = \begin{pmatrix} 4 \\ 5 \\ 6 \end{pmatrix}.$$

   a. Show that $x \geq y$.
   b. Show that $u \geq y$.
   c. Is there any relationship between x and u?
   d. Show that $v \geq x$, $v \geq y$, and $v \geq u$.

21. If $x \geq y$ and $y \geq u$, prove that $x \geq u$.

22. If $x^{(1)}, x^{(2)}, \ldots, x^{(n)}$ is a set of n vectors, show how to find a vector u such that $u \geq x^{(i)}$ for all i. Also show how to find a vector v such that $v \leq x^{(i)}$ for all i.

2. THE PRODUCT OF VECTORS; EXAMPLES

The reader may wonder why it is necessary to introduce both column and row vectors when their properties are so similar. This question can be answered in several different ways. First, in many applications two kinds of quantities are studied simultaneously, and it is convenient to represent one of them as a row vector and the other as a column vector. Second, there is a way of combining row and column vectors that is very useful for certain types of calculations. To bring out these points let us look at the following simple economic example.

Example 1. Suppose a man named Smith goes into a grocery store to buy a dozen each of peaches and oranges, a half dozen each of apples and pears, and three lemons. Let us represent his purchases by means of the following row vector:

$$x = [6 \text{ (apples)}, 12 \text{ (peaches)}, 3 \text{ (lemons)}, 12 \text{ (oranges)}, 6 \text{ (pears)}]$$
$$= (6, 12, 3, 12, 6).$$

Suppose that apples are 4 cents each, peaches 6 cents, lemons 9 cents, oranges 5 cents, and pears 7 cents. We can then represent the prices of these items as a column vector

$$y = \begin{pmatrix} 4 \\ 6 \\ 9 \\ 5 \\ 7 \end{pmatrix} \quad \begin{matrix} \text{cents per apple} \\ \text{cents per peach} \\ \text{cents per lemon} \\ \text{cents per orange} \\ \text{cents per pear.} \end{matrix}$$

The obvious question is, what is the total amount that Smith must pay for his purchases? We would like to multiply the quantity vector x by the price vector y, and we would like the result to be Smith's bill. We see that our multiplication should have the following form:

$$x \cdot y = (6, 12, 3, 12, 6) \begin{pmatrix} 4 \\ 6 \\ 9 \\ 5 \\ 7 \end{pmatrix}$$

$$= 6 \cdot 4 + 12 \cdot 6 + 3 \cdot 9 + 12 \cdot 5 + 6 \cdot 7$$
$$= 24 + 72 + 27 + 60 + 42$$
$$= 225 \text{ cents or } \$2.25.$$

This is, of course, the computation that the cashier performs in figuring Smith's bill.

We shall adopt in general the above definition of multiplication of row times column vectors.

DEFINITION. Let u be a row vector and v a column vector each having the same number n of components; then we shall define the product $u \cdot v$ to be

$$u \cdot v = u_1 v_1 + u_2 v_2 + \cdots + u_n v_n.$$

Notice that we always write the row vector first and the column vector second, and this is the only kind of vector multiplication that we consider. Some examples of vector multiplication are

$$(2, 1, -1) \cdot \begin{pmatrix} 3 \\ -1 \\ 4 \end{pmatrix} = 2 \cdot 3 + 1 \cdot (-1) + (-1) \cdot 4 = 1,$$

$$(1, 0) \cdot \begin{pmatrix} 0 \\ 1 \end{pmatrix} = 1 \cdot 0 + 0 \cdot 1 = 0 + 0 = 0.$$

Note that the result of vector multiplication is always a *number*.

Example 2. Consider an oversimplified economy that has three industries, which we call coal, electricity, and steel, and three consumers 1, 2, and 3. Suppose that each consumer uses some of the output of each industry and also that each industry uses some of the output of each other industry. We assume that the amounts used are positive or zero, since using a negative quantity has no immediate interpretation. We can represent the needs of each consumer and industry by a three-component demand (row) vector, the first component measuring the amount of coal needed by the consumer or industry; the second component the amount of electricity needed; and the third component the amount of steel needed, in some convenient units. For example, the demand vectors of the three consumers might be

$$d_1 = (3, 2, 5), \quad d_2 = (0, 17, 1), \quad d_3 = (4, 6, 12)$$

and the demand vectors of each of the industries might be

$$d_C = (0, 1, 4), \qquad d_E = (20, 0, 8), \qquad d_S = (30, 5, 0),$$

where the subscript C stands for coal; the subscript E, for electricity; and the subscript S, for steel. Then the total demand for these goods by the consumers is given by the sum

$$d_1 + d_2 + d_3 = (3, 2, 5) + (0, 17, 1) + (4, 6, 12) = (7, 25, 18).$$

Also, the total industrial demand for these goods is given by the sum

$$d_C + d_E + d_S = (0, 1, 4) + (20, 0, 8) + (30, 5, 0) = (50, 6, 12).$$

Therefore the total overall demand is given by the sum

$$(7, 25, 18) + (50, 6, 12) = (57, 31, 30).$$

Suppose now that the price of coal is \$1 per unit, the price of electricity is \$2 per unit, and the price of steel is \$4 per unit. Then these prices can be represented by the column vector

$$p = \begin{pmatrix} 1 \\ 2 \\ 4 \end{pmatrix}.$$

Consider the steel industry: it sells a total of 30 units of steel at \$4 per unit so that its total income is \$120. Its bill for the various goods is given by the vector product

$$d_S \cdot p = (30, 5, 0) \cdot \begin{pmatrix} 1 \\ 2 \\ 4 \end{pmatrix} = 30 + 10 + 0 = \$40.$$

Hence the profit of the steel industry is \$120 − \$40 = \$80. In the exercises below the profits of the other industries will be found.

This model of an economy is unrealistic in two senses. First, we have not chosen realistic numbers for the various quantities involved. Second, and more important, we have neglected the fact that the more an industry produces the more inputs it requires. The latter complication will be introduced in Section 13.

Example 3. Consider the rectangular coordinate system in the plane shown in Figure 1. A two-component row vector $x = (a, b)$ can be regarded as a point in the plane located by means of the coordinate axes as shown. The point x can be found by starting at the origin of coordinates O and moving a distance a along the x_1 axis; then moving a distance b along a line parallel to the x_2 axis. If we have two such points, say $x = (a, b)$ and $y = (c, d)$, then the points $x + y$, $-x$, $-y$, $x - y$, $y - x$, $-x - y$ have the geometric significance shown in Figure 2.

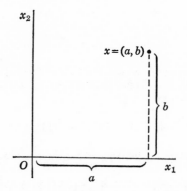

Figure 1

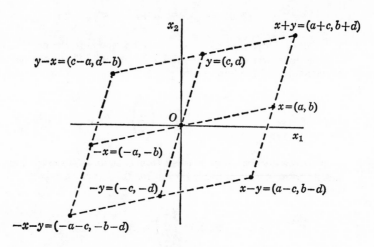

Figure 2

The idea of multiplying a row vector by a number can also be given a geometric meaning (see Figure 3). There we have plotted the point corresponding to the vector $x = (1, 2)$, and $2x$, $\frac{1}{2}x$, $-x$, and $-2x$. Observe that all these points lie on a line through the origin of coordinates. Another vector quantity that has geometrical significance is the vector $z = ax + (1 - a)y$, where a is any number between 0 and 1. Observe in Figure 4 that the points z all lie on the line segment between the points x and y. If $a = \frac{1}{2}$, the corresponding point on the line segment is the midpoint of the segment. Thus, if $x = (a, b)$ and $y = (c, d)$, then the point

$$\tfrac{1}{2}x + \tfrac{1}{2}y = \tfrac{1}{2}(a, b) + \tfrac{1}{2}(c, d)$$

$$= \left(\frac{a + c}{2}, \frac{b + d}{2} \right)$$

is the midpoint of the line segment between x and y.

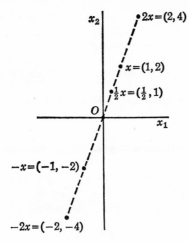

Figure 3

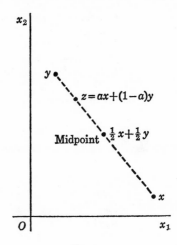

Figure 4

EXERCISES

1. Compute the quantities (*a*) through (*d*) for the following vectors:

$$u = (1, -1, 4), \qquad x = (0, 1, 2)$$

$$v = \begin{pmatrix} 5 \\ 0 \\ 1 \end{pmatrix}, \qquad y = \begin{pmatrix} -1 \\ -1 \\ 2 \end{pmatrix}.$$

a. $u \cdot v + x \cdot y = ?$ [*Ans.* 12.]
b. $(-u + 5x) \cdot (3v - 2y) = ?$
c. $5u \cdot v + 10[x \cdot (2v - y)] = ?$ [*Ans.* 55.]
d. $2[(u - x) \cdot (v + y)] = ?$

2. Plot the points corresponding to the row vectors $x = (3, 4)$ and $y = (-2, 7)$. Then compute and plot the following vectors.
a. $\frac{1}{2}x + \frac{1}{2}y$.   b. $x + y$.   c. $x - 2y$.
d. $\frac{4}{5}x + \frac{1}{5}y$.   e. $3x - 2y$.   f. $4y - 3x$.

3. If $x = (1, -1, 2)$ and $y = (0, 1, 3)$ are points in space, what is the midpoint of the line segment joining x to y?   [*Ans.* $(\frac{1}{2}, 0, \frac{5}{2})$.]

4. If u is a three-component row vector, v is a three-component column vector having the same number of components, and a is a number, prove that $a(u \cdot v) = (au) \cdot v = u \cdot (av)$.

5. Suppose that Brown, Jones, and Smith go to the grocery store and purchase the following items:

> Brown: two apples, six lemons, and five pears;
> Jones: two dozen peaches, two lemons, and two dozen oranges;
> Smith: ten apples, one dozen peaches, two dozen oranges, and a half dozen pears.

a. How many different kinds of items did they purchase?   [*Ans.* 5.]
b. Write each of their purchases as row vectors with as many components as the answer found in *a*.

    c. Using the price vector given in Example 1, compute each man's grocery bill.   [*Ans.* $0.97; $2.82; $2.74.]

    d. By means of vector addition find the total amount of their purchases as a row vector.

    e. Compute in two different ways the total amount spent by the three men at the grocery store.   [*Ans.* $6.53.]

6. Prove that vector multiplication satisfies the following two properties:

$$\text{(i)} \qquad u \cdot (av) = a(u \cdot v),$$
$$\text{(ii)} \qquad u \cdot (v + w) = u \cdot v + u \cdot w,$$

where u is a three-component row vector, v and w are three-component column vectors, and a is a number.

7. The production of a book involves several steps: first it must be set in type, then it must be printed, and finally it must be supplied with covers and bound. Suppose the typesetter charges $6 an hour, paper costs $\frac{1}{4}$ cent per sheet, the printer charges 11 cents for each minute that his press runs, the cover costs 28 cents, and the binder charges 15 cents to bind each book. Suppose now that a publisher wishes to print a book that requires 300 hours of work by the typesetter, 220 sheets of paper per book, and 5 minutes of press time per book.

    a. Write a five-component row vector that gives the requirements for the first book. Write another row vector that gives the requirements for the second, third, . . . copies of the book. Write a five-component column vector whose components give the prices of the various requirements for each book, in the same order as they are listed in the requirement vectors above.

    b. Using vector multiplication, find the cost of publishing one copy of a book.   [*Ans.* $1801.53.]

    c. Using vector addition and multiplication, find the cost of printing a first-edition run of 5000 copies.   [*Ans.* $9450.]

    d. Assuming that the type plates from the first edition are used again, find the cost of printing a second edition of 5000 copies.

          [*Ans.* $7650.]

8. Perform the following calculations for Example 2.

    a. Compute the amount that each industry and each consumer has to pay for the goods it receives.

    b. Compute the profit made by each of the industries.

    c. Find the total amount of money that is paid out by all the industries and consumers.

    d. Find the proportion of the total amount of money found in *c.* paid out by the industries. Find the proportion of the total money that is paid out by the consumers.

9. A building contractor has accepted orders for five ranch style houses, seven Cape Cod houses, and twelve Colonial style houses. Write a three-component row vector x whose components give the numbers of each type of house to be built. Suppose that he knows that a ranch style house requires 20 units of wood; a Cape Cod, 18 units; and a Colonial style, 25 units of wood. Write a column vector u whose components give the various quantities of wood needed for each type of house. Find the total amount of wood needed by computing the vector product xu.

          [*Ans.* 526.]

10. Let $x = (x_1 \quad x_2)$ and let a and b be the vectors

$$a = \begin{pmatrix} 3 \\ 4 \end{pmatrix}, \qquad b = \begin{pmatrix} 2 \\ 3 \end{pmatrix}.$$

If $x \cdot a = -1$ and $x \cdot b = 7$, determine x_1 and x_2.

[*Ans.* $x_1 = -31$; $x_2 = 23$.]

11. Let $x = (x_1 \quad x_2)$ and let a and b be the vectors

$$a = \begin{pmatrix} 4 \\ 8 \end{pmatrix}, \qquad b = \begin{pmatrix} 1 \\ 2 \end{pmatrix}.$$

If $x \cdot a = x_1$ and $x \cdot b = x_2$, determine x_1 and x_2.

12. Consider the vectors

$$x = (5, 8), \qquad y = (3, 7), \qquad f = \begin{pmatrix} 1 \\ 1 \end{pmatrix}.$$

    a. Compute $\frac{1}{2}xf$ and $\frac{1}{2}yf$, and show that these numbers are the averages of the components of x and y, respectively.   [*Ans.* 6.5, 5.]

    b. Compute $\frac{1}{4}(x + y)f$ and give an interpretation for this number.

[*Partial Ans.* 5.75.]

13. Let x and y be two n-component row vectors, and let f be an n-component column vector all of whose entries are 1's.

    a. Compute $(1/n)xf$ and $(1/n)yf$ and interpret the result.

    b. Compute $(1/2n)(x + y)f$ and interpret the result.

[*Hint:* Exercise 12 is a special case.]

14. Consider an experiment in which there are two outcomes; we get \$2 with probability $\frac{1}{3}$ and \$3 with probability $\frac{2}{3}$. Let

$$a = (2, 3) \quad \text{and} \quad p = \begin{pmatrix} \frac{1}{3} \\ \frac{2}{3} \end{pmatrix}.$$

Show that the expected outcome of the experiment is ap.

15. If an experiment has outcomes $a_1, a_2, \ldots, a_n$ occurring with probabilities $p_1, p_2, \ldots, p_n$, define the vectors

$$a = (a_1, \ldots, a_n) \quad \text{and} \quad p = \begin{pmatrix} p_1 \\ p_2 \\ \vdots \\ p_n \end{pmatrix}.$$

Show that the expected outcome is ap.

16. Consider the vectors

$$a = (a_1, a_2), \qquad x = \begin{pmatrix} x_1 \\ x_2 \end{pmatrix}$$

and a number c. Show that the equation $ax = c$ is a single equation in two variables.

17. Consider the vectors

$$a = (a_1, a_2), \qquad b = (b_1, b_2), \qquad x = \begin{pmatrix} x_1 \\ x_2 \end{pmatrix}$$

and two numbers c_1 and c_2. Show that the equations

$$ax = c_1, \qquad bx = c_2$$

represent two simultaneous equations in two unknowns.

18. Show that every set of two simultaneous equations in two unknowns can be written as in Exercise 17.

3. MATRICES AND THEIR COMBINATION WITH VECTORS

A matrix is a rectangular array of numbers written in the form

$$A = \begin{pmatrix} a_{11} & a_{12} & \cdots & a_{1n} \\ a_{21} & a_{22} & \cdots & a_{2n} \\ \cdot & \cdot & \cdots & \cdot \\ a_{m1} & a_{m2} & \cdots & a_{mn} \end{pmatrix}.$$

Here the letters a_{ij} stand for real numbers and m and n are integers. Observe that m is the number of rows and n is the number of columns of the matrix. For this reason we call it an $m \times n$ matrix. If $m = n$ the matrix is *square*. The following are examples of matrices.

$$(1, 2, 3), \qquad \begin{pmatrix} 1 \\ 2 \\ 3 \end{pmatrix}, \qquad \begin{pmatrix} 1 & -1 \\ -2 & 2 \end{pmatrix},$$

$$\begin{pmatrix} 1 & 0 & 0 & 0 \\ 0 & 1 & 0 & 0 \\ 0 & 0 & 1 & 0 \\ 0 & 0 & 0 & 1 \end{pmatrix}, \qquad \begin{pmatrix} 1 & 7 & -8 & 9 & 10 \\ 3 & -1 & 14 & 2 & -6 \\ 0 & 3 & -5 & 7 & 0 \end{pmatrix}.$$

The first example is a row vector that is a 1×3 matrix; the second is a column vector that is a 3×1 matrix; the third example is a 2×2 square matrix; the fourth is a 4×4 square matrix; and the last is a 3×5 matrix.

Two matrices having the same shape (that is, having the same number of rows and columns) are said to be *equal* if and only if the corresponding entries are equal.

Recall that in Chapter 3, Section 9, we found that a matrix arose naturally in the consideration of a Markov-chain process. To give another example of how matrices occur in practice and are used in connection with vectors we consider the following example.

Example 1. Suppose that a building contractor has accepted orders for five ranch style houses, seven Cape Cod houses, and twelve Colonial style houses. We can represent his orders by means of a row vector $x = (5, 7, 12)$. The contractor is familiar, of course, with the kinds of "raw materials" that go into each type of house. Let us suppose that these raw materials are steel, wood, glass, paint, and labor. The numbers in the matrix below give the amounts of each raw material going into each type of house, expressed in convenient units. (The numbers are put in arbitrarily, and are not meant to be realistic.)

$$
\begin{array}{c}
\\
\text{Ranch:}\\
\text{Cape Cod:}\\
\text{Colonial:}
\end{array}
\begin{array}{ccccc}
\text{Steel} & \text{Wood} & \text{Glass} & \text{Paint} & \text{Labor}\\
\left(\begin{array}{ccccc}
5 & 20 & 16 & 7 & 17\\
7 & 18 & 12 & 9 & 21\\
6 & 25 & 8 & 5 & 13
\end{array}\right) = R
\end{array}
$$

Observe that each row of the matrix is a five-component row vector that gives the amounts of each raw material needed for a given kind of house. Similarly, each column of the matrix is a three-component column vector that gives the amounts of a given raw material needed for each kind of house. Clearly, a matrix is a succinct way of summarizing this information.

Suppose now that the contractor wishes to compute how much of each raw material to obtain in order to fulfill his contracts. Let us denote the matrix above by R; then he would like to obtain something like the product xR, and he would like the product to tell him what orders to make out. The product should have the following form:

$$
xR = (5, 7, 12)\begin{pmatrix}
5 & 20 & 16 & 7 & 17\\
7 & 18 & 12 & 9 & 21\\
6 & 25 & 8 & 5 & 13
\end{pmatrix}
$$

$$
\begin{aligned}
&= (5\cdot5 + 7\cdot7 + 12\cdot6, 5\cdot20 + 7\cdot18 + 12\cdot25,\\
&\quad\ 5\cdot16 + 7\cdot12 + 12\cdot8, 5\cdot7 + 7\cdot9 + 12\cdot5,\\
&\quad\ 5\cdot17 + 7\cdot21 + 12\cdot13)\\
&= (146, 526, 260, 158, 388).
\end{aligned}
$$

Thus we see that the contractor should order 146 units of steel, 526 units of wood, 260 units of glass, 158 units of paint, and 388 units of labor. Observe that the answer we get is a five-component row vector and that each entry in this vector is obtained by taking the vector product of x times the corresponding column of the matrix R.

The contractor is also interested in the prices that he will have to pay for these materials. Suppose that steel costs $15 per unit, wood costs $8 per unit, glass costs $5 per unit, paint costs $1 per unit, and labor costs $10 per unit. Then we can write the cost as a column vector as follows:

$$
y = \begin{pmatrix}
15\\
8\\
5\\
1\\
10
\end{pmatrix}.
$$

Here the product Ry should give the costs of each type of house, so that the multiplication should have the form

$$Ry = \begin{pmatrix} 5 & 20 & 16 & 7 & 17 \\ 7 & 18 & 12 & 9 & 21 \\ 6 & 25 & 8 & 5 & 13 \end{pmatrix} \begin{pmatrix} 15 \\ 8 \\ 5 \\ 1 \\ 10 \end{pmatrix}$$

$$= \begin{pmatrix} 5 \cdot 15 + 20 \cdot 8 + 16 \cdot 5 + 7 \cdot 1 + 17 \cdot 10 \\ 7 \cdot 15 + 18 \cdot 8 + 12 \cdot 5 + 9 \cdot 1 + 21 \cdot 10 \\ 6 \cdot 15 + 25 \cdot 8 + 8 \cdot 5 + 5 \cdot 1 + 13 \cdot 10 \end{pmatrix}$$

$$= \begin{pmatrix} 492 \\ 528 \\ 465 \end{pmatrix}.$$

Thus the cost of materials for the ranch style house is \$492, for the Cape Cod house \$528, and for the Colonial house \$465.

The final question the contractor might ask is what is the total cost of raw materials for all the houses he will build. It is easy to see that this is given by the vector xRy. We can find it in two ways as shown below.

$$xRy = (xR)y = (146, 526, 260, 158, 388) \cdot \begin{pmatrix} 15 \\ 8 \\ 5 \\ 1 \\ 10 \end{pmatrix} = 11{,}736.$$

$$xRy = x(Ry) = (5, 7, 12) \cdot \begin{pmatrix} 492 \\ 528 \\ 465 \end{pmatrix} = 11{,}736.$$

The total cost is then \$11,736.

We shall adopt, in general, the following definitions for the multiplication of a matrix times a row or a column vector.

DEFINITION. Let A be an $m \times n$ matrix, let x be an m-component row vector, and let u be an n-component column vector; then we define the products xA and Au as follows:

$$xA = (x_1, x_2, \ldots, x_m) \begin{pmatrix} a_{11} & a_{12} & \cdots & a_{1n} \\ a_{21} & a_{22} & \cdots & a_{2n} \\ \vdots & & & \\ a_{m1} & a_{m2} & \cdots & a_{mn} \end{pmatrix}$$

$$= (x_1 a_{11} + x_2 a_{21} + \cdots + x_m a_{m1}, x_1 a_{12} + x_2 a_{22} + \cdots + x_m a_{m2}, \ldots, x_1 a_{1n} + x_2 a_{2n} + \cdots + x_m a_{mn})$$

$$Au = \begin{pmatrix} a_{11} & a_{12} & \cdots & a_{1n} \\ a_{21} & a_{22} & \cdots & a_{2n} \\ \cdot & & & \\ \cdot & & & \\ \cdot & & & \\ a_{m1} & a_{m2} & \cdots & a_{mn} \end{pmatrix} \begin{pmatrix} u_1 \\ u_2 \\ \cdot \\ \cdot \\ \cdot \\ u_n \end{pmatrix}$$

$$= \begin{pmatrix} a_{11}u_1 + a_{12}u_2 + \cdots + a_{1n}u_n \\ a_{21}u_1 + a_{22}u_2 + \cdots + a_{2n}u_n \\ \cdot \\ \cdot \\ \cdot \\ a_{m1}u_1 + a_{m2}u_2 + \cdots + a_{mn}u_n \end{pmatrix}.$$

The reader will find these formulas easy to work with if he observes that each entry in the products xA or Au is obtained by vector multiplication of x or u by a column or row of the matrix A. Notice that in order to multiply a row vector times a matrix, the number of rows of the matrix must equal the number of components of the vector, and the result is another row vector; similarly, to multiply a matrix times a column vector, the number of columns of the matrix must equal the number of components of the vector, and the result of such a multiplication is another column vector.

Some numerical examples of the multiplication of vectors and matrices are:

$$(1, 0, -1) \begin{pmatrix} 3 & 1 \\ 2 & 3 \\ 2 & 8 \end{pmatrix} = (1 \cdot 3 + 0 \cdot 2 - 1 \cdot 2, \ 1 \cdot 1 + 0 \cdot 3 - 1 \cdot 8)$$

$$= (1, -7);$$

$$\begin{pmatrix} 3 & 1 & 2 \\ 2 & 3 & 8 \end{pmatrix} \begin{pmatrix} 1 \\ -1 \\ 2 \end{pmatrix} = \begin{pmatrix} 3 - 1 + 4 \\ 2 - 3 + 16 \end{pmatrix} = \begin{pmatrix} 6 \\ 15 \end{pmatrix};$$

$$\begin{pmatrix} 3 & 2 & -1 \\ 1 & 0 & 2 \\ 0 & 3 & 1 \\ 5 & -4 & 7 \\ -3 & 2 & -1 \end{pmatrix} \begin{pmatrix} 1 \\ 0 \\ -2 \end{pmatrix} = \begin{pmatrix} 5 \\ -3 \\ -2 \\ -9 \\ -1 \end{pmatrix}.$$

Observe that if x is an m-component row vector and A is $m \times n$, then xA is an n-component row vector; similarly, if u is an n-component column vector, then Au is an m-component column vector. These facts can be observed in the examples above.

Example 2. In Example 1 of Section 2 assume that Smith has two stores at which he can make his purchases, and let us say that the prices charged at these two stores are slightly different. Let the price vector at the second store be

$$y = \begin{pmatrix} 5 \\ 5 \\ 10 \\ 4 \\ 6 \end{pmatrix} \begin{matrix} \text{cents per apple} \\ \text{cents per peach} \\ \text{cents per lemon} \\ \text{cents per orange} \\ \text{cents per pear.} \end{matrix}$$

Smith now has the option of buying all his purchases at store 1, all at store 2, or buying just the lower-priced items at the store charging the lower price. To help him decide, we form a price matrix, as follows:

$$P = \begin{array}{ccc} \text{Prices} & \text{Prices} & \text{Minimum} \\ \text{store 1} & \text{store 2} & \text{price} \end{array} \begin{pmatrix} 4 & 5 & 4 \\ 6 & 5 & 5 \\ 9 & 10 & 9 \\ 5 & 4 & 4 \\ 7 & 6 & 6 \end{pmatrix}.$$

The first column lists the prices of store 1, the second the prices of store 2, and the third the lesser of these two prices. To compute Smith's bill under the three possible ways he can make his purchases, we compute the product xP, as follows:

$$xP = (6, 12, 3, 12, 6) \begin{pmatrix} 4 & 5 & 4 \\ 6 & 5 & 5 \\ 9 & 10 & 9 \\ 5 & 4 & 4 \\ 7 & 6 & 6 \end{pmatrix} = (225, 204, 195).$$

We thus see that if Smith buys only in store 1 his bill will be \$2.25, if he buys only in store 2 his bill will be \$2.04, but if he buys each item in the cheaper of the two stores (apples and lemons in store 1, the rest in store 2) his bill will be \$1.95.

Exactly what Smith will, or should, do depends on circumstances. If both stores are equally close to him, he will probably split his purchases and obtain the smallest bill. If store 1 is close and store 2 is very far away, he may buy everything at store 1. If store 2 is closer and store 1 is far enough away so that the 9 cents he would save by splitting his purchases is not worth the effort, he may buy everything at store 2.

The example just cited is an example of a *decision problem*. In such problems it is necessary to choose one of several courses of action, or *strategies*. For each such course of action or strategy, it is possible to compute the cost or *worth* of such a strategy. The decision maker will choose a strategy with maximum worth.

Sometimes the worth of an outcome must be measured in psychological units; we then say that we measure the *utility* of an outcome. For the purposes of this book we shall always assume that the utility of an outcome is measured in monetary units, so that we can compare the worths of two different outcomes to the decision maker.

Many of the applications of mathematics to business and industrial problems consist in formulating such problems as decision problems and then choosing a strategy that has maximum worth. We shall discuss such decision problems in greater detail in the next example, and in parts of later chapters of the book.

Example 3. As a second example of a decision problem consider the following. An urn contains 5 red, 3 green, and 1 white ball. One ball will be drawn at random, and then payments will be made to holders of lottery tickets according to the following schedule:

$$
M = \begin{pmatrix} \text{Red} & \text{Green} & \text{White} \\ 1 & 4 & 0 \\ 3 & 1 & 0 \\ 0 & 0 & 16 \end{pmatrix} \begin{matrix} \text{Ticket 1} \\ \text{Ticket 2} \\ \text{Ticket 3} \end{matrix}
$$

Thus, if a red ball is selected, holders of ticket 1 will get $1, holders of ticket 2 will get $3, and holders of ticket 3 will get nothing. If green is chosen, the payments are 4, 1, and 0, respectively. And if white is chosen, holders of ticket 3 get $16, and the others nothing. Which ticket would we prefer to have?

Our decision will depend upon the concept of expected value discussed in the preceding chapter. The statements, "draw a red ball," "draw a green ball," "draw a white ball," have probabilities $\frac{5}{9}$, $\frac{3}{9}$, and $\frac{1}{9}$, respectively. From these probabilities we can calculate the expected value of holding each of the lottery tickets as described in the last chapter. However, a compact way of performing all these calculations is to compute the product Mp, where p is the probability vector

$$
p = \begin{pmatrix} \frac{5}{9} \\ \frac{3}{9} \\ \frac{1}{9} \end{pmatrix}.
$$

From this we have

$$
Mp = \begin{pmatrix} 1 & 4 & 0 \\ 3 & 1 & 0 \\ 0 & 0 & 16 \end{pmatrix} \begin{pmatrix} \frac{5}{9} \\ \frac{3}{9} \\ \frac{1}{9} \end{pmatrix}
$$

$$
= \begin{pmatrix} 1\cdot\frac{5}{9} + 4\cdot\frac{3}{9} + 0\cdot\frac{1}{9} \\ 3\cdot\frac{5}{9} + 1\cdot\frac{3}{9} + 0\cdot\frac{1}{9} \\ 0\cdot\frac{5}{9} + 0\cdot\frac{3}{9} + 16\cdot\frac{1}{9} \end{pmatrix} = \begin{pmatrix} \frac{17}{9} \\ \frac{18}{9} \\ \frac{16}{9} \end{pmatrix}.
$$

It is easy to see that the three components of Mp give the expected values of holding lottery tickets 1, 2, and 3, respectively. From these numbers we can see that ticket 2 is the best one, 1 is the next best, and 3 is third best.

If we have to buy the tickets, then the cost of the tickets will determine which is the best buy. If each ticket costs $3, we would better off by not buying any ticket at all, since we would then expect to lose money. If each ticket costs $1, then we should buy ticket 2, since it would give us a net expected gain of $2 − $1 = $1. If the first two tickets cost $2.10, and the third $1.50, we should buy the third ticket, since it is the only one for which we would have a positive net expectation.

EXERCISES

1. Perform the following multiplications:

a. $\begin{pmatrix} 1 & -1 \\ -2 & 2 \end{pmatrix}\begin{pmatrix} 7 \\ 2 \end{pmatrix} = ?$

b. $(3, -4)\begin{pmatrix} 1 & -1 \\ -2 & 2 \end{pmatrix} = ?$ 　　　　　　　　[Ans. $(11, -11)$.]

c. $\begin{pmatrix} 1 & 3 & 0 \\ 7 & -1 & 3 \\ -8 & 14 & -5 \\ 9 & 2 & 7 \\ 10 & -6 & 0 \end{pmatrix} \cdot \begin{pmatrix} 3 \\ -1 \\ 1 \end{pmatrix} = ?$

d. $(2, 2)\begin{pmatrix} 1 & -1 \\ -1 & 1 \end{pmatrix} = ?$ 　　　　　　　　[Ans. $(0, 0)$.]

e. $\begin{pmatrix} 1 & -1 \\ -1 & 1 \end{pmatrix}\begin{pmatrix} 5 \\ 5 \end{pmatrix} = ?$

f. $(0, 2, -3)\begin{pmatrix} 1 & 7 & -8 & 9 & 10 \\ 3 & -1 & 14 & 2 & -6 \\ 0 & 3 & -5 & 7 & 0 \end{pmatrix} = ?$

g. $(x_1, x_2)\begin{pmatrix} a & b \\ c & d \end{pmatrix} = ?$ 　　　　[Ans. $(ax_1 + cx_2, bx_1 + dx_2)$.]

h. $\begin{pmatrix} a & b \\ c & d \end{pmatrix}\begin{pmatrix} u_1 \\ u_2 \end{pmatrix} = ?$

i. $\begin{pmatrix} 1 & 0 & 0 \\ 0 & 1 & 0 \\ 0 & 0 & 1 \end{pmatrix}\begin{pmatrix} u_1 \\ u_2 \\ u_3 \end{pmatrix} = ?$

j. $(x_1, x_2, x_3)\begin{pmatrix} 1 & 0 & 0 \\ 0 & 1 & 0 \\ 0 & 0 & 1 \end{pmatrix} = ?$

2. What number does the matrix in parts i. and j. above resemble?

3. Notice that in Exercise 1d. above the product of a row vector, none of whose components is zero, times a matrix, none of whose components is zero, yields the zero row vector. Find another example which is similar to this one. Answer the analogous question for Exercise 1(e).

4. When possible, solve for the indicated quantities.

a. $(x_1, x_2)\begin{pmatrix} 0 & -1 \\ 7 & 3 \end{pmatrix} = (7, 0)$. Find the vector x.   [*Ans.* (3, 1).]

b. $(2, -1)\begin{pmatrix} a & b \\ c & d \end{pmatrix} = (6, 3)$. Find the matrix $\begin{pmatrix} a & b \\ c & d \end{pmatrix}$. In this case can you find more than one solution?

c. $\begin{pmatrix} 1 & -1 \\ -1 & 1 \end{pmatrix}\begin{pmatrix} u_1 \\ u_2 \end{pmatrix} = \begin{pmatrix} 3 \\ 4 \end{pmatrix}$. Find the vector u.

d. $\begin{pmatrix} -1 & 4 \\ 2 & -8 \end{pmatrix}\begin{pmatrix} u_1 \\ u_2 \end{pmatrix} = \begin{pmatrix} 3 \\ -6 \end{pmatrix}$. Find u. How many solutions can you find?

$$\left[Ans.\ u = \begin{pmatrix} 4k - 3 \\ k \end{pmatrix},\ \text{for any number } k.\right]$$

5. Solve for the indicated quantities below and give an interpretation for each.

a. $(1, -1)\begin{pmatrix} 0 & 2 \\ -2 & 4 \end{pmatrix} = a(1, -1)$; find a.   [*Ans.* $a = 2$.]

b. $\begin{pmatrix} 1 & 2 \\ 2 & 4 \end{pmatrix}\begin{pmatrix} u_1 \\ u_2 \end{pmatrix} = 5\begin{pmatrix} u_1 \\ u_2 \end{pmatrix}$; find u. How many answers can you find?

$$\left[Ans.\ u = \begin{pmatrix} k \\ 2k \end{pmatrix} \text{ for any number } k.\right]$$

c. $\begin{pmatrix} \frac{5}{8} & \frac{1}{8} \\ \frac{3}{8} & \frac{7}{8} \end{pmatrix}\begin{pmatrix} u_1 \\ u_2 \end{pmatrix} = \begin{pmatrix} u_1 \\ u_2 \end{pmatrix}$; find u. How many answers are there?

6. In Exercise 5 of the preceding section construct the 3×5 matrix whose rows give the various purchases of Brown, Jones, and Smith. Multiply on the right by the five-component price (column) vector to find the three-component column vector whose entries give each person's grocery bill. Multiply on the left by the row vector $x = (1, 1, 1)$ and on the right by the price vector to find the total amount that they spent in the store.

7. In Example 1 of this section, assume that the contractor is to build seven ranch style, three Cape Cod, and five Colonial type houses. Recompute, using matrix multiplication, the total cost of raw materials, in two different ways, as in the example.

8. The following matrix gives the vitamin contents of three food items, in conveniently chosen units:

Vitamin:	A	B	C	D
Food I:	.5	.5	0	0
Food II:	.3	0	.2	.1
Food III:	.1	.1	.2	.5

If we eat 5 units of food I, 10 units of food II, and 8 units of food III, how much of each type of vitamin have we consumed? If we pay only for the vitamin content of each food, paying 10 cents, 20 cents, 25 cents, and 50 cents, respectively, for units of the four vitamins, how much does a unit of each type of food cost? Compute in two ways the total cost of the food we ate.

$$[Ans. \ (6.3, 3.3, 3.6, 5.0); \begin{pmatrix} 15 \\ 13 \\ 33 \end{pmatrix} ; \$4.69.]$$

9. In Example 2, by how much would store 1 have to reduce the price of apples to make Smith's purchases less expensive there than at store 2?

10. In Example 2, find the store at which the total cost to Smith is the least when he wishes to purchase
    a. $x = (4, 1, 2, 0, 1)$.   [Ans. Store 1, cost 47 cents.]
    b. $x = (2, 1, 3, 1, 0)$.
    c. $x = (2, 1, 1, 2, 0)$.

11. In Example 3, let us assume that an individual chooses ticket 1 with probability r_1, ticket 2 with probability r_2, and ticket 3 with probability r_3. Let $r = (r_1, r_2, r_3)$. Give an interpretation for rMp. Compute this for the case that $r_1 = r_2 = r_3 = \frac{1}{3}$.
    $$[Ans. \ rMp = \tfrac{17}{9}, \text{ which is the expected return.}]$$

12. A company is considering which of three methods of production it should use in producing three goods, A, B, and C. The amount of each good produced by each method is shown in the matrix

$$
\begin{array}{cccc}
 & A & B & C & \\
R = & \begin{pmatrix} 2 & 3 & 1 \\ 1 & 2 & 3 \\ 2 & 4 & 1 \end{pmatrix} & \begin{array}{l} \text{Method 1} \\ \text{Method 2} \\ \text{Method 3} \end{array}
\end{array}
$$

Let p be a vector whose components represent the profit per unit for each of the goods. What does the vector Rp represent? Find three different vectors p such that under each of these profit vectors a different method would be most profitable.

$$[Partial \ Ans. \ \text{For } p = \begin{pmatrix} 10 \\ 8 \\ 7 \end{pmatrix} \text{ method 3 is most profitable.}]$$

13. Consider the matrices

$$A = \begin{pmatrix} a_{11} & a_{12} \\ a_{21} & a_{22} \end{pmatrix}, \quad x = \begin{pmatrix} x_1 \\ x_2 \end{pmatrix}, \quad b = \begin{pmatrix} b_1 \\ b_2 \end{pmatrix}.$$

a. Show that the equation $Ax = b$ represents two simultaneous equations in two unknowns.
b. Show that every set of two simultaneous equations in two unknowns can be written in this form for the proper choice of A and b.

14. Consider the matrices

$$P = \begin{pmatrix} \frac{1}{2} & \frac{1}{2} \\ \frac{3}{4} & \frac{1}{4} \end{pmatrix} \quad \text{and} \quad f = \begin{pmatrix} 1 \\ 1 \end{pmatrix}.$$

Show that $Pf = f$. The vector f is called a fixed vector on the right of P.

15. Let P be the matrix of transition probabilities for a Markov chain having n states, and let f be a column matrix all of whose entries are 1's. Show that $Pf = f$. [*Hint:* Exercise 18 provides a special case.]

16. Let $w = (\frac{3}{5}, \frac{2}{5})$ and let P be the matrix in Exercise 14. Show that $wP = w$. For this reason w is called a fixed vector on the left of P.

17. Let A, B, and C be matrices of the same shape, and let h and k be numbers. Use the ordinary rules for numbers plus the definitions of this section to show that the following laws hold.

A1. $A + B = B + A$ (commutative law of addition).
A2. $A + (B + C) = (A + B) + C$ (associative law of addition).
A3. If 0 is the zero matrix of the same shape, then $A + 0 = A$ (additive identity law).
A4. Define $-A = (-1)A$; then $A - A = 0$ (additive inverse law).
S1. $h(kA) = (hk)A$ (mixed associative law).
S2. $1A = A$ for all A (unity law).
S3. $h(A + B) = hA + hB$ (first distributive law).
S4. $(h + k)A = hA + kA$ (second distributive law).

4. THE ADDITION AND MULTIPLICATION OF MATRICES

Two matrices of the same shape—that is, having the same number of rows and columns—can be added together by adding corresponding components. For example, if A and B are two 2×3 matrices, we have

$$A + B = \begin{pmatrix} a_{11} & a_{12} & a_{13} \\ a_{21} & a_{22} & a_{23} \end{pmatrix} + \begin{pmatrix} b_{11} & b_{12} & b_{13} \\ b_{21} & b_{22} & b_{23} \end{pmatrix}$$

$$= \begin{pmatrix} a_{11} + b_{11} & a_{12} + b_{12} & a_{13} + b_{13} \\ a_{21} + b_{21} & a_{22} + b_{22} & a_{23} + b_{23} \end{pmatrix}.$$

Observe that the addition of vectors (row or column) is simply a special case of the addition of matrices. Numerical examples of the addition of matrices are

$$(1, 0, -2) + (0, 5, 0) = (1, 5, -2),$$

$$\begin{pmatrix} 1 & 0 \\ 0 & 1 \end{pmatrix} + \begin{pmatrix} -1 & 0 \\ 0 & -1 \end{pmatrix} = \begin{pmatrix} 0 & 0 \\ 0 & 0 \end{pmatrix},$$

$$\begin{pmatrix} 7 & 0 & 0 \\ -3 & 1 & -6 \\ 4 & 0 & 7 \\ 0 & -2 & -2 \\ 1 & 1 & 1 \end{pmatrix} + \begin{pmatrix} -8 & 0 & 1 \\ 4 & 5 & -1 \\ 0 & 3 & 0 \\ -1 & 1 & -1 \\ 0 & -4 & 2 \end{pmatrix} = \begin{pmatrix} -1 & 0 & 1 \\ 1 & 6 & -7 \\ 4 & 3 & 7 \\ -1 & -1 & -3 \\ 1 & -3 & 3 \end{pmatrix}.$$

Other examples occur in the exercises. The reader should observe that we do *not* add matrices of different shapes.

If A is a matrix and k is any number, we define the matrix kA as

$$kA = k \begin{pmatrix} a_{11} & a_{12} & \cdots & a_{1n} \\ a_{21} & a_{22} & \cdots & a_{2n} \\ & \cdot & \cdots & \cdot \\ a_{m1} & a_{m2} & \cdots & a_{mn} \end{pmatrix} = \begin{pmatrix} ka_{11} & ka_{12} & \cdots & ka_{1n} \\ ka_{21} & ka_{22} & \cdots & ka_{2n} \\ & \cdot & \cdots & \cdot \\ ka_{m1} & ka_{m2} & \cdots & ka_{mn} \end{pmatrix}.$$

Observe that this is merely componentwise multiplication, as was the analogous concept for vectors. Examples of multiplication of matrices by constants are

$$-2 \begin{pmatrix} 7 & -2 & 8 \\ 0 & 5 & -1 \end{pmatrix} = \begin{pmatrix} -14 & 4 & -16 \\ 0 & -10 & 2 \end{pmatrix},$$

$$6 \begin{pmatrix} 1 & 0 \\ 0 & 1 \\ 3 & -4 \end{pmatrix} = \begin{pmatrix} 6 & 0 \\ 0 & 6 \\ 18 & -24 \end{pmatrix}.$$

The multiplication of a vector by a number is, of course, a special case of the multiplication of a matrix by a number.

Under certain conditions two matrices can be multiplied together to give a new matrix. As an example, let A be a 2×3 matrix and B be a 3×2 matrix. Then the product AB is found as

$$AB = \begin{pmatrix} a_{11} & a_{12} & a_{13} \\ a_{21} & a_{22} & a_{23} \end{pmatrix} \begin{pmatrix} b_{11} & b_{12} \\ b_{21} & b_{22} \\ b_{31} & b_{32} \end{pmatrix}$$

$$= \begin{pmatrix} a_{11}b_{11} + a_{12}b_{21} + a_{13}b_{31} & a_{11}b_{12} + a_{12}b_{22} + a_{13}b_{32} \\ a_{21}b_{11} + a_{22}b_{21} + a_{23}b_{31} & a_{21}b_{12} + a_{22}b_{22} + a_{23}b_{32} \end{pmatrix}.$$

Observe that the product is a 2×2 matrix. Also notice that each entry in the new matrix is the product of one of the rows of A times one of the columns of B; for example, the entry in the second row and first column is found as the product

$$(a_{21} \quad a_{22} \quad a_{23}) \begin{pmatrix} b_{11} \\ b_{21} \\ b_{31} \end{pmatrix} = a_{21}b_{11} + a_{22}b_{21} + a_{23}b_{31}.$$

The following definition holds for the general case of matrix multiplication:

DEFINITION. Let A be an $m \times k$ matrix and B be a $k \times n$ matrix; then the product matrix $C = AB$ is an $m \times n$ matrix whose components are

$$c_{ij} = (a_{i1} \quad a_{i2} \quad \cdots \quad a_{ik}) \begin{pmatrix} b_{1j} \\ b_{2j} \\ \cdot \\ \cdot \\ \cdot \\ b_{kj} \end{pmatrix}$$

$$= a_{i1}b_{1j} + a_{i2}b_{2j} + \cdots + a_{ik}b_{kj}.$$

The important things to remember about this definition are: first, in order to be able to multiply matrix A times matrix B, the number of columns of A must be equal to the number of rows of B; second, the product matrix $C = AB$ has the same number of rows as A and the same number of columns as B; finally, to get the entry in the ith row and jth column of AB we multiply the ith row of A times the jth column of B. Notice that the product of a vector times a matrix is a special case of matrix multiplication.

Below are several examples of matrix multiplication:

$$\begin{pmatrix} 2 & -1 \\ 0 & 3 \end{pmatrix}\begin{pmatrix} 7 & 0 \\ -2 & -3 \end{pmatrix} = \begin{pmatrix} 16 & 3 \\ -6 & -9 \end{pmatrix},$$

$$\begin{pmatrix} 3 & 0 & 1 \\ -1 & 2 & 0 \\ 0 & 0 & 2 \end{pmatrix}\begin{pmatrix} 1 & 0 & 0 \\ 0 & -1 & 0 \\ 1 & 1 & 1 \end{pmatrix} = \begin{pmatrix} 4 & 1 & 1 \\ -1 & -2 & 0 \\ 2 & 2 & 2 \end{pmatrix},$$

$$\begin{pmatrix} 3 & 1 & 4 \\ 2 & 0 & 5 \end{pmatrix}\begin{pmatrix} 1 & 3 & 0 & 0 \\ 1 & 1 & 0 & 0 \\ 0 & 0 & 1 & 1 \end{pmatrix} = \begin{pmatrix} 4 & 10 & 4 & 4 \\ 2 & 6 & 5 & 5 \end{pmatrix}.$$

We next ask how we multiply more than two matrices together. Let A be an $m \times h$ matrix, let B be an $h \times k$ matrix, and let C be a $k \times n$ matrix. Then we can certainly define the products $(AB)C$ and $A(BC)$. It turns out that these two products are equal, and we define the product ABC to be their common value; that is,

$$ABC = A(BC) = (AB)C.$$

The rule expressed in the above equation is called the *associative law* for multiplication. We shall not prove the associative law here, although the student will be asked to check an example of it in Exercise 5.

If A and B are square matrices of the same size, then they can be multiplied in either order. It is not true, however, that the product AB is necessarily equal to the product BA. For example, if

$$A = \begin{pmatrix} 1 & 1 \\ 0 & 0 \end{pmatrix} \quad \text{and} \quad B = \begin{pmatrix} 1 & 0 \\ 1 & 0 \end{pmatrix},$$

then we have

$$AB = \begin{pmatrix} 1 & 1 \\ 0 & 0 \end{pmatrix}\begin{pmatrix} 1 & 0 \\ 1 & 0 \end{pmatrix} = \begin{pmatrix} 2 & 0 \\ 0 & 0 \end{pmatrix},$$

whereas

$$BA = \begin{pmatrix} 1 & 0 \\ 1 & 0 \end{pmatrix}\begin{pmatrix} 1 & 1 \\ 0 & 0 \end{pmatrix} = \begin{pmatrix} 1 & 1 \\ 1 & 1 \end{pmatrix},$$

and it is clear that $AB \neq BA$.

1. Perform the following operations.

a. $2\begin{pmatrix} 6 & 1 \\ 0 & -3 \\ -1 & 2 \end{pmatrix} - 3\begin{pmatrix} 4 & 2 \\ 0 & 1 \\ -5 & -1 \end{pmatrix} = ?$ $\left[Ans. \begin{pmatrix} 0 & -4 \\ 0 & -9 \\ 13 & 7 \end{pmatrix}.\right]$

b. $\begin{pmatrix} 6 & 1 & -1 \\ 1 & -3 & 2 \end{pmatrix} - 5\begin{pmatrix} 4 & 0 & -5 \\ 2 & 1 & -1 \end{pmatrix} = ?$

c. $\begin{pmatrix} 6 & 1 \\ 0 & -3 \end{pmatrix}\begin{pmatrix} 4 & 0 & -4 \\ 2 & 1 & -1 \end{pmatrix} = ?$

d. $\begin{pmatrix} 6 & 0 & -1 \\ 1 & -3 & 2 \end{pmatrix}\begin{pmatrix} 4 & 2 \\ 0 & 1 \\ -5 & -1 \end{pmatrix} = ?$ $\left[Ans. \begin{pmatrix} 29 & 13 \\ -6 & -3 \end{pmatrix}.\right]$

e. $\begin{pmatrix} 1 & -1 \\ -1 & 1 \end{pmatrix}\begin{pmatrix} 1 & -1 \\ -1 & 1 \end{pmatrix} = ?$

f. $\begin{pmatrix} 4 & 1 & 4 \\ -1 & -2 & -1 \\ 2 & -1 & -2 \end{pmatrix}\begin{pmatrix} 3 & 0 & 1 \\ -1 & 2 & 0 \\ 0 & 0 & 2 \end{pmatrix} = ?$ $\left[Ans. \begin{pmatrix} 11 & 2 & 12 \\ -1 & -4 & -3 \\ 7 & -2 & -2 \end{pmatrix}.\right]$

g. $\begin{pmatrix} 1 & -2 \\ 0 & 0 \\ 7 & 5 \\ -4 & 8 \\ 0 & -2 \end{pmatrix}\begin{pmatrix} -7 & 9 & -5 & 6 & 0 \\ -1 & 0 & 3 & -4 & 1 \end{pmatrix} = ?$

2. Let A be any 3×3 matrix and let I be the matrix

$$I = \begin{pmatrix} 1 & 0 & 0 \\ 0 & 1 & 0 \\ 0 & 0 & 1 \end{pmatrix}.$$

Show that $AI = IA = A$. The matrix I acts for the products of matrices in the same way that the number 1 acts for products of numbers. For this reason it is called the identity matrix.

3. Let A be any 3×3 matrix and let 0 be the matrix

$$0 = \begin{pmatrix} 0 & 0 & 0 \\ 0 & 0 & 0 \\ 0 & 0 & 0 \end{pmatrix}.$$

Show that $A0 = 0A = 0$ for any A. Also show that $A + 0 = 0 + A = A$ for any A. The matrix 0 acts for matrices in the same way that the number 0 acts for numbers. For this reason it is called the zero matrix.

4. If $A = \begin{pmatrix} 0 & 0 \\ 0 & 1 \end{pmatrix}$ and $B = \begin{pmatrix} 1 & 0 \\ 0 & 0 \end{pmatrix}$, show that $AB = \begin{pmatrix} 0 & 0 \\ 0 & 0 \end{pmatrix}$. Thus the product of two matrices can be the zero matrix even though neither of the matrices is itself zero. Find another example that illustrates this point.

5. Verify the associative law for the special case when

$$A = \begin{pmatrix} -1 & 0 & 5 \\ 7 & -2 & 0 \end{pmatrix}, \quad B = \begin{pmatrix} 1 & 7 & 0 \\ -3 & -1 & 0 \\ 1 & 0 & 5 \end{pmatrix}, \quad C = \begin{pmatrix} -1 & -1 \\ 2 & 0 \\ 0 & 4 \end{pmatrix}.$$

6. Consider the matrices

$$A = \begin{pmatrix} 1 & 0 & 1 \\ -1 & 17 & 57 \end{pmatrix}, \qquad B = \begin{pmatrix} 1 & 1 & 1 \\ 2 & 2 & 2 \\ 3 & 3 & 3 \\ 0 & 0 & 0 \end{pmatrix},$$

$$C = \begin{pmatrix} 1 & 0 & -1 \\ 0 & -1 & 1 \\ -1 & 1 & 0 \end{pmatrix}, \qquad D = \begin{pmatrix} -1 & -1 \\ 2 & 2 \\ 1 & 1 \end{pmatrix}.$$

The shapes of these are 2×3, 4×3, 3×3, and 3×2, respectively. What is the shape of

a. AC.   b. DA.   c. AD.   d. BC.

e. CB.   f. DAC.   g. $BCDA$.   [*Ans.* 4×3.]

7. In Exercise 6 find:

a. The component in the second row and second column of AC.
[*Ans.* 40.]

b. The component in the fourth row and first column of BC.

c. The component in the last row and last column of DA.   [*Ans.* 58.]

d. The component in the first row and first column of CB.

8. If A is a square matrix, it can be multiplied by itself; hence we can define (using the associative law)

$$A^2 = A \cdot A,$$
$$A^3 = A^2 \cdot A = A \cdot A \cdot A,$$
$$\vdots$$
$$A^n = A^{n-1} \cdot A = A \cdot A \cdot \ldots \cdot A \qquad (n \text{ factors}).$$

These are naturally called "powers" of a matrix—the first one being called the square; the second, the cube; and so on. Compute the indicated powers of the following matrices.

a. If $A = \begin{pmatrix} 1 & 0 \\ 3 & 4 \end{pmatrix}$, find A^2, A^3, and A^4.

$$\left[Ans. \ \begin{pmatrix} 1 & 0 \\ 15 & 16 \end{pmatrix} ; \begin{pmatrix} 1 & 0 \\ 63 & 64 \end{pmatrix} ; \begin{pmatrix} 1 & 0 \\ 255 & 256 \end{pmatrix} .\right]$$

b. If I and 0 are the matrices defined in Exercises 2 and 3, find I^2, I^3, I^n, 0^2, 0^3, and 0^n.

c. If $A = \begin{pmatrix} 0 & 0 & 0 \\ 1 & 0 & 0 \\ 2 & -1 & 0 \end{pmatrix}$, find A^2, A^3, and A^n.

d. If $A = \begin{pmatrix} 1 & 1 \\ 1 & 1 \end{pmatrix}$, find A^n.

9. Cube the matrix

$$\begin{pmatrix} 0 & 1 & 0 \\ 0 & \frac{1}{2} & \frac{1}{2} \\ \frac{1}{3} & 0 & \frac{2}{3} \end{pmatrix}.$$

Compare your answer with the matrix $P^{(3)}$ in Example 1, Chapter 3, Section 9, and comment on the result.

10. Consider a two-stage Markov process whose transition matrix is

$$P = \begin{pmatrix} p_{11} & p_{12} \\ p_{21} & p_{22} \end{pmatrix}.$$

a. Assuming that the process starts in state 1, draw the tree and set up tree measures for three stages of the process. Do the same, assuming that the process starts in state 2.

b. Using the trees drawn in a., compute the quantities $p_{11}^{(3)}$, $p_{12}^{(3)}$, $p_{21}^{(3)}$, $p_{22}^{(3)}$. Write the matrix $P^{(3)}$.

c. Compute the cube P^3 of the matrix P.

d. Compare the answers you found in parts b. and c. and show that $P^{(3)} = P^3$.

11. Show that the fifth and all higher powers of the matrix

$$\begin{pmatrix} 0 & 1 & 0 \\ 0 & 0 & 1 \\ 1 & 1 & 0 \end{pmatrix}$$

have all entries positive. Show that no smaller power has this property.

12. In Example 1 of Section 3 assume that the contractor wishes to take into account the cost of transporting raw materials to the building site as well as the purchasing cost. Suppose the costs are as given in the matrix below:

	Purchase	Transport	
	15	4.5	Steel
	8	2	Wood
$Q =$	5	3	Glass
	1	0.5	Paint
	10	0	Labor

Referring to the example:

a. By computing the product RQ find a 3×2 matrix whose entries give the purchase and transportation costs of the materials for each kind of house.

b. Find the product xRQ, which is a two-component row vector whose first component gives the total purchase price and second component gives the total transportation cost.

c. Let $z = \begin{pmatrix} 1 \\ 1 \end{pmatrix}$ and then compute $xRQz$, which is a number giving the total cost of materials and transportation for all the houses being built. [*Ans.* $14,304.]

13. A company has four levels of management executives: top, upper middle, lower middle, and junior. Each year a top management executive entertains 30 very important and 2 important visitors; an upper middle executive entertains 10 very important, 15 important, and 2 ordinary visitors; a lower management executive entertains 1 very important, 28 important, and 20 ordinary visitors; finally, each year a junior executive entertains 3 ordinary visitors. The very important visitors are always taken to the most expensive restaurants; important visitors are half the time taken to the most expensive, a quarter of the time to expensive, and the remainder of the time to medium-priced restaurants; and ordinary visitors go half the time to a medium-priced restaurant and half the time to a snack bar. Dinner in the most expensive restaurants costs $100, in the expensive restaurants, $25, in the medium-priced restaurants, $10, and at the snack bar, $5. If there are 20 top executives, 75 upper middle, 200 lower middle, and 125 junior executives, answer the following.

a. What is the total number of very important, important, and ordinary visitors each year?

b. How many bills are paid at the most expensive, expensive, medium-priced, and snack-bar restaurants?

c. What are the yearly expenses for entertaining for each class of management?

d. What is the total cost of entertaining for the company? Calculate in two ways. [*Ans.* $586,381.]

14. Find three different 2×2 matrices A such that $A^2 = I$.

15. The *commutative law for addition* is

$$A + B = B + A$$

for any two matrices A and B of the same shape. Prove that the commutative law for addition is true from the definition of matrix addition and the fact that it is true for ordinary numbers.

16. The *distributive laws for numbers and matrices* are

$$k(A + B) = kA + kB,$$
$$(h + k)A = hA + kA$$

for any two numbers h and k and any two matrices A and B of the same shape. Prove that this law holds from the definitions of numerical multiplication of matrices, addition of matrices and the ordinary rules for numbers.

17. The *distributive laws for matrix multiplication* are:

$$(A + B)C = AC + BC,$$
$$C(A + B) = CA + CB,$$

where A, B, and C are matrices of suitable shapes. Show that these laws hold from the definitions of matrix multiplication and addition, and the ordinary rules for numbers.

18. A *diagonal matrix* is square and its only nonzero entries are on the main diagonal. For instance, the matrices

$$A = \begin{pmatrix} 1 & 0 \\ 0 & 4 \end{pmatrix}, \qquad B = \begin{pmatrix} 3 & 0 \\ 0 & 2 \end{pmatrix}$$

are 2×2 diagonal matrices.

a. Show that A and B commute—that is, $AB = BA$.

b. Show that any pair of diagonal matrices of the same size commute when multiplied together.

19. Consider the matrices

$$A = \begin{pmatrix} 0 & 1 & 0 \\ 0 & 0 & 1 \\ 1 & 0 & 0 \end{pmatrix} \quad \text{and} \quad B = \begin{pmatrix} 0 & 0 & 1 \\ 1 & 0 & 0 \\ 0 & 1 & 0 \end{pmatrix}.$$

a. Show that $A^2 = B$ and $A^3 = I$. What is A^4?
b. Show that $B^2 = A$ and $B^3 = I$.
c. Show that $A^3 = BA = AB = B^3 = I$, hence A and B commute.

20. For the matrix

$$A = \begin{pmatrix} 0 & 1 & 0 & 0 \\ 0 & 0 & 1 & 0 \\ 0 & 0 & 0 & 1 \\ 1 & 0 & 0 & 0 \end{pmatrix},$$

what is the smallest k such that $A^k = I$?

21. Let $A = \begin{pmatrix} 1 & 1 \\ 0 & 1 \end{pmatrix}$.

a. Find a matrix B such that $AB = \begin{pmatrix} 1 & 0 \\ 0 & 1 \end{pmatrix}$.

b. Find a matrix D such that $AD = \begin{pmatrix} 2 & 0 \\ 4 & 3 \end{pmatrix}$.

$$[Ans. \ (a) \ \begin{pmatrix} 1 & -1 \\ 0 & 1 \end{pmatrix}; \ (b) \ \begin{pmatrix} -2 & -3 \\ 4 & 3 \end{pmatrix}.]$$

5. THE SOLUTION OF LINEAR EQUATIONS

There are many occasions when the simultaneous solutions of linear equations is important. In this section we shall develop methods for finding out whether a set of linear equations has solutions, and for finding all such solutions.

Example 1. Consider the following example of three linear equations in three unknowns.

(1) $x_1 + 4x_2 + 3x_3 = 1$,

(2) $2x_1 + 5x_2 + 4x_3 = 4$,

(3) $x_1 - 3x_2 - 2x_3 = 5$.

Equations such as these, that contain one or more variables, are called *open statements*. Statement (1) is true for some values of the variables (for instance, when $x_1 = 1$, $x_2 = 0$, and $x_3 = 0$), and false for other values of the variables (for instance, when $x_1 = 0$, $x_2 = 1$, and $x_3 = 0$). The truth set of (1) is the set of all vectors $\begin{pmatrix} x_1 \\ x_2 \\ x_3 \end{pmatrix}$ for which (1) is true. Similarly, the truth set of the three simultaneous equations (1), (2), and (3) is the set of all vectors $\begin{pmatrix} x_1 \\ x_2 \\ x_3 \end{pmatrix}$

that make true their conjunction

$$(x_1 + 4x_2 + 3x_3 = 1) \wedge (2x_1 + 5x_2 + 4x_3 = 4)$$
$$\wedge (x_1 - 3x_2 - 2x_3 = 5).$$

When we say that we solve a set of simultaneous equations, we mean that we determine the truth set of their conjunction.

Before we discuss the solution of these equations we note that they can be written as a single equation in matrix form as follows:

$$\begin{pmatrix} 1 & 4 & 3 \\ 2 & 5 & 4 \\ 1 & -3 & -2 \end{pmatrix} \begin{pmatrix} x_1 \\ x_2 \\ x_3 \end{pmatrix} = \begin{pmatrix} 1 \\ 4 \\ 5 \end{pmatrix}.$$

One of the uses of vector and matrix notation is in writing a large number of linear equations in a single simple matrix equation such as the one above. It also leads to the detached coefficient form of solving simultaneous equations that we shall discuss at the end of the present section and in the next section.

The method of solving the linear equations above is the following. First we use equation (1) to eliminate the variable x_1 from equations (2) and (3); that is, we subtract two times (1) from (2) and then subtract (1) from (3), giving

(1')	$x_1 + 4x_2 + 3x_3 = 1,$
(2')	$-3x_2 - 2x_3 = 2,$
(3')	$-7x_2 - 5x_3 = 4.$

Next we divide equation (2') through by the coefficient of x_2, namely, -3, obtaining $x_2 + \frac{2}{3}x_3 = -\frac{2}{3}$. We use this equation to eliminate x_2 from each of the other two equations. In order to do this we subtract four times this equation from (1') and add seven times this equation to (3'), obtaining

(1'')	$x_1 + 0 + \frac{1}{3}x_3 = \frac{11}{3},$
(2'')	$x_2 + \frac{2}{3}x_3 = -\frac{2}{3},$
(3'')	$-\frac{1}{3}x_3 = -\frac{2}{3}.$

The last step is to divide through (3'') by $-\frac{1}{3}$, which is the coefficient of x_3, obtaining the equation $x_3 = 2$; we use this equation to eliminate x_3 from the first two equations as follows:

(1''')	$x_1 + 0 + 0 = 3,$
(2''')	$x_2 + 0 = -2,$
(3''')	$x_3 = 2.$

The solution can now be read from these equations as $x_1 = 3$, $x_2 = -2$, and $x_3 = 2$. The reader should substitute these values into the original equations (1), (2), and (3) above to see that the solution has actually been obtained.

In the example just discussed we saw that there was only one solution to the set of three simultaneous equations in three variables. Example 2 will be one in which there is *more* than one solution, and Example 3 will be one in which there are *no* solutions to a set of three simultaneous equations in three variables.

Example 2. Consider the following linear equations:

(4) $$x_1 - 2x_2 - 3x_3 = 2,$$

(5) $$x_1 - 4x_2 - 13x_3 = 14,$$

(6) $$-3x_1 + 5x_2 + 4x_3 = 0.$$

Let us proceed as before and use equation (4) to eliminate the variable x_1 from the other two equations. We have

(4') $$x_1 - 2x_2 - 3x_3 = 2,$$

(5') $$-2x_2 - 10x_3 = 12,$$

(6') $$-x_2 - 5x_3 = 6.$$

Proceeding as before, we divide equation (5') by -2, obtaining the equation $x_2 + 5x_3 = -6$. We use this equation to eliminate the variable x_2 from each of the other equations—namely, we add twice this equation to (4') and then add the equation to (6').

(4'') $$x_1 + 0 + 7x_3 = -10,$$

(5'') $$x_2 + 5x_3 = -6,$$

(6'') $$0 = 0.$$

Observe that we have eliminated the last equation completely! We also see that the variable x_3 can be chosen completely arbitrarily in these equations. To emphasize this, we move the terms involving x_3 to the righthand side, giving

(4''') $$x_1 = -10 - 7x_3,$$

(5''') $$x_2 = -6 - 5x_3.$$

The reader should check, by substituting these values of x_1 and x_2 into equations (4), (5), and (6), that they are solutions regardless of the value of x_3. Let us also substitute particular values for x_3 to obtain numerical solutions. Thus, if we let $x_3 = 1, 0, -2$, respectively, and compute the resulting numbers, using (4''') and (5'''), we obtain the following numerical solutions.

$$
\begin{aligned}
x_1 &= -17, & x_2 &= -11, & x_3 &= 1, \\
x_1 &= -10, & x_2 &= -6, & x_3 &= 0, \\
x_1 &= 4, & x_2 &= 4, & x_3 &= -2.
\end{aligned}
$$

The reader should also substitute these numbers into (4), (5), and (6) to show that they are solutions. To summarize, our second example has an infinite number of solutions, one for each numerical value of x_3 that is substituted into equations (4''') and (5''').

Example 3. Suppose that we modify equation (6) by changing the number on the righthand side to 2. Then we have

(7) $$x_1 - 2x_2 - 3x_3 = 2,$$

(8) $$x_1 - 4x_2 - 13x_3 = 14,$$

(9) $$-3x_1 + 5x_2 + 4x_3 = 2.$$

If we carry out the same procedure as before and use (7) to eliminate x_1 from (8) and (9), we obtain

(7') $$x_1 - 2x_2 - 3x_3 = 2,$$

(8') $$-2x_2 - 10x_3 = 12,$$

(9') $$-x_2 - 5x_3 = 8.$$

We divide (8') by -2, the coefficient of x_2, obtaining, as before, $x_2 + 5x_3 = -6$. Using this equation to eliminate x_2 from the other two equations, we have

(7'') $$x_1 + 0 + 7x_3 = -10,$$

(8'') $$x_2 + 5x_3 = -6,$$

(9'') $$0 = 2.$$

Observe that the last equation is *logically false*—that is, false for all values of x_1, x_2, x_3. Because our elimination procedure has led to a false result, we conclude that the equations (7), (8), and (9) have *no* solution. The student should always keep in mind that this possibility exists when considering simultaneous equations.

In the examples above the equations we considered had the same number of variables as equations. The next example has more variables than equations and the last has more equations than variables.

Example 4. Consider the following two equations in three variables:

(10) $$-4x_1 + 3x_2 + 2x_3 = -2,$$

(11) $$5x_1 - 4x_2 + x_3 = 3.$$

Using the elimination method outlined above, we divide (10) by -4, and then subtract five times the result from (11), obtaining

(10') $$x_1 - \tfrac{3}{4}x_2 - \tfrac{1}{2}x_3 = \tfrac{1}{2},$$

(11') $$-\tfrac{1}{4}x_2 + \tfrac{7}{2}x_3 = \tfrac{1}{2}.$$

Multiplying (11′) by −4 and using it to eliminate x_2 from (10′), we have

(10″) $x_1 + 0 - 11x_3 = -1,$

(11″) $x_2 - 14x_3 = -2.$

We can now let x_3 take on any value whatsoever and solve these equations for x_1 and x_2. We emphasize this fact by rewriting them as in Example 2 as

(10‴) $x_1 = 11x_3 - 1,$

(11‴) $x_2 = 14x_3 - 2.$

The reader should check that these are solutions and also, by choosing specific values for x_3, find numerical solutions to these equations.

Example 5. Let us consider the other possibility suggested by Example 4, namely, the case in which we have more equations than variables. Consider the following equations:

(12) $-4x_1 + 3x_2 = 2,$

(13) $5x_1 - 4x_2 = 0,$

(14) $2x_1 - x_2 = a,$

where a is an arbitrary number. Using equation (12) to eliminate x_1 from the other two, we obtain

(12′) $x_1 - \tfrac{3}{4}x_2 = -\tfrac{1}{2},$

(13′) $-\tfrac{1}{4}x_2 = \tfrac{5}{2},$

(14′) $\tfrac{1}{2}x_2 = a + 1.$

Next we use (13′) to eliminate x_2 from the other equations, obtaining

(12″) $x_1 + 0 = -8,$

(13″) $x_2 = -10,$

(14″) $0 = a + 6.$

These equations remind us of the situation in Example 3, since we will be led to a false result unless $a = -6$. We see that equations (12), (13), and (14) have the solution $x_1 = -8$ and $x_2 = -10$ only if $a = -6$. If $a \neq -6$, then there is *no* solution to these equations.

The examples above illustrate all the possibilities that can occur in the general case. There may be no solutions, exactly one solution, or an infinite number of solutions to a set of simultaneous equations.

The procedure that we have illustrated above is one that turns any set of linear equations into an equivalent set of equations from which the existence of solutions and the solutions can be easily read. A student who learned other ways of solving linear equations may wonder why we use the procedure above—one that is not always the quickest way of solving equations. The answer is that we use it because it always works; that is, it is a *canonical* procedure to apply to *any* set of linear equations. The faster methods usually work only for equations that have solutions, and even then may not find all solutions.

We next want to describe the computational process illustrated above in terms of a flow diagram. But first let us return to the equations of Example 1. Note that the variables, coefficients, and righthand sides are in columns at the beginning of the solution and are always kept in the same column throughout the computation. It is obvious that the location of a coefficient of a variable is sufficient identification for it, and that it is unnecessary to keep writing the variables. We can start with the following labeled tableau:

(15)

x_1	x_2	x_3	-1	
1	4	3	1	$= 0$
2	5	4	4	$= 0$
1	-3	-2	5	$= 0$

Notice that if we take the variables labeling the columns of the tableau, drop them down, multiply by the corresponding coefficients of the first row of the tableau and set them equal to the label on the right, we obtain the equation

$$x_1 + 4x_2 + 3x_3 - 1 = 0,$$

which is just equation (1) with the 1 on the righthand side moved to the lefthand side (with changed sign). Similarly, dropping the variables down to the second and third rows of the tableau in (15) will give equations (2) and (3).

The flow diagram in Figure 5 gives a precise description of the method illustrated above for solving simultaneous equations but using the tableau of (15) as an initial tableau and then constructing a series of related tableaux that preserve the property just illustrated. That is, in each of the tableaux of the computational process if we drop the labels at the top of the tableau down to any row, multiply as above, and set the result equal to the label on the right, we get a valid equation. At every step the set of equations so obtained is equivalent to the original set. And in the final tableau the answer(s) to the original problem are displayed; or if the original equations do not have a solution, that fact is also discovered.

The tableau of (15) will be called the *detached coefficient tableau* for simultaneous equations. If we originally had m equations in n unknowns, then the tableau will be m by $n + 1$. The final column, column $n + 1$, corresponding to the constants b_i on the righthand side of the original equations, is separated by a vertical line. In the flow diagram of Figure 5 nonzero numbers to the *left of the vertical line* are selected as *pivots*. As we shall see, the pivoting process is just the use of one equation to eliminate a variable from all the other equations, which is exactly what was done in the discussion of the examples previously.

Example 6. Starting with the tableau of (15), we apply the flow diagram of Figure 5. We set $i = 1$ as indicated in box 1 and then move to box 2. Since the first row of the tableau has a nonzero coefficient (in fact, it has three of them), we move to box 3. Choose $j = 1$, since the first entry of the first row is not zero. If we carry out the rest of the steps in box 3 and also in box 4 of Figure 5, we obtain the following tableau:

$$
(16) \quad
\begin{array}{cccc}
0 & x_2 & x_3 & -1 \\
\hline
1 & 4 & 3 & 1 \\
0 & -3 & -2 & 2 \\
0 & -7 & -5 & 4
\end{array}
\quad
\begin{array}{l}
= -x_1 \\
= 0 \\
= 0
\end{array}
$$

In (16) we have also interchanged the labels on the first column and first row as described in box 5 of Figure 5. We now are at box 6, and since $i = 1 < m = 3$, we go to box 7 and set $i = 2$. Then we return to box 2 and carry out the construction of the next tableau. It is

$$
(17) \quad
\begin{array}{cccc}
0 & 0 & x_3 & -1 \\
\hline
1 & 0 & \frac{1}{3} & \frac{11}{3} \\
0 & 1 & \frac{2}{3} & -\frac{2}{3} \\
0 & 0 & -\frac{1}{3} & -\frac{2}{3}
\end{array}
\quad
\begin{array}{l}
= -x_1 \\
= -x_2 \\
= 0
\end{array}
$$

We next set $i = 3$ and construct the final tableau:

$$
(18) \quad
\begin{array}{cccc}
0 & 0 & 0 & -1 \\
\hline
1 & 0 & 0 & 3 \\
0 & 1 & 0 & -2 \\
0 & 0 & 1 & 2
\end{array}
\quad
\begin{array}{l}
= -x_1 \\
= -x_2 \\
= -x_3
\end{array}
$$

Since $i = 3$, we now move from box 6 to box 10 of the flow diagram. The answer to the question in box 10 is No, so we go to box 12. We find that the answer to the problem is unique. If we drop the labels at the top of the final tableau (18) down to each of the rows of the tableau, we obtain the equations

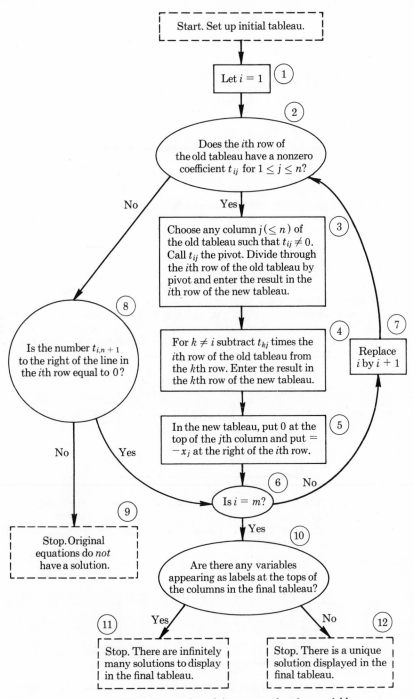

Flow diagram for solving m equations in n variables

Figure 5

$$-3 = -x_1 \quad \text{or} \quad x_1 = 3,$$
$$2 = -x_2 \quad \text{or} \quad x_2 = -2,$$
$$-2 = -x_3 \quad \text{or} \quad x_3 = 2,$$

which were the answers obtained before.

The reader should check that the equations of Example 1 and the tableaux above correspond exactly.

(1), (2), and (3)	correspond to	(15),
(1'), (2'), and (3')	correspond to	(16),
(1''), (2''), and (3'')	correspond to	(17),
(1'''), (2'''), and (3''')	correspond to	(18).

Note that this correspondence is exact in the sense that if we carry out the procedure for obtaining equations from tableaux we obtain the same equations as before (but possibly in a slightly different form). Notice also that it is important to include the zero entries in the tableaux where necessary.

Example 7. Box 3 of Figure 5 states that we can choose *any* column j with $t_{ij} \neq 0$. In the previous example we chose the *first* nonzero entry in each row as we went through the pivoting procedure, and the reader may wonder if that was necessary. To show that it isn't, we rework that example with a different selection of pivots and show that we arrive at exactly the same result. We start again with tableau (15), but this time choose $j = 3$ on the first step. Our second tableau is then

(19)

x_1	x_2	0	-1	
$\frac{1}{3}$	$\frac{4}{3}$	1	$\frac{1}{3}$	$= -x_3$
$\frac{2}{3}$	$-\frac{1}{3}$	0	$\frac{8}{3}$	$= 0$
$\frac{5}{3}$	$-\frac{1}{3}$	0	$\frac{17}{3}$	$= 0$

Now we set $i = 2$ and must select j. Since both entries in the second row of (19) are nonzero, we can choose either—let us take $j = 1$. (The reader should carry out details for the other choice.) Carrying out the pivoting steps, we obtain as the next tableau:

(20)

0	x_2	0	-1	
0	$\frac{3}{2}$	1	-1	$= -x_3$
1	$-\frac{1}{2}$	0	4	$= -x_1$
0	$\frac{1}{2}$	0	-1	$= 0$

Next we have $i = 3$. The only choice is now $j = 2$. After pivoting as in Figure 5, we obtain:

(21)

	0	0	0	-1	
0	0	1	2	$= -x_3$
1	0	0	3	$= -x_1$
0	1	0	-2	$= -x_2$

From the final tableau we read off the answer, $x_1 = 3$, $x_2 = -2$, and $x_3 = 2$, as before.

Example 8. Suppose that we have two sets of simultaneous equations to solve and that they differ only in their righthand sides. For instance, suppose we want to solve

$$(22) \qquad \begin{pmatrix} 1 & 4 & 3 \\ 2 & 5 & 4 \\ 1 & -3 & -2 \end{pmatrix} \begin{pmatrix} x_1 \\ x_2 \\ x_3 \end{pmatrix} = \begin{pmatrix} 1 \\ 4 \\ 5 \end{pmatrix} \quad \text{and} \quad = \begin{pmatrix} -1 \\ 0 \\ 2 \end{pmatrix}.$$

It is obvious that the calculations will be the same regardless of the numbers appearing on the righthand side. Therefore, it is possible to solve both sets of simultaneous equations at once. We illustrate by the following series of tableaux.

(23)

x_1	x_2	x_3	-1		
1	4	3	1	-1	$= 0$
2	5	4	4	0	$= 0$
1	-3	-2	5	2	$= 0$

Notice that the vertical line still separates the coefficients of the variables and the righthand sides. Notice also that the label -1 can now refer to either of the righthand sides, depending upon which set of simultaneous equations we are interested in. We solve the problem using the flow diagram of Figure 5 and being careful to choose pivots to the left of the vertical line in the tableau. The remaining tableaux are as follows.

(24)

0	x_2	x_3	-1		
1	4	3	1	-1	$= -x_1$
0	-3	-2	2	2	$= 0$
0	-7	-5	4	3	$= 0$

$$
\begin{array}{ccccc}
0 & 0 & x_3 & \overbrace{}^{\displaystyle -1} & \\
\end{array}
$$

(25)

1	0	$\frac{1}{3}$	$\frac{11}{3}$	$\frac{5}{3}$	$= -x_1$
0	1	$\frac{2}{3}$	$-\frac{2}{3}$	$-\frac{2}{3}$	$= -x_2$
0	0	$-\frac{1}{3}$	$-\frac{2}{3}$	$-\frac{5}{3}$	$= 0$

$$
\begin{array}{ccccc}
0 & 0 & 0 & \overbrace{}^{\displaystyle -1} & \\
\end{array}
$$

(26)

1	0	0	3	0	$= -x_1$
0	1	0	-2	-4	$= -x_2$
0	0	1	2	5	$= -x_3$

Attaching the label -1 to the fourth column, we read off the answers

$$ x_1 = 3, \qquad x_2 = -2, \qquad x_3 = 2 $$

to the first set of equations. Similarly, attaching the label -1 now to column five, we read off the answers

$$ x_1 = 0, \qquad x_2 = -4, \qquad x_3 = 5 $$

to the second set of equations. The reader should check these answers by substituting into the original equations.

EXERCISES

1. Using the detached coefficient tableau, rework Examples 2–4 using the flow diagram of Figure 5. Show that
   a. in Example 2 the computation ends in box 11.
   b. in Example 3 the computation ends in box 9.
   c. in Example 4 the computation ends in box 11.
2. Find all the solutions of the following simultaneous equations.
   a. $4x_1 \quad + 5x_3 = \quad 6,$
   $\quad x_2 - 6x_3 = -2,$
   $\quad 3x_1 \quad + 4x_3 = \quad 3.$ [Ans. $x_1 = 9, x_2 = -38, x_3 = -6$.]
   b. $3x_1 - \quad x_2 - 2x_3 = \quad 2,$
   $\quad 2x_2 - \quad x_3 = -1,$
   $\quad 3x_1 - 5x_2 \qquad = \quad 3.$ [Ans. No solution.]
   c. $-x_1 + 2x_2 + 3x_3 = 0,$
   $\quad x_1 - 4x_2 - 13x_3 = 0,$
   $\quad -3x_1 + 5x_2 + 4x_3 = 0.$ [Ans. $x_1 = -7x_3, x_2 = -5x_3$.]
3. Find all the solutions of the following simultaneous equations.
   a. $x_1 + \quad x_2 + \quad x_3 = 0,$

$$2x_1 + 4x_2 + 3x_3 = 0,$$
$$4x_2 + 4x_3 = 0.$$

b. $\quad x_1 + \quad x_2 + \quad x_3 = -2,$
$$2x_1 + 4x_2 + 3x_3 = \quad 3,$$
$$4x_2 + 2x_3 = \quad 2.$$

c. $4x_1 \qquad\quad + 4x_3 = \quad 8,$
$$x_2 - 6x_3 = -3,$$
$$3x_1 + \quad x_2 - 3x_3 = \quad 3.$$

4. Find all solutions of the following equations using the detached coefficient tableau and the flow diagram in Figure 5.

a. $\quad 5x_1 - 3x_2 = -7,$
$$-2x_1 + 9x_2 = \quad 4,$$
$$2x_1 + 4x_2 = -2.$$
  [*Ans.* $x_1 = -\frac{17}{13}; x_2 = \frac{2}{13}.$]

b. $\quad\quad x_1 + 2x_2 = \quad 1,$
$$-3x_1 + 2x_2 = -2,$$
$$2x_1 + 3x_2 = \quad 1.$$
  [*Ans.* No solution.]

c. $\quad 5x_1 - 3x_2 - 7x_3 + \quad x_4 = \quad 10,$
$$-x_1 + 2x_2 + 6x_3 - 3x_4 = -3,$$
$$x_1 + \quad x_2 + 4x_3 - 5x_4 = \quad 0.$$

5. Find all solutions of:

$$x_1 + 2x_2 + 3x_3 + \quad 4x_4 = 10,$$
$$2x_1 - \quad x_2 + \quad x_3 - \quad x_4 = 1,$$
$$3x_1 + \quad x_2 + 4x_3 + \quad 3x_4 = 11,$$
$$-2x_1 + 6x_2 + 4x_3 + 10x_4 = 18.$$

[*Ans.* $x_1 = \frac{12}{5} - x_3 - \frac{2}{5}x_4; x_2 = \frac{19}{5} - x_3 - \frac{9}{5}x_4,$ x_3 and x_4 arbitrary.]

6. We consider buying three kinds of food. Food I has one unit of vitamin A, three units of vitamin B, and four units of vitamin C. Food II has two, three, and five units, respectively. Food III has three units each of vitamin A and vitamin C, none of vitamin B. We need to have eleven units of vitamin A, nine of vitamin B, and 20 of vitamin C.

a. Find all possible amounts of the three foods that will provide precisely these amounts of the vitamins.

b. If food I costs 60 cents and the others cost 10 cents each per unit, is there a solution costing exactly \$1?   [*Ans.* (b) Yes; 1, 2, 2.]

7. Solve the following four simultaneous sets whose righthand sides are listed under (a), (b), (c), and (d) below. Use the detached coefficient tableau.

	(a)	(b)	(c)	(d)
$4x_1 \quad + 5x_3 =$	1	1	0	0
$x_2 - 6x_3 =$	2	0	0	1
$3x_1 \quad + 4x_3 =$	3	0	1	0.

[*Ans.* (a) $x_1 = -11, x_2 = 56, x_3 = 9.$]

8. Solve the following four sets of simultaneous equations, which differ only in their righthand sides.

	(a)	(b)	(c)	(d)
$x_1 + x_2 + \quad x_3 =$	3	0	12	0
$x_1 - x_2 + 2x_3 =$	2	-1	7	0
$2x_1 + x_2 - \quad x_3 =$	2	3	11	0.

9. Solve the following three sets of simultaneous equations.

$$
\begin{array}{cccc}
 & (a) & (b) & (c) \\
x_1 + x_2 + x_3 = & 1 & 2 & 0 \\
x_1 - x_2 + 2x_3 = & -2 & 2 & 0 \\
3x_1 - x_2 + 5x_3 = & -3 & 2 & 0.
\end{array}
$$

10. Show that the equations

$$
\begin{aligned}
-4x_1 + 3x_2 + ax_3 &= c, \\
5x_1 - 4x_2 + bx_3 &= d,
\end{aligned}
$$

always have a solution for all values of a, b, c, and d.

11. Find conditions on a, b, and c in order that the equations

$$
\begin{aligned}
-4x_1 + 3x_2 &= a, \\
5x_1 - 4x_2 &= b, \\
-3x_1 + 2x_2 &= c.
\end{aligned}
$$

have a solution   [*Ans.* $2a + b = c$.]

12. *a.* Let $v = (v_1, v_2)$ and let A be the matrix

$$
A = \begin{pmatrix} 3 & -4 \\ 2 & -6 \end{pmatrix}.
$$

Find all solutions of the equation $vA = v$.   [*Ans.* $v = (0, 0)$.]

b. Let $v = (v_1, v_2)$ and let A be the matrix

$$
A = \begin{pmatrix} 3 & 6 \\ -2 & -5 \end{pmatrix}.
$$

Find all solutions of the equation $vA = v$.
                [*Ans.* $v = (k, k)$ for any number k.]

13. Let $v = (v_1, v_2)$ and let P be the matrix

$$
P = \begin{pmatrix} \frac{1}{3} & \frac{2}{3} \\ \frac{4}{5} & \frac{1}{5} \end{pmatrix}.
$$

a. Find all solutions of the equation $vP = v$.

b. Choose the solution for which $v_1 + v_2 = 1$.

14. If $x = (v_1, v_2, v_3)$ and A is the matrix

$$
A = \begin{pmatrix} 1 & -2 & 0 \\ 0 & 5 & 4 \\ 0 & -6 & -4 \end{pmatrix},
$$

find all solutions of the equation $vA = v$.
                [*Ans.* $v = (-k/2, 5k/4, k)$ for any number k.]

15. If $v = (v_1, v_2, v_3)$ and P is the matrix

$$P = \begin{pmatrix} 0 & \frac{1}{2} & \frac{1}{2} \\ \frac{1}{3} & \frac{1}{3} & \frac{1}{3} \\ \frac{1}{5} & 0 & \frac{4}{5} \end{pmatrix},$$

find all solutions of the equation $vP = v$. Select the unique solution for which $v_1 + v_2 + v_3 = 1$.

16. *a.* Show that the simultaneous linear equations

$$\begin{aligned} x_1 + x_2 + x_3 &= 1, \\ x_1 + 2x_2 + 3x_3 &= 0, \end{aligned}$$

can be interpreted as a single matrix-times-column-vector equation of the form

$$\begin{pmatrix} 1 & 1 & 1 \\ 1 & 2 & 3 \end{pmatrix} \begin{pmatrix} x_1 \\ x_2 \\ x_3 \end{pmatrix} = \begin{pmatrix} 1 \\ 0 \end{pmatrix}.$$

b. Show that *any* set of simultaneous linear equations may be interpreted as a matrix equation of the form $Ax = b$, where A is an $m \times n$ matrix, x is an n-component column vector, and b is an m-component column vector.

17. *a.* Show that the equations of Exercise 16(*a*) can be interpreted as a row-vector-times-matrix equation of the form

$$(v_1, v_2, v_3) \begin{pmatrix} 1 & 1 \\ 1 & 2 \\ 1 & 3 \end{pmatrix} = (1 \quad 0).$$

b. Show that *any* set of simultaneous linear equations may be interpreted as a matrix equation of the form $vA = b$, where A is an $m \times n$ matrix, v is an m-component row vector, and b is an n-component row vector.

18. *a.* Show that the simultaneous linear equations of Exercise 16a. can be interpreted as asking for all possible ways of expressing the column vector $\begin{pmatrix} 1 \\ 0 \end{pmatrix}$ in terms of the column vectors $\begin{pmatrix} 1 \\ 1 \end{pmatrix}$, $\begin{pmatrix} 1 \\ 2 \end{pmatrix}$, and $\begin{pmatrix} 1 \\ 3 \end{pmatrix}$.

b. Show that *any* set of linear equations may be interpreted as asking for all possible ways of expressing a column vector in terms of given column vectors.

19. For what value of the constant k does the following system have a unique solution? Find the solution in this case. What is the case if k does not take on this value?

$$\begin{aligned} 2x \qquad + 4z &= 6, \\ 3x + y + z &= -1, \\ 2y - z &= -2, \\ x - y + kz &= -5. \end{aligned}$$

[*Ans.* $k = -2$; $x = -1$, $y = 0$, $z = 2$; no solution.]

20. Consider the following set of simultaneous equations:

$$\begin{aligned}
x_1 + y_1 &= a, \\
x_1 + y_2 &= b, \\
x_2 + y_1 &= c, \\
x_2 + y_2 &= d.
\end{aligned}$$

a. For what conditions on a, b, c, and d will these equations have a solution?

b. Give a set of values for a, b, c, and d for which the equations do *not* have a solution.

c. Show that if there is *one* solution to these equations, then there are *infinitely many* solutions.

21. Which of the following statements are true and which false concerning the solution of m simultaneous linear equations in n unknowns written in the form $Ax = b$?

a. If there are infinitely many solutions, then $n > m$.

b. If the solution is unique, then $n = m$.

c. If $m = n$, then the solution is unique.

d. If $n > m$, then there cannot be a unique solution.

e. If $b = 0$, then there is always at least one solution.

f. If $b = 0$, then there are always infinitely many solutions.

g. If $b = 0$ and $x^{(1)}$ and $x^{(2)}$ are solutions, then $x^{(1)} + x^{(2)}$ is also a solution.   [*Ans. d., e.,* and *g.* are true.]

22. Let

$$A = (a, b, c), \qquad x = \begin{pmatrix} x_1 \\ x_2 \\ x_3 \end{pmatrix},$$

and let d be any number. Consider the open statement $Ax = d$.

a. If $A \neq 0$, show that the truth set of $Ax = d$ is not empty.

b. If $A = 0$ and $d = 0$, show that $Ax = d$ is logically true.

c. If $A = 0$ and $d \neq 0$, show that $Ax = d$ is logically false.

d. Use a., b., and c. to prove the following theorem: A single open statement $Ax = d$ is logically false if and only if $A = 0$ and $d \neq 0$.

6. THE INVERSE OF A SQUARE MATRIX

If A is a square matrix and B is another square matrix of the same size having the property that $BA = I$ (where I is the identity matrix), then we say that B is the *inverse* of A. When it exists, we shall denote the inverse of A by the symbol A^{-1}. To give a numerical example, let A and A^{-1} be the following:

(1)
$$A = \begin{pmatrix} 4 & 0 & 5 \\ 0 & 1 & -6 \\ 3 & 0 & 4 \end{pmatrix},$$

(2)
$$A^{-1} = \begin{pmatrix} 4 & 0 & -5 \\ -18 & 1 & 24 \\ -3 & 0 & 4 \end{pmatrix}.$$

Then we have

$$A^{-1}A = \begin{pmatrix} 4 & 0 & -5 \\ -18 & 1 & 24 \\ -3 & 0 & 4 \end{pmatrix} \cdot \begin{pmatrix} 4 & 0 & 5 \\ 0 & 1 & -6 \\ 3 & 0 & 4 \end{pmatrix} = \begin{pmatrix} 1 & 0 & 0 \\ 0 & 1 & 0 \\ 0 & 0 & 1 \end{pmatrix} = I.$$

If we multiply these matrices in the other order, we also get the identity matrix; thus

$$AA^{-1} = \begin{pmatrix} 4 & 0 & 5 \\ 0 & 1 & -6 \\ 3 & 0 & 4 \end{pmatrix} \cdot \begin{pmatrix} 4 & 0 & -5 \\ -18 & 1 & 24 \\ -3 & 0 & 4 \end{pmatrix} = \begin{pmatrix} 1 & 0 & 0 \\ 0 & 1 & 0 \\ 0 & 0 & 1 \end{pmatrix} = I.$$

In general it can be shown that if A is a square matrix with inverse A^{-1}, then the inverse satisfies the equation

$$A^{-1}A = AA^{-1} = I.$$

It is easy to see that a square matrix can have only one inverse. Suppose that in addition to A^{-1} we also have a B such that

$$BA = I.$$

Then we see that

$$B = BI = B(AA^{-1}) = (BA)A^{-1} = IA^{-1} = A^{-1}.$$

Finding the inverse of a matrix is analogous to finding the reciprocal of an ordinary number, but the analogy is not complete. Every nonzero number has a reciprocal, but there are matrices, not the zero matrix, that have no inverse. For example, if

$$A = \begin{pmatrix} 1 & -1 \\ -1 & 1 \end{pmatrix} \quad \text{and} \quad B = \begin{pmatrix} 1 & 1 \\ 1 & 1 \end{pmatrix},$$

then

$$AB = \begin{pmatrix} 1 & -1 \\ -1 & 1 \end{pmatrix} \cdot \begin{pmatrix} 1 & 1 \\ 1 & 1 \end{pmatrix} = \begin{pmatrix} 0 & 0 \\ 0 & 0 \end{pmatrix} = 0.$$

From this it follows that neither A nor B can have an inverse. To show that A does not have an inverse, let us assume that A had an inverse A^{-1}. Then

$$B = (A^{-1}A)B = A^{-1}(AB) = A^{-1}0 = 0,$$

contradicting the fact that $B \neq 0$. The proof that B cannot have an inverse is similar.

Let us now try to calculate the inverse of the matrix A in (1). Specifically, let's try to calculate the first column of A^{-1}. Let

$$x = \begin{pmatrix} x_1 \\ x_2 \\ x_3 \end{pmatrix}$$

be the desired entries of the first column. Then from the equation $AA^{-1} = I$ we see that we must solve

$$\begin{pmatrix} 4 & 0 & 5 \\ 0 & 1 & -6 \\ 3 & 0 & 4 \end{pmatrix} \begin{pmatrix} x_1 \\ x_2 \\ x_3 \end{pmatrix} = \begin{pmatrix} 1 \\ 0 \\ 0 \end{pmatrix}.$$

Similarly, to find the second and third columns of A^{-1} we want to solve the additional sets of equations,

$$\begin{pmatrix} 4 & 0 & 5 \\ 0 & 1 & -6 \\ 3 & 0 & 4 \end{pmatrix} \begin{pmatrix} x_1 \\ x_2 \\ x_3 \end{pmatrix} = \begin{pmatrix} 0 \\ 1 \\ 0 \end{pmatrix} \quad \text{and} \quad = \begin{pmatrix} 0 \\ 0 \\ 1 \end{pmatrix},$$

respectively. We thus have three sets of simultaneous equations that differ only in their righthand sides. This is exactly the situation described in Example 8 of the previous section. To solve them, we start with the tableau

(3)

x_1	x_2	x_3	-1			
4	0	5	1	0	0	$= 0$
0	1	-6	0	1	0	$= 0$
3	0	4	0	0	1	$= 0$

Pivoting on the 4 in the first row, we get

(4)

0	x_2	x_3	-1			
1	0	$\frac{5}{4}$	$\frac{1}{4}$	0	0	$= -x_1$
0	1	-6	0	1	0	$= 0$
0	0	$\frac{1}{4}$	$-\frac{3}{4}$	0	1	$= 0$

Because the second column has a 1 in the second row and zeros elsewhere, to pivot on the 1 all we need do is to interchange the labels. Then we can pivot on the $\frac{1}{4}$ in the third column to obtain the final tableau:

(5)

	0	0	0		-1		
1	0	0	4	0	5	$= -x_1$
0	1	0	-18	1	24	$= -x_2$
0	0	1	-3	0	4	$= -x_3$

We see that the inverse A^{-1}, which is given in (2), appears to the right of the vertical line in the tableau of (5).

   Of course, we were lucky that we could choose a sequence of pivots down the main diagonal of the matrix. Sometimes, because of the location of zeros in the matrix, or for other reasons, this is not possible. Let us rework the example with a different choice of pivots. Starting with (3), the following tableaux show what happens when we choose pivots down the other diagonal of the matrix.

(6)

	0	0	x_3		-1		
$\frac{4}{5}$	0	1	$\frac{1}{5}$	0	0	$= -x_3$
$\frac{24}{5}$	1	0	$\frac{6}{5}$	1	0	$= 0$
$-\frac{1}{5}$	0	0	$-\frac{4}{5}$	0	1	$= 0$

Again we can relabel the second row and column and proceed to the last pivot.

(7)

	0	0	0		-1		
0	0	1	-3	0	4	$= -x_3$
0	1	0	-18	1	24	$= -x_2$
1	0	0	4	0	-5	$= -x_1$

Now we do not find the inverse of A to the right of the vertical because we did not obtain the identity matrix to the left of the line. However, we can achieve the latter by simply interchanging the first and third rows, and we obtain the inverse matrix A^{-1} given in (2).

   The procedure just illustrated will find the inverse of any square matrix A, *providing A has an inverse*. We summarize it as follows:

RULE FOR INVERTING A MATRIX. Let A be a matrix that has an inverse. To find the inverse of A start with the tableau

$$(A \mid I)$$

and change it by row transformations (as described in Section 5) into the tableau

$$(I \mid B).$$

The resulting matrix B is the inverse A^{-1} of A.

Even if A has no inverse, the procedure just outlined can be started. At some point in the procedure a tableau will be found that is not of the desired final form and from which it is impossible to change by row transformations of the kind described.

Example 1. Show that the matrix

$$A = \begin{pmatrix} 4 & 0 & 8 \\ 0 & 1 & -6 \\ 2 & 0 & 4 \end{pmatrix}$$

has no inverse.

We set up the initial tableau as follows:

	x_1	x_2	x_3		-1		
(8)	4	0	8	1	0	0	$= 0$
	0	1	-6	0	1	0	$= 0$
	2	0	4	0	0	1	$= 0$

Pivoting on the 4 in the first row, we obtain

	0	x_2	x_3		-1		
(9)	1	0	2	$\frac{1}{4}$	0	0	$= -x_1$
	0	1	-6	0	1	0	$= 0$
	0	0	0	$-\frac{1}{2}$	0	1	$= 0$

We can pivot on the 1 in the second row and column by merely interchanging the labels. But we cannot pivot on the third row, because all its entries to the left of the vertical line are zero. In other words, we ended in Box 9 of the flow diagram in Figure 5. Hence we conclude that A has no inverse.

Because of the form of the final tableau in (7), we see that it is impossible to solve the equations

$$\begin{pmatrix} 4 & 0 & 8 \\ 0 & 1 & -6 \\ 2 & 0 & 4 \end{pmatrix} \begin{pmatrix} x_1 \\ x_2 \\ x_3 \end{pmatrix} = \begin{pmatrix} 0 \\ 0 \\ 1 \end{pmatrix},$$

since these equations are inconsistent, as is shown by the tests developed in Section 5. In other words, it is not possible to solve for the third column of the inverse matrix.

It is clear that an $n \times n$ matrix A has an inverse if and only if the following sets of simultaneous equations,

$$Ax = \begin{pmatrix} 1 \\ 0 \\ \vdots \\ 0 \end{pmatrix}, \quad Ax = \begin{pmatrix} 0 \\ 1 \\ \vdots \\ 0 \end{pmatrix}, \quad \dots, \quad Ax = \begin{pmatrix} 0 \\ 0 \\ \vdots \\ 1 \end{pmatrix},$$

can all be uniquely solved. And these sets of simultaneous equations, since they all share the same lefthand sides, can be solved uniquely if and only if the transformation of the rule for inverting a matrix can be carried out. Hence we have proved the following theorem.

THEOREM. A square matrix A has an inverse if and only if the tableau

$$(A \mid I)$$

can be transformed by row transformations into the tableau

$$(I \mid A^{-1}).$$

Example 2. Let us find the inverse of the matrix

$$A = \begin{pmatrix} 1 & 4 & 3 \\ 2 & 5 & 4 \\ 1 & -3 & -2 \end{pmatrix}.$$

The initial tableau is

	x_1	x_2	x_3	-1			
(10)	1	4	3	1	0	0	= 0
	2	5	4	0	1	0	= 0
	1	-3	-2	0	0	1	= 0

Transforming it by row transformations—that is, pivoting—we obtain the following series of tableaux:

	0	x_2	x_3		-1		
(11)	1	4	3	1	0	0	$= -x_1$
	0	-3	-2	-2	1	0	$= 0$
	0	-7	-5	-1	0	1	$= 0$

0	0	x_3		-1		
1	0	$\frac{1}{3}$	$-\frac{5}{3}$	$\frac{4}{3}$	0	$= -x_1$
0	1	$\frac{2}{3}$	$\frac{2}{3}$	$-\frac{1}{3}$	0	$= -x_2$
0	0	$-\frac{1}{3}$	$\frac{11}{3}$	$-\frac{7}{3}$	1	$= 0$

0	0	0		-1		
1	0	0	2	-1	1	$= -x_1$
0	1	0	8	-5	2	$= -x_2$
0	0	1	-11	7	-3	$= -x_3$

The inverse of A is then

$$A^{-1} = \begin{pmatrix} 2 & -1 & 1 \\ 8 & -5 & 2 \\ -11 & 7 & -3 \end{pmatrix}.$$

The reader should check that $A^{-1}A = AA^{-1} = I$.

EXERCISES

1. Compute the inverse of each of the following matrices.

$$A = \begin{pmatrix} 1 & 0 & 0 \\ 3 & 1 & 5 \\ -2 & 0 & 1 \end{pmatrix}, \qquad B = \begin{pmatrix} 4 & 3 & 2 \\ 0 & 1 & -1 \\ 0 & 0 & 7 \end{pmatrix},$$

$$C = \begin{pmatrix} 9 & -1 & 0 & 0 \\ 0 & 8 & -2 & 0 \\ 0 & 0 & 7 & -3 \\ 0 & 0 & 0 & 6 \end{pmatrix}, \qquad D = \begin{pmatrix} 1 & 0 & 0 \\ \frac{1}{3} & 4 & 0 \\ \frac{1}{2} & 3 & 2 \end{pmatrix}.$$

[*Partial Ans.* $A^{-1} = \begin{pmatrix} 1 & 0 & 0 \\ -13 & 1 & -5 \\ 2 & 0 & 1 \end{pmatrix}$; $D^{-1} = \begin{pmatrix} 1 & 0 & 0 \\ -\frac{1}{12} & \frac{1}{4} & 0 \\ -\frac{1}{8} & -\frac{3}{8} & \frac{1}{2} \end{pmatrix}$.]

2. Show that each of the following matrices fails to have an inverse.

$$A = \begin{pmatrix} 1 & 2 & 3 \\ -1 & 1 & 0 \\ 0 & 3 & 3 \end{pmatrix}, \qquad B = \begin{pmatrix} 1 & 1 & 0 \\ 2 & 0 & 5 \\ -1 & 1 & -5 \end{pmatrix},$$

$$C = \begin{pmatrix} 1 & 1 & 2 & 3 \\ 0 & 5 & 4 & 2 \\ -1 & -3 & 1 & 0 \\ 0 & 3 & 7 & 5 \end{pmatrix}, \qquad D = \begin{pmatrix} 1 & 1 & 1 \\ 1 & 1 & 1 \\ 1 & 1 & 1 \end{pmatrix}.$$

3. Let A, B, and D be the matrices of Exercise 1; let

$$x = \begin{pmatrix} x_1 \\ x_2 \\ x_3 \end{pmatrix} \quad \text{and} \quad w = (w_1, w_2, w_3);$$

let b, c, d, e, and f be the following vectors:

$$b = \begin{pmatrix} 3 \\ -1 \\ 0 \end{pmatrix}, \quad c = \begin{pmatrix} -1 \\ 2 \\ -3 \end{pmatrix}, \quad d = (3, 7, -2), \quad e = (1, 1, 1), \quad f = \begin{pmatrix} 1 \\ 1 \\ 1 \end{pmatrix}.$$

Use the inverses you computed in Exercise 1 to solve the following equations.

a. $Ax = b$.   b. $Bx = c$.   c. $wD = e$.
d. $wB = d$.   e. $wA = e$.   f. $Dx = f$.

[*Partial Ans.* a. $x = \begin{pmatrix} 3 \\ -40 \\ 6 \end{pmatrix}$; e. $w = (-10, 1, -4)$; f. $x = \begin{pmatrix} 1 \\ \frac{1}{6} \\ 0 \end{pmatrix}$.]

4. Rework Exercise 7 of Section 5 by first writing the equations in the form $Ax = b$, and finding the inverse of A.

5. Solve the following problem by first inverting the matrix. (Assume $ad \neq bc$.) If a grinding machine is supplied with x pounds of meat and y pounds of scraps (meat scraps and fat) per day, then it will produce $ax + by$ pounds of ground meat and $cx + dy$ pounds of hamburger per day. In other words, its production vector is

$$\begin{pmatrix} a & b \\ c & d \end{pmatrix}\begin{pmatrix} x \\ y \end{pmatrix}.$$

What inputs are necessary in order to get 25 pounds of ground meat and

70 pounds of hamburger? In order to get 20 pounds of ground meat and 100 pounds of hamburger?

6. For each of the matrices A and D in Exercise 2 find a nonzero vector whose product with the given matrix is 0.

7. Show that if A has no inverse, then neither does any of its positive powers A^k.

8. The formula $(A^{-1})^{-1} = A$ states that if A has an inverse A^{-1}, then A^{-1} itself has an inverse, and this inverse is A. Prove both parts of this statement.

9. Expand the formula $(AB)^{-1} = B^{-1}A^{-1}$ into a two-part statement analogous to the one in the exercise above. Then prove both parts of your statement.

10. *a.* Show that $(AB)^{-1} \neq A^{-1}B^{-1}$ for the matrices

$$A = \begin{pmatrix} 1 & 1 \\ 0 & 1 \end{pmatrix} \quad \text{and} \quad B = \begin{pmatrix} 1 & 0 \\ 2 & 1 \end{pmatrix}.$$

b. Find $(AB)^{-1}$ in two different ways. [*Hint:* Use Exercise 9.]

11. Give a criterion for deciding whether the 2×2 matrix $\begin{pmatrix} a & b \\ c & d \end{pmatrix}$ has an inverse. [*Ans.* $ad \neq bc$.]

12. Give a formula for $\begin{pmatrix} a & b \\ c & d \end{pmatrix}^{-1}$, when it exists.

13. If $\begin{pmatrix} a & b \\ c & d \end{pmatrix}$ has an inverse and has integer components, what condition must it fulfill in order that $\begin{pmatrix} a & b \\ c & d \end{pmatrix}^{-1}$ have integer components?

14. Let A be the matrix $\begin{pmatrix} 2 & -5 \\ -1 & 3 \end{pmatrix}$.

a. Find A^{-1}.

b. Use the result of (*a*) to solve the matrix equation $A^2x = b$, where

$$x = \begin{pmatrix} x_1 \\ x_2 \end{pmatrix} \quad \text{and} \quad b = \begin{pmatrix} -1 \\ 2 \end{pmatrix}$$

[*Ans.* $x = \begin{pmatrix} 36 \\ 13 \end{pmatrix}$.]

15. Let A be a square matrix that has an inverse. Show that the inverse of A^2 is $(A^{-1})^2$. What is the inverse of A^n?

Exercises 16 through 21 refer to the problem of computing $(I - Q)^{-1}$ where Q is a lower triangular matrix.

16. A matrix is *lower triangular* if it has zeros on and above its main diagonal. For instance,

$$Q = \begin{pmatrix} 0 & 0 & 0 \\ 4 & 0 & 0 \\ 10 & 5 & 0 \end{pmatrix}$$

is lower triangular.

a. Compute Q^2, saving the result for later exercises.

b. Show that $Q^3 = 0$, and also that $Q^k = 0$ for $k \geq 3$.

17. Consider the equation $w = wQ + d$ where Q is as in Exercise 16, and

$$w = (w_1, w_2, w_3), \qquad d = (20, 5, 3).$$

Solve symbolically for w.   [*Ans.* $w = d(I - Q)^{-1}$.]

18. *a.* Establish the identity

$$(I - Q)(I + Q + Q^2) = I - Q^3 = I$$

where Q is as in Exercise 16.

b. Show from (*a*) that $(I - Q)^{-1} = I + Q + Q^2$.

c. Use (*b*) to compute $(I - Q)^{-1}$.

$$\left[Ans.\ (I - Q)^{-1} = \begin{pmatrix} 1 & 0 & 0 \\ 4 & 1 & 0 \\ 30 & 5 & 1 \end{pmatrix} . \right]$$

d. Use (*c*) to solve for the w of Exercise 17.   [*Ans.* $w = (130, 20, 3)$.]

19. Let Q be any $n \times n$ lower triangular matrix.

a. Show that $Q^k = 0$ for $k \geq n$.

b. Show that $(I - Q)(I + Q + \cdots + Q^{n-1}) = I - Q^n = I$.

c. Show that $(I - Q)^{-1} = I + Q + \cdots + Q^{n-1}$.

20. Find $(I - Q)^{-1}$ for Q being each of the following.

a. $\begin{pmatrix} 0 & 0 & 0 & 0 \\ 7 & 0 & 0 & 0 \\ 2 & 0 & 0 & 0 \\ 3 & 4 & 5 & 0 \end{pmatrix}.$

b. $\begin{pmatrix} 0 & 0 & 0 & 0 & 0 \\ 2 & 0 & 0 & 0 & 0 \\ 5 & 3 & 0 & 0 & 0 \\ 0 & 1 & 8 & 0 & 0 \\ 10 & 5 & 0 & 3 & 0 \end{pmatrix}.$

$$\left[Ans.\ (a) \begin{pmatrix} 1 & 0 & 0 & 0 \\ 7 & 1 & 0 & 0 \\ 2 & 0 & 1 & 0 \\ 41 & 4 & 5 & 1 \end{pmatrix} . \right]$$

*7. THE PARTS-REQUIREMENTS LISTING PROBLEM

Consider a factory that produces parts, subassemblies and assemblies made from these parts, and subassemblies and assemblies made from parts and subassemblies. The assemblies are finished goods that are shipped to other factories, while the parts and subassemblies are constructed to go into assemblies. Suppose that the factory has received an order for a certain number of each of the assemblies; how many of each kind of part must be made to construct all the parts and subassemblies needed to fulfill the order?

For simple assemblies involving only a few parts this is a simple task. But for orders involving thousands of assemblies each involving thousands of parts and subassemblies the task becomes formidable. We shall develop matrix methods for solving this problem completely.

Let us assume that there are n different parts, subassemblies, and assemblies manufactured by the company. Denote these items by a_1, a_2, ..., a_n. It will be convenient to list these items in a certain order.

DEFINITION. We say that the manufactured items a_1, a_2, ..., a_n are listed in *technological order* if it is true that an item a_i does not appear on the list until all of the parts and subassemblies that must go into it have already appeared on the list.

For instance, a gasoline engine cannot appear on the list until all of its parts (such as pistons, rings, valves, connecting rods, block, head) have already appeared on the list.

It is also true that for any list of items that can actually be manufactured it must be possible to list them in technological order. For otherwise there would be a group of parts, no one of which could be listed until all others were listed, or in other words, no one of which could be produced until all the others were finished. And this would lead to an impossible manufacturing situation.

DEFINITION. Let q_{ij} be the number of units of items a_j directly needed to assemble one item a_i. Let Q be the matrix with components q_{ij}. We call Q the *quantity matrix*.

When we say that items are directly needed in the assembly of another item we mean that if we had on hand q_{i1} units of item a_1, q_{i2} units of item a_2, ..., and q_{in} units of a_n then we could immediately assemble one unit of a_i and have no parts left over. From this it is obvious that $q_{ii} = 0$, since an item cannot be required in the assembly of the same item without its being impossible to list the parts in technological order. Hence all entries *on* the main diagonal of Q are 0. Also, all entries *above* the main diagonal of Q are 0, since the technological order of listing the parts means that if a_j is needed to assemble a_i then a_j is listed before a_i and hence $j < i$.

> **Example 1.** A tripod mast of the type shown in Figure 6 is to be constructed. Each leg is assembled by bolting together (using 6 bolts) two rods to form a half leg, and then bolting together two half legs (again using 6 bolts) to form a leg. The three legs are bolted together at the top (using 15 bolts) to a plate to form the completed mast. Of course we can easily count the various parts requirements. But let us first set up the quantity matrix. From the foregoing description we see that Q is as given in Figure 7. For ease of reading, zero entries above the main diagonal are omitted from the matrix. We note that all the nonzero entries appear below the main diagonal.

Because of the lower-triangular structure of the Q matrix it enjoys a special property asserted in the following theorem.

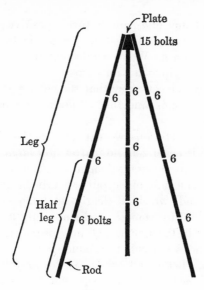

Figure 6

$$
Q = \begin{array}{l} \\ a_1 \text{ rods} \\ a_2 \text{ bolts} \\ a_3 \text{ half legs} \\ a_4 \text{ legs} \\ a_5 \text{ plate} \\ a_6 \text{ mast} \end{array}
\begin{array}{cccccc}
a_1 & a_2 & a_3 & a_4 & a_5 & a_6 \\
0 & & & & & \\
0 & 0 & & & & \\
2 & 6 & 0 & & & \\
0 & 6 & 2 & 0 & & \\
0 & 0 & 0 & 0 & 0 & \\
0 & 15 & 0 & 3 & 1 & 0
\end{array}
$$

Figure 7

THEOREM 1. If Q is a lower-triangular $n \times n$ matrix, then $Q^k = 0$ for $k \geq n$.

Proof. From the definition of matrix multiplication we note that Q^2 has a 0 diagonal below the main diagonal, Q^3 has two such diagonals, and so on. Hence $Q^n = 0$, and thus if $k \geq n$, $Q^k = Q^{k-n}Q^n = 0$.

The powers of the matrix Q have interesting interpretations. To see what these are let $q_{ij}^{(2)}$ be the i, jth entry of Q^2. Then, using the rule for matrix multiplication, we see that

$$(1) \qquad q_{ij}^{(2)} = q_{i1}q_{1j} + q_{i2}q_{2j} + \cdots + q_{i,i-1}q_{i-1,j},$$

where the sum in (1) is terminated at $i - 1$, since $q_{ij} = 0$ when $j \geq i$. If we remember that all the entries q_{ij} are nonnegative integers, we see from (1) that the only way $q_{ij}^{(2)}$ can be nonzero is for one or more products of the form $q_{ik}q_{kj}$ to be nonzero. But such a product is nonzero only if both terms are. And if $q_{ik} > 0$ and $q_{kj} > 0$, then a positive number of units of a_j are needed to produce one unit of a_k, and in turn a positive number of units of a_k are needed to produce one unit of a_i. We say in this case that a_i has *two-stage* requirements for a_j. We conclude that the entries of Q^2 give the number of two-stage requirements for items.

In the same way one can show that the entries of Q^3 give the three-stage requirements for items, and that Q^4 gives the number of four-stage requirements, and so on.

From these interpretations we can get another intuitive proof of Theorem 1. For if Q^k is never zero no matter how large k is, then the production process has nonzero k-stage demands for items for every k. Hence, in order to produce one unit of output, an arbitrarily large number of parts must be on hand, which is clearly an impossible manufacturing situation. Hence $Q^k = 0$ for some k, and since only $n - 1$ items precede the final one, Q^n must be 0. Of course, Q^k may be 0 already for a smaller k.

Now suppose that we decide to produce x_1 units of a_1, x_2 units of a_2, ..., and x_n units of a_n. Let us call $x = (x_1, x_2, \ldots, x_n)$ the *production vector*. How many units of each item must we plan to produce? To be more specific, let us ask the question, how many units of a_j must we produce? The answer can be obtained from the quantity matrix Q and the production vector x. Thus, in order to produce x_1 units of a_1, we will need to produce $x_1 q_{1j}$ units of a_j; to produce x_2 units of a_2, we need to produce $x_2 q_{2j}$ units of a_j; ... ; and to produce x_n units of a_n, we need to produce $x_n q_{nj}$ units of a_j. Adding these together, we get

$$(2) \qquad\qquad x_1 q_{1j} + x_2 q_{2j} + \cdots + x_n q_{nj}$$

as the total number of units of a_j that must be produced to manufacture the production vector x. It is easy to see that (2) is just the jth component of the vector xQ. Hence the vector xQ gives the internal production requirements for the factory when it produces the amounts given in the production vector x. We shall call the vector xQ the *internal demand vector*, since it measures the quantities of parts that must be manufactured and used internally by the factory in order to maintain production x.

Suppose now that the factory wants to ship d_1 units of a_1, d_2 units of a_2, ..., and d_n units of a_n. We call $d = (d_1, d_2, \ldots, d_n)$ the *outside demand vector*, since it measures the quantities of each part that are produced by the factory and shipped away, instead of being used internally by the factory for further production.

The question now is, what should the production vector x be in order to supply both the inside demand xQ and the outside demand d? It is easy to see that x must satisfy the following equation:

$$(3) \qquad\qquad x = xQ + d.$$

We now have the purely mathematical question of solving equation

(3) for x. If we take the xQ term to the lefthand side and factor out x, we get

$$(4) \qquad\qquad x(I - Q) = d.$$

If the matrix $I - Q$ has an inverse, it is easy to solve (4) by multiplying on the right by $(I - Q)^{-1}$. We get

$$(5) \qquad\qquad x = d(I - Q)^{-1}$$

as the desired solution. We now show that the inverse does exist.

THEOREM 2. Let Q be any matrix that satisfies the statement of Theorem 1. Then $I - Q$ has an inverse given by the equation

$$(6) \qquad\qquad (I - Q)^{-1} = I + Q + Q^2 + \cdots + Q^{k-1},$$

where k is the smallest number such that $Q^k = 0$.

Proof. For any r the following identity can be established by multiplying out the lefthand side:

$$(7) \qquad\qquad (I - Q)(I + Q + Q^2 + \cdots + Q^{r-1}) = I - Q^r.$$

If we now let k be the smallest number such that $Q^k = 0$, we see that

$$(8) \qquad\qquad (I - Q)(I + Q + Q^2 + \cdots + Q^{k-1}) = I,$$

which proves that the inverse exists and is given as stated in equation (6).

It can be shown from (6) that if the entries of Q are nonnegative integers, then so are the entries of $(I - Q)^{-1}$ (see Exercise 6).

The computation of the inverse of $I - Q$ can be carried out using the technique of Section 6, and the lower-triangular structure of Q makes it particularly easy to do this.

Example 1 (continued). For the Q matrix given above, the matrices $I - Q$ and $(I - Q)^{-1}$ are given in Figures 8 and 9. The computation of $(I - Q)^{-1}$, by the algorithm of Section 6, is very easy and is left to the reader as an exercise.

$$I - Q = \begin{pmatrix} 1 & & & & & \\ 0 & 1 & & & & \\ -2 & -6 & 1 & & & \\ 0 & -6 & -2 & 1 & & \\ 0 & 0 & 0 & 0 & 1 & \\ 0 & -15 & 0 & -3 & -1 & 1 \end{pmatrix}$$

Figure 8

$$(I - Q)^{-1} = \begin{pmatrix} 1 & & & & & \\ 0 & 1 & & & & \\ 2 & 6 & 1 & & & \\ 4 & 18 & 2 & 1 & & \\ 0 & 0 & 0 & 0 & 1 & \\ 12 & 69 & 6 & 3 & 1 & 1 \end{pmatrix}$$

Figure 9

Suppose now that a telephone company orders 10 of the tripod masts for use in setting up temporary transmission lines, and also orders 1000 bolts, 6 half legs, and 2 plates as spare parts in case of damage to the original masts. What are the production requirements on the factory to fulfill this order? We see that

$$d = (0, 1000, 6, 0, 2, 10);$$

hence the required production is given by

$$x = d(I - Q)^{-1} = (132, 1726, 66, 30, 12, 10),$$

as the reader can easily verify by carrying out the matrix multiplication. Thus the factory must produce 132 rods, 1726 bolts, 66 half legs, 30 legs, 12 plates, and 10 masts. It then has exactly the items needed to fulfill the order.

It may be argued that the problem above can be solved directly by having a clerk simply count the parts requirements, and indeed this is so. [This suggests that $(I - Q)^{-1}$ can be calculated by counting total parts requirements, see Exercise 9.] However, he would have to do the same kind of arithmetic for each different order that came in, and thus he would be doing over and over the same arithmetical calculations. Hence, even though the work of finding $(I - Q)^{-1}$ may be rather extensive, once it is done it can be used repeatedly in calculating the parts requirements for new orders. Then the single matrix multiplication $d(I - Q)^{-1}$ is all the calculation that is needed for each new demand d.

It should also be remarked that high-speed computers can be programmed to carry out these computations very quickly.

EXERCISES

1. The Ajax Electric Company makes a common household convenience called a Shock Unit. A Shock Unit contains two basic components, A and B. These components are connected by a resistor and two electric coils. Component A has in it two resistors and one electric coil. Component B has in it three electric coils and one resistor. To make an electric coil requires 20 units of wire. For every coil or resistor two units of wire

are needed for connections. Set up the technological matrix for producing a Shock Unit.

$$Ans.\ Q = \begin{bmatrix} W \\ C \\ R \\ A \\ B \\ S \end{bmatrix} \begin{pmatrix} 0 \\ 22 & 0 \\ 2 & 0 & 0 \\ 0 & 1 & 2 & 0 \\ 0 & 3 & 1 & 0 & 0 \\ 0 & 2 & 1 & 1 & 1 & 0 \end{pmatrix}.$$

2. Find $(I - Q)^{-1}$ for Exercise 1.

3. Compute the production vector x in Exercise 1 for each of the following demands:

   a. Three Shock Units. [*Ans.* $x = (420, 18, 12, 3, 3, 3)$.]

   b. Two Shock Units, three spare resistors, two spare coils, and ten units of wire.

   c. Two Shock Units, two spare units A, and two spare units B.

                       [*Ans.* $x = (468, 20, 14, 4, 4, 2)$.]

4. Let Q be each of the lower triangular matrices listed below. Find $(I - Q)^{-1}$.

   a.
$$\begin{pmatrix} 0 \\ 2 & 0 \\ 5 & 3 & 0 \\ 0 & 1 & 8 & 0 \\ 10 & 4 & 0 & 3 & 0 \end{pmatrix}.$$
   b.
$$\begin{pmatrix} 0 \\ 7 & 0 \\ 2 & 0 & 0 \\ 3 & 4 & 5 & 0 \end{pmatrix}.$$

5. Find the production vectors needed to satisfy the outside demand vectors given below, if the quantity matrices are as given in the corresponding parts of Exercise 4.

   a. $d = (2, 0, 3, 10, 15)$.   *b.* $d = (0, 1, 5, 8)$.

6. Use Theorem 2 to show that if the entries of a quantity matrix Q are nonnegative integers, then so are the entries of $(I - Q)^{-1}$.

7. If Q is a quantity matrix, show that the entries of Q^3 give the three-stage requirements for items.

8. Write the solution x as a sum of terms dQ^i, using (5) and (6). Interpret the individual terms and verify that the sum does represent the required x.

9. Let Q be any lower-triangular matrix with integer entries such as those in Exercise 4. Devise a method for computing $(I - Q)^{-1}$ by interpreting the entries of Q as parts requirements, and merely counting the total parts requirements. Check your method by using it on the matrices in Exercise 4 and comparing with your previous answers.

10. Compute the production vector, for each of the demands given below, for the production process of Example 1.

   a. $d = (10, 500, 50, 0, 20, 300)$.

   b. $d = (0, 2000, 0, 15, 5, 125)$.

8. APPLICATIONS OF MATRIX THEORY TO MARKOV CHAINS

In this section we shall show applications of matrix theory to Markov chains. For simplicity we shall confine our discussion to three-state Markov chains, but a similar procedure will work for any other Markov chain.

In Section 9 of Chapter 3, we noted that to each Markov chain there was a matrix of transition probabilities. For example, if there are three states, a_1, a_2, and a_3, then

$$P = \begin{array}{c} \\ a_1 \\ a_2 \\ a_3 \end{array} \begin{array}{ccc} a_1 & a_2 & a_3 \\ \begin{pmatrix} p_{11} & p_{12} & p_{13} \\ p_{21} & p_{22} & p_{23} \\ p_{31} & p_{32} & p_{33} \end{pmatrix} \end{array}$$

is the transition matrix for the chain. Recall that the *row sums* of P are all equal to 1. Such a matrix is called a transition matrix.

DEFINITION. A *transition matrix* is a square matrix with nonnegative entries such that the sum of the entries in each row is 1.

In order to obtain a Markov chain we must specify how the process starts. Suppose that the initial state is chosen by a chance device that selects state a_j with probability $p_j^{(0)}$. We can represent these initial probabilities by means of the vector $p^{(0)} = (p_1^{(0)}, p_2^{(0)}, p_3^{(0)})$. As in Exercise 10 of Section 4, we can construct a tree measure for as many steps of the process as we wish to consider. Let $p_j^{(n)}$ be the probability that the process will be in state a_j after n steps. Let the vector of these probabilities be $p^{(n)} = (p_1^{(n)}, p_2^{(n)}, p_3^{(n)})$.

DEFINITION. A row vector p is called a *probability vector* if it has non-negative components whose sum is 1.

Obviously the vectors $p^{(0)}$ and $p^{(n)}$ are probability vectors. Also each row of a transition matrix is a probability vector.

By means of the tree measure it can be shown that these probabilities satisfy the following equations:

$$p_1^{(n)} = p_1^{(n-1)}p_{11} + p_2^{(n-1)}p_{21} + p_3^{(n-1)}p_{31},$$
$$p_2^{(n)} = p_1^{(n-1)}p_{12} + p_2^{(n-1)}p_{22} + p_3^{(n-1)}p_{32},$$
$$p_3^{(n)} = p_1^{(n-1)}p_{13} + p_2^{(n-1)}p_{23} + p_3^{(n-1)}p_{33}.$$

It is not hard to give intuitive meanings to these equations. The first one, for example, expresses the fact that the probability of being in state a_1 after n steps is the sum of the probabilities of being at each of the three possible states after $n - 1$ steps and then moving to state a_1 on the nth step. The interpretation of the other equations is similar.

If we recall the definition of the product of a vector times a matrix, we can write the equations above as

$$p^{(n)} = p^{(n-1)}P.$$

If we substitute values of n, we get the equations: $p^{(1)} = p^{(0)}P$; $p^{(2)} = p^{(1)}P = p^{(0)}P^2$; $p^{(3)} = p^{(2)}P = p^{(0)}P^3$; and so on. In general, it is evident that

$$p^{(n)} = p^{(0)}P^n.$$

Thus we see that, if we multiply the vector $p^{(0)}$ of initial probabilities by the nth power of the transition matrix P, we obtain the vector $p^{(n)}$, whose components give the probabilities of being in each of the states after n steps.

In particular, let us choose $p^{(0)} = (1, 0, 0)$, which is equivalent to letting the process start in state a_1. From the equation above we see that then $p^{(n)}$ is the first row of the matrix P^n. Thus the elements of the first row of the matrix P^n give us the probabilities that after n steps the process will be in a given one of the states, under the assumption that it started in state a_1. In the same way, if we choose $p^{(0)} = (0, 1, 0)$, we see that the second row of P^n gives the probabilities that the process will be in one of the various states after n steps, given that it started in state a_2. Similarly the third row gives these probabilities, assuming that the process started in state a_3.

In Section 9 of Chapter 3, we considered special Markov chains that started in given fixed states. There we arrived at a matrix $P^{(n)}$ whose ith row gave the probabilities of the process ending in the various states, given that it started at state a_i. By comparing the work that we did there with what we have just done, we see that the matrix $P^{(n)}$ is merely the nth power of P, that is, $P^{(n)} = P^n$. (Compare Exercise 10 of Section 4.) Matrix multiplication thus gives a convenient way of computing the desired probabilities.

DEFINITION. The probability vector w is a *fixed point* of the matrix P, if $w = wP$.

Example 1. Consider the transition matrix

$$P = \begin{pmatrix} \frac{2}{3} & \frac{1}{3} \\ \frac{1}{2} & \frac{1}{2} \end{pmatrix} = \begin{pmatrix} .667 & .333 \\ .500 & .500 \end{pmatrix}.$$

If $w = (.6, .4)$, then we see that

$$wP = (.6, .4)\begin{pmatrix} \frac{2}{3} & \frac{1}{3} \\ \frac{1}{2} & \frac{1}{2} \end{pmatrix} = (.6, .4) = w,$$

so that w is the fixed point of the matrix P.

If we had happened to choose the vector w as our initial probability vector $p^{(0)}$, we would have had $p^{(n)} = p^{(0)}P^n = wP^n = w = p^{(0)}$. In this case the probability of being at any particular state is the same at all steps of the process. Such a process is in *equilibrium*.

As seen above, in the study of Markov chains we are interested in the powers of the matrix P. To see what happens to these powers, let us further consider the example.

Example 1 (continued). Suppose that we compute powers of the matrix P in the example above. We have

$$P^2 = \begin{pmatrix} .611 & .389 \\ .583 & .417 \end{pmatrix}, \qquad P^3 = \begin{pmatrix} .602 & .398 \\ .597 & .403 \end{pmatrix}, \qquad \text{and so on.}$$

It looks as if the matrix P^n is approaching the matrix

$$W = \begin{pmatrix} .6 & .4 \\ .6 & .4 \end{pmatrix};$$

and, in fact, it can be shown that this is the case. (When we say that P^n approaches W we mean that each entry in the matrix P^n gets close to the corresponding entry in W.) Note that each row of W is the fixed point w of the matrix P.

DEFINITION. A transition matrix is said to be *regular* if some power of the matrix has only positive components.

Thus the matrix in the example is regular, since every entry in it is positive, so that the first power of the matrix has all positive entries. Other examples occur in the exercises.

THEOREM. If P is a regular transition matrix, then

    i. the powers P^n approach a matrix W,
    ii. each row of W is the same probability vector w,
    iii. the components of w are positive.

We omit the proof of this theorem;* however, we can prove the next theorem.

THEOREM. If P is a regular transition matrix, and W and w are given by the previous theorem, then

    a. if p is any probability vector, pP^n approaches w;
    b. the vector w is the unique fixed-point probability vector of P.

Proof. First let us consider the vector pW. The first column of W has a w_1 in each row. Hence in the first component of pW each component of p is multiplied by w_1, and therefore we have w_1 times the sum of the components of p, which is w_1. Doing the same for the other components, we

---

* For an elementary proof see Kemeny, Mirkil, Snell, and Thompson, *Finite Mathematical Structures* (Englewood Cliffs, N.J.: Prentice-Hall, Inc., 1959), chap. 6, sec. 3.

note that pW is simply w. But pP^n approaches pW; hence it approaches w. Thus if any probability vector is multiplied repeatedly by P, it approaches the fixed point w. This proves part (a).

Since the powers of P approach W, $P^{n+1} = P^n P$ approaches W, but it also approaches WP; hence $WP = W$. Any one row of this matrix equation states that $wP = w$; hence w is a fixed point (and by the previous theorem a probability vector). We must still show that it is unique. Let u be any probability-vector fixed point of P. By part (a) we know that uP^n approaches w. But since u is a fixed point, $uP^n = u$. Hence u remains fixed but "approaches" w. This is possible only if $u = w$. Hence w is the only probability-vector fixed point. This completes the proof of part (b).

The following is an important consequence of this theorem. If we take as p the vector $p^{(0)}$ of initial probabilities, then the vector $pP^n = p^{(n)}$ gives the probabilities after n steps, and this vector approaches w. Therefore, no matter what the initial probabilities are, if P is regular, then after a large number of steps the probability that the process is in state a_j will be very nearly w_j.

We noted for an independent-trials process that if p is the probability of a given outcome a, then this may be given an alternate interpretation by means of the law of large numbers: in a long series of experiments the fraction of outcomes in which a occurs is approximately p, and the approximation gets better and better as the number of experiments increases. For a regular Markov chain the components of the vector w play the analogous role. That is, the fraction of times that the chain is in state a_i approaches w_i, no matter how one starts.

Example 1 (continued). Let us take $p^{(0)} = (.1, .9)$ and see how $p^{(n)}$ changes. Using P as in the example above, we have that $p^{(1)} = (.5167, .4833)$, $p^{(2)} = (.5861, .4139)$, and $p^{(3)} = (.5977, .4023)$. Recalling that $w = (.6, .4)$, we see that these vectors do approach w.

Example 2. As an example let us derive the formulas for the fixed point of a 2×2 transition matrix with positive components. Such a matrix is of the form

$$S = \begin{pmatrix} 1 - a & a \\ b & 1 - b \end{pmatrix},$$

where $0 < a < 1$ and $0 < b < 1$. Since S is regular, it has a unique probability-vector fixed point $w = (w_1, w_2)$. Its components must satisfy the equations

$$w_1(1 - a) + w_2 b = w_1,$$
$$w_1 a + w_2(1 - b) = w_2.$$

Each of these equations reduces to the single equation $w_1 a = w_2 b$. This single equation has an infinite number of solutions. However, since w is a probability vector, we must also have $w_1 + w_2 = 1$, and the new equation gives the point $[b/(a + b), a/(a + b)]$ as the unique fixed-point probability vector of S.

Example 3. Suppose that the President of the United States tells person A his intention either to run or not to run in the next election. Then A relays the news to B, who in turn relays the message to C, and so on, always to some new person. Assume that there is a probability $p > 0$ that any one person, when he gets the message, will reverse it before passing it on to the next person. What is the probability that the nth man to hear the message will be told that the President will run? We can consider this as a two-state Markov chain, with states indicated by "yes" and "no." The process is in state "yes" at time n if the nth person to receive the message was told that the President would run. It is in state "no" if he was told that the President would not run. The matrix P of transition probabilities is then

$$
\begin{array}{c}
\quad\quad \text{yes} \quad\ \text{no} \\
\begin{array}{c} \text{yes} \\ \text{no} \end{array}
\begin{pmatrix} 1 - p & p \\ p & 1 - p \end{pmatrix}.
\end{array}
$$

Then the matrix P^n gives the probabilities that the nth man is given a certain answer, assuming that the President said "yes" (first row) or assuming that the President said "no" (second row). We know that these rows approach w. From the formulas of the last section, we find that $w = (\frac{1}{2}, \frac{1}{2})$. Hence the probabilities for the nth man's being told "yes" or "no" approach $\frac{1}{2}$ independently of the initial decision of the President. For a large number of people, we can expect that approximately one-half will be told that the President will run and the other half that he will not, independently of the actual decision of the President.

Suppose now that the probability a that a person will change the news from "yes" to "no" when transmitting it to the next person is different from the probability b that he will change it from "no" to "yes." Then the matrix of transition probabilities becomes

$$
\begin{array}{c}
\quad\quad \text{yes} \quad\ \text{no} \\
\begin{array}{c} \text{yes} \\ \text{no} \end{array}
\begin{pmatrix} 1 - a & a \\ b & 1 - b \end{pmatrix}.
\end{array}
$$

In this case $w = [b/(a + b), a/(a + b)]$. Thus there is a probability of approximately $b/(a + b)$ that the nth person will be told that the President will run. Assuming that n is large, this probability is independent of the actual decision of the President. For n large we can expect, in this case, that a proportion approximately equal to $b/(a + b)$ will have been told that the President will run, and a proportion $a/(a + b)$ will have been told that he will not run. The important thing to note is that, from the assumptions we have made, it follows that it is not the President but the people themselves who determine the probability that a person will be told "yes" or "no," and the proportion of people in the long run that are given one of these predictions.

Example 4. For this example, we continue the study of Example 2 in Chapter 3, Section 9. The first approximation treated in that example leads to a two-state Markov chain, and the results are similar to those obtained in Example 1 above. The second approximation led to a four-state Markov chain with transition probabilities given by the matrix

$$\begin{array}{c} \\ \text{AA} \\ \text{XA} \\ \text{AX} \\ \text{XX} \end{array} \begin{array}{cccc} \text{AA} & \text{XA} & \text{AX} & \text{XX} \\ \begin{pmatrix} 1-a & 0 & a & 0 \\ b & 0 & 1-b & 0 \\ 0 & 1-c & 0 & c \\ 0 & d & 0 & 1-d \end{pmatrix} \end{array}.$$

If a, b, c, and d are all different from 0 or 1, then the square of the matrix has no zeros, and hence the matrix is regular. The fixed probability vector is found in the usual way (see Exercise 18) and is

$$\left(\frac{bd}{bd + 2ad + ca}, \frac{ad}{bd + 2ad + ca}, \frac{ad}{bd + 2ad + ca}, \frac{ca}{bd + 2ad + ca} \right).$$

Note that the probability of being in state AX after a large number of steps is equal to the probability of being in state XA. This shows that in equilibrium a change from A to X must have the same probability as a change from X to A.

From the fixed vector we can find the probability of purchasing A in the far future. This is found by adding the probability of being in state AA and XA, giving

$$\frac{bd + ad}{bd + 2ad + ca}.$$

Notice that, to find the probability of purchasing A on the purchase preceding some purchase far in the future, we should add the probabilities of being in states AA and AX. That we get the same result corresponds to the fact that predictions far in the future are essentially independent of the particular period being predicted. In other words, the process is acting as if it were in equilibrium.

EXERCISES

1. Which of the following matrices are regular?

a. $\begin{pmatrix} \frac{1}{2} & \frac{1}{2} \\ \frac{1}{2} & \frac{1}{2} \end{pmatrix}$.

b. $\begin{pmatrix} 0 & 1 \\ \frac{1}{4} & \frac{3}{4} \end{pmatrix}$.   [Regular]

c. $\begin{pmatrix} 1 & 0 \\ \frac{1}{3} & \frac{2}{3} \end{pmatrix}$.

d. $\begin{pmatrix} \frac{1}{5} & \frac{4}{5} \\ 1 & 0 \end{pmatrix}$.   [Regular]

e. $\begin{pmatrix} \frac{1}{2} & \frac{1}{2} \\ 0 & 1 \end{pmatrix}$.

f. $\begin{pmatrix} 0 & 1 \\ 1 & 0 \end{pmatrix}$.   [Not regular]

g. $\begin{pmatrix} \frac{1}{2} & \frac{1}{2} & 0 \\ 0 & \frac{1}{2} & \frac{1}{2} \\ \frac{1}{3} & \frac{1}{3} & \frac{1}{3} \end{pmatrix}$.

h. $\begin{pmatrix} \frac{1}{3} & 0 & \frac{2}{3} \\ 0 & 1 & 0 \\ 0 & \frac{1}{5} & \frac{4}{5} \end{pmatrix}$.   [Not regular]

2. Show that the 2×2 matrix

$$S = \begin{pmatrix} 1-a & a \\ b & 1-b \end{pmatrix}$$

is a regular transition matrix if and only if either

(i) $0 < a \leq 1$ and $0 < b < 1$; or
(ii) $0 < a < 1$ and $0 < b \leq 1$.

3. Find the fixed point for the matrix in Exercise 2 for each of the cases listed there. [*Hint:* Most of the cases were covered in the text above.]

4. Find the fixed point w for each of the following regular matrices.

a. $\begin{pmatrix} \frac{3}{4} & \frac{1}{4} \\ \frac{1}{2} & \frac{1}{2} \end{pmatrix}$.   [*Ans.* $w = (\frac{2}{3}, \frac{1}{3})$.]

b. $\begin{pmatrix} .9 & .1 \\ .1 & .9 \end{pmatrix}$.

c. $\begin{pmatrix} \frac{3}{4} & \frac{1}{4} & 0 \\ 0 & \frac{2}{3} & \frac{1}{3} \\ \frac{1}{4} & \frac{1}{4} & \frac{1}{2} \end{pmatrix}$.   [*Ans.* $w = (\frac{2}{7}, \frac{3}{7}, \frac{2}{7})$.]

5. Let $p^0 = (\frac{1}{2}, \frac{1}{2})$ and compute $p^{(1)}$, $p^{(2)}$, and $p^{(3)}$ for the matrices in Exercises 4a. and 4b. Do they approach the fixed points of these matrices?

6. Give a probability-theory interpretation to the condition of regularity.

7. Consider the two-state Markov chain with transition matrix

$$P = \begin{matrix} & a_1 \ a_2 \\ \begin{matrix} a_1 \\ a_2 \end{matrix} & \begin{pmatrix} 0 & 1 \\ 1 & 0 \end{pmatrix} \end{matrix}.$$

What is the probability that after n steps the process is in state a_1 if it started in state a_2? Does this probability become independent of the initial position for large n? If not, the theorem of this section must not apply. Why? Does the matrix have a unique fixed-point probability vector?

8. Prove that, if a regular 3×3 transition matrix has the property that its column sums are 1, its fixed-point probability vector is $(\frac{1}{3}, \frac{1}{3}, \frac{1}{3})$. State a similar result for $n \times n$ transition matrices having column sums equal to 1.

9. Compute the first five powers of the matrix

$$P = \begin{pmatrix} .8 & .2 \\ .2 & .8 \end{pmatrix}.$$

From these, guess the fixed-point vector w. Check by computing what w is.

10. Show that all transition matrices of the form

$$\begin{pmatrix} 1 - a & a \\ a & 1 - a \end{pmatrix},$$

where $0 < a < 1$, have the same unique fixed point.   [*Ans.* $w = (\frac{1}{2}, \frac{1}{2})$.]

11. A professor has three pet questions, one of which occurs on every test he gives. The students know his habits well. He never uses the same question twice in a row. If he used question one last time, he tosses a coin, and uses question two if a head comes up. If he used question two, he tosses two coins and switches to question three if both come up heads. If he used question three, he tosses three coins and switches to question one if all three come up heads. In the long run, which question does he use most often, and how frequently is it used?

[*Ans.* Question two, 40 percent of the time.]

12. A professor tries not to be late for class too often. If he is late one day, he is 90 percent sure to be on time next time. If he is on time, then the next day there is a 30 percent chance of his being late. In the long run, how often is he late for class?

13. The Land of Oz is blessed by many things, but not good weather. They *never* have two nice days in a row. If they have a nice day they are just as likely to have snow as rain the next day. If they have snow (or rain), they have an even chance of having the same the next day. If there is a change from snow or rain, only half of the time is this a change to a nice day. Set up a three-state Markov chain to describe this situation. Find the long-range probability for rain, for snow, and for a nice day. What fraction of the days does it rain in the Land of Oz?

[*Ans.* The probabilities are: nice, $\frac{1}{5}$; rain, $\frac{2}{5}$; snow, $\frac{2}{5}$.]

14. Let S be the matrix

$$S = \begin{pmatrix} 1 & 0 \\ \frac{1}{2} & \frac{1}{2} \end{pmatrix}.$$

Compute the unique probability-vector fixed point of S, and use your result to prove that S is not regular.

15. Show that the matrix

$$S = \begin{pmatrix} 1 & 0 & 0 \\ \frac{1}{2} & 0 & \frac{1}{2} \\ 0 & 0 & 1 \end{pmatrix}$$

has more than one probability-vector fixed point. Find the matrix that S^n approaches, and show that it is not a matrix all of whose rows are the same.

16. Let P be a transition matrix in which all the entries that are not zero have been replaced by x's. Devise a method of raising such a matrix to powers in order to check for regularity. Illustrate your method by showing that

$$P = \begin{pmatrix} 0 & 1 & 0 \\ 0 & 0 & 1 \\ \frac{1}{2} & \frac{1}{2} & 0 \end{pmatrix}$$

is regular.

17. Consider a Markov chain such that it is possible to go from any state a_i to any state a_j and such that p_{kk} is not 0 for at least one state a_k. Prove that the chain is regular. [*Hint:* Consider the times that it is possible to go from a_i to a_j via a_k.]

18. Show that the vector given in Example 4 is the fixed vector of the transition matrix.

19. Determine whether each of the following matrices is regular.

a. $\begin{pmatrix} 0 & 1 \\ \frac{3}{4} & \frac{1}{4} \end{pmatrix}$.

b. $\begin{pmatrix} \frac{1}{2} & 0 & \frac{1}{2} \\ 0 & 1 & 0 \\ \frac{1}{3} & \frac{1}{2} & \frac{1}{6} \end{pmatrix}$.

c. $\begin{pmatrix} 0 & 0 & 1 \\ 0 & 1 & 0 \\ 1 & 0 & 0 \end{pmatrix}$.

d. $\begin{pmatrix} 0 & 0 & 1 \\ \frac{1}{2} & 0 & \frac{1}{2} \\ \frac{1}{2} & \frac{1}{2} & 0 \end{pmatrix}$.

e. $\begin{pmatrix} \frac{1}{2} & \frac{1}{2} & 0 & 0 \\ \frac{3}{4} & \frac{1}{2} & 0 & 0 \\ 0 & 0 & \frac{1}{3} & \frac{2}{3} \\ \frac{1}{4} & 0 & \frac{1}{4} & \frac{1}{2} \end{pmatrix}$.

f. $\begin{pmatrix} 0 & \frac{1}{2} & \frac{1}{2} \\ 1 & 0 & 0 \\ 1 & 0 & 0 \end{pmatrix}$.

[*Ans. a.* and *d.* are regular.]

20. Consider the three-state Markov chain with transition matrix

$$P = \begin{pmatrix} \frac{1}{2} & \frac{1}{3} & \frac{1}{6} \\ \frac{1}{2} & \frac{1}{2} & 0 \\ \frac{1}{2} & \frac{1}{2} & 0 \end{pmatrix}.$$

a. Show that the matrix has a unique fixed probability vector.

[*Ans.* $(\frac{1}{2}, \frac{5}{12}, \frac{1}{12})$.]

b. Approximately what is the entry in the third column of the first row of P^{100}?

c. What is the interpretation of the entry estimated in *b.*?

21. Assume that it is known that of the sons of Harvard alumni, 80 percent go to Harvard and all the rest go to Yale; of the sons of Yale men, 40 percent go to Yale, the remainder split evenly between Harvard and Dartmouth; and of the sons of Dartmouth men, 70 percent go to Dartmouth, 20 percent to Harvard, and 10 percent to Yale.

a. Set up this process as a Markov chain.

b. What is the probability that the grandson of a Harvard man goes to Harvard?

c. What is the long-run fraction expected in each school?

[*Ans. b.* .7; *c.* (Harvard, $\frac{5}{9}$; Yale, $\frac{2}{9}$; Dartmouth, $\frac{2}{9}$.)]

9. ABSORBING MARKOV CHAINS

In this section we shall consider a kind of Markov chain quite different from regular chains.

DEFINITION. A state in a Markov chain is an *absorbing state* if it is impossible to leave it. A Markov chain is *absorbing* if (1) it has at least one absorbing state, and (2) from every state it is possible to go to an absorbing state (not necessarily in one step).

Example 1. A particle moves on a line; each time it moves one unit to the right with probability $\frac{1}{2}$, or one unit to the left. We introduce barriers so that if it ever reaches one of these barriers it stays there. As a simple example, let the states be 0, 1, 2, 3, 4. States 0 and 4 are absorbing states. The transition matrix is then

$$P = \begin{array}{c} \\ 0 \\ 1 \\ 2 \\ 3 \\ 4 \end{array} \begin{pmatrix} \begin{array}{ccccc} 0 & 1 & 2 & 3 & 4 \end{array} \\ \begin{array}{ccccc} 1 & 0 & 0 & 0 & 0 \\ \frac{1}{2} & 0 & \frac{1}{2} & 0 & 0 \\ 0 & \frac{1}{2} & 0 & \frac{1}{2} & 0 \\ 0 & 0 & \frac{1}{2} & 0 & \frac{1}{2} \\ 0 & 0 & 0 & 0 & 1 \end{array} \end{pmatrix}.$$

The states 1, 2, 3 are all nonabsorbing states, and from any of these it is possible to reach the absorbing states 0 and 4. Hence the chain is an absorbing chain. Such a process is usually called a *random walk*.

When a process reaches an absorbing state we shall say that it is *absorbed*.

THEOREM. In an absorbing Markov chain the probability that the process will be absorbed is 1.

We shall indicate only the basic idea of the proof of the theorem. From each nonabsorbing state, a_j, it is possible to reach an absorbing state. Let n_j be the minimum number of steps required to reach an absorbing state, starting from state a_j. Let p_j be the probability that, starting from state a_j, the process will *not* reach an absorbing state in n_j steps. Then $p_j < 1$. Let n be the largest of the n_j and let p be the largest of the p_j. The probability of not being absorbed in n steps is less than p, in $2n$ steps is less than p^2, and so on. Since $p < 1$, these probabilities tend to zero.

For an absorbing Markov chain we consider three interesting questions: (a) What is the probability that the process will end up in a given absorbing state? (b) On the average, how long will it take for the process to be absorbed? (c) On the average, how many times will the process be in each nonabsorbing state? The answer to all these questions depends, in general, on the state from which the process starts.

Consider then an arbitrary absorbing Markov chain. Let us renumber the states so that the absorbing states come first. If there are r absorbing states and s nonabsorbing states, the transition matrix will have the following *canonical* (or standard) *form*.

(1)
$$P = \begin{array}{c} \\ r \\ s \end{array} \left(\begin{array}{c|c} \overset{r\ \text{states}}{I} & \overset{s\ \text{states}}{O} \\ \hline R & Q \end{array} \right).$$

Here I is an r-by-r identity matrix, O is an r-by-s zero matrix, R is an s-by-r matrix, and Q is an s-by-s matrix. The first r states are absorbing and the last s states are nonabsorbing.

In Section 8 we saw that the entries of the matrix P^n gave the probabilities of being in the various states starting from the various states. It is easy to show that P^n is of the form

(2)
$$P^n = \begin{pmatrix} I & O \\ * & Q^n \end{pmatrix}$$

where the asterisk stands for the s-by-r matrix in the lower lefthand corner of P^n, which we do not compute here. The form of P^n shows that the entries of Q^n give the probabilities for being in each of the nonabsorbing states after n steps for each possible nonabsorbing starting state. (After zero steps the process must be in the same nonabsorbing state in which it started. Hence $Q^0 = I$.) By our first theorem, the probability of being in the nonabsorbing states after n steps approaches zero. Thus every entry of Q^n must approach zero as n approaches infinity; that is, $Q^n \to 0$.

Consider then the infinite series

$$I + Q + Q^2 + Q^3 + \cdots.$$

Suppose that Q were a nonnegative number x instead of a nonnegative matrix. To correspond to the fact that $Q^n \to O$ we take x to be less than 1. Then

$$1 + x + x^2 + \cdots = (1 - x)^{-1}.$$

By an argument similar to that of Theorem 2, Section 7, it can be proved that the matrix series behaves in exactly the same way. That is,

$$I + Q + Q^2 + \cdots = (I - Q)^{-1}.$$

The matrix $(I - Q)^{-1}$ will be called the *fundamental matrix* for the given absorbing chain. It has the following important interpretation:

Let n_{ij} be the mean number of times that the chain is in state a_j if it starts in state a_i, for nonabsorbing states a_i and a_j. Let N be the matrix whose components are n_{ij}. We will show that $N = (I - Q)^{-1}$. If we take into account the contribution of the original (which is 1 if $i = j$ and 0 otherwise), we may write the equation

$$n_{ij} = d_{ij} + (p_{i,r+1}n_{r+1,j} + p_{i,r+2}n_{r+2,j} + \cdots + p_{i,r+s}n_{r+s,j}),$$

where d_{ij} is 1 if $i = j$ and 0 otherwise. (Note that the sum in parentheses is merely the sum of the products $p_{ik}n_{kj}$ for k running over the nonabsorbing states.) This equation may be written in matrix form:

$$N = I + QN.$$

Then $(I - Q)N = I$, and hence $N = (I - Q)^{-1}$, as was to be shown. Thus we have found a probabilistic interpretation for our fundamental matrix; its i, j entry is the mean number of times that the chain is in state a_j if it starts at a_i. The fact that $N = I + Q + Q^2 + \cdots$ also has a probabilistic interpretation. Since the i, j entry of Q^n is the probability of being in a_j

on the nth step if we start at a_i, we have shown that the mean of the number of times in state a_j may be written as the sum of the probabilities of being there on particular steps. Thus we have answered question (c) as follows.

THEOREM. Let $N = (I - Q)^{-1}$ be the fundamental matrix for an absorbing chain. Then the entries of N give the mean number of times in each nonabsorbing state for each possible nonabsorbing starting state.

Example 1 (continued). In Example 1 the transition matrix in canonical form is

$$
\begin{array}{c}
 \\
0 \\
4 \\
\\
1 \\
2 \\
3
\end{array}
\begin{array}{cc}
\begin{array}{cccccc}
0 & 4 & 1 & 2 & 3
\end{array} \\
\left(\begin{array}{cc|ccc}
1 & 0 & 0 & 0 & 0 \\
0 & 1 & 0 & 0 & 0 \\
\hline
\frac{1}{2} & 0 & 0 & \frac{1}{2} & 0 \\
0 & 0 & \frac{1}{2} & 0 & \frac{1}{2} \\
0 & \frac{1}{2} & 0 & \frac{1}{2} & 0
\end{array}\right).
\end{array}
$$

From this we see that the matrix Q is

$$
Q = \begin{pmatrix} 0 & \frac{1}{2} & 0 \\ \frac{1}{2} & 0 & \frac{1}{2} \\ 0 & \frac{1}{2} & 0 \end{pmatrix}
$$

and

$$
I - Q = \begin{pmatrix} 1 & -\frac{1}{2} & 0 \\ -\frac{1}{2} & 1 & -\frac{1}{2} \\ 0 & -\frac{1}{2} & 1 \end{pmatrix}.
$$

Computing $(I - Q)^{-1}$, we find

$$
N = (I - Q)^{-1} = \begin{array}{c} 1 \\ 2 \\ 3 \end{array}\begin{pmatrix} \frac{3}{2} & 1 & \frac{1}{2} \\ 1 & 2 & 1 \\ \frac{1}{2} & 1 & \frac{3}{2} \end{pmatrix}.
$$

Thus, starting at state 2, the mean number of times in state 1 before absorption is 1, in state 2 it is 2, and in state 3 it is 1.

We next answer question (b). If we add all the entries in a row, we will have the mean number of times in any of the nonabsorbing states for a given starting state—that is, the mean time required before being absorbed. This may be described as follows:

THEOREM. Consider an absorbing Markov chain with s nonabsorbing states. Let c be an s-component column vector with all entries 1. Then the vector $t = Nc$ has as components the mean number of steps before being absorbed for each possible nonabsorbing starting state.

Example 1 (continued). For Example 1 we have

$$
t = Nc = \begin{matrix} 1 \\ 2 \\ 3 \end{matrix} \begin{matrix} 1 & 2 & 3 \end{matrix} \\
\begin{pmatrix} \frac{3}{2} & 1 & \frac{1}{2} \\ 1 & 2 & 1 \\ \frac{1}{2} & 1 & \frac{3}{2} \end{pmatrix} \begin{pmatrix} 1 \\ 1 \\ 1 \end{pmatrix}
$$

$$
= \begin{matrix} 1 \\ 2 \\ 3 \end{matrix} \begin{pmatrix} 3 \\ 4 \\ 3 \end{pmatrix}.
$$

Thus the mean number of steps to absorption starting at state 1 is 3, starting at state 2 it is 4, and starting at state 3 it is again 3. Since the process necessarily moves to 1 or 3 from 2, it is clear that it requires one more step starting from 2 than from 1 or 3.

We now consider question (a). That is, what is the probability that an absorbing chain will end up in a particular absorbing state? It is clear that this probability will depend upon the starting state and be interesting only for the case of a nonabsorbing starting state. We write as usual our matrix in the canonical form

$$
P = \left(\begin{array}{c|c} I & O \\ \hline R & Q \end{array} \right).
$$

THEOREM. Let b_{ij} be the probability that an absorbing chain will be absorbed in state a_j if it starts in the nonabsorbing state a_i. Let B be the matrix with entries b_{ij}. Then

$$
B = NR
$$

where N is the fundamental matrix and R is as in the canonical form.

Proof. Let a_i be a nonabsorbing state and a_j be an absorbing state. If we compute b_{ij} in terms of the possibilities on the outcome of the first step, we have the equation

$$
b_{ij} = p_{ij} + \sum_k p_{ik} b_{kj}
$$

where the summation is carried out over all nonabsorbing states a_k. Writing this in matrix form gives

$$
B = R + QB
$$
$$
(I - Q)B = R
$$

and hence
$$
B = (I - Q)^{-1}R = NR.
$$

Example 1 (continued). In the random-walk example we found that

$$N = \begin{pmatrix} \frac{3}{2} & 1 & \frac{1}{2} \\ 1 & 2 & 1 \\ \frac{1}{2} & 1 & \frac{3}{2} \end{pmatrix}.$$

From the canonical form we find that

$$R = \begin{pmatrix} \frac{1}{2} & 0 \\ 0 & 0 \\ 0 & \frac{1}{2} \end{pmatrix}.$$

Hence

$$B = NR = \begin{pmatrix} \frac{3}{2} & 1 & \frac{1}{2} \\ 1 & 2 & 1 \\ \frac{1}{2} & 1 & \frac{3}{2} \end{pmatrix}\begin{pmatrix} \frac{1}{2} & 0 \\ 0 & 0 \\ 0 & \frac{1}{2} \end{pmatrix}$$

$$= \begin{matrix} 1 \\ 2 \\ 3 \end{matrix}\begin{pmatrix} \frac{3}{4} & \frac{1}{4} \\ \frac{1}{2} & \frac{1}{2} \\ \frac{1}{4} & \frac{3}{4} \end{pmatrix}.$$

Thus, for instance, starting from a_1, there is probability $\frac{3}{4}$ of absorption in a_0 and $\frac{1}{4}$ for absorption in a_4.

Let us summarize our results. We have shown that the answers to questions (a), (b), and (c) can all be given in terms of the fundamental matrix $N = (I - Q)^{-1}$. The matrix N itself gives us the mean number of times in each state before absorption depending upon the starting state. The column vector $t = Nc$ gives us the mean number of steps before absorption, depending upon the starting state. The matrix $B = NR$ gives us the probability of absorption in each of the absorbing states, depending upon the starting state.

EXERCISES

1. Which of the following transition matrices are from absorbing chains?

   $a.$ $P = \begin{pmatrix} 1 & 0 \\ \frac{1}{2} & \frac{1}{2} \end{pmatrix}.$

   $b.$ $P = \begin{pmatrix} 1 & 0 & 0 \\ 0 & \frac{1}{2} & \frac{1}{2} \\ 0 & \frac{1}{3} & \frac{2}{3} \end{pmatrix}.$

   $c.$ $P = \begin{pmatrix} 1 & 0 & 0 & 0 & 0 \\ 0 & \frac{1}{2} & 0 & \frac{1}{2} & 0 \\ \frac{1}{5} & \frac{1}{5} & \frac{1}{5} & \frac{1}{5} & \frac{1}{5} \\ 0 & \frac{1}{3} & 0 & \frac{2}{3} & 0 \\ 0 & 0 & 0 & 0 & 1 \end{pmatrix}.$

   $d.$ $P = \begin{pmatrix} 1 & 0 & 0 & 0 \\ \frac{1}{2} & 0 & 0 & \frac{1}{2} \\ \frac{1}{4} & \frac{1}{4} & \frac{1}{4} & \frac{1}{4} \\ 0 & 0 & 0 & 1 \end{pmatrix}.$

   [*Ans. a.* and *d.*]

2. Consider the two-state transition matrix

$$P = \begin{pmatrix} 1 - a & a \\ b & 1 - b \end{pmatrix}.$$

For what choices of a and b do we obtain an absorbing chain?

3. In the random-walk example (Example 1) of the present section, assume that the probability of a step to the right is $\frac{2}{3}$ and of a step to the left is $\frac{1}{3}$. Find N, t, and B. Compare these with the results for probability $\frac{1}{2}$ for a step to the right and $\frac{1}{2}$ to the left.

4. In the Land of Oz example (see Exercise 13, Section 8) let us change the transition matrix by making R an absorbing state. This gives

$$
\begin{array}{c}
 & \begin{array}{ccc} R & N & S \end{array} \\
\begin{array}{c} R \\ N \\ S \end{array} &
\begin{pmatrix}
1 & 0 & 0 \\
\frac{1}{2} & 0 & \frac{1}{2} \\
\frac{1}{4} & \frac{1}{4} & \frac{1}{2}
\end{pmatrix}.
\end{array}
$$

Find the fundamental matrix N, and also t and B. What is the interpretation of these quantities?

5. An analysis of a recent hockey game between Dartmouth and Princeton showed the following facts: If the puck was in the center (C) the probabilities that it next entered Princeton territory (P) or Dartmouth territory (D) were .4 and .6, respectively. From D it went back to C with probability .95 or into the Dartmouth goal ($\overline{D}$) with probability .05 (Princeton scores one point). From P it next went to C with probability .9 and to Princeton's goal $\overline{P}$ with probability .1 (Dartmouth scores one point). Assuming that the puck begins in C after each point, find the transition matrix of this five-state Markov chain. Calculate the probability that Dartmouth will score. [*Ans.* $\frac{4}{7}$.]

6. A number is chosen at random from the integers 1, 2, 3, 4, 5. If x is chosen, then another number is chosen from the set of integers less than or equal to x. This process is continued until the number 1 is chosen. Form a Markov chain by taking as states the largest number that can be chosen. Show that

$$
\begin{array}{c}
 & \begin{array}{cccc} 2 & 3 & 4 & 5 \end{array} \\
N = \begin{array}{c} 2 \\ 3 \\ 4 \\ 5 \end{array} &
\begin{pmatrix}
1 & 0 & 0 & 0 \\
1 & \frac{1}{2} & 0 & 0 \\
1 & \frac{1}{2} & \frac{1}{3} & 0 \\
1 & \frac{1}{2} & \frac{1}{3} & \frac{1}{4}
\end{pmatrix} + I,
\end{array}
$$

where I is the 4×4 identity matrix. What is the mean number of draws? [*Ans.* $\frac{25}{12}$.]

7. Using the result of Exercise 6, make a conjecture for the form of the fundamental matrix if we start with integers from 1 to n. What would the mean number of draws be if we started with numbers from 1 to 10?

8. Three tanks fight a three-way duel. Tank A has probability $\frac{1}{2}$ of destroying the tank it fires at. Tank B has probability $\frac{1}{3}$ of destroying, and Tank C has probability $\frac{1}{6}$ of destroying. The tanks fire together and each tank fires at the strongest opponent not yet destroyed. Form a Markov chain by taking as state the tanks that survive any one round. Find N, t, B, and interpret your results.

9. The following is an alternative method of finding the probability of absorption in a particular absorbing state, say a_j. Find the column vector d such that the jth component of d is 1, all other components corresponding to absorbing states are 0, and $Pd = d$. There is only one such vector. Component d_i is the probability of absorption in a_j if the process starts in a_i. Use this method to find the probability of absorption in state 0 in the random-walk example given in this section.

10. The following is an alternative method for finding the mean number of steps to absorption. Let t_i be the mean number of steps to absorption starting at state a_i. This must be the same as taking one more step and then adding $p_{ij}t_j$ for every nonabsorbing state a_j.
   a. Give reasons for the claim above that

$$t_i = 1 + \sum_j p_{ij}t_j,$$

   where the summation is over the nonabsorbing states.
   b. Solve for t for the random-walk example.
   c. Verify that the solution agrees with that found in the text.

11. Peter and Paul are matching pennies, and each player flips his (fair) coin before revealing it. They initially have three pennies between them and the game ends whenever one of them has all the pennies. Let the states be labeled with the number of pennies that Peter has.
   a. Write the transition matrix.
   b. What kind of a Markov chain is it?
   c. If Peter initially has two pennies, what is the probability that he will win the game?

12. Peter and Paul are matching pennies as in Exercise 11, except that whenever one of the players gets all three pennies, he returns one to his opponent, and the game continues.
   a. Set up the transition matrix.
   b. Identify the kind of Markov chain that results.   [*Ans.* Not regular.]
   c. Find the long-run probabilities of being in each of the states.

13. Peter and Paul are matching pennies as in Exercise 11, except that if Peter gets all the pennies, the game is over, while if Paul gets all the pennies, he gives one back to Peter, and the game continues.
   a. Set up the transition matrix.
   b. Identify the resulting Markov chain.   [*Ans.* Absorbing.]
   c. If Peter initially has one penny, what is the probability of his winning the game? If he has two pennies?

14. A rat is put into the maze of the figure below. Each time period, it chooses at random one of the doors in the compartment it is in and moves into another compartment.

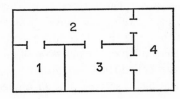

a. Set up the process as a Markov chain (with states being the compartments) and identify it.   [*Ans.* Regular.]

b. In the long run, what fraction of his time will the rat spend in compartment 2?   [*Ans.* $\frac{3}{8}$.]

c. Make compartment 4 into an absorbing state by assuming the rat will stay in it once it reaches it. Set up the new process and identify it as a kind of Markov chain.   [*Ans.* Absorbing.]

d. In part (c), if the rat starts in compartment 1, how many steps will it take him, on the average, to reach compartment 4?

[*Ans.* $4\frac{1}{3}$ steps.]

*10. AN EXAMPLE FROM WAITING-LINE THEORY

In this section we are going to treat the following problem. Customers arrive at a service station, which has a single server. If the server is not busy the customer is given service. But if the server is busy the customer joins a line.

Examples of such a problem are people arriving at a post office window, airplanes arriving at an airport waiting in a "stack" to obtain a runway, people lining up at a theater window for tickets, people waiting at checkout counters in a supermarket, and mechanics waiting for service at a tool crib.

To make the problem more precise we must specify how the customers arrive and how much time is required for their service. A great variety of assumptions might be made; we shall consider only one simple set of assumptions. We shall choose some convenient, small interval of time and assume that in a single interval of time at most one customer can arrive. The probability that a customer does arrive is p, independent of whether a customer arrived in any other time interval. We shall assume further that when a customer is being served there is a fixed probability r that he finishes his service in any one interval, independent of the number of previous time units of service. Let $\bar{p} = 1 - p$ and $\bar{r} = 1 - r$.

We shall treat this problem by Markov-chain theory. We shall form a Markov chain by taking as the state the number of individuals in line at the beginning of a time interval (including the customer being served). Naturally, the line cannot be greater than some preassigned number. This number could be taken to be the number of people in the world. But usually people are turned away when the line gets longer than a certain size. This is certainly the case for theater tickets. In the case of airplanes, when the traffic gets too heavy the planes must be sent to another airport, and so on. We suppose that n is the maximum possible length of a line.

We shall see that much of the behavior of our system can be described in terms of a quantity called the traffic intensity, denoted by u. This is the product of p and the mean service time of a customer. To find the mean service time we note first that the probability that a customer ends his service on the jth time period is $\bar{r}^{j-1}r$. Hence the mean service time is

$$
\begin{aligned}
1 \cdot r + 2 \cdot \bar{r}r + 3 \cdot \bar{r}^2 r + \cdots &= r(1 + 2\bar{r} + 3\bar{r}^2 + 4\bar{r}^3 + \cdots) \\
&= r[(1 + \bar{r} + \bar{r}^2 + \cdots) + (\bar{r} + \bar{r}^2 + \bar{r}^3 + \cdots) \\
&\qquad + (\bar{r}^2 + \bar{r}^3 + \bar{r}^4 + \cdots) + \cdots] \\
&= r\left(\frac{1}{1 - \bar{r}} + \frac{\bar{r}}{1 - \bar{r}} + \frac{\bar{r}^2}{1 - \bar{r}} + \cdots\right) \\
&= r\frac{1}{(1 - \bar{r})^2} = \frac{1}{r}.
\end{aligned}
$$

Thus the traffic intensity is $u = p/r$. We will assume that $p \neq r$—that is, that $u \neq 1$. (See Exercises 6–9.)

A convention is needed to cover the case of an empty line. We assume that a customer does *not* get served during the period in which he arrives, even if the line is empty. We now have all the necessary information to obtain the transition probabilities. We consider three cases depending upon the number of people waiting in line. The number waiting may be 0, or more than 0 but less than n, or n.

If there is no one in line, then during the next time unit there will be one person in line with probability p and no one in line with probability $\bar{p}$.

If the line is neither empty nor full, then the number can increase by one, stay the same, or decrease by one. It will increase by one if the customer being served is not finished and if a new customer arrives. The probability that this happens is $p\bar{r}$. In order that the line decrease by one it is necessary that the customer being served finish his service and no new customer arrive. The probability that this happens is $\bar{p}r$. Finally, the probability that the line stays the same is the probability that neither of these happens or $1 - p\bar{r} - \bar{p}r$.

When there are n customers in line the line decreases by one if the customer being served finishes and it remains the same if he does not finish; these have probabilities r and $\bar{r}$, respectively. Any new customer arriving in this period would be turned away.

For the case $n = 4$, we have then the transition matrix

$$
P = \begin{array}{c c}
 & \begin{array}{ccccc} 0 & 1 & 2 & 3 & 4 \end{array} \\
\begin{array}{c} 0 \\ 1 \\ 2 \\ 3 \\ 4 \end{array} &
\left(\begin{array}{ccccc}
\bar{p} & p & 0 & 0 & 0 \\
\bar{p}r & 1 - \bar{p}r - p\bar{r} & p\bar{r} & 0 & 0 \\
0 & \bar{p}r & 1 - \bar{p}r - p\bar{r} & p\bar{r} & 0 \\
0 & 0 & \bar{p}r & 1 - \bar{p}r - p\bar{r} & p\bar{r} \\
0 & 0 & 0 & r & \bar{r}
\end{array}\right)
\end{array}.
$$

To find the fixed vector we shall make use of an important property of the special nature of our chain. We have a chain that has integer states and can move at most one unit in each step. We know further that our chain is regular. (See Exercise 17, Section 8.) Hence for any state a_i it returns over and over again to this state. The fraction of the time in a large number of periods that it is in a_i is given by w_i. The fraction of the time that it moves from i to $i+1$ is $w_i p_{i,i+1}$. The fraction of times it moves from $i+1$ to i is $w_{i+1} p_{i+1,i}$. However, these fractions must be the same since every time it moves from i to $i+1$ it must later move from $i+1$ to i, since there is no other way of returning to i. Hence

$$w_i p_{i,i+1} = w_{i+1} p_{i+1,i} \quad \text{or} \quad \frac{w_i}{w_{i+1}} = \frac{p_{i+1,i}}{p_{i,i+1}}.$$

Using this fact we can find the fixed vector of our five-state chain to be

$$(1) \qquad\qquad w = \frac{r-p}{r\bar{r} - p\bar{p}s^4} \, (\bar{r}, s, s^2, s^3, \bar{p}s^4)$$

where $s = p\bar{r}/r\bar{p}$.

Example 1. Let $p = .25$ and $r = .50$. Then the transition matrix is

$$
P = \begin{array}{c@{\quad}c}
 & \begin{array}{ccccc} 0 & 1 & 2 & 3 & 4 \end{array} \\
\begin{array}{c} 0 \\ 1 \\ 2 \\ 3 \\ 4 \end{array} &
\left(\begin{array}{ccccc}
.75 & .25 & 0 & 0 & 0 \\
.375 & .500 & .125 & 0 & 0 \\
0 & .375 & .500 & .125 & 0 \\
0 & 0 & .375 & .500 & .125 \\
0 & 0 & 0 & .5 & .5
\end{array} \right)
\end{array}
$$

and

$$w = \tfrac{1}{107}(54, 36, 12, 4, 1)$$

$$\approx (.505, .336, .112, .037, .009).$$

Example 2. Let $p = .8$ and $r = .4$. Then the transition matrix is

$$
P = \begin{array}{c@{\quad}c}
 & \begin{array}{ccccc} 0 & 1 & 2 & 3 & 4 \end{array} \\
\begin{array}{c} 0 \\ 1 \\ 2 \\ 3 \\ 4 \end{array} &
\left(\begin{array}{ccccc}
.2 & .8 & 0 & 0 & 0 \\
.08 & .44 & .48 & 0 & 0 \\
0 & .08 & .44 & .48 & 0 \\
0 & 0 & .08 & .44 & .48 \\
0 & 0 & 0 & .4 & .6
\end{array} \right)
\end{array}
$$

and

$$w = \tfrac{1}{5178}(6, 60, 360, 2160, 2592)$$

$$\approx (.001, .012, .070, .417, .501).$$

We note in these two examples quite a different long-range prediction. In the first example, we see that a person would be turned away very infrequently. Also, approximately half the time the server would not be occupied. In the second example, over half the time a person is turned away and the server is almost always busy. We see from the form of the fixed vector that these two different types of behavior correspond to the case $s < 1$ and $s > 1$. Let us see what these conditions mean in terms of u. If

$$\frac{p\bar{r}}{r\bar{p}} < 1,$$

then $p\bar{r} < r\bar{p}$ or $p - pr < r - pr$. That is, $p < r$, or $u < 1$. Similarly, $s > 1$ corresponds to the case $r < p$ or $u > 1$. That is, our two types of behavior correspond to whether the traffic intensity is greater than one or less than one.

We consider now the general case where we allow a line of length n. The fixed vector for this case is

$$(2) \qquad w = \frac{r - p}{r\bar{r} - p\bar{p}s^n} \, (\bar{r}, s, s^2, s^3, \ldots, s^{n-1}, \bar{p}s^n).$$

Two components of the fixed vector are particularly interesting. These are w_0 and w_n. The component w_0 tells the fraction of the time in the long run that the server will be unoccupied. One would not want this to be too large in practice. The component w_n tells us how frequently the line is full and customers will have to be turned away in the long run. This should also be small. Let us examine these quantities when n is very large. If the traffic intensity is less than one and n is sufficiently large, then s^n is very small. Hence w_n is small, and w_0 is approximately

$$\frac{r - p}{r\bar{r}} \cdot \bar{r} = 1 - u.$$

Thus the traffic intensity tells us how much time on the average the server will be busy. When u is near one this time is small, and when u is small it is large.

Similarly, when the traffic intensity is greater than one and n is large, s^n will be large. Thus w_0 will be very small, and w_n may be approximated by neglecting $r\bar{r}$ in comparison to $p\bar{p}s^n$. If we do this we obtain

$$w_n \approx \frac{p - r}{p} = 1 - \frac{1}{u}.$$

Again, the traffic intensity tells us how often in the long run customers will be turned away. When it is near one this will be rare, and when it is large this will happen often. We may therefore conclude that if n is large and the objective is (1) to keep the server busy and (2) to turn away few people, then u should be near one. Observe that this will almost surely mean that the average waiting time [see equation (3) below] for a customer will be large. If we also have the objective of keeping customer waiting time low (see, for instance, Example 1 of Chapter 3, Section 14), it is not so easy to state the requirements of a well-designed system.

Another quantity of interest in the study of queues is the average length of the queue after the system has reached its equilibrium. From w we obtain the mean line length:

$$m = w_0 \cdot 0 + w_1 \cdot 1 + w_2 \cdot 2 + \cdots + w_n \cdot n$$

$$= \frac{r - p}{r\bar{r} - p\bar{p}s^n} (s + 2s^2 + 3s^3 + \cdots + (n - 1)s^{n-1} + n\bar{p}s^n).$$

If we assume that the traffic intensity is less than one, and not too near one, and n is large, this sum may be approximated by

$$m \approx \frac{r - p}{r\bar{r}} (s + 2s^2 + 3s^3 + \cdots).$$

Using the same method as for the mean service time, we find that

(3)
$$m \approx \frac{r - p}{r\bar{r}} \frac{s}{(1 - s)^2} = \bar{p} \frac{u}{1 - u}.$$

EXERCISES

In Exercises 1 through 3 consider the case $n = 4$, $p = .2$, and $r = .6$.

1. Find the transition matrix P and the fixed vector w. Check w against equation (1).
2. Find the fraction of times in the long run that the server is free and the fraction of times that a customer is turned away.
3. Find the mean length of the line in equilibrium, and compare it to equation (3).
4. Compute the mean length of the line in equilibrium for the case $p = .25$, $r = .50$, and compare the result to equation (3).
5. Give an intuitive argument to show that if u is significantly greater than one, then the mean length of the line is near n. Check this in the case $p = .8$, $r = .4$.

Exercises 6 through 9 refer to the case $u = 1$, $n = 4$.

6. Set up P, making use of the fact that $p = r$.
7. Find the fixed vector w. What form will w take for general n if $u = 1$?
$$\left[Ans. \ w = \frac{1}{n - 1 + 2\bar{p}} (\bar{p}, 1, \ldots, 1, \bar{p}). \right]$$
8. Find the fraction of times in the long run that the server is free, and the fraction of times the line is full.
9. Find the mean length of the line in equilibrium. $[Ans. \ m = \frac{1}{2}n]$
10. Compare results for the cases (a) $p = .25$, $r = .50$, (b) $p = .8$, $r = .4$, (c) $p = r = .50$. Which seems most satisfactory?

When the probability that a customer finishes his service in a given time interval depends upon the number of previous time units of service he has had, the length of the line at each time is no longer a Markov chain. However, if the line is observed only when a customer finishes service, a Markov chain is obtained. Exercises 11 through 15 relate to this chain when the service time is a constant time of two units for each customer. The probability of an arrival is p for each time interval as before.

11. If the maximum line length is 4, show that the transition matrix is

$$
P = \begin{array}{c} \\ 0 \\ 1 \\ 2 \\ 3 \\ 4 \end{array}
\begin{array}{c}
\begin{array}{ccccc} 0 & 1 & 2 & 3 & 4 \end{array} \\
\left(\begin{array}{ccccc}
\overline{p}^2 & 2p\overline{p} & p^2 & 0 & 0 \\
\overline{p}^2 & 2p\overline{p} & p^2 & 0 & 0 \\
0 & \overline{p}^2 & 2p\overline{p} & p^2 & 0 \\
0 & 0 & \overline{p}^2 & 2p\overline{p} & p^2 \\
0 & 0 & 0 & 1 & 0
\end{array} \right).
\end{array}
$$

12. Verify that the fixed vector is

$$
w = \frac{1-s}{1-2ps^3}\,(\overline{p}^2,\, 1 - \overline{p}^2,\, s,\, s^2,\, \overline{p}^2 s^3),
$$

where $s = (p/\overline{p})^2$.

13. Give the form of the transition matrix for the general case where the maximum line allowed is n, and show that the fixed vector is

$$
w = \frac{1-s}{1-2ps^{n-1}}\,(\overline{p}^2,\, 1 - \overline{p}^2,\, s,\, s^2,\, \ldots,\, s^{n-2},\, \overline{p}^2 s^{n-1}),
$$

where $s = (p/\overline{p})^2$.

14. Find the traffic intensity. For what value of r do we obtain the same intensity in the model discussed in this section?

15. Show that if $u < 1$, and n is sufficiently large, the fraction of time that the server is busy in the long run is again approximately u.

*11. CHARGE ACCOUNTS

The purpose of this section is to analyze some actual data of the history of charge accounts in a certain department store.

A given customer may charge items over a period of months, and his payments often lag several months behind the charges. Our store classifies accounts according to the "oldest unpaid dollar." This is most simply explained in terms of an example. Suppose that a customer has three unpaid bills, $30 from two months ago, $50 from 3 months ago, and $16 left from a charge 5 months ago. This account is then classified as "5 months old." If he pays $10 on his account, this is credited against his oldest purchase, but this still leaves him with a 5-months-old account, since he owes $6 more on his 5-months-old debt. However, if he pays at least $16, the account is reclassified as "3 months old," if he pays at least $66 it is classified as "2 months old," and upon payment of $96 the account is labeled as "paid up." Any account that has 6-months-old items on it is labeled as a "bad debt" in our store.

We may analyze the change of status of any one account as a stochastic process. Until the account is settled, it is in one of six states, being labeled 0, 1, 2, 3, 4, or 5 months old. (A 0-months-old account has only current charges on it.) It can move up no more than one step, since debts age only one month during a month, but it may stay where it is or move down any number of steps. The account may be settled in one of two ways, either by being paid up, or by being written off as a bad debt. The former may occur at any time, but the latter only happens to an account that was 5 months old the step before.

Let us assume that it is reasonable to analyze this stochastic process as a Markov chain. Then we have an absorbing chain with the six non-absorbing states 0, 1, 2, 3, 4, and 5, and the two absorbing states I (paid up) and II (bad debt). The transition probabilities for our store, as observed over a period of time, were as follows:

	I	II	0	1	2	3	4	5
I	1	0	0	0	0	0	0	0
II	0	1	0	0	0	0	0	0
0	.21	0	.67	.12	0	0	0	0
1	.14	0	.19	.44	.23	0	0	0
2	.13	0	.08	.20	.36	.23	0	0
3	.11	0	.01	.04	.17	.29	.38	0
4	.15	0	.02	0	.09	.20	.42	.12
5	.08	.21	.01	.02	.01	.10	.11	.46

$P = $ (the above matrix).

By means of a computing machine we can compute the following approximate quantities:

	0	1	2	3	4	5
0	3.68	.94	.40	.16	.11	.03
1	1.80	2.60	1.10	.45	.31	.07
2	1.33	1.20	2.34	.97	.66	.15
3	.86	.74	1.08	2.24	1.53	.34
4	.73	.55	.85	1.07	2.53	.56
5	.47	.39	.46	.67	.82	2.04

$N = $ (the above matrix),

$t = $			$B = $	I	II
0	5.33		0	.995	.005
1	6.32		1	.99	.01
2	6.65		2	.97	.03
3	6.80		3	.93	.07
4	6.29		4	.88	.12
5	4.85		5	.57	.43

The interpretation of t is perfectly straightforward. It is the mean number of months until the account is settled one way or another. It is interesting to note that all of these times are around 5 or 6 months, and that there is surprisingly little variation.

Equally interesting is the interpretation of B. Let us look at the probabilities of absorption in II—that is, the probability that the debt will turn out to be bad. It is not surprising that the older the debt is the higher the chance that it will turn bad. But it is interesting to see how rapidly the probability increases with age.

We will use this example to illustrate a new application of the N matrix. It is based on the following result.

Suppose that a number of individuals are started out in a Markov chain, at various states. We then introduce new individuals after one step, etc. At each stage we have all the previous individuals (unless they have been absorbed) and a number of new ones. We are interested in the number of individuals in a given state in the long run.

THEOREM. Suppose that P is an absorbing chain, and Q its nonabsorbing part. Suppose that at time 0 there are z_i individuals in state i. On all future steps x_i individuals are added at state i. Then, introducing the vectors x, y, and z, with components x_i, y_i, and z_i, respectively,

1. the mean number of individuals in state i approaches y_i, where $y = xN$. This is independent of z.
2. $z = y$ is the unique starting distribution under which the system is in equilibrium.

Proof. Let $z^{(n)}$ be the distribution after n steps. Then $z^{(n+1)} = z^{(n)}Q + x$. Thus, $z^{(1)} = zQ + x$, $z^{(2)} = zQ^2 + x(I + Q)$, and so on. Thus we find that

$$z^{(n)} = zQ^n + x(I + Q + \cdots + Q^{n-1}).$$

Since Q^n tends to 0, so does zQ^n. And the series $I + Q + \cdots + Q^{n-1}$ converges to N, hence $z^{(n)}$ tends to xN, proving the first part of the theorem.

A system is said to be in equilibrium if $z^{(1)} = z$ (and hence all $z^{(n)}$ are the same). This means that

$$z = zQ + x \quad \text{or} \quad z(I - Q) = x.$$

But we can multiply this equation by $N = (I - Q)^{-1}$ to find that it is equivalent to $z = xN$. This proves the second part of the theorem.

Let us suppose that in our store m new accounts are opened each month. More precisely, m is the number of the customers who make a charge who do not have active balances, since once an account is paid up, a new charge is just like a new account in our model. Then

$x = (m, 0, 0, 0, 0, 0)$. The theorem tells us that no matter what the present distribution of accounts is, this distribution will, in the long run, approach $xN = mN_1$, where N_1 is the first row of the N-matrix. Thus if 1000 new accounts are added to the list each month, then the long-run distribution will roughly be that of Figure 10. The total number of accounts on the

Months old	0	1	2	3	4	5
Number of accounts	3680	940	400	160	110	30

Figure 10

books in the long run will be the sum of these, or approximately 5320. Since a new account is expected to stay on the books for an average of 5.33 months (see t), we would expect 1000×5.330 accounts. This checks, except for a rounding error. Similarly, from B we find that approximately 995 accounts will be paid up each month, and that 5 will be declared bad.

Furthermore, the distribution of Figure 10 is an (approximate) equilibrium distribution for the model. That is, if the present distribution should happen to be exactly $y = xN$, and 1000 new accounts are added monthly, then the number of accounts of a given age will be the same in the future as it is now.

Let us now consider what we can say about the amounts of money tied up in charge accounts. The store finds over a long period that 0 or 1 month accounts average $40, 2 or 3 months accounts average $60, and older accounts average $80. Weighting y by these amounts, we find that the amounts of money in the long run in accounts of various lengths are

$$(147.2, 37.6, 24, 9.6, 8.8, 2.4) \text{ thousands of dollars.}$$

Thus in the long run the store will have about $229,600 tied up in charge accounts. This vector times R is (41864, 504). The first number gives the value of the accounts each month that are completely paid up, while the second gives the monthly average for debts newly declared bad.

EXERCISES

Exercises 1 through 6 refer to the following model. A retail store extends short-range credit to its customers. It classifies accounts according to the oldest unpaid dollar, but if there is any sum unpaid for three months, then the account is turned over to a collection agency. For simplicity we assume that if a customer pays an account, he pays all of it. Experience shows that there is probability $\frac{1}{2}$ that a current account is paid off, $\frac{1}{3}$ for a month-old account, and $\frac{1}{4}$ for a two-months-old account.

1. Set up the transition matrix. [*Hint:* There are 3 nonabsorbing and 2 absorbing states.]

2. Compute N, t, and B, and interpret the last two.

3. Suppose that each month 210 new accounts are added to the books. What will the long-range distribution of accounts be? How many will be paid off each month, and how many turned over to the collection agency in the long run?

[*Partial Ans.* An average of 157.5 will be paid and 52.5 will be bad debts.]

4. Suppose that we modify the basic assumption that a customer always pays his entire account. Instead let us assume that he incurs a charge every month and is equally likely in any one month to pay off all of it or just the oldest charge (in which case the "age" of the account will be the same next month). Set up the new transition matrix.

5. Compute N, t, and B for the transition matrix of Exercise 4. Interpret t and B.

6. In Exercise 4 suppose again that 210 new accounts come in each month. Find the long-range distribution of accounts, the number paid off each month, and the number turned over to the collection agency.

[*Partial Ans.* An average of 114 will be paid off and 96 will be bad debts.]

7. Suppose that P is an absorbing Markov chain. We move from state to state according to the transition probabilities, and receive a reward f_i when in state i. If we receive such a reward on all steps (including the original position), then show that using the column vectors f and g with components f_i and g_i respectively, the expected amount gained before reaching an absorbing state is g_i if we start in state i, where $g = Nf$.

Exercises 8 through 12 refer to the following model. A man buys a store. The profits of the store vary from month to month. For simplicity we suppose that he earns either \$5000 or \$2000 a month ("high" or "low"). The man may sell his store at any time, and there is a 10 percent chance of his selling during a high-profit month, and a 40 percent chance during a low-profit month. If he does not sell, with probability $\frac{2}{3}$ the profits will be the same next month, with $\frac{1}{3}$ they will change.

8. Set up the transition matrix. [*Hint:* There are two nonabsorbing and one absorbing states.]

9. Compute N, t, and B. Interpret t and B.

10. Set up the vector f (see Exercise 7) and compute g. Interpret the two components.

11. Suppose that the man switches his strategy, and sells the store during a high month with 40 percent probability, and in a low month with 10 percent probability. How are the answers in Exercises 8 through 10 changed?

12. In Exercise 11, how must the \$5000 profit item change so that his expected total gain is the same whether he starts with a high or low month?

The remaining exercises refer to the following problem. A small college has a thesis requirement for graduation besides four years of course work that must be completed. Some of the students are able to finish their thesis by the end of the fourth year, but others require an additional year. Each year some of the students drop out, and if any student does not finish his thesis by the end of the fifth year he is dropped from the rolls. From his records the dean of the college estimates the probabilities of a given student's returning each year or dropping out to be as indicated below:

	1	2	3	4	5	D	G
1	0	.8				.2	0
2		0	.7			.3	0
3			0	.9		.1	0
4				0	.1	.1	.8
5					0	.2	.8

13. Set up the problem as an absorbing Markov chain with two absorbing states. Find Q and R.

14. Find directly Q^2, Q^3, and Q^4. Show that $Q^5 = 0$. Prove that $N = I + Q + Q^2 + Q^3 + Q^4$. Calculate N.

15. Compute t and B. Interpret each of these.

16. What is the probability that an entering student will graduate? What is the mean time that he is in college? [*Ans.* .444; 2.91 years.]

*12. FURTHER APPLICATIONS OF MARKOV CHAINS

Example 1. The techniques of the last section may be applied to the analysis of the work load in a given company. We will illustrate this in terms of a small company with four employees, consisting of a president, a vice-president, and a secretary for each. We suppose that some piece of business comes in, and we observe the way it passes through the company. It comes to a specific employee, who may carry out the task himself, or pass it on to another employee. We also allow for the possibility that the task may be laid aside and never carried out.

Adopting a Markov-chain model, we will have four nonabsorbing states, corresponding to the four employees, P, V, PS, VS, and two absorbing states, I (done) and II (laid aside). The nature of the work is such that the president is equally likely to pass an item to his secretary or to the vice-president. The vice-president is in the habit of passing $\frac{3}{4}$ of his work on to his secretary. The remainder is equally likely to be done by him or laid aside. Each secretary does $\frac{3}{8}$ of her tasks personally, lays aside $\frac{1}{8}$, and the rest of the items are split evenly between items sent to the other secretary or returned to her boss for further instructions. The resulting R and Q matrices are

$$R = \begin{array}{c} P \\ V \\ PS \\ VS \end{array}\begin{pmatrix} 0 & 0 \\ \frac{1}{8} & \frac{1}{8} \\ \frac{3}{8} & \frac{1}{8} \\ \frac{3}{8} & \frac{1}{8} \end{pmatrix}, \qquad Q = \begin{array}{c} P \\ V \\ PS \\ VS \end{array}\begin{pmatrix} 0 & \frac{1}{2} & \frac{1}{2} & 0 \\ 0 & 0 & 0 & \frac{3}{4} \\ \frac{1}{4} & 0 & 0 & \frac{1}{4} \\ 0 & \frac{1}{4} & \frac{1}{4} & 0 \end{pmatrix}.$$

the column headers for R being I, II and for Q being P, V, PS, VS.

From this we find:

$$N = \begin{array}{c} P \\ V \\ PS \\ VS \end{array}\begin{pmatrix} 1.2 & .8 & .8 & .8 \\ .075 & 1.3 & .3 & 1.05 \\ .325 & .3 & 1.3 & .55 \\ .1 & .4 & .4 & 1.4 \end{pmatrix}$$

with column headers P, V, PS, VS.

$$
t = \begin{matrix} P \\ V \\ PS \\ VS \end{matrix} \begin{pmatrix} 3.6 \\ 2.725 \\ 2.475 \\ 2.3 \end{pmatrix}, \qquad
B = \begin{matrix} \\ P \\ V \\ PS \\ VS \end{matrix}
\begin{matrix} \text{I} & \text{II} \\ \begin{pmatrix} .7 & .3 \\ .67 & .33 \\ .73 & .27 \\ .725 & .275 \end{pmatrix} \end{matrix}.
$$

Again, the interpretation of t and B is direct and enlightening. If we want to take some business to the company, it is safest to hand it to the president's secretary, and it is least likely to get done if it is handed to the vice-president. As far as time is concerned, it is fastest to hand it to one of the secretaries, and slowest to take it directly to the president.

Let us suppose that 60 items of business come in daily, and $\frac{2}{3}$ go to the president's secretary and the rest to the vice-president's secretary. Thus $x = (0, 0, 40, 20)$. We find

$$
y = xN = (15, 20, 60, 50).
$$

This is a fairly realistic distribution of labor in a small company. We should note in particular that although the president's secretary may complain that twice as much work comes to her each morning as to the other secretary, by the end of the day the vice-president's secretary has nearly as much work to do.

The total work load, measured in terms of number of items times people handling each item, is the sum of the components of y, or 145. We obtain the same answer by computing xt. And the components of $xB = (43.7, 16.3)$ show us that about 44 of the tasks get done and 16 are laid aside on an average day.

Suppose that the company wishes to redistribute its work load, by controlling where the 60 items of business are received. That is, the company wishes to specify y and to determine x suitably (subject to the condition that $xc = 60$). Since $y = xN$, we must have $x = y(I - Q)$. The restriction yields

$$
xc = y(I - Q)c = 60.
$$

Let $h = (I - Q)c$; then the company may specify any distribution of labor subject to the condition that $yh = 60$. In our example

$$
h = (I - Q)c = \begin{pmatrix} 0 \\ \frac{1}{4} \\ \frac{1}{2} \\ \frac{1}{2} \end{pmatrix}.
$$

Suppose that our company decides on a completely democratic work load, so that y should be of the form $y = (a, a, a, a)$. The restriction yields $(\frac{5}{4})a = 60$, or $a = 48$. That is, each employee will have a load of 48. Then

$$
x = y(I - Q) = (36, 12, 12, 0).
$$

Thus 60 percent of the work should come to the president, and 20 percent each to his secretary and to the vice-president.

Example 2. Let us study the changes in personnel need in a given department in a large industry. For simplicity we will consider only whether these needs increase, decrease, or stay the same in a given year. This will lead to a three-state regular Markov chain, with the three possibilities represented by $+$, $-$, and 0, respectively.

In our particular industry there is a fixed probability p that last year's trend will continue. Furthermore, the president of the company disapproves of a department's making a change in one year and making the opposite change in the next year. Thus our transition matrix has the form

$$P = \begin{array}{c} \\ + \\ 0 \\ - \end{array} \overset{\displaystyle + \quad 0 \quad -}{\begin{pmatrix} p & q & 0 \\ r & p & s \\ 0 & q & p \end{pmatrix}}, \qquad p + q = 1, \quad p + r + s = 1.$$

In particular, therefore, $q = r + s$. It is a simple computation to find the fixed vector $w = (r/2q, \frac{1}{2}, s/2q)$.

The components of the fixed vector give the long-run average for the number of years in which a certain trend holds. It is very interesting to note that although the numbers p, q, r, and s have not been specified, we can predict that in half the years the personnel need will be unchanged.

We can also compute the long-run rise or fall in employment, if we know the average size of an increase or decrease in staff. Suppose that in an increasing year an average of a people are hired, while in a decreasing year an average of b employees are let go. Then the average change in employment per year is

$$\left(\frac{r}{2q}\right) a + \left(\frac{1}{2}\right) 0 - \left(\frac{s}{2q}\right) b$$

or

(1)
$$\frac{ra - sb}{2(r + s)}.$$

In particular, there will be a long-range expansion if $ra > sb$, a decline if $ra < sb$, and a rough equilibrium if $ra = sb$.

Example 3. A man is interested in investing in one of two companies. Of a potential of 12,000 customers, company A now attracts 10,000 while company B attracts only 2000. On the other hand, from a sample survey he notes that 20 percent of A's customers switch to B in the next month, while only 10 percent of B's customers switch to A. Assuming that this trend continues, what advice can we give him for his investment?

If we formulate the problem as a two-state Markov chain, we obtain the transition matrix

$$P = \begin{array}{c} \\ A \\ B \end{array} \overset{\displaystyle A \quad B}{\begin{pmatrix} .8 & .2 \\ 1 & .9 \end{pmatrix}}$$

and the fixed vector $w = (\frac{1}{3}, \frac{2}{3})$. This means that in the long run the customers will split $\frac{1}{3}$ to $\frac{2}{3}$, or 4000 for A and 8000 for B. But how long is this long run? Which is more important, the present highly favorable position of company A, or the long-run advantage of B? If we let $x = (10000, 2000)$, and if $x^{(n)}$ is the distribution of customers after n months, then $x^{(n)} = xP^n$. Or for computational purposes we let $x^{(0)} = x$, and $x^{(n+1)} = x^{(n)}P$, and we can compute the distributions step by step. The results for two years are shown in Figure 11.

No. of Months	Number of Customers for A	B
0	10,000	2,000
3	6,058	5,942
6	4,706	7,294
9	4,242	7,758
12	4,083	7,913
18	4,010	7,990
24	4,001	7,999

Figure 11

We see that the "long-run" effect shows up very quickly. If the present trend continues, company B will catch up with A in about three months, far exceed it in six months, and then make small gains towards the 8000 figure. By the end of two years the long-range estimate is for all practical purposes exact. Hence the man should certainly invest in B. Of course in a more complex problem, with a larger number of states, the convergence to the long-range distribution will be slower, but the very same type of computation will show us the relative advantages of possible investments.

EXERCISES

Exercises 1 through 6 refer to the following problem. A car rental agency operates in three cities. The following table shows the transition of cars during a typical month:

	Go to A	Go to B	Go to C	Lost
From A:	.5	.2	.2	.1
From B:	.2	.5	.2	.1
From C:	.1	.3	.4	.2

For example, a car in city A stays there with probability .5, ends up at B or C with probability .2, and is lost (sold or destroyed) with probability .1.

1. Set up a Markov-chain model.
2. Compute N, t, and B, and interpret your results.
3. Suppose that the agency supplies 70 new cars to each city each month. What is the long-run distribution of cars? How many are lost per month in the long run?   [*Ans.* A has 490, B 630, C 490; 210 are lost.]
4. How many cars should the agency supply to the various cities each month so that in the long run each city has 500 cars?
     [*Ans.* 100 to A and C, none to B.]

5. How many cars should the agency supply to the various cities each month so that in the long run there will be 600 cars in each of cities A and C, and 400 in B?   [*Ans.* Impossible.]

6. Prove that a long-run distribution vector y with components y_i is achievable if and only if $y \geq yQ$. Give a simple condition on Q for the possibility of achieving a uniform distribution (all y_i the same) in this type of model.

Exercises 7 through 10 refer to the following problem. Two manufacturers have competing products, A and B. If the present trend continues, customers will shift from product to product according to the following matrix:

$$\begin{array}{c} \\ A \\ B \end{array} \begin{array}{cc} A & B \\ \begin{pmatrix} .9 & .1 \\ .2 & .8 \end{pmatrix} \end{array}.$$

To improve his share of the market, manufacturer A considers the introduction of an additional product, which may be either X or Y. Pretesting indicates that the trends would then be as follows:

$$\begin{array}{c} \\ A \\ B \\ X \end{array} \begin{array}{ccc} A & B & X \\ \begin{pmatrix} .8 & .1 & .1 \\ .1 & .7 & .2 \\ .1 & .4 & .5 \end{pmatrix} \end{array} \quad \text{or} \quad \begin{array}{c} \\ A \\ B \\ Y \end{array} \begin{array}{ccc} A & B & Y \\ \begin{pmatrix} .8 & .1 & .1 \\ .1 & .6 & .3 \\ .2 & .2 & .6 \end{pmatrix} \end{array}.$$

7. Under the present arrangement, what fraction of the market would buy product A in the long run?

8. What fraction of the market could the manufacturer count on in the long run if he produced both A and X?

9. What fraction of the market could the manufacturer count on if he produced both A and Y?

10. Use the results of Exercises 7 through 9 to advise the manufacturer.

*13. TWO EXAMPLES FROM ECONOMICS AND FINANCE

Markov-chain models are probabilistic in nature. However, it turns out that sometimes the mathematics used to analyze them can also be used in analyzing deterministic models. In the present section we shall discuss two deterministic models that can be solved by imbedding them in absorbing Markov chains and using the mathematical results of the previous section. The reader will also observe a close connection with the parts-requirements problem solved in Section 7.

In what we are going to do the question of whether a given Markov chain is absorbing is crucial. Hence we need an algorithm for determining the answer to this question. Such an algorithm is given in Figure 12. The proof that the algorithm works is given in Exercises 1 and 2.

Example 1. Apply the method in Figure 12 to the transition matrix:

$$P = \begin{pmatrix} 1 & 0 & 0 & 0 \\ 0 & 0 & \frac{1}{3} & \frac{2}{3} \\ \frac{1}{2} & \frac{1}{2} & 0 & 0 \\ 0 & 0 & 1 & 0 \end{pmatrix}.$$

We carry out the checking process indicated by the algorithm, marking the checks in the order in which they were made. We obtain

$$\begin{array}{c} \quad\quad 1\checkmark\ 3\checkmark\ 2\checkmark\ 3\checkmark \\ \begin{array}{c} 1\checkmark \\ 3\checkmark \\ 2\checkmark \\ 3\checkmark \end{array} \begin{pmatrix} 1 & 0 & 0 & 0 \\ 0 & 0 & \frac{1}{3} & \frac{2}{3} \\ \frac{1}{2} & \frac{1}{2} & 0 & 0 \\ 0 & 0 & 1 & 0 \end{pmatrix}. \end{array}$$

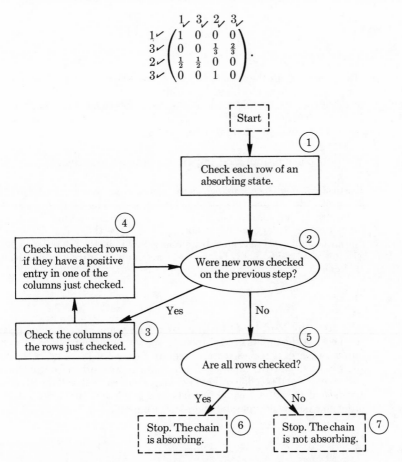

Flow diagram for testing to see whether a Markov chain is absorbing

Figure 12

Since all rows are checked, the Markov chain is absorbing. The reader should find the paths from each state to the absorbing state. The numbers of the checks will help in this regard (see Exercise 3).

Example 2. Let us apply the method of Figure 12 to the transition matrix:

$$P' = \begin{pmatrix} 1 & 0 & 0 & 0 \\ 0 & \frac{1}{3} & 0 & \frac{2}{3} \\ \frac{1}{2} & 0 & \frac{1}{2} & 0 \\ 0 & \frac{3}{4} & 0 & \frac{1}{4} \end{pmatrix}.$$

The checks produced by the algorithm are:

$$\begin{array}{c} \quad 1\checkmark \quad 2\checkmark \\ \begin{array}{c} 1\checkmark \\ \\ 2\checkmark \\ \\ \end{array} \begin{pmatrix} 1 & 0 & 0 & 0 \\ 0 & \frac{1}{3} & 0 & \frac{2}{3} \\ \frac{1}{2} & 0 & \frac{1}{2} & 0 \\ 0 & \frac{3}{4} & 0 & \frac{1}{4} \end{pmatrix}. \end{array}$$

Here, since not all the rows are checked, the Markov chain whose transition matrix is P' is not absorbing. The reader should check that the states $\{2, 4\}$ form a closed set, in the sense that it is impossible to leave them once entered. In particular it is impossible to go from either of these states to the absorbing state (1), so that the chain is not absorbing.

We now consider our first important applied example.

Example 3. *The Open Leontief Model.* Consider an economy with r industries and each industry produces just one kind of good. These industries are interconnected in the sense that each must buy a nonnegative amount of the other industries' products in order to operate. Let q_{ij} be the dollar amount of the output of industry j that must be purchased by industry i in order to produce \$1 of its own goods. Let Q be the $r \times r$ matrix with entries q_{ij}. By definition we have

(1) $$Q \geq 0.$$

It is not hard to see that for fixed i the sum $q_{i1} + \cdots + q_{ir}$ gives the total cost of the inputs needed by industry i in order to produce \$1 worth of output. Clearly it makes sense to require that $q_{i1} + \cdots + q_{ir} \leq 1$; that is, the total value of the inputs going into a dollar's worth of output must be less than or equal to a dollar. For obvious reasons we shall call the ith industry *profitable* if the strict inequality holds, and *profitless* if the equality holds. In order to rule out unprofitable industries we require

(2) $$Qf \leq f,$$

where f is the r-component column vector of all 1's.

Suppose now that the total economy is to be run so that a vector $d = (d_1, \ldots, d_r)$ of goods can be supplied for consumption. Here d_j is the amount of good j to be consumed. At what levels shall we run each industry in order to supply total demand? Let x_i be the level at which industry i is to be run. To make economic sense, $x_i \geq 0$. Then $x = (x_1, \ldots, x_r)$ is the *activity vector* for the industries, and $x \geq 0$. The jth component of xQ is $x_1 q_{1j} + \cdots + x_r q_{rj}$, and this is the total output of industry j demanded by all the other industries when the economy uses the activity vector x. In the same manner one can see that xQ is the vector of internal demands when the economy uses the activity vector x.

Now the vector x must be chosen so as to provide the sum of the internal plus the external demand. That is,

$$(3) \qquad\qquad x = xQ + d.$$

The reader should observe that this is the same as equation (3) of Section 7, although the definition of Q is quite different there. Equation (3) implies

$$(4) \qquad\qquad x(I - Q) = d.$$

If the matrix $(I - Q)$ has a nonnegative inverse, we can solve for (4) as

$$(5) \qquad\qquad x = d(I - Q)^{-1},$$

and the result will be economically meaningful. If this inverse does not exist or if it has negative entries, then there will be some kinds of outside demand vectors d for which there is no nonnegative solution activity vector x.

Thus we need conditions on the matrix Q that $(I - Q)$ have a nonnegative inverse. Here we apply the theory of absorbing Markov chains. We imbed the matrix Q into a Markov chain P having $r + 1$ states as follows:

$$(6) \qquad\qquad P = \left(\begin{array}{c|c} 1 & 0 \\ \hline R & Q \end{array}\right),$$

where the first state is absorbing, and R is an $r \times 1$ matrix with components $r_i = 1 - (q_{i1} + \cdots + q_{ir})$ for $i = 1, \ldots, r$. (We label the first state 0.) We now apply the flow diagram of Figure 12. If we end up in box 6, we know that P is an absorbing Markov chain with fundamental matrix $N = (I - Q)^{-1}$. And the fundamental matrix is nonnegative. If we end up in box 7 of Figure 12, it can be shown (see Exercise 5) that $I - Q$ is singular and has no inverse. Hence in this case there is no economic solution to the economy as it stands.

We summarize our results in a theorem.

THEOREM. Let Q be the input matrix of an open Leontief economy satisfying (1) and (2); then equation (3) can be solved for all demand vectors d if and only if the Markov chain P of (6) is an absorbing chain.

As an example suppose that there are three industries and

$$(7) \qquad\qquad Q = \begin{pmatrix} 0 & \frac{1}{2} & 0 \\ \frac{1}{3} & \frac{1}{3} & \frac{1}{3} \\ \frac{1}{6} & 0 & \frac{1}{2} \end{pmatrix}.$$

Then the Markov chain P is given by

(8)
$$P = \begin{pmatrix} 1 & 0 & 0 & 0 \\ \frac{1}{2} & 0 & \frac{1}{2} & 0 \\ 0 & \frac{1}{3} & \frac{1}{3} & \frac{1}{3} \\ \frac{1}{3} & \frac{1}{6} & 0 & \frac{1}{2} \end{pmatrix}.$$

Applying the algorithm of Figure 12, we easily find that the Markov chain is absorbing. Hence $(I - Q)^{-1}$ exists. It is

(9)
$$(I - Q)^{-1} = \begin{pmatrix} 1 & -\frac{1}{2} & 0 \\ -\frac{1}{3} & \frac{2}{3} & -\frac{1}{2} \\ -\frac{1}{6} & 0 & \frac{1}{2} \end{pmatrix}^{-1} = \begin{pmatrix} \frac{3}{2} & \frac{9}{8} & \frac{3}{4} \\ 1 & \frac{9}{4} & \frac{3}{2} \\ \frac{1}{2} & \frac{3}{8} & \frac{9}{4} \end{pmatrix}.$$

Thus for a demand vector $d = (400, 200, 300)$ we have activity vector

(10)
$$x = d(I - Q)^{-1} = (400, 200, 300) \begin{pmatrix} \frac{3}{2} & \frac{9}{8} & \frac{3}{4} \\ 1 & \frac{9}{4} & \frac{3}{2} \\ \frac{1}{2} & \frac{3}{8} & \frac{9}{4} \end{pmatrix}$$

$$= (950, 1012.5, 1275),$$

so that industry 1 must produce $950 worth of output, industry 2, $1012.50 worth of output, and industry 3, $1275 worth of output in order that consumptions of $400, $200, and $300 of each industry's output may be realized.

> **Example 4.** *A Cost Accounting Model.* Consider a company that has r departments. It has adopted accounting conventions that if department i performs services for department j then it charges a fraction q_{ij} of its costs to department j. It requires $q_{ii} = 0$, since it does not make sense for a department to charge costs to itself. It also requires $q_{ij} \geq 0$, so that (1) holds. No department is permitted to charge more than 100 percent of its costs to other departments, so that $q_{i1} + \cdots + q_{ir} \leq 1$, and (2) holds as well. Departments for which the equality holds are called *service departments*, since they charge away all of their costs, and departments for which the inequality holds are *profit centers*, since they actually pay some of their costs. Let d_i be the dollar amount of external costs charged to department i by outside firms, and let $d = (d_1, \ldots, d_r)$ be the corresponding vector. Finally, let x_i be the total costs assigned to department i and let $x = (x_1, \ldots, x_r)$ be the corresponding vector.
>
> Since the costs assigned to a department must be the sum of the internally charged costs plus the external costs, it is easy to see by the same kind of analysis as for the Leontief model that equation (3) must be satisfied by the x's. Therefore we have the same problem as before of determining whether the inverse of $(I - Q)$ exists. The same solution technique of imbedding the matrix Q in a Markov chain and using Figure 12 to see if it is absorbing provides the solution technique.

It is remarkable that from two quite different interpretations in the Leontief input-output model and the cost accounting model we have arrived at exactly the same mathematical model and corresponding solution technique.

As a numerical example consider the matrix

$$Q = \begin{pmatrix} 0 & 0 & 0 & 0 & 0 \\ 0 & 0 & 0 & 0 & 0 \\ \frac{1}{2} & 0 & 0 & \frac{1}{3} & \frac{1}{6} \\ \frac{1}{4} & \frac{1}{4} & \frac{1}{4} & 0 & \frac{1}{4} \\ 0 & \frac{1}{3} & \frac{1}{3} & \frac{1}{3} & 0 \end{pmatrix}.$$

Here the first two departments are profit centers, since they do not charge any of their costs to other departments of the company. The last three departments are service centers, since they charge off all their costs to other departments. It is easy to show that the Markov chain P obtained by (6) is absorbing, hence $(I - Q)^{-1}$ exists. A computer gave the following values for this inverse:

$$(I - Q)^{-1} = \begin{pmatrix} 1 & 0 & 0 & 0 & 0 \\ 0 & 1 & 0 & 0 & 0 \\ -\frac{1}{2} & 0 & 1 & -\frac{1}{3} & -\frac{1}{6} \\ -\frac{1}{4} & -\frac{1}{4} & -\frac{1}{4} & 1 & -\frac{1}{4} \\ 0 & -\frac{1}{3} & -\frac{1}{3} & -\frac{1}{3} & 1 \end{pmatrix}^{-1}$$

$$= \begin{pmatrix} 1 & 0 & 0 & 0 & 0 \\ 0 & 1 & 0 & 0 & 0 \\ .7547 & .2453 & 1.2453 & .5283 & .3396 \\ .5472 & .4528 & .4528 & 1.2830 & .3962 \\ .4340 & .5660 & .5660 & .6038 & 1.2453 \end{pmatrix}.$$

If we assume that $d_i = 10,000$ for $i = 1, \ldots, 5$—that is, each department incurs outside expenses of $10,000—then from (5) we find that

$$x = (27,359 \quad 22,641 \quad 22,641 \quad 24,151 \quad 19,811).$$

Notice that the sum of the costs of the first two departments, which are profit centers, is $27,359 + $22,641 = $50,000. In other words, the profit centers end up paying all the outside costs. This is always true (see Exercise 7).

EXERCISES

1. In Figure 12 show that each time we check a new row when we are in box 4 of the flow diagram, there is a way of getting from state i to an absorbing state. Hence show that if we end up in box 6, the chain is absorbing.

2. In Figure 12 show that if we end up in box 7, there is at least one state that cannot reach an absorbing state.

3. In Example 1 show that if we number each check as it is made, then the numbers on the rows are equal to 1 plus the minimum number of steps to go from that state to an absorbing state.

4. Apply the flow diagram of Figure 12 to the following examples of Markov chains to see if they are absorbing.

a. $\begin{pmatrix} 0 & 1 & 0 \\ 1 & 0 & 0 \\ 0 & 1 & 0 \end{pmatrix}.$

b. $\begin{pmatrix} \frac{1}{2} & 0 & \frac{1}{2} & 0 \\ \frac{1}{4} & 0 & \frac{1}{4} & \frac{1}{2} \\ 0 & 0 & 1 & 0 \\ 0 & \frac{1}{2} & 0 & \frac{1}{2} \end{pmatrix}.$

c. $\begin{pmatrix} 0 & \frac{1}{2} & \frac{1}{2} \\ 1 & 0 & 0 \\ 1 & 0 & 0 \end{pmatrix}.$

d. $\begin{pmatrix} 1 & 0 & 0 & 0 \\ 0 & \frac{1}{2} & \frac{1}{2} & 0 \\ 0 & 0 & 0 & 1 \\ \frac{1}{2} & \frac{1}{2} & 0 & 0 \end{pmatrix}.$

5. Assume that we started with an $r \times r$ matrix Q satisfying (1) and (2), defined the Markov chain P as in (6), and applied the flow diagram of Figure 12, ending up in box 7.
   a. Let $h_i = 0$ when i is a checked row and $h_i = 1$ when i is an unchecked row. Let h be the r-component column vector with components h_i. Show that $h \neq 0$.
   b. Show that $Qh = h$, and hence $(I - Q)h = 0$.
   c. If $(I - Q)^{-1}$ exists, use (b) to show that $h = 0$.
   d. Use a. and c. to prove that $(I - Q)^{-1}$ does not exist.

6. Let Q and d be as given below for Leontief input-output models. When possible, solve for x as in (5).

a.
$$Q = \begin{pmatrix} \frac{1}{2} & 0 & \frac{1}{2} \\ \frac{1}{4} & 0 & \frac{1}{4} \\ 0 & \frac{1}{2} & 0 \end{pmatrix}, \qquad d = (5000, 8000, 2000).$$

b.
$$Q = \begin{pmatrix} 0 & \frac{1}{2} & \frac{1}{2} \\ \frac{1}{2} & 0 & \frac{1}{2} \\ \frac{1}{2} & \frac{1}{2} & 0 \end{pmatrix}, \qquad d = (100, 500, 300).$$

c.
$$Q = \begin{pmatrix} 0 & 1 & 0 \\ 0 & 0 & 1 \\ \frac{1}{2} & 0 & 0 \end{pmatrix}, \qquad d = (1000, 2000, 3000).$$

7. In the cost accounting model of Example 4 show that no service center can pay any outside cost. Use this to show that the profit centers must ultimately pay all outside costs.

8. Let Q and d be as given below for cost accounting models. When possible, solve for x as in (5).

a.
$$Q = \begin{pmatrix} 0 & \frac{1}{2} & \frac{1}{4} \\ \frac{1}{3} & 0 & \frac{1}{3} \\ 1 & 0 & 0 \end{pmatrix}, \qquad d = (200, 500, 700).$$

b.
$$Q = \begin{pmatrix} 0 & 1 & 0 \\ \frac{1}{2} & 0 & \frac{1}{2} \\ \frac{2}{3} & \frac{1}{3} & 0 \end{pmatrix}, \qquad d = (3000, 7000, 5000).$$

c.
$$Q = \begin{pmatrix} 0 & \frac{1}{5} & \frac{3}{5} \\ \frac{1}{6} & 0 & \frac{1}{3} \\ \frac{1}{6} & \frac{2}{3} & 0 \end{pmatrix}, \qquad d = (1000, 1000, 1000).$$

SUGGESTED READING

Birkhoff, G., and S. MacLane, *A Survey of Modern Algebra*, third ed., Macmillan, New York, 1965.

Johnson, R. E., *First Course in Abstract Algebra*, Prentice-Hall, Englewood Cliffs, N. J., 1953.

Beaumont, R. A., and R. W. Ball, *Introduction to Modern Algebra and Matrix Theory*, Rinehart, New York, 1954, Chaps. I, II, III, IV.

Hadley, G., *Linear Algebra*, Addison-Wesley, Reading, Mass., 1961, Chaps. 1–5.

Kemeny, John G., and J. Laurie Snell, *Finite Markov Chains*, Van Nostrand, Princeton, N. J., 1960.

Cyert, R. M., H. J. Davidson, and G. L. Thompson, "Estimation of the Allowance for Doubtful Accounts by Markov Chains," *Management Science*, **8** (1962), p. 287–303.

Cyert, R. M., and G. L. Thompson, "Selecting a Portfolio of Credit Risks by Markov Chains," *Journal of Business*, **41** (1968), pp. 39–46.

Thompson, G. L., "On the Parts Requirements Problem," *Operations Research*, **13** (1965), pp. 453–461.

Vaszonyi, A., *Scientific Programming in Business and Industry*, Wiley, New York, 1958, Chap. 13.

CHAPTER

5

LINEAR PROGRAMMING

1. POLYHEDRAL CONVEX SETS

Recall that an equation containing one or more variables is called an *open statement*. For instance,

(a) $$-2x_1 + 3x_2 = 6$$

is an example of an open statement. If we let $A = (-2, 3)$, $x = \begin{pmatrix} x_1 \\ x_2 \end{pmatrix}$, and $b = 6$, we can write (a) in matrix form as

$$Ax = (-2, 3)\begin{pmatrix} x_1 \\ x_2 \end{pmatrix} = -2x_1 + 3x_2 = 6 = b.$$

For some two-component vectors x the statement $Ax = b$ is true and for others it is false. For instance, if $x = \begin{pmatrix} 3 \\ 4 \end{pmatrix}$, it is true, since $-2\cdot 3 + 3\cdot 4 = 6$; and if $x = \begin{pmatrix} 2 \\ 4 \end{pmatrix}$, it is false, since $-2\cdot 2 + 3\cdot 4 = 8$. The set of all two-component vectors x that make the open statement $Ax = b$ true is defined to be the *truth set* of the open statement.

> **Example 1.** In plane geometry it is usual to picture in the plane the truth sets of open statements such as (a). Thus we can regard each two-component vector x as being the components of a point in the plane in the usual way. Then the truth set or *locus* (which is the geometric term for truth set) of (a) is the straight line plotted in Figure 1. Points on this line may be obtained by assuming values for one of the variables and computing the corresponding values for the other variable. Thus, setting $x_1 = 0$, we find $x_2 = 2$, so that the

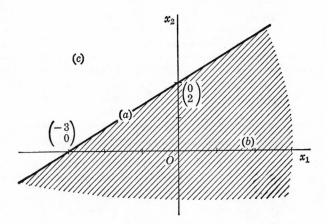

Figure 1

point $x = \begin{pmatrix} 0 \\ 2 \end{pmatrix}$ lies on the locus; similarly, setting $x_2 = 0$, we find $x_1 = -3$,

so that the point $\begin{pmatrix} -3 \\ 0 \end{pmatrix}$ lies on the locus; and so on.

In the same way inequalities of the form $Ax \leq b$ or $Ax < b$ or $Ax \geq b$ or $Ax > b$ are open statements and possess truth sets. And in the case that x is a two-component vector, these can be plotted in the plane.

Example 2. Consider the inequalities (b) $Ax < b$, (c) $Ax > b$, (d) $Ax \leq b$, and (e) $Ax \geq b$, where A, x, and b are as in Example 1. They may be written as

(b) $\qquad\qquad\qquad\qquad -2x_1 + 3x_2 < 6,$

(c) $\qquad\qquad\qquad\qquad -2x_1 + 3x_2 > 6,$

(d) $\qquad\qquad\qquad\qquad -2x_1 + 3x_2 \leq 6,$

(e) $\qquad\qquad\qquad\qquad -2x_1 + 3x_2 \geq 6.$

Consider (b) first. What points $\begin{pmatrix} x_1 \\ x_2 \end{pmatrix}$ satisfy this inequality? By trial and error we can find many points on the locus. Thus the point $\begin{pmatrix} 1 \\ 2 \end{pmatrix}$ is on it, since $-2 \cdot 1 + 3 \cdot 2 = 4 < 6$; on the other hand the point $\begin{pmatrix} 1 \\ 3 \end{pmatrix}$ is not on the locus, because $-2 \cdot 1 + 3 \cdot 3 = -2 + 9 = 7$, which is not less than 6. In between these two points we find $\begin{pmatrix} 1 \\ \frac{8}{3} \end{pmatrix}$, which lies on the boundary—that is, on the locus of (a). We note that, starting with $\begin{pmatrix} 1 \\ \frac{8}{3} \end{pmatrix}$ on locus (a), by increasing x_2 we went outside the locus (b); by decreasing x_2 we came into the locus (b) again. This holds in general. Given a point on the locus of (a), by increasing its second coordinate we get more than 6, but by decreasing the second coordinate we get less than 6, and hence the latter gives a point in the truth set of (b). Thus we find that the locus of (b) consists of all points of the plane *below* the line (a)—in other words, the shaded area in Figure 1. The area on one side of a straight line is called an *open half plane.*

We can apply exactly the same analysis to show that the locus of (c) is the open half plane above the line (a). This can also be deduced from the fact that the truth sets of statements (a), (b), and (c) are disjoint and have as union the entire plane.

Since (d) is the disjunction of (a) and (b), the truth set of (d) is the union of the truth sets of (a) and (b). Such a set, which consists of an open half plane together with the points on the line that define the half plane, is called a *closed half plane.* Obviously, the truth set of (e) consists of the union of (a) and (c) and therefore is also a closed half plane.

Frequently we want to assert several different open statements at once—that is, we want to assert the conjunction of several such statements. The easy way to do this is to let A be an $m \times n$ matrix, x an n-component column vector, and b an m-component column vector. Then the statement $Ax \leq b$ is the conjunction of the i statements $A_i x \leq b_i$, where A_i is the ith row of A and b_i is the ith entry of b.

Example 3. A box manufacturer makes small and large boxes from a single kind of cardboard. The small boxes require 2 square feet of cardboard each and the large boxes 3 square feet each. If the manufacturer has 60 square feet of cardboard on hand, what are the possible combinations of small and large boxes that he can make?

In order to set up this problem let x_1 be the number of small boxes and x_2 the number of large boxes to be made. Since it is impossible to make negative numbers of boxes, we have the obvious constraints

(f) $$x_1 \geq 0,$$

(g) $$x_2 \geq 0.$$

Also, because of the constraint on the total amount of cardboard on hand, we have

(h) $$2x_1 + 3x_2 \leq 60.$$

If we now want to state these three inequality constraints simultaneously in the form $Ax \leq b$, we must first change (f) and (g) into $\leq$ constraints. This can be done by multiplying through by -1, so that (f) becomes $-x_1 \leq 0$ and (g) becomes $-x_2 \leq 0$. If we now define

$$A = \begin{pmatrix} -1 & 0 \\ 0 & -1 \\ 2 & 3 \end{pmatrix}, \qquad x = \begin{pmatrix} x_1 \\ x_2 \end{pmatrix}, \qquad b = \begin{pmatrix} 0 \\ 0 \\ 60 \end{pmatrix},$$

we see that $Ax \leq b$ is a matrix way of asserting the conjunction of (f), (g), and (h). The truth set of $Ax \leq b$ is the intersection of the three individual truth sets. The truth set of (f) is the right half plane; the truth set of (g) is the upper half plane; and the truth set of (h) is the half plane below and on the line $2x_1 + 3x_2 = 60$. The intersection of these is the triangle (including the sides and corners) shaded in Figure 2. The area shaded in Figure 2 contains all those and only those points that simultaneously satisfy (f), (g), and (h), or, equivalently, $Ax \leq b$.

In the examples considered so far we have restricted ourselves to open statements with two variables. Such statements have truth sets that can be sketched in the plane. In the same way open statements with three variables have truth sets that can be visualized in three-dimensional space. Open statements with four or more variables have truth sets in four or more dimensions, which we can no longer visualize. However, applied problems frequently lead to such statements. Fortunately, we will develop methods (in Section 4) for handling them without having to visualize the truth sets geometrically.

In order to have a notation that will enable us to talk in general about conjunctions of several open statements in any number of dimensions, we shall, for the remainder of this chapter, consider b to be an m-component column vector, x an n-component column vector, and A an $m \times n$ matrix. The ith row of A will be denoted by A_i. Similarly, the ith component of b will be denoted by b_i. Of course, A_i is an n-component row vector and b_i is a number. We shall let $\mathfrak{X}_n$ denote the set of all n-component column vectors x. Thus in Example 3 we had $m = 3$ and $n = 2$. A was a 3×2 matrix, x a two-component column vector, and b a three-component column vector. The set of all two-component column vectors x is denoted by $\mathfrak{X}_2$.

We now set up some definitions that will be used in the later exposition.

DEFINITION. The truth set of $A_ix = b_i$ is called a *hyperplane* in $\mathfrak{X}_n$. The truth sets of inequalities of the form $A_ix < b_i$ or $A_ix > b_i$ are called *open half spaces*, while the truth sets of the inequalities $A_ix \leq b_i$ or $A_ix \geq b_i$ are called *closed half spaces* in $\mathfrak{X}_n$.

When we assert the conjunction of several open statements, the resulting truth set is the intersection of the truth sets of the individual open statements. Thus in Example 3 we have the conjunction of $m = 3$ open statements in $\mathfrak{X}_2$. In Figure 2 we show this geometrically as the intersection

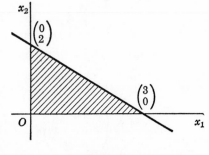

Figure 2

of $m = 3$ closed half spaces (planes) in $n = 2$ dimensions. Such intersections of closed half spaces are of special importance.

DEFINITION. The intersection of a finite number of closed half spaces is a *polyhedral convex set*.

THEOREM. Any polyhedral convex set is the truth set of an inequality statement of the form $Ax \leq b$.

Proof. A closed half space is the truth set of an inequality of the form $A_i x \leq b_i$. (An inequality of the form $A_i x \geq b_i$ can be converted into one of this form by multiplying by -1.) Now a polyhedral convex set is the truth set of the conjunction of several such statements. Since A is the matrix whose ith row is A_i and b is the column vector with components b_i, then the inequality statement $Ax \leq b$ is a succinct way of stating the conjunction of the inequalities $A_1 x \leq b_1, \ldots, A_m x \leq b_m$. This completes the proof.

The terminology polyhedral *convex* sets is used because these sets are special examples of convex sets. A convex set C is a set such that whenever u and v are points of C, the entire line segment between u and v also belongs to C. This is equivalent to saying that all points of the form $z = au + (1 - a)v$ for $0 \leq a \leq 1$ belong to C whenever u and v do. In this chapter we shall be concerned primarily with polyhedral convex sets.

EXERCISES

1. Draw pictures of the truth sets of $Ax \leq b$, where A and b are as given below. (Construct the truth sets of the individual statements first and then take their intersection.)

$a.$ $A = \begin{pmatrix} 1 & 0 \\ 0 & 1 \\ -2 & -3 \end{pmatrix}$, $b = \begin{pmatrix} 3 \\ 2 \\ 0 \end{pmatrix}$.

$b.$ $A = \begin{pmatrix} -2 & -3 \\ -1 & 1 \\ 1 & 1 \end{pmatrix}$, $b = \begin{pmatrix} -6 \\ 2 \\ 3 \end{pmatrix}$.

$c.$ $A = \begin{pmatrix} 2 & 3 \\ -1 & 1 \\ 1 & 1 \end{pmatrix}$, $b = \begin{pmatrix} 6 \\ 2 \\ 3 \end{pmatrix}$.

$d.$ $A = \begin{pmatrix} 0 & -1 \\ -1 & 0 \\ 1 & 0 \end{pmatrix}$, $b = \begin{pmatrix} 0 \\ 0 \\ 2 \end{pmatrix}$.

$e.$ $A = \begin{pmatrix} 1 & 0 \\ -1 & 0 \\ 0 & 1 \\ 0 & -1 \end{pmatrix}$, $b = \begin{pmatrix} 2 \\ 2 \\ 3 \\ 3 \end{pmatrix}$.

$f.$ $A = \begin{pmatrix} 3 & 2 \\ 3 & 2 \end{pmatrix}$, $b = \begin{pmatrix} -6 \\ 6 \end{pmatrix}$.

$g.$ $A = \begin{pmatrix} -3 & -2 \\ 3 & 2 \end{pmatrix}$, $b = \begin{pmatrix} -6 \\ 6 \end{pmatrix}$.

$h.$ $A = \begin{pmatrix} -1 & 1 \\ 1 & 1 \end{pmatrix}$, $b = \begin{pmatrix} 0 \\ 0 \end{pmatrix}$.

i. $A = \begin{pmatrix} 1 & 0 \\ -1 & 0 \end{pmatrix}, \quad b = \begin{pmatrix} 2 \\ -5 \end{pmatrix}.$

j. $A = \begin{pmatrix} -3 & -2 \\ -2 & -3 \\ -1 & 0 \\ 0 & -1 \end{pmatrix}, b = \begin{pmatrix} -6 \\ -6 \\ 0 \\ 0 \end{pmatrix}.$

k. $A = \begin{pmatrix} -2 & -1 \\ 1 & 0 \\ 0 & 1 \end{pmatrix}, \quad b = \begin{pmatrix} -7 \\ 0 \\ 0 \end{pmatrix}.$

2. In the cardboard-box problem of Example 3 consider the following additional constraints:

   a. "At least as many small as large boxes should be made." Write a constraint involving x_1 and x_2 that expresses this and find A and b. Draw the picture of the resulting convex set.
   [Partial Ans. $-x_1 + x_2 \leq 0.$]

   b. In addition to the constraints above add a constraint expressing, "at most 20 small boxes should be made." Find A and b and sketch the convex set.
   [Partial Ans. $x_1 \leq 20.$]

3. Of the polyhedral convex sets constructed in Exercise 1, which have a finite area and which have infinite area?
   [Partial Ans. c., d., f., h., and j. are of infinite area; g. is a line; i. and k. are empty.]

4. For each of the following half planes give an inequality of which it is the truth set.

   a. The open half plane above the x_1 axis.   [Ans. $x_2 > 0.$]

   b. The closed half plane on and above the straight line making angles of 45° with the positive x_1 and x_2 axis.

Exercises 5 through 9 refer to a situation in which a retailer is trying to decide how many units of items X and Y he should keep in stock. Let x be the number of units of X and y be the number of units of Y. X costs \$4 per unit and Y costs \$3 per unit.

5. One cannot stock a negative number of units of either X or Y. Write these conditions as inequalities and draw their truth sets.

6. The maximum demand over the period for which the retailer is contemplating holding inventory will not exceed 600 units of X or 600 units of Y. Modify the set found in Exercise 5 to take this into account.

7. The retailer is not willing to tie up more than \$2400 in inventory altogether. Modify the set found in Exercise 6.

8. The retailer decides to invest at least twice as much in inventory of item X as he does in inventory of item Y. Modify the set of Exercise 7.

9. Finally, the retailer decides that he wants to invest \$900 in inventory of item Y. What possibilities are left?   [Ans. None.]

10. Assume that a pound of meat contains 80 units of protein and 10 units of calcium while a quart of milk contains 15 units of protein and 60 units of calcium. If an adult's minimum daily requirements are 40 units of protein and 30 units of calcium, what consumption quantities of meat and milk will yield at least these minimum daily requirements? A convenient way to summarize the data is by the following *data box*:

	Protein	Calcium
Meat	$80\,\dfrac{\text{units protein}}{\text{lb. meat}}$	$10\,\dfrac{\text{units calcium}}{\text{lb. meat}}$
Milk	$15\,\dfrac{\text{units protein}}{\text{qt. milk}}$	$60\,\dfrac{\text{units calcium}}{\text{qt. milk}}$
Requirements	$40\,\dfrac{\text{units protein}}{\text{day}}$	$30\,\dfrac{\text{units calcium}}{\text{day}}$

a. Let w_1 be the number of pounds of meat and w_2 be the number of quarts of milk consumed per day, and let $w = (w_1, w_2)$. Write inequality constraints that will solve the above problem. Find A and c so that they can be written $wA \geq c$.

b. Sketch the set of feasible vectors. Show that it is unbounded (that it has infinite area).

c. Show that another way of indicating units in the data box is as follows:

	Protein	Calcium	
Meat	80	10	(per pound)
Milk	15	60	(per quart)
Requirements	40	30	(per day)
	(units)	(units)	

2. EXTREME POINTS; MAXIMA AND MINIMA OF LINEAR FUNCTIONS

In the present section we first discuss the problem of finding the extreme points of a bounded convex polyhedral set. Then we find out how to compute the maximum and minimum values of a linear function defined on such a set.

We use the following notation: The polyhedral convex set C is the truth set of the statement $Ax \leq b$, where A is an $m \times n$ matrix, x is an n-component column vector, and b is an m-component column vector. We let $A_1, A_2, \ldots, A_m$ denote the rows of A. Hence A_i is an n-component row vector and

$$A = \begin{pmatrix} A_1 \\ A_2 \\ \vdots \\ A_m \end{pmatrix}.$$

The statement $Ax \leq b$ is then the conjunction of the statements

$$A_1 x \leq b_1, \quad A_2 x \leq b_2, \quad \ldots, \quad A_m x \leq b_m.$$

DEFINITION. We shall call the truth set of the statement $A_i x = b_i$ the *bounding hyperplane* of the half space $A_i x \leq b_i$.

Thus, in Figure 1 of the preceding section the slanting line (a) is the bounding hyperplane of the half space (b).

We found in the previous section that a convex set C was the intersection of a finite number of half spaces. The bounding hyperplanes of these half spaces that also contain points of C are called *bounding hyperplanes* of C. Thus in Example 3 of Section 1 the bounding hyperplanes of the polyhedral convex set given there are the three boundary lines of the triangle shaded in Figure 2. Note that these lines intersect in pairs in three points, the vertices of the triangle.

DEFINITION. Let C be the polyhedral convex set defined by $Ax \leq b$, where x is an n-component vector. Then a point T is an *extreme* (or *corner*) *point* of C if it

    a. belongs to C, and
    b. is the intersection of n bounding hyperplanes of C.

Example 1. Find the extreme points of the polyhedral convex set $Ax \leq b$, where

$$A = \begin{pmatrix} 2 & 3 \\ -2 & -1 \\ 0 & -1 \end{pmatrix}, \quad x = \begin{pmatrix} x_1 \\ x_2 \end{pmatrix}, \quad b = \begin{pmatrix} 60 \\ -32 \\ -2 \end{pmatrix}.$$

The corresponding inequalities are:

$$\begin{aligned} 2x_1 + 3x_2 &\leq 60, \\ 2x_1 + x_2 &\geq 32, \\ x_2 &\geq 2. \end{aligned}$$

The last two inequalities have been multiplied through by -1, and can be regarded as managerial constraints added to the box-manufacturer problem of Example 3 of Section 1. A sketch of the three half planes (Figure 3) shows that the set of feasible solutions is a triangle. Hence we can find the extreme points by changing the inequalities to equalities in pairs and solving three sets of simultaneous equations. We obtain in this way the points

$$\begin{pmatrix} 9 \\ 14 \end{pmatrix}, \quad \begin{pmatrix} 15 \\ 2 \end{pmatrix}, \quad \begin{pmatrix} 27 \\ 2 \end{pmatrix},$$

which are the extreme points of the set.

We can now give an interpretation for the various points of the polyhedral convex set in terms of the system of inequalities. An extreme

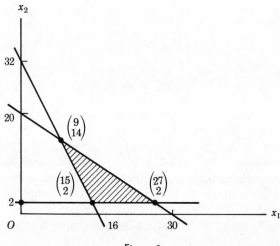

Figure 3

point lies on two boundaries, which means that two of the inequalities are actually equalities. A point on a side, other than an extreme point, lies on one boundary and hence one inequality is an equality. An interior point of the polygon must, by a process of elimination, correspond to the case where the inequalities are all strict inequalities—that is, not only $\leq$ but $<$ holds.

There is a mechanical (but lengthy) method for finding all the extreme points of a polyhedral convex set C defined by $Ax \leq b$. Consider the bounding hyperplanes $A_1x = b_1, \ldots, A_mx = b_m$ of the half spaces that determine C. Select a subset of n of these hyperplanes and solve their equations simultaneously. If the result is a unique point x^0 (and only then) check to see whether or not x^0 belongs to C. If it does, by the above definition, x^0 is an extreme point of C. Moreover, all extreme points of C can be found in this manner.

Example 2. Let

$$A = \begin{pmatrix} -1 & 0 \\ 0 & -1 \end{pmatrix} \quad \text{and} \quad b = \begin{pmatrix} 0 \\ 0 \end{pmatrix}.$$

Then the polyhedral convex set C defined by $Ax \leq b$ is the first quadrant of the x_1, x_2 plane, shaded in Figure 4. The only extreme point is the origin, which is the intersection of the lines $x_1 = 0$ and $x_2 = 0$. This is an example of an *unbounded* polyhedral convex set.

Notice that the set C contains the *ray* or half line that starts at the origin of coordinates and extends upward to the right making a 45-degree angle with the axes. This ray is dotted in Figure 4. Of course, this set also contains many other rays; two others are shown in the figure.

We shall say that a polyhedral convex set is *bounded* if it does not contain a ray. A set, such as the one in Figure 4, that does contain rays will be called *unbounded*. For simplicity we shall restrict our discussion in most of this chapter to bounded convex sets.

Example 3. Consider the box-manufacturer problem of Example 1, and suppose that the manufacturer makes a profit of $1 on small and $2 on large boxes. Hence, if he makes x_1 small and x_2 large boxes, his profit function is $x_1 + 2x_2$, and the inequalities limiting the choice of x_1 and x_2 are given in Example 1. What is the most and what the least profit he can make?

We must find the maximum and the minimum value of $x_1 + 2x_2$ for point (x_1, x_2) in the triangle shaded in Figure 3. Let us first try the extreme points. At $(15, 2)$ we have a profit of 19, at $(27, 2)$ a profit of 31, and at $(9, 14)$ a profit of 37. Clearly the last extreme point is most profitable. But what can we say about the remainder of the triangle? If we start at $(9, 14)$ and try to move to other points in the triangle, clearly the best thing to do is to move along the bounding hyperplane $2x_1 + 3x_2 = 60$, since in this way we can get the most favorable tradeoff between x_1 and x_2. However, for each unit we decrease x_2 along this line we can increase x_1 by only $\frac{3}{2}$ units, with a net loss of profit. Hence the maximum profit is taken on at the extreme point $(9, 14)$. A similar argument shows that the minimum profit is taken on at the extreme point $(15, 2)$. Thus for this example the maximum and minimum profits are observed at extreme points. We will show that this is true in general.

Given a convex polyhedral set C and a linear function

$$cx = c_1x_1 + c_2x_2 + \cdots + c_nx_n,$$

where $c = (c_1, c_2, \ldots, c_n)$, we want to show in general that the maximum and minimum values of the function cx always occur at extreme points of C. We shall carry out the proof for the planar case in which $n = 2$, but our results are true in general.

First, we will show that the values of the linear function $c_1x_1 + c_2x_2$ on any line segment lie *between* the values the function has at the two end points (possibly equal to the value at one end point). We represent the

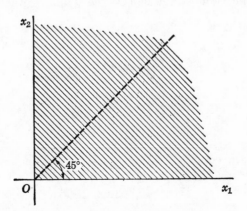

Figure 4

points as column vectors $\begin{pmatrix} x_1 \\ x_2 \end{pmatrix}$ and then we see that our linear function is represented by the row vector (c_1, c_2). Let the end points of the segment be

$$p = \begin{pmatrix} x_1' \\ x_2' \end{pmatrix} \quad \text{and} \quad q = \begin{pmatrix} x_1'' \\ x_2'' \end{pmatrix}.$$

We have seen in Chapter 4 (see Figure 4) that the points in between p and q can be represented as $tp + (1 - t)q$, with $0 \le t \le 1$. If the values of the function at the points p and q are P and Q, respectively (assume that $P \ge Q$), then at a point in between the value will be $tP + (1 - t)Q$, since the function is linear. This value can also be written as

$$tP + (1 - t)Q = Q + (P - Q)t,$$

which (for $0 \le t \le 1$) is at least Q and at most P.

We are now in a position to prove the result illustrated in Example 3.

THEOREM. A linear function cx defined over a convex polyhedral set C takes on its maximum (and minimum) value at an extreme point of C.

Proof. The proof of the theorem is illustrated in Figure 5. We shall suppose that at the extreme point p the function takes on a value P greater than or equal to the value at any other extreme point, and at the extreme point q it takes on its smallest extreme-point value, Q. Let r be any point of the polygon. Draw a straight line between p and r and continue it until it cuts the polygon again at a point u lying on an edge of the polygon, say the edge between the corner points s and t. (The line may even cut the edge at one of the points s and t; the analysis remains unchanged.) By hypothesis the value of the function at any corner point must lie between Q and P. By the above result the value of the function at u must lie between its values at s and t, and hence must also lie between Q and P. Again by the above

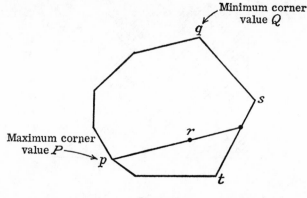

Figure 5

result the value of the function at r must lie between its values at p and u, and hence must also lie between Q and P. Since r was any point of the polygon, our theorem is proved.

Suppose that in place of the linear function $c_1x_1 + c_2x_2$ we had considered the function $c_1x_1 + c_2x_2 + k$. The addition of the constant k merely changes every value of the function, including the maximum and minimum values of the function, by that amount. Hence the analysis of where the maximum and minimum values of the function are taken on is unchanged. Therefore, we have the following theorem.

THEOREM. The function $cx + k$ defined over a convex polyhedral set C takes on its maximum (and minimum) value at an extreme point of C.

A method of finding the maximum or minimum of the function $cx + k$ defined over a convex set C is then the following: find the extreme points of the set; there will be a finite number of them; substitute the coordinates of each into the function; the largest of the values so obtained will be the maximum of the function and the smallest value will be the minimum of the function. The method is illustrated in Example 3 above.

In Section 5 we will describe the so-called *simplex method*, which is considerably more efficient for solving the problem above.

EXERCISES

1. Consider the cardboard-box problem of Exercise 2 of Section 1. Assuming that both constraints stated in (f) and (g) are in effect and the profit function is $x_1 + 2x_2$, find the extreme point (or points) that give maximum and minimum profit.

2. Rework Exercise 1 with profit function $2x_1 + 3x_2$. Show that in this case there is more than one solution for maximum profit.

3. Consider the diet problem of Exercise 10 of Section 1. Suppose that meat costs $1 per pound and milk costs 30 cents per quart. Find the lowest-cost diet that will meet minimum requirements.
   [*Ans.* $w = (\frac{13}{31}, \frac{40}{93})$, cost is $\$\frac{17}{31}$.]

4. The owner of an oil truck with a capacity of 500 gallons hauls gasoline and oil products from city to city. On any given trip he wishes to load his truck with at least 200 gallons of regular gasoline, at least 100 gallons of high-test gasoline, and at most 150 gallons of kerosene. Assuming that he always fills his truck to capacity, find the convex set of ways that he can load his truck. Interpret the extreme points of the set. [*Hint:* There are four extreme points.]

5. An advertiser wishes to sponsor a half-hour television comedy and must decide on the composition of the show. The advertiser insists that there be at least three minutes of commercials, while the television network requires that the commercial time be limited to at most 15 minutes. The comedian refuses to work more than 22 minutes each half-hour show. If a band is added to play while neither the comedian nor the commercials

are on, construct the convex set C of possible assignments of time to the comedian, the commercials, and the band that use up the 30 minutes. Find the extreme points of C.

[*Ans.* If x_1 is the comedian time, x_2 the commercial time, and $30 - x_1 - x_2$ the band time, the extreme points are

$$\begin{pmatrix} 0 \\ 3 \end{pmatrix}, \begin{pmatrix} 22 \\ 3 \end{pmatrix}, \begin{pmatrix} 22 \\ 8 \end{pmatrix}, \begin{pmatrix} 15 \\ 15 \end{pmatrix} \text{ and } \begin{pmatrix} 0 \\ 15 \end{pmatrix}.]$$

6. In Exercise 4 suppose that the oil truck operator gets 3 cents per gallon for delivering regular gasoline, 2 cents per gallon for high test, and 1 cent per gallon for kerosene. Write the expression that gives the total amount he will get paid for each possible load that he carries. How should he load his truck in order to earn the maximum amount?
[*Ans.* He should carry 400 gallons of regular gasoline, 100 gallons of high test, and no kerosene.]

7. In Exercise 6, if he gets 3 cents per gallon of regular and 2 cents per gallon of high-test gasoline, how high must his payment for kerosene become before he will load it on his truck in order to make a maximum profit? [*Ans.* He must get paid at least 3 cents per gallon of kerosene.]

8. In Exercise 5 let x_1 be the number of minutes the comedian is on and x_2 the number of minutes the commercial is on the program. Suppose the comedian costs \$200 per minute, the commercials cost \$50 per minute, and the band is free. How should the advertiser choose the composition of the show in order that its cost be a minimum?

9. Consider the polyhedral convex set P defined by the inequalities

$$-1 \leq x_1 \leq 4,$$
$$0 \leq x_2 \leq 6.$$

Find four different sets of conditions on the constants a and b that the function $\mathbf{F}(x) = ax_1 + bx_2$ should have its maximum at one and only one of the four corner points of P. Find conditions that $\mathbf{F}$ should have its minimum at each of these points.

[*Ans.* For example, the maximum is at $\begin{pmatrix} 4 \\ 6 \end{pmatrix}$ if $a > 0$ and $b > 0$.]

10. A well-known nursery rhyme says, "Jack Sprat could eat no fat. His wife (call her Jill) could eat no lean. . . ." Suppose Jack wishes to have at least one pound of lean meat per day, while Jill needs at least .4 pound of fat per day. Assume they buy only beef having 10 percent fat and 90 percent lean, and pork having 40 percent fat and 60 percent lean. Jack and Jill want to fulfill their minimal diet requirements at the lowest possible cost.
   a. Let x be the amount of beef and y the amount of pork they purchase per day. Construct the convex set of points in the plane representing purchases that fulfill both persons' minimum diet requirements.
   b. Suggest necessary restrictions on the purchases, that will change this set into a convex polygon.
   c. If beef costs \$1 per pound, and pork costs 50 cents per pound, show that the diet of least cost has only pork, and find the minimum cost.
      [*Ans.* \$.83.]
   d. If beef costs 75 cents and pork costs 50 cents per pound, show that there is a whole line segment of solution points and find the minimum cost. [*Ans.* \$.83.]

   e. If beef and pork each cost \$1 a pound, show that the unique minimal cost diet has both beef and pork. Find the minimum cost.

                                     [*Ans.* \$1.40.]

   f. Show that the restriction made in part *b.* did not alter the answers given in *c.–e.*

11. In Exercise 10*d.* show that for all but one of the minimal-cost diets Jill has more than her minimum requirement of fat, while Jack always gets exactly his minimal requirement of lean. Show that all but one of the minimal-cost diets contains some beef.

12. In Exercise 10*e.* show that Jack and Jill each get exactly their minimal requirements.

13. In Exercise 10 if the price of pork is fixed at \$1 a pound, how low must the price of beef fall before Jack and Jill will eat only beef?   [*Ans.* \$.25.]

14. In Exercise 10, suppose that Jack decides to reduce his minimal requirement to .6 pound of lean meat per day. How does the convex set change? How do the solutions in 3(*c*), (*d*), and (*e*) change?

3. LINEAR PROGRAMMING PROBLEMS

An important class of practical problems are those that require the determination of the maximum or the minimum of a linear function $cx + k$ defined over a polyhedral convex set of points C. We illustrate these so-called *linear programming problems* by means of the following examples. In the next section we shall discuss the simplex method for solving these examples.

   Example 1. An automobile manufacturer makes automobiles and trucks in a factory that is divided into two shops. Shop 1, which performs the basic assembly operation, must work 5 man-days on each truck but only 2 man-days on each automobile. Shop 2, which performs finishing operations, must work 3 man-days for each automobile or truck that it produces. Because of men and machine limitations shop 1 has 180 man-days per week available while shop 2 has 135 man-days per week. If the manufacturer makes a profit of \$300 on each truck and \$200 on each automobile, how many of each should he produce to maximize his profit?

   Before proceeding, let us summarize the problem in the *data box* of Figure 6. (The term *data box* is due to A. W. Tucker.) Notice that the num-

	Trucks	Autos	Capacities
Shop 1	$5\,\dfrac{\text{S1-man-hr}}{\text{truck}}$	$2\,\dfrac{\text{S1-man-hr}}{\text{auto}}$	$180\,\dfrac{\text{S1-man-hr}}{\text{week}}$
Shop 2	$3\,\dfrac{\text{S2-man-hr}}{\text{truck}}$	$3\,\dfrac{\text{S2-man-hr}}{\text{auto}}$	$135\,\dfrac{\text{S2-man-hr}}{\text{week}}$
Profits	$300\,\dfrac{\$}{\text{truck}}$	$200\,\dfrac{\$}{\text{auto}}$	

Figure 6

bers above appear in the data box with their physical dimensions attached. When doing dimensional analysis, in the sense of physics, we may manipulate these dimension quantities just like algebraic quantities. We shall see in Section 6 that we can obtain interpretations for dual variables by means of dimensional analysis. The reader is strongly advised to set up a similar data box for every linear programming example he works.

An alternate and slightly more elegant way of indicating the units in the data box is shown in Figure 7. The reader should compare it with Figure 6

	Trucks	Autos	Capacities	
Shop 1	5	2	180	(Man-hours)
Shop 2	3	3	135	(Man-hours)
Profits	300	200		($)
	(per truck)	(per auto)	(per week)	

Figure 7

to see the correspondence between them. When in doubt, use the more explicit indications of Figure 6.

A dimensional fraction such as "S1-manhr/truck" is read "shop 1 manhours per truck." Suppose we now introduce two variables x_1 with dimensions "trucks/week," which will become the number of trucks per week we should produce, and x_2 with dimensions "autos/week." Then the first constraint of the data box of Figure 6 becomes:

$$\left(5 \frac{\text{S1-manhr}}{\text{truck}}\right)\left(x_1 \frac{\text{trucks}}{\text{week}}\right) + \left(2 \frac{\text{S1-manhr}}{\text{auto}}\right)\left(x_2 \frac{\text{autos}}{\text{week}}\right) \leq 180 \frac{\text{S1-manhr}}{\text{week}}.$$

Now, by canceling the common term "truck" from numerator and denominator of the first term, and similarly canceling the common dimension "auto" from the numerator and denominator of the second term, we see that the resulting dimensions of each term are "S1-manhr/week"—the same as the dimensions of the capacity term on the righthand side of the inequality. A similar dimensional analysis can be carried out for the second capacity constraint. Dropping dimensions, we have the following restrictions:

$$5x_1 + 2x_2 \leq 180,$$
$$3x_1 + 3x_2 \leq 135,$$

together with the obviously necessary nonnegative constraints $x_1 \geq 0$ and $x_2 \geq 0$.

Subject to these constraints we want to maximize the profit function:

$$\left(300 \frac{\$}{\text{truck}}\right)\left(x_1 \frac{\text{trucks}}{\text{week}}\right) + \left(200 \frac{\$}{\text{auto}}\right)\left(x_2 \frac{\text{autos}}{\text{week}}\right).$$

Canceling out the common terms, we see that the dimensions of this function are simply "$/week."

In order to state the problem as a linear programming problem we define the quantities:

$$A = \begin{pmatrix} 5 & 2 \\ 3 & 3 \end{pmatrix}, \quad b = \begin{pmatrix} 180 \\ 135 \end{pmatrix}, \quad \text{and} \quad c = (300, 200),$$

which are immediately evident from the data boxes in Figures 6 and 7. Then our problem is:

Maximum problem: Determine the vector $x = \begin{pmatrix} x_1 \\ x_2 \end{pmatrix}$ so that the weekly profit, given by the quantity cx, is a maximum subject to the inequality constraints $Ax \leq b$ and $x \geq 0$. The inequality constraints insure that the weekly number of available man-hours is not exceeded and that nonnegative quantities of automobiles and trucks are produced.

The graph of the convex set of possible x vectors is pictured in Figure 8.

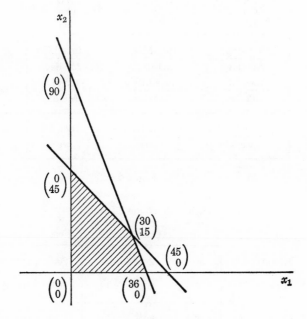

Figure 8

Clearly this is a problem of the kind discussed in the previous section. The extreme points of the convex set C are

$$T_1 = \begin{pmatrix} 0 \\ 0 \end{pmatrix}, \quad T_2 = \begin{pmatrix} 36 \\ 0 \end{pmatrix}, \quad T_3 = \begin{pmatrix} 0 \\ 45 \end{pmatrix}, \quad \text{and} \quad T_4 = \begin{pmatrix} 30 \\ 15 \end{pmatrix}.$$

Following the solution procedure outlined in the previous section, we test the function $cx = 300x_1 + 200x_2$ at each of these extreme points. The values taken on are 0, 10800, 9000, and 12000. Thus the maximum weekly profit is \$12,000, achieved by producing 30 trucks and 15 automobiles per week.

Example 2. A mining company owns two different mines that produce a given kind of ore. The mines are located in different parts of the country and have different production capacities. After crushing, the ore is graded into three classes: high-grade, medium-grade, and low-grade ores. There is some demand for each grade of ore. The mining company has contracted to provide a smelting plant with 12 tons of high-grade, 8 tons of medium-grade, and 24 tons of low-grade ore per week. It costs the company $200 per day to run the first mine and $160 per day to run the second. However, in a day's operation the first mine produces 6 tons of high-grade, 2 tons of medium-grade, and 4 tons of low-grade ore, while the second mine produces daily 2 tons of high-grade, 2 tons of medium-grade, and 12 tons of low-grade ore. How many days a week should each mine be operated in order to fulfill the company's orders most economically?

Before proceeding, we again summarize the problem in the data boxes of Figures 9 and 10. The reader should compare these two figures to see the

	High-Grade Ore HG	Medium-Grade Ore MG	Low-Grade Ore LG	Cost
Mine 1	$6\dfrac{\text{tons-HG}}{\text{M1-day}}$	$2\dfrac{\text{tons-MG}}{\text{M1-day}}$	$4\dfrac{\text{tons-LG}}{\text{M1-day}}$	$200\dfrac{\$}{\text{M1-day}}$
Mine 2	$2\dfrac{\text{tons-HG}}{\text{M2-day}}$	$2\dfrac{\text{tons-MG}}{\text{M2-day}}$	$12\dfrac{\text{tons-LG}}{\text{M2-day}}$	$160\dfrac{\$}{\text{M2-day}}$
Requirements	$12\dfrac{\text{tons-HG}}{\text{week}}$	$8\dfrac{\text{tons-MG}}{\text{week}}$	$24\dfrac{\text{tons-LG}}{\text{week}}$	

Figure 9

	High-Grade Ore	Medium-Grade Ore	Low-Grade Ore	Cost	
Mine 1	6	2	4	200	(per day)
Mine 2	2	2	12	160	(per day)
Requirements	12	8	24		(per week)
	(tons)	(tons)	(tons)	($)	

Figure 10

correspondence between them. We shall make use of these dimensions when we give interpretations of the dual variables in Section 6.

Let $v = (v_1, v_2)$ be the 2-component row vector whose component v_1 gives the number of days per week that mine 1 operates and v_2 gives the number of days per week that mine 2 operates. If we define the quantities

$$A = \begin{pmatrix} 6 & 2 & 4 \\ 2 & 2 & 12 \end{pmatrix}, \quad c = (12, 8, 24), \quad \text{and} \quad b = \begin{pmatrix} 200 \\ 160 \end{pmatrix},$$

which are immediately evident from the data box of Figure 9, we can state the problem above as a minimum problem.

Minimum problem: Determine the vector w so that the weekly operating cost, given by the quantity vb, is a minimum subject to the inequality restraints $vA \geq c$ and $v \geq 0$. The inequality restraints insure that the weekly output requirements are met and the limits on the components of v are not exceeded.

It is clear that this is a minimum problem of the type discussed in detail in the preceding section. In Figure 11 we have graphed the convex

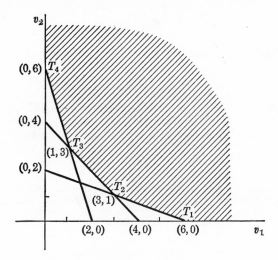

Figure 11

polyhedral set C defined by the inequalities $vA \geq c$.

The extreme points of the convex set C are

$$T_1 = (6, 0), \quad T_2 = (3, 1), \quad T_3 = (1, 3), \quad T_4 = (0, 6).$$

Testing the function $vb = 200v_1 + 160v_2$ at each of these extreme points, we see that it takes on the values 1200, 760, 680, and 960, respectively. We see that the minimum operating cost is \$680 per week and it is achieved at T_3— that is, by operating the first mine one day a week and the second mine three days a week.

Observe that if the mines are operated as indicated, then the combined weekly production will be 12 tons of high-grade ore, 8 tons of medium-grade ore, and 40 tons of low-grade ore. In other words, for this solution low-grade ore is overproduced. If the company has no other demand for the low-grade ore, then it must discard 16 tons of it per week in this minimum-cost solution of its production problem. We shall discuss this point further in Section 6.

Example 3. As a variant of Example 2, assume that the cost vector is

$$b = \begin{pmatrix} 160 \\ 200 \end{pmatrix};$$

in other words, the first mine now has a lower daily cost than the second. By the same procedure as above we find that the minimum cost level is again $680 and is achieved by operating the first mine three days a week and the second mine one day a week. In this solution 20 tons of high-grade ore, instead of the required 12 tons, are produced, while the requirements of medium- and low-grade ores are exactly met. Thus eight tons of high-grade ore must be discarded per week.

Example 4. As another variant of Example 2, assume that the cost vector is

$$b = \begin{pmatrix} 200 \\ 200 \end{pmatrix};$$

in other words, both mines have the same production costs. Evaluating the cost function vb at the extreme points of the convex set, we find costs of $1200 on two of the extreme points (T_1 and T_4) and costs of $800 on the other two extreme points (T_2 and T_3). Thus the minimum cost is attained by operating either one of the mines three days a week and the other one one day a week. But there are other solutions, since if the minimum is taken on at two distinct extreme points it is also taken on at each of the points on the line segment between. Thus any vector w where $1 \le v_1 \le 3$, $1 \le v_2 \le 3$, and $v_1 + v_2 = 4$ also gives a minimum-cost solution. For example, each mine could operate two days a week.

It can be shown (see Exercise 2) that for any solution v with $1 < v_1 < 3$, $1 < v_2 < 3$, and $v_1 + v_2 = 4$, both high-grade and low-grade ore are overproduced.

EXERCISES

1. In Example 1, assume that profits are $200 per truck and $300 per automobile. What should the factory now produce for maximum profit?

2. In Example 4, show that both high- and low-grade ore are overproduced for solution vectors w with $1 < v_1 < 3$, $1 < v_2 < 3$, and $v_1 + v_2 = 4$.

3. A manufacturer has two machines, M_1 and M_2, which he uses to manufacture two products, P_1 and P_2. To produce one unit of P_1, three hours of time on M_1 and six hours on M_2 are needed. And to produce one unit of P_2 takes six hours on M_1 and five hours on M_2. Each machine can run a maximum of 2100 hours per year. If the manufacturer sells product P_1 for a net profit of $40 and P_2 for a net profit of $50 each, what production mix shall he produce to maximize his total profit?

   a. Set up the data box for the problem, marking the dimensions of all numbers.

   b. Find A, b, and c.

   c. Draw the set of possible production vectors and find the optimum profit point.

$$[Ans. \ x^0 = \begin{pmatrix} 100 \\ 300 \end{pmatrix} \text{ with yearly profit of } \$19{,}000.]$$

4. Two breakfast cereals, Krix and Kranch, supply varying amounts of vitamin B and iron; these are listed together with one-third of the daily minimum requirements (MDR) in the table below.

	Vitamin B	Iron
Krix	.15 mg/oz.	1.67 mg/oz.
Kranch	.10 mg/oz.	3.33 mg/oz.
$\frac{1}{3}$ MDR	.12 mg/day	2.0 mg/day

Krix costs 8 cents an ounce and Kranch 10 cents an ounce. How can we satisfy $\frac{1}{3}$ MDR at minimum cost?
   a. Let v_1 be the amount of Krix eaten and v_2 the amount of Kranch eaten. Write a minimizing linear programming problem for the above. Set up the data box and find A, b, and c.
   b. Draw the convex set of possible amounts eaten defined by the inequalities in (a).
   c. What is the lowest-cost feasible diet?

   [*Ans.* $v^0 = (.6, .3)$ with cost 7.8 cents.]

5. A farmer owns a 200-acre farm and can plant any combination of two crops I and II. Crop I requires one man-day of labor and $10 of capital for each acre planted, while crop II requires 4 man-days of labor and $20 of capital for each acre planted. Crop I produces $40 of net revenue per acre and crop II $60. The farmer has $2200 of capital and 320 man-days of labor available for the year. What is the optimal planting strategy?

   $\left[\textit{Ans. } x^0 = \begin{pmatrix} 180 \\ 20 \end{pmatrix} \text{ with \$8400 revenue.}\right]$

6. In Exercise 5 assume that the revenue from crop II is $90 per acre.
   a. Find the new maximum-revenue scheme, and show that now the best thing for the farmer to do is to leave 30 acres unplanted.
   b. Explain why the farmer should leave part of his land fallow in this case.

7. Suppose that a pound of meat contains 1 unit of carbohydrates, 3 units of vitamins, and 12 units of proteins and costs $1. Suppose also that one pound of cabbage contains 3, 4, and 1 units of these items, respectively, and costs 25 cents per pound. If these are the only foods available and the minimum daily requirements are 8 units of carbohydrates, 19 units of vitamins, and 7 units of protein, what is the minimum-cost diet?

   [*Ans.* $v^0 = (.2, 4.6)$ with cost $1.35.]

8. Suppose that the minimum-cost diet found in Exercise 7 is unpalatable. In order to increase its palatability, add a constraint requiring that at least a half pound of meat be eaten, and resolve the problem. How much is the cost of the minimum-cost diet increased owing to this palatability constraint?   [*Ans.* $.244.]

9. In Exercise 8 suppose that we add a different kind of palatability constraint—namely, that at most two pounds of cabbage be eaten. Now how much is the cost of the minimum-cost diet increased?

   [*Ans.* $2.82.]

10. A manufacturer produces two types of bearings, A and B, utilizing three types of machines, lathes, grinders, and drill presses. The machinery requirements for one unit of each product, in hours, are expressed in the following table.

	Bearing	Lathe	Grinder	Drill Press
	A	.01	.03	.03
	B	.02	.01	.015
Weekly machine capacity (hr)		400	450	480

He makes a profit of 10 cents per type A bearing and 15 cents per type B bearing. What should his weekly production of each bearing be in order to maximize his profits?

$$[Ans. \quad x = \begin{pmatrix} 8000 \\ 16000 \end{pmatrix} \text{ with weekly profits of \$3200.}]$$

4. THE DUAL PROBLEM

As the examples of the preceding sections have shown, some linear programming problems are maximizing and some are minimizing. Thus we might be interested in maximizing profits, production, or market share—or we might want to minimize costs, completion times, or raw-material usage. We shall show that to each maximizing problem there is a well-defined minimizing problem that uses the same data and whose solution has important mathematical implications concerning the original maximizing problem. Similarly, to each minimizing problem there is a well-defined maximizing problem that uses the same data and is similarly related.

First, we recall that every linear programming problem can be put into one of the two following forms:

$$(1) \qquad \left. \begin{array}{ll} \text{Max} & cx \\ \text{subject to} & Ax \le b \\ & x \ge 0 \end{array} \right\} \quad \text{the MAXIMUM problem}$$

or

$$(2) \qquad \left. \begin{array}{ll} \text{Min} & vb \\ \text{subject to} & vA \ge c \\ & v \ge 0 \end{array} \right\} \quad \text{the MINIMUM problem}$$

If the components of A, b, c are the same, then the two problems (1) and (2) are called *dual linear programming problems*. Every linear programming problem, whether of the maximum or minimum type, has a dual that can be formally stated as above. The dual of a given problem frequently has important economic meaning and always has mathematical significance—see the discussion in Section 6.

To set up a MAXIMUM PROBLEM proceed as follows: Let the variables to be determined be $x_1, \ldots, x_n$; set up the data box as in Figure 12, with the x-variables appearing as labels on the top of the box. It then

$$\begin{array}{cccc}
x_1 & x_2 & \cdots & x_n
\end{array}$$

a_{11}	a_{12}	$\cdots$	a_{1n}	b_1
a_{21}	a_{22}	$\cdots$	a_{2n}	b_2
$\cdot$	$\cdot$	$\cdots$	$\cdot$	$\cdot$
a_{m1}	a_{m2}	$\cdots$	a_{mn}	b_m
c_1	c_2	$\cdots$	c_n	

Figure 12

follows that, taking A, b, and c from the data box, the maximum problem is in form (1) above.

To set up a MINIMUM PROBLEM proceed as follows: Let the variables to be determined by $v_1, \ldots, v_m$; set up the data box as in Figure 13 with the v-variables appearing as labels to the left of the box. It then

	x_1	x_2		x_n	
v_1	a_{11}	a_{12}	$\cdots$	a_{1n}	b_1
v_2	a_{21}	a_{22}	$\cdots$	a_{2n}	b_2
$\cdot$	$\cdot$	$\cdot$	$\cdots$	$\cdot$	$\cdot$
v_m	a_{m1}	a_{m2}	$\cdots$	a_{mn}	b_m
	c_1	c_2	$\cdots$	c_n	

Figure 13

follows that, taking A, b, and c from the data box, the minimum problem is in form (2) above.

We now make two important observations. First, the dual problem to a maximum problem with data box as in Figure 12 can be obtained by merely labeling the rows $v_1, \ldots, v_m$; and the dual problem to the minimum problem whose data box is in Figure 13 can be obtained by labeling the columns $x_1, \ldots, x_n$. Second, the dimensions of the dual variables in either case can be obtained by dividing the dimensions of the b's or c's by the corresponding a's, as the following examples will make clear. We shall see that the interpretations of the dual variables are easy, once their physical dimensions are determined.

The reader may wonder why we introduce the dual problem instead of concentrating on the original problem alone. The reason is that the simplex method to be discussed later automatically produces the optimum solution to both problems simultaneously. Also the solution to the dual problem always has important managerial and economic interpretations.

Before we can describe how the simplex method works, we must make a change in the formulation of the dual programs. What we shall do is to add *slack* variables to the inequalities stated in expressions (1) and (4) of this section in such a way as to make them into equations. To see how this is done, consider as an example the system of inequalities

$$-u + 2v \leq 5, \qquad u \geq 0 \quad \text{and} \quad v \geq 0.$$

We now add a new slack variable w and obtain a new system of expressions:

$$-u + 2v + w = 5, \qquad u \geq 0, \quad v \geq 0, \quad w \geq 0.$$

Thus we obtain the equation

$$-u + 2v + w = 5$$

in nonnegative variables. Notice that the new system of expressions is equivalent to the old system, since any solution of the new system that has $w = 0$ represents a case for which $-u + 2v = 5$, and a solution of the new system for which $w > 0$ represents a case for which $-u + 2v < 5$. Moreover, it is obvious that we can write any solution of the old system as a solution of the new system by properly choosing a nonnegative value of w. Thus the truth sets of the two systems are identical.

Now we want to reformulate the constraints of problems (1) and (2). Let y be an m-component vector of *slack variables* y_i, and let f be a number; then (1) is equivalent to

$$\begin{array}{lll} \text{Max} & cx = f \\ \text{(3)} \qquad \text{Subject to} & Ax + y = b, \\ & x, y \geq 0. \end{array}$$

To see this, rewrite the constraint of (3) as follows:

$$\text{(4)} \qquad\qquad Ax - b = -y;$$

then it is obvious that $y \geq 0$ is equivalent to $-y \leq 0$, and the latter is, from (4), the same as $Ax \leq b$. The number $f = cx$ measures the current value of the objective function of the maximum problem.

Similarly, let u be an n-component row vector of *slack* variables u_j, and let g be a number; then (2) is equivalent to

$$\begin{array}{lll} \text{Minimize} & vb = g \\ \text{(5)} \qquad \text{subject to} & vA - u = c, \\ & u, v \geq 0. \end{array}$$

To see the equivalence rewrite the equality constraint of (5) as

(6) $$vA - c = u;$$

then it is obvious that $u \geq 0$ and $vA \geq c$ are the same. The number $g = vb$ measures the current value of the objective function of the minimizing problem.

Next we show that the pair of dual problems in (3) and (5) can both be represented in the same tableau, and that the tableau can be obtained by extending either of the data boxes in Figure 12 or 13. Consider the (Tucker) tableau, which we shall later call the *initial simplex tableau*, in Figure 14.

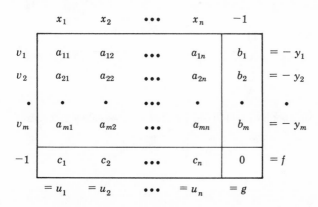

Figure 14

Notice that Figure 14 can be obtained from Figure 12 by adding the 0 entry in the lower righthand corner, putting variables $v_1, \ldots, v_m$ and -1 along the left margin, putting -1 above the $(n + 1)$st column, marking the righthand side with $= -y_1, \ldots, = -y_m$, and $= f$, and marking the bottom of the matrix with $= u_1, \ldots, = u_n$, and $= g$. Figure 14 can be obtained in a similar manner from Figure 13. The reason for this labeling is as follows: if we drop the x's and -1 down to the first row of the matrix, multiply by the coefficients there, and set equal to the label on the right, we have

$$a_{11}x_1 + a_{12}x_2 + \cdots + a_{1n}x_n - b_1 = -y_1,$$

which is just exactly the first equation of (4). Dropping the labels at the top down to the other rows will give the other equations of (4). Finally, dropping the labels down to the last row gives

$$c_1x_1 + c_2c_2 + \cdots + c_nx_n = f,$$

which is just the definition of f.

In a similar manner, if we move the labels on the left of Figure 10 into each column of the tableau, multiply, and set equal to the label at the bottom, we have the various equations of (6) together with the definition of g.

Example 1. The data box for the automobile/truck example of the last section is shown in Figures 6 and 7; hence its initial simplex tableau is as given in Figure 15.

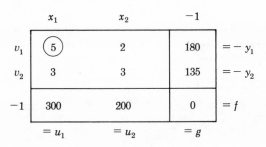

Figure 15

The primal equations for this problem corresponding to (4) are

$$\begin{aligned}
5x_1 + \quad 2x_2 - 180 &= -y_1, \\
3x_1 + \quad 3x_2 - 135 &= -y_2, \\
300x_1 + 200x_2 \qquad &= f.
\end{aligned}$$

The dual equations for this problem corresponding to (6) are

$$\begin{aligned}
5v_1 + \quad 3v_2 - 300 &= u_1, \\
2v_1 + \quad 3v_2 - 200 &= u_2, \\
180v_1 + 135v_2 \qquad &= g.
\end{aligned}$$

These are obtained in the manner described above.

Example 2. The data box for the mining example of the last section is shown in Figures 9 and 10; hence its initial simplex tableau is as given in Figure 16.

	x_1	x_2	x_3	-1	
v_1	⑥	2	4	200	$= -y_1$
v_2	2	2	12	160	$= -y_2$
-1	12	8	24	0	$= f$
	$= u_1$	$= u_2$	$= u_3$	$= g$	

Figure 16

The primal equations for this problem corresponding to (6) are

$$6v_1 + \quad 2v_2 - 12 = u_1,$$
$$2v_1 + \quad 2v_2 - \quad 8 = u_2,$$
$$4v_1 + \quad 12v_2 - 24 = u_3,$$
$$200v_1 + 160v_2 \qquad = g,$$

and the dual equations corresponding to (4) are

$$6x_1 + 2x_2 + \quad 4x_3 - 200 = -y_1,$$
$$2x_1 + 2x_2 + 12x_3 - 160 = -y_2,$$
$$12x_1 + 8x_2 + 24x_3 \qquad = f.$$

The reader should set up in an analogous way the initial simplex tableaux for Examples 3 and 4 of Section 3.

We next show that from equations (4) and (6) we can immediately derive *Tucker's duality equation*:

(7) $$g - f = vy + ux.$$

This follows easily since

$$g - f = vb - cx = v(Ax + y) - (vA - u)x = vy + ux,$$

where we used the substitutions $b = Ax + y$ from (4) and $c = vA - u$ from (6).

Nonnegative vectors x, y, u, and v that satisfy (4) and (6) will be called *feasible vectors* for the equality form of the linear programming problem. Note that the duality relation (7) is true for *all* solutions x, y, u, and v satisfying (4) and (6) whether nonnegative or not. However, the following theorem shows that a pair of feasible vectors for one of the problems implies a bound on the objective function of the other problem.

THEOREM. (a) Let x^0, y^0, and f^0 be *optimal* solutions to maximizing problem (3), and let u, v, and g be *feasible* solutions to the dual minimizing problem (5); then $cx^0 = f^0 \leq g = vb$; in other words, for any feasible vector v, the value $g = vb$ is an *upper bound* to the maximum value $f^0 = cx^0$ of the maximizing problem (3).

(b) Let u^0, v^0, and g^0 be *optimal* solutions to the minimizing problem (5), and let x, y, and f be *feasible* solutions to the dual maximizing problem (3); then $v^0 b = g^0 \geq f = cx$; in other words, for any feasible vector x, the value $f = cx$ is a *lower bound* to the minimum value $g^0 = v^0 b$ of the minimizing problem (5).

Proof. (a) If u, v, x^0, and y^0 are all nonnegative vectors, then it follows that $vy^0 \geq 0$ and $ux^0 \geq 0$, so that, from (7), we have

$$g - f^0 = vy^0 + ux^0 \geq 0,$$

or, in other words, $g \geq f^0$, as asserted.

The proof of (b) is similar.

We illustrate the theorem by returning to the previous examples.

Example 1 (continued). If we consider the automobile/truck example whose initial tableau is given in Figure 15, we can easily check that the following quantities solve the primal problem: $x_1 = 10$, $x_2 = 10$, $y_1 = 110$, $y_2 = 75$. These were obtained by selecting arbitrary but not too large values for x_1 and x_2 and then solving for y_1 and y_2. From this feasible solution we calculate $cx = 300 \cdot 10 + 200 \cdot 10 = 3000 + 2000 = 5000$; hence we know that $5000 \leq g^0 = v^0 b$; that is, we have found a lower bound to the optimum value g^0 of the dual minimizing problem.

Similarly, we can select v_1 and v_2 to be fairly large, but otherwise arbitrary, and solve for u_1 and u_2. For instance, $v_1 = 50$, $v_2 = 40$, $u_1 = 70$, and $u_2 = 20$ are a feasible choice for these quantities. From them we know that $f^0 = cx^0$ is definitely not greater than $vb = 180 \cdot 50 + 135 \cdot 40 = 9000 + 5400 = 14,400$.

Since we know that the optimum values are $f^0 = 12,000 = g^0$, we see that, in fact, the lower and upper bounds are correct in this instance. The reader should try several other feasible solutions for this example.

Example 2 (continued). Let us check the theorem for the mining example shown in Figure 16. Suppose we choose $x_1 = 20$, $x_2 = 20$, $x_3 = 5$, so that $y_1 = 20$ and $y_2 = 20$. We thus obtain the lower bound on g^0 as $cx = 12 \cdot 20 + 8 \cdot 20 + 24 \cdot 5 = 240 + 160 + 120 = 520$.

Similarly, we can choose $v_1 = 2$, $v_2 = 2$, and correspondingly $u_1 = 4$, $u_2 = 0$, and $u_3 = 8$, so an upper bound for f^0 is $vb = 200 \cdot 2 + 160 \cdot 2 = 720$.

Since the true value is 680, we see that the upper and lower bounds again are correct.

EXERCISES

1. Illustrate the theorem of this section by finding other feasible solutions to the primal and dual problems for the automobile/truck example, and show that the upper and lower bounds so obtained are correct.

2. Do the same for the mining example.

3. For Example 3 of Section 3:
   a. Set up and label the initial tableau.
   b. Write the primal and dual equations.
   c. Find feasible solutions to the primal equations and determine a bound to the dual problem.
   d. Find feasible solutions to the dual problem and derive a bound on the primal problem.

4. Repeat Exercise 3 for Exercise 4 of Section 3.

5. Repeat Exercise 3 for Exercise 5 of Section 3.

6. Repeat Exercise 3 for Exercise 7 of Section 3.

7. Repeat Exercise 3 for Exercise 10 of Section 3.

*8. Let x^0 and v^0 be nonnegative vectors such that $f^0 = cx^0 = v^0b = g^0$, $Ax^0 \le b$, and $v^0A \ge c$.

  a. Show that if x is any other feasible vector, then

$$cx \le v^0Ax \le v^0b = cx^0,$$

  so that x^0 solves the maximum problem.

  b. Similarly, show that v^0 solves the minimum problem.

  c. Show that $cx^0 = v^0b = v^0Ax^0$.

9. Use (7) to show that if x, y, u, and v are vectors related as in (4) and (6), then $ux \ge 0$ and $vy \ge 0$ imply $g \ge f$. (Note that this is true whether or not x, y, u, and v are nonnegative.)

  If x, y, u, and v are vectors related as in (4) and (6), then they are said to have the *complementary slackness property* if and only if

$$ux = 0 \quad \text{and} \quad vy = 0.$$

The remaining exercises refer to this property.

10. Use (7) to show that if x, y, u, and v satisfy the complementary slackness property, then $g = f$. Is the converse true?

*11. If x, y, u, and v are nonnegative vectors, show that $g = f$ if and only if they have the complementary slackness property.

*12. Use Exercises 8, 10, and 11 to show that nonnegative vectors related as in (4) and (6) are optimal if and only if they satisfy the complementary slackness property.

5. THE SIMPLEX METHOD

In Section 3 we solved simple linear programming problems having two variables by sketching convex sets in the plane. To solve such problems in more than two variables by the same method would require visualizing convex sets in more than two dimensions, which is extremely difficult. But fortunately there is an algorithm, called the *simplex algorithm*, that permits us to solve such large-scale linear programming problems without such visualizations. The reader will recall that in Chapter 4 we developed an algorithm for solving simultaneous linear equations that was algebraic (not geometric) in nature and avoided similar visualization problems.

For simplicity we shall make the following two assumptions in the present and next sections:

I. THE NONNEGATIVITY ASSUMPTION. We shall assume $b \ge 0$; that is, every component of b is nonnegative.

II. THE NONDEGENERACY ASSUMPTION. The extreme points of the convex set of feasible vectors are each the intersection of *exactly* n bounding hyperplanes, where n is the number of components of the vectors involved.

In Section **7** we shall indicate how these two assumptions can be dropped. We emphasize, however, that for linear programming problems derived from actual applications both assumptions will be satisfied, or else the problem can be reformulated so that they are. Moreover, when codes are written for computers to solve linear programming problems, precautions are taken to insure that these assumptions hold.

We now proceed to discuss the simplex method. Later we shall give motivations for each of the steps of the method.

After the data box has been set up for either a maximizing or minimizing problem, the simplex method begins with the initial simplex tableau (the Tucker tableau) of Figure 14. Note that it was derived from the data box as described in the previous section. The simplex algorithm will change the initial tableau into a second one, that into a third, and so on, until finally a tableau is obtained that displays the optimum answers to both the primal and dual problems. A typical tableau in this computational process is shown in Figure 17. Note that the variables have been identified

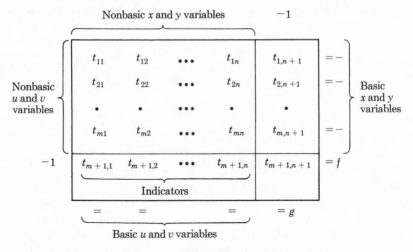

Figure 17

as being of two kinds: *basic* and *nonbasic*; the basic variables appear on the bottom and righthand sides of the tableau and the nonbasic variables on the left and top. As we shall see, in any tableau, if we set the nonbasic variables equal to zero then the corresponding values of the basic variables can be read from the last row and last column of the tableau. The other important thing to note is that the entries of the first n columns of the last row are called *indicators*.

The flow chart in Figure 18 describes how the simplex method works. Look at box 1 in the upper lefthand corner. We see that for the automobile/truck and mining examples of the previous section we have already carried out the directives there: the problems are set up and the initial tableaux formed. We now discuss in detail the rest of the computation for these two examples.

Example 1. The initial tableau for the automobile/truck example appears in Figure 15. To solve this problem using the simplex method we go next to box 2 of the flow chart in Figure 18. We note that in the initial simplex

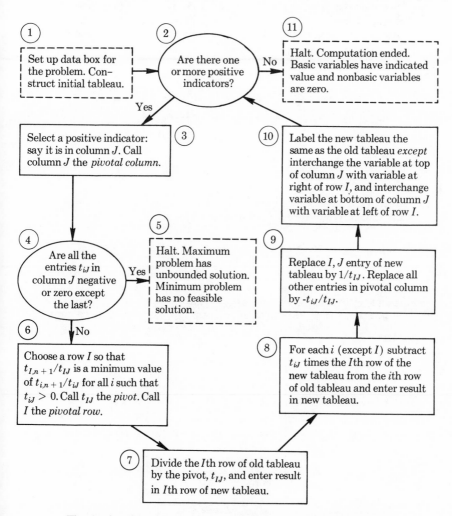

The simplex algorithm for problems with nonnegative righthand sides

Figure 18

tableau of Figure 15 there are positive indicators, so the answer to the question in box 2 is "yes." Hence we proceed to box 3, which says "select a positive indicator." Suppose we select 300, which makes column 1 the pivotal column and $J = 1$. We now go to box 4 and observe that there are positive entries in column 1, so that the answer to the question there is "no," and we go on to box 6. We must now find the pivotal row. For this we examine the ratios $t_{i,n+1}/t_{i1}$ for $i = 1$ and 2. These ratios are $180/5 = 36$ and $135/3 = 45$. Since the smaller ratio occurs in the first row, we see that the 5 entry in the first column of Figure 15 is the pivot and $I = 1$, so that the first row is pivotal. The pivot is circled in Figure 15.

Next we carry out the directives in boxes 7 and 8 of Figure 18, which construct the rows of the new tableau. In box 7 we find we must divide through the pivotal row of the old tableau by the pivot and insert it in the new tableau (Figure 19). Then we multiply this new row by 3 and subtract

1	$\frac{2}{5}$	36
0	$\frac{9}{5}$	27
0	80	$-10,800$

Figure 19

it from the second row of the old tableau to form the second row of the new tableau. In vector form, this computation is

$$-3(1 \quad \tfrac{2}{5} \quad 36) + (3 \quad 3 \quad 135) = (0 \quad \tfrac{9}{5} \quad 27).$$

Similarly, we multiply the new row by 300 and subtract from the third row of the old tableau to form the third row of the new tableau as shown. To complete the new tableau we must replace the pivotal column as described in box 9 of Figure 18; the result is given in Figure 20. Also we must inter-

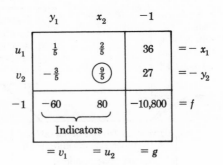

Figure 20

change the labels of the variables at both ends of the pivot row with the variables at both ends of the pivot column as described in box 10 of Figure 18. The completed new second tableau appears in Figure 20.

We now find ourselves back at box 2 of the flow chart of Figure 18. Since the 80 in the second column, last row of Figure 20 is positive, the answer to the question in box 2 is "yes," so we go to box 3. Clearly we must choose $J = 2$. The answer to question in box 4 is "no," so we go on to box 6 to choose the pivot. The two ratios to be considered are $36/\tfrac{2}{5} = 90$ and

$27/\frac{9}{5} = 15$, so that the second row is pivotal and $\frac{9}{5}$ (circled in Figure 20) is the new pivot. Carrying out the instructions in boxes 7 and 8 of the flow diagram gives the tableau in Figure 21, and finishing up with boxes 9 and 10 gives the completed third tableau (Figure 22).

$\frac{1}{3}$	0	30
$-\frac{1}{3}$	1	15
$-\frac{100}{3}$	0	$-12{,}000$

Figure 21

	y_1	y_2	-1	
u_1	$\frac{1}{3}$	$-\frac{2}{9}$	30	$= -x_1$
u_2	$-\frac{1}{3}$	$\frac{5}{9}$	15	$= -x_2$
-1	$-\frac{100}{3}$	$-\frac{400}{9}$	$-12{,}000$	$= f$
	$= v_1$	$= v_2$	$= g$	

Indicators

Figure 22

We again find ourselves in box 2 of the flow diagram. But this time we find no positive indicators for the tableau of Figure 22; hence the answer to the question there is "no" and we go to box 11, which says that the computation is ended. The answers to both the primal and dual problems are displayed in the final tableau. To see what they are, we first set the nonbasic variables equal to zero as instructed in box 11 of the flow diagram. Hence we have $u_1 = u_2 = y_1 = y_2 = 0$, since the nonbasic variables appear on the left and top of the final tableau. Knowing that $y_i = 0$ for $i = 1, 2$, we drop the variables at the top of the final tableau down to the first row and multiply, obtaining $-30 = -x_1$ or simply $x_1 = 30$. Dropping these down one row further gives $x_2 = 15$. And dropping them down to the last row gives $f = 12{,}000$, which is the final value of the objective function. Thus the optimal solution vectors to the maximizing problem are:

$$x^0 = \begin{pmatrix} 30 \\ 15 \end{pmatrix}, \quad y^0 = \begin{pmatrix} 0 \\ 0 \end{pmatrix}, \quad \text{and} \quad f^0 = 12{,}000.$$

Note that this is the same solution that we found in the previous section.

We can also find the optimal solution to the dual problem. (The interpretation of this solution will be given in the next section.) Knowing $u_j = 0$ for $j = 1, 2$, we move the variables on the left of Figure 22 into the first column, multiply, and obtain $v_1 = \frac{100}{3}$. Moving them to the second column gives $v_2 = \frac{400}{3}$, and moving them to the third column gives $g = 12{,}000$, the value of the objective function of the minimizing problem. Hence the optimal solution vectors to the minimizing problem are:

$$v^0 = \left(\tfrac{100}{3}, \tfrac{400}{3}\right), \quad u^0 = (0, 0), \quad \text{and} \quad g^0 = 12{,}000.$$

The reader should substitute x^0 and y^0 into the primal, and v^0 and u^0 into the dual equations written down previously and show that they are satisfied. Note also that $f^0 = v^0 b = cx^0 = g^0$ at an optimum solution. This is always true, and will be discussed further in the next section.

Example 2. Let us solve the mining example using the simplex method. The initial tableau is in Figure 16. The first indicator 12 was selected so that the first column is pivotal. The pivot is 6, which is circled in the figure, and was chosen because the two ratios involved are $\tfrac{100}{3}$, which is smaller than $\tfrac{160}{2} = 80$, hence the first row is pivotal and the pivot is 6. Carrying out steps 7 through 10 of the flow diagram (Figure 18), we construct the second tableau in Figure 23. There are two positive indicators, and we choose the

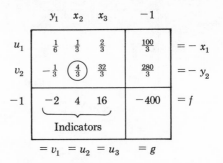

Figure 23

first one, 4, so that the second column is pivotal. The new pivot is $\tfrac{4}{3}$, which is circled in the second (pivotal) row. Carrying out the rest of the steps of the flow diagram, we obtain the third tableau (Figure 24). All indicators in this

$$\begin{array}{ccccc}
 & y_1 & y_2 & x_3 & -1 \\
u_1 & \tfrac{1}{4} & -\tfrac{1}{4} & -2 & 10 & = -x_1 \\
u_2 & -\tfrac{1}{4} & \tfrac{3}{4} & 8 & 70 & = -x_2 \\
-1 & -1 & -3 & -16 & -680 & = f \\
\end{array}$$

Indicators

$$= v_1 \quad = v_2 \quad = u_3 \qquad = g$$

Figure 24

tableau are negative, so the computation is complete. We read off the optimum answers to the primal minimizing problem as

$$v^0 = (1, 3), \quad u^0 = (0, 0, 16), \quad \text{and} \quad g^0 = 680,$$

and the final minimum operating cost for the mines is \$680 per week. These are the same answers as the graphical procedure gave.

The optimum answers to the dual maximizing problem can also be obtained as

$$x^0 = \begin{pmatrix} 10 \\ 70 \\ 0 \end{pmatrix}, \quad y^0 = \begin{pmatrix} 0 \\ 0 \end{pmatrix}, \quad \text{and} \quad f^0 = 680.$$

Interpretations for these will be given in the next section.

Example 3. Our next example illustrates the fact that a given variable may first be basic, become nonbasic, then become basic again, and so on, several times during the course of the simplex computation. Figures 25 through 28

	x_1	x_2	-1	
v_1	2	(1)	3	$= -y_1$
v_2	3	1	4	$= -y_2$
-1	17	5	0	$= f$
	$= u_1$	$= u_2$	$= g$	

Figure 25

	x_1	y_1	-1	
u_2	2	1	3	$= -x_2$
v_2	(1)	-1	1	$= -y_2$
-1	7	-5	-15	$= f$
	$= u_1$	$= v_1$	$= g$	

Figure 26

	y_2	y_1	-1	
u_2	-2	(3)	1	$= -x_2$
u_1	1	-1	1	$= -x_1$
-1	-7	2	22	$= f$
	$= v_2$	$= v_1$	$= g$	

Figure 27

	y_2	x_2	-1	
v_1	$-\frac{2}{3}$	$\frac{1}{3}$	$\frac{1}{3}$	$= -y_1$
u_1	$\frac{1}{3}$	$\frac{1}{3}$	$\frac{4}{3}$	$= -x_1$
-1	$-\frac{17}{3}$	$-\frac{2}{3}$	$-22\frac{2}{3}$	$= f$
	$= v_2$	$= u_2$	$= g$	

Figure 28

give the necessary tableaux, and the pivots are circled there. There is another way of working this problem that requires only two tableaux. It starts with a pivot in the first column instead of the second (see Exercise 9). This illustrates the rule that it is frequently (but not invariably) better to start the simplex method with a column having the most positive indicator. Note that y_1 started out basic, became nonbasic, then became basic again. And x_2 was initially nonbasic, became basic, and ended up nonbasic. The final optimal answers are:

$$v^0 = (0, \tfrac{17}{3}), \quad u^0 = (0, \tfrac{2}{3}), \quad g^0 = 22\tfrac{2}{3},$$
$$x^0 = \begin{pmatrix} \frac{4}{3} \\ 0 \end{pmatrix}, \quad y^0 = \begin{pmatrix} \frac{1}{3} \\ 0 \end{pmatrix}, \quad f^0 = 22\tfrac{2}{3}.$$

Example 4. The reader has undoubtedly wondered about box 5 of the flow diagram in Figure 18, since we have not yet ended in it. Actually, if we are solving an applied problem that is correctly formulated so that it has a solution, we will never end in it. Consider, however, the problem whose initial tableau is in Figure 29. Both the first two columns have positive in-

	x_1	x_2	-1	
v_1	-1	1	1	$= -y_1$
v_2	1	-1	1	$= -y_2$
-1	1	1	0	$= f$
	$= u_1$	$= u_2$	$= g$	

Figure 29

dicators. If we choose the first one and pivot, we obtain the tableau of Figure 30. Now there is one positive indicator in the second column, so $J = 2$. But the answer to the question in box 4 of Figure 18 is "yes," so we arrive at box 5, which says that the maximum problem has an unbounded solution and the minimum problem has no feasible solution.

It is easy to verify that these assertions are correct for the problem at hand. For instance, the constraints for the minimizing problem displayed in Figure 30 are

$$v_1 + u_1 + 1 = v_2,$$
$$-u_1 - 2 = u_2,$$

and it is easy to see that the second equation can never be solved with non-negative values of u_1 and u_2. Similarly, the constraints of the maximizing problem displayed in Figure 30 are

$$y_2 \qquad -2 = -y_1,$$
$$y_2 - x_2 - 1 = -x_1,$$

and these can be solved with nonnegative solutions as follows: $y_2 = 0$, $y_1 = 2$, $x_2 = k$, and $x_1 = 1 + k$, where k is an arbitrarily large positive number. Thus $x_1 + x_2 = 1 + 2k$ can be made arbitrarily large, and the maximizing problem has an unbounded solution.

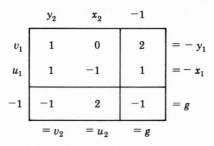

Figure 30

For practical purposes, however, we can ignore the no-solution possibility, since we will be dealing with well-formulated problems that have solutions.

EXERCISES

1. Use the simplex method to solve Example 3 of Section 3.
2. Use the simplex method to solve Example 4 of Section 3 even though the nondegeneracy hypothesis is not satisfied. Show that there are two ways to proceed, each one leading to a different solution of the minimum problem.
3. Use the simplex method to solve Exercise 3 of Section 3.
4. Use the simplex method to solve Exercise 4 of Section 3.
5. Use the simplex method to solve Exercise 5 of Section 3.
6. Use the simplex method to solve Exercise 6 of Section 3.
7. Use the simplex method to solve Exercise 7 of Section 3.
8. Use the simplex method to solve Exercise 8 of Section 3.
9. Solve the problem in Example 3 by choosing the first pivot in the first column. Show that the answer can be obtained in one step.
10. Use the simplex method to solve Exercise 10 of Section 3.
11. A nut packager has on hand 121 pounds of peanuts and 49 pounds of cashews. He can sell two kinds of mixtures of these nuts: a cheap mix

that has 80 percent peanuts and 20 percent cashews, or a party mix that has 30 percent peanuts and 70 percent cashews. If he can sell the party mix at 80 cents a pound and the cheap mix at 50 cents a pound, how many pounds of each mix should he make in order to maximize the amount he can obtain?

[*Ans.* Let x_1 be the number of pounds of party mix and x_2 the number of pounds of the cheap mix. Then the data are

$$A = \begin{pmatrix} .3 & .8 \\ .7 & .2 \end{pmatrix}, \quad b = \begin{pmatrix} 121 \\ 49 \end{pmatrix}, \quad \text{and} \quad c = (80, 50).$$

The packager should make 30 pounds of the party mix and 140 pounds of the cheap mix. His income is $94.]

12. The operator of an oil refinery can buy light crude oil at $6 per barrel and heavy crude at $5 per barrel. The refining process produces the following quantities of gasoline, kerosene, and fuel oil from one barrel of each type of crude:

	Gasoline	Kerosene	Fuel Oil
Light crude	.5	.25	.2
Heavy crude	.4	.3	.25

Note that in each case 5 percent of the barrel of crude is lost in the form of gases (which have to be burned) and unusable sludge. During the summer months the operator has contracted to deliver 50,000 barrels of gasoline, 30,000 barrels of kerosene, and 10,000 barrels of fuel oil per month. How many barrels of each type of crude should he process in order to meet his production quotas at minimum possible cost?

13. During the winter months the refinery operator of Exercise 12 contracts to deliver 36,000 barrels of gasoline, 12,000 barrels of kerosene, and 18,000 barrels of fuel oil. What is his optimal winter production plan?

14. In Exercises 12 and 13 show that there is an excess production of at least one of the goods during each time of the year. Discuss practical ways in which this excess production can be used.

15. In the tableau of Figure 16 make the pivot be the 2 entry in the first column rather than the circled 6 entry shown. Show that this leads to a negative value of x_1, and hence explain the reasons in box 6 of Figure 18 for the special choice of the pivot.

6. DUALITY INTERPRETATIONS AND RESULTS

As we saw in the previous section, the simplex method is the same for both maximizing and minimizing problems. The only difference in setting up the two problems is the choice of row or column vectors for the various quantities involved. In either case we ended up with a data box containing a matrix A, a column vector b, and a row vector c. Using these data we stated both a maximizing and a minimizing problem—only one of which initially interested us. The other problem is called the *dual* linear programming problem. The dual of a maximizing problem is a minimizing problem and vice versa. And the dual of the dual problem is, in either case, the original problem.

We saw that the simplex method solved both the original problem and its dual simultaneously. It is therefore of interest to see what interpretation, if any, can be given to the dual of a linear programming problem. We shall see that we can always give the dual problem mathematical and economic or managerial interpretations that are of considerable interest.

The first step in interpreting the solution to the dual problem is that of determining the dimensions of the variables involved. Recall that in Section 3 we set up for each linear programming problem a data box, and the numbers in the data box had dimensions. We now need to determine the dimensions of the variables of both the primal and dual problems. The following rule tells how to do this.

RULE FOR DETERMINING DIMENSIONS OF VARIABLES

a. The dimension of x_j is the ratio of the dimension of b_j divided by the dimension of a_{ij} for any i.
b. The dimension of v_i is the ratio of the dimension of c_j divided by the dimension of a_{ij} for any j.

In working with dimensions we use the rules of ordinary algebra for canceling and so on, as explained earlier in Section 3.

Example 1. Let us return to the auto/truck example; its data box is given in Figure 6. We have already found the dimensions of the primal variables x_1 (trucks/week) and x_2 (autos/week). Let us use rule (b) above to determine the dimensions of the dual variables v_1 and v_2. For v_1 we have

$$\text{dimension of } v_1 = (\text{dimension of } c_1)/(\text{dimension } a_{11})$$

$$= \frac{\$}{\text{truck}} \bigg/ \frac{\text{S1-manhr}}{\text{truck}}$$

$$= \frac{\$}{\text{truck}} \cdot \frac{\text{truck}}{\text{S1-manhr}}$$

$$= \frac{\$}{\text{S1-manhr}}.$$

In Exercise 1 the reader is asked to show that we would have obtained the same result if we had divided the dimension of c_2 by the dimension of a_{12}. In the same manner we have

$$\text{dimension of } v_2 = (\text{dimension of } c_1)/(\text{dimension } a_{21})$$

$$= \frac{\$}{\text{truck}} \cdot \frac{\text{truck}}{\text{S2-manhr}}$$

$$= \frac{\$}{\text{S2-manhr}}.$$

Figure 31 summarizes the complete data box for the auto/truck example, indicating the dimensions of all variables and constants.

	$x_1 \dfrac{\text{trucks}}{\text{week}}$	$x_2 \dfrac{\text{autos}}{\text{week}}$	Capacities
$v_1 \dfrac{\$}{\text{S1-man-hr}}$	$5 \dfrac{\text{S1-man-hr}}{\text{truck}}$	$2 \dfrac{\text{S1-man-hr}}{\text{auto}}$	$180 \dfrac{\text{S1-man-hr}}{\text{week}}$
$v_2 \dfrac{\$}{\text{S2-man-hr}}$	$3 \dfrac{\text{S2-man-hr}}{\text{truck}}$	$3 \dfrac{\text{S2-man-hr}}{\text{auto}}$	$135 \dfrac{\text{S2-man-hr}}{\text{week}}$
Profits	$300 \dfrac{\$}{\text{truck}}$	$200 \dfrac{\$}{\text{auto}}$	

Figure 31

Example 2. The data box for the mining example is given in Figure 9. We already know that the dimensions of v_1 and v_2 are mine 1-days/week and mine 2-days/week, respectively. Let us use rule (a) above to find the dimensions of x_1.

$$\text{dimension of } x_1 = (\text{dimension of } b_1)/(\text{dimension of } a_{11})$$

$$= \frac{\$}{\text{M1-day}} \bigg/ \frac{\text{tons-HG}}{\text{M1-day}}$$

$$= \frac{\$}{\text{tons-HG}}.$$

A similar application of rule (a) gives the dimensions of x_2 and x_3 as \$/ton-MG and \$/ton-LG, respectively.

	$x_1 \dfrac{\$}{\text{ton-HG}}$	$x_2 \dfrac{\$}{\text{ton-MG}}$	$x_3 \dfrac{\$}{\text{ton-LG}}$	Costs
$v_1 \dfrac{\text{M1-days}}{\text{week}}$	$6 \dfrac{\text{tons-HG}}{\text{M1-day}}$	$2 \dfrac{\text{tons-MG}}{\text{M1-day}}$	$4 \dfrac{\text{tons-LG}}{\text{M1-day}}$	$200 \dfrac{\$}{\text{M1-day}}$
$v_2 \dfrac{\text{M2-days}}{\text{week}}$	$2 \dfrac{\text{tons-HG}}{\text{M2-day}}$	$2 \dfrac{\text{tons-MG}}{\text{M2-day}}$	$12 \dfrac{\text{tons-LG}}{\text{M2-day}}$	$160 \dfrac{\$}{\text{M2-day}}$
Requirements	$12 \dfrac{\text{tons-HG}}{\text{week}}$	$8 \dfrac{\text{tons-MG}}{\text{week}}$	$24 \dfrac{\text{tons-LG}}{\text{week}}$	

Figure 32

Figure 32 shows the data box for the mining example, indicating dimensions for all variables and constants.

Determining the dimensions of the dual variables is the first step in their interpretation. The next step is to look at the optimal dual solutions for the examples above and give their interpretations.

Example 1 (continued). In Example 1 of Section 5 we found the optimal solution to the auto/truck example was

$$x^0 = \begin{pmatrix} 30 \\ 15 \end{pmatrix}, \quad v^0 = (\tfrac{100}{3}, \tfrac{400}{9}), \quad f^0 = g^0 = 12{,}000.$$

We know that $v_1^0 = \tfrac{100}{3}$ has dimensions \$/S1-manhr, which sound like a *value* for shop-1 man-hours. We shall show that this is in fact the case. Suppose we increase the number of shop-1 man-hours from 180 to 183. Our problem is then summarized in the data box of Figure 33, where the dimensions are the

	x_1	x_2	Capacities
v_1	5	2	183
v_2	3	3	135
Profits	300	200	

Figure 33

same as in Figure 31 and are therefore omitted. The reader will be asked to show in Exercise 2 that the optimal solution to this problem is

$$x^0 = \begin{pmatrix} 31 \\ 14 \end{pmatrix} \quad \text{and} \quad v^0 = (\tfrac{100}{3}, \tfrac{400}{9})$$

with objective value 12,100. Notice that the objective value has increased by 100, which is just three times the dual variable $v_1^0 = \tfrac{100}{3}$. Hence we see that $v_1^0 = 33.33$ is the *imputed value* of an additional hour of shop-1 man-hours. It should be remarked right away that the imputed-value interpretation holds over only a limited range of changes in shop-1 man-hours. Hence we should more properly say that $v_1^0 = 33.33$ is the *imputed value* of an additional hour in shop 1 *provided the dual solution is not changed by* adding this extra capacity.

Note also that the imputed value is determined independently of the *cost* of providing the extra man-hours in shop 1. In order to provide extra man-hours it would be necessary to pay workers overtime, or else do subcontracting, or the like. What the optimal dual variables tell us is the cost of providing extra hours in shop 1 should not be more than their imputed value, or else it is not optimal to get them.

In Exercise 3 the reader will be asked to show that the optimal dual variable $v_2^0 = \tfrac{400}{9} = 44.44$, which has dimensions \$ per shop-2 man-hour, is the imputed value of an additional hour in shop 2 provided the optimal dual solution does not change after the extra time is added. As before, it is the maximum amount one should be willing to pay to obtain the extra time.

Example 2 (continued). In Example 2 of Section 5 we found the optimal solutions to the mining example were

$$v^0 = (1, 3), \quad x^0 = \begin{pmatrix} 10 \\ 70 \\ 0 \end{pmatrix}, \quad \text{and} \quad f^0 = g^0 = 680.$$

We know that $x_1^0 = 10$ has dimensions \$ per ton of high-grade ore, which sounds like the *imputed cost* of producing an additional ton of high-grade ore, and we shall show that this is the case. Suppose we increase the requirements for high-grade ore production from 12 to 16 tons. The new data box is shown in Figure 34, dimensions being the same as in Figure 32. In Exercise 4

	x_1	x_2	x_3	Costs
v_1	6	2	4	200
v_2	2	2	12	160
Requirements	16	8	24	

Figure 34

the reader will be asked to show that the optimal solution to the new problem is

$$w^0 = (2, 2), \quad x^0 = \begin{pmatrix} 10 \\ 70 \\ 0 \end{pmatrix}, \quad \text{and} \quad f^0 = g^0 = 720.$$

Notice that the costs of production have increased from 680 to 720, which is $4 \cdot x_1^0 = 4 \cdot 10 = 40$. Hence $x_1^0 = 10$ was the per-ton cost of each of the additional four units of high-grade ore.

In Exercise 5 you will be asked to show that x_2^0 can be similarly interpreted as the *imputed or marginal cost* of producing an additional ton of medium-grade ore, *provided the* additional production does *not* cause a new dual solution to appear.

Now let us look at $x_3^0 = 0$, which has dimension \$ per ton of low-grade ore. What this says is that low-grade ore is free in the sense that producing an additional ton has zero cost. What does this mean? If we look at the slack vector $u^0 = (0, 0, 16)$ found in Section 5, we observe that there is an overproduction of low-grade ore by 16 tons beyond the requirements. In other words we have already overproduced, so the additional ton will cost zero to produce since it already exists. However, this is true only within limits. For suppose we change the requirement for low-grade ore to 56 tons, giving the data box of Figure 35. In Exercise 6 the reader will be asked to show that the optimal solution to the problem in Figure 35 is

$$v^0 = (.5, 4.5), \quad x^0 = \begin{pmatrix} 27.5 \\ 0 \\ 8.75 \end{pmatrix}, \quad \text{and} \quad f^0 = g^0 = 820.$$

	x_1	x_2	x_3	Costs
v_1	6	2	4	200
v_2	2	2	12	160
Requirements	12	8	56	

Figure 35

Note that we now have a new dual solution, so that the old dual variable $x_3 = 0$ did not hold for the entire range of changes in the requirements for low-grade ore.

Let us try to give general interpretations to a pair of dual linear programming problems. For either problem the matrix A will be called the matrix of technological coefficients, since it indicates how activity vectors are combined into the constraining inequalities. Then we can give different interpretations to the vectors c, b, x, and v, depending on whether our original problem is a maximizing or a minimizing one.

If the original problem is maximizing, we interpret x as the *activity vector*. Then the vector b is interpreted as the *capacity-constraint vector*, whose components give the amounts of the various "scarce resources" that can be demanded by a given activity vector. The vector c is the *profit vector*, whose entries give the unit profits for each component of the activity vector x. Finally, the vector v is the *imputed-value vector*, whose entries give the imputed values of each of the scarce resources that enter into the production process, provided the changes in scarce resources are sufficiently small that the dual solution remains optimal.

If the original problem is minimizing, we interpret v as the *activity vector*. Then c is interpreted as the *requirements vector*, whose components give the minimum amounts of each good that must be produced. The vector b is the *cost vector*, whose entries give the unit costs of each of the activities. Finally, the vector x is the *imputed-cost* vector, whose components give the imputed costs of producing additional amounts of each of the required goods, *provided* the changes in requirements are sufficiently small that the dual solution remains optimal.

Next we shall briefly discuss two important theorems in linear programming. First we restate the dual problems:

The *MAXIMUM Problem*	The *MINIMUM Problem*
Max: $\qquad cx = f$	Min: $\qquad vb = g$
Subject to: (1) $Ax + y = b$,	Subject to: (3) $vA - u = c$,
$\qquad$ (2) $x \geq 0, y \geq 0$.	$\qquad$ (4) $v \geq 0, u \geq 0$.

Vectors x and y satisfying (1) and (2) and vectors v and u satisfying (3) and (4) are called *feasible vectors*.

In all the examples solved above we found that $f = g$ at the optimum solution. It is no accident that the dual problems share common values. The next theorem, which is the principal theorem of linear programming, shows that this will always happen whenever the problems have solutions.

THE DUALITY THEOREM. The maximum problem has as a solution a feasible vector x^0, such that $cx^0 = \max cx$, if and only if the minimum problem has a solution that is a feasible vector v^0, such that $v^0b = \min vb$. Moreover, the equality $cx^0 = v^0b$ holds if and only if x^0 and v^0 are solutions to their respective problems.

The duality theorem is extremely powerful, for it says that if one of the problems has a (finite) solution, then the other one necessarily also has a (finite) solution, and both problems share a common value. Another consequence of the theorem is that if one of the problems does *not* have a solution, then neither does the other.

The proof of the duality theorem is beyond the scope of this book, but some parts of it are indicated in Exercises 25 and 26, and in Exercise 8 of Section 4. We saw an example of a linear programming problem without a solution in Example 4 of Section 4. Another example is in Exercise 27.

The duality theorem states that $g^0 = f^0$ at the optimum solution. Applying this to Tucker's duality equation [(7) in Section 4], we obtain:

$$(5) \qquad\qquad 0 = g^0 - f^0 = v^0y^0 + u^0x^0.$$

However, since v^0, y^0, u^0, and x^0 are all feasible optimal vectors, they are, in particular, nonnegative. Hence $v^0y^0 \geq 0$ and $u^0x^0 \geq 0$. But the only way that two nonnegative numbers can add up to zero is for both of them to be zero. Therefore

$$(6) \qquad\qquad v^0y^0 = 0,$$

$$(7) \qquad\qquad u^0x^0 = 0.$$

If we now simply restate (6) and (7), we obtain the following important theorem.

THE COMPLEMENTARY SLACKNESS THEOREM

A. For each i *either* $v_i^0 = 0$ *or* $y_i^0 = b_i - \sum_{j=1}^{n} a_{ij}x_j^0 = 0$.

B. For each j *either* $x_j^0 = 0$ *or* $u_j^0 = \sum_{i=1}^{m} v_i^0 a_{ij} - c_j = 0$.

Proof. The proof of this theorem is simple because (6) says that the sum of the products $v_i^0 y_i^0$ must equal zero, but each term of the product is nonnegative so each product must itself be zero, which gives (A). The proof of (B) follows similarly from (7).

Example 2 (continued). From the final tableau in Figure 24 of the previous section we found that the complete solution to the mining problem was

$$v^0 = (1, 3), \quad u^0 = (0, 0, 16), \quad x^0 = \begin{pmatrix} 10 \\ 70 \\ 0 \end{pmatrix}, \quad y^0 = \begin{pmatrix} 0 \\ 0 \end{pmatrix}.$$

We see that since $u_3^0 = 16$—that is, in the optimal solution low-grade ore is overproduced—the imputed cost of low-grade ore must be zero; and it is, since $x_3^0 = 0$. Also, since both v_1^0 and v_2^0 are positive, both components of y^0 must be zero, which they are. The reader should state the other consequences of the complementary slackness theorem for this example.

Let us conclude by discussing the reasons for the various steps of the simplex method. If we always think of the nonbasic variables, which appear at the left and on the top of the tableaus (see Figures 14 and 17), as being set equal to zero, then in the initial tableau of Figure 14 we see the initial solution vectors

$$(8) \qquad\qquad x = 0, \quad y = b, \quad v = 0, \quad \text{and} \quad u = -c.$$

Since we have assumed $b \geq 0$, we see that the first three vectors are non-negative, but u is nonnegative only if c was initially nonpositive. In the latter case the initial tableau is optimal (see Exercise 11). Since this is not normally the case, there is usually at least one positive indicator, so that the first answer to the question in box 2 of Figure 18 is yes. Thus we must go around the loop and carry out at least one pivot. As we do so, the simplex method systematically changes the tableau in order to make u into a nonnegative vector without destroying the nonnegativeness of x, y, or v, and also keeping $f = cx = vb = g$ at all times.

In step 6 of Figure 18 the pivot was chosen in order to have the smallest ratio $t_{I,n+1}/t_{IJ}$ so that no current x_i or y_j should become negative. The reader may verify that if the pivot is chosen not to have this property, then some such variable is made negative (see Exercise 15 of the preceding section). The nondegeneracy assumption made in Section 4 can be used to show (see Exercise 25) that on each pivot step the value of the current f will actually increase. In Exercise 26 you will be asked to show that at most a finite number of pivot steps can be made. Hence, if the problem has a solution, we must arrive in a finite number of steps at a tableau having all positive indicators. At each step the current solution in a tableau satisfies equations (1), (2), and (3) above, and when all indicators are positive we have also satisfied (4), so that $v \geq 0$ and $u \geq 0$. By the duality theorem if we have found x^0, y^0, v^0, and u^0 satisfying (1)–(4) and also $f^0 = cx^0 = v^0b = g^0$, then an optimum solution to the programming problem has been found.

EXERCISES

1. In Example 1 show that the same answer for the dimension of v_1 can be obtained by dividing the dimension of c_2 by the dimension of a_{12}.

2. Show that the vectors

$$x^0 = \binom{31}{14} \quad \text{and} \quad v^0 = (\tfrac{100}{3}, \tfrac{400}{9})$$

solve the problem in Figure 33. [*Hint:* Substitute into the primal and dual problems.]

3. *a.* Use the optimal solution to the automobile/truck problem in Figure 31 to predict how the objective function, which measures profit, will change if the capacity of shop 2 is changed from 135 to 144 man-hours per week.

    b. Solve the problem in Figure 31 with the 135 changed to 144 and use its solution to show that your prediction in (*a*) was correct.

$$[\textit{Ans.} \text{ Profit } 12,400, \ x^0 = \binom{28}{20}, \ v^0 = (\tfrac{100}{3}, \tfrac{400}{9}).]$$

4. Show that the solution to the mining example in Figure 34 is

$$v = (2, 2), \quad x^0 \text{ as before}, \quad f = g = 720.$$

5. *a.* Use the solution to Exercise 4 to predict what will happen in the mining problem if the requirement for medium-grade ore is increased from 8 to 10.

    b. Solve the mining problem in Figure 34 with the 8 replaced by 10 and show that your prediction in (*a*) was correct.

$$[\textit{Ans.} \ v^0 = (1.5, 3.5), \ x^0 \text{ as before}, f = g = 860.]$$

6. Show that the solution to the problem in Figure 35 is

$$v^0 = (.5, 4.5), \quad x^0 = \begin{pmatrix} 27.5 \\ 0 \\ 8.75 \end{pmatrix}, \quad f = g = 820.$$

Interpret the solution.

7. In the automobile/truck example of Figure 31, suppose that the manufacturer can subcontract up to 18 of either shop 1 or shop 2 man-hours at $38 per hour. What is his optimal action? [*Hint:* You can answer this question without solving a linear programming problem.]

8. In the mining example of Figure 32 suppose the mining owner can sell 10 more tons of medium-grade ore at $55 per ton. Should he do so?

9. Consider again the general interpretation of a maximizing problem in which x is an activity vector, b the capacity-constraint vector, and c the profit vector. Let v^0 be the optimum dual solution vector. Discuss the following managerial interpretation of the components v_i^0 of v^0. "Additional amounts of scarce resource i should be acquired only if its cost is less than the component v_i^0 that gives the imputed value of an additional (sufficiently small) quantity."

10. Consider again the general interpretation of a minimizing problem in which v is the activity vector, c the requirements vector, and b the cost vector. Let x^0 be the optimum dual solution vector. Discuss the following managerial interpretations of the components x_i^0 of x. "Additional amounts of the jth good should be produced only if they can be sold with gross profit at least as large as the component x_j^0, which gives the imputed cost of producing an additional (sufficiently small) quantity."

11. Consider the dual maximum and minimum problems in equality form as expressed above. If $c \leq 0$, prove that the initial solution (8) is optimal. [*Hint:* Use the duality theorem.]

12–20. For each of Exercises 1–9 of Section 3 carry out the following steps:
    a. Find the dimensions of the dual variables.
    b. Set up the initial tableau with the dimensions of all variables and numbers indicated.
    c. Read the answers to both primal and dual problems from the final tableau.
    d. Interpret the dual solutions for the specific problems in each case.
    e. State the complementary slackness theorem for each problem and interpret.

21–24. Repeat for Exercises 10–13 of Section 5.

*25. The assumption of nondegeneracy stated in Section 5 can be shown to be equivalent to the following: at no time in the pivoting process of the simplex method are any of the entries in the first m rows of the last column of the tableau ever zero. Use this fact to show that on each pivot step the value of $f = cx$ *increases.*

*26. Show that there are only a finite number of ways that the components of the x and y vectors can be used to label the top and righthand side of the various tableaus during the pivoting process. Use the result of Exercise 25 to show that no tableau can ever be repeated in the course of solving a nondegenerate problem by the simplex method. Hence, conclude that the simplex method described in Figure 18 must stop in a finite number of steps with the optimal solution to the linear programming problem, or else with proof that the problem has no finite solution.

27. Use the flow diagram of Figure 18 to show that the problem whose initial tableau is

-1	1	4
2	-4	8
2	3	0

does not have a solution. Verify algebraically and geometrically the statements in box 5 of that flow diagram.

*7. EQUALITY CONSTRAINTS AND THE GENERAL SIMPLEX METHOD

In this (optional) section we shall discuss the removal of the nonnegativity and nondegeneracy assumptions that we imposed at the beginning of Section 5 on linear programming problems. As stated there, most problems will automatically satisfy these assumptions. If not, they can usually be changed so that they do. We illustrate the latter first.

> **Example 1.** Consider again the automobile/truck example of Figure 6. Suppose we add the managerial constraint that at least 20 automobiles should be produced—perhaps because we have orders for them. The inequality that will do this is $x_2 \geq 20$, but it is a $\geq$ inequality instead of a $\leq$ inequality as is required for a maximizing problem. Multiplying through by -1 gives $-x_3 \leq -20$. Hence the maximizing problem is

$$\text{Maximize} \quad 300x_1 + 200x_2$$

(1)
$$\begin{aligned} \text{Subject to} \quad & 5x_1 + 2x_2 \leq 180, \\ & 3x_1 + 3x_2 \leq 135, \\ & -x_2 \leq -20, \\ & x_1, x_2 \geq 0. \end{aligned}$$

We see that the b vector is

(2)
$$b = \begin{pmatrix} 180 \\ 135 \\ -20 \end{pmatrix},$$

which does not satisfy the nonnegativity assumption. However, let us set up the initial tableau and see what we can do with it. It is shown in Figure 36.

	x_1	x_2	-1	
v_1	5	2	180	$= -y_1$
v_2	3	3	135	$= -y_2$
v_3	0	(-1)	-20	$= -y_3$
-1	300	200	0	$= f$
	$= u_1$	$= u_2$	$= g$	

Figure 36

Notice that in the third row where the -20 entry is, there is also a -1. If we were to pivot on the -1, using the usual rules as given in Figure 18, we could change the -20 into a $+20$. Carrying out this pivot operation gives the tableau of Figure 37, which *has* a positive b vector. Hence we can now proceed in the usual way. Choosing the most positive indicator, which is 300,

	x_1	y_3	-1	
v_1	5	2	140	$= -y_1$
v_2	③	3	75	$= -y_2$
v_3	0	1	20	$= -x_2$
-1	300	200	-4000	$= f$
	$= u_1$	$= v_3$	$= g$	

Figure 37

we determine that the pivot should be the 3 circled in the first column. Carrying out the rest of the pivot steps as in Figure 18 gives the tableau in Figure 38. Since all indicators there are negative, we have determined the optimal solution, namely

$$x^0 = \begin{pmatrix} 25 \\ 20 \end{pmatrix}, \quad {}_{\ast}v^0 = (0, 100, 100), \quad \text{and} \quad f^0 = g^0 = 11{,}500.$$

	y_2	y_3	-1	
v_1	$-\frac{5}{3}$	-3	65	$= -y_1$
u_1	$\frac{1}{3}$	1	25	$= -x_1$
u_2	0	1	20	$= -x_2$
-1	-100	-100	$-11{,}500$	$= f$
	$= v_2$	$= v_3$	$= g$	

Figure 38

In other words, the optimum decision now is to produce 25 trucks and 20 automobiles for a gross profit of \$11,500. Notice that the gross profit has gone down, which is not surprising since we are satisfying an additional constraint. Notice also that the dual solution indicates that for each automobile less that we require to be made, an additional \$100 profit can be realized. Notice also that the imputed value of shop 1 man-hours has gone to zero! This is because $y_1 = 65$, indicating that we are not using all of the shop 1 man-hours. Also the imputed value of shop 2 man-hours has jumped from \$44.44 to \$100 per hour, which indicates that shop 2 has become a more important "bottleneck" in the production process.

The previous example shows one way of deriving a problem that has negative b vector coefficients—namely, by imposing a $\geq$ constraint with positive righthand side on the maximizing problem. Another way is to impose an equality constraint. For example, consider the equation

(3) $$2x_1 + 5x_2 - 7x_3 = 12.$$

We can clearly replace it by the two inequalities

(4) $2x_1 + 5x_2 - 7x_3 \leq 12$ and $2x_1 + 5x_2 - 7x_3 \geq 12,$

but the second of these is a $\geq$ constraint. We can change it into a $\leq$ constraint by multiplying by a -1, obtaining

(5) $2x_1 + 5x_2 - 7x_3 \leq 12$ and $-2x_1 - 5x_2 + 7x_3 \leq -12$

as a pair of $\leq$ inequalities that are equivalent to the single equality (3).

When solving simple examples such as Example 1 by hand it is usually quite easy to see how to pivot on negative numbers in the tableau in such a way that the problem becomes one having nonnegative righthand sides. However, for large problems, and particularly for computing-machine computation, it is necessary to have a set of rules that will always work, without depending upon the ingenuity of the user. Such an algorithm is presented in Figure 39. It is usually called "phase I" of the simplex method, and what it does is to put the tableau in the standard form so that the flow diagram of Figure 18 can be applied. We illustrate it with an example.

Example 2. Consider the linear programming problem

$$\text{Maximize}\quad 2x_1 + x_2$$

(6) $$\text{Subject to}\quad \begin{aligned} x_1 + x_2 &\leq 20, \\ x_1 + 2x_2 &= 30, \\ x_1, x_2 &\geq 0. \end{aligned}$$

The set of feasible x-vectors is the line segment between the points $\begin{pmatrix} 0 \\ 15 \end{pmatrix}$ and $\begin{pmatrix} 10 \\ 10 \end{pmatrix}$ shown darkened in Figure 40. In order to solve (6) we replace the equality constraint by a pair of inequalities and obtain the problem:

$$\text{Maximize}\quad 2x_1 + x_2$$

(7) $$\text{Subject to}\quad \begin{aligned} x_1 + x_2 &\leq 20, \\ x_1 + 2x_2 &\leq 30, \\ -x_1 - 2x_2 &\leq -30, \\ x_1, x_2 &\geq 0. \end{aligned}$$

Thus we obtain a problem that does not satisfy the nonnegativity assumption.

Let us solve the problem by following the flow diagram of Figure 39. We set up the initial tableau with the negative b_i's last as instructed in box 1 of that figure. The initial tableau is given in Figure 41. The answer to the question in box 2 of Figure 39 is yes, so we go to box 3, where we must choose $K = 3$. The answer to the question in box 4 is no, so we go on to box 6. Since both entries in the first two columns of the third row of Figure 41 are negative, J can be either 1 or 2; we choose $J = 1$. Then the ratio rule in box 6

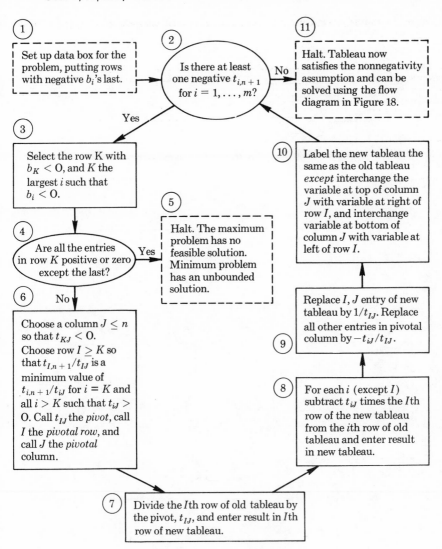

(1)
Set up data box for the problem, putting rows with negative b_i's last.

(2)
Is there at least one negative $t_{i,n+1}$ for $i = 1, \ldots, m$?

No

(11)
Halt. Tableau now satisfies the nonnegativity assumption and can be solved using the flow diagram in Figure 18.

Yes

(3)
Select the row K with $b_K < 0$, and K the largest i such that $b_i < 0$.

(10)
Label the new tableau the same as the old tableau *except* interchange the variable at top of column J with variable at right of row I, and interchange variable at bottom of column J with variable at left of row I.

(4)
Are all the entries in row K positive or zero except the last?

Yes

(5)
Halt. The maximum problem has no feasible solution. Minimum problem has an unbounded solution.

(6)
No

Choose a column $J \leq n$ so that $t_{KJ} < 0$. Choose row $I \geq K$ so that $t_{I,n+1}/t_{IJ}$ is a minimum value of $t_{i,n+1}/t_{iJ}$ for $i = K$ and all $i > K$ such that $t_{iJ} > 0$. Call t_{IJ} the *pivot*, call I the *pivotal row*, and call J the *pivotal column*.

(9)
Replace I, J entry of new tableau by $1/t_{IJ}$. Replace all other entries in pivotal column by $-t_{iJ}/t_{IJ}$.

(8)
For each i (except I) subtract t_{iJ} times the Ith row of the new tableau from the ith row of old tableau and enter result in new tableau.

(7)
Divide the Ith row of old tableau by the pivot, t_{IJ}, and enter result in Ith row of new tableau.

Phase I of the simplex method for problems having at least one negative righthand side

Figure 39

gives $I = 3$. Carrying out the pivot steps in boxes 7–10 of Figure 39 gives the next tableau shown in Figure 42. Notice that a new negative has appeared in the third column of the first row! So the answer to the question in box 2 of Figure 39 is again yes, and we must go around the main loop of the flow diagram again. We find that $K = 1$ and $J = 2$ are the only possible choices, and these give $I = 1$, so that we must pivot on the -1 circled in the first row of Figure 42. After pivoting, the new tableau is as shown in Figure 43.

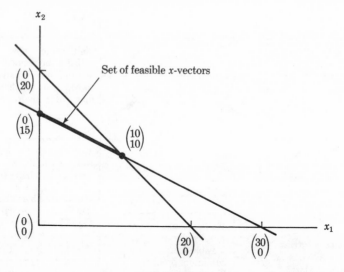

Figure 40

	x_1	x_2	-1	
v_1	1	1	20	$= -y_1$
v_2	1	2	30	$= -y_2$
v_3	$\boxed{-1}$	-2	-30	$= -y_3$
-1	2	1	0	$= f$
	$= u_1$	$= u_2$	$= g$	

Figure 41

	y_3	x_2	-1	
v_1	1	$\boxed{-1}$	-10	$= -y_1$
v_2	1	0	0	$= -y_2$
u_1	-1	2	30	$= -x_1$
-1	2	-3	-60	$= f$
	$= v_3$	$= u_2$	$= g$	

Figure 42

	y_3	y_1	-1	
u_2	-1	-1	10	$= -x_2$
v_2	1	0	0	$= -y_2$
u_1	1	2	10	$= -x_1$
-1	-1	-3	-30	$= f$
	$= v_3$	$= v_1$	$= g$	

Figure 43

Since both indicators are negative, we have obtained the optimal solution without further pivoting. It is

$$x^0 = \begin{pmatrix} 10 \\ 10 \end{pmatrix}, \quad v^0 = (3, 0, 1), \quad \text{and} \quad f^0 = g^0 = 30.$$

The reader should locate the solution on the diagram of Figure 40.

The last topic of this section is the question of removing the non-degeneracy assumption stated in Section 5. A complete discussion of the problem is beyond the scope of this book, but an interested reader may wish to refer to one of the more advanced texts listed at the end of this chapter. We shall indicate the essential ideas here, however. An example will suffice for this purpose.

Example 3. Consider the problem:

(8)
$$
\begin{aligned}
\text{Maximize} \quad & x_1 + x_2 \\
\text{Subject to} \quad & x_1 \qquad\;\; \le 4, \\
& \qquad x_2 \le 4, \\
& 2x_1 + x_2 \le 8, \\
& x_1, x_2 \ge 0.
\end{aligned}
$$

The set of feasible x-vectors is shown shaded in Figure 44. Notice that the

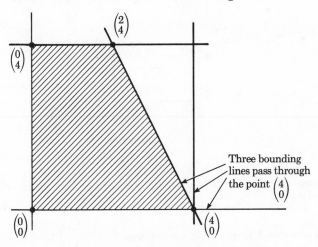

Figure 44

set has four extreme points and that each is the intersection of exactly two bounding lines *except* for the point $\begin{pmatrix} 4 \\ 0 \end{pmatrix}$, which has three bounding lines through it. We shall show that this can lead to the appearance of a zero in the b area of the tableau after some pivoting, and when this happens it is possible to pivot without improving the objective function. The initial tableau for the problem is given in Figure 45.

	x_1	x_2	-1	
v_1	① 1	0	4	$= -y_1$
v_2	0	1	4	$= -y_2$
v_3	2	1	8	$= -y_3$
-1	1	1	0	$= g$
	$= u_1$	$= u_2$	$= g$	

Figure 45

Since both indicators are positive, suppose we choose the first one. The minimum-ratio rule then selects the first row to be pivotal, and we pivot on the one circled. (Note that we could also pivot on the 2 in the third column, first row, and the results will be similar; see Exercise 10.) The new, tableau is given in Figure 46. Notice that a zero did appear in the third row, third column of Figure 46. In order to make it into something positive a small

	y_1	x_2	-1	
u_1	1	0	4	$= -x_1$
v_2	0	1	4	$= -y_2$
v_3	-2	① 1	$0 + \epsilon$	$= -y_3$
-1	-1	1	-4	$= f$
	$= v_1$	$= u_2$	$= g$	

Figure 46

amount ϵ is added to it. This is called a *perturbation*. Geometrically it corresponds in Figure 44 to moving the line $2x_1 + x_2 = 8$ parallel to itself upward slightly. This makes the extreme point $\begin{pmatrix} 4 \\ 0 \end{pmatrix}$ have just two bounding lines through it, and adds a new extreme point $\begin{pmatrix} 4 \\ \epsilon \end{pmatrix}$ nearby. We will find it on the next iteration. The second column has a positive indicator, and the minimum-ratio rule selects the third row to be pivotal and 1 the pivot, circled in Figure 46. The new tableau is given in Figure 47.

Now we observe that column 1 has a positive indicator, so we must still pivot again. The ratio rule selects as pivot the 2 in the first column, circled in Figure 47. The next tableau is given in Figure 48.

Since both indicators in Figure 48 are negative, we have the optimal solution. Notice that if we replace ϵ by 0 we still have an optimal tableau,

	y_1	y_3	-1	
u_1	1	0	4	$= -x_1$
v_2	(2)	-1	$4 - \epsilon$	$= -y_2$
u_2	-2	1	$0 + \epsilon$	$= -x_2$
-1	1	-1	$-4 - \epsilon$	$= f$
	$= v_1$	$= v_3$	$= g$	

Figure 47

	y_2	y_3	-1	
u_1	$-\frac{1}{2}$	$-\frac{1}{2}$	$2 + \left(\frac{\epsilon}{2}\right)$	$= -x_1$
v_1	1	$-\frac{1}{2}$	$2 - \left(\frac{\epsilon}{2}\right)$	$= -y_1$
u_2	-1	0	4	$= -x_2$
-1	$-\frac{1}{2}$	$-\frac{1}{2}$	$-6 - \left(\frac{\epsilon}{2}\right)$	$= f$
	$= v_2$	$= v_3$	$= g$	

Figure 48

hence our perturbation did not affect the original problem enough to change the solution, which is

$$x^0 = \begin{pmatrix} 2 \\ 4 \end{pmatrix}, \quad v^0 = (0, \tfrac{1}{2}, \tfrac{1}{2}), \quad \text{and} \quad f^0 = g^0 = 6.$$

Actually, if we had ignored the 0 in the last column of Figure 47 and just gone ahead with the simplex method as given in Figure 18, we would have arrived at the same solution without difficulty. But notice that in going from tableau 46 to 47 we then would not have increased the objective function f at all. It can happen with larger problems that the computation could go from one tableau to the next several times in a row without changing f, and after a finite number of pivots return to a tableau constructed earlier. From then on the computational process will go through the same sequence of tableaus indefinitely without changing f. This is called *cycling*. Actually it rarely happens in practice. The smallest known example in which it can occur has seven variables. For small problems that can be worked by hand it never occurs.

There are several ways of avoiding cycling for computer codes that handle large problems. One way is the process of perturbation illustrated above. There only one 0 was found and it was made positive by adding $+\epsilon$ to it. If a second zero were found, then $+\epsilon^2$ would be added; and if a third were found, then $+\epsilon^3$ would be added; and so on. The final tableau will then have numbers plus polynomials in ϵ in the last column. By selecting ϵ *not* to be equal to any of the finite number of zeros of these polynomials and also very small, we can prove that there always is a perturbation of the components of the b-vectors that will avoid cycling, and that has the same solution as the original problem when ϵ is replaced by 0 in the final tableau.

Still another (practical) way of avoiding cycling is the following. Whenever a zero is about to appear in a tableau, there will be more than one choice of pivotal row in box 6 of the flow diagram of Figure 18. This can be seen in Figure 45, in which, given the pivotal column $J = 1$, we can choose *either $I = 1$ or $I = 3$* when applying the test. Suppose now we choose between these two at random, instead of always choosing the first one. It can be shown that if this method is used to "break ties" when selecting pivotal rows, then the simplex method will not cycle with probability 1. For practical purposes this provides an adequate safeguard against the very rare possibility of cycling in computations.

EXERCISES

1. Write pairs of $\leq$ inequalities that are equivalent to each of the following = constraints.
   a. $12x_1 + 3x_2 - 7x_3 = 15$.
   b. $3x_1 - 2x_2 + 4x_3 = 0$ and $-4x_1 + x_2 - 2x_3 = 7$.

2. Consider the mining example (Example 2 of Section 3) again with the additional constraint that exactly 16 tons of high-grade ore should be produced per week. Show that the tableau has a nonnegative b vector.

3. Show that a minimizing problem with $b \geq 0$ can always be solved using Figure 18 regardless of the form of the additional constraints that may be imposed on the minimizing problem.

4. In Example 1 of Section 3 show that the additional constraint $x_1 \leq 15$ can be imposed and the problem solved using Figure 18.

5. Show that a maximizing problem with only $\leq$ constraints and positive b vector can be solved using Figure 18 regardless of how many additional $\leq$ constraints are added, as long as the righthand sides of such additional constraints are nonnegative.

6. Use the results of Exercises 3–5 to show that the phase I computation of Figure 39 is needed only when a $\leq$ constraint with negative righthand side is added to the maximizing problem.

7. Apply the phase I simplex method of Figure 39 to the following examples.

   a. Maximize $\quad 2x_1 + x_2$

   Subject to $\quad x_1 + x_2 \leq 10$,
   $\qquad\qquad\quad x_1 + x_2 \geq 6$,
   $\qquad\qquad\quad x_1 \quad\;\; \leq 8$,
   $\qquad\qquad\quad x_1, x_2 \geq 0$.

   b. Maximize $\quad x_1$

   Subject to $\quad x_1 \qquad\quad \geq 2$,
   $\qquad\qquad\qquad\quad\; x_2 \geq 3$,
   $\qquad\qquad\quad 3x_1 + 2x_2 \leq 24$.

8. Apply the phase I computation to the problem whose initial tableau is given by

1	1	20
-1	-2	-50
2	1	0

and show that the computation ends up in box 5 of Figure 39. Draw the constraint sets of the primal and dual problems and give a geometric interpretation to the statements in box 5 of Figure 39.

*9. Show in general that if the computation of Figure 39 ends up in box 5, then the statements given there are correct.

*10. Show that phase I is needed if and only if $x = 0$ is *not* a feasible vector for the maximizing problem.

11. Start with Figure 45 and carry out pivoting steps, starting with the pivot in the third row, first column. Show that equivalent results are obtained.

12. Show that even if we do not add $+\epsilon$ in the third row, third column of Figure 46, the simplex method will yield the correct solution.

13. Add the constraint $-x_1 + x_2 \leq 4$ to the problem in (8) and show that no matter which column is chosen for the first pivot, a 0 is still produced in the b-vector after one pivot. Show that the simplex method still works.

*14. *a.* Show that the phase I simplex method will eventually make the last inequality with negative righthand side into one with positive (or zero) righthand side without making the righthand sides of later inequalities negative.

   b. Show that in a finite number of steps all negative righthand sides will be made nonnegative, or else the computation will end up in box 5 of the flow diagram in Figure 39.

8. TRANSPORTATION PROBLEMS

One of the first kinds of linear programming problems to be stated and solved was the so-called *transportation problem*, which is the problem of shipping at lowest cost a homogeneous good, such as steel, wood, wheat, oil, from m different warehouse locations to n different markets. As we shall see in the next section, this model has applications to many problems that have nothing to do with transportation. For this reason, and others, the transportation model is extremely important.

Example 1. As our first example of a transportation problem consider Figure 49. There we consider the shipment from three warehouses W_1, W_2,

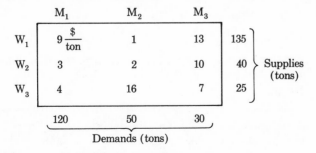

Figure 49

and W_3 to three markets M_1, M_2, and M_3. The *cost* of shipping from warehouse W_i to market M_j is given in the ith row and jth column of the matrix. Thus the cost of shipping from W_1 to M_1 is $c_{11} = 9$ \$/ton; the cost of shipping from W_2 to M_3 is $c_{23} = 10$ \$/ton; and so on. On the righthand side of the cost matrix are listed the supplies in each warehouse; thus the supply in W_1 is $a_1 = 135$ tons, the supply in W_2 is $a_2 = 40$ tons, and the supply in W_3 is 25 tons. Similarly, on the bottom of the cost matrix are listed the demands at each of the markets: the demand in M_1 being $b_1 = 120$ tons, in M_2 50 tons, and in M_3 30 tons. Note that the total supplies add up to the total demands, since

$$135 + 40 + 25 = 200 = 120 + 50 + 30,$$

and this assumption will be necessary at first.

The data for an arbitrary transportation problem are shown in Figure 50. Here we assume that there are m warehouses and n markets; c_{ij} is

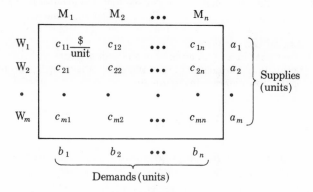

Figure 50

the unit cost of shipping from warehouse W_i to market M_j; a_i is the number of units of supply in warehouse W_i and b_j is the number of units demanded in market M_j. We assume that the sum of the supplies equals the sum of the demands—that is,

$$(1) \qquad \sum_{i=1}^{m} a_i = \sum_{j=1}^{n} b_j.$$

Later we will show how to alter a problem that does not satisfy this assumption so that we have an equivalent problem that does satisfy it.

In order to state the problem mathematically we define the variables v_{ij} to be the amount to be shipped from warehouse W_i to market M_j, for $i = 1, \ldots, m$ and $j = 1, \ldots, n$. It follows that the cost of shipping from W_i to M_j is then $c_{ij}v_{ij}$, and the total cost would be the sum of all these products for all i and j. Also the total amount shipped from W_i is $v_{i1} + v_{i2} + \cdots + v_{in}$ and the total amount shipped to M_j is $v_{1j} + v_{2j} + \cdots + v_{mj}$. Hence the following linear programming problem is to be solved: Minimize

$$(2) \qquad \sum_{i=1}^{m} \sum_{j=1}^{n} c_{ij}v_{ij} = g$$

subject to

(3) $$\sum_{j=1}^{n} v_{ij} = a_i \qquad \text{for } i = 1, \ldots, m,$$

(4) $$\sum_{i=1}^{m} v_{ij} = b_j \qquad \text{for } j = 1, \ldots, n,$$

(5) $$v_{ij} \geq 0 \qquad \text{for all } i \text{ and } j.$$

To recapitulate the meaning of these expressions, note that in (2) we are trying to minimize the total shipping cost subject to (3), which says that the total amount shipped *from* warehouse W_i is equal to the supply a_i there, (4) which says that the total amount shipped *to* market M_j is equal to the demand b_j there, and (5) which is the obvious requirement that shipments should be nonnegative, since negative shipments would have no meaning in the problem at hand.

The matrix C whose entries are c_{ij} for $i = 1, \ldots, m$ and $j = 1, \ldots, n$ will be called the *cost matrix*. The quantities a_i for $i = 1, \ldots, m$ and b_j for $j = 1, \ldots, n$ will be called the *supplies* and *demands*, respectively. Sometimes we will call the a_i's and b_j's the *rim conditions*.

Example 1 (continued). Let us write the data box for the problem in Figure 49. Since $m = n = 3$, we have 9 variables, and since the primal problem is minimizing, we write them on the lefthand side. Also note that (3) and (4) are equations; however, we shall treat them as if they were $\geq$ inequalities. In Exercise 19 you will be asked to show that, because of assumption (1), the optimal solution will make these inequalities into equalities. Since there are m equations of type (3) and n of type (4), we will have $m + n = 3 + 3 = 6$ such inequalities. The resulting 9×6 linear programming problem has the data box shown in Figure 51. Note that all the coefficients in the A matrix are 0's or 1's. Note also the way in which the 1's make a pattern in the matrix. This kind of pattern holds good even for larger transportation problems. In fact, whenever such a pattern exists one should suspect that a transportation problem is involved.

Although we could solve this linear programming problem by the simplex method, we shall instead derive a special version of the method that uses (for the example) the 3×3 data matrix of Figure 49 as the tableau instead of the 9×6 data box of Figure 51. Because this tableau is much smaller and the corresponding calculations easier, we shall see that this method—called the *stepping stone method*—is much more efficient for this problem than the usual simplex method would be.

Any set of mn variables v_{ij} that solve equations (3), (4), and (5) is said to be a *feasible solution* to the problem. A feasible solution that has at most $m + n - 1$ positive entries is said to be a *basic feasible solution*. By *cell* (i, j) we shall mean the (i, j)th entry of the cost matrix. We shall indicate a positive shipment, $v_{ij} > 0$, by putting a circle around c_{ij} and the amount v_{ij} above the circle.

v_{11}	1	0	0	1	0	0	9
v_{12}	1	0	0	0	1	0	1
v_{13}	1	0	0	0	0	1	13
v_{21}	0	1	0	1	0	0	3
v_{22}	0	1	0	0	1	0	2
v_{23}	0	1	0	0	0	1	10
v_{31}	0	0	1	1	0	0	4
v_{32}	0	0	1	0	1	0	16
v_{33}	0	0	1	0	0	1	7
	135	40	25	120	50	30	

Figure 51

We now discuss the so-called *minimum-entry method* for finding an initial basic feasible solution. We outline it in a series of steps as follows:

1. Find the cell (p, q) such that c_{pq} is the smallest cost in the unchecked part of the matrix.
2. Ship as much as possible by cell (p, q); that is, let v_{pq} be the smaller of a_p and b_q and adjust a_p and b_q accordingly. In formula form this is:

$$\text{let} \quad v_{pq} = \text{minimum } (a_p, b_q),$$
$$\text{replace} \quad a_p \text{ by } a_p - v_{pq},$$
$$\text{replace} \quad b_q \text{ by } b_q - v_{pq}.$$

(Note that at the end of this step either a_p or b_q, or both, will be zero.)

3. a. If $a_p = 0$ and $b_q > 0$, check row p. (In this case we have emptied warehouse p but not yet satisfied the demand at market q.)
   b. If $a_p > 0$ and $b_q = 0$, check column q. (In this case we have satisfied market q but not yet emptied warehouse p.)
   c. If both $a_p = 0$ and $b_q = 0$ (the degenerate case), check row p *unless* it is the only unchecked row remaining, in which case check column q.
4. If there are two or more unchecked rows and columns, return to step 1. Otherwise halt, since the starting basic feasible solution will be obtained.

Before we prove that the method above does find an initial solution, we illustrate it on the example of Figure 49.

Example 1 (continued). The smallest entry in the cost matrix of Figure 49 is the 1 in cell $(1, 2)$. Since $a_1 = 135$ and $b_2 = 50$, we make $v_{12} = 50$ as indicated in step 2 above. After carrying out the rest of step 2, we see that $b_2 = 0$, so that in step 3b. we check column 2. The resulting partial solution is indicated in Figure 52. Note that at this step we have completely satisfied the demand at market 2 by using just part of the supply at warehouse 1. Since all three rows and the first and third columns are unchecked, we go back to step 1 as indicated in step 4. The remaining unchecked part of the matrix is in columns 1 and 3, and the smallest entry there is the 3 in cell $(2, 1)$. Since $a_2 = 40$ and $b_1 = 120$, we set $v_{21} = 40$, $a_2 = 0$, $b_1 = 80$, and check row 2, leading to the partial solution in Figure 53. Since we still have

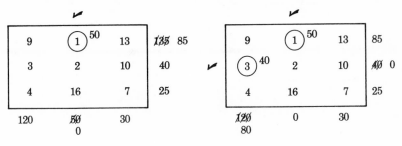

Figure 52   Figure 53

two unchecked rows and columns, we continue the process at step 1 of the method. The smallest entry in the unchecked part of the matrix (rows 1 and 3 and columns 1 and 3) is the 4 entry in cell $(3, 1)$. Since $a_3 = 25$, and $b_1 = 80$, we set $v_{31} = 25$, $a_3 = 0$, $b_1 = 55$, and check row 3. The result is in Figure 54. We still have one unchecked row and two unchecked columns, so we go back to step 1. The unchecked matrix consists now of just cells $(1, 1)$ and $(1, 3)$. The smaller cost, 9, occurs in cell $(1, 1)$, so, upon examining $a_1 = 85$ and $b_1 = 55$, we make $v_{11} = 55$, $a_1 = 30$, and $b_1 = 0$, and check column 1, giving the result in Figure 55. At this point the unchecked part of the matrix consists

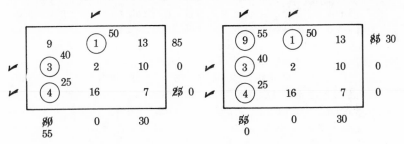

Figure 54   Figure 55

of only cell $(1, 3)$. Since $a_1 = 30 = b_3$, we set $v_{13} = 30$ and make $a_1 = 0$ and $b_1 = 0$. In step 3 we see that we now have the degenerate case (c), and 1 is the only unchecked row, so we check column 3. The new partial solution is shown in Figure 56. In step 4 of the computational scheme we now are instructed to stop, since all the rows have been checked. The reader should now check that the solution given in Figure 56 is a feasible solution. Note that the complete solution is:

$$v_{11} = 55, \qquad v_{12} = 50, \qquad v_{13} = 30,$$
$$v_{21} = 40, \qquad v_{22} = 0, \qquad v_{23} = 0,$$
$$v_{31} = 25, \qquad v_{32} = 0, \qquad v_{33} = 0,$$

since the uncircled cells are assumed to have zero shipments.

By working a few of the exercises, the reader will find this method for finding an initial feasible solution very easy to apply in practice.

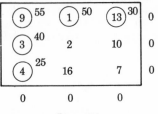

Figure 56

Next we find the cost of the shipping pattern indicated by the initial feasible solution in Figure 56. To do this all we do is multiply each shipping amount by the unit cost, obtaining

$$9 \cdot 55 + 1 \cdot 50 + 13 \cdot 30 + 3 \cdot 40 + 4 \cdot 25 = 495 + 50 + 390 + 120 + 100$$
$$= \$1155.$$

Later we will see that this is not the lowest possible shipping cost.

THEOREM. The minimum-entry method produces a basic feasible solution to any transportation problem.

Proof. Consider the $m \times n$ transportation problem in Figure 50. Initially it has $m + n$ unchecked rows. Each time we go through steps 2 and 3 of the minimum-entry method we check either a row or a column, but not both. We never return to step 1 unless at least one unchecked row and one unchecked column remain. If a single column is left unchecked, we will always check one of the remaining rows if more than two such remain. Finally, we never check a row if it is the only one remaining—hence at the end of the process there is always one unchecked row and no unchecked column (see Figure 56). Hence we will have checked exactly $m + n - 1$ rows and columns, and so we have chosen at most that many nonzero values of the v_{ij}'s. Therefore we have produced a basic feasible solution.

We shall call the set B of $m + n - 1$ cells corresponding to the possible nonnegative shipments of any basic feasible solution the *basis* for the solution. Thus the basis for the solution in Figure 56 consists of the cells

$$B = \{(1, 1), (1, 2), (1, 3), (2, 1), (3, 1)\}.$$

It is easy to see that every row and every column has at least one basis cell in it.

Example 1 (continued). Suppose now we return to Figure 56 and see if there is any way we can improve on the shipping pattern indicated there.

There are nine cells in the matrix, and our initial basic feasible solution has used five of them. Hence we might consider whether or not it would be better to have used one of the four remaining cells instead of the basis cells actually used. For instance, suppose we try to use cell $(2, 2)$, which has a cost of 2. In particular, suppose we try to ship an amount x by this route. We indicate this in Figure 57 by putting a square box around the 2 and an x above it.

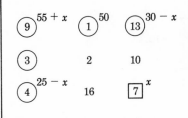

Figure 57

In order to make the shipments along each row and each column add up the rim requirements we must decrease the amount shipped by the basis cells in the same row and column. Hence we must *subtract* x from the amounts shipped by cells $(2, 1)$ and $(1, 2)$. Finally, to correct for these changes in row 1 and column 1 we must *add* x to the amount shipped in cell $(1, 1)$. The reader should now check that for any x the row and column rim requirements of Figure 49 are satisfied. Clearly we will want $x \geq 0$, since we don't want to ship a negative amount by way of cell $(2, 2)$. Also we will want $40 - x$ and $50 - x$ both to be positive, so that we don't ship negative amounts by cells $(2, 1)$ and $(1, 2)$. Hence $0 \leq x \leq 40$ is a possible range of x. For x in this range how will the total shipping cost change? It is easy to see that the change will be found by multiplying $\pm x$ by each of the costs in each cell in which it occurs; that is, the change in cost is

$$2x - 1x + 9x - 3x = (2 - 1 + 9 - 3)x = 7x.$$

This is the addition to the cost over the 1155 already incurred. Since we are minimizing the total costs, it is clear that we should choose $x = 0$; that is, we shouldn't use cell $(2, 2)$ at all, since it will only increase total costs and lead to a worse solution than that already obtained.

Suppose we try the same thing at cell $(3, 3)$. The resulting shipping changes are shown in Figure 58. Here the change in shipping cost will be given by

$$7x - 13x + 9x - 4x = (7 - 13 + 9 - 4)x = -x,$$

Figure 58

so that now it pays to make x positive. Since the expressions $30 - x$ and $25 - x$ must be nonnegative, we see that x is confined in the interval $0 \leq x \leq 25$, and since we want to make it as large as possible we choose $x = 25$. Now we see that the amount shipped by cell $(3, 1)$ is zero, so we can remove it from the basis. Hence, if we introduce cell $(3, 3)$ into the basis to the largest extent possible, we will remove cell $(3, 1)$ from the basis. Setting $x = 25$ leads to the tableau in Figure 59. Note that this solution still has five basis cells and costs $1155 - 25 = 1130$.

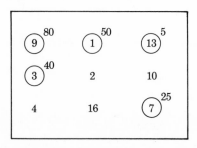

Figure 59

The obvious question now is, is there any way to still further reduce the shipping cost? In Exercise 6 the reader will be asked to show that introducing each of the cells $(2, 2)$, $(2, 3)$, $(3, 1)$, and $(3, 2)$ only *increases* the total shipping cost. We shall shortly state a theorem asserting that when this is the case, we have found the optimum (lowest-cost) shipping solution. We shall also give another proof of this same fact in the next section.

Let us look again at Figure 57. When we tried to introduce cell $(2, 2)$ into the basis, we found that a closed loop or *cycle* was formed as follows: $(2, 2)$, $(1, 2)$, $(1, 1)$, and $(2, 1)$. These four cells have the property that each row and each column of the matrix contains either 0 or 2 of them.

DEFINITION. A *cycle* S is a subset of cells of the cost matrix with the property that each row and each column contains either 0 or 2 cells of S.

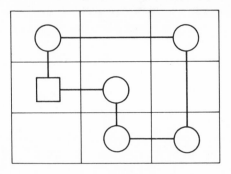

Figure 60

Another example of a cycle is shown in Figure 58 and consists of cells (1, 1), (1, 3), (3, 3), (3, 1). Two other examples are shown in Figures 60 and 61; lines have been drawn to emphasize the cycles.

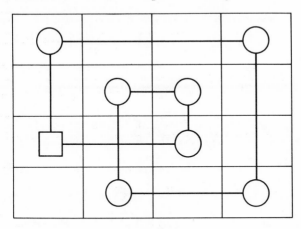

Figure 61

In working small problems by hand, one can easily find cycles by trial and error. In Exercise 8 a method is described that will always find the cycle. Still other, faster, ways available for computers are described in some of the references at the end of the chapter.

LEMMA 1. (a) The basis B of a basic feasible solution is a set of $m + n - 1$ cells, and among these cells there are no cycles.

(b) If any cell not in B is added to B, then a unique cycle is created.

Proof. The proofs of these intuitively obvious facts are outlined in Exercises 24 and 25.

In working Example 1 we tried to add each of the cells not in the basis B to the basis and see what changes would be made in the feasible solution, and also to see if this change would reduce the cost of the shipping pattern. We found that in order to evaluate the cycle we had to go around the cycle and combine the costs in each of the cells in the cycle with alternating plus and minus signs, beginning with a plus sign on the cell being added to the basis.

DEFINITION. Let S be the cycle formed when cell (p, q) is added to the basis B. Start with (p, q) and go around the cycle in either direction, calling the cells alternately "getter" and "giver" cells, with (p, q) being a getter cell. Then the *value of the cycle* is the sum of the costs in the cells in S, with the costs in getter cells having a plus sign and the costs in giver cells having a minus sign.

For instance, in Figure 57 the value of the cycle shown is

$$c_{22} - c_{12} + c_{11} - c_{21} = 2 - 1 + 9 - 3 = 8.$$

And in Figure 58 the value of the cycle is

$$c_{33} - c_{13} + c_{11} - c_{31} = 7 - 13 + 9 - 4 = -1.$$

We found that if a cycle has a negative value, it pays to introduce the cell that created the cycle into the basis and remove some other cell, in the sense that we could reduce the total shipping cost if we did so. But if the value of the cycle is positive or zero, then it does not pay, since we can only increase (or leave the same) the shipping cost.

> **Example 1 (continued).** Let us consider again Figure 58. There we have a unique cycle created when cell $(3, 3)$ is added to the basis. If we go around the cycle, we see that cell $(3, 3)$ is a getter cell, cell $(1, 3)$ is a giver cell, cell $(1, 1)$ is a getter cell, and cell $(3, 1)$ is a giver cell. Since the value of the cycle is negative, it pays to bring cell $(3, 3)$ into the basis to the maximum extent possible. How did we find the maximum extent?—by looking at the *giver* cells around the cycle. In this case there are just two giver cells: $(1, 3)$ can give up to 30 units, and cell $(3, 1)$ can give up to 25 units. Hence we can introduce $(3, 3)$ up to the amount the smallest giver can give, which in this case is 25. When we set $x = 25$, we can readjust the shipments around the cycle as indicated in Figure 58 and then remove cell $(3, 3)$ from the basis, since it now does not ship a positive amount.

DEFINITION. We shall say that a transportation problem is *nondegenerate* if for every feasible solution v_{ij} with basis B we have $v_{ij} > 0$ for all (i, j) in B.

In Exercise 18 you will be asked to show how every problem can be transformed into an equivalent nondegenerate problem.

THEOREM. Let v_{ij} be a solution with basis B to a nondegenerate transportation problem. Then this solution is optimal if and only if the cycle determined when each cell (p, q) not in B is added to B has nonnegative value.

Proof. The proof of this theorem may be sketched as follows. Assume that there is a cell (p, q) not in B that has a negative value. Then, proceeding as in the example above, we can introduce it into the basis and remove the minimum giver cell on the cycle from the basis. Since the minimum giver cell will give a positive amount by the assumption of nondegeneracy, this transformation will actually decrease the total cost of shipping, hence the original solution was not optimal. On the other hand, suppose every cell not in the basis B determines a cycle with nonnegative value. We know that introducing each such cell into the solution by itself can only increase the shipping cost (or leave it the same). And if we introduce two or more cells simultaneously, it is easy to show that their effects are additive, so that such changes can only increase or leave unchanged the total shipping cost. Since we can go from the current shipping solution to any other feasible solution by adding cells to B and adjusting the amounts shipped accordingly, there is no other feasible solution better than the current one, and therefore the current solution v_{ij} is optimal.

The procedures and results above can now be formalized into the so-called *stepping-stone method* for solving transportation problems. The flow diagram for this method appears in Figure 62. In box 2 it is suggested

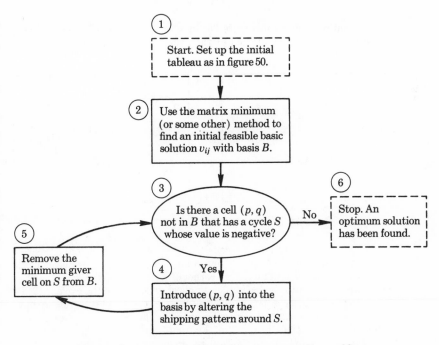

The stepping-stone method for solving transportation problems

Figure 62

that there are other methods for finding initial basic feasible solutions. Another method is given in Exercises 21 and 22.

Example 2. Let us apply Figure 62 to the problem whose initial tableau is given in Figure 63. The matrix minimum method introduces cell $(2, 1)$, which ships 20, then cell $(3, 2)$, shipping 20 also, then cell $(2, 2)$, shipping 10, and then cells $(2, 3)$ and $(2, 1)$, which ship 25 each. The initial solution, which costs 525, is shown in Figure 64.

Cell $(1, 1)$ creates cycle $(1, 1)$, $(1, 2)$, $(2, 2)$, $(2, 1)$ in the basis B (which consists of the circled cells in Figure 64). The value of this cycle is $4 - 1 + 4 - 9 = -4$, so that it pays to bring it into the basis. In the cycle the giver

cells are (2, 1) and (1, 2) and the smallest giver is (1, 2), which can give 20.
Hence we bring (1, 1) into the basis and remove (1, 2) by alternately adding
and subtracting 20 from the shipments around the cycle. The resulting basic

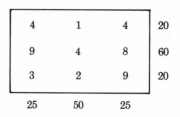

4	1	4	20
9	4	8	60
3	2	9	20
25	50	25	

Figure 63

feasible solution is given in Figure 65; its cost is $525 - 4 \cdot 20 = 485$. To see
if it is optimal we evaluate each of the cycles determined by the nonbasic
cells.

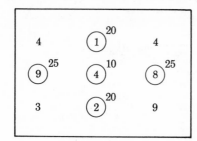

Figure 64

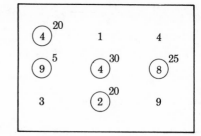

Figure 65

The cycles determined by cells (1, 2), (1, 3), and (3, 3) have positive
value, but the value of the cycle determined by cell (3, 1) (which consists
of the four cells in the lower lefthand corner of Figure 65) is $3 - 2 + 4 - 9 = -4$, so we bring it into the basis. The smallest giver cell on the cycle is (2, 1),
which can give 5; hence, after readjusting shipments around the cycle we have
the basic feasible solution of Figure 66, which costs $485 - 4 \cdot 5 = 465$. Again
we follow the directions in box 3 of Figure 62 to see if we can improve on
this solution. Cells (1, 2), (2, 1), and (3, 3) have positive values. The cycle
for cell (1, 3) is connected by lines in Figure 66. The value of this cycle is
$4 - 8 + 4 - 2 + 3 - 4 = -3$, so that it pays to bring (1, 3) into the basis.

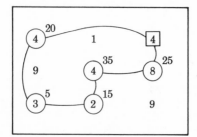

Figure 66

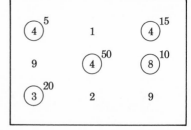

Figure 67

The smallest giver on the cycle is cell (3, 2), which can give 15. Hence we rearrange shipments around the cycle by alternately adding and subtracting 15, and we arrive at the feasible solution of Figure 67. The cost of the shipping solution in Figure 67 is $465 - 3 \cdot 15 = 420$. The reader should now check that each of the four nonbasic cells in that figure has positive value, so that the solution given there is the optimal solution to the problem stated in Figure 63.

Each time we go around the loop of the flow diagram in Figure 62 we make a change just like the pivoting operation in linear programming method previously described. We also shall call the process illustrated here of adding a cell to the basis and removing another cell from the basis *pivoting*. Hence in Example 2 it was necessary to pivot three times from the initial solution to solve the problem. But in Example 1 only one pivot was needed.

Example 3. We consider another example that will show what happens when the problem is degenerate. Consider the tableau in Figure 68. Note that

9	1	13	50
3	2	5	120
4	16	7	30
120	50	30	

Figure 68

the supply in warehouse 1 equals the demand in market 2, the supply in warehouse 2 equals the demand in market 1, and the supply in warehouse 3 equals the demand in market 3. Applying the minimum-entry method to the problem, we see that the smallest entry is the 1 in cell (1, 2), so we ship the maximum amount by this route, which is 50. The result is shown in Figure 69.

Note that we have simultaneously emptied warehouse 1 and supplied all the demand in market 2. We cross out row 1 according to step 3(c) of the minimum-entry method. The next available smallest entry is the 2 in cell

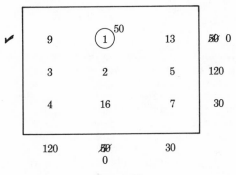

Figure 69

$(2, 2)$. Here we compare the amount in warehouse 2, which is 120, with the amount demanded in market 2, which is now 0! So we can ship only zero by this route. We do this and cross out column 2, giving the result in Figure 70.

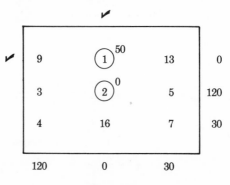

Figure 70

The appearance of a zero shipment in a basis cell means that we have a degenerate solution, but this will not cause difficulty in finding the initial basic feasible solution. On the next step we choose the next lowest cost, which is the 3 in cell $(2, 1)$, and ship the maximum amount, leading to the result in Figure 71.

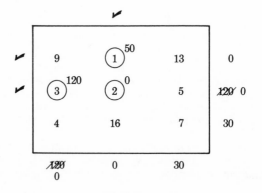

Figure 71

Again we have simultaneously emptied warehouse 2 and satisfied market 1, which is indicative of a degenerate problem. We cross out row 2 according to the rule in step 3(c) of the minimum-entry method. On the next step we consider smallest remaining cost, the 4 in cell $(3, 1)$, and ship 0 by it, and on the step after that we ship 30 by the cell $(3, 3)$, leading to the initial feasible basic solution given in Figure 72.

The cost of this solution is $1 \cdot 50 + 3 \cdot 120 + 7 \cdot 30 = 620$. We now apply box 3 of the flow diagram in Figure 62 and check the nonbasis cells to see if any has negative value. It is easy to see that cell $(2, 3)$ has value $5 - 7 + 4 - 3 = -1$, so that it should be brought into the basis. If it is brought into the basis the smallest giver cell on the cycle $S = \{(2, 3), (3, 3), (3, 1), (2, 3)\}$

is cell (3, 3), which can give 30. Adding and subtracting 30 around the cycle and removing (3, 3) from the basis leads to the final tableau in Figure 73.

The cost of this solution is $620 - 1 \cdot 30 = 590$, and a check of each nonbasis cell shows that they all have positive value. Hence the shipping solution in Figure 73 is the optimum one for the problem.

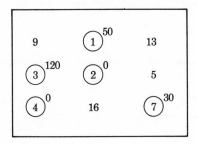

Figure 72   Figure 73

EXERCISES

1. Use the minimum-entry method to find initial basic feasible solutions to the following problems.

   a.

3	5	50
9	4	50
40	60	

   [*Ans.* $v_{11} = 40$, $v_{12} = 10$, $v_{22} = 50$, cost $= 370$.]

   b.

11	14	13	16	95
18	20	24	14	118
63	31	26	93	

   [*Ans.* $v_{11} = 63$, $v_{12} = 6$, $v_{13} = 26$, $v_{22} = 25$, $v_{24} = 93$, cost $= 2917$.]

   c.

11	12	24	90
21	18	5	61
9	8	16	49
52	68	80	

   [*Ans.* $v_{11} = 52$, $v_{12} = 19$, $v_{13} = 19$, $v_{23} = 61$, $v_{32} = 49$, cost $= 1953$.]

2. For each problem in Exercise 1 apply the stepping-stone method in Figure 62 to find the optimal solution.

[*Ans.* (*a*) Initial solution is optimal. (*b*) Initial solution is optimal. (*c*) One pivot is needed. Optimal solution is: $v_{11} = 52$, $v_{12} = 38$, $v_{23} = 61$, $v_{32} = 30$, $v_{33} = 19$, cost $= 1877$.]

3. For a certain problem the initial tableau is as follows:

6	9	8	48
6	21	18	30
9	17	10	68
38	64	44	

a. Find the initial solution when cell (1, 1) is brought into the basis first.   [*Partial Ans.* The cost is 1856.]

b. Find the initial solution when cell (2, 1) is brought into the basis first.   [*Partial Ans.* Cost $= 1676$.]

c. Show that with the starting solution in (*a*) three pivots are needed to get the optimum answer, which is $v_{12} = 48$, $v_{21} = 30$, $v_{31} = 8$, $v_{32} = 16$, $v_{33} = 44$, cost $= 1396$.

d. Show that with the starting solution in (*b*) only two pivots are needed.

4. Given the problem:

15	6	7	17	27
9	8	13	9	45
8	17	20	14	54
45	23	7	51	

a. Show that the initial basic solution costs 1075

b. Show that the optimum solution can be obtained in one pivot.

[*Ans.* $v_{12} = 20$, $v_{13} = 7$, $v_{22} = 3$, $v_{24} = 42$, $v_{31} = 45$, $v_{34} = 9$, cost $= 1057$.]

5. Given the 3 × 4 problem:

12	24	22	21	75
5	15	9	8	66
12	13	18	21	57
68	36	42	52	

a. Show that the initial basic solution costs 2754.

b. Show that three pivots are needed to get the optimum answer.

[*Ans.* $v_{11} = 68$, $v_{14} = 7$, $v_{23} = 21$, $v_{24} = 45$, $v_{32} = 36$, $v_{33} = 21$, cost $= 2358$.]

    c. Show that another basic optimal solution is: $v_{11} = 68$, $v_{13} = 7$, $v_{23} = 14$, $v_{24} = 52$, $v_{32} = 36$, $v_{33} = 21$.

6. Refer to Figure 59.
    a. Show that the value of the cycle determined by cell $(2, 2)$ is $+7$.
    b. The value of the cycle for cell $(2, 3)$ is $+3$.
    c. The value of the cycle for cell $(3, 1)$ is $+1$.
    d. The value of the cycle for cell $(3, 2)$ is $+21$.
    e. Use these results to show that the solution indicated in the figure is the optimum.

7. *a.* In Figure 60 show that the value of the cycle shown is

$$c_{21} - c_{11} + c_{13} - c_{33} + c_{32} - c_{22}.$$

    b. In Figure 61 show that the value of the cycle shown is

$$c_{31} - c_{11} + c_{14} - c_{44} + c_{42} - c_{22} + c_{23} - c_{33}.$$

8. Consider a transportation problem with initial basic solution and basis B, and suppose we are adding a cell (p, q) to B and trying to find the unique cycle it determines. The following *crossing-out* algorithm will find the cycle:

    0. Start with the (unchecked) cost matrix and basis B and set $B^* = B \cup \{(p, q)\}$.
    1. If there is a cell in the unchecked region of the matrix that is unique in its row (that is, it is the only cell of B^* in its row), check that row and remove the cell from B^*; similarly, if there is a cell that is unique in its column, check that column and remove the cell from B^*.
    2. Stop when there are no more cells that are unique in their row or column. The remaining cells of B^* form a cycle (see Exercise 11.)

Apply this algorithm to find the cycle in Figure 57.
    [*Ans.* Column 3 and row 3 are checked in either order, leaving the cells in the upper lefthand corner of the matrix, which do form a cycle.]

9. Apply the crossing-out routine to determine the cycle in Figure 58.

10. Apply the crossing-out routine to the tableaus you generated in the solutions of Exercises 1–5.

11. Prove that the crossing-out routine of Exercise 8 does produce the required cycle by carrying out the following steps:
    a. Show that initially we have $m + n$ rows and columns in the cost matrix, and $m + n$ cells in B^*.
    b. Show that each time we check a row or column in the matrix and remove a cell from B^* we keep the equality between the number of remaining rows and columns and the number of cells of B^*.
    c. Show that at the conclusion of step 2 of the algorithm each remaining (unchecked) row or column has at least two cells of B^* in it.
    d. By a counting argument, show that each remaining row or column cannot have more than two cells of B^* in it.
    e. Use *c.* and *d.* to show that the remaining cells form a cycle.

12. Draw a flow diagram for the minimum-entry start method described in the text.

13. Consider the following problem:

	M_1	M_2	M_3	M_4	
W_1	9	1	13	0	150
W_2	3	2	10	0	50
W_3	4	16	7	0	40
	120	50	30	40	

a. Show it is just the problem in Figure 49 but with warehouse supplies increased.
b. Show that M_4 can be regarded as a "dummy" market and that shipments to it correspond to surplus amounts retained in warehouses.
c. Give a rationale for the 0 costs in column 4. Can you think of other costs that would be reasonable here?
d. Show that the solution to this problem is: $v_{11} = 60$, $v_{12} = 50$, $v_{14} = 40$, $v_{21} = 50$, $v_{31} = 10$, $v_{33} = 30$, cost = 990. Interpret the v_{14} shipment.

14. Rework Exercise 13 with the following problem (see Figure 63):

4	1	4	0	40
9	4	8	0	70
3	2	9	0	30
25	50	25	40	

[*Ans.* $v_{12} = 15$, $v_{13} = 25$, $v_{22} = 30$, $v_{24} = 40$, $v_{31} = 25$, $v_{32} = 5$, cost = 320.]

15. Consider the following problem:

	M_1	M_2	M_3	
W_1	9	1	13	135
W_2	3	2	10	40
W_3	4	16	7	25
W_4	0	0	0	30
	135	55	40	

a. Show that it is just the problem in Figure 49 but with market demands increased.
b. Show that W_4 can be regarded as a "dummy" warehouse and that shipments by it correspond to amounts withheld from or rationed to the various markets.
c. Give a rationale for the 0 costs in row 4. Can you think of other costs that would be reasonable here?

   d. Show that the solution to this problem is: $v_{11} = 80$, $v_{12} = 55$, $v_{21} = 40$, $v_{31} = 15$, $v_{33} = 10$, $v_{43} = 30$, cost $= 1025$. Interpret the v_{43} shipment.

16. Rework Exercise 15 with the following problem (see Figure 63):

4	1	4	20
9	4	8	60
3	2	9	20
0	0	0	25
35	60	30	

[*Ans.* $v_{11} = 15$, $v_{13} = 5$, $v_{22} = 60$, $v_{31} = 20$, $v_{43} = 25$, cost $= 380$.]

17. Replace the problem in Figure 68 by the following:

9	1	13	0	50.1
3	2	5	0	120.1
4	16	7	0	30.1
120	50	30	.3	

   a. Show that the initial feasible solution has positive shipments on all basis cells, so that it is not degenerate.
   b. Solve the problem completely.
   c. Round off the answers to the nearest integer you got in *b.* and show they are just those in Figure 73.

*18. For the problem in Figure 50 show that by adding a small amount to each warehouse supply and adding a dummy market to make the sum of the supplies add up to the sum of the demands it is always possible to replace the problem given there by an equivalent problem that is not degenerate.

*19. Consider the problem in (2), (3), (4), and (5). Show that if we treat (3) and (4) as $\geq$ constraints, then:
   a. The minimum-cost solution to the problem will force the $\geq$ constraints corresponding to (4) to be $=$ constraints.
   b. Because of assumption (1) the result of (*a*) will force the $\geq$ constraints corresponding to (3) to become $=$ constraints also.
   c. Use this result to show that the solution to Figure 51 will also be the solution to the problem in Figure 49.

*20. *a.* Write the dual problem to the problem in Figure 51.
   b. Write the dual problem to the one given in expressions (2)–(5).

*21. The so-called "northwest-corner rule" for finding an initial feasible basic solution is:

   0. Start with the unchecked cost matrix and rim conditions.
   1. Ship the maximum amount by the northwest-corner (upper lefthand) cell and change the rim conditions accordingly.

2. If this shipment empties the warehouse, check the first row of the unchecked matrix; otherwise check the first column.
3. If there are unchecked rows and columns of the matrix, go to step (1). Otherwise stop.

Show that this procedure leads to the following initial solution for the problem in Figure 49.

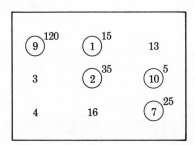

The cost of this solution is 1390.

22. Apply the northwest-corner rule to the problem in Figure 62.

[*Partial Ans.* Cost = 545.]

23. Based on your experience with the northwest-corner rule in Exercises 21 and 22, criticize its effectiveness. What are its advantages and disadvantages?

*24. Prove Lemma 1(a) by carrying out the following steps:

   i. Since a basic feasible solution has $m + n - 1$ cells and there are $m + n$ rows and columns, at least one row or column has a unique cell in it.
   ii. If we cross out the row or column found in (i), we obtain another problem with one fewer row or column and one fewer basis cell.
   iii. Iterate the process in (ii) and show that we will cross out all cells. Hence show that there can be no cycles.

*25. Prove Lemma 1(b) by showing that the crossing-out routine of Exercise 8 leads to a unique result.

9. APPLICATIONS OF TRANSPORTATION PROBLEMS

Many practical problems can be formulated as transportation problems and solved by the methods developed in the previous section. We shall illustrate a few of the wide variety of such problems here.

Example 1. *The Assignment Problem.* Suppose that we have n men and n jobs, and we have determined for the ith man and the jth job the training cost, c_{ij}, to make the ith man ready for the jth job. How can we assign one man to each of the jobs in order to minimize the overall training cost? This is the so-called assignment problem.

We have illustrated this problem in Figure 74, in which five men are to be assigned to five jobs. The training costs of assigning each man to each of the jobs appear in each row of the matrix. Around the sides of the matrix the rim conditions are all set equal to 1, since each man is available for one job, and each job needs one man.

Job Number

	1	2	3	4	5	
John	10	65	32	29	14	1
Joe	58	26	92	12	17	1
Bill	39	16	43	13	29	1
Jack	14	37	42	60	15	1
Henry	45	12	14	35	20	1
	1	1	1	1	1	

Figure 74

The minimum-cost solution (obtained by a computer) to the problem is to ship one unit by each of cells $(1, 1)$, $(2, 4)$, $(3, 2)$, $(4, 5)$, and $(5, 3)$. In other words, the minimum-cost solution assigns John to job 1, Joe to job 4, Bill to job 2, Jack to job 5, and Henry to job 3. The cost of the optimum solution is 67 units. The reader can easily verify by trial and error that there is no lower-cost solution.

More generally, any square transportation problem in which all the rim conditions are 1's is called an assignment problem. These occur very often in practice; other applications that present them are given in the exercises. Very fast computer methods have been devised to solve assignment problems.

Example 2. *Production Scheduling.* The Acme Widget company is planning its production scheduling for the months of November, December, and January, during which time it grants extra vacation for the Christmas holidays. Each widget requires one man-hour of labor, which costs the company $1.60 in regular wages or $2.40 in overtime wages. The company expects demands for 900 widgets in November, 1500 in December, and 1200 in January. It costs the company $.50 per month to store a widget made in advance. If it has 1000 regular-time hours in November, 600 in December, and 1000 in January, and never allocates more than half as many overtime hours as regular-time hours, how shall the company meet its production demands at minimum total cost?

The transportation problem in Figure 75 is set up to solve this production scheduling problem. Notice that the six rows are labeled November regular, November overtime, December regular, December overtime, January regular, and January overtime. Opposite each row is the number of regular or overtime hours available in the corresponding month. The four columns are labeled November, December, January, and Surplus. The first three columns indicate the monthly demands for widgets, which are listed on the bottom, and the Surplus column represents surplus hours, and is needed since the sum of all the regular and overtime hours is 300 larger than the total number of widgets demanded over the three-month period. Let us look at the costs in the first column. The 1.6 entry in the first row is the unit cost of making a widget in November for November's demand, and the 2.4 entry in the second row is the overtime cost of making the widget in November for use then. The remaining entries are each 100, which is simply a sufficiently large number that the corresponding cell cannot be used in any optimum solution. The reason we don't want to use December or January regular or overtime for producing for November demand is, of course, that it is an infeasible way to meet such demand.

	November	December	January	Surplus	
Nov. Regular	1.6	2.1	2.6	0	1000
Nov. Overtime	2.4	2.9	3.4	0	500
Dec. Regular	100	1.6	2.1	0	600
Dec. Overtime	100	2.4	2.9	0	300
Jan. Regular	100	100	1.6	0	1000
Jan. Overtime	100	100	2.4	0	500
	900	1500	1200	300	

Hours (to the right of the 600/300 rows)

Demand for Widgets   Surplus Hours

Figure 75

The costs in the second column have a similar interpretation. The 2.1 cost in the first row of the second column represents the per-unit cost of producing the widget in November, which is $1.60, plus the storage cost of $.50 needed to hold the unit for one month. The 2.9 cost in the second row is similarly the overtime cost of 2.4 plus $.50 storage cost. The 1.6 and 2.4 entries in the next two rows are just the regular and overtime costs of producing in December's demand. The entries in the last two rows are 100 to prevent satisfying December's demand from January's production. The entries in the third column can be explained similarly. The zero entries in the fourth column are simply to indicate that extra hours may remain unused at zero cost wherever they may occur.

The optimum solution, again found by a computer, appears in Figure 76. Note that we supply all of November's demand by regular time work in November, and we also use 100 hours of regular time in November to make 100 widgets to be put in inventory for December's demand. We also use 500 hours of overtime in November to store widgets for December's demand. Then in December we use all the regular and overtime to fulfill the rest of December's demand. Notice that the unit cost of production for December varies from 1.6 to 2.9 dollars per unit. This happens because we simultaneously have a large demand and a small labor supply during that month. All of the demand for January is supplied by use of the regular time of 1000 hours plus 200 of the overtime hours. The remaining 300 overtime hours are not used by the solution, which is indicated by the use of the (6, 4) cell.

The total cost of the solution appearing in Figure 76 is $6,860; and this is the cheapest way of supplying demand for widgets during the three-month period, given the constraints on the labor supply.

	November	December	January	Surplus	
Nov. Regular	(1.6) 900	(2.1) 100	2.6	0	1000
Nov. Overtime	2.4	(2.9) 500	3.4	0	500
Dec. Regular	100	(1.6) 600	2.1	0	600
Dec. Overtime	100	(2.4) 300	2.9	(0) 0	300
Jan. Regular	100	100	(1.6) 1000	0	1000
Jan. Overtime	100	100	(2.4) 200	(0) 300	500
	900	1500	1200	300	

Figure 76

Obviously the model can be extended to cover periods of several months (or other time units such as weeks) and to handle more than two kinds of labor. It is clear that such extensions quickly lead to quite large transportation problems for which a computer is essential.

Example 3. *The Caterer Problem.* A certain caterer knows that he will need 80, 40, 110, and 70 napkins for the next four days. He has no napkins on hand, but he can buy them new for $.40 each. Two kinds of laundry services are available to wash dirty napkins: a fast one-day service costs $.20 per napkin, while a slow two-day service costs $.12 per napkin. How many napkins should he buy, and how many should he have laundered by each of the services in order to minimize his costs?

It is easy to think of other interpretations of this problem. For instance, instead of napkins we can think of mechanical equipment such as an engine, and instead of laundry services we can think of maintenance and repair services.

	Day 1	Day 2	Day 3	Day 4	Surplus	
Napkins Bought New	.4	.4	.4	.4	0	300
Dirty Napkins from Day 1	100	.2	.12	.12	0	80
Dirty Napkins from Day 2	100	100	.2	.12	0	40
Dirty Napkins from Day 3	100	100	100	.2	0	110
	80	40	110	70	230	

Figure 77

Figure 77 gives a transportation-problem tableau that will solve the present problem. On the lefthand side are listed the various sources of supply for napkins: first napkins bought new; then dirty napkins from day 1 that can be laundered and used for later needs, then dirty napkins from days 2 and 3. On the right are the supplies from each of these "sources." The 300 in the first row indicates the maximum number of napkins that would ever be bought—namely the total demand on all four days, which is 300. In the second-row rim condition we have the dirty napkins from the first day, in the third and fourth rows the dirty napkins from the second and third days. On the top are listed days 1 through 4, which play the role of the "markets" in the problem. The various needs for each day are listed in the rim conditions on the bottom.

Now let us explain the cost entries. The costs in the Surplus column on the right are all zero, meaning that unused supplies can be stored at zero cost. In the first column the entry in the first row is .4, which is the unit cost of new napkins purchased to meet the first day's demands. The rest of the costs in the first column are all 100, meaning that it is very expensive to wash dirty napkins from days 1, 2, or 3 to be used on day 1! In fact, of course, no optimal solution will make use of these cells with large costs. In column 2 the first entry is again the cost of new napkins, the second entry is the cost, .2, of laundering a dirty napkin from day 1 by the fast laundry service so that it will be ready for use on day 2, and the rest of the entries are large costs to prevent physically impossible plans. In the third column the first entry is the cost of new napkins, the second entry the cost of laundering dirty napkins from the first day by the slow laundry service for use on the third day, and the last two entries have the same explanation as before. The entries in column 4 are explained similarly. The rim condition for column 5, which is 230, is just the difference between the sum of all the supplies and the sum of all the demands.

The problem was solved by a computer; the solution is displayed in Figure 78. Notice that 80 new napkins were bought new for the first day's

	Day 1	Day 2	Day 3	Day 4	Surplus	
Napkins Bought New	(.4)80	(.4)30	.4	.4	(0)190	300
Dirty Napkins from Day 1	100	(.2)10	(.12)70	.12	0	80
Dirty Napkins from Day 2	100	100	(.2)40	.12	0	40
Dirty Napkins from Day 3	100	100	100	(.2)70	(0)40	110
	80	40	110	70	230	

Figure 78

demand. To meet the second day's demand 30 new napkins were purchased, and 10 dirty napkins from the first day were laundered by the fast service. To meet the third day's demand, 70 napkins from the first day were laundered by the slow laundry service and all 40 dirty napkins from the second day were washed by the fast laundry service. Demand for the fourth day was supplied by washing 70 dirty napkins from the third day by means of the fast laundry service. It is also interesting to interpret the two entries in the Surplus column. The 190 entry in the first row means that of the total demand for 300 napkins, 190 of the demand was supplied by washed rather than new napkins; or to put it differently, 110 new napkins were purchased, and the remaining demand was supplied by rewashed napkins. The entry of 40 in the (4, 5) cell means that 40 of the dirty napkins from day 3 were not washed and used for day 4's demand.

Notice that at the end of day 4 there are 70 dirty napkins from day 4 plus 40 dirty napkins left over from day 3, making a total of 110 dirty napkins.

In other words this solution leaves all the napkins dirty. In Exercise 12 a way is suggested to extend the problem and end up with all napkins clean.

EXERCISES

1. Fred, Charlie, and Pete all work for the same company and are to be assigned to handle three one-day jobs in each of three cities. Their distances from the cities are:

	City 1	City 2	City 3
Fred	10	8	40
Charlie	30	20	18
Pete	14	12	30

If each man is to be assigned one job, find the assignment that minimizes total travel time.

[*Ans.* Fred—city 1, Pete—city 2, Charlie—city 3.]

2. Show that there is another optimal solution in which Fred and Pete change assignments.

3. Consider the following project diagram:

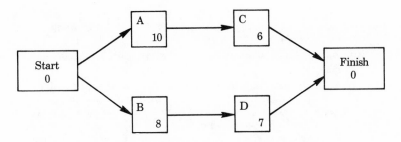

Show that the solution of the assignment problem below will find the *shortest path* from Start to Finish.

	A	B	C	D	Finish	
Start	10	8	100	100	100	1
A	0	100	6	100	100	1
B	100	0	100	7	100	1
C	100	100	0	100	0	1
D	100	100	100	0	0	1
	1	1	1	1	1	

4. Show that if the times in the assignment problem above are changed from positive to negative, the solution will locate the *longest path* from Start to Finish. Show that the cost of the optimum solution will be the negative of the length of the longest path.

5. Rework Exercise 3 if arrows are added between jobs A and D, and between jobs B and C. [*Hint:* Change the cost in cell (2, 4) from 100 to 7, and change the cost in cell (3, 3) from 100 to 6.]

6. Rework Exercise 4 with the same changes as in Exercise 5.

7. In Figure 76 show that the average cost of widget production is 1.6 in November, 2.23 in December, and 1.73 in January. If the manufacturer could subcontract widget production at a unit cost of 2.5 per widget, how would the solution change?

8. In Figure 75 suppose the demands are 1200, 1000, and 1200 for November, December, and January, respectively. Rework the problem by inspection and verify that your answer is optimal.

9. The widget manufacturer also has a vacation problem during the summer months of June, July, and August. The monthly demands and available hours for these months are:

	June	July	August
Demand	900	1200	900
Hours	1000	600	600

The hours shown are for regular time, and the overtime hours available are half of the regular-time hours. Set up the new problem and solve it by inspection.

10. Set up the caterer problem for demands of 70, 100, 60, and 90 on the next four days. If you are ambitious, solve it.

11. *a.* In the caterer problem show that it is necessary to buy at least as many napkins as are needed on the highest-demand day.

  b. Show that it does not pay to buy more than the number demanded on the highest-demand day.

  c. Conclude that the number bought will equal the highest number demanded on any one day.

12. Use the result of Exercise 11 to show that the solution to the following problem will wash all napkins and have them ready by day 6.

	Day 1	Day 2	Day 3	Day 4	Day 6	
Napkins Bought	.4	.4	.4	.4	100	110
Dirty Napkins from Day 1	100	.2	.12	.12	.12	80
Dirty Napkins from Day 2	100	100	.2	.12	.12	40
Dirty Napkins from Day 3	100	100	100	.2	.12	110
Dirty Napkins from Day 4	100	100	100	100	.12	70
	80	40	110	70	110	

*13. Set up a general tableau for the production smoothing problem over a period of n months, with arbitrary regular-time, overtime, and storage costs.

*14. Set up a general tableau for a caterer problem over n days with arbitrary purchase price, and fast and slow laundering costs.

*15. Consider an arbitrary transportation problem with an optimal solution having a basis B. If a cell (p, q) not in B determines a cycle with *zero* value, show that (p, q) can be brought into the basis, and some other cell taken out, and that the resulting solution is an *alternate optimal solution* to the problem. [*Hint:* See Exercises 1 and 2.]

SUGGESTED READING

Charnes, A., and W. W. Cooper, *Management Models and Industrial Applications of Linear Programming*, Wiley, New York, 1961, 2 vols.

Dantzig, G. B., *Linear Programming and Extensions*, Princeton University Press, Princeton, N. J., 1963.

Hillier, F. S., and G. J. Lieberman, *Introduction to Operations Research*, Holden-Day, San Francisco, 1967.

Spivey, W. A., and R. M. Thrall, *Linear Optimization*, Holt, Rinehart and Winston, New York, 1970.

Tucker, A. W., "Combinatorial Algebra of Matrix Games and Linear Programming," in E. F. Beckenbach, ed., *Applied Combinatorial Mathematics*, Wiley, New York, 1964, pp. 320–347.

Wagner, H. M., *Principles of Operations Research with Applications to Managerial Decisions*, Prentice-Hall, Englewood Cliffs, N. J., 1969.

6

DECISION THEORY
AND ANALYSIS

1. INTRODUCTION

Some business decision problems can be thought of as a sequence of "acts" and "events." The decision maker first chooses an act out of a set of possible alternatives, then one out of a set of possible events occurs "by chance," then another act can be chosen from a set of alternatives made available by the preceding act-event sequence, then another event occurs, and so on. Sometimes two or more choices of act can occur without an intervening event, and sometimes two or more events can occur without an intervening act, but for descriptive purposes we can treat such sequences as "compound" acts or events. Sometimes the entire "sequence" can be simply a choice of one out of a set of acts followed by the realization of one out of a set of events. Where no substantial uncertainty is involved, the whole decision problem may consist simply in the choice of a single (possibly compound) act; many mathematical programming problems (Chapter 5) are of this sort. In the present chapter, however, we shall discuss problems in which the consequences of at least some acts are uncertain events.

> **Example 1.** The Loan Department of the Tenth National Bank has received a request for an 18-month loan of $1000 from Mr. I. M. Broke. Mr. Broke is asked to fill out a credit application, which he hands to a loan officer who has three initial acts among which to choose: (1) grant the loan immediately, (2) refuse the loan immediately, (3) obtain direct information from Mr. Broke's credit references. If he chooses the third act, the loan officer will receive information (an event) which, for present purposes, we can classify into one of three categories: (1) favorable, (2) unfavorable, (3) mixed. For each of these outcomes he is then free to (1) grant the loan, (2) refuse the loan, (3) verify additional statements on Mr. Broke's application. (It would appear to be foolish for the loan officer to grant the loan if the information were unfavor-

able and to refuse it if it were favorable, and indeed it can be proved under some very reasonable assumptions that such a strategy would be foolish. We lose nothing at this stage, however, by keeping all options—even foolish ones —open.) If the third act is chosen, the loan officer will receive additional information (an event): the statements on the application are either (1) true, or (2) false. In either case, he must now decide whether (1) to grant or (2) to refuse the loan. Following a decision to grant the loan at any stage in the process, some one out of a large number of possible events will occur: either the loan will be paid back on schedule, or it will be paid back in full but on a delayed schedule with additional interest (notice that this gross description has many detailed realizations depending on which one of the thousands of possible specific repayment rates actually occurs), or Mr. Broke will go bankrupt and a settlement will be made (again many possibilities), or Mr. Broke will skip town without repaying anything.

Even in an example as straightforward as this one, it is apparent that the purely structural aspects of a business decision problem may be hard to define. It is seldom a simple task to think out all the alternatives available at a given stage, to anticipate all the possible events emanating from a given choice of act, and to specify correctly the time sequence of acts and events. And even if the structuring is correctly done, the subsequent analysis may tax our computing capabilities, even when those capabilities include the use of large-scale computers. As a result, in applications of decision theory and analysis to real business problems, a purely formal mathematical approach must frequently be supplemented by some informal common sense to cut the problem down to tractable size.

In order to get started on the mathematical aspects of decision theory without getting bogged down in structural detail, we shall look first at problems in which the act-event sequence is as simple as possible. That is, we shall look at decision problems in which an initial choice of act is followed by one out of a set of possible events, after which the problem terminates. As we shall see, this simplification is less restrictive than we might at first believe: problems involving longer act-event sequences can always be analyzed using small extensions of the procedures we develop here.

In the framework described, a decision problem can be characterized by a set of acts $A = \{a_1, \ldots, a_j, \ldots, a_n\}$ that we can perform, a set of possible events $E = \{e_1, \ldots, e_i, \ldots, e_m\}$ representing chance events or actions over which we have no control, and for each act-event pair a consequence $c(e_i, a_j)$ that describes what happens when event e_i occurs after the choice of act a_j.

Sometimes a consequence involves only cash flows, so that $c(e_i, a_j) = c_{ij}$ is an ordinary matrix as in Example 2 below. But in other cases $c(e_i, a_j)$ may also involve a number of intangibles such as good will, share of market, steadiness of earnings growth, leadership position in the community, and so on. Example 3 below is such a case.

Even in situations where only cash flows are involved, such flows may occur over time in ways that require them to be distinguished. For instance, a decision maker would certainly want to distinguish between (a) a two-year cash flow resulting in a loss of $10 million in year 1 followed by a gain of $11 million in year 2, and (b) a flow consisting of a gain of $.5 million in each of the two years, even though the total net flow over the two years is the same in both cases.

Example 2. The XYZ company has been invited by the ABC company to submit a bid to produce 10,000 units of a product. XYZ already owns the necessary machinery, has the required capacity available, and can produce the 10,000 units at a total variable cost of $100,000. The company has been instructed to submit bids at an integral number of dollars per unit, with the understanding that only one other company is bidding against XYZ, and that the contract will go to the lowest bidder. If both bids are identical, the contract will go to XYZ's rival. The management of XYZ believes that a bid in excess of $14 per unit is virtually certain to lose; a bid of $10 per unit or less would result in no net profit; so that the set of feasible acts consists of bids of $11, $12, $13, or $14 per unit. From XYZ's point of view, the possible events are its rival's possible bids. These bids can be classified as $11 or less, $12, $13, $14, or $15 or more. The other bidder can be sure to win the contract by bidding $11 or less, no matter what XYZ does; XYZ will surely win if its rival bids $15 or more. In Figure 1 a so-called "payoff table," which in this case is a matrix, shows the consequences (in terms of net profit to XYZ) for every relevant act-event combination.

In problems where the number of possible acts and/or events is really very large—for example, if bids could be submitted in integral numbers of cents instead of dollars—the size of a payoff table may become impractically large. It may, nevertheless, be perfectly practical to express the entries in such a table symbolically, by means of a mathematical formula. (See Exercise 4.)

Acts: XYZ Bids

		a_1: $11	a_2: $12	a_3: $13	a_4: $14
Events:	e_1: $\leq$$11	$ 0	$ 0	$ 0	$ 0
Rival	e_2: $12	10,000	0	0	0
Bids	e_3: $13	10,000	20,000	0	0
	e_4: $14	10,000	20,000	30,000	0
	e_5: $\geq$$15	10,000	20,000	30,000	40,000

Figure 1

Example 3. Number Crunchers, Inc. (NCI) is a computer service bureau that sells time on its leased batch-processing computer. NCI has entered into an agreement with the Gigo Company, which will pay NCI $5000 a month for two years starting two months hence to process certain data and produce a number of reports for Gigo. NCI plans to obtain a new computer at the termination of the Gigo contract.

Since the contract was signed NCI has received information about a new remote job-entry (RJE) station that could be installed on Gigo's premises and that could eliminate the inconvenience and time delay involved in physically transporting the input data from Gigo to NCI and the output reports in the other direction. For this convenience Gigo has agreed to pay NCI an additional $1250 a month over and above the $1750 a month cost of the RJE equipment and the communications costs. Gigo has stated certain perform- ance specifications, however, that must be satisfied before these additional payments are made. NCI must decide now whether to commence the neces- sary systems work to permit operation of the RJE station. The cost (one- time) of this systems work would be $5000, but NCI has been unable to obtain any assurance from the manufacturer that the RJE equipment will perform to Gigo's stated specifications. "It all depends on the mix of jobs you are running, which differs from one installation to another."

If they fail to meet specifications in two months, NCI must pay the rental of $1750 a month on Gigo's RJE equipment, in addition to foregoing the $1250 a month additional payment for RJE service. NCI believes that at that time a three-month additional systems effort costing $3000 will in- crease the chances of succeeding; if it does not work, a new release of the operating system, scheduled for eight months hence, will still further increase NCI's chances of meeting specifications. (Specifications will surely be met with the new operating system if they are met with the existing system.) If even this fails, however, the attempt to provide RJE service will be aban- doned six months after the commencement of the contract, all RJE equip- ment being returned to the manufacturer. Gigo has given NCI the option of waiting until the new operating system is released before attempting to pro- vide RJE service. If this is done, NCI will still have to invest the initial $5000 in systems development, but can avoid the $3000 cost of additional systems work as well as the payment for Gigo's RJE equipment if the system does not work.

Despite the risks, NCI's management is interested in trying to develop this facility as a feature that may serve other customers as well. A survey of existing customers has not revealed intense interest, but there is some hope that the ability to provide RJE will bring in new customers. The expertise obtained by installing RJE on the present computer will be transferable in part to the new computer.

NCI has three acts among which to choose: undertake initial systems work to try to make installation of the RJE station possible in two months (a_1); undertake initial systems work to try to make installation of the RJE station possible eight months hence, when the new operating system is re- leased (a_2); do not undertake efforts to install RJE system (a_3). NCI's man- agement has decided that if they reject this contract, they will not try to develop RJE expertise until they replace their present computer. There are four possible events: the RJE system will work (that is, satisfy Gigo's speci- fications) in two months if systems work is started immediately (e_1); the RJE system will work in five months after additional systems effort (e_2); the RJE system will work with the new operating system (e_3); Gigo's specifications cannot be met even with the new operating system (e_4).

Figure 2 is a payoff table showing consequences of the various act-event combinations. Consequences are described in terms of cash flow (over and above the basic $5000 per month) in each of the two years of the contract, as well as a qualitative statement of NCI's position regarding RJE expertise. Of course, most of the cash flows in the first year do not represent a constant rate of flow; for some purposes, a finer breakdown (perhaps into three-month periods) might be desirable. (See Exercise 5.)

Events \ Acts	a_1: Try now	a_2: Try with new op. system	a_3: Don't try
e_1: Works immediately	10,000 15,000 Early expertise	2,500 15,000 Latest expertise	0 0 No expertise
e_2: Works 3 months later	−2,000 15,000 Later expertise	2,500 15,000 Latest expertise	0 0 No expertise
e_3: Works only with new op. system	−11,000 15,000 Latest expertise	2,500 15,000 Latest expertise	0 0 No expertise
e_4: Doesn't work	−18,000 0 No expertise	−5,000 0 No expertise	0 0 No expertise

Meaning of entries

> Cash flow first year
> Cash flow second year
> Amount of expertise

Figure 2

EXERCISES

1. Verify the entries in Figure 1.
2. Verify the entries in Figure 2.
3. In Example 2, suppose identical bids by XYZ and the rival bidder were to result in XYZ's obtaining the contract. What changes would be required in the payoff table of Figure 1 to reflect this fact?
4. In Example 2, let x represent XYZ's bid and let r represent the rival's bid. Write a formula to express the consequence (in terms of net profit to XYZ)
   a. if $r \leq x$,
   b. if $r > x$.
5. In Example 3, what is the cash flow in each quarter of year 1 for each consequence? Let the first quarter begin two months hence.

6. In Example 2, suppose it cost \$5000 to perform the analysis necessary to submitting a bid. Modify the entries in Figure 1 accordingly. Should any other acts be considered? If so, describe them and compute the appropriate consequences.

7. A retailer must decide how many units of a certain item to stock daily. Demand for the item will be between 0 and 3 units inclusive. Any units remaining unsold at the end of the day will be thrown away. The units cost the retailer \$1 each and sell for \$3. List the relevant acts and events and prepare a payoff table for the problem.

8. In Exercise 7, let q be the number of units stocked and let d be the number demanded. Write a formula to express the consequence to the retailer
a. if $d < q$,
b. if $d \geq q$.

9. Suppose the retailer of Exercise 7 would be able to scrap any units left over at the end of the day for \$.25. Modify your answer to Exercise 7 accordingly.

10. Suppose that whenever the retailer of Exercise 7 ran out of stock he would fill demands in excess of his stock by purchasing units for \$4. Modify your answer to Exercise 7 accordingly.

11. Baker is a hot-dog salesman who owns a stand near a baseball stadium. For each game he buys Q hot dogs. He makes a profit of 10 cents on each hot dog sold. The unsold hot dogs, if any, are returned to the manufacturer at a loss of 2 cents each. From his past records, Baker estimates the following probabilities for selling hot dogs:

d = number of hot dogs demanded	10	20	30	40	50
p = probability of that demand	.1	.2	.4	.2	.1

(For simplicity his sales have been rounded off to the nearest multiple of 10.) How many hot dogs should Baker buy in order to maximize his net profit? Solve this problem by carrying out the following steps:
a. The payoff table below shows profits in cents. Fill in the remaining entries.

Number of hot dogs ordered

		10	20	30	40	50	
	10	100			40	20	
	20	100	200	180	160	140	
Number of hot dogs demanded	30			300		260	$= M$
	40	100			400		
	50					500	

b. Let p be the demand probability vector. Calculate pM and find its maximum entry in order to determine the decision that maximizes expected net profit.

12. In Exercise 11 suppose that Baker's records show the following probabilities of selling various numbers of hot dogs for fair, cloudy, and rainy
days:

Number of Hot Dogs Demanded	10	20	30	40	50
Demand probability on a fair day	.1	.1	.2	.3	.3
Demand probability on a cloudy day	.1	.2	.4	.2	.1
Demand probability on a rainy day	.4	.3	.2	.1	0

How many hot dogs should he order if the day is fair? cloudy? rainy?
[*Ans.* Fair: order 50; cloudy: order 40; rainy: order 30.]

2. UTILITY THEORY

How can a decision maker make a choice among acts any one of which
may result in one of several events and its associated consequence? As a
start, he must be able to order the possible consequences from least desirable to most desirable. Sometimes this is very easy to do. When the consequences are completely expressible in terms of net profit, for example, any
reasonable decision maker would order them according to the rule "the
more, the better." In Example 2 of Section 1 there is no question that
$10,000 is better than $0, $20,000 is better than $10,000, and so on. When
the consequences are not completely expressible in terms of a single measure (such as net profit) whose desirability increases as the value of the
measure increases, it is not so easy to order consequences in terms of their
desirability. In Example 3 of Section 1, for instance, although it is clear
that $c(e_2, a_2)$ is more desirable than $c(e_3, a_1)$ (that is, $2500 in year 1,
$15,000 in year 2, and latest expertise is preferable to $-$11,000 in year 1,
$15,000 in year 2, and latest expertise), the relative desirabilities of $c(e_2, a_1)$
and $c(e_2, a_2)$ are not so easy to establish. Whether (a) sustaining a $2000
loss in year 1 in order to obtain expertise three months after the start of
the contract is better than (b) obtaining a $2500 net profit in year 1 and
achieving expertise six months after the start depends on a complicated
series of judgments regarding NCI's cash-flow needs, reported profits, and
competitive position. With the help of decision analysis it may be possible
to explore more fully the possible consequences of acquiring expertise at
various times and the consequences of different cash flows in year 1, but
any additional analysis rests ultimately on the judgment of the decision
maker. We shall return to this problem in Section 3.

Even when we can order consequences in terms of desirability, doing
so does not necessarily solve the decision problem, except under unusual
circumstances. In comparing the consequences of any two acts, it will
usually be the case that for some events one of the acts will be better and
for other events the other will be better. In Example 2 of Section 1, for

instance, a_3 (XYZ bids \$13) is better than a_2 (XYZ bids \$12) if the rival's bid is \$14 or more, worse if the bid is \$13, and identical with a_2 if the bid is \$12 or less. (See Exercise 1 for a case in which one act is worse for all events.)

To have a basis for choosing among acts under all circumstances the decision maker must be able to assess the probabilities of the various possible events, and he must also have a way of calibrating his *liking* of various consequences. Referring again to Example 2 of the previous section, it is clear that a_3 will increase in desirability relative to a_2 as the probability of e_4 or e_5 increases, but probabilities alone do not provide any analytical basis of choice between the two acts. Even if $\mathbf{Pr}[e_4 \vee e_5] = .99$ and $\mathbf{Pr}[e_3] = .01$ in XYZ's judgment, XYZ's management *might* find a_2 preferable to a_3 because \$20,000 is vitally needed to stay in business, and even a small chance of getting nothing is too great a risk to offset the very probable outcome of \$30,000 if a_3 is chosen.

Before discussing how to express a decision maker's liking for various consequences in a meaningful way in a complicated decision problem, first consider the problem whose payoff table is given in Figure 3, where there

Events	Probabilities	Acts	
		a_1	a_2
e_1	$\mathbf{Pr}[e_1]$	c^*	c^*
e_2	$\mathbf{Pr}[e_2]$	c_*	c^*
e_3	$\mathbf{Pr}[e_3]$	c^*	c_*
e_4	$\mathbf{Pr}[e_4]$	c_*	c_*

Figure 3

are two acts, any number of events, but only two possible consequences, c_* and c^*, and suppose that c^* is preferred to c_*. Observe that in addition to acts, events, and consequences, we also show in the payoff table the probability assigned to each event. If the probabilities of the events are given, then it is easy, without any further assessment, to decide which act is better: it is simply the act with the higher probability of c^* (and consequently the lower probability of c_*). The purpose of *utility theory* is to find methods of reducing real-world problems to problems like that of Figure 3, in which there are only two consequences.

To see how this can be done, consider any decision problem in which there are a number of possible consequences (cf. Examples 2 and 3 of Section 1). Choose two *reference consequences*, c_* and c^*, such that any possible real consequence in the decision problem is at least as desirable as c_*, and c^* is at least as desirable as any possible real consequence. In Example 2 of Section 1, for instance, we could let c_* be any specified negative net profit and c^* be any net profit in excess of \$40,000; in Example 3, c_* might be $-\$40,000$ in year 1, \$0 in year 2, and no expertise, while c^* might be \$20,000 in year 1, \$35,000 in year 2, and early expertise.

Having decided on c_* and c^*, the decision maker can now assess his *utility* for any consequence c of his decision problem by imagining he is faced with the following *subsidiary* decision problem. There are two acts: "sure thing" (a_1) and "gamble" (a_2), and two events: "win" (e_1) and "lose" (e_2). If a_1 is chosen, the decision maker gets c with certainty; if a_2 is chosen, he gets c^* if "win" occurs and c_* if "lose" occurs. A payoff table for the subsidiary decision problem is shown in Figure 4.

		Acts	
Events	*Probability*	a_1: *Sure thing*	a_2: *Gamble*
e_1: Win	$\mathbf{Pr}[e_1]$	c	c^*
e_2: Lose	$\mathbf{Pr}[e_2]$	c	c_*

Figure 4

Let $\mathbf{Pr}[e_1] = p$ (and hence $\mathbf{Pr}[e_2] = 1 - p$) and suppose c is less desirable than c^* and more desirable than c_*. Clearly if $p = 1$ the decision maker prefers a_2, since by supposition he prefers c^* for sure to c for sure. Similarly, if $p = 0$ he prefers a_1, since c_* is less desirable than c. As p decreases from 1 to 0, he should like a_2 less and less, and hence there should be some breakeven value of p, say u, such that if $p > u$ he prefers the gamble (a_2) and if $p < u$ he prefers the sure thing (a_1). If $p = u$ exactly, he is indifferent between a_1 and a_2. If this indifference in the subsidiary decision problem is carried over to the real-world problem, it means that the decision maker is indifferent between facing a real-world problem that involves a consequence c and facing a substitute problem in which in place of c a gamble occurs with consequence c^* having probability u and c_* having probability $1 - u$. To show its dependence on a particular consequence c, we shall sometimes denote this breakeven probability u by $u(c)$ and refer to it as the utility of c (relative to reference consequences c_* and c^*). If c is just as desirable as (or identical with) c^*, the breakeven probability is, of course, $u = 1$; if c is just as desirable as c_*, then $u = 0$.

How does the ability to find the utility of a consequence help us solve a real-world problem? It does so by permitting us to substitute for the real-world problem an equivalent problem with consequences c_* and c^* only. Consider a decision problem with n acts, m events, as shown in Figure 5. Assume that probabilities for the events and utilities for the consequences c_{ij} relative to reference consequences c_* and c^* have been assessed. Consider act a_j. Event e_i occurs with probability $\mathbf{Pr}[e_i]$ and results

Acts

Events	Probabilities	a_1	...	a_j	...	a_n
e_1	$\mathbf{Pr}[e_1]$	c_{11}	...	c_{1j}	...	c_{1n}
$\vdots$	$\vdots$	$\vdots$		$\vdots$		$\vdots$
e_i	$\mathbf{Pr}[e_i]$	c_{i1}	...	c_{ij}	...	c_{in}
$\vdots$	$\vdots$	$\vdots$		$\vdots$		$\vdots$
e_m	$\mathbf{Pr}[e_m]$	c_{m1}	...	c_{mj}	...	c_{mn}

Figure 5

in consequence c_{ij}. By the definition of utility, the decision maker is indifferent between c_{ij} for sure and a probability $u(c_{ij})$ of obtaining c^* and $1 - u(c_{ij})$ of obtaining c_*, and in view of the fact that a gamble involving c_* and c^* can be substituted for c_{ij} in his real-world problem, he is indifferent between (1) receiving c_{ij} with probability $\mathbf{Pr}[e_i]$ and (2) receiving c^* with probability $\mathbf{Pr}[e_i]u(c_{ij})$ and c_* with probability $\mathbf{Pr}[e_i](1 - u(c_{ij}))$. Making similar substitutions for all consequences associated with act a_j, it follows that the decision maker is indifferent between (1) receiving c_{1j} with probability $\mathbf{Pr}[e_1], \ldots, c_{ij}$ with probability $\mathbf{Pr}[e_i], \ldots, c_{mj}$ with probability $\mathbf{Pr}[e_m]$, and (2) receiving c^* with probability $\sum_{i=1}^{m} \mathbf{Pr}[e_i]u(c_{ij})$ and c_* with probability $\sum_{i=1}^{m} \mathbf{Pr}[e_i](1 - u(c_{ij}))$. Thus in place of the real-world act a_j an equally desirable act can be constructed; the substitute act has only two consequences, each with computable probabilities. Any other real-world act can be similarly reduced to an equivalent substitute act with the same two consequences, having possibly different probabilities. Thus the entire decision problem can be reduced to one in which there are only two consequences, and the principle we used to find the better act in the problem whose payoff table is given in Figure 3 can be used here: choose the act with the highest probability of c^*. We shall call the numerical value of the expression $\sum_{i=1}^{m} \mathbf{Pr}[e_i]u(c_{ij})$ the utility of act a_j, and symbolize its value by $\bar{u}(a_j)$.

Example 1. Figure 6 is a payoff table for a two-act three-event problem.

Acts

Events	Probabilities	a_1	a_2
e_1	.3	c_{11}	c_{12}
e_2	.5	c_{21}	c_{22}
e_3	.2	c_{31}	c_{32}
	1.0		

Figure 6

In Figure 7, breakeven probabilities assessed by the decision maker

Consequence	Breakeven Probability
c_{11}	.9
c_{21}	.4
c_{31}	.1
c_{12}	.8
c_{22}	.7
c_{32}	.2

Figure 7

relative to reference consequences c_* and c^* are listed for each of the six consequences in Figure 6. For example, the fact that the decision maker has assessed for c_{11} a breakeven probability .9 means that in choosing between (1) a gamble involving c^* and c_* as consequences and (2) c_{11} for sure, he would prefer the gamble if the probability of winning c^* exceeded .9, he would prefer the sure thing if the probability of c^* were less than .9, and he would be indifferent between the gamble and the sure thing if the probability of c^* were .9 exactly.

In analyzing a_1, we can now say that a .3 probability of c_{11} is equivalent to a $.3 \times .9 = .27$ probability of c^* and a $.3 \times .1 = .03$ probability of c_*; that a .5 probability of c_{21} is equivalent to a $.5 \times .4 = .20$ probability of c^* and a $.5 \times .6 = .30$ probability of c_*; and that a .2 probability of c_{31} is equivalent to a $.2 \times .1 = .02$ probability of c^* and a $.2 \times .9 = .18$ probability of c_*. The act is thus equivalent to a $.27 + .20 + .02 = .49$ probability of c^* and a $.03 + .30 + .18 = .51$ probability of c_*. Briefly, the utility of a_1 is .49, or $\bar{u}(a_1) = .49$. By similar analysis, a_2 is equivalent to a $.3 \times .8 + .5 \times .7 + .2 \times .2 = .63$ probability of c^* and a $.3 \times .2 + .5 \times .3 + .2 \times .8 = .37$ probability of c_*; that is, $\bar{u}(a_2) = .63$. Clearly, a_2 is more desirable than a_1 because its equivalent substitute problem offers a larger chance at c^* than does the equivalent substitute problem for a_1; more briefly, $\bar{u}(a_2) = .63 > \bar{u}(a_1) = .49$.

Example 2. Consider a company facing the possibility of a catastrophic risk that will leave it bankrupt. Very expensive safety precautions can reduce the probability of the risk by a fixed amount. Suppose it costs \$d to reduce the risk of catastrophe by .1—for example, from .9 to .8, or from .5 to .4, or from .1 to 0. Consider two problems: (1) the present risk of catastrophe is .5; (2) the present risk of catastrophe is .1. Suppose in Problem 1 analysis reveals that it pays to spend \$d to reduce the risk to .4. Does this mean that with the same utilities it will necessarily pay to spend \$d to reduce the risk from .1 to 0 in Problem 2? Most people think that a reduction in risk from .1 to 0 is "worth more" than a reduction from .5 to .4, but we shall show in the context of the present problem that this is not so. Figure 8 shows payoff tables for Problems 1 and 2, where we decompose the event "catastrophe" in Problem 1 to permit different probabilities to be assigned to it for the two acts. Observe that in Problem 1 if the catastrophe occurs even though safety precautions are taken, the company will have first spent \$d and then gone bankrupt, but "bankruptcy" is nevertheless a sufficient description of the consequence.

Let c_* be "bankrupt" and let c^* be "no change." Then $u(\text{bankrupt}) = 0$, $u(\text{no change}) = 1$. Suppose the decision maker is asked to

PROBLEM 1

		Acts	
Events	Probabilities	a_1: No Safety	a_2: Safety
Catastrophe	.4	Bankrupt	Bankrupt
Catastrophe	.1	Bankrupt	$d poorer
No catastrophe	.5	No change	$d poorer
	1.0		

PROBLEM 2

		Acts	
Events	Probabilities	a_1: No Safety	a_2: Safety
Catastrophe	.1	Bankrupt	$d poorer
No catastrophe	.9	No change	$d poorer
	1.0		

Figure 8

assess his utility (relative to c_* and c^*) for being $d poorer (but not bankrupt), and suppose he said that he would be indifferent between (1) a gamble that resulted in no change with probability .85 and bankruptcy with probability .15 and (2) being $d poorer for sure. Then $u(\$d$ poorer$) = .85$.
In Problem 1,

$$\bar{u}(a_1) = .4 \times 0 + .1 \times 0 + .5 \times 1 = .5$$
$$< \bar{u}(a_2) = .4 \times 0 + .1 \times .85 + .5 \times .85 = .51,$$

and hence a_2 is better. In Problem 2,

$$\bar{u}(a_1) = .1 \times 0 + .9 \times 1 = .9$$
$$> \bar{u}(a_2) = .1 \times .85 + .9 \times .85 = .85,$$

so that a_1 is better. Thus it pays to reduce the risk of catastrophe from .5 to .4, but it does not pay to reduce the risk from .1 to 0.

EXERCISES

1. In Example 2 of Section 1 list the consequences associated with the act a_0: XYZ bids $10, and the five events listed in the payoff table (Figure 1). Show that no matter what probabilities are assigned to the events, a_0 cannot be the best act because there are acts whose consequences are at least as good as those of a_0 for every possible event.
2. Consider the following payoff table where consequences are measured in

	Acts		
Events	a_1	a_2	a_3
e_1	10	9	5
e_2	15	19	20
e_3	5	9	10

dollars of net profit. There is no event for which a_2 is the best act. Can a_2 therefore be eliminated for every possible set of probabilities assigned to the events?

3. Give a set of probabilities for events e_1, e_2, and e_3 for which a_2 is the better act in Figure 3.

4. Suppose that the XYZ company of Example 2, Section 1, considers as reference consequences c_*: net loss of \$10,000; c^*: net profit of \$90,000. XYZ's management has decided it is indifferent between (1) a gamble giving a .316 probability of obtaining c^* and a .684 probability of obtaining c_* and (2) obtaining a net profit of \$0 for certain. It is also indifferent between (1) a gamble giving a .548 probability of c^* and a .452 probability of c_* and (2) obtaining a net profit of \$20,000 for certain. Suppose that the probabilities assigned to the events e_1 through e_5 are .2, .1, .2, .2, .3, respectively.
   a. Show that XYZ's stated indifferences and assessed probabilities imply that the act a_2: bid \$12 is indifferent to an artificial substitute act in which with probability .4784, c^* will occur and with probability .5216, c_* will occur.
   b. What is the utility of a_2 relative to the reference consequences c_* and c^*?

5. In the situation of Exercise 4, suppose that XYZ's management has also decided it is indifferent between (1) a gamble giving a .632 probability of c^* and a .368 probability of c_* and (2) a net profit of \$30,000 for certain.
   a. Substitute for the act a_3: bid \$13 an equivalent act involving only the reference consequences c_* and c^*.
   b. What is the utility of a_3?
   c. Which act is better, a_2 or a_3?

6. In Example 1, suppose we define a new "utility" $u^*(c_{ij}) = 7u(c_{ij}) + 6$. Then $u^*(c_{ij})$ does not have a probabilistic interpretation as does $u(c_{ij})$.
   a. Compute $u^*(c_{ij})$ from $u(c_{ij})$ for the six consequences.
   b. Compute $\bar{u}^*(a_j) = \sum_{i=1}^{3} \mathbf{Pr}[e_i] u^*(c_{ij})$ for $j = 1, 2$.
   c. Show that

$$\bar{u}^*(a_2) = 7\bar{u}(a_2) + 6 = 7 \times .63 + 6 = 10.41$$
$$> \bar{u}^*(a_1) = 7\bar{u}(a_1) + 6 = 7 \times .49 + 6 = 9.43,$$

and hence that if we treat u^* as a utility, it ranks acts in the same order as u.

7. Generalize the results of Exercise 6 as follows. Consider two acts, m events, and the appropriate consequences, and suppose utilities $u(c_{ij})$ have been assessed for all the consequences and probabilities $\mathrm{Pr}[e_i]$ for all the events. Let

$$\bar{u}(a_j) = \sum_{i=1}^{m} \mathbf{Pr}[e_i]u(c_{ij})$$

be the utility of act j, $j = 1$, 2, and suppose $\bar{u}(a_1) > \bar{u}(a_2)$. Now consider new "utilities" $u^*(c_{ij}) = ku(c_{ij}) + K$, where $k > 0$, and let

$$\bar{u}^*(a_j) = \sum_{i=1}^{m} \mathbf{Pr}[e_i]u^*(c_{ij}).$$

Show that $\bar{u}^*(a_j) = k\bar{u}(a_j) + K$, and hence that $\bar{u}^*(a_1) > \bar{u}^*(a_2)$.

8. Consider five consequences, $c_1, \ldots, c_5$, ranked in order of preference, with c_5 most preferred. If c_1 and c_5 are reference consequences, then $u(c_1) = 0$, $u(c_5) = 1$. Suppose utilities have been assessed relative to c_1 and c_5 for the intermediate consequences, and $u(c_2) = .2$, $u(c_3) = .3$, $u(c_4) = .6$. Now let $u^*(c_3)$ be the utility of c_3 relative to reference consequences c_2 and c_4. Show that $u^*(c_3) = .25$ by showing that a .25 probability of winning c_2 is equivalent to a $.25 \times .6 + .75 \times .2 = .3$ probability of winning c_5 and a .7 probability of winning c_1.

9. Generalize the results of Exercise 8 to show that if $0 < u(c_2) < u(c_3) < u(c_4) < 1$, then $u^*(c_3)$ must satisfy

$$[1 - u^*(c_3)]u(c_2) + u^*(c_3)u(c_4) = u(c_3),$$

or

$$u^*(c_3) = \frac{u(c_3) - u(c_2)}{u(c_4) - u(c_2)}.$$

10. Consider a decision problem involving a choice between two acts, a_1 and a_2. The consequences of either act are expressible as net cash flows, and for either act one of just four possible cash flows will result: \$100, \$200, \$300, or \$400. For act a_1 the respective probabilities of these four consequences are .20, .20, .40, and .20, while for a_2 the probabilities are .05, .30, .35, and .30. Summarize the problem in the form of a payoff table involving acts, events, probabilities, and consequences. Show that for any utilities that increase as cash flow increases, a_2 is better than a_1, since for each event in the payoff table the consequence associated with a_2 is as good as, or better than, that associated with a_1. [*Hint:* List not four but seven events, $e_1, e_2, \ldots, e_7$, which represent the seven possible combinations of these consequences with respective probabilities .05, .15, .15, .05, .30, .10, .20.]

11. Let c_d stand for the statement "the consequence is a net cash flow of d dollars or less" and let a_j stand for the statement "act a_j was chosen." Show that in the problem of Exercise 10,

$$\mathbf{Pr}[c_d \mid a_2] \leq \mathbf{Pr}[c_d \mid a_1] \qquad \text{for all } d.$$

(When this condition is satisfied, a_2 is said to dominate a_1 probabilistically.)

12. Show that in the problem of Exercise 10 if for act a_2 the probability of the \$200 cash flow were increased from .30 to .45 and the probability

of the $300 flow were reduced from .35 to .20, then (a) there is no way of listing events so that for every event a_2 is at least as good as a_1; (b) the probabilistic relation shown to hold in Exercise 11 no longer holds for all d. (It can be shown in general that if a_2 dominates a_1 probabilistically, then a_2 is better than a_1 for any utilities assigned so as to increase as the consequences increase in value.)

3. UTILITY CURVES

When consequences must be described in terms of more than one measure (cf. Example 3 of Section 1), directly assessing the utility of each consequence is sometimes the most efficacious way to proceed. At other times it may be possible to reduce the various measures to a single measure. Consequences that are spread out over time (for example, cash flows in year 1 and year 2) may sometimes be reduced to a single "present value," but in problems involving large potential swings of money, the idea of discounting at some constant rate that is independent of either the time or the amount of cash flow may be very dangerous. A person who discounted future cash flows at the rate of 10 percent per year would quite reasonably conclude that a $100 cash outflow followed by a $120 inflow a year later has a positive net present value, and hence is desirable, but he would also conclude that a $1,000,000 outflow followed by a $1,200,000 inflow a year later is desirable, even though he might run the risk of starving to death during the year in which he paid out the $1,000,000.

Consequences that are more or less "intangible" can also sometimes be converted into equivalent values measurable on a more easily interpreted scale, but again we must exercise care in trying to do so. In Example 3 of Section 1, for instance, we might try to assess a differential immediate cash value for obtaining "latest" expertise on RJE (remote job entry) as against no expertise at all, but this value may depend on other cash flows. Following a loss of $11,000 in the first year, this expertise might be worth nothing, because the company would not then have the capital to exploit it. Following a profit of $2500, expertise might have substantial value, however.

> **Example 1.** In the problem of Example 3, Section 1, suppose the president of NCI says the company is currently in a fairly strong cash position, and that NCI could absorb the loss if the worst possible act-event combination (a_1, e_4) occurred, although it would be seriously weakened financially. If he came close to breaking even in the first year on the Gigo venture—that is, if his first-year cash flow were within $\pm$$3000—he would be indifferent between (1) receiving $15,000 from Gigo in the second year and (2) receiving an additional $12,500 in the first year and nothing in the second. If he suffered a major cash drain in the first year, however—for example, if the combination (a_1, e_3) occurred—then a hypothetical opportunity to divert the second-year cash flow to the first year would be so attractive that he would settle for just $9000 in the first year in place of $15,000 in the second. If the best possible act-event combination (a_1, e_1) occurred, and he received $10,000 in the first

year, then although he would prefer to receive the second-year cash flow of $15,000 sooner than later, he would require more than $12,500 in the first year to make the diversion from the second year to the first worthwhile. After some thought, he decides that he would be indifferent between $13,500 in the first year and $15,000 in the second year under these circumstances.

As regards when, if ever, NCI achieves expertise on RJE, he feels that he would be just willing to trade early expertise for $10,000 cash in the first year, that later expertise would be worth $5000 in cash in the first year, and that latest expertise would be worth $2500 if first-year cash flow were $2500 and second-year cash flow were $15,000, but that it would be impossible to exploit it, and hence it would be worth nothing, if the cash flows were −$11,000 and $15,000.

His decision problem can now be reduced to an equivalent problem involving only first-year cash flows and no expertise with the payoff table shown in Figure 9.

		Acts	
Events	a_1: *Try Now*	a_2: *Try with New Operating System*	a_3: *Don't Try*
e_1: Works immediately	$33,500	$17,500	$0
e_2: Works three months later	15,500	17,500	0
e_3: Works only with new op. system	−2,000	17,500	0
e_4: Doesn't work	−18,500	−5,000	0

Figure 9

When consequences can be described in terms of a single measure, as in Example 2 of Section 1, or when they can be reduced to a single measure, as we have done in Example 3 of that section, it may be very much easier to assess the utility of various consequences. Often the most natural unit in which to measure or to convert consequences is money. If we assess utilities not on differential cash flows, but rather on some aggregate monetary measure such as individual "wealth" or corporate "liquid assets" we can, furthermore, obtain utilities that are real numbers for all possible positions in which we may find ourselves within a certain specified period of time. These utilities can then be applied not to just a single decision problem but to all problems the individual or company faces that will be resolved within that time period.

In principle, the job of assessing a company's utility for assets can proceed exactly as in the preceding section. We shall symbolize consequences measured in terms of assets by a capital A with appropriate sub- or superscripts, rather than using the more general symbol c. As reference consequences asset positions A_* and A^* are selected that are respectively no better than and no worse than any position the corporation expects to be in during the time period over which the utilities will be used. Then for any intermediate asset position a "breakeven" probability can be assessed, such that a gamble with a probability u of obtaining the better reference consequence and a probability $1 - u$ of obtaining the worse is indifferent to having the intermediate asset position for sure.

To do this kind of assessment for a few asset positions is a reasonable task. To do it for very many asset positions between A_* and A^* is clearly impractical. Fortunately, if the utilities for a few asset positions have been carefully assessed, they can be plotted as points on a graph having asset position on the horizontal axis and utility on the vertical axis, and a smooth curve drawn through the plotted points may provide a reasonable representation of the utility for intermediate asset positions. In Section 5 we shall discuss in detail the implications of such curves and their application to the problem of assessment. But first we shall see how such curves can be used in solving and interpreting the solution of decision problems. In the remainder of this chapter, all asset positions will be expressed in thousands of dollars.

Example 2. In Figure 10 we have drawn a utility curve that might represent the utility for assets relative to reference consequences $A_* = 0$, $A^* = 100$

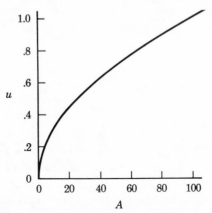

Figure 10

(thousands of dollars) that the XYZ company of Example 2, Section 1, has assessed. Suppose XYZ currently has assets of $A = 10$ and is contemplating the bidding situation described in Example 2 of Section 1. In Figure 11 we compute the utility of a_2: bid \$12, under the assumption that the probabilities assigned to the events $e_1, \ldots, e_5$ are as shown in Figure 11.

The computations in column 6 of Figure 11 simply form the product of probability times utility for each event and sum these products. The resulting sum of .4784 (see Exercise 4 of Section 2) is by definition the utility of act a_2 and has the following interpretation. If the XYZ company is willing to act on the basis of the utility curve in Figure 10 and the probabilities in Figure 11, then the company should be indifferent between (1) a_2: bid \$12, which will result in an asset position of 10 (thousands of dollars) with probability

.3 and 30 with probability .7 and (2) a gamble that will result in an asset position of 100 with probability .4784 and 0 with probability .5216. It can be shown (see Exercise 1) that the utilities of acts a_1, a_3, and a_4 are respectively .4208, .4745, and .4336. Thus a_2 is the best act, in the sense that all four acts have been reduced to equivalent gambles involving the reference consequences, with a_2 having the highest probability of achieving A^*. In short, a_2 is best because its utility is highest.

(1)	(2)	(3)	(4)	(5)	(6)
		Net	Asset		
Events—	Probability	Profit	Position	Utility	Product
Rival Bids	of Event	($000)	($000)	for Assets	(2) × (5)
e_1: $11	.2	$ 0	$10	.316	.0632
e_2: 12	.1	0	10	.316	.0316
e_3: 13	.2	20	30	.548	.1096
e_4: 14	.2	20	30	.548	.1096
e_5: 15	.3	20	30	.548	.1644
	1.0				$\bar{u}(a_2) =$ .4784

Figure 11

In addition to finding the best choice of act in a given decision problem, a utility curve can be used to translate utilities back into more meaningful units. We have already seen that for any "sure thing" A whose desirability is greater than the lower reference consequence A_* and less than the highest A^*, a decision maker can assess a *breakeven probability* u such that he is indifferent between A for sure and a gamble on the reference consequences with probability u of getting A^*. Conversely, for any fixed probability u of getting A^* in a gamble on the reference consequences, there must be a consequence A between A_* and A^* such that the decision maker is indifferent between A and the gamble. If we have a utility curve, it is easy to obtain this value by reading the curve "inversely"—that is, by finding the given value of u on the vertical axis, reading over to the curve and down to the horizontal axis to obtain the corresponding value of A. Using the utility curve of Figure 10, a utility of .4784 corresponds to an asset position of about 22.8; that is, the curve implies that a decision maker would be indifferent between 22.8 for sure and a gamble on the reference consequences having probability .4784 of getting A^*. We have now established that the act a_2 is indifferent to a gamble on the reference consequences having probability .4784 of getting A^*, and that this gamble is in turn indifferent to 22.8 for sure. Thus the act a_2 having uncertain consequences corresponding to events e_1 through e_5 is equivalent to an asset position of 22.8 for sure. This equivalent "sure thing" is called a *certainty equivalent*.

It is sometimes interesting to look at the difference between the *expected value* (see Chapter 3, Section 7) of an act and its *certainty equivalent*.

This difference is called the *risk premium*. The expected value of assets for a_2 is

$$.2 \times 10 + .1 \times 10 + .2 \times 30 + .2 \times 30 + .3 \times 30 = 24 \ (\$000),$$

and the risk premium for a_2 with this particular utility curve is thus $24 - 22.8 = 1.2$. As we shall see in the next section, some utility curves can imply negative risk premiums.

Utility curves can often be expressed in terms of mathematical formulas. The properties of such curves can then be analyzed mathematically (by calculus), and it is thus possible to specify classes of curves defined by mathematical formulas that have certain desirable properties. We shall discuss in Section 5 just what kinds of properties may be desirable. Defining utility curves by mathematical formulas also permits more accurate hand computation of utilities and certainty equivalents, although this frequently requires the use of auxiliary mathematical tables. It also makes it very easy to perform utility computations in a digital computer program.

To conduct a complete analysis using a utility curve defined by a mathematical formula, we need one formula to compute the utility of any asset position and an "inverse" formula to compute the asset position corresponding to a given utility. In general, a formula for computing the utility of assets may not have an easily expressible inverse, but the curves in Example 3 below all have simple formulas both to obtain utilities from assets and assets from utilities.

Example 3. Figures 12, 13, and 14 show utility curves that can be expressed in terms of mathematical formulas. Below each figure two formulas are given. The first converts an asset position A (expressed in thousands of dollars) into the corresponding utility; the second converts a utility u into the corresponding asset position (expressed in thousands of dollars). In all three figures the

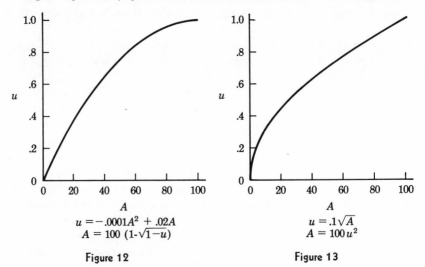

$$u = -.0001A^2 + .02A$$
$$A = 100 \ (1 - \sqrt{1-u})$$

Figure 12

$$u = .1\sqrt{A}$$
$$A = 100 \, u^2$$

Figure 13

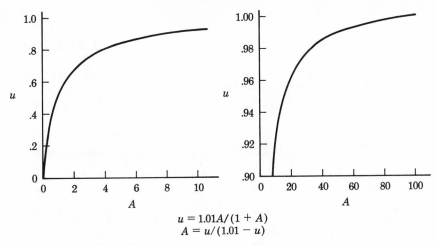

$$u = 1.01A/(1 + A)$$
$$A = u/(1.01 - u)$$

Figure 14 (a)   Figure 14 (b)

reference consequences are 0 and 100 ($000). The utility curve for Figure 14 is shown in two parts, in order to make it more legible. Part (a) stretches out part of the horizontal axis, while part (b) stretches out part of the vertical axis.

Using the formulas for the utility curve in Figure 12, for example, an asset position of 20 corresponds to a utility of

$$-.0001 \times 20^2 + .02 \times 20 = .36,$$

and conversely a utility of .36 corresponds to an asset position of

$$100(1 - \sqrt{1 - .36}) = 100(1 - \sqrt{.64}) = 100(1 - .8) = 20$$

($000). These values, can, of course, be verified by reading the graph. A table of square roots is included as Appendix Table V.

Using the formulas for the utility curve of Figure 13, the utility of an asset position of 36 is

$$.1\sqrt{36} = .6,$$

and conversely a utility of .6 corresponds to an asset position of

$$100(.6)^2 = 36.$$

This utility curve is identical with the curve graphed as Figure 10.

For Figure 14 the utility of an asset position of 4 is

$$1.01(\tfrac{4}{5}) = .808,$$

and conversely the asset position corresponding to a utility of .808 is

$$\frac{.808}{1.01 - .808} = \frac{.808}{.202} = 4.$$

1. Verify the utilities for a_1, a_3, and a_4 given at the end of Example 2 using the utility curve drawn in Figures 10 and 13.

2. Compute the expected asset values of a_1, a_3, and a_4 in Exercise 1. Which act results in the highest expected assets?

3. Compute the risk premiums for a_1, a_3, and a_4 in Exercise 1.

4. Suppose in Example 2 of Section 1 that instead of knowing it will definitely cost 100 ($000) to produce 10,000 units, XYZ's management assesses a .5 probability that the cost will be 80 and a .5 probability that it will be 120, and that these probabilities are independent of the rival's bid. Construct a payoff table for the problem.

5. In the situation of Exercise 4 compute the utilities, certainty equivalents, and risk premiums of acts a_1 through a_4, using the utility curve of Figure 10, assuming that XYZ has initial assets of $10(000). Compare the utilities of each act with the corresponding utilities computed in Exercise 1. Which act is best?

6. Suppose that in Example 1, NCI currently has net liquid assets of 40 ($000), and its utility curve for assets one year hence (assuming no RJE expertise) is the one graphed as Figure 10 and also as Figure 13. Compute the utility, certainty equivalent, expected assets, and risk premium of each act given the payoff table of Figure 9 and probabilities of .5, .2, .1, and .2 for the events e_1, e_2, e_3, and e_4, respectively. Which act is best?

7. Repeat Exercise 6, but assume that in the course of NCI's two-year contract with Gigo, NCI's other business has a .5 probability of increasing its asset position by 20 and a .5 probability of decreasing it by 20, and that these probabilities are independent of the outcomes of the RJE venture.

8. Suppose you were offered a gamble that would pay you $1000 if you won and require you to pay $1000 if you lost. Would you accept the gamble if the probability of winning were .4? .5? .6? .8? .9? What is the *lowest* probability of winning for which you will still accept the gamble? Suppose your current asset position (in $000) is A_0. If you accepted the gamble at this lowest probability, what would be its utility, certainty equivalent, expected value, and risk premium relative to reference consequences (in $000) of $A_* = A_0 - 1$, $A^* = A_0 + 1$?

9. Repeat Exercise 8, except that you get $2000 if you win, nothing if you lose, and your reference consequences are $A_* = A_0$, $A^* = A_0 + 2$.

10. Suppose you were facing a risk with probability .5 of winning $1000 and probability .5 of losing $1000. To be relieved of this risk would you *pay* $100? $200? $300? What is the *most* that you would pay, or the *least* that you would accept to be relieved of this risk? If you were relieved of the risk at this price, what are your implied utility, certainty equivalent, expected value, and risk premium of the gamble relative to reference consequences (expressed in $000) of $A_* = A_0 - 1$, $A^* = A_0 + 1$, where A_0 is your current asset position?

11. Repeat Exercise 10, except that you get $2000 if you win, nothing if you lose, and your reference consequences are $A_* = A_0$, $A^* = A_0 + 2$.

12. Compute utilities for the following asset positions by using the formulas for the curves in Figures 12, 13, and 14, and verify your computations by reading the curves.
    a. 40.
    b. 80.

13. Compute the asset positions corresponding to the following utilities by using the formulas for the curves in Figures 12, 13, and 14, and verify your computations by reading the curves.
    a. .8.
    b. .2.

14. Consider a decision problem with the following payoff table, where the consequences are asset positions expressed in $000. Compute the utility,

Events	Probabilities	a_1	a_2
e_1	.25	0	20
e_2	.25	40	40
e_3	.50	.50	100	60
	1.00		

certainty equivalent, expected value, and risk premium for each act and decide which act is better if the utility curve is the one shown as
    a. Figure 12.
    b. Figure 13.
    c. Figure 14.

15. *a.* In Exercise 14, using the utility curve of Figure 13, compute the certainty equivalent of act a_1 conditional on knowing that event e_3 will not occur.
    b. Consider an artificial act having just two events—e_3 of the original act and a second event whose consequence is an asset position equal in value to that computed in part (*a*) above; let the probability of each event be .5. Show that the utility computed for the artificial act is the same as the utility computed for act a_1 in part (*b*) of Exercise 14.

16. Using the method of Exercise 15, show how an act having more than two events whose consequences can be fully described as asset positions can be evaluated by computing utilities and certainty equivalents for a succession of artificial acts each having just two events.

17. Consider any act all of whose consequences can be fully described in terms of asset positions, and suppose that A_1 is no more desirable and A_m is no less desirable than any of the asset positions to which the act can lead. Show that the certainty equivalent for the act must lie between A_1 and A_m.

4. RISK AVERSION AND RISK REDUCTION

A utility curve for assets for which every possible gamble involving consequences within a specified interval has a positive risk premium is said to be *risk averse* over that interval. A curve for which all gambles over an interval have negative risk premiums is said to be *risk seeking* in that interval. A curve for which all gambles in a given interval have precisely zero risk premiums is said to be *risk neutral* in that interval. Utility curves can be risk averse for all gambles within a certain interval and risk seeking or risk neutral for gambles in some other interval, or they can have just one form of risk behavior for all possible consequences.

What does a utility curve look like if it is risk neutral over an interval? Let $u = K + kA$ for $A_1 < A < A_m$, where $k > 0$. The formula for u is the equation of a straight line. Now consider a decision problem having m events in which an act a has consequences $A_1, \ldots, A_i, \ldots, A_m$ between A_1 and A_m, and respective probabilities $p_1, \ldots, p_i, \ldots, p_m$ adding to 1. What is the utility of that act? It is simply

$$
\begin{aligned}
\bar{u}(a) &= p_1(K + kA_1) + \cdots + p_i(K + kA_i) + \cdots + p_m(K + kA_m) \\
&= (p_1 + \cdots + p_i + \cdots + p_m)K \\
&\qquad\qquad + k(p_1A_1 + \cdots + p_iA_i + \cdots + p_mA_m) \\
&= K + k\bar{A},
\end{aligned}
$$

where $\bar{A}$ is the expected value of A. What is the certainty equivalent of that act? It is the value of A that, for fixed K and k, satisfies

$$ u = K + kA = K + k\bar{A}; $$

that is, the certainty equivalent is $\bar{A}$. What is the expected value of the act? It is simply $\bar{A}$, the expected value of A. Thus both the expected value and the certainty equivalent of the act have value $\bar{A}$, and their difference—the risk premium—is, therefore, zero, as was to be shown.

We can now ask what a utility curve must look like if it is risk averse over an interval. The answer is that it must be concave over that interval; that is, the curve must lie above any straight line connecting two points lying within that interval. Figure 15 shows a utility curve that is concave over the interval from A_0 to A_3. Let us first consider an act with only two possible consequences, A_1 and A_2, both between A_0 and A_3. The values of A_1 and A_2 and their corresponding utilities u_1 and u_2 are shown in Figure 15, as is $\bar{u} = p_1u_1 + p_2u_2$, the utility of the act. We have just seen that the expected value of an act is numerically equal to its certainty equivalent in the special case where the utility curve is linear. The straight line connecting the points (A_1, u_1) and (A_2, u_2) thus permits us to obtain $\bar{A}$, the expected value of the act, by reading from $\bar{u}$ to the straight line and then down to the horizontal axis, as shown in the figure. The certainty equivalent (labeled CE) is obtained by reading from $\bar{u}$ to the utility curve and then down. Because the utility curve is above the connecting straight line, the certainty equivalent falls to the left of the expected value, and the risk premium is positive. Because the utility curve is concave between A_0 and A_3, and therefore by definition above any straight line connecting any two points on the curve in this interval, the risk premium is positive for any act having just two consequences in this interval. But any act

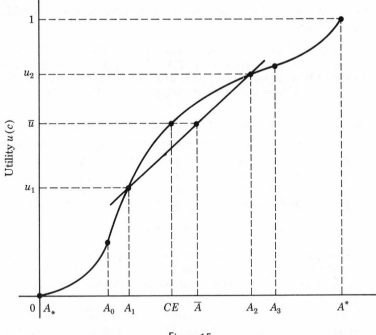

Figure 15

having more than two consequences can be evaluated by evaluating a succession of two-valued acts all of whose consequences are included in the interval that contained the original act's consequences (see Exercises 16 and 17 of Section 3). Thus any act whose consequences all fall within a concave portion of a utility curve will have a positive risk premium, so that by definition a concave portion of a utility curve is risk averse over the interval of concavity.

By a similar argument, it is easy to show that a risk-seeking portion of a utility curve is convex; that is, the curve lies *below* any straight line connecting two points on that portion of the curve. The portions of the curve in Figure 15 to the right of A_3 and to the left of A_0 are both convex and hence risk seeking.

For acts involving consequences that are confined to a very narrow interval it seems reasonable that even a concave or convex utility curve will behave as if it were approximately linear over that interval, and indeed it can be proved (by calculus) that this is so. In fact, it can be shown that for gambles resulting in assets with a fixed expected value, the risk premium under any utility curve is approximately proportional to the variance (see Chapter 3, Section 7) of the outcomes when the variance itself is small. When the standard deviation is halved, for example, the risk premium is reduced by a factor of approximately 4. Thus decisions whose consequences have small variance may often be analyzed by choosing the act whose expected value is highest, without ever explicitly considering one's utility curve.

Example 1. Consider a gamble whose outcome will result in either asset position A_1 or A_2; the probability of A_1 is .75, of A_2 .25, and A_1 and A_2 are chosen so that the expected value of assets following the gamble is 25; that is, $.75A_1 + .25A_2 = 25$. In Figure 16(a) we show the expected value and

Gamble	A_1	A_2	Expected Value	Variance	Variance/.75
1	0	100	25	1875	2500
2	10	70	25	675	900
3	20	40	25	75	100
4	24	28	25	3	4
5	24.5	26.5	25	.75	1

Figure 16(a)

variance for five gambles having this set of characteristics. We also show the ratio of the variance of each gamble to the variance of the fifth gamble.

In Figure 16(b) we show the utility, certainty equivalent, and risk pre-

Gamble	Utility	Certainty Equivalent	Risk Premium	Ratio
1	.2500	13.3975	11.6025	2320.5854
2	.3700	20.6275	4.3725	874.5370
3	.4300	24.5017	.4983	99.6722
4	.4372	24.9800	.0200	3.9996
5	.4374	24.9950	.0050	1.0000

Figure 16(b)

mium computed using the utility curve of Figure 12 for each of the gambles of Figure 16(a). We also show the ratio of the risk premium of each gamble to the risk premium of the fifth. Figures 16(c) and (d) show the same data when

Gamble	Utility	Certainty Equivalent	Risk Premium	Ratio
1	.2500	6.2500	18.7500	2549.0192
2	.4463	19.9216	5.0784	690.4012
3	.4935	24.3566	.6434	87.4685
4	.4997	24.9711	.0289	3.9274
5	.4999	24.9926	.0074	1.0000

Figure 16(c)

computations are performed using the utility curves of Figures 13 and 14, respectively. In Figure 16(b) the ratios in the fifth column are quite close to the ratios in the last column of Figure 16(a), indicating that the risk premium is nearly proportional to the variance over a very wide range of gambles. In Figure 16(c) the ratios match quite well except for gamble 2. Using the

Gamble	Utility	Certainty Equivalent	Risk Premium	Ratio
1	.2500	.3289	24.6711	888.1579
2	.9376	12.9464	12.0536	433.9286
3	.9678	22.9167	2.0833	75.0000
4	.9710	24.8929	.1071	3.8571
5	.9711	24.9722	.0278	1.0000

Figure 16(d)

extremely risk-averse utility curve of Figure 14, the results of Figure 16(d) show that the ratios match those of Figure 16(a) moderately well for small gambles, though quite poorly for the larger gambles.

Risk aversion pervades a great deal of business practice. Some examples follow. In all of them, we shall refer to the risk-averse utility curve in Figures 10 and 13.

Example 2. *Insurance.* A company having assets of 100 (in $000) believes that there is one chance in ten of a disastrous fire's occurring in the next year, which would cost 100 and leave the company with zero assets. For 10 a fire insurance policy can be purchased under which, in the event of such a fire, the company will be paid 70. A payoff table in terms of assets is shown in Figure 17.

		Acts	
Events	Probabilities	a_1: Do not buy insurance	a_2: Buy insurance
e_1: No fire	.9	100	90
e_2: Fire	.1	0	60
	1.0		

Figure 17

In analyzing act a_1, we observe that the utility of 100 is 1.0, the utility of 0 is 0, and therefore $\bar{u}(a_1) = .9 \times 1.0 + .1 \times 0 = .9$; from Figure 13 we see that the certainty equivalent corresponding to a utility of .9 is 81, while the expected value is $.9 \times 100 + .1 \times 0 = 90$ so that the risk premium is 9. In analyzing act a_2, the utility of 90 is .949, that of 60 is .775, and $\bar{u}(a_2) = .9 \times .949 + .1 \times .775 = .9316$; the certainty equivalent is about 86.8, the expected value is $.9 \times 90 + .1 \times 60 = 87$, and the risk premium is .2. Clearly, a_2 is better than a_1 even though its expected value is considerably less. The insurance costs a lot and does not provide complete protection, but it guarantees the company against the catastrophic results that it cannot afford. Observe that from the point of view of the insurance company, which is presumably less risk averse, a formal evaluation in terms of the insurance company's utility curve of the acts "sell the policy" and "don't sell" will almost certainly rate "sell" as better.

Example 3. *Risk-sharing: Syndicates.* A company with 50 in assets (in $000) can invest in a venture that, if successful, will result in 50 net profit, and if a failure will result in a loss of 50. It assesses the probability of success as .7. It can (1) keep its full share of the venture, or (2) form a syndicate whereby it sells fractions of the venture to other companies and individuals, or (3) not enter into the venture at all. Suppose the company offers 1 percent shares for $100 each, and can sell 50 such shares. Should it do so? Figure 18 shows the payoff table for the problem.

		Acts		
Events	*Probabilities*	a_1: *Do Not Syndicate*	a_2: *Syndicate*	a_3: *Do Nothing*
Succeeds	.7	100	80	50
Fails	.3	0	30	50

Figure 18

The utility of act a_1 is $.7 \times 1.0 + .3 \times 0 = .7$, the certainty equivalent is 49, the expected value 70, and the risk premium 21. The utility of act a_2 is $.7 \times .894 + .3 \times .548 = .7902$, the certainty equivalent is about 62.5, the expected value is $.7 \times 80 + .3 \times 30 = 65$, and the risk premium is 2.5. The utility of act a_3 is .707, and its certainty equivalent and expected value are both 50, so that the risk premium is 0. Clearly, act a_2 is best, while a_1 is worse than doing nothing, even though its expected value is highest. The units offered for syndication may be attractive to many purchasers who, even though possibly highly risk averse, face relatively small risks when the scale of the venture is reduced to 1 percent; that is, the range of consequences for them is sufficiently narrow so that their utility curves are virtually linear over the range.

Example 4. *Test Information.* Computermatik, Inc., a vendor of time-sharing computer services, is negotiating a contract with a user whereby Computermatik will supply the user time-sharing services for one year during off-peak hours at a fixed price of 70 ($000). The user will install his own computer system at the termination of the contract. Computermatik's computer itself would be idle during this time if the contract were not signed, so that the direct cost of supplying the service would be virtually zero, but the cost of systems and communications development to meet the needs of the contract would be 20. The contract calls for a certain level of service which, if not achieved, will result in cancellation with no payment to Computermatik. The vendor is not certain whether the system he proposes to design can handle the mix of problems that the user will supply, and he assesses the probability of failure as .4.

A second computer vendor has already developed a system something like the one that Computermatik proposes, and the user is willing to cooperate in running a test on this system to simulate a day's usage, provided Computermatik pays the cost of the test. Because of communications costs and the special arrangements required, the test will cost Computermatik 5. Because the systems are somewhat different and the test only simulates the real environment in which Computermatik's proposed system will operate, the vendor is by no means certain either that good performance on the test will mean that the contract specifications can be satisfied, or that bad performance means they cannot be satisfied. In fact, Computermatik believes that if its proposed system would work satisfactorily, the test would nevertheless give an *unfavorable* result with probability .1, while if the proposed system would perform unsatisfactorily, the test would give a *favorable* result with probability .1.

Because of the special nature of the contract, the system that Computermatik proposes to design in order to satisfy it will have no value for future contracts, whether it works or not. Computermatik's assets are currently 30. A payoff table for the problem in terms of assets is shown in Figure 19. Observe that the events are described in terms of both the success or

	Events	Proba-	Acts		
System	*Test*	*bilities*	a_1: *Sign Contract*	a_2: *First Test*	a_3: *Do Nothing*
Satisfactory	Favorable	.54	100	95	30
Satisfactory	Unfavorable	.06	100	25	30
Unsatisfactory	Favorable	.04	10	5	30
Unsatisfactory	Unfavorable	.36	10	25	30
		1.00			

Figure 19

failure of the system and the outcome of the test. The joint probabilities of the two events are shown. For instance, if we let s stand for the statement "the system is satisfactory" and u for "the test is unfavorable," then we are given that $\Pr[s] = .6$, $\Pr[u \mid s] = .1$, from which we can compute that $\Pr[u \wedge s] = .06$, as shown in Figure 19. The dollar entries in Figure 19 are computed as follows. If the contract is signed without testing and the system works, Computermatik's assets will increase by 70 to 100; if the system fails, they will suffer a loss of 20 and their assets will decrease to 10. If they first test and the test is favorable and the system works, their assets will increase by 70 less the 5 cost of the test, to 95; if the test is favorable but the system fails, they will suffer a loss of 20 on the system plus the 5 cost of the test, so that their assets will be reduced to 5; if the test is unfavorable (whether or not the system would in fact work) they will not sign the contract but will have reduced their assets by 5 because of the cost of the test.

In analyzing act a_1, the utility of 100 is 1.0 and that of 10 is .316, so that the utility of the act is

$$.54 \times 1.0 + .06 \times 1.0 + .04 \times .316 + .36 \times .316 = .7264;$$

the certainty equivalent of the act is about 52.8, the expected value is

$$.54 \times 100 + .06 \times 100 + .04 \times 10 + .36 \times 10 = 64,$$

and the risk premium is $64 - 52.8 = 11.2$. For act a_2 the utilities of 95, 25, and 5 are respectively .975, .500, and .224, so that

$$\bar{u}(a_2) = .54 \times .975 + .06 \times .500 + .04 \times .224 + .36 \times .500 = .7455;$$

the certainty equivalent is about 55.6, the expected value is

$$.54 \times 95 + .06 \times 25 + .04 \times 5 + .36 \times 25 = 62,$$

and the risk premium is $62 - 55.6 = 6.4$. For a_3 the utility is .548, the certainty equivalent and expected value are both 30, and the risk premium is 0. Even though the expected value of a_2 is less than that of a_1, it is clearly the best alternative. Observe that although in Examples 2 and 3 insurance and syndication effectively replaced very unfavorable consequences with less unfavorable consequences (at the cost of replacing very favorable consequences with less favorable consequences), the test in the present example creates a consequence even less favorable than the most unfavorable consequence without testing. The value of the test, however, is in reducing probabilistically one's exposure to unfavorable consequences. Without the test there is a .4 probability of the contract's resulting in assets of 10; with the test, there is a .04 probability of assets being reduced to 5, but a .42 probability that they will be reduced only to 25. With the utility curve of Figure 10, these consequences favor the test.

Another very important way of reducing risk is through diversification. This is such an important topic that we shall consider it in detail in Section 6.

EXERCISES

1. Analyze the insurance problem (Example 2) if the probability of a fire next year is only .05.

2. Analyze the syndicate problem (Example 3) under the assumption that the shares are given away for nothing.

3. Under the original assumption that shares are sold for $100 each, compute utilities for the syndicate problem (Example 3) assuming 20 percent, 40 percent, . . . , 100 percent of the venture was sold. Draw a graph showing utilities on the vertical axis corresponding to percentage sold shown on the horizontal axis. What percentage maximizes the utility?

4. Analyze the testing problem (Example 4) under the assumption that if the proposed system performed unsatisfactorily, the test would give a favorable result with probability .2.

5. A person with $30,000 assets is offered a gamble that will pay him $20,000 if he wins but will require him to pay $10,000 if he loses. His utility for assets is given by Figure 14. If the probability of winning the gamble is .7, what are its utility, certainty equivalent, expected value, and risk premium? Should the gamble be accepted?

6. Suppose the gamble offered in Exercise 5 must be risked twice or not at all, and suppose the possible outcomes on the second trial are independent of the outcomes on the first trial. What are the possible asset positions following the second gamble, and what are their probabilities? What are the possible asset positions and their probabilities following a third gamble if three gambles must be risked or none at all?

7. Compute the utility, certainty equivalent, expected value, and risk premium for the problem of Exercise 5 if the person to whom the gamble is offered must agree in advance to play twice. Do the same if he must agree to play three times.

8. It is often asserted that while a person may be risk averse for a single gamble, he will be less and less so as the number of gambles increases, because the "law of averages" makes a sequence of very unfavorable events unlikely. Comment in the light of your answers to Exercises 5–7.

9. Consider 50-50 gambles that will result in asset positions of $A_1 = A - 10$ following a loss, $A_2 = A + 10$ following a win. Clearly, expected assets following such a gamble are A. Complete the accompanying table show-

A	A_1	u_1	A_2	u_2	$\bar{u}$	Certainty Equivalent	Risk Premium
10	0	0	20	.36	.18	9.45	.55
30	20	.36	40	.64	.50	29.29	—
50	40	.64	60	.84	.74	—	—
70	60	.84	80	.96	—	—	—
90	80	—	100	—	—	—	—

ing the utilities (based on the curve of Figure 12 above) of a number of such gambles, their certainty equivalents, and their risk premiums. How does the risk premium behave as A increases?

10. Repeat Exercise 9 for the table below and the utility curve graphed in

A	A_1	u_1	A_2	u_2	$\bar{u}$	Certainty Equivalent	Risk Premium
10	0	0	20	.9619	.4810	.91	9.09
30	20	.9619	40	.9854	.9736	26.77	—
50	40	.9854	60	.9934	.9894	—	—
70	60	.9934	80	.9975	—	—	—
90	80	—	100	—	—	—	—

Figure 14. How does the risk premium behave as A increases?

11. A decision maker has \$30,000 in assets. Show that if his utility curve is given by Figure 14, he should not pay \$5000 to acquire a lottery ticket that will give him a .9 probability of winning \$20,000 and a .1 probability of losing \$20,000.

12. A decision maker has a lottery ticket that gives him a .9 probability of winning \$20,000 and a .1 probability of losing \$20,000. If, in addition to the lottery ticket, he has \$30,000 in assets, and if his utility curve is given by Figure 14, show that he should not sell the ticket for \$5000. Are your answers to Exercises 11 and 12 inconsistent? Explain.

13. Compute the expected values and variances of the five gambles shown in Figure 16(a), and verify the entries in the fourth and fifth columns of that figure.

14. Compute the utility, certainty equivalent, and risk premium for gamble 1 of Figure 16(a) under the assumption that the utility curve is that of
    a. Figure 12.
    b. Figure 13.
    c. Figure 14.
    Using the results of your computations, verify the entries in the first row of Figures 16(b), (c), and (d).

15. It can be shown that an approximation to the risk premium of any gamble can be obtained from the formula $\frac{1}{2}RV$, where R depends on the utility curve and on the expected value of the gamble, and V is the variance of the gamble. The approximation improves as V decreases. In the case where the expected value of a gamble is 25, the value of R for the utility curves of Figures 12, 13, and 14 can be shown to be $\frac{1}{75}$, $\frac{1}{50}$, $\frac{1}{13}$, respectively. Compute approximations to the risk premiums of the five gambles of Figures 16(b), (c), and (d), and compare the approximate with the actual risk premiums.

16. Characterize the following company policies as risk averse or risk seeking.
    a. A fire insurance company will not accept a policy with face value of more than $50,000 on a house, but it is willing to join a group of two or more companies in insuring such houses.
    b. In a certain large company a division manager can by himself authorize expenditures of up to $25,000. Larger expenditures must be authorized by the central management.
    c. Some firms are organized to provide "venture capital" to small or new businesses with especially promising ideas. In return they require ownership of a fairly sizable percentage of the outstanding stock of the company.

5. ASSESSMENT OF UTILITY CURVES

In principle, as we have noted, a utility curve defined on assets relative to asset positions A_* and A^* can be assessed by considering for each of several asset positions the breakeven probability of winning A^* that makes a gamble on the reference consequences indifferent to a given asset position for certain. Some people object to the direct assessment of breakeven probabilities —that is, utilities—as is shown by the following typical dialogue between an imaginary decision maker (DM) and a decision analyst (DA). Again, we will treat all monetary figures as if they were measured in thousands of dollars.

Example 1.

DA. I'd like you to try to assess your utility curve for assets relative to reference consequences of 0 and 100. By 0 I mean that you are totally broke—you have no assets but the clothes that you and your family are wearing, the sympathy of friends and relatives, and your ability to work. No insurance, no pension fund, no hidden bank accounts, no car. You could survive on welfare until you found work. Now consider having 50 in assets for sure. Would you trade that for a gamble giving you a .99 chance at 100 and a .01 chance at 0?

DM. Sure. That's easy. The outcome of 0 is pretty grim, but I could survive. Anyone who is afraid to take a .01 chance of losing everything when he has a .99 chance of doubling his assets is too chickenhearted to be in business.

DA. Suppose you had only a .3 chance of winning the 100. Now what would you prefer, the gamble or the sure thing?

DM. The sure thing—no question about it. I wouldn't even think of accepting the gamble unless its expected value were greater than 50—that is, the probability of winning has to be more than .5—but it's pretty hard to pin down just how much more than .5 it ought to be.

DA. How about .6?

DM. Now it's starting to get hard to answer. Let's see, the expected value is 60: I guess I'd like more of a risk premium than 10 when I have a .4 probability of losing everything.

DA. How about .7?

DM. Well, naturally the gamble is more attractive now than it was a moment ago, but whether it's more attractive than 50 for sure is hard for me to say. I guess it's just awfully hard for me to internalize a .7 probability of success. I know what a 50-50 probability feels like—I can visualize an outcome being dependent on the toss of a coin—but there is no chance device to simulate a probability of .6 or .7 that I feel as comfortable with.

DA. Okay, let me switch my questioning strategy and ask you to imagine that you are confronted with a 50-50 gamble on the reference consequences and could exchange the gamble for some fixed asset position for sure. Would you take 60?

DM. That's easy. I'd certainly take 60. In fact, because I am risk averse, I'd settle for something less than the expected value of the gamble.

DA. How about 10?

DM. No, that's not enough. I guess I'd have an awfully hard time deciding whether I preferred the gamble to the sure thing if the sure thing were about 30 in assets.

We shall resume the dialogue in a moment, but let us interrupt to recapitulate what has happened so far. DM was unhappy assessing a breakeven probability that made a gamble on the reference consequences indifferent to a fixed "sure thing" (50 in assets for sure): that is, he felt uncomfortable assessing his utility for 50 directly. DA has now switched the assessment method so that DM is being asked to find not a breakeven probability of winning a gamble when the "sure thing" is fixed, but a breakeven level of the "sure thing" when the probability of winning the gamble is fixed at the "internalizable" level of .5. That is, DM has been asked to assess his certainty equivalent for a 50-50 gamble on the reference consequences, or, more simply, the asset position corresponding to a utility of .5. Let us continue with the dialogue.

Example 1 (continued).

DA. It sounds to me as if you can cope with 50-50 gambles, so let's try to obtain some more points on your utility curve in roughly the same way. Suppose now that you have a choice between a 50-50 gamble that will leave you with assets of either 0 or 30 and having assets of 10 for sure. Which would you prefer?

DM. The 10 sounds better to me. In fact, I guess I'd accept 5 or more in order to have a little nest egg to get started with again, rather than having a 50-50 chance of ending up with nothing.

We interrupt once more to analyze what has happened. DM has said that he is indifferent between (1) confronting a 50-50 gamble resulting in assets of either 30 or 0 and (2) having 5 for sure; that is, his certainty equivalent for the gamble is 5. Figure 20 shows a payoff table for this problem.

		Acts	
Events	Probabilities	a_1: Gamble	a_2: Sure Thing
e_1: Win	.5	30	5
e_2: Lose	.5	0	5
	1.0		

Figure 20

By DM's own assessment, the utilities of a_1 and a_2 are identical. But we have already established that $u(30) = .5$, $u(0) = 0$, so that the utility of a_1 is $.5 \times .5 + .5 \times 0 = .25$. Since the only consequence emanating from choice of a_2 is 5, it follows that $u(5) = .25$. Thus we now have found asset positions corresponding to utilities of 0, .25, .5, and 1. In the accompanying table we show systematically how DM can assess asset positions corre-

Consequences of 50-50 Gamble ($000)	Certainty Equivalent ($000)	Implied Utility
$ 0, $100	$30	.5
0, 30	5	.25
30, 100	60	.75
0, 5	1	.125
5, 30	12	.375
30, 60	40	.625
60, 100	75	.875

Figure 21

sponding to these utilities and others as well. The procedure could be continued to obtain utilities halfway between 0 and .125, between .125 and .250, and so on, but we have now gone far enough to resume the dialogue.

Example 1 (continued).

DA. I see that for every one of the gambles I have asked you to consider, your certainty equivalent is less than the expected value of the gamble. Is it reasonable to say that you want your utility curve to be risk averse throughout the interval from 0 to 100?

DM. Precisely. I chose my certainty equivalents by backing off from expected value in a way that seemed reasonable to me. While I'm willing to take chances, I certainly don't want to undertake risks whose expected values are less than standing pat.

DA. If that is your objective—and it seems like a very reasonable one to me —then I think you're in trouble. Look at what your certainty equivalents imply regarding a 50-50 gamble with consequences of 12 and 40. Your utilities are .375 and .625, your utility of the gamble is $.5 \times .375 + .5 \times .625 = .5$, and your asset position corresponding to a utility of .5 is 30, so that your certainty equivalent for the gamble is 30. But the expected value of the gamble is only $.5 \times 12 + .5 \times 40 = 26$, so that you actually have a *negative* risk premium for this gamble.

DM. Well, I guess I can change some of my certainty equivalents. In the gamble resulting in either 5 or 30 my certainty equivalent ought to be less than the expected value of 17, and in the gamble resulting in 30 or 60 it ought to be less than 45. Well, I guess I could be convinced to change my certainty equivalent in the first case to 15 and in the second to 44; but that would still leave me with a negative risk premium for a 50-50 gamble on those consequences, and I can't, in good conscience, push those numbers up any higher. I guess that maybe I ought to change my original 30 certainty equivalent for a 50-50 gamble on the reference consequences, but that will throw every other assessment out of kilter.

It should be clear from this example that it may be very hard to assess a large number of independent certainty equivalents and reconcile them with generally desirable properties of a utility curve. For this reason it is often preferable first to state generally desirable properties of a utility curve, and then to try to find a specific curve that has these properties and that passes through a few very carefully assessed points whose consistency with one another has been thoroughly checked out.

What properties should utility curves for assets have? Everyone agrees that utility should increase as assets increase; if it did not, it would pay—or at least not hurt—to throw assets away.

As we saw in Section 4, a great deal of business practice is based on risk aversion—that is, on concave utility curves. There is no law against risk-seeking behavior, but people and companies who buy insurance, share risks, diversify, and obtain expensive test information are acting inconsistently with risk-seeking utility curves. Such people and companies will generally be willing to say that risk aversion is a desirable property of their utility curves.

One other property of a risk-averse utility curve that is worth considering is the behavior of risk premiums as one's asset position changes. Consider a two-valued 50-50 gamble that will make your asset position $A + d$ if you win, $A - d$ if you lose. Clearly, your expected assets following this gamble will be A. Suppose that the difference between your initial assets A and the certainty equivalent for this gamble is a positive constant K that may depend on d but not on A. Then your utility curve is said to have the property of constant risk aversion. Suppose, for example, that your current asset position is A and you face a 50-50 gamble that would change your wealth by 1 (\$000)—that is, make your asset position $A + 1$ if you won and $A - 1$ if you lost, so that $d = 1$. Suppose your certainty equivalent in assets for this gamble were $A - .2$—that is, $K = .2$. Then if you had constant risk aversion and your initial assets were A', your certainty equivalent in assets for this same gamble would be $A' - .2$. Many people feel that this is an undesirable property of a utility curve.

Now consider a 50-50 gamble that will make your asset position Ar

if you win and A/r if you lose, where $r > 1$. Suppose that the ratio between your certainty equivalent and your initial assets is a positive constant k that may depend on r but not on A. Then your utility curve is said to have the property of constant proportional risk aversion. Suppose, for example, that your initial assets were $A = 10$ and you faced a 50-50 gamble that would leave you with assets of 20 if you won and with 5 if you lost, so that $r = 2$. Suppose your certainty equivalent for assets following this gamble were 11.25; that is, the ratio of certainty equivalent to initial assets were $11.25/10 = 1.125$. Then if you had constant proportional risk aversion, and had initial assets $A' = 50$ instead of $A = 10$, your certainty equivalent assets for a 50-50 gamble that would leave you in an asset position of 100 if you won, 25 if you lost, would be $1.125 \times 50 = 56.25$. Some people find that their attitude toward risk is consistent with constant proportional risk aversion (see Exercise 5).

> **Example 2.** The utility curve graphed in Figure 13 has the property of constant proportional risk aversion, which can be shown algebraically as follows. Using the formula to compute utilities from assets, the utility of a 50-50 gamble that will result in an asset position Ar following win, A/r following loss, is
>
> $$\bar{u} = .5 \times .1\sqrt{Ar} + .5 \times .1 \sqrt{\frac{A}{r}}$$
>
> $$= .05\sqrt{A}\left(\sqrt{r} + \frac{1}{\sqrt{r}}\right).$$
>
> Using the formula to compute certainty equivalents from assets, the certainty-equivalent value is
>
> $$CE = 100\left[.05\sqrt{A}\left(\sqrt{r} + \frac{1}{\sqrt{r}}\right)\right]^2$$
>
> $$= .25A\left(\sqrt{r} + \frac{1}{\sqrt{r}}\right)^2.$$
>
> The ratio
>
> $$\frac{CE}{A} = .25\left(\sqrt{r} + \frac{1}{\sqrt{r}}\right)^2$$
>
> is independent of A, as was to be shown.

One reason for considering these special properties of utility curves is that if the decision maker thinks his attitude toward risk has one of these properties, then his whole utility curve can be assessed by directly assessing either his certainty equivalents or breakeven probabilities for just one hypothetical gamble.

A property of utility curves that is less constraining than constant or constant proportional risk aversion is simply decreasing positive risk aversion. If a 50-50 gamble yields an asset position $A + d$ following win, $A - d$ following loss, and if a utility curve is such that for any fixed d the risk premium for such a gamble is always positive but decreases as A increases, the utility curve is said to have the property of decreasing positive risk aversion. Many people find this property very desirable. Such curves can match a decision maker's own attitudes toward risk quite flexibly; at the same time, their specification does not require very many assessments of breakeven probabilities or certainty equivalents by the decision maker. It can be shown that the utility curve graphed in Figure 14 has decreasing positive risk aversion (see Exercise 10 of Section 4). The curve graphed in Figure 12, on the contrary, has increasing positive risk aversion (see Exercise 9 of Section 4). The implication of a curve with decreasing positive risk aversion is that a decision maker who uses it will never take risks with negative expected values, but as his assets increase he will be more and more likely to self-insure, not to share risky ventures that have positive expected valued, not to undertake expensive risk-reducing tests, and not to seek diversification for risk reduction.

EXERCISES

1. Consider reference consequences of 0 and 10 in thousands of dollars of assets. Assess your certainty equivalent for a 50-50 gamble on the reference consequences. Call this certainty equivalent $A_{.5}$.

2. Assess your certainty equivalent for a 50-50 gamble resulting either in 0 or in the consequence $A_{.5}$ assessed in Exercise 1. Call this new certainty equivalent $A_{.25}$. Similarly, assess your certainty equivalent on a 50-50 gamble with consequences $A_{.5}$ and 10; call this new certainty equivalent $A_{.75}$.

3. Assess your certainty equivalent for a 50-50 gamble resulting in the consequences $A_{.25}$ and $A_{.75}$ assessed in Exercise 2. Compare your answer with the value $A_{.5}$ assessed in Exercise 1. Reconcile any inconsistencies by reassessing $A_{.25}$, $A_{.50}$, and $A_{.75}$ if necessary.

4. Using the utility curve graphed in Figure 13, compute certainty equivalents for the following 50-50 gambles:
   a. 10, 90.
   b. 20, 80.
   c. 40, 90.

5. Consider 50-50 gambles that will result in asset positions of $2A$ following a win, $A/2$ following a loss. Complete the table below for utilities computed from the curve shown in Figure 13.

A	A_1	u_1	A_2	u_2	$\bar{u}$	Certainty Equivalent	Risk Premium	CE/A
10	5	.2236	20	.4472	.3354	11.25	1.25	1.125
20	10	.3162	40	.6325	.4743	22.50	—	—
30	15	.3873	60	.7746	.5809	—	—	—
40	20	.4472	80	.8944	—	—	—	—
50	25	—	100	—	—	—	—	—

6. Consider 50-50 gambles that will result in asset positions of $A + 10$ following a win, $A - 10$ following a loss. Complete the table below for

A	A_1	u_1	A_2	u_2	$\bar{u}$	Certainty Equivalent	Risk Premium
10	0	0	20	.4472	.2236	5.00	5.00
20	10	.3162	30	.5477	.4320	18.66	1.34
30	20	.4472	40	.6325	.5398	29.14	.86
40	30	.5477	50	.7071	.6274	39.36	—
50	40	.6325	60	.7746	.7035	49.49	—
60	50	.7071	70	.8367	.7719	—	—
70	60	.7746	80	.8944	—	—	—
80	70	—	90	—	—	—	—
90	80	—	100	—	—	—	—

utilities computed from the curve shown in Figure 13. (It can be shown that this utility curve has not only the property of constant proportional risk aversion but that of decreasing positive risk aversion as well.)

7. Utilities can be computed relative to reference consequences $A_* = 10$, $A^* = 100$ according to the formula

$$u = \log A - 1,$$

where the logarithm is taken to the base 10. Certainty equivalents corresponding to utilities between 0 and 1 can be computed according to the formula

$$A = 10^{u+1}.$$

Show algebraically that this utility curve has the property of constant proportional risk aversion.

8. Utilities for reference consequences $A_* = 0$, $A^* = 100$ can be computed according to the formula

$$u = \frac{1 - 10^{-.02A}}{.99}.$$

Conversely, for any utility u, the corresponding certainty equivalent can be computed according to the formula

$$A = -50 \log (1 - .99u),$$

where the logarithm is taken to the base 10.

a. Show that the utility for a 50-50 gamble that will result in assets of either $A + d$ or $A - d$ is given by the formula

$$\frac{1 - .5 \times 10^{-.02A}(10^{-.02d} + 10^{.02d})}{.99}.$$

 b. By using the formula for certainty equivalents, show that the certainty equivalent for the gamble in part (*a*) above is given by the formula

$$-50 \log [.5 \times 10^{-.02A}(10^{-.02d} + 10^{.02d})] = A - 50 \log [.5(10^{-.02d} + 10^{.02d})].$$

 c. Show that the risk premium for the gamble in part (*a*) above is given by the formula

$$50 \log [.5(10^{-.02d} + 10^{.02d})],$$

which is positive and independent of *A*. What have we proved about the properties of this utility curve?

6. PORTFOLIO SELECTION: STATEMENT OF THE PROBLEM

We have seen that a decision maker who is risk averse may often want to avoid "putting all his eggs in one basket," even though the "basket" may be an excellent one. He may find that it pays to spread his assets over a number of different investments—to put his eggs in several different baskets—to reduce even a small risk of catastrophe. This general strategy often motivates companies to merge with dissimilar companies or to introduce totally new product lines. A conglomerate company may be able to survive a crisis in one industry if its subsidiary companies are spread over a variety of industries; similarly, failure of a given product line can be absorbed by a company that has a large variety of product lines.

 Desirable though this kind of diversification may be, however, it may entail some offsetting costs. A company that acquires a dissimilar company through a merger may be less skilled in managing its new acquisition than it was in managing its original business. Similarly, the risks of launching a new product line may be high enough to make such a move undesirable when viewed in isolation. Whether or not a given diversifying strategy makes sense, however, depends on its possible effects viewed not in isolation but in the context of all the other uncertainties that already exist.

 Much of the spirit of diversification is captured in portfolio analysis, which is an important subject in its own right. Mutual funds and trusts are required by law to diversify their funds into a number of securities, and virtually all investors choose to diversify rather than invest all their money in a single security.

 Portfolio analysis starts with the assumption that an investor initially owns no securities, but has an amount A_0 of liquid assets on hand and a list of securities under consideration. These "securities" may be stocks, bonds, "risk-free" securities, or just plain cash. It is assumed that the investor will invest all his funds today in a portfolio of securities chosen from the list, hold the portfolio for some specified period of time (a year, say), and then sell it out completely.

The investor is assumed to have thought seriously about the uncertainties in the future values of the securities under consideration. We shall calculate the future value of a security as the selling price a year hence, augmented by the value of dividends received during the year, and diminished by any taxes incurred, and shall express this value as a fraction of the purchase price. We shall call this fraction the "return." If, for example, a security cost $50 today, were sold for $60 a year hence, and paid $4 in dividends, and if the investor's tax rate on dividends were 60 percent and on capital gains 25 percent, then his total taxes would be ($60 − $50) × .25 + $4 × .6 = $4.90, the "value" at the end of the year would be $60 + $4 − $4.90 = $59.10, and the "return" would be $59.10/$50 = 1.182. Observe that the return will be 1.0 (*not* 0) if the value at the end of the year happens to be exactly equal to the value today.

The analysis further assumes that the investor has not only thought about every possible return of every security on his list, but has actually assessed the joint probability of every combination of returns of all such securities. If he has three securities on his list, for example, and believes he can adequately represent his uncertainty about returns by considering 10 possible values for each security, then there are 1000 possible combinations of returns, and for each such combination we assume that he has assessed the probability of its occurrence. Clearly, assessments of this sort cannot be made directly, and we shall consider later how the assessment problem can be handled practically. For the moment, we shall simply assume that the required probabilities have been obtained in one way or another.

We shall assume that the investor is interested only in purchasing securities for straight cash; he cannot borrow money and he cannot engage in short selling of securities. He can invest any fraction of his cash whatsoever in a given security by obtaining, if necessary, fractional shares. Transaction costs (which in fact are about 2 percent of the amount of transaction) will be treated as negligible. We also assume that the market is sufficiently broad relative to the investor's cash on hand that the return on any security will be unaffected by the amount he buys or sells.

In order to keep the level of examples reasonably simple, we shall assume that the possible returns on each security can be adequately described by just two possible values of returns. Actual portfolio analysis makes much more sophisticated assumptions about the probabilistic nature of returns, but many of the problems, methods, and interpretations of more general portfolio analysis can be captured, at the sacrifice of some realism, by our assumption of two-valued returns.

Example 1. Mr. Jones has $A_0 = \$50,000$ in liquid assets available for investment. He is considering two securities, X and Y. Security X is a speculative growth stock with possible returns of 2.0 (that is, it will double its value)

or .3 (its value will decrease by 70 percent). Security Y is also a very specu-
lative stock, but it has less growth potential and more risk; its possible returns
are 1.9 or .05. The probabilities of all possible combinations of returns are as
shown in Figure 22.

		Security Y	
	Returns	*1.9*	*.05*
	2.0	.05	.45
Security X			
	.3	.45	.05

Figure 22

Mr. Jones is considering various portfolios: investing all $50,000 in X,
all $50,000 in Y, splitting his funds evenly between X and Y, or investing all
his funds in a riskless security (such as a high-grade government bond that
will mature in one year) whose return will be 1.05 (that is, it will pay 5
percent interest) with certainty. The problem and the potential outcomes of
the various portfolios are summarized in a payoff table (Figure 23), where,

	Events			*Acts*		
Return on X	*Return on Y*	*Proba-bilities*	*a_1: 50 in X*	*a_2: 50 in Y*	*a_3: 25 in X, 25 in Y*	*a_4: 50 in riskless security*
2.0	1.90	.05	100	95.0	97.50	52.5
2.0	.05	.45	100	2.5	51.25	52.5
.3	1.90	.45	15	95.0	55.00	52.5
.3	.05	.05	15	2.5	8.75	52.5
		1.00				

Figure 23

as usual, we express all monetary figures in units of thousands of dollars.

Mr. Jones' utility curve for liquid assets A relative to reference consequences $A_* = 0$, $A^* = 100$ (thousands of dollars) is shown in Figure 13.
Because his utility curve is risk averse over the entire interval between the
reference consequences, Mr. Jones is inclined to rule out security Y, whose
purchase would leave him with expected net assets of less than 50, and whose
certainty equivalent would therefore be still less. He proceeds, nevertheless,
to analyze his problem formally, as shown in Figure 24. The consequences
of each portfolio are given in thousands of dollars; the utilities and certainty
equivalents are computed by formula, instead of being read from the curve
in Figure 13.

Clearly, a_4: investing in the riskless security, is the best of the four
acts. As expected, a_2: investing 50 in security Y, results in a very unfavorable
asset position, while a_1: investing 50 in security X, is not too bad, although
not as good as a_4. Surprisingly, however, a_3, the portfolio consisting of a 50-50
split of Jones' liquid assets between securities X and Y, turns out to be
better than investing everything in X. Why does it make sense to buy some
of a clearly inferior security? The worst consequence resulting from a_3 is 8.75,
while the worst resulting from a_1 is 15, and similarly the best consequence

	a_1: 50 in X			a_2: 50 in Y			a_3: 25 in X, 25 in Y			a_4: 50 in Riskless		
Prob.	*Cons.*	*Util.*	*Prod.*	*Cons.*	*Util.*	*Prod.*	*Cons.*	*Util.*	*Prod.*	*Cons.*	*Util.*	*Prod.*
.05	100	1.000	.050	95.0	.975	.049	97.50	.987	.049	52.5	.725	.036
.45	100	1.000	.450	2.5	.158	.071	51.25	.716	.322	52.5	.725	.326
.45	15	.387	.174	95.0	.975	.439	55.00	.742	.334	52.5	.725	.326
.05	15	.387	.019	2.5	.158	.008	8.75	.296	.015	52.5	.725	.036
1.00		$\bar{u}(a_1) = .693$			$\bar{u}(a_2) = .567$			$\bar{u}(a_3) = .720$			$\bar{u}(a_4) = .724$	
Certainty equivalents:	48.1			32.1			51.8			52.5		

Figure 24

resulting from mixing X and Y is only 97.5, whereas the best from X alone is 100. Nevertheless, a_3 is better because it substantially reduces the probability of the worst consequence: under a_3, the probability of the consequence 8.75 is only .05, while under a_1 the probability of the consequence 15 is .50. To be sure, the probability of the best consequence is also reduced under a_3, but a risk-averse utility curve may prefer less probability on the extremes, as it does in this case.

The reduction in the probability of extreme consequences is attributable to the fact that, according to the probabilities assessed in Figure 22, when X goes down, Y tends to go up, and when Y goes down, X tends to go up. In fact, if we let x stand for "X went up" and y stand for "Y went up," then

$$\mathbf{Pr}[\sim x \mid y] = \frac{\mathbf{Pr}[\sim x \wedge y]}{\mathbf{Pr}[y]} = \frac{.45}{.5} = .9,$$

while $\mathbf{Pr}[\sim y \mid x]$ similarly is .9. Thus a loss on X is frequently offset in part by a gain on Y and vice versa. In fact, it is easy to show (see Exercise 6) that if X and Y *always* moved in opposite directions—that is, if

$$\mathbf{Pr}[x \wedge y] = \mathbf{Pr}[\sim x \wedge \sim y] = 0 \quad \text{and} \quad \mathbf{Pr}[\sim x \wedge y] = \mathbf{Pr}[x \wedge \sim y] = .5$$

—then the mixed portfolio (a_3) would be better even than the riskless portfolio (a_4). Notice that this improvement is a result of changing the probability assigned to $x \wedge y$ (and the other possible conjunctions). The probability that x is true and the probability that y is true each are .5, as in the original statement of the problem.

While Jones cannot in fact do anything to change the probabilities assigned to the possible returns, he can explore other investment strategies. A portfolio consisting of a mixture of securities X and Y need not be restricted to a 50-50 mixture.

In Figure 25 we explore two new portfolios—a_5: invest 30 in X and 20 in Y; and a_6: invest 30 in the risk-free security and 20 in X. Both of these portfolios are better than any of those shown in Figure 24. Observe that a_5 simply mixes X and Y in different proportions from those in a_3, while a_6 causes X and the risk-free security to be mixed. The effect of this latter strategy is to make unfavorable extremes less severe at the cost of reducing favorable extremes; this, in the setting of the present example, increases utility if not carried too far.

Acts

Prob.	a_5: 30 in X, 20 in Y			a_6: 20 in X, 30 in Riskless		
	Cons.	Util.	Prod.	Cons.	Util.	Prod.
.05	98	.990	.049	71.5	.846	.042
.45	61	.781	.351	71.5	.846	.381
.45	47	.686	.309	37.5	.612	.276
.05	10	.316	.016	37.5	.612	.031
1.00		$\bar{u}(a_5) = .725$			$\bar{u}(a_6) = .730$	

Certainty equivalents: 52.6   53.1

Figure 25

Is it possible to do better with a mixture of all three securities than with combinations of only two? What is the best portfolio for this list of securities and this utility curve? Precise answers to these questions can be obtained only by obtaining utilities and certainty equivalents for a large number of possible portfolios, and this can most easily be done on a computer. Figure 26(a) shows a set of six curves, each one representing a different frac-

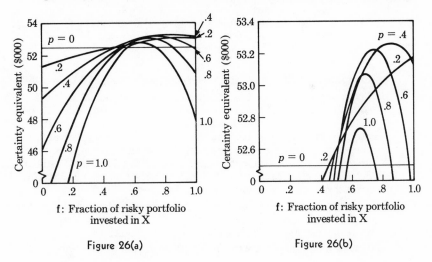

f: Fraction of risky portfolio invested in X

Figure 26(a)

f: Fraction of risky portfolio invested in X

Figure 26(b)

tion p invested in risky (as distinguished from risk-free) securities. The horizontal axis gives the fraction f invested in security X as a fraction of the total amount invested in risky securities. The vertical axis shows the certainty equivalent corresponding to each computed portfolio. Figure 26(b) shows results in greater detail for those portfolios having high certainty equivalents. As can be seen, a portfolio involving all three securities is best. Figure 27 shows a computation of the utility and certainty equivalent for the portfolio (a_7) that consists of investing 28.5 in the riskless security, and of the remaining 21.5, investing 17.85, or 83 percent, in X.

a_7: Invest 28.5 in Riskless, 17.85 in X, 3.65 in Y

Probability	Consequence	Utility	Product
.05	72.56	.852	.043
.45	65.80	.811	.365
.45	42.22	.650	.292
.05	35.46	.595	.030
1.00			$\bar{u}(a_7) = .730$

Certainty equivalent = 53.3

Figure 27

EXERCISES

1. Verify the entries in Figures 23 and 24.

2. Verify the computations in Figures 25 and 27.

3. Suppose Mr. Jones had only $A_0 = 10$ in liquid assets, and were considering the following portfolios:

a_1:   10 in X;
a_2:   10 in Y;
a_3:   5 in X, 5 in Y;
a_4:   10 in riskless security.

Compute the utility and certainty equivalent of each of these portfolios.

4. Verify that the four portfolios in Exercise 3 are ranked in utility and certainty equivalent in the same order as are the four portfolios designated as a_1, a_2, a_3, and a_4 in Example 1 of this section. With Mr. Jones' utility curve, will it be true in general that the value of A_0 will have no effect on the ranking of various possible portfolios? [*Hint:* What are the properties of this utility curve, as revealed by Exercises 5 and 6 of Section 5?] Would the value of A_0 have an effect on the ranking of portfolios if Mr. Jones had some other utility curve? Why?

5. Compute the utility and certainty equivalent of the four portfolios shown in Figure 23 on the assumption that Mr. Jones' utility curve was the one shown in Figure 12 instead of the one in Figure 13.

6. Letting x stand for "X went up" and y stand for "Y went up," suppose

$$\mathbf{Pr}[x \wedge y] = \mathbf{Pr}[\sim x \wedge \sim y] = 0 \quad \text{and} \quad \mathbf{Pr}[\sim x \wedge y] = \mathbf{Pr}[x \wedge \sim y] = .5.$$

Using Mr. Jones' original utility curve, compute the utilities and certainty equivalents of the portfolios whose possible consequences are shown in Figure 23. [*Hint:* Do you have to perform any new computations for portfolios a_1, a_2, and a_4?]

7. Repeat Exercise 6 under the assumption that

$$\mathbf{Pr}[x \wedge y] = \mathbf{Pr}[\sim x \wedge y] = \mathbf{Pr}[x \wedge \sim y] = \mathbf{Pr}[\sim x \wedge \sim y] = .25.$$

8. Repeat Exercise 6 under the assumption that

$$\mathbf{Pr}[x \wedge y] = \mathbf{Pr}[\sim x \wedge \sim y] = .5, \qquad \mathbf{Pr}[\sim x \wedge y] = \mathbf{Pr}[x \wedge \sim y] = 0.$$

What is the effect on the utility and certainty equivalent of a_3 as X and Y tend to move more and more in the same direction?

9. *a.* Compute e_x, the expected value of the return on security X, the probabilities of whose returns are shown in Figure 22.

    b. Compute e_y, the expected value of the return on security Y.

10. *a.* Compute v_{xx}, the variance of the return on security X.

    b. Compute v_{yy}, the variance of the return on security Y.

11. Consider a portfolio consisting of n securities in which a fraction f_1 of the investor's initial liquid assets A_0 is invested in the first security, a fraction f_2 in the second, . . . , a fraction f_n in the nth, where the sum of the f's is 1. If the return on the first security is r_1, the return on the second is r_2, . . . , the return on the nth is r_n, then the return on the portfolio is

$$r^* = f_1 r_1 + f_2 r_2 + \cdots + f_n r_n.$$

    a. Compute the return on a portfolio consisting of a 50-50 mixture of securities X and Y of Example 1 given the event that X and Y both went up.

    b. Repeat *a.* given the event X went up and Y went down.

    c. Repeat *a.* given the event X went down and Y went up.

    d. Repeat *a.* given the event X and Y both went down.

12. *a.* Compute the expected value e^* of the return on the portfolio of Exercise 11 given the probabilities of the various possible events shown in Figure 22. Show that $e^* = .5e_x + .5e_y$, where e_x and e_y were defined in Exercise 9.

    b. Compute the variance v^* of the return on the portfolio of Exercise 11.

13. If an experiment produces pairs of numbers (a_1, b_1), (a_2, b_2), . . . , (a_k, b_k) with probabilities p_1, p_2, . . . , p_k whose sum is 1, then the *covariance* is defined as

$$(a_1 - E_a)(b_1 - E_b)p_1 + (a_2 - E_a)(b_2 - E_b)p_2 + \cdots \\ + (a_k - E_a)(b_k - E_b)p_k,$$

where E_a is the expected value of the a's, and E_b is the expected value of the b's. Compute v_{xy}, the covariance of returns on securities X and Y.

14. Show that the variance v^* of the return computed directly in Exercise 12 can also be computed according to the formula

$$v^* = .25v_{xx} + .25v_{yy} + .5v_{xy},$$

where v_{xx} and v_{yy} were previously defined and computed in Exercise 10, and v_{xy} in Exercise 13.

15. It can be shown that if a portfolio consists of a mixture of securities X and Y, with a fraction f in security X and $(1 - f)$ in security Y, then the expected value e^* of the return on the portfolio is

$$e^* = fe_x + (1 - f)e_y,$$

while the variance is

$$v^* = f^2 v_{xx} + (1 - f)^2 v_{yy} + 2f(1 - f)v_{xy}.$$

a. Show that the results obtained in Exercises 12 and 14 for the case $f = .5$ agree with this formula.

b. Compute directly the expected value e^* and variance v^* of return on a portfolio consisting of a fraction .6 invested in security X and a fraction .4 invested in security Y. Check your results by using the formulas given above.

16. a. Compute the expected values of liquid assets for the portfolios designated as a_3 (Figure 23) and a_5 (Figure 25). Show that these expected values can be computed indirectly by multiplying the values of e^* computed in Exercises 12(a) and 15(b) by A_0.

b. Compute the variances of liquid assets for the two portfolios designated in part (a). Show that these variances can be computed indirectly by multiplying the values of v^* computed in Exercises 12(b) and 15(b) by A_0^2.

c. Show that the standard deviations of liquid assets for the two portfolios can be computed from the standard deviations of their returns by multiplying the latter by A_0.

17. Consider a mixture of risky securities having a return with an expected value e^* and a variance v^*. Suppose an investor forms a portfolio consisting of a fraction p invested in the mixture of risky securities described above and a fraction $1 - p$ invested in a riskless security having a return of e_0.

a. Show that the return on this portfolio has expected value

$$e = e_0(1 - p) + e^*p,$$

a variance

$$v = p^2 v^*,$$

and a standard deviation

$$d = p\sqrt{v^*}.$$

b. Show that liquid assets for this portfolio will have expected value, variance, and standard deviation of $A_0 e$, $A_0^2 v$, and $A_0 d$, respectively.

18. a. Compute the expected value and variance of return on a risky portfolio consisting of a fraction .83 invested in security X and .17 invested in security Y. [*Hint:* Use the formulas given in Exercise 15.]

b. Use your answer to part (a) and the formulas given in Exercise 17 to compute the expected value, variance, and standard deviation of liquid assets for the portfolio evaluated in Figure 27.

c. Compute directly the expected value, variance, and standard deviation of liquid assets for the portfolio of Figure 27, and verify the formulas of Exercise 17.

19. Suppose two securities, X and Y, have possible joint returns, with probabilities as follows:

| | Returns | Security Y | |
		2.0	.5
Security X	1.5	.42	.28
	.8	.18	.12

a. Show that the returns on security X are independent of the returns on security Y (see Chapter 3, Section 6) and that, conversely, the returns on Y are independent of those on X.

b. Show that the covariance of returns on X and Y is 0.

20. Suppose two securities, X and Y, have possible joint returns with probabilities as follows:

| | Returns | Security Y | |
		1.8	.2
Security X	1.5	.25	0
	1.0	0	.5
	.5	.25	0

a. Show that the returns on security X are dependent on the returns on security Y, and vice versa.

b. Show that the covariance of returns on X and Y is 0. [In general, it can be shown that if pairs of numbers are independent, their covariance is necessarily 0, but if their covariance is 0, they are not necessarily independent.]

7. PORTFOLIO SELECTION: OPTIMIZATION AND ASSESSMENT

The problem of selecting an optimal portfolio, while straightforward when there are only three securities under consideration, becomes extremely cumbersome when the number of securities under consideration becomes even a little bit larger. There are two reasons for this. First, it becomes very difficult to assess the required probabilities. Even with only ten securities and with possible returns on each described by just two values (as in Section 6), there would be $2^{10} - 1 = 1023$ joint probabilities to assess, and with 20 securities there would be over 1 million. Second, it becomes extremely time-consuming to search for the optimal portfolio, even with a computer. If, for example, we wanted to examine up to ten different levels of investment for each of ten different securities, we would have to compute 10^{10} utilities and certainty equivalents—a major task for even the fastest computers. We shall discuss the second of these problems first.

Consider any act whatsoever that results in uncertain consequences having expected value E and standard deviation D. If D is not too large, then the certainty equivalent of the act can be shown to be approximately

(1) $$CE \approx E - \tfrac{1}{2}RD^2,$$

where the constant R depends on the decision maker's utility curve and may also depend on the expected value E. For risk-averse utility curves, $R > 0$. The approximation improves as D decreases (see Example 1 of Section 4).

In situations where this approximation holds reasonably well, it follows that for *any* risk-averse decision maker facing two acts having the same expected value, the act with the smaller standard deviation will have the larger certainty equivalent and thus will be better. This suggests that the optimal act can be found by examining only the subset of possible acts that minimize the standard deviation for given expected value. Because (1) is only an approximation, it is possible to find situations in which, for some given risk-averse utility curve, an act with a smaller expected value and a larger standard deviation than some other act nevertheless has a higher certainty equivalent (see Exercises 4 through 6), but such situations are unusual unless D is very large.

The approximation (1) has some very interesting and far-reaching consequences for portfolio theory in general. Most of these general consequences can be illustrated in terms of a very special case, in which there are just two risky securities, X and Y, and a riskless security. We shall show how this very special problem can be solved, and indicate how the solution method generalizes to the case where there are any number of risky securities.

Suppose that the return on security X has expected value e_x, variance v_{xx}, and standard deviation d_x, and suppose that e_y, v_{yy}, and d_y are similarly defined for security Y. The riskless security has return e_0. We can assume without loss of generality that the return on security X has at least as high an expected value as the return on security Y—that is, that $e_x \geq e_y$; in order to have a nontrivial problem, we must also assume that $e_x > e_0$ (see Exercise 1). We also define for the combination of returns of securities X and Y the covariance (see Exercise 13 of Section 6) v_{xy}.

Let p be the fraction of the investor's liquid assets that he invests in risky securities; the remaining fraction $1 - p$ will be invested in the riskless security. Of the amount invested in risky securities, let f be the fraction invested in security X and let $1 - f$ be the fraction invested in security Y. Let e, v, and d be the expected value, variance, and standard deviation of return on such a portfolio. Of course, e, v, and d depend on p and f as well as on the values of e_x, e_y, e_0, v_{xx}, v_{yy}, and v_{xy}; we shall sometimes formally indicate their dependence on p by writing $e(p)$, $v(p)$, and $d(p)$. Our initial objective is to find the subset of possible acts that minimize the standard deviation for given expected value—that is, to find the values of p and f that minimize d for given e. We shall start, however, with an even more specialized problem in which all liquid assets are invested in risky securities —that is, $p = 1$.

If $p = 1$, then the return on a portfolio consisting of a fraction f of liquid assets invested in security X and a fraction $1 - f$ invested in security Y has expected value

$$(2) \qquad e(1) = fe_x + (1 - f)e_y,$$

variance

$$(3) \qquad v(1) = f^2 v_{xx} + (1 - f)^2 v_{yy} + 2f(1 - f)v_{xy},$$

and standard deviation

$$(4) \qquad d(1) = \sqrt{f^2 v_{xx} + (1 - f)^2 v_{yy} + 2f(1 - f)v_{xy}}$$

(see Exercise 15 of Section 6). The optimization problem with $p = 1$ can then be stated mathematically as follows:

For given e, find f to

$$(5) \qquad \text{Minimize } d(1) = \sqrt{f^2 v_{xx} + (1 - f)^2 v_{yy} + 2f(1 - f)v_{xy}},$$

where f is constrained by

$$(6) \qquad fe_x + (1 - f)e_y = e,$$

$$(7) \qquad 0 \leq f \leq 1.$$

The constraint (7), together with the assumption that $e_x \geq e_y$, implies that e is constrained by

$$(8) \qquad e_y \leq e \leq e_x.$$

Solving (6) for f, we obtain

$$(9) \qquad f = \frac{e - e_y}{e_x - e_y} ;$$

substituting (9) in (5), and using the new constraint (8) derived from (7), we can express $d(1)$ in terms of e and restate the problem as follows:

For given e,

$$(10) \quad \text{Minimize } d(1) = \frac{\sqrt{(e - e_y)^2 v_{xx} + (e_x - e)^2 v_{yy} + 2(e - e_y)(e_x - e)v_{xy}}}{e_x - e_y},$$

where e is constrained by

$$(11) \qquad e_y \leq e \leq e_x.$$

If e is given, however, the value of $d(1)$ given by (10) is unique; that is, there is no longer a minimization problem, so that we can finally formulate the problem as:

Find $d(1)$, as given by (10), for values of e constrained by (11).

These values of $d(1)$, together with the value of e to which they correspond, will define what we shall call the *efficient set of risky portfolios*, and such portfolios will be called "efficient."

> **Example 1.** We continue with Mr. Jones' problem of Section 6. In Exercise 9 of that section, we found that $e_x = 1.15$, $e_y = .975$; in Exercise 10 we found that $v_{xx} = .7225$, $v_{yy} = .855625$; and in Exercise 13 we found that $v_{xy} = -.629$. Then the problem is to find, for values of e constrained by

(12) $$.975 \leq e \leq 1.15,$$

> the corresponding values of

(13)

$$d(1) = \sqrt{(e-.975)^2(.7225)+(1.15-e)^2(.855625)+2(e-.975)(1.15-e)(-.629)}/.175.$$

> Figure 28 is a graph showing for values of e satisfying (12) the values of $d(1)$ that satisfy (13); that is, it is a graph of the efficient set of risky portfolios. Observe that all values on the graph to the left of its minimum, which occurs at $e = 1.067$, represent portfolios having higher standard deviation and lower expected value than the portfolio for which $e = 1.067$, and hence we need consider only those points in the efficient set corresponding to values of $e \geq 1.067$.

Let us now return to the original problem, in which p, the fraction invested in risky securities, can be less than 1. If the return on the risky part of such a portfolio has expected value $e(1)$ and standard deviation $d(1)$, then, as we saw in Exercise 17 of Section 6, the return on the portfolio consisting in part of the riskless security has expected value

(14) $$e(p) = (1 - p)e_0 + pe(1),$$

and standard deviation

(15) $$d(p) = pd(1).$$

This means that if we represent a given "efficient" risky portfolio by a point on a graph of the efficient set for risky portfolios like that of Figure 28, then any portfolio consisting of a mixture of this risky portfolio and the riskless security can be represented by a point on a straight-line segment like the dashed line in Figure 29 connecting the point $(e_0, 0)$ with the point representing the risky portfolio (see Exercises 7 and 8). Any point on such a line segment will represent a portfolio containing some of the riskless asset, and it will have less standard deviation than a point on the curve directly

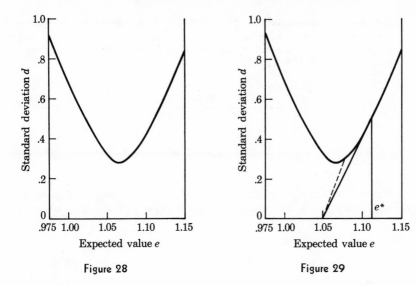

Figure 28   Figure 29

above it; hence any part of the curve to the left of the point where the line segment intersects it can be replaced by the line segment itself.

But if we could move the point of intersection between the curve and the line segment further to the right, we could do even better; points on this new segment will have lower standard deviation than points directly above them either on the old segment or on the curve. Thus we are encouraged to draw a line from $(e_0, 0)$ to a point on the curve as far to the right as possible; this is done in Figure 29 for the problem of Example 1, where the straight line is just tangent to the curve at $e^* = 1.118$.

We call the set of points on this straight-line segment and on the curve to the right of e^* the efficient set when both risky and riskless securities are considered. The portfolio that is optimal given the approximation (1) can now be selected from those portfolios represented by points on the efficient set as follows. Points at and to the right of e^* represent portfolios containing the two risky securities X and Y only—that is, points for which $p = 1$. For any such points on this part of the curve, the fraction invested in X can be computed using formula (9); once any such fraction is determined, the utility and certainty equivalent can be computed as in Section 6. Points to the left of e^* all lie on the straight-line segment, and represent portfolios whose risky part is divided between X and Y in a way determined by formula (9) when $e = e^*$; for any such point the fraction p in risky securities is proportional to the distance between its expected return e and the riskless return e_0. More precisely,

(16)
$$p = \frac{e - e_0}{e^* - e_0}.$$

Example 1 (continued). The point at $e = 1.13$ represents a portfolio for which $p = 1, f = (1.13 - .975)/(1.15 - .975) = .155/.175 = .886$—that is, for which 44.3 is invested in X and 5.7 in Y, while the point at $e = 1.07$ represents a portfolio for which

$$p = \frac{1.07 - .975}{1.118 - .975} = \frac{.095}{.143} = .296,$$

$$f = \frac{1.118 - .975}{1.15 - .975} = .815$$

—that is, a portfolio for which 35.2 is invested in the riskless security, 12.1 in X, and 2.7 in Y. These two portfolios are evaluated in Figure 30.

	44.3 in X, 5.7 in Y			35.2 in Riskless, 12.1 in X, 2.7 in Y		
Probability	*Consequence*	*Utility*	*Product*	*Consequence*	*Utility*	*Product*
.05	99.4	.997	.050	66.3	.814	.041
.45	88.9	.943	.424	61.2	.782	.352
.45	24.1	.491	.221	45.8	.677	.304
.05	13.6	.368	.018	40.7	.638	.032
1.00			.713			.729
Certainty equivalents:			50.9			53.2

Figure 30

If we systematically evaluate portfolios represented by points on the efficient set, we find that the best portfolio corresponds to a point for which $e = 1.08$, $d = .137$, $p = .444$, and $f = .815$; this is a portfolio for which 27.8 is invested in the riskless security, 18.1 in X, and 4.1 in Y. The portfolio is evaluated in Figure 31. The utility and certainty equivalent ob-

	27.8 in Riskless, 18.1 in X, 4.1 in Y		
Probability	*Consequence*	*Utility*	*Product*
.05	73.2	.855	.043
.45	65.6	.810	.364
.45	42.4	.651	.293
.05	34.8	.590	.030
1.00			.730

Certainty equivalent = 53.3

Figure 31

tained by using the approximate method of analysis should be compared with the utility and certainty equivalent shown in Figure 27. Even when the computations are carried to eight significant figures on a computer, the differences are negligible.

Where has all of this analysis taken us? It has enabled us to reduce the problem of finding the optimal portfolio from that of examining all (p, f) pairs to that of examining all values of e from e_0 to e_x. That is, we have reduced a two-dimensional search to a one-dimensional search.

How does the problem generalize when there are more than two—say n—risky securities? The general portfolio problem is to find the optimal $(p, f_1, f_2, \ldots, f_n)$ combination (where $f_1 + f_2 + \cdots + f_n = 1$). Using the approximate method of solution, we first try to obtain an efficient set for risky securities only. We can obtain an expression for the variance of return of any mixture of risky securities from knowledge of the variances of return of each security and knowledge of the covariances of return of every possible pair of securities, and from this information we can easily compute the standard deviation of return. The problem of minimizing the standard deviation of return for given expected value of return is no longer trivial when there are more than two risky securities—in fact, it becomes a rather complicated mathematical programming problem. But ultimately we obtain an efficient set for risky portfolios, which is a curve relating e to d. When we finally introduce the riskless security, we may be able to replace all or part of that curve with a straight-line segment. As before, the task of finding the portfolio that is optimal for this approximate method of analysis involves examining portfolios corresponding to various values of e, rather than examining all possible combinations of risky and riskless securities represented by $(p, f_1, f_2, \ldots, f_n)$. We have reduced a multidimensional search, which is virtually impossible to conduct if the number of dimensions (that is, risky securities) exceeds three, to a one-dimensional search.

One additional point of great importance in the administration of portfolios arises from the theory we have developed. If two or more investors assess the same probability distribution on returns, and if each of their portfolios should include some of the same riskless security, then even if the investors have different utility curves, their portfolios should all consist of precisely the same mix of risky securities; that is, the only differences between the mixes of the investors' portfolios, reflecting differences in their utility curves, should be the fraction invested in the riskless security. This follows from the fact that if the investors all have some of the riskless security in their portfolios, then the only part of the efficient set of interest is the straight-line segment, and any point on this segment represents a portfolio with the same mix of risky securities as any other point on the segment. From a practical point of view a portfolio manager, who in effect supplies the probability assessments for his clients, can optimize his clients' portfolios by combining a standard mixture of stocks with the riskless security in proportions dictated by each client's attitude toward risk.

We turn next to the first problem of practical implementation of portfolio theory mentioned at the beginning of this section. How can we assess a joint probability distribution of returns on tens or hundreds of different securities?

It would be convenient if we could assume that returns on all securities under consideration were independent (cf. Chapter 3, Section 6). Then, instead of having to assess the joint probabilities of all possible combinations of returns, we could assess the probabilities of returns on each security separately and compute the probabilities of various combinations by formula. If there are three securities, X, Y, and Z, if each has just two possible returns, and if x stands for the statement "The higher return occurred for security X," and similarly for y and z, then under the assumption of independence we would have to make just three probability assessments: $\mathbf{Pr}[x]$, $\mathbf{Pr}[y]$, and $\mathbf{Pr}[z]$. We could then compute the probability of any joint outcome as the product of the individual outcomes; for example,

$$\mathbf{Pr}[x \wedge \sim y \wedge \sim z] = \mathbf{Pr}[x] \times \mathbf{Pr}[\sim y] \times \mathbf{Pr}[\sim z]$$
$$= \mathbf{Pr}[x] \times (1 - \mathbf{Pr}[y]) \times (1 - \mathbf{Pr}[z]).$$

In general, instead of making $2^n - 1$ assessments for n securities, we could make just n probability assessments, again assuming only two possible returns for each security.

Unfortunately, the assumption of independence of returns is patently false. Anyone who has even a glimmer of experience watching stock-price movements knows that stocks tend to move in the same direction, and stocks picked from within a particular industry group tend to behave more nearly alike than stocks picked from among different industries. Stock-market forecasters, in fact, typically try to forecast how the market as a whole will behave, then how a particular industry group will behave relative to the market, and finally how a particular stock within an industry group will behave relative to the industry.

While the fact of market and industry effects on individual stock returns means that these returns tend to be mutually *dependent*, it also suggests a *structure* for this dependence, which can greatly ease the task of assessment. In particular, it suggests that *conditional* on a given market and industry level, it might make sense to assess the returns of all stocks within an industry as being independent.

Example 2. Consider three stocks, X, Y, and Z. Suppose an analyst decides to assess their possible returns as independent conditional on the level of the stock and suppose he assumes three possible levels of the market (Up, Down, and No change). Again, we assume that for each stock there are just two possible returns, but that the probabilities assigned to these returns depend on the market level. Figure 32 shows the assessment made by the analyst conditional on the various states of the market.

	Probability Assigned to Higher Value of		
State of Market	X	Y	Z
Up	.9	.8	.4
No change	.7	.8	.2
Down	.3	.7	.1

Figure 32

If, in addition, the analyst assesses probabilities for the three different levels of the market as .5 for Up, .3 for No change, and .2 for Down, then it is possible, assuming that the returns on X, Y, and Z are conditionally independent given the market level, to compute the joint probability of any combination of returns of X, Y, and Z. Letting u, n, and d stand for the statements "the market went up," "there was no change," "the market went down," respectively, we can compute, for example,

$$\mathbf{Pr}[x \wedge y \wedge z] = \mathbf{Pr}[x \wedge y \wedge z \mid u]\mathbf{Pr}[u] + \mathbf{Pr}[x \wedge y \wedge z \mid n]\mathbf{Pr}[n]$$
$$+ \mathbf{Pr}[x \wedge y \wedge z \mid d]\mathbf{Pr}[d]$$
$$= (.9 \times .8 \times .4) \times .5 + (.7 \times .8 \times .2) \times .3$$
$$+ (.3 \times .7 \times .1) \times .2$$
$$= .1440 + .0336 + .0042 = .1818,$$

$$\mathbf{Pr}[{\sim}x \wedge y \wedge {\sim}z] = \mathbf{Pr}[{\sim}x \wedge y \wedge {\sim}z \mid u]\mathbf{Pr}[u]$$
$$+ \mathbf{Pr}[{\sim}x \wedge y \wedge {\sim}z \mid u]\mathbf{Pr}[u]$$
$$+ \mathbf{Pr}[{\sim}x \wedge y \wedge {\sim}z \mid d]\mathbf{Pr}[d]$$
$$= (.1 \times .8 \times .6) \times .5 + (.3 \times .8 \times .8) \times .3$$
$$+ (.7 \times .7 \times .9) \times .2$$
$$= .0240 + .0576 + .0882 = .1698,$$

Joint Event	Probability
$x \wedge y \wedge z$	.1818
$x \wedge y \wedge {\sim}z$	.3882
$x \wedge {\sim}y \wedge z$	.0462
$x \wedge {\sim}y \wedge {\sim}z$	.1038
${\sim}x \wedge y \wedge z$	.0402
${\sim}x \wedge y \wedge {\sim}z$	.1698
${\sim}x \wedge {\sim}y \wedge z$	.0118
${\sim}x \wedge {\sim}y \wedge {\sim}z$	.0582
	1.0000

Figure 33

and so forth. Figure 33 shows the set of all joint probabilities based on the conditional assessments of Figure 32 and the probabilities of u, n, and d.

Again, we can ask what we have accomplished by decomposing assessments in this fashion. With only three securities, we actually had to assess nine conditional probabilities in Figure 32, plus the probabilities assigned to the state of the market (two independent assessments), making a total of eleven; we were able to compute from these eleven assessed probabilities the probabilities that should be assigned to the eight possible joint events, as shown in Figure 33. It does not at first appear as though we have substantially reduced the task of assessment.

But suppose we had four stocks instead of three. Then we would have to make three additional assessments, for a total of fourteen, in order to compute the probabilities to assign to the sixteen possible joint events. And if we had ten stocks, we would have to make a total of thirty-two assessments to obtain the probabilities to be assigned to the 1024 possible joint events. With just twenty stocks the number of possible joint events exceeds one million, and yet the number of assessments required is only sixty-two.

Of course, we are still working with only two possible levels of each stock, with only one "factor"—the state of the market, and with only three possible states of that factor. Much more sophisticated probabilistic assumptions, which give the effect of many possible levels of each stock and which use several factors, each having many possible states, are employed in actual portfolio analysis. But, as we have already seen, the number of values assigned to the possible states and returns is not crucial to the analysis; the approximate optimization method involves knowledge of only the expected values, variances, and covariances of returns. And the way of obtaining the covariances in the realistic situation where the returns on securities are not independent still involves the kind of decomposition we have illustrated in this section.

EXERCISES

1. In the problem of Example 1, suppose that there were a riskless security with return $e_0 = 1.20$. What would the optimal portfolio be for Mr. Jones?

2. Use formula (13) to compute values of $d(1)$ on the efficient set for risky portfolios corresponding to the following values of e:
   a. $e = .975$.
   b. $e = 1.15$.
   c. $e = 1.118$.
   Verify that the values of $d(1)$ so computed lie on the curve graphed in Figure 28.

3. Use formula (9) to compute values of f corresponding to the following values of e for the problem of Example 1:
   a. $e = .975$.
   b. $e = 1.15$.
   c. $e = 1.118$.

4. a. Compute Mr. Jones' utility and certainty equivalent for a portfolio in which 24.75 is invested in security X, 2.75 in Y, and the rest in the riskless security.
   b. Repeat (a), but 28 is invested in X, 7 in Y, and the rest in the riskless security.

5. a. Compute the expected value, variance, and standard deviation for the portfolio of Exercise 4(a).
   b. Repeat (a) for the portfolio of Exercise 4(b).

6. Show that the portfolio of Exercise 4(a) has higher utility and certainty equivalent than that of 4(b), but lower mean and higher standard deviation. Which portfolio is really better? Which portfolio is better based on the approximation given by equation (1)?

7. In Figure 28, consider the point on the efficient set for riskless securities whose e-coordinate is 1.10.
   a. Using equation (9), show that this point represents a portfolio having $f = \frac{5}{7}, p = 1$.
   b. Compute the expected value and standard deviation of return on a portfolio of which five-sevenths consists of security X and two-sevenths of Security Y. Verify that these values correspond to the coordinates of the point.

8. In Figure 28, draw a line from (1.05, 0) to the point on the efficient set for risky securities whose e-coordinate is 1.10. Consider the point on this line whose e-coordinate is 1.08.
   a. Plot the point and record its d-coordinate.
   b. Using equations (9) and (16), show that this point represents a portfolio having $f = \frac{5}{7}, p = .6$.
   c. Compute the expected value $e(.6)$ and standard deviation $d(.6)$ of a portfolio four-tenths of which is invested in the riskless asset, while five-sevenths of the remaining six-tenths is invested in X and the rest in Y. Verify that these values correspond to the (e, d) coordinates of the point plotted in part (a).

9. In the situation of Example 1, suppose that the return on the riskless security were 1.03 instead of 1.05.
   a. Show that if $e > 1.09$, the strategy that minimizes d for given e is to invest a fraction

$$f = \frac{e - .975}{.175}$$

   in security X and the rest in Y.
   b. Show that if $1.03 \leq e \leq 1.09$, the strategy that minimizes d for given e is to invest a fraction

$$p = \frac{e - 1.03}{1.09 - 1.03}$$

   in risky assets and the remainder in the riskless asset. Of the amount in risky assets, a fraction

$$f = \frac{1.09 - .975}{1.15 - .975} = .656$$

   should be invested in security X and the remainder in Y.

10. Suppose Mr. Jones of Example 1 could not only invest money in a riskless security providing a return of 1.05, but could also borrow money at a cost of 5 percent and invest the proceeds in risky securities. Suppose that he in fact borrows 10 and invests it, along with his original liquid assets of 50, in a portfolio consisting of securities X and Y, with $f = .815$.
   a. Show that the amounts invested in X and Y are 48.9 and 11.1, respectively.
   b. Show that Jones' net liquid assets if both securities go up are 118.39.

    c. Compute Jones' net liquid assets for the other possible outcomes of his investment.

    d. Compute Jones' return for every possible outcome of his investment.

11. *a.* In the problem of Exercise 10, compute the expected value, variance, and standard deviation of return.

    b. Plot a point in Figure 29 corresponding to the expected value and standard deviation that you have just computed.

    c. Show that the point plotted in part (*b*) can be obtained by extending the straight-line segment drawn between (e_0, 0) and the point on the efficient set for risky securities at $e^* = 1.118$ upwards and to the right.

    d. How should the efficient set for both riskless and risky securities be modified if funds can be borrowed at the same rate of interest as the risky security provides?

12. Suppose that Mr. Jones of Example 1 could borrow funds at 5 percent interest but that the best interest rate he could obtain by investing in a riskless security was only 3 percent (that is, his return was 1.03) instead of 5 percent.

    a. Show that for any given expected return *e*, if $e > 1.118$, the strategy that minimizes *d* is to borrow, investing 81.5 percent of the total of borrowed funds and original liquid assets in security X and the remaining 18.5 percent in Y.

    b. Show that for any given expected return *e*, if $1.03 < e < 1.09$, the strategy that minimizes *d* is not to borrow, but to invest some liquid assets in the riskless security and, of the remainder, invest 65.6 percent in security X and the remaining 34.4 percent in Y.

    c. Show that if $1.09 \le e \le 1.118$, the strategy that minimizes *d* for given *e* is not to borrow, but to invest all liquid assets in risky securities, the proportions in X and Y depending on the value of *e*.

    d. Describe the efficient set for both riskless and risky securities when money can be borrowed, but at a higher rate of interest than that provided by the riskless security.

13. Verify the entries in Figure 33.

14. Suppose the possible returns on security X of Example 2 are 1.5 and .8, that the possible returns on Y are 2.0 and .5, and that the possible returns on Z are 1.3 and .9. Compute the expected value, variance, and standard deviation of return on a portfolio 50 percent of which is invested in X, 30 percent in Y, and 20 percent in Z.

15. *a.* Letting e_x be the expected return of security X and similarly for e_y and e_z, compute e_x, e_y, and e_z for the securities of Example 2 under the assumptions of Exercise 14.

    b. Show that the expected return on the portfolio of Exercise 14 can be computed as $.5e_x + .3e_y + .2e_z$.

16. Letting v_{xx} be the variance of return for security X, v_{xy} the covariance of returns for securities X and Y, and so on, compute the following variances and covariances of returns for the securities of Example 2 under the assumptions of Exercise 14: v_{xx}, v_{yy}, v_{zz}, v_{xy}, v_{xz}, v_{yz}.

17. Show that the variance of return on the portfolio of Exercise 14 can be computed as

$$.5^2 v_{xx} + .3^2 v_{yy} + .2^2 v_{zz} + 2 \times .5 \times .3 v_{xy} + 2 \times .5 \times .2 v_{xz} + 2 \times .3 \times .2 v_{yz}.$$

SUGGESTED READING

Markowitz, Harry, "Portfolio Selection," *Journal of Finance*, vol. 7, 1952.

Pratt, John W., "Risk Aversion in the Small and in the Large," *Econometrica*, vol. 32, 1964.

Raiffa, Howard, *Decision Analysis*, Addison-Wesley, Reading, Mass., 1968.

Schlaifer, Robert, *Analysis of Decisions Under Uncertainty*, McGraw-Hill, New York, 1969.

Sharpe, William, "A Simplified Model for Portfolio Selection," *Management Science*, vol. 9, 1963.

Tobin, James, "Liquidity Preference as Behavior Toward Risk," *Review of Economics and Statistics*, 1958.

CHAPTER

7

MATHEMATICS OF FINANCE

1. A FINITE DIFFERENCE EQUATION

We will consider a class of problems from the mathematics of finance, all of which may be treated by the same mathematical tool.

> **Example 1.** A person has $5000 in a savings account. He adds $300 to this each year. The account earns 4 percent interest, compounded annually. How much money will he have at the end of 10 years?
>
> The direct way of computing the answer to this problem is to find, step-by-step, the balance after each year. Let x_j be the balance after j years. Suppose that we have already found this; how would we find the next year's balance? First of all, the balance x_j earns 4 percent interest during the year, which increases the balance by $.04x_j$. Second, $300 is added during the year. Hence
>
> $$x_{j+1} = x_j + .04x_j + 300 = (1.04)x_j + 300.$$
>
> We also know that $x_0 = 5000$ is the original balance, and from these two equations we may compute the balance x_{10} in ten steps.

Let us state the problem of Example 1 in more general form. Consider a fund with starting balance P, where $P \geq 0$. At the end of each period a "payment" p is made *to* the fund. (If the "payment" has the effect of increasing the balance, $p > 0$; if it decreases the balance, $p < 0$; if no payment is made, $p = 0$.) The balance bears interest in each period at a rate r. Then, as in Example 1, the next balance

$$x_{j+1} = x_j + rx_j + p.$$

Or, more simply,

(1) $$x_{j+1} = (1 + r)x_j + p, \qquad r > 0,$$

and

(2)
$$x_0 = P.$$

Our problem is to find the final balance S after n periods. If we discover a formula for x_j, then $S = x_n$. As we shall see in the next section, this formulation has a wide variety of applications. It can be used, for example, to determine the accumulation of an annuity, or the accumulation of a deposit subject to compound interest, or the repayment of a loan or mortgage. In accumulating an annuity, for instance, we start with an initial balance $P = 0$ and make payments of amount $p > 0$ to the fund for n periods; we ask for the balance at the end of the nth period. If an amount $P > 0$ is deposited and earns compound interest, then $p = 0$ and we ask for the balance at the end of the nth period. In repaying a mortgage, P is the amount of the mortgage and the payments p reduce this amount, hence $p < 0$. The number of periods n is so selected that the mortgage is repaid at the end of it, hence $S = 0$.

We may also choose the periods to suit the problem. They may be monthly, quarterly, or annual computations. We simply let n be the number of months, or the number of quarters, or the number of years; r is the interest rate per period. So far we have assumed that the period of compounding and the period of payment are the same. For instance, we assumed in Example 1 that interest was compounded annually and that payments were made once a year. In Section 4 we shall show how to deal with situations where the period of compounding is different from the period of payment, but we shall assume in the remainder of this section and in Sections 2 and 3 that the two periods are the same.

Our immediate task is to find a general formula that will tell us the balance x_j after j periods. For this we must solve the *finite difference equation* (1), subject to the *initial condition* (2). It will be convenient to introduce new variables by the definition

(3)
$$y_j = \frac{x_j + \dfrac{p}{r}}{(1 + r)^j}.$$

The economic interpretation of the variables y_j is asked for in Exercise 9 of the next section. Let us now reformulate (1) in an equivalent form in terms of the variables y_j. For this we solve (3) for x_j as follows:

(4)
$$x_j = (1 + r)^j y_j - \frac{p}{r}$$

and substitute into (1).

$$(1 + r)^{i+1}y_{j+1} - \frac{p}{r} = (1 + r)\left[(1 + r)^{i}y_j - \frac{p}{r}\right] + p$$

$$= (1 + r)^{i+1}y_j - p\frac{1 + r}{r} + p$$

$$= (1 + r)^{i+1}y_j - \frac{p}{r}.$$

We now add p/r to both sides of the equation, and divide through by $(1 + r)^{i+1}$. This leads to the very simple equivalent form for (1),

(5) $$y_{j+1} = y_j.$$

We must also reformulate (2) in terms of the y's. From (3) we find

$$y_0 = \frac{x_0 + \dfrac{p}{r}}{(1 + r)^0} = x_0 + \frac{p}{r},$$

remembering that any number to the 0th power is 1. Thus (2) becomes

$$y_0 = P + \frac{p}{r}.$$

However equation (5) states that each y is equal to the previous one; hence they must all be equal, so each has the same value as y_0. Thus our solution in terms of the y's is

(6) $$y_j = P + \frac{p}{r}.$$

We can now obtain the desired formula by substituting this into (4). The solution of our general problem is

(7) $$x_j = \left(P + \frac{p}{r}\right)(1 + r)^i - \frac{p}{r}.$$

Hence

(8) $$S = \left(P + \frac{p}{r}\right)(1 + r)^n - \frac{p}{r}.$$

For convenience in using this formula, Table III shows the values of $(1 + r)^n$ for several possible combinations of r and n.

Example 1 (continued). In our problem, $P = 5000$, $p = 300$, $n = 10$, and $r = .04$. Hence from (8),

$$S = \left(5000 + \frac{300}{.04}\right)(1.04)^{10} - \frac{300}{.04}.$$

From Table III we find that $(1.04)^{10} = 1.4802$; hence

$$S = (12,500)(1.4802) - 7500 = 11,002.50,$$

and our balance at the end of 10 years will be \$11,002.50.

Example 2. We place \$100 in a savings account. The bank pays 4 percent interest compounded quarterly; that is, 1 percent interest is paid each quarter. What will our balance be after 5 years?

Here $P = 100, r = 1$ percent $= .01$, and $n = 20$, since our basic period is $\frac{1}{4}$ of a year. Since there are no additional payments, $p = 0$. From (8) we find

$$S = (100 + 0)(1 + r)^{20} - 0 = 100(1 + r)^{20}.$$

From Table III we find that $(1 + r)^{20} = 1.2202$; hence $S = 122.02$. Our balance will be \$122.02.

Example 3. Mr. Jones would like an income of \$6000 per year, paid in equal annual installments for 20 years. How much must he invest in order to obtain this income if the invested balance earns 5 percent per year?

In this case P is the unknown amount to be invested. The yearly payments decrease the balance, hence $p = -6000$. Also, $n = 20, r = .05$, hence $p/r = -120,000$ according to the information given. If the capital invested is just barely enough to provide the desired installments, then S will be 0. Hence from (8) we obtain

$$0 = (P - 120,000)(1.05)^{20} + 120,000.$$

From Table III we find that $(1.05)^{20} = 2.6533$; hence

$$0 = 2.6533P - 198,396; \qquad P = \frac{198,396}{2.6533} = 74,773.$$

Thus \$74,773 must be invested by Mr. Jones.

Example 4. A company can construct a factory building for \$800,000, or it can lease an equivalent building for \$75,000 a year for 25 years with the option of purchasing the building for \$100,000 at the end of the 25-year period. The company can earn 14 percent per year before taxes on its invested capital. What should it do?

Here we want to make a comparison between a lump-sum payment now and a series of equal payments over 25 years. We can proceed by either (a) finding the lump-sum equivalent of the 25 lease payments, or (b) finding the equal annual installment equivalent of the \$800,000 lump-sum payment. We shall do the former, leaving the latter procedure as an exercise (see Exercise 10).

Let L be the lump-sum equivalent of the rent-buy option. Then $p = -75,000, S = 100,000, n = 25$, and $r = .14$. However, there is a slight additional complication in that lease payments must be made at the beginning of each year rather than at the end. Hence we must take $P = L - 75,000$ and correct (8) by recalling that no payment is made at the end of the last period. Thus,

$$100,000 = \left(L - 75,000 - \frac{75,000}{.14} \right)(1.14)^{25} + \frac{75,000}{.14} + 75,000.$$

From Table III we find that $(1.14)^{25} = 26.462$. Solving for L, we obtain $L = \$591,414$.

Thus \$591,414 invested in a fund that earned interest at the rate of the company's own operations would produce earnings sufficient to meet the lease payments and purchase the building after 25 years. For \$591,414, the company would have exactly the same facilities that would cost \$800,000 if the company were to build. Clearly, leasing is preferable.

EXERCISES

1. If \$20,000 is invested in a company that earns 6 percent per year on invested capital, and if the earnings are reinvested, how much is the investment worth at the end of 10 years?

2. If Mr. Jones lends Mr. Smith \$2000 at 6 percent interest compounded quarterly (that is, 1.5 percent interest is paid each quarter), how much must Mr. Smith pay at the end of 6 years?   [*Ans.* \$2859.]

3. An annuity is set up into which \$100 per year is paid for 16 years. If the money paid in bears interest at 5 percent per year, what will be the value of the annuity at the end of the sixteenth year?

4. A company can invest in a project that will raise its revenues by \$10,000 per year. The project costs \$30,000 initially and has an anticipated life of 4 years. If the company can earn 20 percent on capital invested in other projects, should it invest in the proposed project?

5. In Exercise 4 what is the present value of a fund that earns 20 percent on its balance each year, from which \$10,000 a year must be paid for 4 years, after which the balance of the fund will be 0?   [*Ans.* \$25,887.]

6. In Exercise 5 prepare a schedule showing the balance of the fund, the amount it earns each year, and the amount it pays out each year. Prepare a flow diagram showing how to compute the balance at the end of each year.

7. In Exercises 4 and 5, find the present value of the fund by working backward from the facts that (*a*) the balance of the fund at the end of year 4 is 0; (*b*) the fund pays out \$10,000 per year; (*c*) neglecting the \$10,000 paid out each year, the balance at the beginning of a year is 1/1.2 times the balance at the end. Prepare a flow diagram to compute the present value of the fund.

8. A sum of money deposited at compound interest earns interest on the previous period's balance. A sum deposited at *simple* interest, however, earns interest only on the original deposit, and not on any additions to the original deposit which result from interest payments. Write the difference equation for the balance in the jth period of a sum P deposited at simple interest at the rate r. Solve the difference equation and write a flow diagram for computing its values.
   [*Partial Ans.* $x_j = x_{j-1} + r\,x_0$, where $x_0 = P$.]

9. Recompute Example 1 assuming that the \$5000 original deposit as well as the \$300 annual deposits earn 4 percent simple interest rather than compound interest. Over the 10-year period, how much extra interest did the compounding yield?

10. In Example 4 suppose the $800,000 were to be invested in a fund from which 25 equal annual installments would be made starting at the *beginning* of year 1. If the fund earns 14 percent per year on its current balance, and if we want $100,000 left at the *end* of the twenty-fifth year, what size payments will be made? Compare these with the lease payments. To what decision does this method of analysis lead?

11. Show that the following flow diagram describes the computational process needed to compute the entries of Table III.

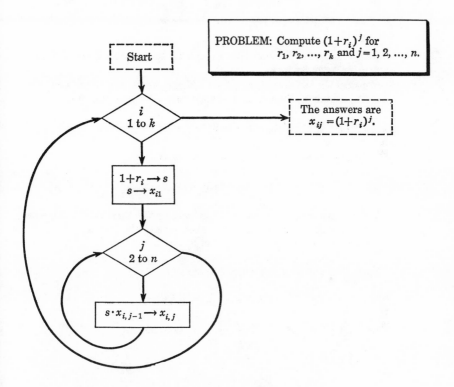

PROBLEM: Compute $(1+r_i)^j$ for $r_1, r_2, \ldots, r_k$ and $j = 1, 2, \ldots, n$.

Start

i
1 to k

The answers are $x_{ij} = (1+r_i)^j$.

$1+r_i \longrightarrow s$
$s \longrightarrow x_{i1}$

j
2 to n

$s \cdot x_{i,j-1} \longrightarrow x_{i,j}$

12. Draw a flow diagram for computing $x_1, x_2, \ldots, x_n$ if $x_0 = P$ and $x_{j+1} = (1 + r)x_j + p$, where $r, n, p,$ and P are given numbers.

13. Consider the sequence $1, \frac{2}{3}, \frac{4}{9}, \frac{8}{27}, \frac{16}{81}, \ldots$. Let x_j be the sum of the first j terms of the sequence. Show that

$$x_{j+1} = x_j + (\tfrac{2}{3})^j$$

subject to $x_1 = 1$. Show that the solution is

$$x_j = 3[1 - (\tfrac{2}{3})^j]$$

by showing that it satisfies both the difference equation and the initial condition $x_1 = 1$. Calculate x_5 (*a*) by summing the terms in the sequence and (*b*) by using the formula.

14. Generalize the result of Exercise 13 by letting x_j be the sum of the first j terms of any geometric sequence $a, ar, ar^2, ar^3, \ldots$, where $r \neq 1$. Show that

$$x_{j+1} = x_j + ar^j$$

subject to $x_1 = a$. Show that the solution is

$$x_j = a \frac{1 - r^j}{1 - r}.$$

Derive the formula for x_j by first writing out the sum that it represents, then writing out the sum for rx_j, and finally performing the subtraction $x_j - rx_j$ term by term.

15. Consider the sequence $1, 2, 3, 4, \ldots$. Let x_j be the sum of the first j terms of the sequence. Show that x_j satisfies the difference equation

$$x_{j+1} = x_j + j + 1$$

subject to $x_1 = 1$. Show that the solution is

$$x_j = \tfrac{1}{2}j(j + 1).$$

Derive the formula for x_j by first writing the sum that it represents term by term in ascending order, then writing the sum term by term in descending order, and adding term by term.

16. Let x_j be the sum of the first j terms of the sequence $r, 2r^2, 3r^3, \ldots, r \neq 1$. Show that the resulting difference equation

$$x_{j+1} = x_j + (j + 1)r^{j+1}$$

with initial condition $x_1 = r$ has as its solution

$$x_j = \frac{r}{(1 - r)^2} [1 - r^j(1 + j - rj)].$$

Derive the formula for x_j by writing the sum it represents and also by writing the sum for rx_j, performing the subtraction $x_j - rx_j$ term by term, and finally applying the results of Exercise 14.

2. SOME IMPORTANT SPECIAL CASES

In Section 1 we solved the following problem: If P dollars are invested, interest is paid on the current balance at a rate of r per period for n periods, and a sum p is added to the fund each period, then the final balance S is given by (8). Also, we could rewrite the result as

(9)
$$S = (1 + r)^n P + \left[\frac{(1 + r)^n - 1}{r}\right] p.$$

In Section 1 we assumed that r, n, P, and p were known, and that S was to be found. We will again assume that the interest rate r and the number of periods n are known, but we will consider various assumptions concerning S, P, and p. Particularly interesting and useful formulas are obtained if one variable is known to be 0, another is also known—but not 0—and the third is to be found. The solutions of (9) for the six such possible combinations are shown in Figure 1. Each is a formula frequently

Name of Formula	Zero Variable	Given Variable	Unknown Variable	Formula
Single payment compound amount:	p	P	S	$S = [(1 + r)^n]P$
Single payment present value:	p	S	P	$P = \left[\dfrac{1}{(1 + r)^n} \right] S$
Uniform payment compound amount:	P	p	S	$S = \left[\dfrac{(1 + r)^n - 1}{r} \right] p$
Uniform payment sinking fund:	P	S	p	$p = \left[\dfrac{r}{(1 + r)^n - 1} \right] S$
Uniform payment capital recovery:	S	P	p	$p = -\left[\dfrac{r(1 + r)^n}{(1 + r)^n - 1} \right] P$
Uniform payment present value:	S	p	P	$P = -\left[\dfrac{(1 + r)^n - 1}{r(1 + r)^n} \right] p$

Figure 1

used in the mathematics of finance. However, it is important to recall that each is but a special case of (9), and the solutions of our problems could be obtained directly from (9) without the use of Figure 1.

The expressions in brackets in the formulas of Figure 1 are called investment formula "factors." Thus $(1 + r)^n$ is the single-payment compound-amount factor, $[(1 + r)^n - 1]/[r(1 + r)^n]$ is the uniform-payment present-value factor, and so on. In books that deal with this subject, these six factors are sometimes tabulated in terms of r and n (see, for example, Grant and Ireson, *Principles of Engineering Economy*). A table of $(1 + r)^n$, however, is actually sufficient to permit the computation of each of the factors with ease.

For reasons that will be made apparent in the next section, the present-value factor has been tabulated separately as Table IV. This makes the computation of the various factors easier still. If we represent the numbers tabulated in Tables III and IV for given r and n by [III] and [IV], respectively, then the investment formula factors are related to these tabulated values according to Figure 2.

Example 1. In Example 3 of Section 1, p was given and we wanted to find the value of P that made $S = 0$ after $n = 20$ years. This is, therefore, a

	Relation to
Factor	*Tabulated Factors*
Single payment compound amount	[III]
Single payment present value	1/[III]
Uniform payment compound amount	[III]·[IV]
Uniform payment sinking fund	1/([III]·[IV])
Uniform payment capital recovery	1/[IV]
Uniform payment present value	[IV]

Figure 2

uniform-payment present-value problem. Using Table III in conjunction with the formula of Figure 1, with $p = -6000$, $r = .05$, $n = 20$, we obtain

$$P = \left[\frac{(1.05)^{20} - 1}{.05(1.05)^{20}}\right] 6000 = \left[\frac{2.6533 - 1}{(.05)(2.6533)}\right] 6000 = 74{,}773$$

as before. Using Table IV, we look up the uniform-payment present-value factor for $r = .05$, $n = 20$, obtaining 12.46, and compute

$$P = (12.462)(6000) = 74{,}772,$$

which agrees with the previous result except for rounding.

Example 2. In Example 2 of the previous section we were given $P = 100$ and wanted to find S after $n = 20$ quarter years, when no further payments were made ($p = 0$). From Figure 1 this is a single-payment compound-amount problem, the solution to which is given by

$$\begin{aligned} S &= (1 + r)^n P \\ &= (1 + .01)^{20}(100) \\ &= 122.02 \end{aligned}$$

as before.

Example 3. It is desired to repay a loan of $100,000 in 12 equal annual installments, where the loan earns interest at the rate of 6 percent per year. How much should be paid each year? In this problem $S = 0$, $P = \$100{,}000$, and p is unknown. It is, therefore, a capital recovery problem. From Table III we find $(1.06)^{12} = 2.0122$, and apply the formula of Figure 1 to obtain

$$p = \left[\frac{(.06)(2.0122)}{2.0122 - 1}\right](-100{,}000),$$

$$(.11928)(-100{,}000) = -11{,}928.$$

Thus payments of $11,928 per year for 12 years will liquidate a fund of $100,000 that earns 6 percent per year. Hence $11,928 per year will repay a $100,000 loan in 12 years at 6 percent interest per year.

Using Table IV, we find that the uniform-payment present-value factor for $n = 12$, $r = .06$ is 8.3838. From Figure 2 we conclude that

$$p = \frac{1}{8.3838}(-100{,}000) = -11{,}928,$$

as before.

It should be observed that the single-payment compound-amount and present-value formulas can be applied to each of a series of nonuniform payments.

Example 4. A machine can be purchased for $10,000. It will permit a company to manufacture a new product that is expected to increase the company's profits by the following amounts over the next 5 years:

Year	Profit Increase
1	$1000
2	3000
3	4000
4	4000
5	5000

After 5 years the machine will be scrapped. The company can earn 10 percent per year on alternative investments. Should the machine be purchased?

We may think of this as a series of single-payment present-value problems. Let S_j be the balance in a fund at the end of the jth year, and let us find the value of P_j that, if invested now, will accumulate to S_j in j years at 10 percent interest. Clearly,

$$P_j = \frac{S_j}{(1 + .10)^j} .$$

If we consider 5 such funds, then the present value of the sum of them will be $P = P_1 + P_2 + P_3 + P_4 + P_5$. If the present value P exceeds the present cost of the machine ($10,000), the machine should be acquired; otherwise it should not. We summarize the necessary calculations in Figure 3.

j	S_j	P_j
1	1000	909
2	3000	2,479
3	4000	3,005
4	4000	2,732
5	5000	3,105
		12,230 = P

Figure 3

Since $P = \$12,230 > \$10,000$, the machine should be purchased.

EXERCISES

1. How much must be paid back on a loan of $1000 for 2 years if 6 percent interest a year is charged and (*a*) if the loan is repaid at the end of the 2-year period? (*b*) if the loan is repaid in two equal annual installments?

2. A man has a son who will enter college in 15 years. He wants to set up an annuity that will yield $5000 toward the expenses of the college

education at that time. If an insurance company will pay him 4 percent, compounded quarterly (that is, 1 percent per quarter on his balance), what must his quarterly payments be?   [*Ans.* $61.22.]

3. Find the uniform payment that has to be made each year to accumulate to $1,000,000 in 30 years if one can earn 30 percent per year on the balance.

4. An investment of $100,000 will yield savings for a company of $20,000 per year for 10 years. If the company can earn 10 percent per year on investment of its capital elsewhere, find the net present value of this investment—that is, the present value of the savings less the cost of the investment. Should the investment be made?   [*Ans.* $22,890; yes.]

5. What sum of money invested today will yield $10,000 thirty years from now if interest is paid at 6 percent per year and is compounded quarterly (that is, $1\frac{1}{2}$ percent interest is paid each quarter)?

6. Compute the present value of $10,000 to be received in 30 years, if interest of 6 percent per year is compounded (*a*) annually, (*b*) quarterly, or (*c*) monthly.

7. An investment of $100,000 will yield savings of $25,000 a year for 5 years, and $10,000 per year for an additional 5 years. If a company can earn 14 percent per year on alternative investments, calculate the net present value of the investment (*a*) by adding the present value of each year's savings and subtracting the initial investment cost; (*b*) by taking the uniform-payment present value for the first five years and for the second five years, discounting the latter value to the present, adding the results, and subtracting the initial investment cost; (*c*) by taking the present value of a series of uniform $10,000 payments for 10 years, adding to this the present value of a series of uniform payments of $15,000 for 5 years, and subtracting the initial investment cost. Justify these three methods, and show that they all yield the same answer. Should the investment be made?

8. An initial deposit P that earns interest at a rate r per year will yield a stream of payments $p = Pr$ forever. Thus, if one can obtain earnings at a rate r on capital invested elsewhere, the present value of a stream of earnings of p per year forever (a *perpetuity* of p per year) is $P = p/r$. Verify this by showing that as n approaches infinity the present-value formula approaches $P = -p/r$.

9. Using the results of Exercise 8, give an economic interpretation to the variable

$$y_i = \frac{x_i + \dfrac{p}{r}}{(1 + r)^i}$$

defined in equation (3) of Section 1. Use this economic interpretation to show why $y_{i+1} = y_i$.

10. Machine A can be purchased for $6000. It will produce earnings of $1000 per year for 10 years, after which it will be sold. Salvage value will be $2000 at that time. Should the machine be purchased if 10 percent can be obtained on alternative investments? What is the net present value of purchasing?   [*Ans.* Yes; $916.]

11. Consider machine B. It can be purchased to perform the same task as machine A described in the preceding exercise. It costs $10,000, will last

14 years, will produce earnings of $1500 per year, and will have no salvage value at the end of its life.

a. If the choice were only between purchasing machine B and doing nothing, would it pay to purchase machine B? What is its net present value? [*Ans.* Yes; $1050.]

b. Between machines A and B, what is the better investment? Why?

12. A machine is purchased for $20,000. After 5 years its salvage value will be $8000, at which time a new $20,000 machine will have to be purchased. If 10 percent can be earned on capital invested elsewhere, what uniform series of payments must be made into a sinking fund to accumulate the $12,000 needed in addition to the salvage value of the old machine in order to purchase the new machine at the end of the fifth year?

13. An oil well is currently producing earnings at the rate of $100,000 per year. The well is believed to have reserves that will last an additional 10 years at the present rate of recovery. For a cost of $160,000, a pump can be installed that will double the rate of recovery (and thereby halve the anticipated life of the well).

a. Find the incremental effect on earnings over the next 10 years of installing the new pump now.

b. Find the net present value of the pump if capital can be invested in alternative projects that will return 10 percent per year. Should the investment be made? [*Ans.* $-$16,300; no.]

c. Repeat (*b*) if alternative investments return 20 percent per year.
[*Ans.* $+$18,870; yes.]

d. Repeat (*b*) if alternative investments return 50 percent.
[*Ans.* $-$9210; no.]

14. A trucking company purchases trucks for $10,000 each. The annual operating cost and the salvage value for a truck j years old is given in the table below for $j = 1, 2, 3, 4,$ and 5.

j	Annual Operating Cost	Salvage Value
1	$1500	$6000
2	2000	5000
3	2500	4000
4	3000	2000
5	4000	1000

The annual operating cost may be treated as occurring at the *end* of the year. Consider a policy of replacing the trucks every 3 years. If the company can earn 20 percent on invested capital, show that a fund of $17,940 will (*a*) provide the annual operating costs at the end of years 1, 2, and 3; (*b*) provide the $6000 capital needed in addition to the salvage value of the old truck to buy a new truck for $10,000 at the end of year 3; (*c*) have a balance of $17,940 at the end of year 3.

15. Generalize the result of Exercise 14 as follows: An asset has a cost of C. Its salvage value at the end of j years is S_j, where $0 \leq S_j \leq C$ and $S_{j+1} \leq S_j$. Operating expenses incurred at the end of the jth year are given by p_j, where $p_{j+1} \geq p_j > 0$. Invested capital earns interest at a rate r per year. How large a sum P must be invested at the beginning to meet all the operating expenses, to allow replacement of the asset at

the end of n years, and still have P left over at the end of n years? Show that the solution of this problem is characterized by the following equations for the balance x_j after j years.

(i) $$x_0 = P,$$
(ii) $$x_{j+1} = (1 + r)x_j - p_{j+1},$$
(iii) $$x_n = C - S_n + P.$$

16. In Exercise 15, let $q_j = p_j/(1 + r)^j$ be the present value of the operating expense in year j. Prove that the solution of (i) and (ii) is given by

(iv) $$x_j = (1 + r)^j[P - (q_1 + q_2 + \cdots + q_j)].$$

17. From (iii) and (iv) in Exercises 15 and 16, show that the sum to be invested is

(v) $$P = \frac{1}{(1 + r)^n - 1} [C - S_n + (1 + r)^n(q_1 + q_2 + \cdots + q_n)].$$

Obtain the result of Exercise 14 by use of this formula.

18. Use formula (v) to find the necessary investment P in Exercise 14 if $n = 1, 2, 4,$ and 5. What is the optimal replacement policy?
    [*Partial Ans.* For $n = 2$, $P = \$20{,}000$; for $n = 4$, $P = \$18{,}138$.]

19. Given that the present value of a payment $-p$ to be made j years hence is $-p/(1 + r)^j$, derive the uniform-payment present-value formula for a series of n such payments that start in one time period from now, by summing the appropriate series using the results of Exercise 14, Section 1.

20. Given that the compound amount of a payment p is $p(1 + r)^j$ j years after the date of payment, derive equation (8) by summing the appropriate series, using the results of Exercise 14, Section 1.

3. SOLVING FOR INTEREST RATE AND NUMBER OF PAYMENTS

In equation (9) there are five variables: P, S, p, n, and r. In Section 2 we have shown, given r and n and two of the three other variables, how to find the fifth variable. In this section we shall assume that P, S, p, and either r or n are given and shall discuss methods of finding the other. We shall also give interpretations of these solutions to equation (9).

We start first with the problem of finding n given P, S, p, and r. To do this we solve (9) for $(1 + r)^n$, thereby obtaining

(10) $$(1 + r)^n = \frac{Sr + p}{Pr + p}, \qquad r > 0.$$

We can readily find the conditions under which (10) has a solution. For fixed r, the lefthand side of (10) increases as n increases. Since $(1 + r)^0 = 1$, as n increases $(1 + r)^n$ takes on all values greater than 1. Hence (10) will have a solution $n > 0$ provided the righthand side is greater than 1—that is,

(11a) $$\frac{Sr + p}{Pr + p} > 1.$$

Recalling the rules for working with inequalities, it is easy to show that this condition will be satisfied under the following circumstances: either

(11b)
$$P + \frac{p}{r} > 0 \quad \text{and} \quad S > P$$

or

(11c)
$$P + \frac{p}{r} < 0 \quad \text{and} \quad S < P.$$

Either of these conditions will guarantee a solution $n > 0$, but the solution will usually not be an integer.

That these conditions make economic sense can be seen by observing that p/r is (see Exercise 8, Section 2) the present value of a perpetuity of p per year at interest r per year. Thus, if $P + (p/r) < 0$, the balance of the fund can never increase, and therefore we can never obtain a final balance S greater than the initial balance P. Accordingly, we must have $S < P$, as given by (11c). A similar argument applies to the condition (11b).

Example 1. A mortgage of \$30,000 is to be paid off in annual installments of \$2000. If interest of 5 percent per year is charged on the unpaid balance, how many years will it take until the unpaid balance is \$10,000? We are given that $P = 30,000$, $S = 10,000$, $r = .05$, and $p = -2000$. We must find n.
The problem has a solution, since

$$P + \frac{p}{r} = \$30,000 - \frac{\$2000}{.05} = -\$10,000 < 0$$

and

$$S = \$10,000 < P = \$30,000$$

so that (11c) is satisfied. We compute

$$\frac{Sr + p}{Pr + p} = \frac{(10,000)(.05) + (-2000)}{(30,000)(.05) + (-2000)} = 3$$

and find in Table III that

$$(1 + .05)^{20} = 2.6533 \quad \text{and} \quad (1 + .05)^{25} = 3.3864.$$

Interpolating roughly, we find n is about 22 years.

Example 2. A machine can be purchased that will produce earnings of \$1000 per year. The machine costs \$6000 and will have a salvage value at the end of its useful life of \$2000 regardless of the number of years that it is used. If 12 percent can be earned on alternative investments, how many years must the machine last to make it equally attractive with alternative investments? We can phrase the problem as follows: $P = 6000$, $p = -1000$, $r = .12$ per year; in how many years will the balance become $S = 2000$?

There is a solution, since

$$P + \frac{p}{r} = \$6000 + \frac{-\$1000}{.12} = -\$2333 < 0$$

and $S = 2000 < P = 6000$, so that (11c) is satisfied. We compute

$$\frac{Sr + p}{Pr + p} = \frac{(2000)(.12) - 1000}{(6000)(.12) - 1000} = 2.71$$

and find in Table III that

$$(1 + .12)^8 = 2.4760 \quad \text{and} \quad (1 + .12)^9 = 2.7731.$$

Hence n is just less than 9 years. If the machine lasts more than 9 years, it is more attractive than alternative investments; if it lasts less than 9 years, it is less attractive than alternative investments.

In decision problems in which a choice is made whether or not to invest in an asset and in which P, S, p, and r are given, the n that satisfies (10) is called the *payback period*. It is a kind of "breakeven value." If the anticipated life of the asset exceeds the payback period, the asset is preferable to alternative investments and should be purchased; if it is less, the asset should not be purchased.

We now return to (10), and assume that r is the unknown quantity. This is a harder problem than those previously considered, and first we will solve the important special case in which $S = 0$. Here we have an original principal P that is reduced to 0 (as in the case of a loan), and hence p is always negative. Let $Z = -P/p$ be the number of payments needed if no interest were charged. We then deduce from (10) that

$$(12) \qquad\qquad Z = -\frac{P}{p} = \frac{(1 + r)^n - 1}{r(1 + r)^n}.$$

However, the righthand side of (12) is the present-value factor, which is given in Table IV. Hence the problem may be solved by means of that table. We know Z and n. We look in the row corresponding to n until we find Z, which gives us the desired r; or, if Z does not occur exactly in this row, we perform a rough interpolation. Since the present value decreases with r, the answer will be unique.

Example 3. A bank offers to make an "auto-loan" of $2000 for 2 years, and it sets the monthly payments at $92.62. What interest is the bank charging? Here $Z = 2000/92.62 = 21.6$, and $n = 24$ months. In the line $n = 24$ of Table IV we find that $r = .0075$ yields 21.89 while $r = .01$ yields 21.24. Roughly interpolating, we obtain $r = .0086$, or an interest rate of .86 percent a month (compounded monthly), or more than 10 percent annually. For the effective annually compounded annual interest rate, see Exercise 1 of Section 4.

If S is not 0, then we must adopt a trial-and-error method. We must substitute a sequence of values for r in (10), compute the ratio of the two sides for each r, and find the $r > 0$ for which the ratio is 1.

Example 4. In Example 2, suppose the machine will last 7 years and it is desired to find the rate of interest that will permit the fund, starting with a balance of \$6000, to pay out \$1000 for 7 years and end with a balance of \$2000. In Figure 4 are listed values of $(1 + r)^7$ and

$$\frac{Sr + p}{Pr + p} = \frac{2000r - 1000}{6000r - 1000}$$

for various values of $r \geq 0$.

r	$(1+r)^n$	$\dfrac{Sr + p}{Pr + p}$	$\dfrac{Sr + p}{Pr + p} \div (1+r)^n$
0	1.000	1.000	1.00
.02	1.149	1.091	.95
.04	1.316	1.211	.92
.06	1.504	1.375	.91
.08	1.714	1.615	.94
.09	1.828	1.783	.98
.10	1.949	2.000	1.03
.12	2.211	2.714	1.23

Figure 4

Hence the required interest rate is between 9 and 10 percent.

When P is the price paid for a bond, S is the maturity value of the bond, p is the periodic coupon payment, and n is the number of periods to maturity, the interest rate r calculated above is called the *yield* per period to maturity. We shall give an example of a bond-yield calculation after discussing nominal and equivalent interest rates (see Example 4, Section 4).

In investment decision problems, where P is the price paid for an asset, S is its salvage value n years hence, and p is the annual earnings of the asset (see Example 4), the interest rate r that satisfies (10) or (11) is called the *internal rate of return*. Like the payback period, it is a kind of break-even value. If the internal rate of return on an asset is greater than the rate that can be earned on other investments, then the asset should be acquired; otherwise it should not be acquired.

Even when payments are not uniform, or when an investment is made in some way other than a lump sum at the beginning, we may *define* the internal rate of return as that interest rate r which makes the net present value of all the cash flows (investment, annual returns, and salvage) equal to zero. Under some circumstances there will be *two* rates of return that satisfy this condition (see Exercise 2). To find the internal rate of return under these conditions we must almost always proceed by trial-and-error.

Example 5. By investing $3400 now and $2000 two years from now, earnings of $1000 + 200j$ dollars a year can be obtained in the jth year, where $j = 1, 2, \ldots, 6$, after which the investment will earn no more and have no salvage value. What is the internal rate of return?

In Figure 5 we show the net cash flows in years 0 through 6.

Year	Net Cash Flow
0	$-3400
1	+1200
2	-600
3	+1600
4	+1800
5	+2000
6	+2200

Figure 5

In Figure 6 we show the present value of these cash flows for various values of $r \geq 0$. The internal rate of return is just below 25 percent.

r	Present Value of Net Cash Flow
.001	$4800
.05	3271
.10	2111
.20	518
.25	-36
.30	-479
.35	-839
.40	-1133

Figure 6

EXERCISES

1. In Exercise 4 of Section 2, find the payback period and the internal rate of return.

2. In Exercise 13 of Section 2, find the internal rates of return. Show that there are two such rates. Interpret your results.

3. In Exercise 13 of Section 2, is there a "payback period"? Discuss.

4. In Exercise 10 of Section 2, find the payback period under the assumption that the machine will have a salvage value of $2000 regardless of when it is retired. Under the same assumption about the salvage value, find the internal rate of return.

5. In Exercise 11 of Section 2, find the payback period and the internal rate of return. Compare the ranking of the machines in Exercises 10 and 11 of that section when one ranks according to (a) net present value; (b) net present value per dollar invested; (c) payback period; (d) internal rate of return.   [*Partial Ans.* (a) B better; (b) A; (c) A; (d) A.]

6. A person may borrow $500 from the New York Finance Company and repay the loan in 24 equal monthly installments of $26.19. What monthly

compounded monthly interest rate is the finance company implicitly charging?

7. Consider the following two problems:

   a. From a fund with initial balance of $100,000, five annual payments of $10,000 each are to be made. What rate of interest must be earned on the balance in the fund in order for its balance at the end of the fifth year to be $20,000?

   b. Ten annual payments of $10,000 per year are made into a fund whose initial balance is $50,000. What rate of interest must be earned on the balance in the fund in order for its balance at the end of the tenth year to be $120,000?

   In both problems, show that there is no $r \geq 0$ that satisfies the required conditions.

8. Show that for given P, S, n, and p, there can be a solution for $r \geq 0$ in (10) only if $S \geq P + np$. Did the problems of Exercise 7 satisfy this condition?

9. Show that the following flow diagram describes a computational process for finding the payback period.

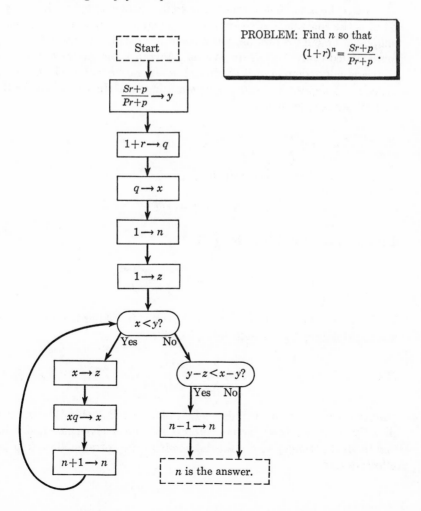

PROBLEM: Find n so that
$$(1+r)^n = \frac{Sr+p}{Pr+p}.$$

10. Construct a flow diagram for computing the rate of return r if P, n, and p are given, and if $S = 0$. Assume that a subroutine for computing $(1 + r)^i$ exists.

4. NOMINAL AND EFFECTIVE INTEREST RATES

So far we have assumed that the payment period coincides with the compounding period. This assumption is not at all necessary; we can easily establish a relationship among interest rates subject to different periods of compounding. When we talk of an interest rate of 6 percent per year compounded quarterly, we really mean an interest rate of $\frac{1}{4} \cdot 6$ percent = 1.5 percent compounded four times per year. The 6 percent is called the *nominal* interest rate; there is in fact an *effective* annually compounded interest rate greater than 6 percent that is equivalent to the nominal 6 percent compounded quarterly.

Let r' be a *nominal* interest rate that is compounded m times a year. What is the equivalent *effective* rate r compounded annually? Consider the compound amount S of a deposit P after N years at an interest rate r'/m compounded every $1/m$ years. We may then ask the equivalent question, what annually compounded effective interest rate r will produce from the same initial deposit the same compound amount? In the first case there are mN periods, so that

$$S = P\left(1 + \frac{r'}{m}\right)^{mN};$$

in the second, there are N periods, and

$$S = P(1 + r)^N.$$

Thus we want to find the r for which

$$P(1 + r)^N = P\left(1 + \frac{r'}{m}\right)^{mN}.$$

Dividing both sides of the equation above by P, taking the Nth root, and then subtracting 1 from both sides, we obtain

(13) $$r = \left(1 + \frac{r'}{m}\right)^m - 1.$$

Observe that this result is independent of N and P. Table III can be used directly to obtain the effective interest rate for a given nominal rate. It can be used inversely to obtain the nominal rate corresponding to a given effective rate.

Example 1. Suppose that 6 percent annual interest is to be compounded monthly. Then 6 percent is the nominal rate r', and $m = 12$. Thus the effective annual rate is

$$r = \left(1 + \frac{.06}{12}\right)^{12} - 1 = (1 + .005)^{12} - 1.$$

From Table III we find that $(1.005)^{12} = 1.0617$, hence $r = .0617$, or about $6\frac{1}{6}$ percent.

A good approximate answer for the effective rate r may be obtained by applying the binomial theorem (see Chapter 2, Section 3) to (13). We obtain

$$r = 1 + \binom{m}{1}\left(\frac{r'}{m}\right)^1 + \binom{m}{2}\left(\frac{r'}{m}\right)^2 + \cdots - 1$$

$$= r' + \left(\frac{m-1}{2m}\right)r'^2 + \cdots.$$

Hence

(14)
$$r \approx r' + \frac{m-1}{2m}r'^2.$$

(For a discussion of the accuracy of this approximation see Exercises 6 and 7.) Note that the estimate given in (14) is always *less* than the true value of r, since the approximation was obtained by ignoring positive terms in the binomial expansion.

Example 1 (continued). If we use (14) instead of (13), we obtain

$$r \approx .06 + (\tfrac{11}{24})(.0036) = .06165,$$

whereas the correct answer to the same number of decimal places is .06168, an excellent agreement.

Example 2. A bank pays 4 percent interest compounded quarterly. What is the equivalent (effective) annual compounding interest rate?
Here $r' = .04$ and $m = 4$. Hence $r = (1.01)^4 - 1 = .0406$, from Table III. Therefore the effective rate is 4.06 percent. The approximate formula (14) yields $.04 + (\tfrac{3}{8})(.0016) = .0406$, which is correct to four decimal places.

Example 3. A mortgage of $50,000 is to be liquidated over 12 years in 48 equal quarterly installments. If interest is charged on the unpaid balance at the annual rate of 8.2 percent compounded annually, how large should the payments be?
Using equation (13) and Table III, we see that

$$.082 = \left(1 + \frac{.08}{4}\right)^4 - 1$$

so that $r' = .08$ and $r'/m = .02$. Now treating the problem in terms of quarter years, we apply the capital-recovery formula. From Table IV, the uniform-payment present-value factor for 48 payments with interest of 2 percent is 30.67. Hence, from Figure 2,

$$p = \frac{1}{30.67} (-50{,}000) = -1630.$$

Thus payments of $1630 per quarter will liquidate the mortgage in 12 years.

Example 4. An investor can purchase a bond for $846.63. At maturity 24 years later, the investor will receive the face value of $1000. The "coupon rate" of the bond is 3 percent payable semiannually; that is, the investor receives "interest" on the bond of $15 twice each year. What is the yield to maturity?

We take as our standard time period a half year; we will determine the semiannually compounded yield, and then translate this into an annually compounded yield. Thus $P = 846.63$, $S = 1000$, $p = -15$, and $n = mN = 2 \cdot 24 = 48$. There is a solution, since

$$S = 1000 > P + np = 846.63 + (48)(-15) = 126.63$$

and $S > P$ (see Exercise 8, Section 3). After trying various values of r in (10), we find that

$$(1 + .02)^{48} = \frac{(1000)(.02) - 15}{(846.63)(.02) - 15},$$

hence $r'/m = r'/2 = .02$. Then

$$r = (1 + .02)^2 - 1 = .0404 = 4.04 \text{ percent.}$$

EXERCISES

1. In Example 3 of Section 3, find the effective annually compounded annual interest rate. [*Ans.* $r \approx .108$.]

2. In Exercise 6 of Section 3, find the effective interest rate.

3. Find the effective interest rate equivalent to 12 percent compounded (*a*) monthly, (*b*) quarterly, (*c*) semiannually.
   [*Ans.* (*a*) 12.68 percent; (*b*) 12.55 percent; (*c*) 12.36 percent.]

4. Find the effective interest rate equivalent to 100 percent compounded (*a*) twice per year, (*b*) five times per year, (*c*) ten times per year, (*d*) 20 times per year, (*e*) 100 times per year. Does the effective interest rate appear to increase without limit as the period of compounding becomes smaller and smaller? (It can be shown that as the period of compounding decreases, the effective interest rate approaches $e^{r'} - 1$, where r' is the nominal interest rate and $e = 2.718 \ldots$ is the number previously encountered in Chapter 3, Section 4. Thus, with $r' = 1.00$, r approaches 1.718 . . . .)
   [*Partial Ans.* (*e*) $r = 1.01^{100} - 1 = 1.01^{96} \cdot 1.01^4 - 1 = (2.5993)(1.0406) - 1 = 1.7048$.]

5. Find the nominal quarterly compounded interest rates equivalent to the following effective rates: (*a*) 4.06 percent, (*b*) 6.14 percent, (*c*) 8.24 percent, (*d*) 10.38 percent.

6. Use the binomial theorem to obtain a better approximation for r than (14). [*Hint:* Carry out the expansion to one more term.]

7. What is the maximum size of improvement obtained in Exercise 6 if r' is at most 10 percent?

8. Use the binomial theorem to show that if $n\epsilon$ is small, then

(vi) $$[(1+r)+\epsilon]^n \approx (1+r)^{n-1}[1+r+n\epsilon].$$

9. Find an approximate value for $(1.0617)^{20}$, using Table III and formula (vi).

10. Use the result of Example 1 and of Exercise 9 to find the compound amount of \$1 compounded monthly at a nominal annual rate of 6 percent for 20 years. Compare your answer with that obtained by compounding \$1 at .5 percent interest per period for 240 periods.

11. Use (14) and the result of Exercise 8 to find the value of an annuity at the end of 24 years if \$100 per quarter is paid into a fund that bears interest at a nominal rate of 6 percent compounded quarterly.

SUGGESTED READING

Bierman, H., and S. Smidt, *The Capital Budgeting Decision*, Macmillan, New York, 1960, Chapters III, VIII.

Goldberg, S., *Introduction to Difference Equations*, Wiley, New York, 1958, Chapter II.

Grant, E. L., and W. G. Ireson, *Principles of Engineering Economy*, 4th Ed., Ronald, New York, 1960, Chapters IV, XV, XVI.

8

MARKOV DECISION PROCESSES

1. REGULAR AND SUPERREGULAR VECTORS

Let P be the transition matrix of an absorbing Markov chain having s (≥ 2) states. We assume as usual that the matrix P is put into the normal form

$$P = \left(\begin{array}{c|c} I & 0 \\ \hline R & Q \end{array}\right)$$

in which the r absorbing states are listed first, and the remaining $s - r$ nonabsorbing states, which we shall call *transient states*, are listed last. Throughout this chapter we shall denote the entries of the matrix P by P_{ij}.

A column vector v will be called a *regular vector* if it satisfies $v = Pv$. In other words, a regular vector v is a fixed vector on the right of the transition matrix P. If v_i is the ith component of a regular vector v, then it satisfies

(1) $$v_i = \sum_{k=1}^{s} P_{ik}v_k$$

for $i = 1, \ldots, s$. We shall also say that a vector v is *regular at state i* if (1) is true for state i. A vector v is then regular if and only if it is regular at all states. Note that in order to decide whether a vector is regular we need only examine the transient states, since for absorbing states $P_{ii} = 1$, hence $v_i = P_{ii}v_i = 1v_i = v_i$, so any vector is automatically regular at an absorbing state.

Let us call the *neighbors* of a state i the states that can be reached from i in one step. Thus, state j is a neighbor of state i if $P_{ij} > 0$. Then to say that a vector is regular at state i, meaning it satisfies (1), is merely to say that its value at i is the average of its values at neighboring states, where we mean the average with respect to the probability measure $p_i = \{P_{i1}, P_{i2}, \ldots, P_{is}\}$.

If we regard the states as situations a player can be in when playing a certain game, and v_i as the player's fortune when in state i, then (1) states that the player's expected fortune after the next play is also v_i. That is, the *game* is *fair* when v is a regular vector.

We shall say that a vector v is *superregular* if it satisfies $v \geq Pv$—that is, if

$$(2) \qquad v_i \geq \sum_{k=1}^{s} P_{ik}v_k$$

for $i = 1, \ldots, s$. Vector v is *superregular at state i* if (2) holds for state i.

With the same interpretations as above a superregular but not regular vector v represents an *unfavorable game*, since a player in state i with fortune v_i must move to a neighboring state, and by (2) his expected fortune on the next step decreases or stays the same.

Example 1. Consider the simple random walk with six states shown in Figure 1. The process moves among the integers (states) 0, 1, 2, 3, 4, and 5. If

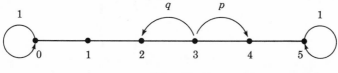

Figure 1

the process is in states 1, 2, 3, or 4 it moves one step to the right with probability p and one step to the left with probability $q = 1 - p$. And if the process ever reaches states 0 or 5, it stays there. Thus we have an absorbing Markov chain in which states 0 and 5 are absorbing and 1, 2, 3, 4 are transient. The transition matrix in normal form is in Figure 2.

$$P = \begin{array}{c} \\ 0 \\ 5 \\ \\ 1 \\ 2 \\ 3 \\ 4 \end{array} \begin{array}{c} \begin{array}{cccccc} 0 & 5 & 1 & 2 & 3 & 4 \end{array} \\ \left(\begin{array}{cc|cccc} 1 & 0 & 0 & 0 & 0 & 0 \\ 0 & 1 & 0 & 0 & 0 & 0 \\ \hline q & 0 & 0 & p & 0 & 0 \\ 0 & 0 & q & 0 & p & 0 \\ 0 & 0 & 0 & q & 0 & p \\ 0 & p & 0 & 0 & q & 0 \end{array}\right) \end{array}$$

Figure 2

Let us consider this process as a game in which the position represents a player's fortune. Then, when the player is in a transient state i, his fortune is $v_i = i$ and his expected fortune after the next play is

$$pv_{i+1} + qv_{i-1} = p(i + 1) + q(i - 1) = i(p + q) + p - q = i + p - q.$$

Thus the game is fair if $p = q = \frac{1}{2}$, and the vector

$$v = \begin{matrix} 0 \\ 5 \\ 1 \\ 2 \\ 3 \\ 4 \end{matrix} \begin{pmatrix} 0 \\ 5 \\ 1 \\ 2 \\ 3 \\ 4 \end{pmatrix}$$

is regular. (The reader should check that $Pv = v$ when $p = q = \frac{1}{2}$ in Figure 2.) On the other hand if $p < \frac{1}{2}$, the game is unfavorable and the vector v is superregular. (Show that $v \geq Pv$ for this case.)

Consider now the case $p > 0$; define $u = q/p$ and let $v_i = u^i$. Then for a transient state i we have for the expected fortune on the next play

$$pv_{i+1} + qv_{i-1} = p\left(\frac{q}{p}\right)^{i+1} + q\left(\frac{q}{p}\right)^{i-1} = \left(\frac{q}{p}\right)^i (q + p) = u^i = v_i.$$

Therefore the vector

$$v = \begin{matrix} 0 \\ 5 \\ 1 \\ 2 \\ 3 \\ 4 \end{matrix} \begin{pmatrix} 1 \\ u^5 \\ u \\ u^2 \\ u^3 \\ u^4 \end{pmatrix}$$

is regular, provided $p > 0$.

As a specific numerical example, let $p = \frac{1}{3}$ so that $q = \frac{2}{3}$ and $u = 2$. Then the vector

$$v = \begin{pmatrix} 1 \\ 32 \\ 2 \\ 4 \\ 8 \\ 16 \end{pmatrix}$$

is regular, as the reader can easily check.

Let P be an arbitrary absorbing Markov chain in canonical form, let $N = (I - Q)^{-1}$ be its fundamental matrix, and let $B = NR$ (see Chapter 4). In Exercise 4 you will be asked to show that P^n approaches the matrix

$$(3) \qquad \bar{B} = \left(\begin{array}{c|c} I & 0 \\ \hline B & 0 \end{array}\right)$$

as n approaches infinity.

Now let v be a vector of the form

(4) $$v = \overline{B}\overline{b},$$

where $\overline{b}$ has the form $\overline{b} = \begin{pmatrix} b \\ 0 \end{pmatrix}$ with b an arbitrary column vector with r components and 0 an $(s - r)$-zero column vector. Then we can prove the following theorem.

THEOREM. Let P be the transition matrix of an arbitrary absorbing Markov chain, b an arbitrary r-component column vector, and $\overline{B}$ and v defined by (3) and (4); then v is a regular vector.

Proof. The proof of this is easy, since

$$Pv = \begin{pmatrix} I & 0 \\ R & Q \end{pmatrix} \begin{pmatrix} I & 0 \\ NR & 0 \end{pmatrix} \begin{pmatrix} b \\ 0 \end{pmatrix}$$

$$= \begin{pmatrix} I & 0 \\ (I + QN)R & 0 \end{pmatrix} \begin{pmatrix} b \\ 0 \end{pmatrix}$$

$$= \begin{pmatrix} I & 0 \\ B & 0 \end{pmatrix} \begin{pmatrix} b \\ 0 \end{pmatrix}.$$

In the last step we used the identity $QN = N - I$, which is established in Exercise 5.

If we take for b a vector with a 1 in the component corresponding to absorbing state a and 0 in all other states, we obtain for $v = \overline{B}\overline{b}$ the column of $\overline{B}$ corresponding to state a—that is, the probabilities of being absorbed in state a. Thus the absorption probability vectors are regular vectors. In Exercise 6 you will be asked to show that any linear combination of regular vectors is regular. Later in this section we will show that all regular vectors can be obtained as linear combinations of the absorption probability vectors.

Example 2. Consider the transition matrix of Figure 2 with $p = q = \frac{1}{2}$. Then

$$N = \begin{pmatrix} 1 & -\frac{1}{2} & 0 & 0 \\ -\frac{1}{2} & 1 & -\frac{1}{2} & 0 \\ 0 & -\frac{1}{2} & 1 & -\frac{1}{2} \\ 0 & 0 & -\frac{1}{2} & 1 \end{pmatrix}^{-1} = \begin{array}{c} \\ 1 \\ 2 \\ 3 \\ 4 \end{array} \begin{pmatrix} 1.6 & 1.2 & .8 & .4 \\ 1.2 & 2.4 & 1.6 & .8 \\ .8 & 1.6 & 2.4 & 1.2 \\ .4 & .8 & 1.2 & 1.6 \end{pmatrix}$$

$$\begin{array}{cccc} 1 & 2 & 3 & 4 \end{array}$$

and therefore

$$B = NR = \begin{matrix} & 0 & 5 \\ 1 \\ 2 \\ 3 \\ 4 \end{matrix} \begin{pmatrix} .8 & .2 \\ .6 & .4 \\ .4 & .6 \\ .2 & .8 \end{pmatrix}.$$

We have already noted that the position vector

$$v = \begin{pmatrix} 0 \\ 5 \\ 1 \\ 2 \\ 3 \\ 4 \end{pmatrix}$$

is a regular vector. We can obtain this vector from $\bar{B}$ as follows:

$$\bar{B}\bar{b} = \begin{pmatrix} 1 & 0 & 0 & 0 & 0 & 0 \\ 0 & 1 & 0 & 0 & 0 & 0 \\ .8 & .2 & 0 & 0 & 0 & 0 \\ .6 & .4 & 0 & 0 & 0 & 0 \\ .4 & .6 & 0 & 0 & 0 & 0 \\ .2 & .8 & 0 & 0 & 0 & 0 \end{pmatrix} \begin{pmatrix} 0 \\ 5 \\ 0 \\ 0 \\ 0 \\ 0 \end{pmatrix} = \begin{pmatrix} 0 \\ 5 \\ 1 \\ 2 \\ 3 \\ 4 \end{pmatrix}.$$

We next describe a way to construct superregular vectors. Let $\bar{N}$ be

(5) $$\bar{N} = \left(\begin{array}{c|c} 0 & 0 \\ \hline 0 & N \end{array} \right),$$

where we have replaced Q by N in the normal form for P and we have also replaced I and R by zero matrices of the same shapes. We now let w be a nonnegative $(s - r)$-component column vector and define $\bar{w} = \begin{pmatrix} 0 \\ w \end{pmatrix}$, where 0 is an r-component column zero vector. Next we define a vector v by

(6) $$v = \bar{N}\bar{w} = \begin{pmatrix} 0 \\ Nw \end{pmatrix}$$

and make the following definition.

DEFINITION. If v and w are related as in (6), then v is said to be a *potential* with *charge w*.

THEOREM. (a) A potential v is a superregular vector.
(b) If v is a potential with charge w, then

(7) $$\bar{w} = (I - P)v.$$

Proof. If (b) is true, then (a) is obviously also true, since $\bar{w} \geq 0$. Hence we need only prove (7). To do this observe that

$$(I - P)v = \begin{pmatrix} 0 & 0 \\ -R & I-Q \end{pmatrix}\begin{pmatrix} 0 & 0 \\ 0 & N \end{pmatrix}\begin{pmatrix} 0 \\ w \end{pmatrix}$$

$$= \begin{pmatrix} 0 & 0 \\ 0 & I \end{pmatrix}\begin{pmatrix} 0 \\ w \end{pmatrix} = \begin{pmatrix} 0 \\ w \end{pmatrix} = \bar{w},$$

which proves (7).

Example 3. As an example of a potential consider the case where we put a charge of 1 on each transient state. Then the potential is determined by Nc, where c is a column vector of all ones. But this is t, the mean number of times in each transient state before absorption for each possible transient starting state.

In the random walk of Example 2 this is

$$t = Nc = \begin{pmatrix} 1.6 & 1.2 & .8 & .4 \\ 1.2 & 2.4 & 1.6 & .8 \\ .8 & 1.6 & 2.4 & 1.2 \\ .4 & .8 & 1.2 & 1.6 \end{pmatrix}\begin{pmatrix} 1 \\ 1 \\ 1 \\ 1 \end{pmatrix} = \begin{pmatrix} 4 \\ 6 \\ 6 \\ 4 \end{pmatrix}.$$

Thus the vector

$$v = \begin{pmatrix} 0 \\ 0 \\ 4 \\ 6 \\ 6 \\ 4 \end{pmatrix} \quad \text{is a potential with charge} \quad \begin{pmatrix} 0 \\ 0 \\ 1 \\ 1 \\ 1 \\ 1 \end{pmatrix}.$$

There is a simple interpretation of potentials and regular vectors. Consider a system whose movement through a set of states is determined by an absorbing Markov chain with transition matrix P. Assume that every time the system is in a transient state i we receive a reward w_i, and if it ends in the absorbing state a we receive a bonus b_a and the system stops. Then $\bar{N}\bar{w}$ represents the expected amount that we will receive by the rewards obtained from transient states, and $\bar{B}\bar{b}$ is the expected final bonus upon stopping. Thus our total expected reward is $v = \bar{N}\bar{w} + \bar{B}\bar{b}$, which is the sum of a potential and a regular vector and hence is a superregular vector.

Example 4. A man buys a stock for \$70 and decides to sell if it reaches either \$50 or \$100. He believes that the price of the stock, rounded to the nearest \$10, will follow the transition matrix of Figure 3, which is just the random

$$
\begin{array}{cccccc}
& 50 & 100 & 60 & 70 & 80 & 90
\end{array}
$$

$$
\begin{array}{c}
50 \\
100 \\
\\
60 \\
70 \\
80 \\
90
\end{array}
\left(
\begin{array}{cc|cccc}
1 & 0 & 0 & 0 & 0 & 0 \\
0 & 1 & 0 & 0 & 0 & 0 \\
\hline
\frac{1}{2} & 0 & 0 & \frac{1}{2} & 0 & 0 \\
0 & 0 & \frac{1}{2} & 0 & \frac{1}{2} & 0 \\
0 & 0 & 0 & \frac{1}{2} & 0 & \frac{1}{2} \\
0 & \frac{1}{2} & 0 & 0 & \frac{1}{2} & 0
\end{array}
\right)
$$

Figure 3

walk of Example 2. The normal dividend is $.50 per share per quarter, but the man believes that the stock will not get into the $90's unless this dividend is doubled.

How can he evaluate the worth of owning the stock, given his decision on when to sell it? We treat the dividends as charges in the above sense and calculate Nb as follows:

$$
\begin{pmatrix}
1.6 & 1.2 & .8 & .4 \\
1.2 & 2.4 & 1.6 & .8 \\
.8 & 1.6 & 2.4 & 1.2 \\
.4 & .8 & 1.2 & 1.6
\end{pmatrix}
\begin{pmatrix}
.5 \\
.5 \\
.5 \\
1.0
\end{pmatrix}
=
\begin{pmatrix}
2.2 \\
3.4 \\
3.6 \\
2.8
\end{pmatrix}.
$$

The bonus part of this process is just the final selling price. Hence the expected value of owning the stock is the sum of a regular plus a potential vector.

$$
\begin{pmatrix}
50 \\
100 \\
60 \\
70 \\
80 \\
90
\end{pmatrix}
+
\begin{pmatrix}
0 \\
0 \\
2.2 \\
3.4 \\
3.6 \\
2.8
\end{pmatrix}
=
\begin{pmatrix}
50 \\
100 \\
62.2 \\
73.4 \\
83.6 \\
92.8
\end{pmatrix}.
$$

Note that each component gives the sum of the expected selling price plus the expected dividends received before selling.

Actually it is possible to write any superregular vector as the sum of a potential plus a regular vector as the following theorem shows.

THEOREM. Any superregular vector v can be written as

(8) $$ v = g + h, $$

where g is a potential and h is a regular vector.

Proof. To prove this we first write v as

(9) $$ v = \begin{pmatrix} v_1 \\ v_2 \end{pmatrix}, $$

where v_1 has r components and v_2 has $s - r$ components. Then it follows that

$$(10) \quad \bar{w} = (I - P)v = \begin{pmatrix} 0 & 0 \\ -R & I - Q \end{pmatrix} \begin{pmatrix} v_1 \\ v_2 \end{pmatrix} = \begin{pmatrix} 0 \\ -Rv_1 + (I - Q)v_2 \end{pmatrix}$$

is nonnegative, since v is superregular. Hence the vector $w = -Rv_1 + (I - Q)v_2$ is a charge. The potential determined by charge w is

$$(11) \quad g = \bar{N}\bar{w} = \begin{pmatrix} 0 & 0 \\ 0 & N \end{pmatrix} \begin{pmatrix} 0 \\ -Rv_1 + (I - Q)v_2 \end{pmatrix} = \begin{pmatrix} 0 \\ -NRv_1 + v_2 \end{pmatrix};$$

hence if we let

$$(12) \qquad h = \bar{B}\bar{v}_1 = \begin{pmatrix} I & 0 \\ NR & 0 \end{pmatrix} \begin{pmatrix} v_1 \\ 0 \end{pmatrix} = \begin{pmatrix} v_1 \\ NRv_1 \end{pmatrix},$$

we see that h is a regular vector and also

$$(13) \qquad g + h = \begin{pmatrix} 0 \\ -NRv_1 + v_2 \end{pmatrix} + \begin{pmatrix} v_1 \\ NRv_1 \end{pmatrix} = \begin{pmatrix} v_1 \\ v_2 \end{pmatrix} = v,$$

which is just (8).

EXERCISES

1. Consider Example 2 and state which of the following vectors is regular, superregular, or neither:

$$a. \begin{matrix} 0 \\ 5 \\ 1 \\ 2 \\ 3 \\ 4 \end{matrix} \begin{pmatrix} 20 \\ 10 \\ 18 \\ 16 \\ 14 \\ 12 \end{pmatrix}. \qquad b. \begin{matrix} 0 \\ 5 \\ 1 \\ 2 \\ 3 \\ 4 \end{matrix} \begin{pmatrix} 0 \\ 0 \\ 16 \\ 12 \\ 8 \\ 4 \end{pmatrix}. \qquad c. \begin{matrix} 0 \\ 5 \\ 1 \\ 2 \\ 3 \\ 4 \end{matrix} \begin{pmatrix} 20 \\ 8 \\ 18 \\ 16 \\ 14 \\ 12 \end{pmatrix}.$$

2. Show that each of the following vectors is superregular for the transition matrix of Example 2 and write each as the sum of a potential plus a regular vector:

$$a. \begin{matrix} 0 \\ 5 \\ 1 \\ 2 \\ 3 \\ 4 \end{matrix} \begin{pmatrix} 10 \\ 0 \\ 24 \\ 38 \\ 32 \\ 26 \end{pmatrix}. \qquad b. \begin{matrix} 0 \\ 5 \\ 1 \\ 2 \\ 3 \\ 4 \end{matrix} \begin{pmatrix} 5 \\ 5 \\ 17 \\ 20 \\ 21 \\ 14 \end{pmatrix}.$$

3. In Example 2 with $p = q = \frac{1}{2}$ assume that a reward of \$1 is given every time the process is in states 3 and 4 and these are the only rewards. Find the vector v that represents the total expected reward for each starting state.

4. $a.$ If P is the transition matrix of an absorbing Markov chain in canonical form, show that

$$P^2 = \begin{pmatrix} I & 0 \\ (I + Q)R & Q^2 \end{pmatrix}.$$

$b.$ Show that

$$P^n = \begin{pmatrix} I & 0 \\ (I + Q + \cdots + Q^{n-1})R & Q^n \end{pmatrix}.$$

$c.$ Use the fact that $Q^n \to 0$ and $N = I + Q + \cdots + Q^n + \cdots$ to show that

$$P^n \to \begin{pmatrix} I & 0 \\ B & 0 \end{pmatrix}.$$

5. Use the fact that $N = I + Q + \cdots + Q^n + \cdots$ to show that $QN = N - I$.

6. $a.$ If v and w are regular vectors and a and b are numbers, show that $av + bw$ is also regular.

$b.$ If v and w are superregular and a and b are nonnegative numbers, show that $av + bw$ is superregular.

7. Consider the following model. A man buys a store. The profits of the store vary from month to month. For simplicity we assume that he earns either \$5000 or \$2000 a month ("high" or "low"). The man may sell his store at any time, and there is a 10 percent chance of his selling during a high-profit month, and a 40 percent chance during a low-profit month. If he does not sell, with probability $\frac{2}{3}$ the profits will be the same the next month, and with probability $\frac{1}{3}$ they will change.

$a.$ Set up the transition matrix.

$$[Ans. \quad \begin{matrix} \text{Sell} \\ \text{High} \\ \text{Low} \end{matrix} \begin{pmatrix} 1 & 0 & 0 \\ \frac{1}{10} & \frac{3}{5} & \frac{3}{10} \\ \frac{2}{5} & \frac{1}{5} & \frac{2}{5} \end{pmatrix}.]$$

$b.$ Compute N, Nc, and NR and interpret each.

$c.$ Let $w = \begin{pmatrix} 5000 \\ 2000 \end{pmatrix}$ and compute the vector $g = Nw$.

$$[Ans. \quad g = \begin{pmatrix} 20{,}000 \\ 10{,}000 \end{pmatrix}.]$$

$d.$ Interpret the vector g.

8. Let P be the transition matrix of a regular Markov chain with states $1, 2, \ldots, r$ and a fixed vector α such that $\alpha P = \alpha$. Assume that every time the system is in state i the player receives a reward of $w_i \geq 0$ with at least one $w_i > 0$. What happens to the expected total reward after n steps as n tends to infinity? What happens to the average winnings as n tends to infinity?

9. Consider the same situation as in Exercise 8 but assume that winning an amount w_i on the nth step is worth to the player only $\beta^n w_i$ because of a discount factor β with $0 < \beta < 1$. Let $\bar{P}$ be the following transition matrix:

$$
\bar{P} = \begin{array}{c} \\ 0 \\ 1 \\ 2 \\ \vdots \\ r \end{array}
\begin{array}{c}
\begin{array}{ccccc} 0 & 1 & 2 & \cdots & r \end{array} \\
\left(\begin{array}{c|cccc}
1 & 0 & 0 & \cdots & 0 \\
\hline
1-\beta & \beta P_{11} & \beta P_{12} & \cdots & \beta P_{1r} \\
1-\beta & \beta P_{21} & \beta P_{22} & \cdots & \beta P_{2r} \\
\vdots & \vdots & & & \\
1-\beta & \beta P_{r1} & \beta P_{r2} & \cdots & \beta P_{rr}
\end{array} \right)
\end{array}.
$$

Show that $\bar{P}$ is the transition matrix of an absorbing Markov chain and that the matrix N for this chain represents the expected total discounted reward before absorption.

10. Let A be any subset of transient states of an absorbing Markov chain. Let v_i be the probability starting at state i that the process ever reaches any member of the set A. Show that v is superregular.

11. Let v be a superregular vector written as in equation (9).
  a. If $v_1 = 0$, show that v is a potential.
  b. If $v_2 \geq NRv_1$, show that v is regular.

12. Use the results of Exercise 11*a.* to show that the vector v of Exercise 10 is a potential.

13. Show that if $\bar{w}$ is the charge of the potential v defined in Exercise 10, then
  a. $\bar{w}_i = 0$ if i is not in A.
  b. If i is in A, $\bar{w}_i$ is the probability that the process leaves A on the first step and does not return. (This is called the *escape probability*.)

14. Consider the random walk on the integers 0 through 7 with probability $\frac{1}{2}$ of moving up or down one step, and with 0 and 7 as absorbing states. Let $A = \{2, 3, 4\}$ and find v_i, the probability of ever reaching A starting in state i, for all i. Verify that v is a potential and find its charge.

2. A FAIR GAME REMAINS FAIR

Recall that for an absorbing Markov chain

$$
P = \left(\begin{array}{c|c} I & 0 \\ \hline R & Q \end{array} \right)
$$

the powers P^n converge to a matrix

$$
\bar{B} = \left(\begin{array}{c|c} I & 0 \\ \hline B & 0 \end{array} \right),
$$

where $B = NR$. Because of the latter condition it follows from our earlier interpretation for NR that for a transient state i and an absorbing state

a, $\overline{B}_{ia}$ is the probability of ending up in absorbing state a given that we started in transient state i.

Assume now that v is a regular vector for P—that is, $v = Pv$. Multiplying both sides of this equation by P, we see that $Pv = P^2v$, so that $v = P^2v$. Repeating this procedure, we find that $v = P^nv$. And passing to the limit we have

(1) $$v = \overline{B}v.$$

Thus for a transient state i

(2) $$v_i = \sum_a B_{ia}v_a,$$

where the sum is taken over all absorbing states. Equation (2) tells us that the values of a regular vector are completely determined by their values on the absorbing states.

The fact that $v = P^nv$ means that a fair game is fair if n plays are made, for any n. We have just seen that it is fair if it is played until an absorbing state is reached. We can also modify the game so that it stops also when it reaches some state in a subset T of the transient states.

To see how this can be done let P be the transition matrix of an absorbing Markov chain with a set A of absorbing states. Let v be a regular vector for P and let T be an arbitrary subset of transient states. Then a *stopping rule* for P is the same chain as P but stopped with payoff v_i whenever a state j in $A \cup T$ is reached for the first time.

THEOREM. *If vector v is regular for absorbing chain P with absorbing states A, then it is also regular for chain P with absorbing states $A \cup T$.*

Proof. To prove this we simply note that for each transient state i in P, v_i is still the average of its neighbors regardless of whether some of them have been changed from transient into absorbing states.

In exactly the same way if v is a superregular vector for P we have $v \geq Pv \geq P^2v \geq \cdots \geq \overline{B}v$, and for i a transient state

(3) $$v_i \geq \sum_a B_{ia}v_a,$$

where the sum is over absorbing states. Thus all the remarks and the theorem above remain true with regular replaced by superregular and fair replaced by unfavorable. Thus, an unfavorable game remains unfavorable to the end, and also under stopping rules.

Example 1. Consider again Example 2 of the previous section, where $A = \{0, 5\}$. Suppose we make $T = \{1\}$. Then the modified chain P^* with this stopping rule is given in Figure 4.

$$P^* = \begin{array}{c} \\ 0 \\ 1 \\ 5 \\ \\ 2 \\ 3 \\ 4 \end{array} \begin{array}{c} \begin{array}{cccccc} 0 & 1 & 5 & 2 & 3 & 4 \end{array} \\ \left(\begin{array}{ccc|ccc} 1 & 0 & 0 & 0 & 0 & 0 \\ 0 & 1 & 0 & 0 & 0 & 0 \\ 0 & 0 & 1 & 0 & 0 & 0 \\ \hline 0 & \frac{1}{2} & 0 & 0 & \frac{1}{2} & 0 \\ 0 & 0 & 0 & \frac{1}{2} & 0 & \frac{1}{2} \\ 0 & 0 & \frac{1}{2} & 0 & \frac{1}{2} & 0 \end{array} \right) \end{array}$$

Figure 4

The reader should check that the vectors

$$v = \begin{pmatrix} 0 \\ 1 \\ 5 \\ 2 \\ 3 \\ 4 \end{pmatrix}, \qquad v' = \begin{pmatrix} 0 \\ 0 \\ 4 \\ 6 \\ 6 \\ 4 \end{pmatrix},$$

which were regular and superregular, respectively, for the original chain, still have these properties with the stopping rule.

Example 2. In the gambler's-ruin example of Section 12 of Chapter 3 if we let $r = q/p$, then $v_i = r^i$ gives a regular vector v, as was proved in the previous section. This vector will remain regular regardless of any stopping rule that the gambler might employ.

Example 3. Consider the more complicated game corresponding to the random walk in Figure 5. The circles represent transient states, and from each

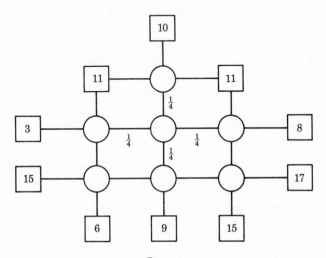

Figure 5

such transient state the chain moves with equal probabilities to the four neighboring states. The game begins in a transient state and continues until an absorbing state, marked with a square, is reached. The amounts received at each absorbing state are marked in the squares.

Consider a transient state A with neighbors B, C, D, and E (some of which may be absorbing states) as shown in Figure 6. Since payoffs are made

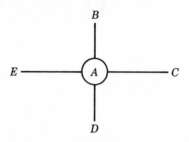

Figure 6

only on the absorbing states, if we let v_i be the expected value of the game starting in state i, then v is a regular vector so that

$$v_A = \tfrac{1}{4}v_B + \tfrac{1}{4}v_C + \tfrac{1}{4}v_D + \tfrac{1}{4}v_E.$$

We can also find the components of v by using formula (2). But (2) involves $B = NR = (I - Q)^{-1}R$, and since inverting a matrix is equivalent to solving simultaneous linear equations, we see that the first method of solving the problem given in Figure 5 is by means of linear equations. We shall indicate other solution techniques in Examples 4, 5, and 6.

The problem in Example 3 is sometimes called a *boundary-value problem*. For this interpretation think of the absorbing states as boundary states, and the transient states as interior states. The boundary values are given and the problem is to find the interior values, knowing only that they satisfy an averaging property.

When such a boundary-value problem can be shown to have a unique solution, as is true in our case, it is often possible to use the method of solving one problem to solve an entirely different kind of problem.

Example 4. Consider the electrical network given in Figure 7. The various points are connected by equal resistances of magnitude R. The circles marked with circles are interior points, and the points indicated by squares are boundary points. Each of the boundary points is kept at a fixed voltage as indicated by the number inside the square. The boundary problem is to find the voltages at the interior points. Let V_i be the voltage at point i. Consider an interior point A with neighbors B, C, D, and E (as in Figure 6). By Kirchhoff's laws the total current coming into and going out of point A is 0. Furthermore the current flowing between two points, such as B and A, is equal to the voltage difference between these points divided by the resistance R. Thus we have

$$\frac{V_B - V_A}{R} + \frac{V_C - V_A}{R} + \frac{V_D - V_A}{R} + \frac{V_E - V_A}{R} = 0,$$

or, by multiplying through by R and solving for V_A,

$$V_A = \tfrac{1}{4}V_B + \tfrac{1}{4}V_C + \tfrac{1}{4}V_D + \tfrac{1}{4}V_E,$$

which is exactly the same equation we have in Example 3. Since it has the same values on absorbing states, both problems must have the same values on interior states.

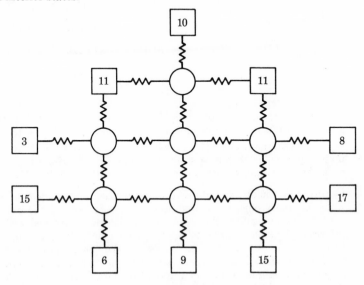

Figure 7

What this means is that we can use the matrix-inversion method of Example 3 to solve the electrical problem of Example 4. Or, conversely, we could build the electrical circuit of Figure 7 and measure the interior voltages in order to solve the Markov chain of Example 3.

Example 5. Still another way of solving the Markov chain of Example 3 is to use a Monte Carlo method. We do this by having a computer start at a random interior state, and by choosing random numbers move from state to state according to the transition probabilities of the Markov chain, stopping as soon as an absorbing state is reached. Then the computer finds the average winnings for each starting state. By the law of large numbers those averages will be approximations for the values v_i. Figure 8 shows the average results

Approximate values found by the Monte Carlo method

		10		
	11	10.534	11	
3	8.583	10.046	10.593	8
15	9.968	10.576	13.27	17
	6	9	15	

Figure 8

of 10,000 such simulations for each starting state. Figure 9 gives the correct values, correct to three decimal places.

Exact values of voltages

		10		
	11	10.514	11	
3	8.521	10.054	10.587	8
15	10.029	10.595	13.295	17
	6	9	15	

Figure 9

Comparison shows that the Monte Carlo results are not spectacularly good. We know from the central limit theorem that in 10,000 trials we can expect an error as large as $1/\sqrt{10,000} = \frac{1}{100}$ for the probability B_{ia} of ending up in a particular absorbing state. Thus it is not surprising that we cannot even obtain two-place accuracy in the answer with the Monte Carlo method.

Example 6. Finally we indicate another method, *the value-iteration method*, which is a very efficient computation method for solving the problem. We start by assigning 0 as the value of each interior point and assigning the prescribed boundary values to the boundary points. It is easy to show that this gives in initial superregular vector $v^{(0)}$. We now go successively through the interior states in some order, replacing the corresponding component of $v^{(0)}$ by the weighted average of values at the neighboring points. Because $v^{(0)}$ was superregular, $v^{(1)}$ will be also, and $v^{(1)} \geq v^{(0)}$. We repeat the process, obtaining $v^{(2)}$ with $v^{(2)} \geq v^{(1)}$. It can be shown that if this process is continued, we obtain a sequence of superregular vectors $v^{(0)} \leq v^{(1)} \leq \cdots \leq v^{(n)} \leq \cdots$ that increases monotonically to a regular vector with the correct entries.

The value-iteration method was carried out for the chain in Example 3. After only 15 iterations it gave answers correct to three places. And the computation time was less than one second, as compared to 32 seconds for the Monte Carlo method.

The example above shows how ideas arising in one kind of application can lead to interesting concepts for quite different applications. The ideas of regular and superregular vectors and potentials were developed for application to physical models such as the electrical circuit of Example 4. However, as we shall see later, these concepts are important for studying quite different problems of considerable importance in social and managerial science.

EXERCISES

1. An urn has nine white balls and eleven black balls. A ball is drawn and replaced. If it is white, you win 5 cents, if black, you lose 5 cents. You have a dollar to gamble with, and your opponent has 50 cents. If you keep on playing till one of you loses all his money, what is the probability that you will lose your dollar?   [*Ans.* .868.]

2. Suppose that you are shooting craps, and you always hold the dice. You have $20, your opponent has $10, and $1 is bet on each game; estimate your probability of ruin.

3. Two government agencies, A and B, are competing for the same task. A has 50 positions, and B has 20. Each year one position is taken away from one of the agencies, and given to the other. If 52 percent of the time the shift is from A to B, what do you predict for the future of the two agencies?
   [*Ans.* One agency will be abolished. B survives with probability .8, A with probability .2.]

4. In the gambler's-ruin problem what is the approximate value of x_A if you are rich, and the gambler starts with $1?

5. Consider a simple model for evolution. On a small island there is room for 1000 members of a certain species. One year a favorable mutant appears. We assume that in each subsequent generation either the mutants take one place from the regular members of the species, with probability .6, or the reverse happens. Thus, for example, the mutation disappears in the very first generation with probability .4. What is the probability that the mutants eventually take over? [*Hint:* See Exercise 4.]   [*Ans.* $\frac{1}{3}$.]

6. In the gambler's-ruin problem show that if $p > \frac{1}{2}$, and both parties have a substantial amount of money, your probability of ruin is approximately $1/r^A$.

7. You are matching pennies. You have 25 pennies to start with, and your opponent has 35. What is the probability that you will win all his pennies?

8. Mr. Jones lives on a short street, about 100 steps long. At one end of the street is his home, at the other a lake, and in the middle a bar. One evening he leaves the bar in a state of intoxication, and starts to walk at random. What is the probability that he will fall into the lake if
   a. He is just as likely to take a step to the right as to the left?
   [*Ans.* $\frac{1}{2}$.]
   b. If he has probability .51 of taking a step towards his home?
   [*Ans.* .119.]

9. You are in the following hopeless situation: You are playing a game in which you have only $\frac{1}{3}$ chance of winning. You have $1, and your opponent has $7. What is the probability of your winning all his money if
   a. You bet $1 each time?   [*Ans.* $\frac{1}{255}$.]
   b. You bet all your money each time?   [*Ans.* $\frac{1}{27}$.]

10. Repeat Exercise 9 for the case of a fair game, where you have probability $\frac{1}{2}$ of winning.

Exercises 11 through 16 refer to the plane grid shown in Figure 10. A game is played on this grid by choosing a starting (interior) point, and moving with equal probability to one of the four neighboring points, till a boundary point is reached.

11. Set up the Q and R matrices. [*Hint:* Q is 3-by-3 and R is 3-by-7.]

12. Find the N matrix. If we start at point 1, how many times on the average can we expect to be in points 2 and 3?   [*Ans.* $\frac{2}{7}$, $\frac{1}{14}$.]

13. For each possible starting position calculate the mean number of steps needed to reach the boundary.   [*Ans.* $\frac{10}{7}$, $\frac{12}{7}$, $\frac{10}{7}$.]

14. For each possible starting point find the probability of ending up at the various boundary points.

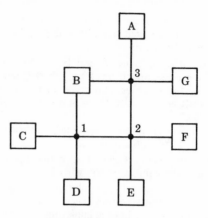

Figure 10

15. We choose point 1 as the starting position. Player I wins if the marker ends up at points C or D, and player II wins otherwise. Show that the game is favorable to player I and find the odds in his favor.

[*Ans.* 15:13.]

16. Suppose that the starting position is decided by tossing two coins. If we get two heads we start at point 1, if two tails at point 2, otherwise at point 3. What is the probability of ending up at B? [*Ans.* $\frac{1}{4}$.]

Exercises 17 through 22 refer to the plane grid shown in Figure 11. The rules of the game are as for Figure 10.

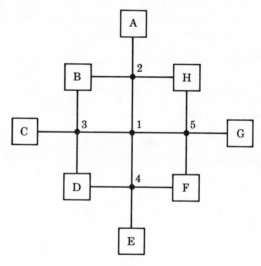

Figure 11

17. Set up the Q and R matrices.

18. Find the N matrix. If we start at the center, and we do *not* count the original position, show that we can expect to be the same number of times in each of the five interior positions.

19. Let us assume that from point 2 it takes an average of $\frac{5}{3}$ steps to reach the boundary. Use common-sense arguments to find the mean number of steps needed from each of the other interior points. Use the N matrix to verify your answers.

20. Find the probabilities of ending up at each boundary point if we start at the center.

21. Find the probability of ending up at each boundary point if we start at point 2.   [Ans. $\frac{13}{48}$ $\frac{7}{24}$ $\frac{1}{48}$ $\frac{1}{24}$ $\frac{1}{48}$ $\frac{1}{24}$ $\frac{1}{48}$ $\frac{7}{24}$.]

22. Using the grid in Figure 11, set up rules for three players so that they have equal chance of winning.

Exercises 23 through 26 deal with the following ruin problem: A and B play a game in which A has probability $\frac{2}{3}$ of winning. They keep playing until either A has won six times or B has won three times.

23. Set up the process as a Markov chain whose states are (a, b), where a is the number of times A won, and b the number of B wins.

24. For each state compute the probability of A winning from that position. [$Hint$: Work from higher a- and b-values to lower ones.]

25. What is the probability that A reaches his goal first?   [Ans. $\frac{1024}{2187}$.]

26. Suppose that payments are made as follows: If A wins six games, he receives \$1, if B wins three games, then A pays \$1. What is the expected value of the payment, to the nearest penny?

3. OPTIMAL STOPPING

We consider now the problem in which we are given an absorbing Markov chain and a *reward vector* w. We start the system as usual but have the option of stopping it at any time we are in a transient state. If we stop in transient state i, we receive the reward w_i. If we do not stop until an absorbing state a is reached, then we must stop and accept the reward w_a. In order to describe a stopping rule we use the procedure of the previous section and specify a subset T of transient states such that whenever we reach a state T we will stop. In particular, $T = \varepsilon$ means that we will continue to play until an absorbing state is reached.

Let P be the transition matrix and A the subset of absorbing states of the Markov chain. Then with stopping rule T we have a new absorbing chain P^T with absorbing states $A \cup T$. Then with stopping rule T, the expected value of the game starting in transient state i is

$$(1) \qquad\qquad v_i = \sum_a \bar{B}^T_{ia} w_a,$$

where the sum is over states a in $A \cup T$, and $\bar{B}^T_{ia}$ is the limiting matrix for this chain. We will show that there is a rule, the *optimal stopping rule*, that makes v_i as large as possible and that the same rule applies for all starting states.

Let $\mathfrak{F}$ be the set of all vectors v satisfying

(2) $$v \geq Pv,$$

(3) $$v \geq w.$$

That is, $\mathfrak{F}$ is the set of all P superregular vectors that dominate w.

THEOREM. The set $\mathfrak{F}$ of all vectors satisfying (2) and (3) is nonempty, and has a unique smallest element g such that

(4) $$g_a = w_a \qquad\qquad \text{for } a \text{ in } A,$$

(5) $$g_i = \text{maximum } (w_i, \Sigma\, P_{ij} g_j) \qquad \text{otherwise.}$$

Proof. Let f be an s-component column vector of all ones and let k be a number. Then $v = kf$ satisfies (2), and if we choose k to be larger than the largest component of w it will satisfy (3) as well; hence $\mathfrak{F}$ is not empty.

For fixed i, consider the set of all numbers of the form v_i for a v in $\mathfrak{F}$. Since each $v_i \geq w_i$, it follows that w_i is a lower bound for these numbers. Therefore they have a greatest lower bound g_i. In other words, g_i is a number that is a lower bound for this set, and such that if r is any other lower bound, then $r \leq g_i$. Carrying out this process for each i, we obtain a vector g.

From the definition of g, if v is in $\mathfrak{F}$, then

$$\sum_j P_{ij} g_j \leq \sum_j P_{ij} v_j \leq v_i,$$

where the last inequality follows since v is superregular. Thus the number $\Sigma\, P_{ij} g_j$ is a lower bound for all v_i for v in $\mathfrak{F}$. Therefore

$$\sum_j P_{ij} g_j \leq g_i,$$

so that g is a superregular vector that dominates w. Therefore g is in $\mathfrak{F}$. By its construction $g \leq v$ for any v in $\mathfrak{F}$. In other words g is the smallest superregular vector that dominates the payoff vector w.

Condition (4) follows from the fact that if $g_a > w_a$ we could replace g_a by w_a and obtain a smaller superregular vector that dominates w. To prove (5) assume that $g_i > w_i$ and also that $g_i > \Sigma\, P_{ij} g_j$. Then obviously we can reduce g_i slightly and these would still be true, and by increasing g_j for $j \neq i$ if necessary we can obtain a contradiction to the fact that g_i is the greatest lower bound of all elements of. This completes the proof.

Let T be the set of all transient states such that

(6) $$g_i = w_i.$$

We shall show that the optimal stopping rule is to stop the first time a state in $T \cup A$ is reached.

THEOREM. The vector g is regular for P^T with absorbing states $A \cup T$.

Proof. This follows easily from (4) and (5) since $g_a = w_a$ for a in $A \cup T$, and $g_i = \Sigma P_{ij} g_j$ for transient i in the chain P^T.

THEOREM. If U is the set and u the value vector associated with any other stopping rule, then $g \geq u$.

Proof. By (1) the expected value of the game depends upon the values w_a for a in $A \cup U$. Since $g_i \geq w_i$ for all states, we have

$$u_i = \Sigma_a \overline{B}^U_{ia} w_a \leq \Sigma_a \overline{B}^U_{ia} g_a \leq g_i,$$

where the sum is over a in $A \cup U$, and the last inequality comes from the fact that g is superregular for P^U since it is superregular for P. Hence $u \leq g$, completing the proof.

Notice that this theorem says that the optimal stopping rule defined by the set T such that (6) holds is the best that one can do *regardless of the starting state*. It is for this reason that we call it the optimal stopping rule. In Exercise 10 you will be asked to show that the superregular vector g is unique, and is completely determined by (4) and (5). This fact will be proved again in a more general setting later.

In Exercise 10 you will be asked to derive a linear programming method for calculating the vector g. This method is useful if the number of states is not too large.

Let us now show that we can use *dynamic programming* methods to solve the problem. First let us modify the problem by adding the additional restriction that we must stop sometime during the first N steps. That is, if we have not stopped by time N, then we must stop and accept reward w_i if we are in state i.

Define a sequence of vectors $g^1, g^2, \ldots, g^N$ by means of the following relations:

(7) $\qquad g^N = w,$

(8) $\qquad g^n = \max(w, Pg^{n+1}) \qquad$ for $n = N - 1, N - 2, \ldots, 2, 1.$

Clearly g^N_i is the value of the game to the player if he is in state i and has already taken N steps. Similarly, $g^{N-1}_i = \max(w_i, \Sigma P_{ij} g^N_j)$ represents the value to him if he is in state i and has already taken $N - 1$ steps and has the choice between w_i and making one more step with expected value $\Sigma P_{ij} g^N_j$. By continuing this analysis backward we can see that g^n_i is the value of the game after n steps have been made and the player is in state i, for $n = N - 1, N - 2, \ldots, 2, 1$.

The procedure of "going to the end and computing backwards" is typical of dynamic programming techniques. Notice that in order to do this we first had to stop the game at N, for if we let it go on, it has no end. However, we are going to let N become large and in this way approach the true game.

From (8) it is clear that the vectors g^n satisfy the conditions:

(9) $g_a^n = w_a$ for a an absorbing state,

(10) $g^n = \max(w, Pg^{n+1})$ for $n = N - 1, \ldots, 2, 1$.

If we now let N increase, it is clear from the interpretation of g^n that its components can only increase, since we can play for a longer time if it is advantageous to do so. Since the expected values are clearly bounded, g^n converges to a limiting vector $\bar{g}$. Since g^n satisfies (9) and (10) for every n, it follows that $\bar{g}$ will also; that is, $\bar{g}$ satisfies (4) and (5). But this means that $\bar{g} = g$, the unique smallest superregular vector that dominates w.

We can use the vectors g^n as approximate values for the vector g. For instance, if we approximate g by g^1, then the optimal strategy can be approximated by stopping the first time that $g_i^1 = w_i$. The approximations will improve as N is increased. It turns out in practice that one often finds the optimal stopping rule by this method for quite small values of N (see Exercise 2). It may, however, require large values of N in order that the components of g^1 be close to the true components of g. In any case it should be remembered that the approximations for a given N are optimal for the game when it is restricted to at most N plays.

Example. Consider the random walk on the integers $0, 1, 2, \ldots, N$ as shown in Figure 12. It turns out that we can solve this problem in a simple special

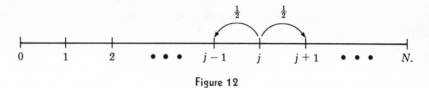

Figure 12

way by noting that a vector v is superregular if for a transient state i we have

(11) $v_i \geq \tfrac{1}{2}v_{i-1} + \tfrac{1}{2}v_{i+1}.$

We shall use this property to solve an example with $N = 6$ and w as given in Figure 13. What property (11) means is that if we plot the w_i values, which are shown as dark vertical lines in Figure 14, then the v_i (and hence g_i)

State i	w_i	g_i
0	2	2
1	1	3
2	4	4
3	3	$4\frac{1}{3}$
4	2	$4\frac{2}{3}$
5	5	5
6	4	4

Figure 13

values must lie on or above the dotted lines that connect the tallest of the w_i values. Using this property that g_i values, which lie *on* the dotted broken lines in Figure 14, are easily found to be as in the last column of Figure 14.

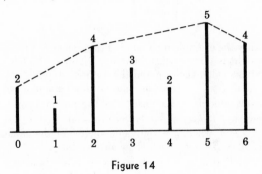

Figure 14

Given this vector g we find the set T to be $T = \{2, 5\}$. Therefore the optimal stopping rule is:

i. If you are in states $A \cup T = \{0, 2, 5, 6\}$, accept w_a and stop.
ii. If you start in state 3 or 4, continue until state 2 or 5 is reached; and if you start in state 1, continue until state 0 or 2 is reached (which, in fact, will be on the next step).

We can check that the components of g are correct as follows: if we start in state 3, we will reach state 2 before reaching state 5 with probability $\frac{2}{3}$; hence the value g_3 under the optimal stopping rule is $g_3 = \frac{2}{3} \cdot 4 + \frac{1}{3} \cdot 5 = 4\frac{1}{3}$.

We have here considered stopping rules that do not depend on time. In Section 6 we shall show the intuitively obvious fact that permitting stopping rules to depend upon time is of no advantage.

EXERCISES

Problems 1 through 4 refer to the random-walk example of the text.

1. Find the value vector g and the optimal stopping rule for the cases:

$$a. \ w = \begin{pmatrix} 2 \\ 3.5 \\ 4 \\ 3 \\ 3 \\ 5 \\ 6 \end{pmatrix} \cdot \quad b. \ w = \begin{pmatrix} 1 \\ 0 \\ 0 \\ 0 \\ 0 \\ 0 \\ 0 \end{pmatrix} \cdot \quad c. \ w = \begin{pmatrix} 1 \\ 0 \\ 0 \\ 0 \\ 0 \\ 0 \\ -3 \end{pmatrix} \cdot$$

2. Find the functions g_1, g_2, g_3, g_4, g_5 defined by (3) and (4) for $N = 5$. Use g_1 as an approximation for g and determine the optimal strategy by it.

$$[Ans. \ g_1 = \begin{pmatrix} 2 \\ 3 \\ 4 \\ 4.25 \\ 4.5 \\ 5 \\ 4 \end{pmatrix} . \ \text{Optimal stopping set determined by } g_1 \text{ is } T = \{0, 2, 5, 6\}.]$$

3. Modify the example by assuming that when in a transient state a step to the right is taken with probability $\frac{2}{3}$ and to the left with probability $\frac{1}{3}$. Find the value vector g and the optimal stopping set.
   [*Partial Ans.* Optimal stopping set is $T = \{0, 5, 6\}$.]
4. Do the same as in Exercise 2 for the modification given in Exercise 3.
5. Show that if h is a regular vector such that (a) $h_a = w_a$, (b) $h \geq w$, then $h = g$, where g is the value vector for the game. [*Hint:* Show that $g \geq \bar{B}g = \bar{B}h = h$. Then show also that $g \leq h$.]
6. Assume that $w_i = 0$ for all transient states. Is it true that

$$g = \max (0, \bar{B}w)?$$

7. Assume that w is a superregular vector. What can you say about g and the optimal stopping rule?
8. Assume that w has the property that $w_i < \sum P_{ij}w_j$ for every transient state. Show that the optimal stopping rule is to play until an absorbing state is reached.
9. Suppose vectors u and v are superregular for P. Let z be the vector with components $z_i = \min (u_i, v_i)$. Show that z is also superregular for P.
10. a. With v, w, and P defined as in the text and e the row vector with all component ones, show that the linear programming problem

$$\begin{aligned} \text{Minimize:} \quad & ev \\ \text{Subject to:} \quad & (I - P)v \geq 0, \\ & v \geq w, \end{aligned}$$

   has a solution.
   b. If v is superregular for P, show $g \leq v$. [*Hint:* Use Exercise 9.]

c. Use b. to show that the solution to the linear programming problem in a. is unique, and gives another way to solve (4) and (5).

4. SPECIAL CASES OF OPTIMAL STOPPING

We consider now a class of optimal stopping problems that have important applications as well as a special form that makes them easy to solve by computers. Further discussion may be found in the references by Dynkin-Yushkevich and Robbins—see "Suggested Reading," at the end of this chapter.

We shall consider Markov chains of the following kind: as states they have pairs (n, i), for $n = 0, 1, \ldots, N$ and index i belonging to some finite set S; the states of the form (N, i) are absorbing and the remaining states are transient; n can be interpreted as time and i as a position; from transient state (n, i) with $n < N$ it is possible to go only to a state of the form $(n + 1, j)$, and we write the transition probability as $P_{(n,i),(n+1,j)}$.

One easy way to obtain a Markov chain of this form is to use the procedure of the last section. That is, take any Markov chain with state space S and transition matrix P; form a new Markov chain with state space the pairs (n, i) for $0 \leq n \leq N$ and i an element of S; for transition probabilities define

$$P_{(N,i),(N,i)} = 1 \quad \text{and} \quad P_{(n,i),(n+1,j)} = P_{ij} \quad \text{for } n < N.$$

Recall that this corresponds to "stopping the chain at time N." In other words we are simply observing the Markov chain for N steps but giving more information when giving the state of the chain. In this way we can consider stopping problems in which the *reward* for stopping in state i depends upon the *time* at which the system is in i.

Example 1. Consider an experiment in which a subject is asked to demonstrate his extrasensory perception. He is given N experiments. On each experiment he is shown two cards face down. One card bears a circle and the other a square. The subject is asked to identify the card with the square.

Assume for the moment that the subject has no ESP ability and is just guessing. Let us set up a Markov chain by taking as a state the pair (n, i), where i gives the number of correct responses out of n trials. Assuming the subject is just guessing, we take as transition probabilities:

$$P_{(n,i),(n+1,i+1)} = \tfrac{1}{2} \quad \text{and} \quad P_{(n,i),(n+1,i)} = \tfrac{1}{2}.$$

Suppose we allow the subject to stop at any time during the N trials. If he stops at the nth trial having made i correct identifications, we shall say that his score, or reward, is i/n. We assume that the subject wants to stop in such a way as to maximize his expected score. In other words, we can interpret the problem as an optimal stopping problem with the payoff vector w given by $w_{n,i} = i/n$.

Before solving this example we shall describe the procedure in the general case. Recall that we must find the smallest superregular vector $g \geq w$ and stop the first time that $g_i = w_i$.

In the last section we showed that the vector g was determined by the two conditions (4) and (5) of that section. In the present case these conditions become:

(1) $\quad g_{(N,1)} = w_{(N,i)},$

(2) $\quad g_{(n,i)} = \max \left[w_{(n,i)}, \sum_j P_{(n,i),(n+1,j)} g_{(n+1,j)} \right]$

$$\text{for } n = 1, 2, \ldots, N - 1.$$

Thus, given $g_{(N,i)}$ from (1), we can substitute into (2) and find the values $g_{(N-1,i)}$, then use these to find $g_{(N-2,i)}$, and so on. Continuing backwards, we eventually find all the values for g.

Example 1 (continued). Consider the case of four trials, $N = 4$. The state space (n, i) and reward vector $w_{(n,i)} = i/n$ are shown in Figure 15.

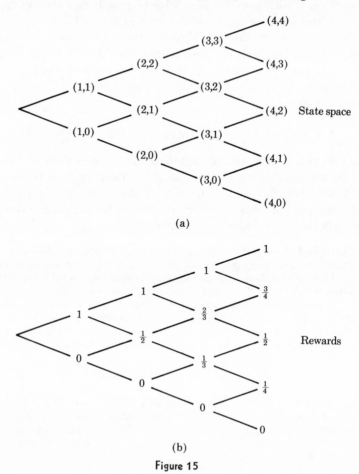

(a)

(b)

Figure 15

We know that $g_{(4,i)} = w_{(4,i)} = i/4$. Using (2), we obtain

$$g_{(3,3)} = \max\left(1, \tfrac{7}{8}\right) = 1,$$
$$g_{(3,2)} = \max\left(\tfrac{2}{3}, \tfrac{5}{8}\right) = \tfrac{2}{3},$$
$$g_{(3,1)} = \max\left(\tfrac{1}{3}, \tfrac{3}{8}\right) = \tfrac{3}{8},$$
$$g_{(3,0)} = \max\left(0, \tfrac{1}{8}\right) = \tfrac{1}{8}.$$

The rest of the g values are computed similarly, and the complete set is shown in Figure 16. From this figure we see that the value of optimal stopping

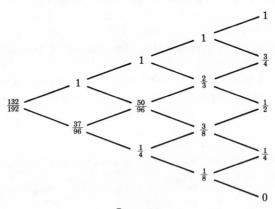

Figure 16

$\frac{132}{192} = .693$. The optimal stopping strategy is indicated in Figure 17, which shows the optimal stopping strategy (here a circle means continue playing and a square means stop).

Without optional stopping the subject could obtain only an expected score of $\tfrac{1}{2}$ by guessing. In our example with four trials optional stopping has

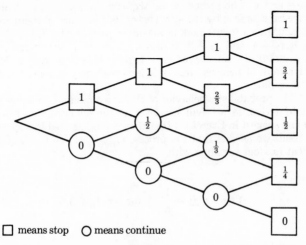

□ means stop   ○ means continue

Figure 17

improved this to .693. If we had allowed 100 trials, then the optional stopping strategy gives an expected score of .784. However, most of the advantage of optional stopping is obtained by being able to stop early in the sequence of trials. For instance, if in 100 trials the subject is permitted to stop only after the first 50 trials have been completed, the expected score is only .515.

Note that the optimal stopping strategy in Figure 17 can be described by saying, "Continue playing until for the first time the number of successes i is large enough that $i/n > \frac{1}{2}$, or until $n = N$."

The situation for the general problem is more complicated than this. The general rule for optional stopping can be stated as follows: for any N there is a sequence $a_1, a_2, \ldots, a_N$ such that the optimal strategy says, "Continue to play until the first time that the number of successes equals a_n or until $n = N$." The sequence $a_1, a_2, \ldots, a_N$ changes as N is increased. More generally, if we imagine being able to play indefinitely, then there is again an optimal stopping sequence $a_1, a_2, \ldots$, but the exact values of these numbers are not known.

Example 2. The next example is a famous problem that has been called the *secretary selection problem* or the *problem of the suitor*. We can state it as follows: A firm is interviewing N candidates for a secretarial job. The candidates arrive for interviews in a random order. There is an absolute ranking of the abilities of the candidates, but as they are interviewed it is possible to establish only a relative ranking of the persons already interviewed. It is assumed that if a candidate is not hired at the end of his interview, he cannot be hired at all; it is not possible to return and select him later. The problem is then to decide when to stop and accept the candidate just interviewed on the basis of all candidates previously interviewed.

Two processes play a central role in analyzing this problem. The first is the sequence $x_1, x_2, \ldots, x_n$ representing the absolute rank of the candidates as they arrive. The second is the sequence $y_1, y_2, \ldots, y_n$ representing the relative rank as seen by the interviewer. For instance, if there are four candidates and their absolute rank in the order they arrive is 3, 1, 4, 2, then $x_1 = 3$, $x_2 = 1$, $x_3 = 4$, and $x_4 = 2$. However, from the interviewer's point of view they are ranked relatively as $y_1 = 1$, $y_2 = 1$, $y_3 = 3$, $y_4 = 2$. Note that the relative rank of persons already interviewed may change, but the absolute rank does not.

The probabilistic behavior of these two random processes is rather difficult to derive, so we shall simply state the following two basic results we need and suggest in Exercise 4 that they can be verified in a special case. The first result we need is that the process $y_1, y_2, \ldots, y_N$ is a sequence of independent random variables with

$$(3) \qquad \Pr[y_n = j] = \frac{1}{n} \qquad \text{for } j = 1, 2, 3, \ldots, n.$$

The second result we need is

(4) $\Pr[x_n = k \mid y_1 = a_1 \wedge y_2 = a_2 \wedge \cdots \wedge y_n = j] = \Pr[x_n = k \mid y_n = j]$

$$= \frac{\binom{k-1}{j-1}\binom{N-k}{n-j}}{\binom{N}{n}}.$$

In other words, only the relative rank of the person just interviewed is important in predicting the absolute rank [equation (3)], and we can give a simple formula [equation (4)] for the probability of the absolute rank of the next candidate.

We now formulate the problem as a Markov chain. We let the states be the pairs (n, j), where j is the relative ranking of the nth candidate who is interviewed. Clearly $j \leq n$, and from state (n, j) we can move only to states $(n + 1, k)$ with $k \leq n + 1$. From (3) we have

(5) $\qquad P_{(n,j),(n+1,k)} = \dfrac{1}{n+1} \qquad$ for $k = 1, 2, \ldots, n + 1$.

We would like to make this an optimal stopping problem, but to do so we need a reward vector. We shall consider two interesting ways of assigning the rewards depending on the criteria of the person doing the interviewing.

For the first way, which we shall call problem 1, we choose the reward for stopping in state (n, j) to be the probability that we have chosen the best candidate. From (4) we determine the payoffs to be

$$w_{(n,j)} = 0 \qquad \text{if } j \neq 1,$$

(6)

$$w_{(n,1)} = \Pr[x_n = 1 \mid y_n = 1] = \frac{n}{N}.$$

For the second way, which we shall call problem 2, we have the objective of minimizing the expected rank of the candidate selected. We shall take the reward for stopping in (n, j) to be the expected rank of the candidate being interviewed. This may also be obtained from (4) and is

(7) $$w_{(n,j)} = j \cdot \frac{N+1}{n+1}.$$

In the solution of the second problem we shall be interested in minimizing the expected reward, since we want a small rank. This involves only minor changes in the solution procedure.

Let us consider now problem 1. We note first that if we just choose the first candidate, our expected reward is $1/N$. As N increases, this tends to zero. It might be guessed that the same thing would be true even with an optimal stopping rule. But the following strategy does better: Assume there are an even number $2N$ of candidates. Let the first N be interviewed without accepting any of them, and then accept the first candidate that is better than any of the first N, or accept the last candidate if none such appears. Clearly if the second best candidate is in the first N interviewed and the best is in the second N interviewed, we will obtain the best candidate. The probability that this happens is

$$\frac{N}{2N} \cdot \frac{N}{2N-1} > \frac{1}{4},$$

regardless of how large N is. Hence there is a strategy that does significantly better than 0. Thus we can achieve a probability of at least $\frac{1}{4}$ by the strategy of passing over the first half of the candidates and then choosing the first candidate better than the best seen so far, or else the last candidate. The optimal strategy has this same form, except that the number that we pass over is not just one-half the total number N. We will illustrate this presently.

For problem 2 the corresponding question to ask is whether as N increases the expected rank of the person chosen increases indefinitely under the optimal stopping rule. The answer to this question is no; in fact the expected rank tends to a finite limiting value. The latter fact has been proved, but there is no known simple form for the optimal strategy as there is in problem 1. We shall indicate a special case shortly.

Of course in practice we are interested in only a finite number N of candidates, and for reasonably small N the optimal strategy and value can easily be found for either problem by using equations (1) and (2). Using the transition matrix and reward vectors given in (5), (6), and (7), these equations become:

(8) $$g_{(N,i)} = w_{(N,i)},$$

(9) $$g_{(n,i)} = \max \left[w_{(n,i)}, \frac{1}{n+1} \sum_{j=1}^{n+1} g_{(n+1,j)} \right],$$

where w is defined by (6) for problem 1 and (7) for problem 2. Also in the solution of problem 2, since we are interested in minimizing the payoff, we replace max by min in using (9).

For $N = 5$ the payoff functions and optimal strategies for the two

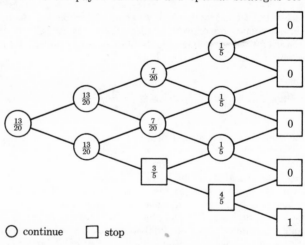

O continue   □ stop

Optimal stopping rule for problem 1 for $N = 5$

Figure 18

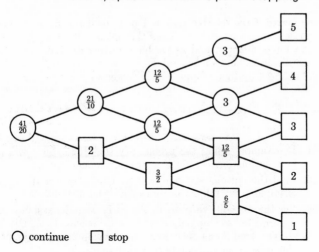

O continue □ stop

Optimal stopping rule for problem 2 for $N = 5$

Figure 19

problems are shown in Figures 18 and 19. As usual a square means to stop
and a circle means to continue.

In the solution for problem 1 we stop only at times when the relative
rank is 1. This is obvious, since if we have relative rank different from 1 for
a candidate being interviewed we know he is not the best, and our objective
is only to get the best. Note also that the optimal strategy can be described
as follows: pass over the first two candidates and then accept the first candidate that is better than all previous candidates or, if necessary, choose the
last candidate. It can be shown that the optimal strategy is always of this
form—that is, for any N there is a number r_n such that the optimal stopping
rule consists of passing over the first $r_n - 1$ candidates and then choosing
the first candidate that is better than all of those previously seen. Again, if
we do not find such a candidate we must choose the last one. The number r_n
can be characterized as follows: it is the smallest number k such that

$$\frac{1}{k} + \frac{1}{k+1} + \cdots + \frac{1}{N-1} \leq 1.$$

For instance, in the case $N = 5$ that we have considered,

$$\frac{1}{2} + \frac{1}{3} + \frac{1}{4} = \frac{13}{12} > 1,$$

$$\frac{1}{3} + \frac{1}{4} = \frac{7}{12} < 1,$$

so that $r_n = 3$, giving the rule that we obtained by direct calculation above.
The limiting value for the probability of selecting the best candidate as N
increases has been shown to have the value $1/e \doteq .368$.

In Figure 19 we see that in the solution for problem 2 we pass over the
first candidate, accept the second or third if they have relative rank 1 and

the fourth if the relative rank is 1 or 2; or if this does not happen we must choose the last candidate. Thus the optimal strategy is more complicated than for problem 1, and as we have mentioned there is no simple way to describe the strategy in general. However, it has been proved that the limiting value under optimal stopping as N increases is approximately 3.87.

EXERCISES

1. In Example 1 find the probability that the subject will get more than half the answers correct if he uses optional stopping. [*Ans.* $\frac{5}{8}$.]

2. Find the optimal stopping rule and the value of the game in the ESP example if the subject is allowed at least 5 trials.

3. For the case of five trials in the ESP example, assume that the subject is permitted to stop only after making at least two trials (that is, he can stop on trial 2 or later). Find the value and the optimal strategy under this restriction and compare with Exercise 2.

4. In the secretary problem of Example 2 consider the case of four applicants. Assume that they arrive in random order. Set up a tree and tree measure to describe the process x_1, x_2, x_3, and x_4. From this find $\Pr[y_3 = j]$ for $j = 1, 2, 3$. Also find $\Pr[x_3 = k \mid y_3 = 2]$ for $k = 1, 2, 3, 4$. Check your answers using (3) and (4).

5. Make a Monte Carlo simulation of 20 experiments of the ESP problem in Example 1 using the optimal stopping rule. Compare the observed average of the number of correct answers with the predicted number.

6. Repeat Exercise 5 for the secretary selection problem in Example 2 for each of the reward vectors.

5. CONDITIONED MARKOV CHAINS

In the conditional probability theory we studied in Chapter III we started with a probability measure on an outcome space, but then modified the measure on the basis of new information. In the present section we shall see how to do this for absorbing Markov chains, and in the next section we shall consider an application of the idea.

Consider an absorbing Markov chain that is started in a particular state 0. Then the theory previously developed leads us to predict that we will end in a given absorbing state a with probability $\overline{B}_{0a}$.

Suppose now that we obtain information that causes us to change these probabilities to a new set of probabilities p_a with $\sum_a p_a = 1$. How can we change the original Markov chain to take into account the new information? We shall permit some p_a's to be 0, just as we may have had $\overline{B}_{0a} = 0$ for certain a. However, if $\overline{B}_{0a} = 0$, we shall require $p_a = 0$. Let us define a vector h by the formula:

$$h_i = \sum_a \frac{\overline{B}_{ia} p_a}{\overline{B}_{0a}},$$

where the sum is taken over all absorbing states a with $p_a > 0$. We note that since h is a linear combination of regular vectors (recall that each column of B is regular), it is also regular. Also it is easy to show that $h_0 = 1$.

We now define a new Markov chain called the *conditional chain* as follows: if $h_i > 0$, then define

$$\overline{P}_{ij} = \frac{P_{ij}h_j}{h_i}.$$

We note that $\overline{P}_{0j}$ is defined, and that we can never go from a state with $h_i > 0$ to a state with $h_j = 0$. Hence we need not define $\overline{P}_{ij}$ for states with $h_i = 0$. Since $h \geq 0$, $\overline{P}_{ij} \geq 0$. Also if $h_i > 0$, since h is regular,

$$\sum_j \overline{P}_{ij} = \sum_j \frac{P_{ij}h_j}{h_i} = \frac{h_i}{h_i} = 1.$$

Assume now that $h_i > 0$ and a is an absorbing state. Then

$$\overline{P}_{ia}^{(n)} = \frac{P_{ia}^{(n)}h_a}{h_i} \to \frac{B_{ia}h_a}{h_i} = \frac{B_{ia}p_a}{h_i B_{0a}}.$$

From this we see

$$\sum_a \overline{P}_{ia}^{(n)} = \frac{1}{h_i}\sum \frac{B_{ia}p_a}{B_{0a}} = \frac{h_i}{h_i} = 1.$$

Thus if we restrict ourselves to the states where $h_j > 0$, we obtain a new absorbing Markov chain, and further

$$\overline{P}_{0a}^{(n)} = \frac{P_{0a}^{(n)}h_a}{h_0} \to B_{0a}h_a = p_a.$$

That is, the final prediction now agrees with the given probabilities p_a.

Example. We introduce an example that we will consider later in more detail. Assume that we take initially a very crude model for the behavior of a stock or bond in a series of five days. We assume that the price on each successive day will rise by one unit or fall by one unit with equal probability. The increase over the next five days could be predicted using the possibility tree in Figure 20.

We shall be interested in the price fluctuation during the five days, and so we shall form a Markov chain by taking as state the time n and increase j. We indicate such a state by a pair (n, j). We shall make the states $(5, 5)$, $(5, 3)$, $(5, 1)$, $(5, -1)$, $(5, -3)$, $(5, -5)$ absorbing states. For the other states the transition probabilities are given by

$$P_{(n,i),(n+1,i+1)} = \tfrac{1}{2}, \qquad P_{(n,i),(n+1,i-1)} = \tfrac{1}{2}.$$

Note that for the transient states we can be in a state at most once.

Assume now that our stock advisor predicts that after five days the stock will have dropped one point. Let us interpret this to mean that with

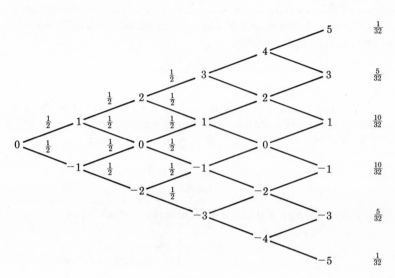

Day	1	2	3	4	5	W_j

Figure 20

probability one the chain will end in the state $(5, -1)$. Then for $\bar{a} = (5, -1)$, $p_{\bar{a}} = 1$ and all other $p_a = 0$. Then

$$h_{(n,i)} = \frac{\overline{B}_{(n,i),(5,-1)}}{\overline{B}_{(0,0),(5,-1)}},$$

and the appropriate values of B are easily calculated from tree measure. We note in defining the new transition matrix $\overline{P}$ that only the ratio of the h values matters. Hence we can use just as well

$$h_{(n,i)} = \overline{B}_{(n,i),(5,-1)}.$$

These values and appropriate new state space are shown in Figure 21.
From these values of h we obtain the new transition probabilities

$$\overline{P}_{(n,i),(n+1,i+1)} = \frac{1}{2} \frac{h(n+1, i+1)}{h(n, i)}$$

and

$$\overline{P}_{(n,i),(n+1,i-1)} = \frac{1}{2} \frac{h(n+1, i-1)}{h(n, i)}.$$

These values are indicated in Figure 22.
We shall consider the problem of optimal stopping—or, better, optimal selling—for this type of example. We assume that we must sell sometime during the next five days. We can see in the initial model without the pre-

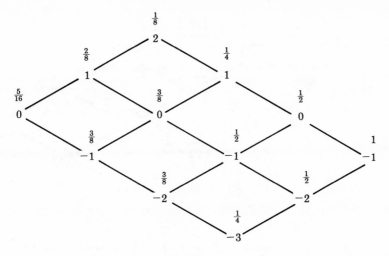

Figure 21

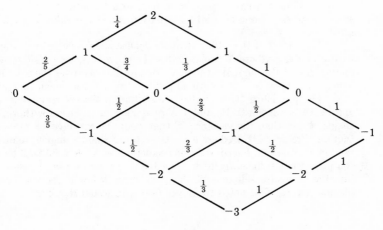

Figure 22

diction that the game is fair, and so we cannot do any better than the initial value 0 by optimal stopping.

Interestingly enough, even in the face of a negative prediction, if we accept the prediction we shall see that we can achieve an expectation greater than 0 by optimal stopping.

We can proceed as in our previous example using the equation

$$(1) \qquad g_{n,i} = \max \left(w_{n,i}, \; P_{n,i+1} g_{n+1,i+1} + P_{n,i-1} g_{n+1,i-1} \right).$$

We know in this example that $w_{n,i} = i$, and the probabilities $P_{n,i+1}$ and $P_{n,i-1}$ are given in Figure 22. We start with $n = 5$. We have only one value for $g_{5,i}$, which is $g_{5,-1} = -1$. We then compute using (1) the other values of $g_{n,i}$, taking $n = 4, 3, 2, 1, 0$ in that order. The results are shown in Figure 23. The points marked by circles are points where $g_{n,i} > w_{n,i}$. We can interpret

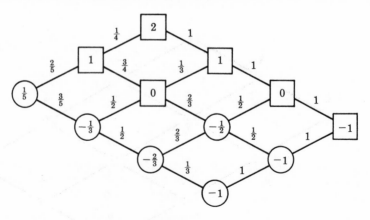

Figure 23

such a point as one at which we should wait. At points marked by squares, $g_{n,i} \leq w_{n,i}$; at these points we should sell. Thus in this example we sell if the price is high and not if it is low. The expected value is $\frac{1}{5}$ under the optimal strategy. Thus a negative prediction has turned a situation where optimal stopping gives a value of 0 into a situation where the value is greater than zero!

The nature of the selling strategy depends in a very critical way on the nature of the predictor's probabilities. To show this, we consider two predictors, A and B, who make the prediction for increase over the next 10 days. Their predictions and the optimal selling strategy are shown in Figure 24.

The predictors both predict a distribution that is symmetric about 0 and hence has mean 0. Predictor A predicts a distribution with variance 8 slightly lower than the variance 10 that would be expected by random fluctuation. Predictor B predicts a variance of 12 slightly higher than that of random fluctuation. Faced with the predictions of A, we would sell only when the price went sufficiently high. Faced with predictions of B, we would do just the opposite: sell only if the price went below a certain level. This phenomena was first noted by Boyce (see "Suggested Reading").

EXERCISES

1. Consider two four-day stock schemes with the following (relative) final h-values:

    a. $h_{(4,4)} = 4,$ b. $h_{(4,4)} = 12,$
       $h_{(4,2)} = 8,$ $h_{(4,2)} = 8,$
       $h_{(4,0)} = 12,$ $h_{(4,0)} = 4,$
       $h_{(4,-2)} = 8,$ $h_{(4,-2)} = 8,$
       $h_{(4,-4)} = 4.$ $h_{(4,-4)} = 12.$

    Find the optimal strategy and value for each, and describe the qualitative change observed.   [*Partial Ans.* Value is *a.* $\frac{7}{36}$ and *b.* $\frac{1}{4}$.]

2. A broker predicts that after $2k$ days a certain stock will be $+2k$ with probability $\frac{1}{2}$, and $-2k$ with probability $\frac{1}{2}$. What is the optimal selling strategy and its value, in face of this prediction?

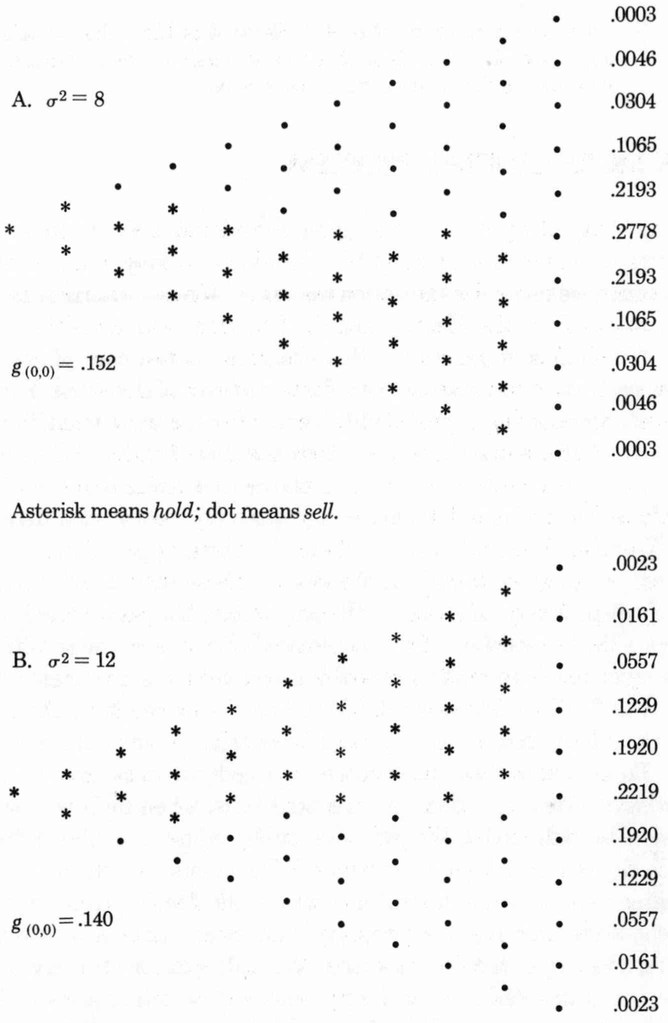

A. $\sigma^2 = 8$

$g_{(0,0)} = .152$

```
                                              •    .0003
                                         •
                               •    •    •    .0046
                          •    •    •    •    .0304
                     •    •    •    •    •    .1065
                •    •    •    •    •    •    .2193
    *    *    *    •    •    •    •    •    .2778
      *    *    *    *    *    *    *    .2193
        *    *    *    *    *    *    *    .1065
          *    *    *    *    *    •    .0304
            *    *    *    •         .0046
              *    •                   .0003
```

Asterisk means *hold*; dot means *sell*.

B. $\sigma^2 = 12$

$g_{(0,0)} = .140$

```
                                    *    •    .0023
                               *    *    •    .0161
                     *    *    *    *    •    .0557
                *    *    *    *    *    •    .1229
           *    *    *    *    *    *    •    .1920
      *    *    *    *    *    *    *    •    .2219
        *    *    •    •    •    •    •    .1920
          •    •    •    •    •    •    .1229
            •    •    •    •    •    •    .0557
              •    •    •    •         .0161
                •         •              .0023
```

Qualitative switch in optimal strategies from $\sigma^2 < n$ to $\sigma^2 > n$

Figure 24

3. Show that if we sell at $(i + 1, j + 1)$ and $(i + 1, j - 1)$, then we sell at (i, j).

4. Show that a sufficient condition for continuing at (i, j) is

$$h_{(i+1, j+1)} > h_{(i+1, j-1)}.$$

Show that this condition is not necessary for continuing.

*5. What four-day prediction distribution with mean 0 and variance 4 when played optimally assures maximum value?

*6. Suppose that after $2k$ days a stock will have the same price as today with probability 1. Suppose also that we adopt a strategy of selling as soon as our stock reaches $+1$. Show that the value of this strategy is $v_{(0,0)} = k/(k + 1)$. Show that this strategy is not in general optimal by computing the optimal value for $k = 8$.

6. A MORE GENERAL PROBLEM

In our study of optimal stopping we considered a situation where at any one time a player had at most two decisions, to stop and accept a reward or to continue using the transition matrix P. We can interpret this as choosing a row of P or the identity matrix I for the next transition.

We shall now generalize this situation to the case where the player has in each state to make one of a finite number of decisions. Each decision amounts to choosing a probability vector for the next transition.

We shall assume there are a finite number of states. When in any state i the player is confronted with the choice of a finite number of decisions. Each possible decision determines a probability vector that determines the next position. We shall assume there are three types of states: *absorbing*, *optimal stopping*, or *transient*. We denote these subsets of states by A, S, and T, respectively. If a is in A the only choice the player has is to stop and accept a final reward w_a. If s is an element of S, one of the possible decisions the player has is to make s absorbing and obtain a final reward w_s. For a state i in T all decisions available to the player result in the game's continuing at least one more play, and he obtains no immediate reward.

To determine how the process proceeds we must give a strategy for the player—that is, a decision rule that tells, when he is in a state, which decision he will make. We will eventually allow the player to make his choice depend on all past outcomes if he wishes. At the moment we will consider a special class of strategies where the decision depends only on the present state and has the property that every time a particular state i occurs, the same decision is made. We call such a strategy a *stationary strategy* and denoted it by π. Every such π determines a transition matrix P, where the ith row of P is the probability vector p associated with the decision made by π when in state i.

We make the basic assumption that every P determined by a stationary strategy is the matrix of an absorbing Markov chain. Thus for any stationary strategy π we have an absorbing chain P with an associated matrix $\bar{B}$. The expected value of the game using π starting in i is given by

$$x_i = \sum_a B_{ia} w_a,$$

where the sum is extended over all a that π makes absorbing.

Example. A player has r dollars. He has a desperate need for N dollars. He has a chance to make a sequence of bets. He wins s with probability .4 and loses s with probability .6. When he has x dollars he can bet any number $t \leq x$

dollars. We assume that he only wants to get N dollars and hence never bets more than necessary to reach this goal. Assume, for example, that $N = 6$. Then there are seven states for the system. The states 0 and 6 are absorbing.

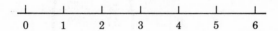

We shall assign $w_0 = 0$, $w_6 = 1$, indicating that the player only wants to get to 6. Also we shall assume that all other states 1, 2, 3, 4, 5 are transient. When in state 1 the player has only one possible decision, namely to bet 1. If in state 2 he has two possible decisions, bet 1 or bet 2. Similarly in state 3 he has three possible decisions. In 4 he has only two, and so on.

We can identify two interesting stationary strategies for this game. One, we shall call *timid play*. In this case the player bets as little as possible, namely \$1 each time. The transition matrix associated with timid play is:

Timid Play

$$D = \begin{array}{c} \\ 0 \\ 1 \\ 2 \\ 3 \\ 4 \\ 5 \\ 6 \end{array} \begin{array}{cccccccc} 0 & 1 & 2 & 3 & 4 & 5 & 6 \\ \left(\begin{array}{ccccccc} 1 & 0 & 0 & 0 & 0 & 0 & 0 \\ .6 & 0 & .4 & 0 & 0 & 0 & 0 \\ 0 & .6 & 0 & .4 & 0 & 0 & 0 \\ 0 & 0 & .6 & 0 & .4 & 0 & 0 \\ 0 & 0 & 0 & .6 & 0 & .4 & 0 \\ 0 & 0 & 0 & 0 & .6 & 0 & .4 \\ 0 & 0 & 0 & 0 & 0 & 0 & 1 \end{array}\right) \end{array}.$$

The other strategy we call *bold play*. In this case the player bets as much as possible. In this case the transition matrix would be:

Bold Play

$$P = \begin{array}{c} \\ 0 \\ 1 \\ 2 \\ 3 \\ 4 \\ 5 \\ 6 \end{array} \begin{array}{cccccccc} 0 & 1 & 2 & 3 & 4 & 5 & 6 \\ \left(\begin{array}{ccccccc} 1 & 0 & 0 & 0 & 0 & 0 & 0 \\ .6 & 0 & .4 & 0 & 0 & 0 & 0 \\ .6 & 0 & 0 & 0 & .4 & 0 & 0 \\ .6 & 0 & 0 & 0 & 0 & 0 & .4 \\ 0 & 0 & .6 & 0 & 0 & 0 & .4 \\ 0 & 0 & 0 & 0 & .6 & 0 & .4 \\ 0 & 0 & 0 & 0 & 0 & 0 & 1 \end{array}\right) \end{array}.$$

We can compare the values of these two strategies by finding in each case the absorption probabilities. A strategy is better for a transient state i if it has a higher probability of ending in state 6 if it starts in i. Finding matrix B by the standard techniques, we find for the two cases:

$$Timid\ Play$$

$$
B = \begin{array}{c} 1 \\ 2 \\ 3 \\ 4 \\ 5 \end{array}
\begin{array}{cc} 0 & 6 \\ \left(\begin{array}{cc} .952 & .048 \\ .880 & .120 \\ .771 & .229 \\ .609 & .391 \\ .365 & .635 \end{array}\right) \end{array} .
$$

$$Bold\ Play$$

$$
B = \begin{array}{c} 1 \\ 2 \\ 3 \\ 4 \\ 5 \end{array}
\begin{array}{cc} 0 & 6 \\ \left(\begin{array}{cc} .916 & .084 \\ .789 & .211 \\ .6 & .4 \\ .474 & .526 \\ .284 & .716 \end{array}\right) \end{array} .
$$

We see from this that the bold strategy is better against the timid strategy for every starting state. To prove that bold strategy is optimal we would have to compare it with every other strategy, stationary and time dependent. Our goal is to prove that there is indeed always a stationary strategy that is as good as any other strategy no matter what the starting state is.

We proceed in a way very similar to the special case we have already considered of optimal stopping.

A vector v is said to be superregular if

$$v \geq \max_{\pi} Pv.$$

Here the maximum is taken over all stationary strategies π with associated transition matrices P. Let $\mathcal{F}$ be the class of all superregular vectors such that $v_i \geq w_i$ for i in $S \cup A$. For each state i let g_i be the greatest lower bound for all v_i, with $v \in \mathcal{F}$. Consider any state i and let

$$(1) \qquad \bar{g}_i{}' = \max_{\pi} (Pg)_i.$$

For any v in $\mathcal{F}$ and any π

$$(Pg)_i \leq (Pv)_i \leq v_i.$$

Hence $\bar{g}_i \leq v_i$. Thus $\bar{g}_i$ is a lower bound for v_i, v in $\mathcal{F}$. Hence $\bar{g}_i \leq g_i$. If $g_i > \bar{g}_i$ we could replace the value of g at i by $\bar{g}_i$ and obtain a superregular vector. For i in $S \cup A$, one choice of π in (1) makes $(Pg)_i = \bar{g}_i \geq w_i$. Thus $\bar{g}_i \geq w_i$. But this means $\bar{g}$ is in $\mathcal{F}$ and hence $\bar{g}_i \geq g_i$. Thus we cannot have $\bar{g}_i < g_i$. Thus $g_i = \max_{\pi} (Pg)_i$. Thus g has the following two properties:

$$(2a) \qquad g_a = w_a \text{ for } a \text{ absorbing,}$$

$$(2b) \qquad g = \max_{\pi} Pg.$$

We now choose a stationary strategy π^* as follows. For each state i choose a vector so that using this vector for the ith row of P

(3) $$g_i = \max_\pi \, (Pg)_i.$$

Note that the decision involved in π^* for states other than i plays no role in $(Pg)_i$. Hence we can do this for every state i separately. We make the choice in such a way that we stop at state i if that is the only decision that will achieve (3) for this state. Let P^* be the transition matrix associated with π^* and B^* the absorption probability. By our choice of π^* g is regular for P^*, and hence

(4) $$g_i = \sum_a \overline{B}^*_{ia} g_a.$$

For a in A, $g_a = w_a$. We wish now to show that if π^* makes s absorbing $g_s = w_s$.

Let

(4) $$h_s = \max_{\pi'} \, (Pg)_s,$$

where the maximum is taken over all stationary strategies π' that do not result in making s absorbing. Then by the construction of π^*

$$h_s < g_s.$$

Define h for all states by making $h_i = g_i$ for $i \neq s$. From (4) and the fact that we have only decreased g to obtain h,

$$h_s > \max_{\pi'} \, (Ph)_s.$$

For strategies that make s absorbing, $(Ph)_s = h_s$. Hence

$$h_s > \max_\pi \, (Ph)_s.$$

Thus h is superregular at s. Also, since h was obtained by only lowering the value of g at s and g was superregular, we see that h is superregular. Since $h_s < g_s$, it cannot be in $\mathfrak{F}$. Hence $h_s < w_s$. Let $c = w_s - h_s$. Then $\overline{h} = h + c$ is in $\mathfrak{F}$. Hence $\overline{h} \geq g$. But

$$\overline{h}_s = w_s \geq g_s.$$

Since we already have $g_s \geq w_s$, we see that $g_s = w_s$, as was to be proved. Thus, using π^*, we have

$$g_i = \sum_a B^*_{ia} w_a,$$

where the sum is taken over all a made absorbing by π^*.

Assume now that we adopt any other decision procedure π, which may depend upon time and past outcomes. We assume only that under π the process will be absorbed with probability 1. Let $\bar{B}_{ia}$ be the probability starting in i that the process ends in a. Let $X_0, X_1, X_2, \ldots$ be the position of the process using π and starting in state i. Assume that

$$X_0 = i \wedge X_1 = j \wedge \cdots \wedge X_{n-2} = l \wedge X_{n-1} = m,$$

and π tells us to make a decision that results in transition vector $\bar{p}$ for the next step. Then

$$E[g(X_n) \mid X_{n-1} = m \wedge X_{n-2} = l \wedge \cdots \wedge X_0 = i] = (\bar{p}g)_m \leq g_m = g(X_{n-1}).$$

Thus $g(X_0), g(X_1), \ldots$ represents an unfavorable game and it can be shown that it will remain unfavorable, that is,

$$g_i \geq \sum_a \bar{B}_{ia}g_a \geq \sum \bar{B}_{ia}w_a.$$

Thus for any starting state i the value using π is $\leq g_i$. We have seen, however, that we can realize g_i for every state by a stationary strategy π^*. Hence there is no reason to consider more general strategies. Also, any other stationary strategies cannot improve on π^* for any state. That is, π^* is uniformly as good as we can do.

As in the case of optional stopping the vector g, which we determined as the smallest superregular vector that dominates w on $S \cup A$, can also be described as the unique vector g that satisfies (2a) and (2b). That is,

$$g_a = w_a \quad \text{for } a \text{ absorbing,}$$

$$g = \max_\pi g.$$

To see this we make the following observation. First we used only properties (2a) and (2b) in proving that π^* was optimal. In particular this says that for any g satisfying these properties g_i is the best that we can do among the finite number of time-independent strategies available. But this description shows that g_i is determined by (2a) and (2b).

Again as in the case of optional stopping we can use this fact to obtain approximate solutions for g and for the optimal strategy. We proceed as in the optional-stopping case. We assume that we can play at most N times. If i is in $A \cup S$, we put $g_i^n = w_i$. If not, we arbitrarily assign a value less than the minimum of w_i, since we know that we can at least achieve this much. Then we define g^n backwards by

$$g^{(n)} = \max g^{(n+1)}, \qquad n = 1, 2, 3, \ldots, N - 1.$$

The vector $g^{(1)}$ is an approximation for g, and the choice of π used in the last step is an approximation for the optimal strategy π^*. As $N \to \infty$, $g^{(n)} \to g$, the value of the unlimited game.

It is important to realize that while the vector g is uniquely determined, the choice of the optimal strategy is not. In fact we already know, for example, in optional stopping—which is a special case—that this is not the case. For another example see Exercise 3.

Let us take $N = 5$. We choose $g_0^{(5)} = 0$ and $g_6^{(5)} = 1$, since they are absorbing states. The other values we take to be 0, since we know that we can obtain at least this much. A standard computing routine then gave the following values for the remaining vectors:

State	$g^{(5)}$	$g^{(4)}$	$g^{(3)}$	$g^{(2)}$	$g^{(1)}$
0	0	0	0	0	0
1	0	0	0	.064	.064
2	0	0	.16	.16	.198
3	0	.4	.4	.4	.4
4	0	.4	.4	.496	.496
5	0	.4	.64	.64	.698
6	1	1	1	1	1

It happened that the program chose at every stage the bold strategy. We see that the values of $g^{(1)}$ are approximations to the values for the bold strategy given earlier, but it would take more iterations to get good approximations. It is typical of these problems that one often gets the optimal strategy very soon, even when the approximations are slow.

Further details and examples may be found in the second and fourth items in the "Suggested Reading," page 463.

EXERCISES

1. For the game discussed show that the bold value vector

$$B_{.,6} \geq \max_{\pi} PB_{.,6}$$

—that is,

$$B_{i,6} \geq .4B_{i+s,6} + .6B_{i-s,6}$$

for all $0 \leq i - s < i < i + s \leq 6$. Why does this imply that B is optimal in this example?

2. Consider the bold strategy for $N = 8$, $p = .4$.

   a. At most how many plays does the game last?

   b. Use the relations

   $$B_{i,8} = \begin{cases} .4B_{2i,8}, & i \leq 4, \\ .4 + .6B_{2i-8,8} & i \geq 4, \end{cases}$$

   to calculate B.

3. Consider the strategy for $N = 8$, $p = .4$, where from $i < 4$ we bet min $(i, 4 - i)$, and from $i \geq 4$ we bet according to the bold strategy. How does this compare with the optimal strategy? Are there other optimal strategies for $N = 8$? How many? [*Ans.* Same as optimal strategies. There are four distinct optimal strategies.]

7. AN INVENTORY EXAMPLE

We consider a more complex example of a Markov decision problem, suggested by a store's attempting to decide the most profitable size of stock to choose for a certain product it sells. We assume that the store orders from a central warehouse once a week. To place an order costs a *fixed charge* of a dollars and then a *variable charge* of c dollars per unit ordered. Thus to order j units costs $a + jc$ dollars.

The store receives orders from its customers during the week and delivers the orders at the end of the week at a price of p dollars per unit. We assume that the store can stock at most M units, and if it receives an order after already filling M orders the sale is lost. There is a storage cost of d dollars per unit per week. Finally we assume that during the week the store receives j orders with probability $p_j, j = 0, 1, \ldots$.

We want to consider the optimal ordering policy for the store by considering a period of N weeks. We do this by taking as states of the system the pairs (n, j), where n is the week and j the stock at the beginning of the week before we place the order to the warehouse. If we are in state (n, j), it is possible to make one of $M - j$ decisions corresponding to increasing the stock level from j to any number up to M. If we increase the stock to k, the transition probability for the next step is given by

$$P^{(k)}_{(n,j),(n+1,l)} = p_{k-l}$$

for $l = 1, 2, \ldots, k - 1$ and

$$P^{(k)}_{(n,j),(n+1,0)} = p_k + p_{k+1} + \cdots .$$

The expected profit during the week if the stock is brought up to k is

$$r^{(k)}_{(n,j)} = pE - c(k - j) - a - kd,$$

where

$$E = \sum_{j=0}^{k-1} jp_j + k \sum_{j \geq k} p_j$$

is the expected number of items sold. Thus if $g_{(n,j)} =$ the value of being in state (n, j) under optimal play it satisfies the basic functional equation:

(1) $$g_{(n,j)} = \max_k (g^{(k)}_{(n,j)}),$$

where

$$g^{(k)}_{(n,j)} = r^{(k)}_{(n,j)} + \sum_{l=0}^{k} P^{(k)}_{(n,j),(n+1,l)} g_{(n+1,l)}.$$

To determine the solution we have to make some convention about the value of g at time N. We shall assume that $g_{(N,j)} = c \cdot j$—that is, simply the cost of the items on hand at this time. The states (N, j) are then absorbing, and we assume that these are also the only stopping states.

We can then solve for v by the familiar backwards-iteration (dynamic programming), method. We illustrate with a specific example where

$c = 6$ (cost per unit good),
$a = 1$ (cost to order),
$d = 2$ (storage cost per unit),
$p = 10$ (price to the customer),
$M = 6$ (maximum storage capacity),

and the probabilities p_j for j orders from customers given by

j	0	1	2	3	4	5	6
p_j	$\frac{1}{16}$	$\frac{2}{16}$	$\frac{3}{16}$	$\frac{4}{16}$	$\frac{3}{16}$	$\frac{2}{16}$	$\frac{1}{16}$

We illustrate the appropriate calculations for the case $N = 5$ working back to values $g_{(4,j)}$. By assumption $g_{(5,j)} = 6 \cdot j$. Thus $g_{(5,j)}$ is given by the vector

$$\begin{vmatrix} 36 \\ 30 \\ 24 \\ 18 \\ 12 \\ 6 \\ 0 \end{vmatrix}.$$

Let us find the value of $g_{(4,0)}$. We must consider the effect of raising the stock level to all possible values between 0 and 6. If our stock is 0 and we leave it at 0, nothing will change, so $g_{(4,0)}^{(0)} = 0$. Consider next $g_{(4,0)}^{(1)}$. We start the week with a stock of 1. The expected number sold is $\frac{1}{16} \cdot 0 + \frac{15}{16} \cdot 1 = \frac{15}{16}$. The order cost $1, and we have a $2 storage charge. If we sell one, we move to state $(5, 0)$ with value 0. If we do not sell any, we move to state $(5, 1)$ with value 6. Hence

$$g_{(4,0)}^{(1)} = 10 \cdot \tfrac{15}{16} - 6 - 1 - 2 + \tfrac{1}{16} \cdot 6 = .75.$$

If we increase the stock to 2, the expected number sold will be

$$0 \cdot \tfrac{1}{16} + 1 \cdot \tfrac{2}{16} + 2 \cdot \tfrac{13}{16} = \tfrac{28}{16}.$$

The process moves to the states $(5, 0)$, $(5, 1)$, $(5, 2)$ with probabilities $\frac{13}{16}$, $\frac{2}{16}$, $\frac{1}{16}$, respectively. Hence

$$g_{(4,0)}^{(2)} = 10 \cdot \tfrac{28}{16} - 12 - 1 - 4 + \tfrac{13}{16} \cdot 0 + \tfrac{2}{16} \cdot 6 + \tfrac{1}{16} \cdot 12 = 2.$$

Similar calculations yield $g_{(4,0)}^{(3)} = 2.5$, $g_{(4,0)}^{(4)} = 2$, $g_{(4,0)}^{(5)} = .75$ and $g_{(4,0)}^{(6)} = -1$. We see from these values that if we should increase the stock level to 3, $g_{(4,0)} = 2.5$. Similar calculations show that if we had a stock of 1 we should also raise the stock level to 3. At 2 or higher we are best off by not increasing the stock level at all. We obtain values for $g_{(4,1)}, g_{(4,2)}, \ldots, g_{(4,6)}$. From these we can then obtain optimal policies and values for $g_{(3,j)}$ by (1).

Carrying out the computations back five periods gives the optimal rule for the case of five periods:

Present Stock	Under Optimal Rule; Order to				
	(1)	(2)	(3)	(4)	(5)
0	3	3	3	3	0
1	3	3	3	3	1
2	2	2	2	2	2
3	3	3	3	3	3
4	4	4	4	4	4
5	5	5	5	5	5
6	6	6	6	6	6

Parenthesized numbers indicate period number

The resulting values under optimal ordering for these five periods are given by the next table.

Present Stock	Value Under Optimal Rule in Period					
	1	2	3	4	5	6
0	13	10.4	7.7	5.1	2.5	0
1	19	16.4	13.7	11.1	8.5	6
2	25.4	22.4	20.2	17.5	15	12
3	32	29.4	26.7	24.1	21.5	18
4	37.6	35	32.4	29.8	27	24
5	42.4	40	37.2	34.6	32	30
6	46.6	44	41.3	39	36	36

We note that the optimal rule for all periods is to order up to 3, and if we have 2 or more, not order any more. This is an example of what is called an (s, S) policy; that is, if the stock is $\leq s$, order up to S, and otherwise do not increase the stock. If we consider the final value at 6 as the return on an initial investment, we see that we make about \$12 or \$13 over the five periods for any initial stock of 5 or less—that is, an average of about \$2.5 per period.

The ease of computing an example of this type enables us to see quickly the effect on the optimal ordering policy and value when certain parameters are changed. We shall illustrate this by changing some of the basic quantities. We shall in each case give the optimal policy and value at the beginning of a five-week period only. For example, if the customer distribution is changed to

j	0	1	2	3	4	5	6
p_j	$\frac{4}{19}$	$\frac{3}{19}$	$\frac{2}{19}$	$\frac{1}{19}$	$\frac{2}{19}$	$\frac{3}{19}$	$\frac{4}{19}$

the optimal ordering policy and value under this policy are:

Initial Stock	Optimal Policy: Order to	Value
0	3	14.9
1	3	20.9
2	2	27
3	3	33.9
4	4	39.5
5	5	44.4
6	6	48.5

Thus changing the nature of the probability distribution while keeping the same mean does not affect the optimal policy and has little effect on the value.

Consider next the effect of a decrease in the price to the customer of from \$10 to \$9 per unit. The optimal policy and value are now:

Initial Stock	Optimal Policy: Order to	Value
0	3	1.84
1	1	8.29
2	2	14.8
3	3	20.8
4	4	26.1
5	5	30.7
6	6	34.7

In this case it pays to order new stock only when the level is down to 0, and then we again order up to 3. Also we can expect to make a profit only with an initial order of 1 to 5—and even here the profit has, of course, significantly decreased.

Consider finally a decrease in the storage charge from \$2 to \$1 per unit. Then the optimal policy is:

Initial Stock	Optimal Policy: Order to	Value
0	4	30.5
1	4	36.5
2	4	42.5
3	3	48.9
4	4	55.5
5	5	61.4
6	6	66.8

As could be expected, we order a larger number when we order, and of course the profit has increased significantly because of the decrease in storage charges.

EXERCISES

1. In the example what is the value under the optimum policy starting with a stock of two if we look ahead only two periods?   [*Ans.* 17.5.]
2. Assume the example is changed so that $M = 2$. Then answer the same question as in Exercise 1.
3. Why is the answer to Exercise 2 different from that of Exercise 1?
4. How much should the retailer be willing to pay to expand the size of the warehouse from 2 to 6?

SUGGESTED READING

W. M. Boyce, "Stopping Rules for Selling Bonds," *Bell Journal of Economics and Management Science*, 1 (1970), pp. 27–53.

L. E. Dubbins and L. J. Savage, *How to Gamble If You Must*, McGraw-Hill, N. Y., 1965.

Dynkin, E. B., and A. A. Yushkevich, *Markov Process Theorems and Problems*, Plenum Press, N. J., 1969.

R. A. Howard, *Dynamic Programming and Markov Processes*, Wiley, N. Y., 1960.

H. Robbins, "Optimal Stopping," *American Mathematical Monthly*, 77 (1970), pp. 333–343.

9

THE THEORY OF GAMES

1. STRICTLY DETERMINED GAMES

In Chapter 5 we discussed linear programming problems that involve *optimization*—that is, the maximization or minimization of a (linear) function subject to linear constraints. In order to optimize a function it is necessary to control all relevant variables.

Game theory considers situations in which there are two (or more) persons, each of whom controls some but not all the variables necessary to determine the outcome(s) of a certain event. Depending upon which event actually occurs, the players receive various payments. If for each possible event the algebraic sum of payments to all players is zero, the game is called *zero-sum;* otherwise it is *nonzero-sum.* Usually the players will not agree as to which event should occur, so that their objectives in the game are different. In the case of a matrix game, which is a two-person zero-sum game in which one player loses what the other wins, game theory provides a solution. The solution is based on the principle that each player tries to choose his course of action so that, regardless of what his opponent does, he can assure himself of a certain minimum amount. Matrix games are discussed in Sections 1 through 4. For many-person nonzero-sum games, several solution concepts have been proposed, of which we discuss only a few in Section 5.

Most recreational games such as ticktacktoe, checkers, backgammon, chess, poker, bridge, and other card or board games can be viewed as games of strategy. On the other hand, such gambling games as dice, roulette, and so on are not (as usually formulated) games of strategy, since a person playing one of these games is merely "betting against the odds."

In this chapter we shall formulate simple games that illustrate the theory and are amenable to computation. We shall base these games on applications in business situations and on recreational games.

Example 1. Two stores, R and C, are planning to locate in one of two towns. As in Figure 1, town 1 has 60 percent of the population while town 2 has 40

Town 1   Town 2

Figure 1

percent. If both stores locate in the same town they will split all the business equally, but if they locate in different towns each will get the business of that town. Where should each store locate?

Clearly this is a game situation, since each store can control where it locates but cannot control at all where its competitor locates. Each store has two possible "strategies": "locate in town 1" and "locate in town 2." Let us list all possible outcomes for each store employing each of its strategies. The result is given in the *payoff matrix* of Figure 2. The entries of the matrix

Store C locates in

		1	2
Store R locates in	1	50	60
	2	40	50

Figure 2

represent the percentages of business that store R gets in each case. They can also be interpreted as the percentage losses of business by C for each case. If both stores locate in town 1 or both in town 2, each gets 50 percent of the business, hence the entries on the main diagonal are 50. If store R locates in town 1 and C in 2, then R gets 60 percent of the business as indicated in entry in row 1 and column 2. (This entry also indicates that C *loses* 60 percent.) Similarly, if R locates in 2 and C in 1, then R gets 40 percent (and C loses 40 percent) as indicated in row 2 and column 1.

How should the players play the matrix game in Figure 2? It is easy to see that store R should prefer to locate in town 1 because, regardless of what C does, R can assure himself of 10 percent more business in town 1 than in town 2. Similarly, store C also prefers to locate in town 1 because he will lose 10 percent less business—that is, gain 10 percent more business—in town 1 than in 2. Hence optimal strategies are for each store to locate in town 1; that is, R chooses row 1 and C chooses column 1 in Figure 2. The value of the game is 50, representing the percentage of the business that R gets.

In Example 1 we started with an applied situation and derived from it a matrix game. Actually, we can interpret any matrix as a game, as the following definition shows.

DEFINITION. Let G be an $m \times n$ matrix with entries g_{ij} for $i = 1,$ $\ldots, m$ and $j = 1, \ldots, n$. Then G can be interpreted as the *payoff matrix* of the following matrix game: Player R (the *row* player) chooses any row i, and simultaneously player C (the *column* player) chooses any column j; the outcome of the game is that C pays to R an amount equal to g_{ij}. (If $g_{ij} < 0$, then this should be interpreted as R paying C an amount equal to $-g_{ij}$.)

Example 2. Consider the matrix in Figure 3 as a game. Thus, if R chooses row 1 and C chooses column 1, then C pays 5 units to R; if R chooses row 1

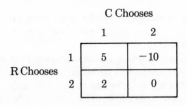

Figure 3

and C chooses column 2, then R pays 10 units to C; and so on. How should the players play this game?

Player R would like to get the 5 payoff in the $(1, 1)$ position, but he knows that if he chooses row 1 he runs the risk that C will choose column 2 and he will lose 10 units. If R chooses row 2, he will either get 2 or break even; hence row 2 is clearly a better choice than row 1 for him. Similarly, if C chooses column 1, then he is certain to have to pay 2 units, and perhaps even 5 units, while if he chooses column 2 he will either break even or gain 10 units. Hence column 2 is best for C. Here optimal strategies are "choose row 2" for R and "choose column 2" for C. The value of the game is the resulting payoff—namely 0.

The 0 entry in the $(2, 2)$ position in the matrix of Figure 3 is said to be a saddle value of the matrix, because it is both the minimum entry of the second row and the maximum entry in the second column.

DEFINITION. Consider a matrix game with payoff matrix G. Entry g_{ij} is said to be a *saddle value* of G if g_{ij} is simultaneously the *minimum* of the ith row and the *maximum* of the jth column. If matrix game G has a saddle value, it is said to be *strictly determined*, and *optimal strategies* for it are:

For player R: "Choose a row that contains a saddle value."
For player C: "Choose a column that contains a saddle value."

The *value* of the game is $v = g_{ij}$, where g_{ij} is any saddle-value entry. The game is *fair* if its value is zero.

In order to justify this definition it must be shown that if there are two or more saddle values then they are all equal. A proof of this fact is outlined in Exercise 10. The next example illustrates it.

Example 3. Let us consider an extension of Example 1 in which the stores R and C are trying to locate in one of the three towns in Figure 4. We shall

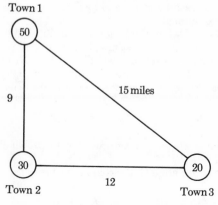

Town 1

50

15 miles

9

30   20

Town 2   Town 3

12

Figure 4

assume that if both stores locate in the same town they split all business equally, but if they locate in different towns then all the business in the town that doesn't have a store will go to the *closer* of the two stores. The percentages of people in each town are marked in the circles. The distances between the towns are marked on the lines connecting them.

The payoff matrix for the resulting game is shown in Figure 5. In

Store C locates in

		1	2	3
Store R locates in	1	50	50	80
	2	50	50	80
	3	20	20	50

Figure 5

Exercise 13 the reader is asked to check that these entries are correct.

Each of the four 50 entries in the 2 × 2 matrix in the upper lefthand corner of Figure 5 is a saddle value of the matrix, since each is simultaneously the minimum of its row and maximum of its column. Hence the game is strictly determined, and optimal strategies are:

For store R: "Locate in either town 1 or town 2."
For store C: "Locate in either town 1 or town 2."

In a real-life location problem one might want to take into account not only present population of cities, but also rate of population growth. In Exercise 14 the reader is asked to criticize these strategies from this point of view.

Instead of the somewhat indefinite description of the optimal strategy for player R as "Locate in either town 1 or 2," we can employ the following device: since we don't care which town we locate in, we can just flip a coin, or use any other chance device, and on the basis of the outcome make the choice between the towns. So we can also use the following strategy: "Select one of the numbers 1 or 2 by means of a random device with arbitrary probabilities for each outcome, and locate in the corresponding town." This strategy is also optimal.

Note that if we multiply the matrix in Figure 5 on the left by the vector $(1, 0, 0)$, we get the first row; hence we shall use this vector to represent the strategy "Locate in town 1" for store R. Similarly, the strategy "Locate in town 2" is represented by the vector $(0, 1, 0)$, since multiplying the matrix on the left by it gives the second row. Then the vector

$$(a, 1 - a, 0) = a(1, 0, 0) + (1 - a)(0, 1, 0) \qquad \text{for } 0 \le a \le 1$$

represents the strategy, "Choose row 1 with probability a and row 2 with probability $1 - a$."

Similarly, for store C, the column vectors

$$\begin{pmatrix} 1 \\ 0 \\ 0 \end{pmatrix}, \quad \begin{pmatrix} 0 \\ 1 \\ 0 \end{pmatrix}, \quad \text{and} \quad \begin{pmatrix} a \\ 1 - a \\ 0 \end{pmatrix} \qquad \text{for } 0 \le a \le 1$$

represent the strategies, "Locate in town 1," "Locate in town 2," and "Locate in town 1 with probability a and in town 2 with probability $1 - a$," respectively.

Player C

	1	5	1	7
Player R	-2	8	0	-9
	1	12	1	3

Figure 6

Example 4. Consider the game G whose matrix is in Figure 6. It is not hard to see that the game is strictly determined with value 1, and there are four saddle values. Optimal strategies are $(1, 0, 0)$ and $(0, 0, 1)$ for player R, and

$$\begin{pmatrix} 1 \\ 0 \\ 0 \\ 0 \end{pmatrix}, \quad \begin{pmatrix} 0 \\ 0 \\ 1 \\ 0 \end{pmatrix}$$

for player C. The four ways we can pair optimal strategies for player R with those for player C give the four saddle values. Besides the optimal strategies above we have their convex combinations

$$a(1, 0, 0) + (1 - a)(0, 0, 1) = (a, 0, 1 - a),$$

which is optimal for R for any a satisfying $0 \le a \le 1$, and

$$a \begin{pmatrix} 1 \\ 0 \\ 0 \\ 0 \end{pmatrix} + (1-a) \begin{pmatrix} 0 \\ 1 \\ 0 \\ 0 \end{pmatrix} = \begin{pmatrix} a \\ 0 \\ 1-a \\ 0 \end{pmatrix},$$

which is optimal for player C for any a in the same range.

As the reader may have already found out for himself, not all matrix games are strictly determined. For instance, the two games shown in Figure 7 are not strictly determined. The solution of such games will be discussed in succeeding sections.

0	1
2	0

(a)

5	−2	3
−5	0	7
3	4	−1

(b)

Figure 7

EXERCISES

1. Determine which of the games given below are strictly determined and which are fair. When the game is strictly determined, find optimal strategies for each player.

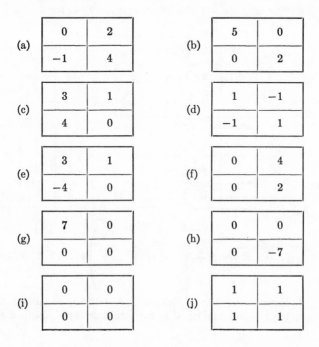

(a)

0	2
−1	4

(b)

5	0
0	2

(c)

3	1
4	0

(d)

1	−1
−1	1

(e)

3	1
−4	0

(f)

0	4
0	2

(g)

7	0
0	0

(h)

0	0
0	−7

(i)

0	0
0	0

(j)

1	1
1	1

[*Ans.* (*a*) Strictly determined and fair; R play row 1, C play column 1; (*b*) nonstrictly determined; (*e*) strictly determined but not fair; R play row 1, C play column 2; (*j*) strictly determined but not fair; both players can use any strategy.]

2. Find the value and all optimal strategies for the following games.

(a)

15	2	−3
6	5	7
−7	4	0

(b)

5	2	−1	−1
1	1	0	1
3	0	−3	7

(c)

0	5	6	−3
1	−1	2	3
1	2	3	4
−1	0	7	5

(d)

1	−12	6
0	−4	1
3	−7	2
3	−4	2
−5	−4	7

$$[Ans. \ (a) \ v = 5; \ (0, 1, 0); \begin{pmatrix} 0 \\ 1 \\ 0 \end{pmatrix}; \ (d) \ (0, a, 0, 1 - a, 0), \begin{pmatrix} 0 \\ 1 \\ 0 \end{pmatrix}, v = -4.]$$

3. Find the values of and all optimal strategies for the following games.

(a)

5	10	6	5
5	7	8	5
0	5	6	5

(b)

−2	0	−1
−5	7	8

(c)

0	0	1	0
1	0	0	0
1	0	1	0

(d)

3	2	3
6	2	7
5	1	4

$$[Ans. \ (a) \ v = 5; \ (a, 1 - a, 0); \begin{pmatrix} a \\ 0 \\ 0 \\ 1 - a \end{pmatrix}; \ (d) \ v = 2; \ (a, 1 - a, 0); \begin{pmatrix} 0 \\ 1 \\ 0 \end{pmatrix}.]$$

4. Each of two players shows one or two fingers (simultaneously) and C pays to R a sum equal to the total number of fingers shown. Write the

game matrix. Show that the game is strictly determined, and find the value and optimal strategies.

5. Each of two players shows one or two fingers (simultaneously) and C pays to R an amount equal to the total number of fingers shown, while R pays to C an amount equal to the product of the numbers of fingers shown. Construct the game matrix (the entries will be the net gain of R), and find the value and the optimal strategies.

   [*Ans.* $v = 1$, R must show one finger, C may show one or two.]

6. Show that a strictly determined game is fair if and only if there is a zero entry such that both entries in its row are nonnegative and both entries in its column are nonpositive.

7. Consider the game

$$G = \begin{array}{|c|c|} \hline 2 & 5 \\ \hline -1 & a \\ \hline \end{array}.$$

   a. Show that G is strictly determined regardless of the value of a.
   b. Find the value of G.   [*Ans.* 2.]
   c. Find optimal strategies for each player.
   d. If $a = 1,000,000$, obviously R would like to get it as his payoff. Is there any way he can assure himself of obtaining it? What would happen to him if he tried to obtain it?
   e. Show that the value of the game is the most that R can assure for himself.

8. Consider the matrix game

$$G = \begin{array}{|c|c|} \hline a & b \\ \hline c & d \\ \hline \end{array}$$

   Show that G is strictly determined for every set of values for a, c, and d. Show that the same result is true if two entries in a given column are always equal.

9. Find necessary and sufficient conditions that the game

$$G = \begin{array}{|c|c|} \hline a & 0 \\ \hline 0 & b \\ \hline \end{array}$$

   should be strictly determined. [*Hint:* These will be expressed in terms of relations among the numbers a and b and the number zero.]

10. a. Show that if there are two saddle values in the same row, then they are equal (to the row minimum).
    b. Show that if there are two saddle values in the same column, then they are equal.
    c. If g_{ij} and g_{hk} are saddle values in different rows and columns, show that $g_{ij} = g_{ik}$. Also show $g_{ik} = g_{hk}$.
    d. Prove that $g_{ij} = g_{hk}$.

11. Two companies, one large and one small, manufacturing the same product, wish to build a new store in one of four towns located on a given highway. If we regard the total population of the four towns as 100 percent, the distribution of population and distances between towns are as shown:

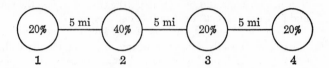

Assume that if the large company's store is nearer a town, it will capture 80 percent of the business, if both stores are equally distant, then the large company will capture 60 percent of the business, and if the small store is nearer, then the large company will capture 40 percent of the business.

a. Set up the matrix of the game.

b. Test for dominated rows and columns.

c. Find optimal strategies and the value of the game and interpret your results.

   [*Ans.* Both companies should locate in town 2; the large company captures 60 percent of the business.]

12. Rework Exercise 11 if the percent of business captured by the large company is 90, 75, and 60, respectively.

13. Show that the entries in Figure 5 are correct.

14. In the store location of Example 3 how do the optimal strategies change if the population of town 1 becomes 51 percent and the population of town 2 29 percent of the total? How might they change if town 2 is growing much faster than town 1?

15. Show that the following game is always strictly determined for nonnegative a and any values of the parameters b, c, d, and e.

$2a$	a	$3a$
b	$-a$	c
d	$-2a$	e

.

16. For what values of a is the following game strictly determined?

   [*Ans.* $-1 \leq a \leq 2$.]

a	6	2
-1	a	-7
-2	4	a

.

2. MATRIX GAMES

As we saw in the numerical examples of the previous section, some matrix games are nonstrictly determined; that is, they have no entry that is simultaneously a row minimum and a column maximum. We can characterize nonstrictly determined 2×2 matrix games as follows:

THEOREM. The matrix game

$$G = \begin{array}{|c|c|} \hline a & b \\ \hline c & d \\ \hline \end{array}.$$

is nonstrictly determined if and only if one of the following two conditions is satisfied:

  i. $a < b$, $a < c$, $d < b$, and $d < c$.
  ii. $a > b$, $a > c$, $d > b$, and $d > c$.

(These equations mean that the two entries on one diagonal of the matrix must each be greater than each of the two entries on the other diagonal.)

Proof. If either of the conditions (i) or (ii) holds, it is easy to check that no entry of the matrix is simultaneously the minimum of the row and the maximum of the column in which it occurs; hence the game is not strictly determined.

To prove the other half of the theorem, recall that, by Exercise 8 of the last section, if two of the entries in the same row or the same column of G are equal, the game is strictly determined; hence we can assume that no two entries in the same row or the same column are equal. Suppose now that $a < b$; then $a < c$ or else a is a row minimum and a column maximum; then also $c > d$ or else c is a row minimum and a column maximum; then also $d < b$ or else d is a row minimum and a column maximum. Hence the assumption $a < b$ leads to case (i) above.

In a similar manner the assumption $a > b$ leads to case (ii). This completes the proof of the theorem.

Example 1. Jones and Smith play the following game: Jones conceals either a \$1 or a \$2 bill in his hand; Smith guesses 1 or 2, winning the bill if he guesses the number. If we make Jones player R (the row player) and Smith player C, the matrix of the game is as in Figure 8. Because the game satisfies condition (i) in the theorem above, the game is nonstrictly determined. Later we will solve it.

Example 2. Mr. Sub works for Mr. Super and frequently must advise him on the acceptability of certain projects. Whenever Mr. Sub can make a clear

Player C
Smith guesses

		1	2
Player R Jones chooses	$1 bill	−1	0
	$2 bill	0	−2

Figure 8

judgment about a given project, he does so honestly. But when he has no reason to either accept or reject a given project, he tries to agree with Mr. Super. If he manages to agree with him he gives himself 10 points; if he is unfavorable when his boss is favorable, he credits himself with 0 points; but when he is favorable and his boss is unfavorable (the worst case), he loses 50 points. The matrix of the game is given in Figure 9. Since the matrix in Figure 9 satisfies condition (ii) of the theorem, it is not strictly determined.

Player C
Mr. Super's opinion

Favorable   Unfavorable

Player R Mr. Sub's opinion	Favorable	10	−50
	Unfavorable	0	10

Figure 9

How should one play a nonstrictly determined game? We must first convince ourselves that no single choice is clearly optimal for either player. In Example 1, R would like to get one of the 0 payoffs. But if he always chooses $1 and C finds this out, C can win $1 by guessing 1. And if R always chooses $2, then C can win $2 by guessing 2. Similarly, if C always guesses 1 or always guesses 2, and R finds this out, then R can always get 0. So our first result is that each player must, in some way, prevent the other player from finding out which choice of alternatives he is going to make.

We also note that for a single play of a nonstrictly determined 2 × 2 game there is no difference between the two strategies, as long as one's strategy is not guessed by the opponent. Let us now consider several plays of the game. What should R do? Clearly, he should not choose the same row all the time, or C will be able to notice and profit by it. Rather, R should choose sometimes one row, sometimes the other. Our key question then is, "How often should R choose each of his alternatives?" In Example 1 it seems reasonable that player R (Jones) should choose the $1 bill about twice as often as the $2 bill, because his losses, if Smith guesses correctly, are half as much. (We will see later that this strategy is, indeed, optimal.) In what order should he do this? For instance, should he select the $1 bill twice in a row and then the $2 bill? That is dangerous, because if player C (Smith) notices the pattern, he can gain by knowing just what R will do next. Thus we see that R should choose the $1 bill two-thirds of the time, but according to some unguessable pattern. The only safe way of doing this is to play it two-thirds of the time at random. He could, for instance, roll a die (without letting C see it) and choose the $1 if one through four turns up, the $2 if five or six turns up. Then his opponent cannot guess what the actual decision will be, since R himself won't know it. We conclude that a rational way of playing is for each player to *mix* his strategies, selecting sometimes one, sometimes the other; and these strategies should be selected at random, according to certain fixed ratios (probabilities) of selecting each.

By a *mixed strategy* in a 2×2 game for player R we shall mean a command of the form, "Play row 1 with probability p_1 and play row 2 with probability p_2," where we assume that $p_1 \geq 0$ and $p_2 \geq 0$ and $p_1 + p_2 = 1$. Similarly, a mixed strategy for player C is a command of the form, "Play column 1 with probability q_1 and play column 2 with probability q_2," where $q_1 \geq 0$, $q_2 \geq 0$, and $q_1 + q_2 = 1$. A mixed strategy vector for player R is the probability row vector (p_1, p_2), and a mixed strategy vector for player C is the probability column vector $\begin{pmatrix} q_1 \\ q_2 \end{pmatrix}$.

Examples of mixed strategies are $(\frac{1}{2}, \frac{1}{2})$ and $\begin{pmatrix} \frac{1}{5} \\ \frac{4}{5} \end{pmatrix}$. The reader may wonder how a player could actually play one of these strategies. The mixed strategy $(\frac{1}{2}, \frac{1}{2})$ is easy to realize, since it is simply the coin-flipping strategy described above. The mixed strategy $\begin{pmatrix} \frac{1}{5} \\ \frac{4}{5} \end{pmatrix}$ is more difficult to realize, since no chance device in common use gives these probabilities. However, suppose a pointer is constructed with a card that is $\frac{4}{5}$ shaded and $\frac{1}{5}$ unshaded, as in Figure 10, and C simply spins the pointer (without letting R see it, of

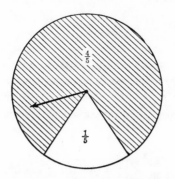

Figure 10

course!). Then, if the pointer stops on the unshaded part he plays the first column, and if it stops on the shaded part he plays the second column, thus realizing the desired strategy. By varying the proportion of shaded area on the card, other mixed strategies can conveniently be realized. An equally effective and less mechanical device for realizing a given mixed strategy is to use a table of random digits (see Table II in the Appendix). For the strategy $\begin{pmatrix} \frac{1}{5} \\ \frac{4}{5} \end{pmatrix}$, for example, we could let the digits 0 and 1 represent a play of column 1, and the remaining digits a play of column 2.

We now want to define what we shall mean by a solution to an $m \times n$ matrix game.

DEFINITION. Let G be an $m \times n$ matrix with entries g_{ij}. An m-component row vector p is a *mixed-strategy vector* for player R if it is a probability vector; similarly, an n-component column vector q is a *mixed-strategy vector for* C if it is a probability vector. (Recall from Chapter 4 that a probability vector is one with nonnegative entries whose sum is 1.) Let v be a number, let e be an m-component row vector all of whose entries are 1, and let f be an n-component column vector all of whose entries are 1. It follows that the vectors ve and vf are

$$ve = \underbrace{(v, v, \ldots, v)}_{m \text{ components}} \quad \text{and} \quad vf = \left. \begin{pmatrix} v \\ v \\ \vdots \\ v \end{pmatrix} \right] n \text{ components}$$

Then v is the *value* of the matrix game G and p^0 and q^0 are *optimal strategies* for the players if and only if the following inequalities hold:

(1) $$p^0 G \geq ve,$$

(2) $$Gq^0 \leq vf.$$

Example 3. In Example 1 of the previous section we had the matrix:

$$G = \begin{pmatrix} 50 & 60 \\ 40 & 50 \end{pmatrix}.$$

We found that the value of this game was $v = 50$ and that optimal strategies were for R to choose row 1, which corresponds to the mixed-strategy vector $p^0 = (1, 0)$, and for C to choose column 1, which corresponds to the mixed-strategy vector $q^0 = \begin{pmatrix} 1 \\ 0 \end{pmatrix}$. Carrying out the calculations in (1) and (2), we have

$$p^0 G = (1, 0) \begin{pmatrix} 50 & 60 \\ 40 & 50 \end{pmatrix} = (50, 60) \geq (50, 50) = 50(1, 1) = ve$$

and

$$Gq^0 = \begin{pmatrix} 50 & 60 \\ 40 & 50 \end{pmatrix} \begin{pmatrix} 1 \\ 0 \end{pmatrix} = \begin{pmatrix} 50 \\ 40 \end{pmatrix} \leq \begin{pmatrix} 50 \\ 50 \end{pmatrix} = 50 \begin{pmatrix} 1 \\ 1 \end{pmatrix} = vf.$$

In a similar manner the solutions to Examples 2, 3, and 4 of Section 1 can be shown to satisfy the definition above (see Exercises 5, 6, and 7). In

Exercise 16 you will be asked to show that optimal strategies to any strictly determined game satisfy the definition above.

Let us return now to the nonstrictly determined 2×2 game. Consider the nonstrictly determined game

$$G = \begin{array}{|c|c|} \hline a & b \\ \hline c & d \\ \hline \end{array} .$$

Having argued, as above, that the players should use mixed strategies in playing a nonstrictly determined game, it is still necessary to decide how to choose an optimal mixed strategy.

If R chooses a mixed strategy $p = (p_1, p_2)$ and (independently) C chooses a mixed strategy $q = \begin{pmatrix} q_1 \\ q_2 \end{pmatrix}$, then player R obtains the payoff a with probability $p_1 q_1$; he obtains the payoff b with probability $p_1 q_2$; he obtains c with probability $p_2 q_1$; and he obtains d with probability $p_2 q_2$; hence his mathematical expectation (see Chapter 3, Section 6) is given by the expression

$$a p_1 q_1 + b p_1 q_2 + c p_2 q_1 + d p_2 q_2$$

By a similar computation, one can show that player C's expectation is the negative of this expression.

To justify this definition we must show that if v, p^0, q^0 exist for G, each player can guarantee himself an expectation of v. Let q be any strategy for C. Multiplying (1) on the right by q, we get

$$p^0 G q \geq (v, v)q = v,$$

which shows that, regardless of how C plays, R can assure himself of an expectation of at least v. Similarly, let p be any strategy vector for R. Multiplying (2) on the left by p, we obtain

$$p G q^0 \leq p \begin{pmatrix} v \\ v \end{pmatrix} = v,$$

which shows that, regardless of how R plays, C can assure himself of an expectation of at most v. It is in this sense that p^0 and q^0 are optimal. It follows further that, if both players play optimally, then R's expectation is exactly v and C's expectation is exactly v. Hence we call v the (expected) *value* of the game.

We must now see whether there are strategies p^0 and q^0 for the game G. For complicated games the finding of optimal strategies will be discussed in Section 4. For a 2×2 nonstrictly determined game the following formulas provide the solution:

$$(3) \qquad\qquad p_1^0 = \frac{d - c}{a + d - b - c},$$

$$(4) \qquad\qquad p_2^0 = \frac{a - b}{a + d - b - c},$$

$$(5) \qquad\qquad q_1^0 = \frac{d - b}{a + d - b - c},$$

$$(6) \qquad\qquad q_2^0 = \frac{a - c}{a + d - b - c},$$

$$(7) \qquad\qquad v = \frac{ad - bc}{a + d - b - c}.$$

It is an easy matter to verify (see Exercise 12) that formulas (3)–(7) satisfy conditions (1)–(2). Actually, the inequalities in (1) and (2) become equalities in this simple case, a fact that is not true in general for nonstrictly determined games of larger size.

The denominator in each formula is the difference between the sums of the entries on the two diagonals. Since, for a nonstrictly determined game, the entries on one diagonal must be larger than those on the other; the denominator cannot be zero.

Let us use these formulas to solve the examples mentioned earlier.

Example 1 (continued). Applying formulas (3)–(7) to the matrix in Figure 8, we have

$$p_1^0 = \frac{-2 - 0}{-1 - 2 - 0 - 0} = \frac{2}{3}, \quad p_2^0 = \frac{-1 - 0}{-3} = \frac{1}{3},$$

$$q_1^0 = \frac{-2 - 0}{-3} = \frac{2}{3}, \quad q_2^0 = \frac{-1 - 0}{-3} = \frac{1}{3}, \quad v = \frac{(-1)(-2) - 0}{-3} = -\frac{2}{3}.$$

Thus the game is biased in favor of player C, since $v = -\frac{2}{3}$, and optimal strategies are

$$p^0 = (\tfrac{2}{3}, \tfrac{1}{3}) \quad \text{and} \quad q^0 = \begin{pmatrix} \tfrac{2}{3} \\ \tfrac{1}{3} \end{pmatrix}.$$

Both Jones and Smith should select their first alternative two-thirds of the time, according to some random pattern.

Example 2 (continued). Let us apply the formulas (3)–(7) to the matrix in Figure 9. We obtain

$$a + d - c - b = 10 + 10 - 0 + 50 = 70$$

so that:

$$p_1^0 = \frac{10 - 0}{70} = \frac{1}{7}, \qquad p_2^0 = \frac{10 + 50}{70} = \frac{6}{7},$$

$$q_1^0 = \frac{10 + 50}{70} = \frac{6}{7}, \quad q_2^0 = \frac{10 - 0}{70} = \frac{1}{7}, \quad v = \frac{10 \cdot 10 - 0}{70} = \frac{10}{7}.$$

Notice that the game is biased in favor of Mr. Sub, not his boss Mr. Super! Also Mr. Sub's optimal strategy is to have an *unfavorable* opinion 6 out of 7 times, while Mr. Super's optimal strategy is to have a *favorable* opinion 6 out of 7 times! Thus, if this game is at all realistic, a subordinate should be much more critical than his superior when judging situations in which there is no clear-cut reason to either accept or reject a project. The conclusion is based on game-theory analysis, not on relative ages, experience, and so on of the two persons.

We conclude this section by proving three theorems that characterize the value and optimal strategies of a game.

THEOREM. If G is a matrix game that has a value and optimal strategies, then the value of the game is unique.

Proof. Suppose that v and w are two different values for the game G. Then let p^0 and q^0 be optimal mixed-strategy vectors associated with the value v such that

(a) $$p^0 G \geq ve,$$

(b) $$Gq^0 \leq vf.$$

Similarly, let p^1 and q^1 be optimal mixed-strategy vectors associated with the value w such that

(c) $$p^1 G \geq we,$$

(d) $$Gq^1 \leq wf.$$

If we now multiply (a) on the right by q^1, we get $p^0 G q^1 \geq (ve)q^1 = v$. In the same way, multiplying (d) on the left by p^0 gives $p^0 G q^1 \leq w$. The two inequalities just obtained show that $w \geq v$.

Next we multiply (b) on the left by p^1 and (c) on the right by q^0, obtaining $v \geq p^1 G q^0$ and $p^1 G q^0 \geq w$, which together imply that $v \geq w$.

Finally we see that $v \leq w$ and $v \geq w$ imply together that $v = w$—that is, the value of the game is unique.

THEOREM. If G is a matrix game with value v and optimal strategies p^0 and q^0, then $v = p^0 G q^0$.

Proof. By definition v, p^0, and q^0 satisfy

$$p^0 G \geq ve \quad \text{and} \quad Gq^0 \leq vf.$$

Multiplying the first of these inequalities on the right by q^0, we get $p^0 G q^0 \geq v$. Similarly, multiplying the second inequality on the left by p^0, we obtain $p^0 G q^0 \leq v$. These two inequalities together imply that $v = p^0 G q^0$, concluding the proof.

The theorems just proved are important because they permit us to interpret the *value* of a game as an *expected value* (see Chapter 3, Section 6). Briefly the interpretation is the following: If the game G is played repeatedly and if each time it is played player R uses the mixed strategy p^0 and player C uses the mixed strategy q^0, then the value v of G is the expected value of the game for R. The law of large numbers implies that, if the number of plays of G is sufficiently large, then the average value of R's winnings will (with high probability) be arbitrarily close to the value v of the game G.

As an example, let G be the matrix of the game of matching pennies:

$$
G = \begin{array}{|c|c|}
\hline
1 & -1 \\
\hline
-1 & 1 \\
\hline
\end{array}.
$$

Using the formulas above, we find that optimal strategies in this game are for R to choose each row with probability $\frac{1}{2}$ and for C to choose each column with probability $\frac{1}{2}$. The value of G is zero. Notice that the only two payoffs that result from a single play of the game are $+1$ and -1, neither of which is equal to the value of the game. However, if the game is played repeatedly, the average value of R's payoffs will approach zero, which is the value of the game.

THEOREM. If G is a game with value v and optimal strategies p^0 and q^0, then v is the largest expectation that R can assure for himself. Similarly, v is the smallest expectation that C can assure for himself.

Proof. Let p be any mixed strategy vector of R and let q^0 be an optimal strategy for C; then multiply the equation $Gq^0 \leq vf$ on the left by p, obtaining $pGq^0 \leq v$. The latter equation shows that, if C plays optimally, the most that R can assure for himself is v. Now let p^0 be optimal for R; then, for every q, $p^0 Gq \geq v$, so that R can actually assure himself of an expectation of v. The proof of the other statement of the theorem is similar.

The theorem above gives an intuitive justification to the definition of value and optimal strategies for a game. Thus the value is the "best" that a player can do, and optimal strategies are the means of assuring this "best."

EXERCISES

1. Find the optimal strategies for each player and the values of the following games:

(a)

1	2
3	4

(b)

1	0
-1	2

(c)

2	3
1	4

(d)

15	3
-1	2

(e)

7	-6
5	8

(f)

3	15
-1	10

$$[Ans. \ (a) \ v = 3; \ (0, 1); \begin{pmatrix} 1 \\ 0 \end{pmatrix}. \quad (b) \ v = \tfrac{1}{2}; \ (\tfrac{3}{4}, \tfrac{1}{4}); \begin{pmatrix} \tfrac{1}{2} \\ \tfrac{1}{2} \end{pmatrix}.$$

$$(d) \ v = 3; \ (1, 0); \begin{pmatrix} 0 \\ 1 \end{pmatrix}. \quad (e) \ v = \tfrac{43}{8}; \ (\tfrac{3}{16}, \tfrac{13}{16}); \begin{pmatrix} \tfrac{7}{8} \\ \tfrac{1}{8} \end{pmatrix}.]$$

2. Set up the ordinary game of matching pennies as a matrix game. Find its value and optimal strategies. How are the optimal strategies realized in practice by players of this game?

3. A version of two-finger Morra is played as follows: Each player holds up either one or two fingers; if the sum of the number of fingers shown is even, player R gets the sum, and if the sum is odd, player C gets it.
   a. Show that the game matrix is

Player C

	1	2
1	2	-3
2	-3	4

Player R (rows labeled 1, 2)

   b. Find optimal strategies for each player and the value of the game.

$$[Ans. \ (\tfrac{7}{12}, \tfrac{5}{12}); \begin{pmatrix} \tfrac{7}{12} \\ \tfrac{5}{12} \end{pmatrix}; v = -\tfrac{1}{12}.]$$

4. Rework Exercise 3 if player C gets the even sum and player R gets the odd sum.

5. Let G be the matrix in Figure 3 described in Example 2 of Section 1. With $v = 0$, $p^0 = (0, 1)$, and $q^0 = \begin{pmatrix} 0 \\ 1 \end{pmatrix}$, show that formulas (1) and (2) are satisfied.

6. Show that the strategies derived in Example 3 of Section 1 satisfy formulas (1) and (2).

7. Show that the strategies derived in Example 4 of Section 1 satisfy formulas (1) and (2).

8. If

$$G = \begin{array}{|c|c|} \hline a & b \\ \hline c & d \\ \hline \end{array}$$

is nonstrictly determined, prove that it is fair if and only if $ad = bc$.

9. In formulas (3)–(7) prove that $p_1 > 0$, $p_2 > 0$, $q_1 > 0$, and $q_2 > 0$. Must v be greater than zero?

10. Find necessary and sufficient conditions that the game

$$G = \begin{array}{|c|c|} \hline a & 0 \\ \hline 0 & b \\ \hline \end{array}$$

be nonstrictly determined. Find optimal strategies for each player and the value of G, if it is nonstrictly determined.

[*Ans.* a and b must be both positive or both negative. $p_1 = b/(a+b)$; $p_2 = a/(a+b)$; $q_1 = b/(a+b)$; $q_2 = a/(a+b)$; $v = ab/(a+b)$.]

11. Suppose that player R tries to find C in one of three towns X, Y, and Z. The distance between X and Y is five miles, the distance between Y and Z is five miles, and the distance between Z and X is ten miles. Assume that R and C can go to one and only one of the three towns and that if they both go to the same town, R "catches" C and otherwise C "escapes." Credit R with ten points if he catches C, and credit C with a number of points equal to the number of miles he is away from R if he escapes.

    a. Set up the game matrix.

    b. Show that both players have the same optimal strategy, namely, to go to towns X and Z with equal probabilities and to go to town Y with probability $\frac{1}{4}$.

    c. Find the value of the game.

12. Verify that formulas (3)–(7) satisfy conditions (1) and (2).

13. Consider the (symmetric) game whose matrix is

$$G = \begin{array}{|c|c|c|} \hline 0 & -a & -b \\ \hline a & 0 & -c \\ \hline b & c & 0 \\ \hline \end{array}$$

    a. If a and b are both positive or both negative, show that G is strictly determined.

   b. If b and c are both positive or both negative, show that G is strictly determined.

   c. If $a > 0$, $b < 0$, and $c > 0$, show that an optimal strategy for player R is given by

$$\left(\frac{c}{a - b + c}, \quad \frac{-b}{a - b + c}, \quad \frac{a}{a - b + c} \right).$$

   d. In part *c.* find an optimal strategy for player C.

   e. If $a < 0$, $b > 0$, and $c < 0$, show that the strategy given in *c.* is optimal for R. What is an optimal strategy for player C?

   f. Prove that the value of the game is always zero.

14. In a well-known children's game each player says "stone" or "scissors" or "paper." If one says "stone" and the other "scissors," then the former wins a penny. Similarly, "scissors" beats "paper," and "paper" beats "stone." If the two players name the same item, then the game is a tie.

   a. Set up the game matrix.

   b. Use the results of Exercise 13 to solve the game.

15. In Exercise 14 let us suppose that the payments are different in different cases. Suppose that when "stone breaks scissors," the payment is one cent; when "scissors cut paper," the payment is two cents; and when "paper covers stone," the payment is three cents.

   a. Set up the game matrix.

   b. Use the results of Exercise 13 to solve the game.

      [*Ans.* $\frac{1}{3}$ "stone," $\frac{1}{2}$ "scissors," $\frac{1}{6}$ "paper"; $v = 0$.]

16. A strictly determined $m \times n$ matrix game G contains a saddle entry g_{ij} that is simultaneously the minimum of row i and the maximum of column j.

   a. Show that by rearranging rows and columns (if necessary) we can assume that g_{11} is a saddle value.

   b. Let $v = g_{11}$ and p^0 and q^0 be probability vectors with first component equal to 1 and all other components equal to 0. Show that these quantities satisfy (1) and (2).

17. Verify that the strategies $p^0 = (\frac{1}{3}, \frac{1}{3}, \frac{1}{3})$ and

$$q^0 = \begin{pmatrix} \frac{1}{3} \\ \frac{1}{3} \\ \frac{1}{3} \end{pmatrix}$$

are optimal in the game G whose matrix is

$$G = \begin{array}{c} \\ \\ \\ \end{array} \begin{array}{|c|c|c|} \hline 1 & 0 & 0 \\ \hline 0 & 1 & 0 \\ \hline 0 & 0 & 1 \\ \hline \end{array}.$$

What is the value of the game?

18. Generalize the result of Exercise 16 to the game G whose matrix is the $n \times n$ identity matrix.

19. Consider the following game:

$$G = \begin{array}{|c|c|c|}
\hline
a & 0 & 0 \\
\hline
0 & b & 0 \\
\hline
0 & 0 & c \\
\hline
\end{array}.$$

a. If a, b, and c are not all of the same sign, show that the game is strictly determined with value zero.

b. If a, b, and c are all of the same sign, show that the vector

$$\left(\frac{bc}{ab + bc + ca}, \ \frac{ca}{ab + bc + ca}, \ \frac{ab}{ab + bc + ca} \right)$$

is an optimal strategy for player R.

c. Find player C's optimal strategy for case b.

d. Find the value of the game for case b. and show that it is positive if a, b, and c are all positive, and negative if they are all negative.

20. Suppose that the entries of a matrix game are rewritten in new units (e.g., dollars instead of cents). Show that the monetary value of the game has not changed.

21. Consider the game of matching pennies whose matrix is

$$\begin{array}{|c|c|}
\hline
1 & -1 \\
\hline
-1 & 1 \\
\hline
\end{array}.$$

If the entries of the matrix represent gains or losses of one penny, would you be willing to play the game at least once? If the entries represent gains or losses of one dollar, would you be willing to play the game at least once? If they represent gains or losses of one million dollars, would you play the game at least once? In each of these cases show that the value is zero and optimal strategies are the same. Discuss the practical application of the theory of games in the light of this example.

3. SOLVING MATRIX GAMES BY A GEOMETRIC METHOD

In Section 1 we found that a strictly determined game of any size could be solved almost by inspection. In Section 2 we found formulas for solving nonstrictly determined 2×2 games. In Section 4 we shall discuss the application of the simplex method to solve arbitrary $m \times n$ matrix games. In the present section we shall discuss special matrix games in which one of the players has just two strategies, and we shall find that a simple geometric method suffices to solve such games rather easily.

Example 1. Suppose that Jones conceals one of the following four bills in his hand: a \$1 or a \$2 United States bill or a \$1 or a \$2 Canadian bill. Smith guesses either "United States" or "Canadian" and gets the bill if his guess is correct. We assume that a Canadian dollar has the same real value as a United States dollar. The matrix of the game is the following:

		Smith guesses U.S.	Can.
U.S.	\$1	−1	0
	\$2	−2	0
Can.	\$1	0	−1
	\$2	0	−2

Jones chooses (U.S. / Can.) at left.

It is obvious that Jones should always choose the \$1 bill of either country rather than the \$2 bill, since by doing so he may cut his losses and will never increase them. This can be observed in the matrix above, since every entry in the second row is less than or equal to the corresponding entry in the first row, and every entry in the fourth row is less than or equal to the corresponding entry in the third row. In effect we can eliminate the second and fourth rows and reduce the game to the following 2×2 matrix game:

		Smith guesses U.S.	Can.
Jones chooses	U.S. \$1	−1	0
	Can. \$1	0	−1

The new matrix game is nonstrictly determined with optimal strategies $(\frac{1}{2}, \frac{1}{2})$ for Jones and $\begin{pmatrix} \frac{1}{2} \\ \frac{1}{2} \end{pmatrix}$ for Smith. The value of the game is $-\frac{1}{2}$, which means that Smith should be willing to pay 50 cents to play it.

DEFINITION. Let A be an $m \times n$ matrix game. We shall say that row i *dominates* row h if every entry in row i is as large as or larger than the corresponding entry in row h. Similarly, we shall say that column j *dominates* column k if every entry in column j is as small as or smaller than the corresponding entry in column k.

Any dominated row or column can be omitted from the matrix game without materially affecting its solution. In the original matrix of Example 1 above, we see that row 1 dominates row 2, and also that row 3 dominates row 4.

Example 2. Consider the game whose matrix is:

$$G = \begin{array}{|c|c|c|c|}
\hline
1 & 0 & -1 & 0 \\
\hline
-3 & -2 & 1 & 2 \\
\hline
\end{array}$$

Observe that column 2 and column 3 each dominate column 4; that is, player C should never play the last column. Thus the game can be reduced to the following 2×3 game:

$$G' = \begin{array}{|c|c|c|} \hline 1 & 0 & -1 \\ \hline -3 & -2 & 1 \\ \hline \end{array}$$

No further rows or columns can be omitted because of domination; hence we must introduce a new technique for the solution of this game.

Suppose that player R announces he is going to use the mixed strategy $p = (p_1, p_2)$. Using the relation $p_1 = 1 - p_2$, we can write this as $p = (1 - p_2, p_2)$. Assume for the moment that player C knows R will use this strategy. Then he can compute his expected payment y from choosing each of his alternatives in G' as follows:

If he chooses column 1:

$$y = 1 \cdot p_1 - 3 \cdot p_2 = (1 - p_2) - 3p_2 = 1 - 4p_2;$$

If he chooses column 2:

$$y = 0 \cdot p_1 - 2 \cdot p_2 = -2p_2;$$

If he chooses column 3:

$$y = -1 \cdot p_1 + 1 \cdot p_2 = -(1 - p_2) + p_2 = -1 + 2p_2.$$

Notice that each of these expectations expresses y as a linear function of p_2. Hence the graphs of these expectations will be a straight line in each case. Since we have the restriction $0 \leq p_2 \leq 1$, we are interested only in the part of the line for which p_2 satisfies the restriction. In Figure 11 we have shown

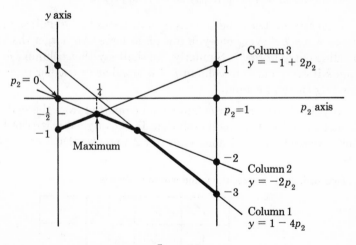

Figure 11

p_2 plotted on the horizontal axis and y on the vertical axis. We have also drawn the vertical line at $p_2 = 1$. The graphs of each of the lines above are shown. Observe that the ordinates of each line when $p_2 = 0$ are just the entries in the first row of G', and the ordinates of each line when $p_2 = 1$ are just the entries in the second row. Since we can easily find these two distinct points on each line, it is easy to draw them.

We now can analyze what C will do. For each value of p_2 that completely determines R's mixed strategy $p = (1 - p_2, p_2)$, player C will minimize his own expectation—that is, he will choose the lowest of the three lines plotted in Figure 11. For each p_2 the lowest line has been drawn in heavily, resulting in the broken-line function shown in the figure. Now R is the maximizing player, so he will try to get the maximum of this function. By visual inspection this obviously occurs at the intersection of the lines corresponding to column 2 and column 3, when $p_2 = \frac{1}{4}$ and the "height" of this function at that point is $-\frac{1}{2}$. From the figure it is clear that $-\frac{1}{2}$ is the maximum R can assure himself, and he can obtain this by using the strategy $p = (\frac{3}{4}, \frac{1}{4})$ corresponding to $p_2 = \frac{1}{4}$. We can find optimal strategies for player C by considering the 2×2 subgame of G (and G') consisting of the second and third columns:

$$G'' = \begin{array}{|c|c|} \hline 0 & -1 \\ \hline -2 & 1 \\ \hline \end{array}$$

Applying the formulas of the preceding section, we obtain as optimal strategies:

$$p^0 = (\tfrac{3}{4}, \tfrac{1}{4}), \qquad q^0 = \begin{pmatrix} \tfrac{1}{2} \\ \tfrac{1}{2} \end{pmatrix}, \qquad v = -\tfrac{1}{2}.$$

We can extend q^0 to an optimal strategy for player C in G by adding two zero entries thus:

$$q^0 = \begin{pmatrix} 0 \\ \tfrac{1}{2} \\ \tfrac{1}{2} \\ 0 \end{pmatrix}.$$

Player R's strategy and the value remain the same, as the reader can easily verify.

Example 3. We have already seen examples where a player has more than one optimal strategy. The game whose matrix is

$$G = \begin{array}{|c|c|c|} \hline 3 & 1 & 0 \\ \hline 0 & 1 & 3 \\ \hline \end{array}$$

is another example. To carry out the same kind of analysis as before, assume that R chooses $p = (p_1, p_2) = (1 - p_2, p_2)$. Then

If C chooses column 1: $\qquad y = 3(1 - p_2) = 3 - 3p_2;$

If C chooses column 2: $\qquad y = (1 - p_2) + p_2 = 1;$

If C chooses column 3: $\qquad y = 3p_2.$

The graphs of these three functions are shown in Figure 12, and the minimum of the three is shown darkened. Since the darkened graph has a flat

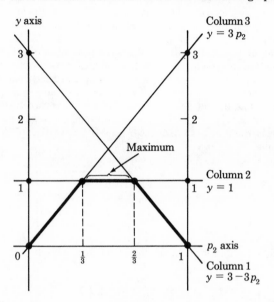

Figure 12

area on the top, the entire flat area represents the maximum of the function. The end points of the flat area are $(\frac{2}{3}, \frac{1}{3})$ and $(\frac{1}{3}, \frac{2}{3})$, and the intervening points that are convex combinations of these, such as

$$a(\tfrac{2}{3}, \tfrac{1}{3}) + (1 - a)(\tfrac{1}{3}, \tfrac{2}{3}) = \tfrac{1}{3}(a + 1, 2 - a),$$

are also optimal strategies, as the reader can verify by inspection. The unique optimal strategy for the column player is to choose the second column, so $q^0 = \begin{pmatrix} 0 \\ 1 \\ 0 \end{pmatrix}$. Of course $v = 1$.

THEOREM. The set of optimal strategies for either player in a matrix game is a convex set. That is, if p^0 and r^0 are optimal for player R, then $ap^0 + (1 - a)r^0$ is also optimal for him, for any a in the range $0 \le a \le 1$. Similarly, if q^0 and s^0 are optimal for player C, then so is $aq^0 + (1 - a)s^0$ for a in the same range.

We shall not give a formal proof of the theorem here, but it is clearly illustrated in Figure 12. In the next section we shall show that a matrix game is equivalent to a linear programming problem, and then the theorem becomes a consequence of the corresponding theorem in linear programming.

Example 4. So far we have illustrated cases in which the row player had just 2 strategies and the column player had 3 or more. A similar method works to solve games in which the column player has just 2 strategies and the row player has more. Consider the game whose matrix is

$$G = \begin{array}{|c|c|} \hline 6 & -1 \\ \hline 0 & 4 \\ \hline 4 & 3 \\ \hline \end{array}$$

Suppose we reverse the analysis above and assume that the column player selects a mixed strategy

$$q = \begin{pmatrix} q_1 \\ q_2 \end{pmatrix} = \begin{pmatrix} 1 - q_2 \\ q_2 \end{pmatrix}$$

and then considers what action R will take. Again there are three choices:

If he chooses row 1: $y = 6q_1 - q_2 = 6(1 - q_2) - q_2 = 6 - 7q_2;$

If he chooses row 2: $y = 4q_2;$

If he chooses row 3: $y = 4q_1 + 3q_2 = 4(1 - q_2) + 3q_2 = 4 - q_2.$

In each case y is the expectation that player R has for each choice. Since he is the maximizing player, he will want to maximize his expectation. In Figure 13 we have shown the three straight lines corresponding to each of these

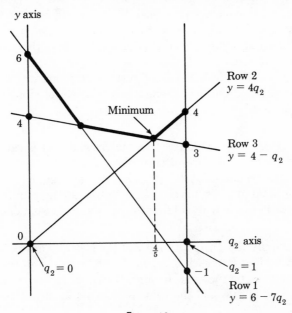

Figure 13

expectations and have darkened the *maximum* of each of these. Player C will want to choose the smallest value on the darkened broken-line function marked in the figure. Since it corresponds to $p_2 = \frac{4}{5}$, the corresponding optimal strategy for the column player is $\begin{pmatrix} \frac{1}{5} \\ \frac{4}{5} \end{pmatrix}$.

To find the corresponding optimal strategy for the row player we consider the 2×2 in the last two rows of the matrix:

0	4
4	3

Using the formulas of the previous section, we have optimal strategies:

$$p^0 = (\tfrac{1}{5}, \tfrac{4}{5}), \qquad q^0 = \begin{pmatrix} \frac{1}{5} \\ \frac{4}{5} \end{pmatrix}, \qquad v = \tfrac{16}{5}.$$

We can extend the optimal row strategy to one optimal for the original game by adding a zero. Thus

$$p^0 = (0, \tfrac{1}{5}, \tfrac{4}{5})$$

is optimal in the game G originally stated.

By using graph paper and a ruler, the reader will be able to solve in a similar manner other games in which one of the players has just two strategies. In principle the graphical method could be extended to larger games, but it is difficult to draw three-dimensional graphs and impossible to draw four- and higher-dimensional graphs, so that this idea has limited usefulness.

The geometric ideas presented in this section are useful conceptually. For instance, the following theorem is intuitively obvious from the geometric point of view.

THEOREM. Let G be an $m \times n$ matrix game with value v; let E be the $m \times n$ matrix each of whose entries is 1; and let k be *any* constant. Then the game $G + kE$ has value $v + k$, and every strategy optimal in the game G is also optimal in the game $G + kE$. (Note that the game $G + kE$ is obtained from the game G by adding the number k to each entry in G.)

If we apply this theorem to any of the previous examples, its truth is clear, since adding k to each entry in G merely moves all the lines in each graph up or down by the same amount. Hence the locations of the optimum points are unchanged, and the value is changed by the amount k.

1. Solve the following games:

(a)

3	0
−2	3
7	5

$[Ans.\ v = 5;\ (0, 0, 1);\ \begin{pmatrix} 0 \\ 1 \end{pmatrix}.]$

(b)

10	5	4	6
18	3	3	4

(c)

1	0	2
0	3	2

$[Ans.\ v = \tfrac{3}{4};\ (\tfrac{3}{4}, \tfrac{1}{4});\ \begin{pmatrix} \tfrac{3}{4} \\ \tfrac{1}{4} \\ 0 \end{pmatrix}.]$

(d)

0	2
1	3
−1	0
2	0

(e)

1	2	3
4	2	1

$[An\ Ans.\ v = 2;\ (\tfrac{3}{5}, \tfrac{2}{5});\ \begin{pmatrix} 0 \\ 1 \\ 0 \end{pmatrix}.]$

(f)

1	0	1	1	2
0	−1	−2	−3	−10

2. Solve the following games:

(a)

0	15
8	0
−10	20
10	12

(b)

-1	-2	0	-3	-4
-2	1	0	2	5

(c)

-1	5	-1	-2	8	10
3	-6	0	8	-9	-8

$$\left[An\ Ans.\ v = -\tfrac{1}{2};\ (\tfrac{1}{2}, \tfrac{1}{2});\ \begin{pmatrix} 0 \\ \tfrac{1}{12} \\ \tfrac{11}{12} \\ 0 \\ 0 \\ 0 \end{pmatrix} .\right]$$

3. Solve the game

1	2	3
3	2	1

.

Since there is more than one optimal strategy for C, find a range of optimal strategies for him.

4. Consider the game whose matrix is:

13	-7
3	8
-1	14
9	-1

a. Find player C's optimal strategy by graphical means.
b. Show that there are six possible subgames that can be chosen by player R.
c. Of the six possible subgames show that two are strictly determined and do not give optimal strategies in the original game.
d. Show that the other four subgames have solutions that can be extended to optimal strategies in the original game.

$$[Ans.\ (\tfrac{1}{5}, \tfrac{4}{5}, 0, 0),\ (\tfrac{3}{7}, 0, \tfrac{4}{7}, 0),\ (0, 0, \tfrac{2}{5}, \tfrac{3}{5}),\ (0, \tfrac{2}{3}, 0, \tfrac{1}{3}).]$$

5. Suppose that Jones conceals in his hand one, two, three, or four silver dollars and Smith guesses "even" or "odd." If Smith's guess is correct, he wins the amount that Jones holds; otherwise he must pay Jones this amount. Set up the corresponding matrix game and find an optimal strategy for each player in which he puts positive weight on all his (pure) strategies. Is the game fair?

6. Consider the following game: Player R announces "one" or "two"; then, independently of each other, both players write down one of these two numbers. If the sum of the three numbers so obtained is odd, C pays R the odd sum in dollars; if the sum of the three numbers is even, R pays C the even sum in dollars.

    a. What are the strategies of R? [*Hint:* He has four strategies.]

    b. What are the strategies of C? [*Hint:* We must consider what C does after "one" is announced or after a "two." Hence he has four strategies.]

    c. Write down the matrix for the game.

    d. Restrict player R to announcing "two," and allow for C only those strategies where his number does not depend on the announced number. Solve the resulting 2 × 2 game.

    e. Extend the above mixed strategies to the original game, and show that they are optimal.

    f. Is the game favorable to R? If so, by how much?

7. Answer the same questions as in Exercise 6 if R gets the even sum and C gets the odd sum [except that, in part (*d*) restrict R to announce "one"]. Which game is more favorable for R? Could you have predicted this without the use of game theory?

8. Two players play five-finger Morra by extending from one to five fingers: If the sum of the number of fingers is even, R gets one, while if the sum is odd, C gets one. Suppose that each player shows only one or two fingers. Show that the resulting game is like matching pennies. Show that the optimal strategies for this game, when extended, are optimal in the whole game.

9. A version of three-finger Morra is played as follows: Each player shows from one to three fingers; R always pays C an amount equal to the number of fingers that C shows; if C shows exactly one more or two fewer fingers than R, then C pays R a positive amount x (where x is independent of the number of fingers shown).

    a. Set up the game matrix for arbitrary x's.

    b. If $x = \frac{1}{2}$, show that the game is strictly determined. Find the value.
    $$[Ans.\ v = -\tfrac{5}{2}.]$$

    c. If $x = 2$, show that there is a pair of optimal strategies in which the first player shows one or two fingers and the second player shows two or three fingers. [*Hint:* Use domination.] Find the value.
    $$[Ans.\ v = -\tfrac{3}{2}.]$$

    d. If $x = 6$, show that an optimal strategy for R is to use the mixed strategy, $(\frac{1}{3}, \frac{1}{2}, \frac{1}{6})$. Show that the optimal mixed strategy for C is to choose his three strategies each with probability $\frac{1}{3}$. Find the value of the game.

10. Another version of three-finger Morra goes as follows: Each player shows from one to three fingers; if the sum of the number of fingers is even, then R gets an amount equal to the number of fingers that C shows: if the sum is odd, C gets an amount equal to the number of fingers that R shows.

    a. Set up the game matrix.

    b. Reduce the game to a 2 × 2 matrix game.

    c. Find optimal strategies for each player and show that the game is fair.

11. Consider the game:

a	b
c	d

a. Draw the graph of expectations for the row player when $a = b$ and prove graphically that the game is strictly determined.

b. Draw the same graph when $a > b, a > c, d > b, d > c$, and show that the game is nonstrictly determined.

c. Draw the same graph when $a < b, a < c, d < b, d < c$, and show that the game is nonstrictly determined.

d. Draw graphs to illustrate cases in which b. and c. do not hold and show that the resulting game is strictly determined.

12. Consider the game of Exercise 11 with the same amount k added to each matrix entry. Show graphically that the value of the game is changed by k and that optimal strategies are the same in both games.

The remaining exercises refer to the *product payoff game* (due to A. W. Tucker). Two sets, S and T, are given, each set containing at least one positive and at least one negative number (but no zeros). Player R selects a number s from set S, and player C selects a number t from set T. The payoff is st.

13. Set up the game for the sets $S = \{1, -1, 2\}$ and $T = \{1, -3, 2, -4\}$.

[*Ans.*

1	−3	2	−4
−1	3	−2	4
2	−6	4	−8

.]

14. Consider the following mixed strategy for either player: "Choose a positive number p and a negative number n with probabilities $-n/(p - n)$ and $p/(p - n)$ respectively." Assume that R uses this strategy.

a. If C chooses a positive number, show that the expected payoff to R is 0.

b. If C chooses a negative number, show that the expected payoff to R is 0.

15. Rework Exercise 14 with R and C interchanged.

16. Use the results of Exercises 14 and 15 to show that the game is fair, and that the strategy quoted in Exercise 14 is optimal for either player.

17. Find all strategies of the kind indicated in Exercise 14 for both players for the game of Exercise 13.

[*Partial Ans.* For R they are $(\frac{1}{2}, \frac{1}{2}, 0)$ and $(0, \frac{2}{3}, \frac{1}{3})$.]

18. By subtracting 10 from each entry, show that the following game is derived from a product payoff game, and find all strategies like those in Exercise 14 for both players. What is the value of the game?

11	7	12	6
9	13	8	14
12	4	14	2

[*Hint:* Use Exercises 13 and 17 and the last theorem.]

19. If a player in the product payoff game has m positive and n negative numbers in his set, show that he has mn strategies like those in Exercise 14.

4. THE SIMPLEX METHOD FOR SOLVING MATRIX GAMES

We have so far restricted our attention to examples of matrix games that were simple enough to be solved by unformalized computations. However, games of realistic size frequently lead to very large matrices for which these simple techniques are not adequate. A clue to a general technique may be found in the fact that the row player is a maximizing player while the column player is a minimizing player. Hence, the problems they are trying to solve sound somewhat like the dual linear programming problems of Chapter 5. So if a matrix game can be formulated as a linear programming problem, it can be solved by the simplex method discussed in the previous chapter.

There are several ways of showing that a matrix game is equivalent to a linear program. We choose a very simple approach here, based on the fact, stated in Section 3, that every matrix game is equivalent to one in which all entries are positive and hence whose value is positive.

Besides finding an equivalent linear programming problem, we shall give a proof, based on the duality theorem of linear programming, that every matrix game has a solution. And we will present a simplex format suitable for the solution of any matrix game.

Let G be an $m \times n$ matrix game and let E be the $m \times n$ matrix all of whose entries are 1's. The second theorem of Section 3 states that G and $G + kE$ have the same optimal strategies, and the value of the second game is k plus the value of the first game. Hence if we start with any game G we can replace it by a game G' all of whose entries are positive, and which has the same optimal strategies. For instance, to get G' we could add 1 minus the most negative entry in G to every entry in G.

Thus without loss of generality we let G be a positive matrix game.

We also let e be the n-component row vector all of whose entries are 1's, and let f be the m-component column vector all of whose entries are 1's. Let z be an m-component row vector and x an n-component column vector. We now consider the following dual linear programming problems:

$$(1) \quad \begin{cases} \begin{array}{cc} \text{Min } zf & \text{Max } ex \\ \text{subject to:} & \text{subject to:} \\ zG \geq e & Gx \leq f \\ z \geq 0 & x \geq 0. \end{array} \end{cases}$$

Note that $x = 0$ satisfies the constraints of the maximizing problem; also, because the entries of G and f are positive, there is at least one nonzero x vector that will satisfy these constraints. Moreover, the set of feasible x vectors is bounded. Because of these facts, and because e has all positive entries, the maximizing problem has solution x^0 such that $ex^0 > 0$. Hence, by the duality theorem, the minimum problem has a solution x^0 and

$$t = z^0 G x^0 = z^0 f = ex^0 > 0.$$

We now set

$$p^0 = \frac{z^0}{t}, \qquad q^0 = \frac{x^0}{t}, \quad \text{and} \quad v = \frac{1}{t},$$

and observe that p^0 and q^0 are probability vectors.

It is easy to see that p^0 is an optimal strategy for player R in G, since x^0 satisfies the constraints of the minimizing problem, and hence

$$p^0 G = \frac{z^0 G}{t} \geq \frac{e}{t} = ve.$$

In Exercise 1 the reader is asked to show similarly that $Gq^0 \leq vf$.

We summarize these results in the following theorem.

THEOREM. (a) Solving the matrix game G with positive entries can be accomplished by solving the dual linear programming problems (1).

(b) Every matrix game has at least one solution; solutions to such games can be found by the simplex method.

Actually, it is not necessary that the matrix game be positive in order that the simplex method work. It is enough that its value is positive. However, in Exercise 3 the reader is asked to work a specific example for which the linear programming problem as described above has no solution if applied to a game with zero value.

Before proceeding to specific examples, let us outline the procedure to be followed in setting up a matrix game for solution by the simplex method.

1. Set up the matrix of the game.
2. Check to see whether the game is strictly determined; if so the solution is already obtained.
3. Check for row and column dominance and remove dominated rows and columns.
4. Make certain that the value of the game is positive. It is sufficient for this to add 1 minus the most negative matrix entry to every entry of the matrix. Let k be the amount added, if any, to each matrix entry.
5. Let G be the matrix of the resulting game; suppose it is $m \times n$. Construct the following matrix tableau:

G	f
e	0

6. Carry out the steps of the simplex algorithm until all indicators are nonpositive. Determine the solutions z^0 and x^0 to the dual linear programming problems, and let $t = z^0 f = ex^0$. We know $t > 0$.
7. The solutions to the original matrix game are given by

$$p^0 = \frac{z^0}{t}, \qquad q^0 = \frac{x^0}{t} \quad \text{and} \quad v = \frac{1}{t} - k.$$

(If dominated rows or columns were removed from the game, the strategy vectors may have to be extended by the addition of some zero components.)

Example 1. We know that the matching pennies game is fair, that is, it has value zero. To make its value positive, we add $k = 2$ to each matrix entry, yielding the following game:

3	1
1	3

Obviously this game is not strictly determined and it does not have dominated rows or columns. We set up the simplex tableau and solve it as shown in Figure 14(a)–(c). (Note that we have called the variables on the left z_1 and z_2 instead of v_1 and v_2, since we are now using v for the value of the game.) From the final tableau in Figure 14(c) we can see that the value of the game is 2 (the reciprocal of $t = \frac{1}{2}$) so that the value of the matching pennies game is 0, which we know already. Also optimal strategies are

$$p^0 = \frac{z^0}{t} = (\tfrac{1}{2}, \tfrac{1}{2}) \quad \text{and} \quad q^0 = \frac{x^0}{t} = \begin{pmatrix} \tfrac{1}{2} \\ \tfrac{1}{2} \end{pmatrix},$$

which we had discovered earlier.

Example 2. Let us solve the two-finger Morra game of Exercise 3 of Section 2. To convert the game into one with positive value let us add 3 to each

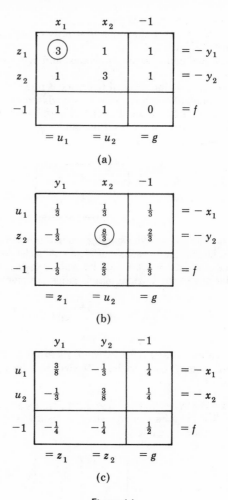

Figure 14

entry of the matrix, noting that this will give two zeros in the resulting game matrix. These zeros will simplify the simplex calculations. The game matrix now is

5	0
0	7

.

Figure 15(a)–(c) shows the initial and two subsequent simplex tableaus. The value of the game, from Figure 16(c), is $\frac{35}{12}$, which means that the value of the original game is $\frac{35}{12} - 3 = -\frac{1}{12}$. Optimal strategies agree with the answer stated in the Exercise.

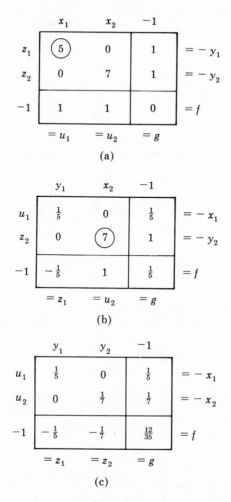

Figure 15

Example 3. Consider the following game: R and C simultaneously display 1, 2, or 3 pennies. If both show the same number of pennies, no money is exchanged; but if they show different numbers of pennies, R gets odd sums and C gets even sums. The matrix of the game is

		C shows		
		1	2	3
	1	0	3	−4
R shows	2	3	0	5
	3	−4	5	0

	x_1	x_2	x_3	-1	
z_1	0	3	-4	1	$=-y_1$
z_2	③	0	5	1	$=-y_2$
z_3	-4	5	0	1	$=-y_3$
-1	1	1	1	0	$=f$
	$=u_1$	$=u_2$	$=u_3$	$=g$	

(a)

	y_2	x_2	x_3	-1	
z_1	0	③	-4	1	$=-y_1$
u_1	$\frac{1}{3}$	0	$\frac{5}{3}$	$\frac{1}{3}$	$=-x_1$
z_3	$\frac{4}{3}$	5	$\frac{20}{3}$	$\frac{7}{3}$	$=-y_3$
-1	$-\frac{1}{3}$	1	$\frac{2}{3}$	$\frac{1}{3}$	$=f$
	$=z_2$	$=u_2$	$=u_3$	$=g$	

(b)

	y_2	y_1	x_3	-1	
u_2	0	$\frac{1}{3}$	$-\frac{4}{3}$	$\frac{1}{3}$	$=-x_2$
u_1	$\frac{1}{3}$	0	$\frac{5}{3}$	$\frac{1}{3}$	$=-x_1$
z_3	$\frac{4}{3}$	$-\frac{5}{3}$	④⓪⁄③	$\frac{1}{3}$	$=-y_3$
-1	$-\frac{1}{3}$	$-\frac{1}{3}$	$\frac{2}{3}$	$\frac{2}{3}$	$=f$
	$=z_2$	$=z_1$	$=u_3$	$=g$	

(c)

	y_2	y_1	y_3	-1	
u_2	$\frac{2}{15}$	$\frac{1}{6}$	$\frac{1}{10}$	$\frac{2}{5}$	$=-x_2$
u_1	$\frac{1}{6}$	$\frac{5}{24}$	$-\frac{1}{8}$	$\frac{1}{4}$	$=-x_1$
u_3	$\frac{1}{10}$	$-\frac{1}{8}$	$\frac{3}{40}$	$\frac{1}{20}$	$=-x_3$
-1	$-\frac{2}{5}$	$-\frac{1}{4}$	$-\frac{1}{20}$	$\frac{7}{10}$	$=f$
	$=z_2$	$=z_1$	$=z_3$	$=g$	

(d)

Figure 16

Since the second row has all nonnegative entries, the game is, if anything, in R's favor. And if R plays the first two rows with equal weight, his expectation is positive. Hence the value of the game is positive, and we do not have to add anything to the matrix entries. The simplex calculations needed to solve the game are shown in Figure 16(a)–(d). From this we see that the value of the game is $1/t = \frac{14}{9}$, and that optimal strategies are

$$p^0 = \frac{z^0}{t} = (\tfrac{5}{14}, \tfrac{4}{7}, \tfrac{1}{14}) \quad \text{and} \quad q^0 = \frac{x^0}{t} = \begin{pmatrix} \frac{5}{14} \\ \frac{4}{7} \\ \frac{1}{14} \end{pmatrix}.$$

The reader should check that these strategies do solve the game.

The examples just solved could have been worked directly, without the use of the simplex method. However, the simplex method works just as well for much larger games for which there is no easy direct method.

EXERCISES

1. If $q^0 = x^0/t$ where x^0 solves the maximum problem stated in (1) and $t = ex^0$, show that q^0 is an optimal strategy for player C in the matrix game G.

2. Solve the following games by the simplex method.

(a)

1	0	3
−2	3	0
−4	5	−6

(b)

−2	3	0	5	−6
3	−4	5	0	7
−4	5	−6	7	0

3. Consider the matching-pennies game with matrix

$$G = \begin{array}{|c|c|} \hline 1 & -1 \\ \hline -1 & 1 \\ \hline \end{array}.$$

   a. Substitute it directly into the simplex format described in rule (5) above, and show that the simplex method breaks down.
   b. Consider the linear programming problem defined in (1) with this G and show directly that it has no solution.

4. Use the simplex method to derive formulas (3)–(7) of Section 2 for optimal strategies in a nonstrictly determined 2×2 game.

5. Work Exercise 19 of Section 2 using the simplex method.

6. Work Exercise 13 of Section 2 using the simplex method.

7. A passenger on a Mississippi river boat was approached by a flashily dressed stranger (the gambler) who offered to play the following game: "You take a red ace and a black deuce and I'll take a red deuce and a black trey; we will simultaneously show one of the cards; if the colors

don't match you pay me and if the colors match I'll pay you; moreover if you play the red ace we will exchange the difference of the numbers on the cards; but if you play the black deuce we will exchange the sum of the numbers. Since you will pay me either $2 or $4 if you lose and I will pay you either $1 or $5 if I lose, the game is obviously fair." Set up and solve the matrix game using the simplex method. Show that the game is not fair. Find the optimal strategies.

[*Partial Ans.* The gambler will win an average of 25 cents per game.]

8. Consider the following game: R chooses 0 or 1 and reveals his choice to C; C chooses 0 or 1, but does not reveal his choice to R; R then chooses 0 or 1 a second time. The sum of the three numbers chosen is computed and R receives odd sums while C receives even sums.

   a. Show that R has four strategies: 00, 01, 10, 11.

   b. Show that C has four strategies: (1) always choose 0, (2) choose the same as R, (3) choose opposite to R, (4) always choose 1.

   c. Show that the payoff matrix is

	(1)	(2)	(3)	(4)
00	0	0	1	1
01	1	1	-2	-2
10	1	-2	1	-2
11	-2	3	-2	3

   d. Solve the game by the simplex method, finding its value and optimal strategies.

   $$[Ans.\ p^0 = (\tfrac{3}{4}, \tfrac{1}{4}, 0, 0),\ q^0 = \begin{pmatrix} \frac{3}{10} \\ \frac{9}{20} \\ \frac{1}{4} \\ 0 \end{pmatrix},\ v = \tfrac{1}{4}.]$$

9. Rework Exercise 8 assuming that the players choose 1 or 2 each time.

10. *The Silent Duel.* Two duelists each have a pistol that contains a single bullet and is equipped with a silencer. They advance toward each other in N steps, and each may fire at his opponent at the end of each step. Neither knows whether his opponent has fired, and each has but one shot in the game. The probability that a player will hit his opponent if he fires after moving k steps is k/N. A player gets 1 if he kills his opponent without being killed himself, -1 if he gets killed without killing his opponent, and 0 otherwise. Each player has N strategies corresponding to firing after steps $1, 2, \ldots, N$. Let i be the strategy chosen by R and j the strategy chosen by C.

   a. If $i < j$, show that the expected payoff to R is given by

   $$\frac{N(i - j) + ij}{N^2}.$$

    b. If $i > j$, show that the expected payoff to R is given by

$$\frac{N(i - j) - ij}{N^2}.$$

    c. If $i = j$, show that the expected payoff to R is 0.

11. In Exercise 10, prove that the game is strictly determined and fair for $N = 2, 3$, and 4. Show that the optimal strategy for $N = 3, 4$ is to fire at the end of the second step in each case. For $N = 2$, show that any strategy is optimal.

12. In Exercise 10, show that the game is nonstrictly determined and fair for $N = 5$, and find the optimal strategies.

    [*Ans.* $p^0 = (0, \frac{5}{11}, \frac{5}{11}, 0, \frac{1}{11})$, and q^0 is the column vector having the same components.]

13. A *symmetric matrix game* G is one for which $g_{ij} = -g_{ji}$ for $i, j = 1, 2, \ldots, n$. In other words, for every payment from C to R there is an equal payment from R to C. Show that every symmetric game is fair. [*Hint:* Show that if x^0 is optimal for R then the column vector y with $y_k = x_k^0$ for $k = 1, \ldots, n$ is optimal for C. From this deduce that the value of the game is zero.]

14. Use Exercise 13 to show that the silent duel is fair for every N.

15. Consider a matrix game G with positive value in which the first row strictly dominates the second row. Show that in the simplex algorithm, no entry in the second row will ever be chosen as a pivot in the first step.

16. Consider a matrix game G with positive value in which the first column dominates the second column. Show that if the pivot is chosen in the first column, after the end of the first simplex calculation the indicator for the second column will be nonnegative.

*5. TWO-PERSON NONZERO-SUM GAMES

The two-person zero-sum games we have discussed so far in the present chapter represent the most orderly and well-developed part of game theory. Unfortunately, it is not always possible to formulate applications of game theory as two-person zero-sum games Instead two- or more-person non-zero-sum games are frequently needed. For such games many solution concepts have been proposed, and there are various arguments for and against each such concept. But no single solution concept is acceptable for all cases.

    In the present section we shall discuss only two-person nonzero-sum games. For these we shall consider four proposed types of solutions: (a) maximin solutions, (b) equilibrium-point solutions, (c) cooperative solutions, and (d) threat solutions. We shall indicate by examples circumstances under which each of these solutions might be applicable. In the exercises, other solution concepts are considered.

    A two-person nonzero-sum game is defined as follows: There are two players R and C as before. Player R has m strategies $1, 2, \ldots, m$, while C has n strategies $1, 2, \ldots, n$. If R chooses strategy i and C chooses strategy j then the players receive the payoff vector (a_{ij}, b_{ij}), where a_{ij} is the amount R receives and b_{ij} is the amount C receives. Let A be the $m \times n$ matrix whose entries are a_{ij}, and let B be the $m \times n$ matrix whose entries are b_{ij}. It is convenient to arrange the payoffs (a_{ij}, b_{ij}) in rectangular form as the following examples illustrate. If $B = -A$—that is, $b_{ij} = -a_{ij}$ for all i and j—then the game is zero-sum and reduces to an ordinary matrix game with matrix A.

Example 1. Suppose there are two firms R and C who are deciding whether or not to enter two different markets, 1 and 2. As the result of market surveys they decide that R is strong in the first market and C is strong in the second market. Their evaluation of the merits of entering these markets is as indicated in the table of Figure 17. The entries in these vectors represent esti-

	C Enters	
	Market 1	Market 2
R Enters Market 1	(15, 10)	(22, 20)
R Enters Market 2	(11, 13)	(10, 15)

Figure 17

mated yearly profit figures, where the first entry is R's profit and the second entry is C's profit. What strategies shall each player choose?

Here the solution is quite obvious since R, looking at his own profits, always prefers to enter market 1 regardless of what C does, while C always prefers to enter market 2. And if they make these choices, each one gets his highest possible profits. Here is a situation in which the players, each acting purely in his own self-interest, arrive at a mutually satisfactory solution.

Suppose now that the results of the survey revealed the payoffs shown in Figure 18. Note that Figure 18 is just like Figure 17 except that the two payoffs of 10 have been changed to 30.

	C Enters	
	Market 1	Market 2
R Enters Market 1	(15, 30)	(22, 20)
R Enters Market 2	(11, 13)	(30, 15)

Figure 18

Note that in Figure 18 there is no domination of the kind observed in Figure 17, and it is not immediately clear what the solution should be. Suppose that R makes the most pessimistic assumption, namely, that C is fully opposed to him and wants to minimize his payoff. Then R would solve the matrix game

$$A = \begin{array}{|c|c|} \hline 15 & 22 \\ \hline 11 & 30 \\ \hline \end{array}$$

which consists of his own payoffs. This is a strictly determined game for which his optimal strategy is "enter market 1." Similarly, if C were pessimistic he would solve the game

$$-B = \begin{array}{|c|c|} \hline -30 & -20 \\ \hline -13 & -15 \\ \hline \end{array}$$

(remember that the b_{ij}'s are payments *to* C), which again is strictly determined and yields the optimal strategy, "enter market 2." If the two players follow these strategies, which we call *maximin* strategies, then they will attain the payoff vector (22, 20) as before.

Before proceeding further with Example 1, we formulate the definition of a maximin strategy.

DEFINITION. Let G be a nonzero-sum game with payoffs (a_{ij}, b_{ij}) for $i = 1, \ldots, m$ and $j = 1, \ldots, n$. Let A be the matrix with entries a_{ij} and B be the matrix with entries b_{ij}. Then a *maximin strategy* for R in G is any optimal strategy for him in the matrix game A, while a *maximin strategy* for C is any optimal strategy for him in the matrix game $-B$.

Example 1 (continued). The maximin strategy for the game of Figure 18 is obtained by solving the matrix games

$$A = \begin{array}{|c|c|} \hline 15 & 22 \\ \hline 11 & 10 \\ \hline \end{array} \quad \text{and} \quad -B = \begin{array}{|c|c|} \hline -10 & -20 \\ \hline -13 & -15 \\ \hline \end{array}$$

which yield the optimal strategies "enter market 1" for R and "enter market 2" for C. Again this gives the payoff vector (22, 20).

Note that the answers obtained for the games of Figures 17 and 18 are the same and yield the same payoff vector, but they have different stability properties. In Figure 17 if the players are at (22, 20) there is no incentive for either of them to change the status quo. But in Figure 18, assume that the players are at the (22, 20) point; if R now makes the assumption that C will keep his choice of strategy fixed, he would prefer to change his strategy from the maximin strategy of "enter market 1" to the more profitable strategy of "enter market 2," since this would lead to the payoff vector of (30, 15) which is better for him (though worse for C). Similarly, if C makes the assumption that R will keep his choice "enter market 1" fixed, C would prefer to switch from "enter market 2" to "enter market 1," since his payoff would be increased from 20 to 30. We see that the (22, 20) point is stable in Figure 17 but unstable in Figure 18.

In order to capture the idea of stability of solutions we define equilibrium-point strategies.

DEFINITION. Let G be a nonzero-sum game and let A and B be the payoff matrices to R and C, respectively. Then the pair of mixed strategies p^0, q^0 are *equilibrium-point strategies* for R and C, respectively, if the following conditions hold:

$$pAq^0 \leq p^0Aq^0 \qquad \text{for all strategies } p \text{ for R, and}$$
$$p^0Bq \leq p^0Bq^0 \qquad \text{for all strategies } q \text{ for C.}$$

The intuitive idea of an equilibrium point is that it is a pair of strategies having the property that neither player can increase his own payoff by changing his strategy, assuming that his opponent keeps his strategy fixed. It can be shown that every nonzero-sum game has equilibrium-point solutions.

Example 1 (continued). In the game of Figure 17 there is a unique equilibrium-point strategy given by the pair $p^0 = (1, 0)$ and $q^0 = \begin{pmatrix} 0 \\ 1 \end{pmatrix}$. The payoff vector for these two strategies is $(22, 20)$. However, in the game of Figure 18 there are two equilibrium points:

i. $p^0 = (1, 0)$, $q^0 = \begin{pmatrix} 1 \\ 0 \end{pmatrix}$ with payoff vector $(15, 30)$,

ii. $p^0 = (0, 1)$, $q^0 = \begin{pmatrix} 0 \\ 1 \end{pmatrix}$ with payoff vector $(30, 15)$.

Thus for the game of Figure 18 we have discovered three possible "solutions" —one maximin solution and two equilibrium-point solutions. And no one of these is clearly preferred by both players to any other one.

When solution concepts are not unique, nothing in the theory of games tells how one of these should be chosen as the solution, or how players should behave so as to reach one of them. Recent experimental work has revealed some experimental conditions under which one or another kind of solution is likely to be reached when such games are played over and over again by the same pair of players. For such games, psychological, historical, legal, or moral factors may dictate which solution would be reached in actual play.

Example 2. We illustrate next a case in which the maximin strategies are mixed and again are not equilibrium-point strategies. Consider the market-entry game whose payoffs are given in Figure 19. To get the maximin strategies

		C Enters	
		Market 1	Market 2
R Enters	Market 1	(10, 10)	(20, 30)
	Market 2	(30, 20)	(15, 15)

Figure 19

we solve the games

$$
A = \begin{array}{|c|c|} \hline 10 & 20 \\ \hline 30 & 15 \\ \hline \end{array}
\qquad \text{and} \qquad
-B = \begin{array}{|c|c|} \hline -10 & -30 \\ \hline -20 & -15 \\ \hline \end{array},
$$

which yield optimal strategies $p^0 = (\tfrac{3}{5}, \tfrac{2}{5})$ for R and $q^0 = \begin{pmatrix} \tfrac{3}{5} \\ \tfrac{2}{5} \end{pmatrix}$ for C. The expected payoff vector for the players if they use these strategies is $(18, 18)$, as the reader can easily compute. There are two equilibrium points, namely,

a. $p^0 = (1, 0)$ and $q^0 = \begin{pmatrix} 0 \\ 1 \end{pmatrix}$ with payoff vector $(20, 30)$,

b. $p^0 = (0, 1)$ and $q^0 = \begin{pmatrix} 1 \\ 0 \end{pmatrix}$ with payoff vector $(30, 20)$.

Note that either of the equilibrium-point strategies yields certain payoffs that are better than the expected payoff for the maximin strategies. However, player R clearly prefers the equilibrium point b. while player C clearly prefers the equilibrium point a. We again have three possible solutions, and any one of them may occur depending on other factors.

In games such as those of Figures 18 and 19 there is a clear tendency for the two players to cooperate and choose strategies that will maximize the sum of their payoffs. This would be particularly desirable if there were some way that they could share the total proceeds. For instance, in Example 2, equilibrium point a. might be satisfactory to both players if C could give a side payment of 5 to R. Or some other division of the proceeds might be agreed upon.

DEFINITION. Let G be a nonzero-sum game. A *cooperative solution* to G is a pair of strategies p^0, q^0 such that the quantity

$$
p^0 A q^0 + p^0 B q^0 = p^0 (A + B) q^0
$$

is a maximum.

Note that nothing in the definition of a cooperative solution tells how the two players will divide their total gains. Various proposals have been made for making this division, but none of them is satisfactory in all cases. It should also be remarked that legal or moral considerations (such as antitrust laws, moral codes) may prevent certain kinds of cooperation in actual games.

Example 3. To point up further difficulties with these solution concepts, we consider the following example. R and C sit on opposite sides of a table. On the table are three one-dollar bills. If they agree on the division of the money (no change is provided), they may have it; otherwise they will get nothing.

We can enumerate the players' strategies as being the demands they make on the money. Each player can demand 0, 1, 2, or 3 dollars. The payoff table is given in Figure 20. In this game every strategy for each player is a maximin strategy, so that solution concept does not limit action. There are four equilibrium points with payoffs (3, 0), (2, 1), (1, 2), and (0, 3). Each is also the payoff of a cooperative solution! How shall we choose among them?

		C Demands			
		0	1	2	3
	0	(0, 0)	(0, 1)	(0, 2)	(0, 3)
	1	(1, 0)	(1, 1)	(1, 2)	(0, 0)
R Demands	2	(2, 0)	(2, 1)	(0, 0)	(0, 0)
	3	(3, 0)	(0, 0)	(0, 0)	(0, 0)

Figure 20

If R and C are able to wait until the conclusion of the game to get change to make some division of their total payoffs, then any of these solutions might be acceptable. But suppose such cooperation is ruled out. It is reasonable then to rule out strategies 0 and 3 for each player, since the first represents too small and the second too large a demand. If we do so, we can consider the reduced game in Figure 21. Here the unique maximin strategy

		C Demands	
		1	2
	1	(1, 1)	(1, 2)
R Demands	2	(2, 1)	(0, 0)

Figure 21

yields the payoffs (1, 1) while the equilibrium-point strategies yield (2, 1) and (1, 2). Thus the maximin strategy, although unique, yields less to each player than either equilibrium-point strategy. We see that the theory of games does not provide a unique answer for this situation.

Example 4. Jones and Smith own gasoline stations on opposite sides of the street. No other stations are nearby. There are only two prices they can charge, high and low, and each day they must decide which price to use for the day. They are not permitted to change prices during the course of the day. Suppose their daily gross receipts are as given in Figure 22.

		Smith Charges	
		High	Low
	High	(10, 10)	(6, 16)
Jones Charges	Low	(16, 6)	(7, 7)

Figure 22

To interpret these numbers observe that if both charge the high price, each receives $10. If both charge the low price (the "gas war"), their income is cut to $7 for the day. Finally, if one charges the high price and the other low, the low-priced man can draw extra business so that his income is $16 while his opponent gets only $6. Let us assume that each station has fixed charges of $8 per day, so that either player will lose money if his opponent charges the low price.

The unique equilibrium and maximin strategies yield the payoff pair (7, 7), as the reader can easily check. Cooperative solutions will yield either the point (16, 6) or the point (6, 16). The total take for the cooperative solution is 22. This could be divided equally by means of side payments. It could also be divided as the game is played day by day, by having the players alternate between high and low prices each day so that their average income is $11.

Still one other solution that has been proposed for such a game is the following: Suppose that Jones is richer than Smith. If Jones charges the low price, Smith will certainly lose money. Hence Jones can make the following type of *threat:* "If you do not agree to a $13–$9 split, I shall lower my price and keep it down until you are bankrupt." Since Jones has more capital than Smith, the threat is effective and, if carried out, would result in the closing of Smith's business. On the other hand, if Smith tried to make a similar threat, he would simply ruin himself, and his threat is therefore suicidal. Here Jones is able to enforce the 13–9 division and has the dominant position in what otherwise appears to be a symmetric game, simply by being richer.

Although we have been deliberately skeptical about these various solution proposals, each has some merit. The fact that none of them fits every conceivable nonzero-sum game is perhaps an indication that such games do not reveal enough of the richness of real-world situations to provide universally satisfactory answers. It also provides avenues for future research.

EXERCISES

1. Consider the following nonzero-sum games:

$$G_1 \quad \begin{array}{|c|c|} \hline (10,\,10) & (5,\,8) \\ \hline (8,\,5) & (3,\,3) \\ \hline \end{array}, \qquad G_2 \quad \begin{array}{|c|c|} \hline (10,\,10) & (12,\,5) \\ \hline (5,\,12) & (7,\,7) \\ \hline \end{array},$$

$$G_3 \quad \begin{array}{|c|c|} \hline (10,\,10) & (18,\,5) \\ \hline (5,\,18) & (7,\,7) \\ \hline \end{array}, \qquad G_4 \quad \begin{array}{|c|c|} \hline (10,\,10) & (25,\,15) \\ \hline (15,\,25) & (5,\,5) \\ \hline \end{array},$$

$$G_5 \quad \begin{array}{|c|c|} \hline (10,\,10) & (20,\,-5) \\ \hline (-5,\,20) & (0,\,0) \\ \hline \end{array}, \qquad G_6 \quad \begin{array}{|c|c|} \hline (0,\,-2) & (15,\,-5) \\ \hline (-5,\,15) & (10,\,10) \\ \hline \end{array}.$$

Complete the following table by filling in the payoffs for each of the three types of solutions to these games.

	Maximin	Equilibrium Point	Cooperative
G_1	(10, 10)	(10, 10)	(10, 10)
G_2			
G_3			(5, 18) or (18, 5)
G_4	(13, 13)	(15, 25) or (25, 15)	
G_5			
G_6	(0, −2)		(10, 10)

2. In Exercise 1, assume that both players are equally rich and that it costs nothing for either of them to play any of the games. In which of the games, if any, might a threat solution be applicable? Why?   [*Ans.* G_6.]

3. Consider the problem in Example 3 with $2 to be divided between R and C this time. Show that there are three equilibrium points, and that there is a strong argument for choosing one of them as the solution. Try an experimental version of the game in which two players play the game over and over again and see if they tend to the distinguished equilibrium point.

4. Consider a general version of the situation of Example 3 in which two players must divide N dollars. Show that if N is even, there is a distinguished equilibrium point, but if N is odd, there is not.

5. By a *competitive solution* to a two-person nonzero-sum game we mean a solution in which R and C choose optimal strategies in the matrix game $A - B$. The rationale for this type of solution is that each player tries to maximize the difference between his own and his opponent's expected payoffs. Find competitive solutions to the six games in Exercise 1.
   [*Partial Ans.* In G_1 it yields the point (3, 3); in G_4 and G_5 it yields (10, 10).]

6. A matrix game can be considered a nonzero-sum game in which $b_{ij} = -a_{ij}$ for every i and j. With this interpretation show that a pair of optimal strategies p^0 and q^0 for a matrix game are equilibrium-point solutions to the corresponding nonzero-sum game.

7. Show that for 2×2 nonzero-sum games, in the definition of a maximin strategy we can replace the phrase "C chooses an optimal strategy in the game $-B$" by "C chooses an optimal strategy in the game B," provided B is not strictly determined. Is the same result true when B is strictly determined?   [*Ans.* No.]

8. By a *vindictive solution* to a two-person nonzero-sum game we mean a solution in which R chooses an optimal strategy in the game $-B$ and C chooses an optimal strategy in the game A. In other words each player tries to minimize his opponent's payoff, regardless of what it does to his own payoff. Find vindictive solutions to the games of Exercise 1.
   [*Partial Ans.* For G_1 it yields (3, 3); for G_4 it yields (13, 13).]

9. Prove that maximin strategies cannot be better for either player than equilibrium-point strategies.

10. Prove that vindictive strategies cannot be better for either player than maximin strategies.

11. Use Exercises 9 and 10 to show that vindictive strategies cannot do better for either player than equilibrium-point strategies.

12. Prove that if there are strategies for both players that are both maxim and vindictive, then they are both competitive.

13. Use the following example to show that a strategy can be both maximin and competitive without being vindictive:

(10, 10)	(9, 9)
(9, 9)	(8, 8)

14. Use the example of Exercise 13 to show that a strategy may be both competitive and vindictive without being maximin.

15. Prove that if there are strategies for both players that are both cooperative and competitive, then they are both maxim.

SUGGESTED READING

Von Neumann, J., and Oskar Morgenstern, *Theory of Games and Economic Behavior*, Princeton University Press, Princeton, N. J., 1944, 3d ed., 1953, Chapter I.

Williams, J. D., *The Compleat Strategyst*, McGraw-Hill, New York, rev. ed., 1966.

Luce, R. Duncan, and Howard Raiffa, *Games and Decisions: Introduction and Critical Survey*, Wiley, New York, 1957.

Shubik, Martin, *Strategy and Market Structure*, Wiley, New York, 1959.

Rapoport, Anatol, *Fights, Games, and Debates*, University of Michigan Press, Ann Arbor, 1960.

Kuhn, H. W., and A. W. Tucker, "Theory of Games," *Encyclopaedia Britannica*, 1956 edition.

Morgenstern, Oskar, "The Theory of Games," *Scientific American*, **180** (1950), pp. 294–308.

Gale, David, *The Theory of Linear Economic Models*, McGraw-Hill, New York, 1960.

McKinsey, J. C. C., *Introduction to the Theory of Games*, McGraw-Hill, New York, 1952.

Bellman, R., and D. Blackwell, "Red Dog, Blackjack, Poker," *Scientific American*, **184** (1951), pp. 44–47.

MacDonald, J., *Strategy in Poker, Business and War*, Norton, New York, 1950·

Dantzig, G. B., *Linear Programming and Extensions*, Princeton University Press, Princeton, N. J., 1963.

Tucker, A. W., "Combinatorial Algebra of Matrix Games and Linear Programming," in *Applied Combinatorial Mathematics*, ed. E. F. Beckenbach, Wiley, New York, 1964, pp. 320–347.

Thompson, G. L., "Game Theory," *McGraw-Hill Encyclopedia of Science and Technology*, 1971 Edition.

APPENDIX TABLES

$$\mathbf{b}(r;\, n,\, p) = \binom{n}{r} p^r (1 - p)^{n-r}$$

n	r	$p = .01$	.02	.05	.10	.15	.20	.25	.30	.40	.50
1	0	.990	.980	.950	.900	.850	.800	.750	.700	.600	.500
	1	.010	.020	.050	.100	.150	.200	.250	.300	.400	.500
2	0	.980	.960	.902	.810	.722	.640	.562	.490	.360	.250
	1	.020	.039	.095	.180	.255	.320	.375	.420	.480	.500
	2			.002	.010	.022	.040	.062	.090	.160	.250
3	0	.970	.941	.857	.729	.614	.512	.422	.343	.216	.125
	1	.029	.058	.135	.243	.325	.384	.422	.441	.432	.375
	2		.001	.007	.027	.057	.096	.141	.189	.288	.375
	3				.001	.003	.008	.016	.027	.064	.125
4	0	.961	.922	.815	.656	.522	.410	.316	.240	.130	.062
	1	.039	.075	.171	.292	.368	.410	.422	.412	.346	.250
	2	.001	.002	.014	.049	.098	.154	.211	.265	.346	.375
	3				.004	.011	.026	.047	.076	.154	.250
	4					.001	.002	.004	.008	.026	.062
5	0	.951	.904	.774	.590	.444	.328	.237	.168	.078	.031
	1	.048	.092	.204	.328	.392	.410	.396	.360	.259	.156
	2	.001	.004	.021	.073	.138	.205	.264	.309	.346	.312
	3			.001	.008	.024	.051	.088	.132	.230	.312
	4					002	.006	.015	.028	.077	.156
	5							.001	.002	.010	.031
6	0	.941	.886	.735	.531	.377	.262	.178	.118	.047	.016
	1	.057	.108	.232	.354	.399	.393	.356	.303	.187	.094
	2	.001	.006	.031	.098	.176	.246	.297	.324	.311	.234
	3			.002	.015	.041	.082	.132	.185	.276	.312
	4				.001	.005	.015	.033	.060	.138	.234
	5						.002	.004	.010	.037	.094
	6								.001	.004	.016
7	0	.932	.868	.698	.478	.321	.210	.133	.082	.028	.008
	1	.066	.124	.257	.372	.396	.367	.311	.247	.131	.055
	2	.002	.008	.041	.124	.210	.275	.311	.318	.261	.164
	3			.004	.023	.062	.115	.173	.227	.290	.273
	4				.003	.011	.029	.058	.097	.194	.273
	5					.001	.004	.012	.025	.077	.164
	6							.001	.004	.017	.055
	7									.002	.008
8	0	.923	.851	.663	.430	.272	.168	.100	.058	.017	.004
	1	.075	.139	.279	.383	.385	.336	.267	.198	.090	.031
	2	.003	.010	.051	.149	.238	.294	.311	.296	.209	.109
	3			.005	.033	.084	.147	.208	.254	.279	.219
	4				.005	.018	.046	.087	.136	.232	.273
	5					.003	.009	.023	.047	.124	.219
	6						.001	.004	.010	.041	.109
	7								.001	.008	.031
	8									.001	.004
9	0	.914	.834	.630	.387	.232	.134	.075	.040	.010	.002
	1	.083	.153	.299	.387	.368	.302	.225	.156	.060	.018
	2	.003	.013	.063	.172	.260	.302	.300	.267	.161	.070
	3		.001	.008	.045	.107	.176	.234	.267	.251	.164
	4			.001	.007	.028	.066	.117	.172	.251	.246
	5				.001	.005	.017	.039	.074	.167	.246
	6					.001	.003	.009	.021	.074	.164
	7							.001	.004	.021	.070
	8									.004	.018
	9										.002

Blank spaces mean $\mathbf{b}(r;\, n,\, p_j) < .0005$.

$$b(r;\, n,\, p)$$

n	r	$p = .01$	.02	.05	.10	.15	.20	.25	.30	.40	.50
10	0	.904	.817	.599	.349	.197	.107	.056	.028	.006	.001
	1	.091	.167	.315	.387	.347	.268	.188	.121	.040	.010
	2	.004	.015	.075	.194	.276	.302	.282	.233	.121	.044
	3		.001	.010	.057	.130	.201	.250	.267	.215	.117
	4			.001	.011	.040	.088	.146	.200	.251	.205
	5				.001	.008	.026	.058	.103	.201	.246
	6					.001	.006	.016	.037	.111	.205
	7						.001	.003	.009	.042	.117
	8								.001	.011	.044
	9									.002	.010
	10										.001
12	0	.886	.785	.540	.282	.142	.069	.032	.014	.002	0
	1	.107	.192	.341	.377	.301	.206	.127	.071	.017	.003
	2	.006	.022	.099	.230	.292	.283	.232	.168	.064	.016
	3		.001	.017	.085	.172	.236	.258	.240	.142	.054
	4			.002	.021	.068	.133	.194	.231	.213	.121
	5				.004	.019	.053	.103	.158	.227	.193
	6					.004	.016	.040	.079	.177	.226
	7					.001	.003	.011	.029	.101	.193
	8						.001	.002	.008	.042	.121
	9								.001	.012	.054
	10									.002	.016
	11										.003
16	0	.851	.724	.440	.185	.074	.028	.010	.003		
	1	.138	.236	.371	.329	.210	.113	.053	.023	.003	
	2	.010	.036	.146	.275	.277	.211	.134	.073	.015	.002
	3		.003	.036	.142	.229	.246	.208	.146	.047	.009
	4			.006	.051	.131	.200	.225	.204	.101	.028
	5			.001	.014	.056	.120	.180	.210	.162	.067
	6				.003	.018	.055	.110	.165	.198	.122
	7					.005	.020	.052	.101	.189	.175
	8					.001	.006	.020	.049	.142	.196
	9						.001	.006	.019	.084	.175
	10							.001	.006	.039	.122
	11								.001	.014	.067
	12									.004	.028
	13									.001	.009
	14										.002
	15										
20	0	.818	.668	.358	.122	.039	.012	.003	.001		
	1	.165	.272	.377	.270	.137	.058	.021	.007		
	2	.016	.053	.189	.285	.229	.137	.067	.028	.003	
	3	.001	.006	.060	.190	.243	.205	.134	.072	.012	.001
	4		.001	.013	.090	.182	.218	.190	.130	.035	.005
	5			.002	.032	.103	.175	.202	.179	.075	.015
	6				.009	.045	.109	.169	.192	.124	.037
	7				.002	.016	.055	.112	.164	.166	.074
	8					.005	.022	.061	.114	.180	.120
	9					.001	.007	.027	.065	.160	.160
	10						.002	.010	.031	.117	.176
	11							.003	.012	.071	.160
	12							.001	.004	.035	.120
	13								.001	.015	.074
	14									.005	.037
	15									.001	.015
	16										.005
	17										.001
	18										
	19										
	20										

APPENDIX TABLE II
Random Numbers

62483	55445	80895	43055	29682
09255	67132	07454	77644	70903
49979	59207	95504	99022	18529
90249	57452	40864	18665	78138
77549	81759	54304	61250	66699
76179	79533	64104	29709	37190
28596	22223	60280	46786	58623
20770	24192	08705	80677	79847
92625	51170	26874	78382	26398
28415	13180	59307	27329	07272
99047	16485	88497	12806	36211
96473	34238	54870	15512	96324
34324	21563	57794	11107	04158
36276	19759	88914	82368	01203
34678	37106	28420	39276	19117
31979	49329	83742	05647	26962
66208	14507	05855	27500	47616
01494	41401	56658	60208	54181
44360	52562	83111	54031	27834
03894	47680	74577	77226	20716
07031	93942	96934	79554	44074
21059	54837	40761	55969	64622
45286	88209	61026	44535	44285
34927	79089	05330	22104	59632
36165	24164	58437	19923	80475
37608	94140	14585	80655	94850
46730	12214	11015	72134	03847
33971	68083	05917	27896	93466
81654	96364	91122	35741	26619
70159	43964	67805	31452	34039
88743	95788	64467	95939	13659
84439	96972	56996	69182	85423
70330	91241	86901	05901	62508
09705	18931	61236	24129	62162
29678	50391	13190	15092	89017
00918	92378	30580	75852	95352
65453	81851	08703	36098	01017
78806	57628	78931	82451	89663
51330	72244	42157	43455	63889
18281	56070	09232	93952	57834
64353	37648	00401	72530	14489
30499	32631	47076	39657	43078
02031	80276	70492	39758	65253
29492	25096	48338	91815	64806
54042	56695	06917	79628	70701
92154	74519	57381	66251	96197
45890	99918	89770	35212	87582
54853	04762	12154	09150	34920
33401	71486	42807	79008	74244
37345	81231	81516	17763	53698

28470	19220	15251	81185	80949
05763	73998	70518	30736	77140
46967	59492	81935	44627	84918
65361	73425	04969	03676	27486
79821	50363	08667	98500	42817
77019	03964	93346	88152	03833
00884	34387	15224	51234	39434
67676	93996	82687	50068	72664
03119	47252	21495	49173	75833
36641	96536	88110	52973	70006
94747	79548	47263	68535	95606
41779	46981	67109	48880	10904
41500	58247	31942	01343	98176
70479	65749	63606	34527	92341
85243	78316	49539	79128	00224
99998	77109	67495	75596	49799
62074	15227	52236	79174	56289
82992	54801	39132	45332	19371
79503	73188	56454	91756	66459
22710	90391	69403	28217	29460
61686	12118	32455	27147	43331
66868	86886	16048	06962	36381
12204	53778	51127	43422	87225
18893	57833	10340	80118	54645
38143	41971	14805	09795	05943
20827	09452	72782	82231	75340
14123	49864	58660	71595	00363
42316	49930	86439	99287	98624
78495	80189	14086	19743	93623
41292	37330	29993	27573	22481
99545	51902	72154	78368	08734
47168	58480	55103	70609	62239
51410	35094	04263	37717	96866
89509	17236	49840	86025	96416
89731	85785	36220	52879	04604
89918	90438	99982	58187	51539
72618	80754	21291	96433	09214
81530	13638	79720	52571	40507
08901	04808	25832	51404	68377
41388	94935	40894	29304	87665
32777	08201	32680	12876	72006
46754	47018	16225	81687	28647
42759	80483	35260	09318	36720
59376	12414	43204	30006	61461
92163	40927	89243	84735	26876
05968	73574	21954	09901	01159
18573	36121	81220	26043	52796
13380	74910	59169	20433	25333
13400	54167	90416	10325	66284
86166	10097	51518	10052	89113

75722	89176	80307	63131	87190
49212	34682	44641	82369	81519
95090	09765	65628	98729	68001
17768	68852	48428	68154	10053
41378	07937	62350	82051	61684
73373	43037	11991	87921	38622
38863	17327	93732	24181	76505
09372	51990	38141	38974	95696
18120	15814	54770	66557	27710
71357	11797	39062	32276	87037
08173	80204	46402	22043	38310
64736	99181	18771	61220	36062
78891	35239	40508	26934	58585
06826	07463	41653	11745	45947
34666	79532	69093	82296	05513
76588	40389	41867	18461	94237
28227	45664	64682	53229	65676
25692	62227	50386	78806	22102
84543	66728	53281	73306	19259
60751	38660	82292	89939	25992
52448	54178	85018	41958	14992
21933	95640	84120	86031	79793
65366	05401	50738	55701	36802
17149	09217	10663	80471	65572
29193	87336	31182	29963	17936
33971	62401	83210	62752	28165
12172	59935	57556	33795	41570
84948	95439	66849	87170	59861
55742	68345	74918	20733	49522
98479	59802	11015	74621	17321
87574	77012	69497	37400	02373
74299	56964	79566	16613	74792
85926	23880	28376	33938	39506
01629	12674	99526	46071	71653
64489	72447	86570	15709	94996
16695	55798	04605	56249	96625
86689	68192	76289	64144	75515
29640	00748	64256	31576	48882
45602	31186	58670	80988	93346
30102	54221	72477	02417	95440
54677	34916	64338	57901	24058
17610	95371	86682	63993	47947
30737	56574	26131	15817	73625
70920	38347	42717	69086	33901
09234	30789	21794	29397	71235
94148	02940	96255	69893	20415
44067	65060	18249	87803	25662
30815	41690	04630	70317	52740
77881	01796	78496	79806	44414
95254	38929	27324	40237	77323

40575	79339	59874	56320	61151
81968	53775	82368	68218	48016
87689	03896	20884	56709	30480
31228	10777	79488	57472	10959
63510	73019	18266	77263	16598
23651	78815	98791	35854	94772
49628	69773	10359	62152	04334
51211	03442	07060	48154	83052
00752	87877	00117	50449	08581
96370	84776	72822	12949	84844
71555	41764	93579	96082	35335
24276	88597	30626	31213	63751
85194	59692	01220	44923	85040
54700	86194	72751	91697	95782
09692	70582	05989	66620	95318
75873	24064	95514	29067	78134
68051	33729	67378	54609	48365
52151	34667	66402	76208	95307
96561	75175	09677	46147	07121
21916	97649	79441	63537	17219
35707	98838	25899	47716	49946
30575	18276	41443	10501	27998
50374	69340	97816	18812	89428
00347	13222	36546	98795	20132
86642	13038	23994	21604	52991
97019	50685	61161	88121	15959
32599	80442	14069	52853	34648
31442	33682	28978	63258	17212
37463	38728	04291	77354	71750
48312	56799	23047	21775	25114
50732	73577	37090	25567	49898
08742	00359	81816	87036	29986
45734	62166	07098	24142	86220
75917	60196	73294	08512	29384
50880	33109	84342	65725	10194
78906	94031	46346	87543	07827
12405	56648	78777	86456	70986
72884	78154	98615	55814	87076
64383	40305	82186	63302	10323
96740	93229	46308	97470	34214
20230	97803	49985	81833	87365
10730	60143	51446	83530	03657
36099	22521	53482	52322	27098
83634	88066	67394	72624	45344
46314	37551	82125	16293	35180
41825	39069	75375	27059	27732
95291	18681	95794	97366	84647
76548	57499	76221	49147	24140
76071	77716	87073	37591	60869
26495	12526	70314	58329	79129

APPENDIX TABLE III

Single Payment Compound Amount Factor

$$(1 + r)^n$$

$n \backslash r$	.0025	.0050	.0075	.010	.015	.020	.025	.030
4	1.0100	1.0202	1.0303	1.0406	1.0614	1.0824	1.1038	1.1255
8	1.0202	1.0407	1.0616	1.0829	1.1265	1.1717	1.2184	1.2668
12	1.0304	1.0617	1.0938	1.1268	1.1956	1.2682	1.3449	1.4258
16	1.0408	1.0831	1.1270	1.1726	1.2690	1.3728	1.4845	1.6047
20	1.0512	1.1049	1.1612	1.2202	1.3469	1.4859	1.6386	1.8061
24	1.0618	1.1272	1.1964	1.2697	1.4295	1.6084	1.8087	2.0328
30	1.0778	1.1614	1.2513	1.3478	1.5631	1.8114	2.0976	2.4273
36	1.0941	1.1967	1.3086	1.4308	1.7091	2.0399	2.4325	2.8983
42	1.1106	1.2330	1.3686	1.5188	1.8688	2.2972	2.8210	3.4607
48	1.1273	1.2705	1.4314	1.6122	2.0435	2.5871	3.2715	4.1323
54	1.1443	1.3091	1.4970	1.7114	2.2344	2.9135	3.7939	4.9341
60	1.1616	1.3489	1.5657	1.8167	2.4432	3.2810	4.3998	5.8916
72	1.1969	1.4320	1.7126	2.0471	2.9212	4.1611	5.9172	8.4000
84	1.2334	1.5204	1.8732	2.3067	3.4926	5.2773	7.9580	11.976
96	1.2709	1.6141	2.0489	2.5993	4.1758	6.6929	10.703	17.076
108	1.3095	1.7137	2.2411	2.9289	4.9927	8.4883	14.394	24.346
120	1.3494	1.8194	2.4514	3.3004	5.9693	10.765	19.358	34.711
180	1.5674	2.4541	3.8380	5.9958	14.584	35.321	85.172	204.50
240	1.8208	3.3102	6.0092	10.893	35.633	115.89	374.74	1204.9
300	2.1150	4.4650	9.4084	19.788	87.059	380.23	1648.8	7098.5
360	2.4568	6.0226	14.731	35.950	212.70	1247.6	7254.2	41822.

$n \backslash r$	.03	.04	.05	.06	.07	.08	.09
1	1.0300	1.0400	1.0500	1.0600	1.0700	1.0800	1.0900
2	1.0609	1.0816	1.1025	1.1236	1.1449	1.1664	1.1881
3	1.0927	1.1249	1.1576	1.1910	1.2250	1.2597	1.2950
4	1.1255	1.1699	1.2155	1.2625	1.3108	1.3605	1.4115
5	1.1593	1.2167	1.2763	1.3382	1.4026	1.4693	1.5386
6	1.1941	1.2653	1.3401	1.4185	1.5007	1.5869	1.6771
7	1.2299	1.3159	1.4071	1.5036	1.6058	1.7138	1.8280
8	1.2668	1.3686	1.4775	1.5938	1.7182	1.8509	1.9926
9	1.3048	1.4233	1.5513	1.6895	1.8385	1.9990	2.1719
10	1.3439	1.4802	1.6289	1.7908	1.9672	2.1589	2.3674
12	1.4258	1.6010	1.7959	2.0122	2.2522	2.5182	2.8127
14	1.5126	1.7317	1.9799	2.2609	2.5785	2.9372	3.3417
16	1.6047	1.8730	2.1829	2.5404	2.9522	3.4259	3.9703
18	1.7024	2.0258	2.4066	2.8543	3.3799	3.9960	4.7171
20	1.8061	2.1911	2.6533	3.2071	3.8697	4.6610	5.6044
25	2.0938	2.6658	3.3864	4.2919	5.4274	6.8485	8.6231
30	2.4273	3.2434	4.3219	5.7435	7.6123	10.063	13.268
35	2.8139	3.9461	5.5160	7.6861	10.677	14.785	20.414
40	3.2620	4.8010	7.0400	10.286	14.974	21.725	31.409
45	3.7816	5.8412	8.9850	13.765	21.002	31.920	48.327
50	4.3839	7.1067	11.467	18.420	29.457	46.902	74.358

APPENDIX TABLE III

Single Payment Compound Amount Factor (concluded)

$n \backslash r$	.10	.12	.14	.16	.18	.20
1	1.1000	1.1200	1.1400	1.1600	1.1800	1.2000
2	1.2100	1.2544	1.2996	1.3456	1.3924	1.4400
3	1.3310	1.4049	1.4815	1.5609	1.6430	1.7280
4	1.4641	1.5735	1.6890	1.8106	1.9388	2.0736
5	1.6105	1.7623	1.9254	2.1003	2.2878	2.4883
6	1.7716	1.9738	2.1950	2.4364	2.6996	2.9860
7	1.9487	2.2107	2.5023	2.8262	3.1855	3.5832
8	2.1436	2.4760	2.8526	3.2784	3.7589	4.2998
9	2.3579	2.7731	3.2519	3.8030	4.4355	5.1598
10	2.5937	3.1058	3.7072	4.4114	5.2338	6.1917
12	3.1384	3.8960	4.8179	5.9360	7.2876	8.9161
14	3.7975	4.8871	6.2613	7.9875	10.147	12.839
16	4.5950	6.1304	8.1372	10.748	14.129	18.488
18	5.5599	7.6900	10.575	14.463	19.673	26.623
20	6.7275	9.6463	13.743	19.461	27.393	38.337
25	10.835	17.000	26.462	40.874	62.669	95.396
30	17.449	29.960	50.950	85.850	143.37	237.38
35	28.102	52.800	98.100	180.31	328.00	590.67
40	45.259	93.051	188.88	378.72	750.38	1469.8
45	72.890	163.99	363.68	795.44	1716.7	3657.3
50	117.39	289.00	700.23	1670.7	3927.4	9100.4

$n \backslash r$	.25	.30	.35	.40	.45	.50
1	1.2500	1.3000	1.3500	1.4000	1.4500	1.5000
2	1.5625	1.6900	1.8225	1.9600	2.1025	2.2500
3	1.9531	2.1970	2.4604	2.7440	3.0486	3.3750
4	2.4414	2.8561	3.3215	3.8416	4.4205	5.0625
5	3.0518	3.7129	4.4840	5.3782	6.4097	7.5938
6	3.8147	4.8268	6.0534	7.5295	9.2941	11.391
7	4.7684	6.2749	8.1722	10.541	13.476	17.086
8	5.9605	8.1573	11.032	14.758	19.541	25.629
9	7.4506	10.604	14.894	20.661	28.334	38.443
10	9.3132	13.786	20.107	28.925	41.085	57.665
12	14.552	23.298	36.644	56.694	86.381	129.75
14	22.737	39.374	66.784	111.12	181.62	291.93
16	35.527	66.542	121.71	217.80	381.85	656.84
18	55.511	112.46	221.82	426.88	802.83	1477.9
20	86.736	190.05	404.27	836.68	1688.0	3325.3
25	264.70	705.64	1812.8	4499.9	10819.	25251.
30	807.79	2620.0	8128.5	24201.	69349.	191750.
35	2465.2	9727.9	36449.	130160.	444510.	1456100.
40	7523.2	36119.	163440.	700040.	2849200.	11057000.
45	22959.	134110.	732860.	3765000.	18262000.	83967000.
50	70065.	497930.	3286200.	20249000.	117060000.	637620000.

APPENDIX TABLE IV

Uniform Payment Present Value Factor

$$\frac{(1+r)^n - 1}{r(1+r)^n}$$

n/r	.0025	.0050	.0075	.010	.015	.020	.025	.030
4	3.9751	3.9505	3.9261	3.9020	3.8544	3.8077	3.7620	3.7171
8	7.9107	7.8230	7.7366	7.6517	7.4859	7.3255	7.1701	7.0197
12	11.807	11.619	11.435	11.255	10.908	10.575	10.258	9.9540
16	15.665	15.340	15.024	14.718	14.131	13.578	13.055	12.561
20	19.484	18.987	18.508	18.046	17.169	16.351	15.589	14.877
24	23.266	22.563	21.889	21.243	20.030	18.914	17.885	16.936
30	28.868	27.794	26.775	25.808	24.016	22.396	20.930	19.600
36	34.386	32.871	31.447	30.108	27.661	25.489	2.3556	21.832
42	39.823	37.798	35.914	34.158	30.994	28.235	25.821	23.701
48	45.179	42.580	40.185	37.974	34.043	30.673	27.773	25.267
54	50.455	47.221	44.269	41.569	36.831	32.838	29.457	26.578
60	55.652	51.726	48.173	44.955	39.380	34.761	30.909	27.676
72	65.817	60.340	55.477	51.150	43.845	37.984	33.240	29.365
84	75.681	68.453	62.154	56.648	47.579	40.526	34.974	30.550
96	85.255	76.095	68.258	61.528	50.702	42.529	36.263	31.381
108	94.545	83.293	73.839	65.858	53.314	44.110	37.221	31.964
120	103.56	90.073	78.942	69.701	55.498	45.355	37.934	32.373
180	144.81	118.50	98.593	83.322	62.096	48.584	39.530	33.170
240	180.31	139.58	111.14	90.819	64.796	49.569	39.893	33.306
300	210.88	155.21	119.16	94.947	65.901	49.869	39.976	33.329
360	237.19	166.79	124.28	97.218	66.353	49.960	39.994	33.333

n/r	.03	.04	.05	.06	.07	.08	.09
1	.9709	.9615	.9524	.9434	.9346	.9259	.9174
2	1.9135	1.8861	1.8594	1.8334	1.8080	1.7833	1.7591
3	2.8286	2.7751	2.7232	2.6730	2.6243	2.5771	2.5313
4	3.7171	3.6299	3.5460	3.4651	3.3872	3.3121	3.2397
5	4.5797	4.4518	4.3295	4.2124	4.1002	3.9927	3.8897
6	5.4172	5.2421	5.0757	4.9173	4.7665	4.6229	4.4859
7	6.2303	6.0021	5.7864	5.5824	5.3893	5.2064	5.0330
8	7.0197	6.7327	6.4632	6.2098	5.9713	5.7466	5.5348
9	7.7861	7.4353	7.1078	6.8017	6.5152	6.2469	5.9952
10	8.5302	8.1109	7.7217	7.3601	7.0236	6.7101	6.4177
12	9.9540	9.3851	8.8633	8.3838	7.9427	7.5361	7.1607
14	11.296	10.563	9.8986	9.2950	8.7455	8.2442	7.7862
16	12.561	11.652	10.838	10.106	9.4466	8.8514	8.3126
18	13.754	12.659	11.690	10.828	10.059	9.3719	8.7556
20	14.877	13.590	12.462	11.470	10.594	9.8181	9.1285
25	17.413	15.622	14.094	12.783	11.654	10.675	9.8226
30	19.600	17.292	15.372	13.765	12.409	11.258	10.274
35	21.487	18.665	16.374	14.498	12.948	11.655	10.567
40	23.115	19.793	17.159	15.046	13.332	11.925	10.757
45	24.519	20.720	17.774	15.456	13.606	12.108	10.881
50	25.730	21.482	18.256	15.762	13.801	12.233	10.962

APPENDIX TABLE IV

Uniform Payment Present Value Factor (concluded)

n/r	.10	.12	.14	.16	.18	.20
1	.9091	.8929	.8772	.8621	.8475	.8333
2	1.7355	1.6901	1.6467	1.6052	1.5656	1.5278
3	2.4869	2.4018	2.3216	2.2459	2.1743	2.1065
4	3.1699	3.0373	2.9137	2.7982	2.6901	2.5887
5	3.7908	3.6048	3.4331	3.2743	3.1272	2.9906
6	4.3553	4.1114	3.8887	3.6847	3.4976	3.3255
7	4.8683	4.5638	4.2883	4.0386	3.8115	3.6046
8	5.3349	4.9676	4.6389	4.3436	4.0776	3.8372
9	5.7590	5.3282	4.9464	4.6065	4.3030	4.0310
10	6.1446	5.6502	5.2161	4.8332	4.4941	4.1925
12	6.8137	6.1944	5.6603	5.1971	4.7932	4.4392
14	7.3667	6.6282	6.0021	5.4675	5.0081	4.6106
16	7.8237	6.9740	6.2651	5.6685	5.1624	4.7296
18	8.2014	7.2497	6.4674	5.8178	5.2732	4.8122
20	8.5136	7.4694	6.6231	5.9288	5.3527	4.8696
25	9.0770	7.8431	6.8729	6.0971	5.4669	4.9476
30	9.4269	8.0552	7.0027	6.1772	5.5168	4.9789
35	9.6442	8.1755	7.0700	6.2153	5.5386	4.9915
40	9.7791	8.2438	7.1050	6.2335	5.5482	4.9966
45	9.8628	8.2825	7.1232	6.2421	5.5523	4.9986
50	9.9148	8.3045	7.1327	6.2463	5.5541	4.9995

n/r	.25	.30	.35	.40	.45	.50
1	.8000	.7692	.7407	.7143	.6897	.6667
2	1.4400	1.3609	1.2894	1.2245	1.1653	1.1111
3	1.9520	1.8161	1.6959	1.5889	1.4933	1.4074
4	2.3616	2.1662	1.9969	1.8492	1.7195	1.6049
5	2.6893	2.4356	2.2200	2.0352	1.8755	1.7366
6	2.9514	2.6427	2.3852	2.1680	1.9831	1.8244
7	3.1611	2.8021	2.5075	2.2628	2.0573	1.8829
8	3.3289	2.9247	2.5982	2.3306	2.1085	1.9220
9	3.4631	3.0190	2.6653	2.3790	2.1438	1.9480
10	3.5705	3.0915	2.7150	2.4136	2.1681	1.9653
12	3.7251	3.1903	2.7792	2.4559	2.1965	1.9846
14	3.8241	3.2487	2.8144	2.4775	2.2100	1.9931
16	3.8874	3.2832	2.8337	2.4885	2.2164	1.9970
18	3.9279	3.3037	2.8443	2.4941	2.2195	1.9986
20	3.9539	3.3158	2.8501	2.4970	2.2209	1.9994
25	3.9849	3.3286	2.8556	2.4994	2.2216	1.9999
30	3.9950	3 3321	2.8568	2.4999	2.2219	2.0000
35	3.9984	3.3330	2.8571	2.5000	2.2222	2.0000
40	3.9995	3.3332	2.8571	2.5000	2.2222	2.0000
45	3.9998	3.3333	2.8571	2.5000	2.2222	2.0000
50	3.9999	3.3333	2.8571	2.5000	2.2222	2.0000

APPENDIX TABLE V
Square Roots

x					$\sqrt{x}$						
	00	01	02	03	04	05	06	07	08	09	10
.1	.3162	.3317	.3464	.3606	.3742	.3873	.4000	.4123	.4243	.4359	.4472
.2	.4472	.4583	.4690	.4796	.4899	.5000	.5099	.5196	.5292	.5385	.5477
.3	.5477	.5568	.5657	.5745	.5831	.5916	.6000	.6083	.6164	.6245	.6325
.4	.6325	.6403	.6481	.6557	.6633	.6708	.6782	.6856	.6928	.7000	.7071
.5	.7071	.7141	.7211	.7280	.7348	.7416	.7483	.7550	.7616	.7681	.7746
.6	.7746	.7810	.7874	.7937	.8000	.8062	.8124	.8185	.8246	.8307	.8367
.7	.8367	.8426	.8485	.8544	.8602	.8660	.8718	.8775	.8832	.8888	.8944
.8	.8944	.9000	.9055	.9110	.9165	.9220	.9274	.9327	.9381	.9434	.9487
.9	.9487	.9539	.9592	.9644	.9695	.9747	.9798	.9849	.9899	.9950	1.0000
1.	1.000	1.049	1.095	1.140	1.183	1.225	1.265	1.304	1.342	1.378	1.414
2.	1.414	1.449	1.483	1.517	1.549	1.581	1.612	1.643	1.673	1.703	1.732
3.	1.732	1.761	1.789	1.817	1.844	1.871	1.897	1.924	1.949	1.975	2.000
4.	2.000	2.025	2.049	2.074	2.098	2.121	2.145	2.168	2.191	2.214	2.236
5.	2.236	2.258	2.280	2.302	2.324	2.345	2.366	2.387	2.408	2.429	2.449
6.	2.449	2.470	2.490	2.510	2.530	2.550	2.569	2.588	2.608	2.627	2.646
7.	2.646	2.665	2.683	2.702	2.720	2.739	2.757	2.775	2.793	2.811	2.828
8.	2.828	2.846	2.864	2.881	2.898	2.915	2.933	2.950	2.966	2.983	3.000
9.	3.000	3.017	3.033	3.050	3.066	3.082	3.098	3.114	3.130	3.146	3.162

INDEX